D1737454

Trees and Shrubs of the Upper Midwest

TREES AND SHRUBS
OF THE UPPER MIDWEST

BY

Carl Otto Rosendahl

UNIVERSITY OF MINNESOTA PRESS · Minneapolis

Fifth Printing 1980

Library of Congress Catalog Card Number: 55-8489
ISBN: 0-8166-0118-6

PREFACE

OVER a quarter of a century has passed since Professor C. O. Rosendahl and the late Professor F. K. Butters published their *Trees and Shrubs of Minnesota*. To the nature lover, the gardener, and the amateur botanist, as well as to the professional botanist, this volume served well as a definitive regional source book on matters pertaining to the woody vegetation of the state.

I feel certain that a similar audience will welcome the present volume, which has been prepared by Professor Rosendahl with great care over the past two years. As its title indicates, the scope of the original work has been broadened. This volume is not only a revision but an enlargement of the earlier one. Changes in the direction of greater usability may be seen in the number of new illustrations, many of which were expertly prepared by Miss Wilma Monserud; the increased prominence given to the common plant names; and the citing of page numbers in the various keys. In bringing the botanical nomenclature up to date, Professor Rosendahl has introduced over a hundred changes of names. Such genera as *Crataegus* (Hawthorn), *Amelanchier* (Juneberry), and *Rubus* (Raspberry) have been revised in the light of more recent intensive studies.

The included map gives an indication of the approximate area (Minnesota, Wisconsin, northern Iowa, and North and South Dakota east of the Missouri River) that is covered in the newly composed notes on plant distribution.

Most of the descriptive material of the previous volume has been retained. The critical reader will value the inclusion of the interpretative discussions of both native and commonly cultivated material, such as are found, for example, in the descriptions of the various species of *Rosa*.

The nature lover who will pause with these pages — and with the trees and shrubs herein described as well — will surely have a truly enriching experience.

A. ORVILLE DAHL
Professor and Chairman of the
Department of Botany

University of Minnesota
May 1955

CONTENTS

Trees and Shrubs of the Upper Midwest

INTRODUCTION

Terminology

In botanical practice the name of a plant is made up of two words, for example, *Quercus alba, Populus tremuloides, Ulmus americana.* The first word represents the *genus*, or group, to which the plant belongs and is always written with a capital letter. The second word indicates the *species*, or kind, and is rarely capitalized.* The meaning of the terms *genus* and *species* and the manner in which they are used can be made clear by the following illustration. In Minnesota there are three native kinds, or species, of pine, namely, the white pine, the Norway pine, and the jack pine. They all belong to the group, or genus, *Pinus* and are known respectively as *Pinus Strobus, Pinus resinosa,* and *Pinus Banksiana.* Somewhat closely related to the pines are other cone-bearing evergreens such as spruces, firs, and hemlocks. These different *genera* (plural of *genus*), together with several others, form a larger relationship that is known as the pine family, or *Pinaceae.* In a similar manner roses, spireas, apples, plums, and many others are grouped into the rose family or *Rosaceae.* The ending *-aceae,* which is generally used to denote a family, is the feminine plural of the Latin suffix *-aceus,* meaning *like* or *related to.* The family name *Pinaceae* is really an adjective agreeing with *plantae* (plants) and meaning *plants related to the pine.*

After families the successively higher categories of plants are *orders, classes,* and *divisions,* each of which in practice is frequently subdivided into *suborders, subclasses,* and *subdivisions.*

The orders are generally named from a characteristic family of a group of families and for the most part have the ending *-ales:* for example, *Fagales, Rosales.* As with family names the ending is in the feminine plural. *Rosales* signifies, for instance, *plants related to the rose family.*

The highest categories, namely, *Subclasses* and *Classes, Subdivisions* and *Divisions,* are designated by names that generally denote some fundamental morphological character upon which the respective category is based; thus *Monocotyledones* and *Dicotyledones* mean respectively plants with one seed

---

* It is capitalized when it is derived from the name of a person, or is the name of a genus or the old substantive name of a plant.

leaf and two seed leaves in the embryo. Similarly the subdivision *Gymnospermae* means the plants with naked seeds, and *Angiospermae*, those with seeds enclosed or hidden in the ovary of the pistil. Lastly, these two subdivisions constitute one of the major *Divisions* of the vegetable kingdom, the *Spermatophyta*, or seed-bearing plants.

The relation of the various categories of the system of classification to each other is made clear by the following scheme:

Division
  (Subdivision)
    Class
      (Subclass)
        Order
          (Suborder)
            Family
              (Subfamily)
              (Tribe)
                Genus
                  (Subgenus)
                    Species
                      (Subspecies, variety, form)

It should be borne in mind in dealing with these various categories that, although essential parts of the scheme of classification, they are only abstractions or concepts and not real entities. This is particularly true of the higher categories, but even the species, which in practice is the unit of classification, is in no wise a definite entity. Only the individuals that compose it have any real existence in nature. Since species are taxonomic concepts, their delimitation becomes to a considerable extent a matter of individual opinion or interpretation. Some workers habitually set very narrow limits to their species, others correspondingly broad ones, with the consequence that there is considerable disparity between different taxonomic treatments. It is obvious, therefore, that knowledge, judgment, and experience, together with due respect for usage and regulations, must be the chief safeguards in avoiding confusion and misunderstanding.

In practice it has long been customary to treat units of lower rank than the species either as *subspecies* or as *varieties*. These are composed of individuals occurring in certain geographical parts of the range of the species and differing in some minor yet constant characters. They are designated by a symbol or a name, preceded by the abbreviation *var.* (L. *varietas*), the whole combination being written in the following form: *Populus nigra* var. *italica*.

If variants show no definite geographical segregation but occur sporadically throughout the range of the species, they are designated as *forms* (L. *forma*). Of similar botanical import are the innumerable horticultural variants and races

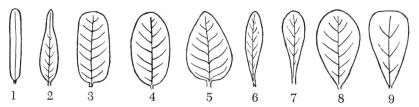

Outlines of simple leaves: 1, Linear. 2, Lanceolate. 3, Oblong. 4, Elliptic.
5, Ovate. 6, Oblanceolate. 7, Spatulate. 8, Obovate. 9, Cuneate.

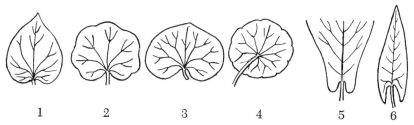

Outlines and bases of simple leaves: 1, Cordate. 2, Orbicular. 3, Reniform.
4, Peltate. 5, Auriculate. 6, Sagittate.

of cultivated species. When such races differ from the normal species in well-marked botanical features they are usually treated as varieties or forms, while minor variation is denoted by strictly horticultural names, such as the "Wealthy" apple or the "Crimson Rambler" rose. In the following pages no attempt has been made to distinguish these minor horticultural variants.

Keys and How to Use Them

In addition to the keys to genera and species under each family throughout the text, two general keys are provided on pages 15 and 19. The first of these, a key to families, is based chiefly upon the structure of the flower and can therefore be used only when flowering specimens are available. The second and more extensive key to genera is based upon vegetative characters almost entirely, particularly the leaves and twigs, and is for use from the time the leaves appear until they fall. It has not seemed desirable to include a key to trees and shrubs in the winter condition, mainly because of the difficulties of differentiating genera and species on characters that often do not lend themselves to brief or even satisfactory description. A number of keys of this kind are available, but most of them prove difficult even for the professional botanist and to the nonprofessional they are hopelessly confusing.

In a publication dealing with as many forms as the present volume, in spite of the valuable aids of numerous illustrations and rather full descriptions, the only sure method by which a plant species can be determined is by tracing it step by step through the family, genus, and species keys. Generally also this way is the quickest, even though one may be tempted to take a short cut by referring at first to the illustrations.

5

To ensure the greatest facility, as well as accuracy, in the use of the keys, they are all based on the methods of alternatives: for example, 1. Petals present; 1. Petals absent. The two alternatives (rarely more) are indicated by being equally indented and by having the same number. (In the two general keys at the

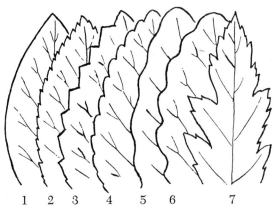

Leaf margins: 1, Entire. 2, Serrate. 3, Dentate.
4, Crenate. 5, Undulate. 6, Sinuate. 7, Incised.

beginning, which are many pages long, it may be necessary to turn over several pages before the second of a pair of numbers is found.) At every step the user should consider both alternatives before making a choice, since one generally throws light upon the other. In the construction of the keys the object has been to make them as simple and direct as accuracy will permit, yet the beginner is sure to encounter terms with which he is not familiar. In addition, he will be faced with the difficulty of deciding how much of a quality, such as pubescence or lobing, a given term or phrase signifies. To aid the beginner in overcoming these difficulties and indeed to make it possible to use the keys successfully at all, explanatory figures and a glossary of terms have been appended. It is strongly urged that these be freely consulted whenever doubt arises. Above all, the temptation to guess at points of structure or the meaning of terms must be avoided; otherwise one is sure to go astray.

For the successful working of a key two rules must be constantly and strictly adhered to: (1) accurate observation of the structure in question, (2) correct interpretation of the descriptive terms. The work of identification will be greatly facilitated by the use of a simple hand lens with magnifying powers of 8–12 diameters. Several makes of such pocket lenses are on the market, but those made by the Bausch and Lomb, Leitz, Spencer, and Zeiss Optical companies are recommended.

Pronunciation

The names of plants are best pronounced according to the so-called English pronunciation of Latin. That is, there are no silent letters; there is a separate

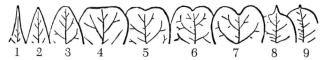

Leaf tips: 1, Acuminate. 2, Acute. 3, Obtuse. 4, Truncate.
5, Retuse. 6, Emarginate. 7, Obcordate. 8, Cuspidate.
9, Mucronate.

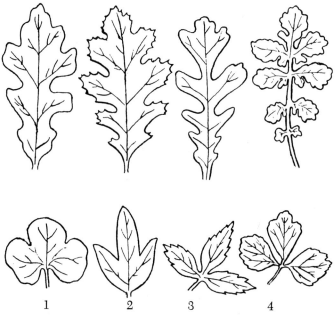

Simple leaves, variously cut or incised (upper series, pinnate;
lower series, palmate): 1, Lobed. 2, Cleft. 3, Parted. 4, Divided.

syllable for each vowel or diphthong; *c* and *g* are soft before *e, i, y, ae,* and *oe,* hard before *a, o,* and *u;* the simple vowels are given the ordinary English sounds, *ae* and *oe* are pronounced like long *e.* The accent for both generic and specific names is indicated throughout the text. Names that are enclosed in brackets are synonyms.

Verification and Determination of Specimens

The beginner will find occasional trees or shrubs that he is unable to name. Even the student of more experience will now and then find very puzzling forms. In such cases it is necessary to make comparisons with authentic material in a good herbarium or else to refer the question to the professional botanist. The Department of Botany of the University of Minnesota is at the service of anyone who wishes to send to it either fresh plants or properly prepared specimens for verification or determination. Fresh specimens may readily be sent through the mails if they are placed in a polyethylene bag or waxed paper and sealed in a small tin box. Empty baking-powder cans or Nabisco wafer boxes make suitable

7

containers for such a purpose. Sometimes it may become necessary to send dried specimens. Then the plants should be pressed between layers of newspapers or blotters while still fresh so that the leaves flatten out and retain their shape. When thoroughly dried they may be placed between cardboards, securely

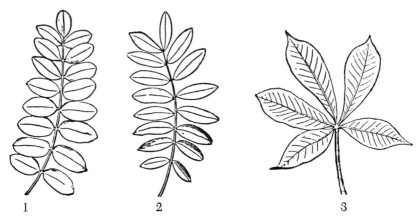

Compound leaves: 1, Odd-pinnate. 2, Abruptly pinnate. 3, Palmate.

wrapped, and sent by parcel post. If plants are bundled up in ordinary paper containers while still fresh or partially wilted, and forwarded by mail, they usually are either decayed or shriveled beyond recognition by the time they reach their destination. For accurate determination flowers and fruits are desirable and sometimes absolutely necessary; this should be kept in mind when collecting specimens.

Measurements and Weight

The metric system of measures has been used throughout this book. For any who are not familiar with this system, it may be stated that the meter (m.) equals 39.37 inches, or approximately 3.3 feet; the decimeter (dm.) is approximately 4 inches; the centimeter (cm.) 2/5 of an inch; and the millimeter (mm.), 1/25 of an inch.

Where weight is given, the figure means pounds per cubic foot of dry wood.

Vegetation Regions

Two principal plant formations, the forest and the prairie, characterize the Upper Midwest. These interdigitate in a diagonal course from southeastern Manitoba in the northwest to northeastern Iowa in the southeast. Their general outline is shown in the map on page 13. These two regions have their characteristic plants, and comparatively few woody species are equally at home in each of them. The forest falls naturally into two regions, the evergreen and the deciduous.

INTRODUCTION

1. *The Evergreen Forests.* The evergreen or coniferous forests originally covered the northeastern third of Minnesota, extending south to a line about halfway between Duluth and the Twin Cities and west nearly as far as the Red River Valley.* They were continuous with those of southeastern Manitoba and Ontario on the north and with those of Wisconsin and the upper peninsula of Michigan on the east. The characteristic trees of the mature upland forest of the region are the three pines, white, red and jack, white spruce, balsam fir, hemlock † and white birch. The bogs harbor black spruce, tamarack, and white cedar.

Deciduous trees, other than white birch, are generally minor or temporary features of the vegetation. Though throughout the region such trees as balsam poplar, aspen, red maple, black ash, pin cherry and mountain ash are more or less frequent, but except where there has been interference with natural conditions they form a subsidiary part of the vegetation. The destruction of the coniferous forest by fire or lumbering is usually followed by a rapid growth of aspen and birch, which for a time form the dominant vegetation. If there is no interference this growth is in time replaced by a return of the conifers unless the original destruction has been so thorough and so widespread that there is no available source of seed. In many places in the northern part of the area, fires have been so frequent as to keep the vegetation more or less permanently in the birch-aspen stage, and finally by consuming most of the soil, so to limit the growth that it is reduced to mere thickets of these species.

Here and there throughout this western section of coniferous forest there are definite inclusions of genuine hardwood forest, characterized by the dominance of such trees as sugar maple, basswood, American elm, and red oak. These patches of hardwood timber are usually found on rich morainic soil and in situations that are relatively free from late spring frosts, adjacent to large lakes or on ridges where there is free air drainage. They are sometimes without admixture of evergreens, but frequently contain some large white pines mingled with the deciduous trees. These scattered stands of hardwoods within the coniferous area may possibly be relics of a former more northerly distribution of the deciduous forest.

Continuous with the evergreen forests of Minnesota the conifers, white, red, and jack pine, hemlock and tamarack, extended southeastward in Wisconsin in an irregular belt of varying width as far as Waucopa and Columbia counties. Here and there within the extensive hardwood region of northeastern Wisconsin occurred isolated areas of pine of considerable extent. As in Minnesota, the great pineries of the state are gone; and where the land has not passed into

---

* According to the classification in E. Lucy Braun, *Deciduous Forests of Eastern North America* (1950), this is the Minnesota Section of the White pine, Hemlock, Northern Hardwoods Region.

† Hemlock is limited to the eastern part of the area, occurring only sporadically along the eastern border of Minnesota.

cultivation, a mixed growth of deciduous trees, mostly oak, aspen, and jack pine has replaced the original forest.

The shrubs as well as the trees of the evergreen forests are, many of them, characteristic. Here are found the white-flowered thimbleberry, the mountain maple, dwarf birches, elders, sweet fern, several kinds of fly-honeysuckle, the hairy climbing honeysuckle, highbush cranberry, *Rosa acicularis,* and, most characteristic of all, numerous heaths such as leatherleaf, Labrador tea, trailing arbutus, wintergreen, dwarf kalmia, and several kinds of blueberries and cranberries.

2. *The Deciduous Forest.* In the northwestern part of the area the deciduous forest occupies a comparatively narrow strip between the coniferous and the prairie. This narrow belt, from about latitude 46° N. northward into Manitoba is a mixed type, the oak being dominant over considerable tracts. In the south there is some admixture of sugar maple and basswood, but northward the growth is less luxuriant, and finally in the region bordering the Red River Valley the deciduous trees are scarcely more than shrubs and the country is locally known as "Brush Prairie." For the most part it is composed of bur oak, choke cherry, black cherry, plum, aspen, elm, balsam poplar, pin cherry, and willows.

South of latitude 46° N. in Minnesota the deciduous forest widens rapidly and, according to the classification of Braun,* falls into two sections of the Maple-Basswood Forest Region, namely, the Big Woods Section and, farther to the east and southeast, the Driftless Section. The former, a tract of pure deciduous forest and known to the early settlers as the "Big Woods," occupied a region of rich calcareous clays in south central Minnesota, extended from about latitude 45° 30″ N. to slightly beyond the bend of the Minnesota River. It was bounded on the east by a line running through Faribault and Northfield, thence northerly, passing about 15 miles west of Minneapolis and northwesterly along the Mississippi River to the vicinity of St. Cloud. The western boundary extended somewhat irregularly from Mankato to southeastern Stearns County. The area thus defined is about 100 miles long from north to south and 40 miles wide at its southern end.

All this area except the bottomlands of the Minnesota River and occasional marshes was occupied by heavy forest. In the less thickly settled parts of this region considerable patches of the original forest are still standing, but, as in general the land is very fertile, there has been more clearing of the forest than in the more rugged country to the east. Throughout the Big Woods the dominant trees are sugar maple, basswood, white and red elms, and red oak. Other oaks are rare, though occasional specimens of bur oak occur and reach large size. There are no conifers except some red cedars on the shores of the numerous lakes, and tamaracks in the bogs of the northeastern part of the area. The com-

* *Deciduous Forests,* p. 329.

10

monest tree of secondary size throughout the Big Woods is the ironwood, and the most abundant shrubs are dogwoods (especially *Cornus racemosa* and *C. rugosa*), sumacs, thorn apples, black haw, and *Rosa blanda*.

On the west, south, and southeast the Big Woods end abruptly along the line of prairies; on the northeast they pass more gradually into a region of open woods, groves, and savannas. This is a region of very mixed soils due to the overlapping of earlier (noncalcareous) and later (calcareous) sheets of glacial drift of the Wisconsin age. In addition there are extensive sandy and gravelly outwash plains and to the northward areas of dune sand. In this region there was much prairie, particularly on gravelly subsoils, with groves of various sizes and some rather large areas of forest. The dominant trees are oaks — bur oak on the more calcareous soils, white oak in great abundance on the heavier acid soils, and Hill's oak on the sandier areas. In some of these the trees reach good size, but often, over considerable areas, they are small and scarcely more than large shrubs. Around some of the lakes and along the bluffs of the Mississippi and the St. Croix rivers, forest of a better type obtains, and locally it may approximate that found in the Big Woods. Northward this country of savannas and poorly developed woodlands extends up the valley of the Mississippi, especially on the east side of the river nearly to the edge of the coniferous forest.

In this area of open woods and groves conifers are rare but somewhat more common than in the region of the Big Woods. Red cedar and, less frequently, juniper and yew occur around lakes and on the bluffs of the Mississippi and St. Croix rivers. White pine is fairly common along the St. Croix and occurs in a few situations along the bluffs of the Mississippi. Tamarack bogs are frequent and may be regarded as local islands of the northeastern forest surrounded by the more southern general vegetation. Finally a larger inclusion of the northern forest, known as the Cedar Creek Forest, occurs in northeastern Anoka County, where there is a considerable area of typical coniferous forest completely isolated from the main body of the formation.

The Driftless Section, in general coextensive with the "Driftless Area," embraces the deciduous forest of southeastern Minnesota, southwestern Wisconsin, northeastern Iowa, and northwestern Illinois. The country is much dissected, with numerous deep river and stream valleys, precipitous bluffs, and rolling uplands. Most of it was not covered by Pleistocene ice. Partly on account of the more southerly location but mainly because of the greater diversity of habitats, the forest of the Driftless Section contains a considerably larger number of woody species than any of the other areas previously discussed. It may conveniently be treated under the headings of bottomland forest, wooded slopes, and forest of the uplands.

On the bottomlands of the Mississippi and the lower reaches of its tributaries, especially subject to frequent overflow, the chief trees are cottonwoods and several species of willow. On slightly higher land the American elm and soft maple are abundant along with such trees as hackberry, green and black ash, box elder, river birch, and occasionally Kentucky coffee tree and swamp white oak. Such woody vines as the Virginia creeper, prickly smilax, and the frost grape are common on the less frequently flooded parts of the bottomlands, the last often attaining great size in such situations.

The forest of the north- and northeast-facing slopes of the high bluffs is composed mainly of red oak, sugar maple, basswood, butternut, large-toothed aspen, pignut hickory, black cherry, and, less frequently, of white birch and black oak. Toward the base of the bluffs and ravines black walnut is common. Scattered groves of white pine occur throughout the region, usually well up the slopes or at the crest of the bluffs. The understory on these slopes is composed mainly of dogwoods (*Cornus rugosa* and *C. alternifolia*), bladdernut, ironwood, and occasionally mountain maple. The south- and west-facing slopes of the region are largely grassland, but on some of the slopes red cedar and juniper are common. In draws or small coulees grow choke cherry, prickly ash, juneberry, smooth sumac, and bittersweet, together with stunted trees of bur oak. The upland forest is composed mainly of oak, in which Hill's oak, white oak, and bur oak predominate, with red oak, shellbark, and pignut hickory and black cherry occupying a secondary position. In abandoned fields and openings trembling aspen is fairly common. The characteristic shrubs of the uplands are hazel, dogwood (*Cornus racemosa*), wild plum, smooth sumac, and arrowwood.

The deciduous forest of northeastern and northern Wisconsin and the adjoining western part of the upper peninsula of Michigan (Superior Upland Section) is a complex formation, "a mosaic of pine, bog and hardwood or hardwood and hemlock communities." [*] As would be expected for so large an area, the topography is greatly varied, the elevation ranging from 602 to 2,023 feet. There are table lands, high morainic ridges and knolls, kettle holes, terraces, outwash plains, talus slopes, stream valleys, and gorges. The soils are of many kinds. Over much of the area sugar maple is the dominant tree species. Usually associated with it are basswood, yellow birch, red oak, and elm, and frequently hemlock and pine. In a number of places hemlock and pine occur in practically pure evergreen stands or with only a minor admixture of deciduous trees. Bogs of tamarack, spruce, and white cedar are common, especially in the northern part of the area, giving the forest a more northern aspect.

3. *The Prairie Region.* The prairie occupied the parts of the Dakotas included in this work, much of western and southern Minnesota, and adjacent Iowa. In addition there are numerous outposts of the prairie (Relic Prairie) well within the area of the deciduous forest in Minnesota, Iowa, and Wisconsin. The native woody vegetation in the prairie region may be considered under

[*] Braun, *Deciduous Forests.*

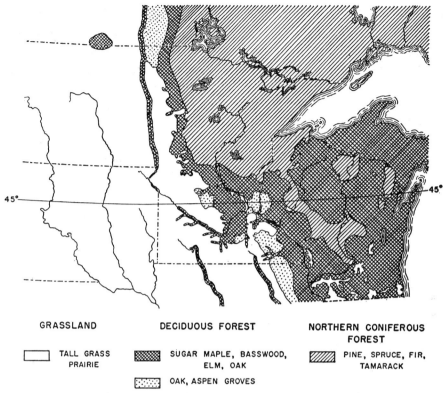

GRASSLAND   DECIDUOUS FOREST   NORTHERN CONIFEROUS FOREST

TALL GRASS PRAIRIE   SUGAR MAPLE, BASSWOOD, ELM, OAK   PINE, SPRUCE, FIR, TAMARACK

OAK, ASPEN GROVES

Vegetation regions of the Upper Midwest. (Adapted from Upham, *Flora of Minnesota*, and Curtis, *Native Vegetation of Wisconsin.*)

three headings: prairie groves, bottomland stream forest, and shrubby plants of the open prairie.

The prairie groves are really detached portions of the general deciduous forests. They are usually found in the vicinity of lakes or where a meandering stream protects a part of the upland. When they are abundant, as in the district about the Twin Cities or in the region between the Big Woods and northern Iowa, the country partakes of the nature of savanna rather than of true prairie, and there is often, but not always, such a savanna-like region between the continuous forests and the open prairie.

The prairie groves partake largely of the character of the adjacent forests, but usually show a greatly diminished number of species both of woody and herbaceous plants. The outer fringe of such groves is usually occupied by bur and Hill's oak, which straggle out into the surrounding prairie often as small trees and even as dwarf shrubs. Generally speaking, the larger the grove, the more species it is likely to display, and even the Big Woods may be considered to be a prairie grove on an unprecedentedly large scale and with a corresponding diversity of flora.

The bottomland woods of the principal streams of the prairie region are not

13

essentially different from those of the deciduous forests, though here again the number of species is apt to be smaller. Cottonwoods and willows are the commonest trees and shrubs along the smaller streams, with the addition of white and rock elm and box elder along the larger streams.

The woody vegetation of the prairie proper consists of certain shrubs scattered through it or characteristically found in clumps. As most of the prairie districts are now under cultivation, these shrubs are found chiefly as fence-row or roadside plants and particularly along railroad right-of-ways. The most characteristic of these are the prairie wild rose, the wolfberry, and lead plant (*Amorpha canescens*).

KEY TO FAMILIES

1. Perianth definitely present, at least in some of the flowers (sometimes very small).
   2. Petals present, i.e., perianth consisting of both calyx and corolla, which are more or less different.*
      3. Petals separate.
         4. Pistils several to many, free.
            5. Stamens numerous, at least more than twice as many as sepals.
               6. Flowers hypogynous.
                  7. Sepals three, smaller than the petals, early deciduous; receptacle elongated ......................MAGNOLIACEAE (p. 138)
                  7. Sepals four, larger than the very small petals, persistent during anthesis; receptacle short..........RANUNCULACEAE (p. 132)
               6. Flowers perigynous ....ROSACEAE (p. 158)
            5. Stamens four or five.......................RUTACEAE (p. 268)
         4. Pistil one, at least as to the ovary, simple or compound.
            8. Ovary superior.
               9. Stamens numerous, at least more than ten.
                  10. Flowers perigynous, hypanthium cup-shaped...............
                      ....*Prunus* in ROSACEAE (p. 246)
                  10. Flowers hypogynous.
                     11. Flowers dioecious; vines.....MENISPERMACEAE (p. 136)
                     11. Flowers perfect.
                        12. Stamens in groups; ovary five-celled; trees.........
                            ....TILIACEAE (p. 308)
                        12. Stamens not grouped; ovary one-celled; low shrubs...
                            ....CISTACEAE (p. 314)
               9. Stamens three to ten.
                  13. Fertile stamens of the same number as the petals (rarely less numerous).
                     14. Stamens standing opposite the petals.
                        15. Stamens and petals six; pistil simple, ovary one-celled..
                            .......................BERBERIDACEAE (p. 134)
                        15. Stamens and petals four or five; pistil compound, ovary two- to four-celled.
                           16. Tendril-bearing vines with palmately lobed or compound leaves. ....VITACEAE (p. 301)
                           16. Erect shrubs or trees with unlobed pinnately veined leaves ....RHAMNACEAE (p. 297)

* In a few forms with inferior ovary, the calyx is greatly reduced and may easily be overlooked (some *Araliaceae*, *Caprifoliaceae*, and *Compositae*).

15

14. Stamens alternating with the petals.
    17. Styles very short, style and stigmas together not over 1.5 mm. long.
        18. Petals four, strap-shaped, 1 cm. or more long; fertile stamens four, staminodes four, opposite the petals . . . . HAMAMELIDACEAE (p. 155)
        18. Petals three to five (mostly five), not strap-shaped, not over 5 mm. long; fertile stamens and staminodes not present in the same flower, staminodes when present in pistillate flowers alternating with the petals.
            19. Leaves simple.
                20. Leaves scale-like or needle-like.
                    21. Styles three, ovary one-celled . . . . TAMARICACEAE (p. 312)
                    21. Style one, stigma much branched, ovary six- to nine-celled . . . . EMPETRACEAE (p. 271)
                20. Leaves not scale-like, ovary three- or four-celled.
                    22. Styles three, lateral . . . . ANACARDIACEAE (p. 272)
                    22. Style or sessile stigma one, terminal.
                        23. Stigma sessile; flowers hypogynous without disk . . . . AQUIFOLIACEAE (p. 278)
                        23. Stigma borne on a short style; stamens inserted on a disk . . . . CELASTRACEAE (p. 281)
            19. Leaves compound.
                24. Leaves with translucent glandular dots; style and stigma one; leaves palmately trifoliolate . . . . RUTACEAE (p. 268)
                24. Leaves not gland-dotted; stigmas and styles three; leaves pinnate, with from three to many leaflets . . . . ANACARDIACEAE (p. 272)
    17. Style and stigma together over 4 mm. long.
        25. Styles and stigmas two, ovary two-celled, flattened and winged at the margin . . ACERACEAE (p. 285)
        25. Style and stigma one, ovary three-celled, not flattened nor winged . . . . . STAPHYLEACEAE (p. 284)
13. Fertile stamens more numerous than the petals.
    26. Leaves compound, flowers usually irregular (nearly regular in two genera of *Leguminosae*).
        27. Pistil simple, ovary one-celled with one parietal placenta; stamens ten except in one genus with strongly perigynous flowers . . . . LEGUMINOSAE (p. 258)
        27. Pistil compound, ovary three-celled; stamens seven or eight; flowers hypogynous . . . . SAPINDACEAE (p. 294)
    26. Leaves simple, flowers regular.
        28. Stamens eight; stigmas two, ovary two-celled, flattened and winged . . . . ACERACEAE (p. 285)

16

28. Stamens ten; ovary three- to five-celled not flattened nor winged.
    29. Ovary three-celled, stigma three-lobed; leaves deciduous .... CLETHRACEAE (p. 332)
    29. Ovary five-celled, stigma disk-shaped, capitate or pointed, leaves evergreen.
        30. Style shorter than the ovary, thick, stigma disk-shaped, orbicular...... PYROLACEAE (p. 332)
        30. Style more or less elongated, slender, stigma capitate or pointed.... ERICACEAE (p. 334)
8. Ovary inferior.
  31. Stamens of the same number as petals and alternate with them.
    32. Petals four, ovary two-celled........ CORNACEAE (p. 323)
    32. Petals five.
        33. Ovary five-celled, hypanthium not extended above top of ovary, sepals minute.......... ARALIACEAE (p. 320)
        33. Ovary one-celled, hypanthium saucer-shaped or tubular, sepals larger than petals..........................
        .... *Ribes* in SAXIFRAGACEAE (p. 144)
  31. Stamens more numerous than the petals.
    34. Leaves opposite or whorled, ovules numerous, minute, fruit a capsule .... SAXIFRAGACEAE (p. 139)
    34. Leaves alternate, ovules mostly two in each cell of the ovary, fruit fleshy........................ ROSACEAE (p. 158)
3. Petals united.
  35. Stamens twice as many as the petals........... ERICACEAE (p. 334)
  35. Stamens equaling the number of petals or fewer.
    36. Ovary superior.
        37. Flowers regular.
            38. Stamens two .... OLEACEAE (p. 352)
            38. Stamens five .... SOLANACEAE (p. 363)
        37. Flowers irregular................. BIGNONIACEAE (p. 364)
    36. Ovary inferior.
        39. Stamens free; ovary two- or three-celled, fruit a berry, capsule, or schizocarp.
            40. Flowers in dense globular heads; stigma long exserted (nearly 1 cm.)................... RUBIACEAE (p. 367)
            40. Flowers not in dense globular heads; stigma slightly if at all exserted................ CAPRIFOLIACEAE (p. 369)
        39. Stamens united by their anthers; ovary one-celled, fruit an achene .... COMPOSITAE (p. 392)
2. Petals absent or not distinguishable from the sepals.
  41. Flowers in catkins or spikes, at least the staminate.
    42. Stamens numerous, at least more than ten.
        43. Flowers dioecious, both kinds in catkins; ovary superior, one-celled................................. SALICACEAE (p. 61)
        43. Flowers monoecious, only staminate in catkins; ovary inferior, two-celled.............................. JUGLANDACEAE (p. 84)
    42. Stamens two to eight.
        44. Staminate flowers in catkin-like spikes, perianth obvious, bracts inconspicuous, a single flower to a bract.
            45. Pistillate flowers in catkin-like spikes, resembling the staminate, ovary superior...................... MORACEAE (p. 129)

17

       45. Pistillate flowers solitary, or in small clusters, ovary inferior...
.... FAGACEAE (p. 110)
     44. Staminate flowers in pendulous catkins, with conspicuous bracts,
       perianth concealed by the bracts, three flowers to a bract........
....BETULACEAE (p. 95)
  41. None of the flowers in catkins or spikes.
    46. Pistils several to many, free.
      47. Stamens numerous; vines...........RANUNCULACEAE (p. 132)
      47. Stamens four or five; prickly shrubs.........RUTACEAE (p. 268)
    46. Pistil strictly one as to the ovary.
      48. Perianth very irregular; ovary inferior.......................
.... ARISTOLOCHIACEAE (p. 131)
      48. Perianth regular or nearly so; ovary superior.
        49. Petals present in the bud, but falling as the flower opens, calyx
          reduced to a collar-like ring............VITACEAE (p. 301)
        49. No perianth parts falling as the flower opens; sepals or calyx
          lobes evident.
          50. Stamens two....................OLEACEAE (p. 352)
          50. Stamens four to eight.
            51. Sepals, four, united into a bell-shaped or funnel-shaped
              perianth; stamens four or eight.
              52. Leaves silvery or scurfy.....................
.... ELAEAGNACEAE (p. 316)
              52. Leaves green, not scurfy...................
.................THYMELAEACEAE (p. 315)
            51. Perianth with five or more sepals or lobes.
              53. Sepals six, entirely free; stamens definitely six,
                stigmas three..............LILIACEAE (p. 60)
              53. Sepals five to eight (if more than five, united into
                a cup-shaped calyx); stamens five to eight; stig-
                mas two.
                54. Ovary two-celled, leaves opposite..........
.... ACERACEAE (p. 285)
                54. Ovary one-celled, leaves alternate..........
....................ULMACEAE (p. 123)
1. Perianth entirely wanting (sometimes represented by very minute scales, glands,
or disks).
  55. True pistils present, ovules enclosed in the ovary, stigmas evident.
    56. Staminate flowers in catkins.
      57. Bracts of the catkin simple, ovary one-celled, superior.
        58. Staminate flower with glands or a cup-shaped disk at the base;
          stigmas short, or expanded, two- to four-lobed, ovules many....
....SALICACEAE (p. 61)
        58. Staminate flower entirely naked at the base; stigmas two, long
          and slender, ovule one..................MYRICACEAE (p. 93)
      57. Bracts of the catkin consisting of several united scales; ovary two-
        celled, mostly inferior.
        59. Scales of the staminate catkin conspicuous, more or less enclosing
          the stamens; pistillate flowers usually in catkins (except *Corylus*)..
....BETULACEAE (p. 95)
        59. Scales of the staminate catkins inconspicuous, the stamens exserted;
          pistillate flowers in groups of one to three....................
.... JUGLANDACEAE (p. 84)
    56. Staminate flowers in heads or panicles.

18

    60. Flowers in globular peduncled heads; stamens expanded at the apex; stigma undivided....................PLATANACEAE (p. 157)

    60. Flowers in panicles; stamens in pairs, pointed; stigma two-lobed....
....OLEACEAE (p. 352)

55. No true pistils present, ovules exposed or borne on the surface of scales, without ovary or stigma.

  61. Ovules and seeds exposed.

    62. Ovules two, at the end of a naked stalk; staminate strobilus elongated; leaves fan-shaped, deciduous..............GINKGOACEAE (p. 33)

    62. Ovules solitary, very short-stalked, surrounded at the base by small scales; staminate strobili nearly spherical; leaves needle-like, evergreen, not aromatic........................TAXACEAE (p. 35)

  61. Ovules borne on the scales of a cone, seeds enclosed between the cone-scales; leaves evergreen (except *Larix*), aromatic.

    63. Foliage leaves linear, needle-like, alternate or in fascicles; ovulate cone with distinct bracts subtending the ovule-bearing scales....
.................................PINACEAE (p. 37)

    63. Foliage leaves often scale-like, opposite or whorled; ovule-bearing scales without obvious bracts..........CUPRESSACEAE (p. 52)

KEY TO GENERA

1. Leaves needle-like or scale-like.

  2. Leaves alternate or fascicled.

    3. Leaves all alternate or scattered.

      4. Trees with fragrant leaves (when crushed).

        5. Leaves four-sided in cross-section, on prominent bases...*Picea* (p. 42)

        5. Leaves flattened.

          6. Leaves bright green on both sides; bract scales projecting from the cones, trifid...........................*Pseudotsuga* (p. 39)

          6. Leaves dark green above, whitish beneath; bract scales included, rounded or mucronate-tipped.

            7. Leaves sessile; cones large (5–10 cm.), erect, scales deciduous...
....*Abies* (p. 38)

            7. Leaves petioled; cones small (1.2–3 cm.), pendent, scales persistent ....*Tsuga* (p. 41)

      4. Shrubs, leaves not fragrant.

        8. Leaves small and scale-like, less than 3 mm. long.

          9. Low shrub, not over 3 dm. high; leaves densely pubescent.......
.... *Hudsonia* (p. 314)

          9. Shrubs 1–3 m. high; leaves nearly or quite glabrous.............
.... *Tamarix* (p. 312)

        8. Leaves more than 3 mm. long, not scale-like.

          10. Leaves strongly involute, blunt............*Empetrum* (p. 271)

          10. Leaves flat, sharp pointed................. *Taxus* (p. 35)

    3. At least some of the leaves fascicled.

      11. Leaves deciduous, many in each fascicle..............*Larix* (p. 46)

      11. Leaves evergreen, two to five in each fascicle..........*Pinus* (p. 48)

  2. Leaves opposite or in whorls of three.

    12. Leaves in whorls of three, needle-like, jointed at the base...............
....*Juniperus* (p. 54)

    12. Leaves opposite, scale-like or needle-like without jointed bases.

      13. Leaves all scale-like, twigs flattened, pairs of leaves of two kinds alternating..*Thuja* (p. 53)

13. Leaves scale-like or needle-like, all alike on the same twig; twigs not flattened ....*Juniperus* (p. 54)

1. Leaves not needle-like or scale-like.
  14. TREES.
    15. Leaves simple.
      16. Leaves not lobed.
        17. Leaves ovate or round, broad.
          18. Leaves entire, mostly very large.
            19. Leaves opposite, mostly cordate at base..*Catalpa* (p. 365)
            19. Leaves alternate, rounded, or narrowed at base.........
                ....*Magnolia* (p. 138)
          18. Leaves serrate to dentate.
            20. Twigs very tough; fruit round, persistent; peduncle winged
                ....*Tilia* (p. 308)
            20. Twigs brittle; fruit disappearing in spring............
                ....*Populus* (p. 61)
        17. Leaves much longer than broad.
          21. Leaves all alternate.
            22. Leaves with three principal ribs from the base.
              23. Sap milky; bark moderately rough or flaky.........
                ....*Morus* (p. 130)
              23. Sap not milky; bark very rough with short corky ridges ....*Celtis* (p. 128)
            22. Veining of leaves strictly pinnate.
              24. Leaves two-ranked or apparently so.
                25. Bark smooth, except when very old, more or less blotched ....*Carpinus* (p. 98)
                25. Bark rough.
                  26. Leaves oblique at base; bark coarsely furrowed ....*Ulmus* (p. 123)
                  26. Leaves not oblique at base; bark finely furrowed....................*Ostrya* (p. 99)
              24. Leaves plainly five-ranked or more.
                27. Young bark with transversely elongated lenticels.
                  28. Bark peeling into papery layers............
                  ....*Betula* (p. 100)
                  28. Bark not peeling into papery layers, inner bark and foliage with smell of bitter almonds ....*Prunus* (p. 246)
                27. Bark without conspicuous transversely elongated lenticels.
                  29. Buds covered by a single scale; fruit dry; seeds with hairs.................*Salix* (p. 69)
                  29. Buds with numerous overlapping scales; fruit fleshy.
                    30. Twigs and branches with definite leafless thorns ....*Crataegus* (p. 235)
                    30. Twigs and branches thornless, or with thorn-like leafy spurs.
                      31. Young twigs tomentose; fruit a pome.
                        32. Leaves mostly subcordate at the base; pomes numerous in panicles, purplish, less than 1 cm. in diameter..*Amelanchier* (p. 224)

32. Leaves narrowed or somewhat rounded at the base, fruit solitary or few in corymbs, bright red or yellowish, more than 12 mm. in diameter . . . . . . *Malus* (p. 219)
31. Young twigs glabrous or puberulent, or scurfy, fruit a drupe.
    33. Foliage white scurfy . . . . *Elaeagnus* (p. 317)
    33. Foliage green . . *Prunus* (p. 246)
21. At least some of the leaves opposite.
    34. Leaves all opposite; lateral veins numerous.
        35. Leaves finely and uniformly serrate . . . . *Viburnum* (p. 373)
        35. Leaves doubly serrate . . . . *Acer* (p. 286)
    34. Some of the leaves alternate; three pairs of lateral veins curving parallel to the margin . . . . *Rhamnus* (p. 297)
16. Leaves lobed.
    36. Leaves fan-shaped, two- or four-lobed, without a midrib . . . . *Ginkgo* (p. 33)
    36. Leaves with an odd number of lobes; midrib prominent.
        37. Leaves palmately veined, at least with three prominent ribs at the base.
            38. Leaves opposite . . . . *Acer* (p. 286)
            38. Leaves alternate.
                39. Mature leaves silvery white beneath . . . . *Populus* (p. 61)
                39. Mature leaves green on both sides.
                    40. Leaves broader than long, lobes entire or with a few coarse teeth . . . . *Platanus* (p. 157)
                    40. Leaves longer than broad, lobes serrate . . . . *Morus* (p. 130)
        37. Veining of leaves strictly pinnate.
            41. Bark white and papery . . . . *Betula* (p. 100)
            41. Bark brown, more or less rough, not papery.
                42. Margin of lobes entire or with a few coarse teeth . . . . *Quercus* (p. 111)
                42. Margin of lobes serrate.
                    43. Twigs and branches with definite leafless thorns . . . . *Crataegus* (p. 235)
                    43. Twigs and branches thornless or with thorn-like leafy spurs . . . . *Malus* (p. 219)
15. Leaves compound.
    44. Leaves palmately compound.
        45. Leaflets three, gland-dotted . . . . *Ptelea* (p. 269)
        45. Leaflets more than three, not gland-dotted . . . . . *Aesculus* (p. 294)
    44. Leaves pinnately compound.
        46. Leaves abruptly pinnate (i.e. without terminal leaflet).
            47. Leaves 4–25 cm. long; leaflets small, elliptical or oblong, rounded at the apex.
                48. Leaves strictly once pinnate; leaflets entire . . . . *Caragana* (p. 265)
                48. Leaves either once or twice pinnate; leaflets crenulate . . . . *Gleditsia* (p. 261)

47. Leaves 3–9 dm. long, twice pinnate; leaflets over 2.5 cm. long, ovate, acuminate...................*Gymnocladus* (p. 259)
46. Leaves odd pinnate (i.e., with a terminal leaflet).
  49. Leaves opposite.
    50. Leaflets entire or finely serrate.......*Fraxinus* (p. 353)
    50. Leaflets lobed or doubly serrate.........*Acer* (p. 286)
  49. Leaves alternate.
    51. Leaflets entire; twigs with paired spines.............
      .... *Robinia* (p. 263)
    51. Leaflets serrate or dissected; twigs not spiny.
      52. Large nut-bearing trees.
        53. Pith in plates, leaflets eleven to twenty-three....
          ....*Juglans* (p. 85)
        53. Pith solid, leaflets five to eleven..............
          ....*Carya* (p. 89)
      52. Small trees with red fleshy fruit.
        54. Sap milky; buds naked.........*Rhus* (p. 273)
        54. Sap not milky; buds scaly......*Sorbus* (p. 215)
14. SHRUBS OR VINES.
  55. Leaves evergreen and leathery.*
    56. Creeping or prostrate shrubs.
      57. Leaves 1–4 cm. wide (mostly over 1.5 cm. wide).
        58. Leaves narrowed to the base, margin serrate; stem puberulent; foliage with wintergreen flavor.........*Gaultheria* (p. 340)
        58. Leaves cordate at the base, margin entire; stem bristly; without evergreen flavor...................*Epigaea* (p. 337)
      57. Leaves 1–10 mm. wide.
        59. Leaves narrowly linear, margin folded back so as to cover the lower surface......................*Empetrum* (p. 271)
        59. Leaves linear-lanceolate to broadly ovate, lower surface exposed.
          60. Stems bristly; leaves broadly ovate, less than 1 cm. long .... *Chiogenes* (p. 343)
          60. Stems not bristly; leaves much longer than wide, mostly more than 1 cm. long.
            61. Leaves glaucous beneath, oblong to lanceolate, mostly less than 5 mm. wide.........*Vaccinium* (p. 344)
            61. Leaves green beneath, obovate to elliptic, mostly over 5 mm. wide.
              62. Lower surface of leaves dotted with dark resinous glands, margin strongly revolute; plant glabrous throughout .... *Vaccinium* (p. 344)
              62. Lower surface of leaves without conspicuous resinous glands, margin of young leaves scarcely revolute; plant pubescent when young......... .... *Arctostaphylos* (p. 341)
    56. Erect shrubs.
      63. Leaves with strongly revolute margins, woolly or whitened beneath.
        64. Leaves woolly beneath..................*Ledum* (p. 335)
        64. Leaves whitened beneath, not woolly.
          65. Leaves opposite..................*Kalmia* (p. 337)
          65. Leaves alternate...............*Andromeda* (p. 339)

* In summer the evergreen character can be determined by the presence of leaves of the previous season's growth.

63. Leaf margin crenulate or serrate, scarcely revolute, leaves green or scurfy beneath.
  66. Shrubs 2–5 dm. high, leaves scurfy beneath, margin crenulate
    . . . . *Chamaedaphne* (p. 338)
  66. Scarcely woody plants, 5–20 cm. high from creeping rhizomes.
    67. Leaves finely serrate, broadly obovate or elliptic, aromatic
    . . . . *Gaultheria* (p. 340)
    67. Leaves coarsely serrate, narrowly obovate or oblanceolate,
    not aromatic. . . . .*Chimaphila* (p. 333)
55. Leaves deciduous.
  68. Leaves, or at least most of them, simple.°
    69. At least some of the leaves opposite or in whorls.
      70. Some alternate leaves present; three pairs of lateral veins curving parallel to the margin. . . . .*Rhamnus* (p.297)
      70. All the leaves opposite or whorled; lateral veins spreading.
        71. Leaf margin entire (rarely some leaves with coarse entire-margined crenations or lobes).
          72. Leaves silvery scurfy. . . . .*Shepherdia* (p. 319)
          72. Leaves green.
            73. Stipules present; leaves often whorled. . . . .
            . . . . *Cephalanthus* (p. 368)
            73. Stipules absent; leaves in pairs.
              74. Leaf scars running together to form a ring.
                75. Stems with a hollow pith.
                  76. Low shrubs 3–10 dm. high. . . . . . .
                  . . . . *Symphoricarpos* (p. 378)
                  76. Tall shrubs over 1 m. high, or twining vines. . . . . . *Lonicera* (p. 381)
                75. Stems with a solid pith.
                  77. Flowers and fruits axillary, in pairs or apparently solitary; leaves very short petioled. . *Lonicera* (p. 381)
                  77. Flowers and fruits in terminal many-flowered clusters; leaves mostly long-petioled . . . .*Cornus* (p. 323)
              74. Leaf scars distinct.
                78. Leaf scars elevated, nearly circular; flower and fruit clusters on short lateral branches . . . . . . *Chionanthus* (p. 356)
                78. Leaf scars not prominently elevated, crescent-shaped to semicircular; flower and fruit clusters at the end of the main shoot . . . .*Syringa* (p. 357)
        71. Leaf margin serrate, dentate, or sharply lobed.
          79. Leaves not lobed.
            80. Bases of petioles meeting, leaf scars usually forming a ring.
              81. Winter buds very small, concealed in the bases of the petioles. . . . .
              . . . . *Philadelphus* (p. 139)
              81. Winter buds obvious while the leaves are still present.

° In a very few species of *Syringa* and *Forsythia* some compound leaves occur in addition to the simple leaves.

82. Leaves sharply doubly serrate with bristle-tipped teeth.................
..............*Rhodotypos* (p. 190)
82. Leaves simply serrate or dentate.
  83. Buds naked or with a single pair of visible bud scales; fruit fleshy.....
  ....*Viburnum* (p. 373)
  83. Buds with several overlapping scales; fruit a dry capsule.
    84. Leaves finely serrate or crenate-serrate; petioles less than 1 cm. long.
      85. Leaves finely serrate; native shrub.............
      ....*Diervilla* (p. 389)
      85. Leaves crenate-serrate; cultivated..*Weigela* (p. 391)
    84. Leaves coarsely serrate; petioles more than 1 cm. long........
    ....*Hydrangea* (p. 142)
80. Bases of petioles manifestly separate, leaf scars not forming a ring.
  86. Pith hollow or chambered, serration of leaves coarse and irregular....*Forsythia* (p. 362)
  86. Pith solid, leaves finely crenate-serrulate...
  ....*Euonymus* (p. 283)
79. Leaves lobed.
  87. Petioles usually with stipules and glands.......
  .... *Viburnum* (p. 373)
  87. Petioles without stipules or glands...........
  ....*Acer* (p. 286)
69. Leaves all alternate or fascicled.
  88. Vines.
    89. Leaves not lobed.
      90. Leaves serrate; stem twining....*Celastrus* (p. 283)
      90. Leaves entire.
        91. Stems twining, unarmed..*Aristolochia* (p. 132)
        91. Stems not twining, armed with prickles or thorns.
          92. Petioles tendril-bearing, stem armed with epidermal prickles........*Smilax* (p. 60)
          92. Petioles not tendril-bearing, stem armed with axillary thorns.........*Lycium* (p. 363)
    89. Leaves palmately lobed.
      93. Margin of lobes entire; stem twining.............
      .... *Menispermum* (p. 137)
      93. Margin of lobes toothed; stem not twining, supported by tendrils.
        94. Tendrils coiling, without disks...*Vitis* (p. 302)
        94. Tendrils attached by disks.................
        ....*Parthenocissus* (p. 302)
  88. Upright shrubs.
    95. Leaves not lobed, pinnatifid, nor dissected.
    96. Leaves fascicled on the older branches.

97. Fascicles of leaves subtended by 1 or more spines or thorns.
    98. Leaves thin, without stipules* . . . .
    . . . . *Berberis* (p. 135)
    98. Leaves thick, those of the young growth with conspicuous rounded stipules . . . .
    . . . . *Chaenomeles* (p. 213)
97. Fascicles not spiny . . . . . *Nemopanthus* (p. 280)
96. Leaves not truly fascicled (sometimes rather crowded on slow-growing shoots).
    99. Buds with a single scale . . . . *Salix* (p. 69)
    99. Buds with several overlapping scales.
        100. Leaves entire.
            101. Leaves silvery scurfy . . . .
            . . . . *Elaeagnus* (p. 317)
            101. Leaves green.
                102. Leaves small (rarely exceeding 2.5 × 5 cm.).
                    103. Leaves thick and leathery, petioles about 5 mm. long . . . . *Cotoneaster* (p. 245)
                    103. Leaves thin, petioles 2 mm. long or less.
                        104. Leaves resinous beneath, short petioled *Gaylussacia* (p. 343)
                        104. Leaves not resinous beneath, almost sessile . . . . *Vaccinium* (p. 344)
                102. Fully developed leaves larger (mostly exceeding 3 × 5 cm.).
                    105. Petioles 1–3 cm. long; bark not especially tough.
                      106. Petioles mostly 2 cm. long; leaves crowded towards the ends of the branches . . . . *Cornus* (p. 323)
                      106. Petioles 1–1.5 cm. long; leaves not crowded.
                        107. Leaves pointed at the apex . . . . *Rhamnus* (p. 297)
                        107. Leaves rounded at the apex . . . . *Cotinus* (p. 278)
                  105. Petioles less than 1 cm.

* *Caragana pygmaea* is likely to be sought here, as the leaflets of the compound fascicled leaves resemble fascicles of simple leaves.

long, bark very tough and
fibrous....*Dirca* (p. 315)

100. Leaves serrate, dentate, or crenate.
    108. Leaves coarsely crenate, crenate-dentate or dentate, the teeth or scallops at least 1 cm. broad.
        109. Leaves cordate, very unequal at the base ....
        ....*Hamamelis* (p. 156)
        109. Leaves narrowed to the equal base ....*Quercus* (p. 111)
    108. Leaves more finely serrate, dentate, or crenate.
        110. Leaves at least twice as long as broad.
            111. Leaves toothed above the middle only, the basal half entire.
                112. Leaves with a few teeth at the rounded apex, otherwise entire, fragrant......
                .... *Myrica* (p. 93)
                112. Leaves serrate or crenate-serrate for at least one-third of their length, apex pointed; not fragrant.
                    113. Serrations sharp, conspicuous, leaves mostly over 2 cm. wide.....
                    ....*Clethra* (p. 332)
                    113. Serrations appressed, somewhat crenate, leaves mostly under 1.5 cm. wide. ..... *Prunus* (p. 246)
            111. Leaves serrate nearly or quite to the base.
                114. Petioles 5 mm. long or less; leaves mostly under 1.5 cm. wide.
                    115. Petioles about 1 mm. long; leaves finely crenate-serru-

late ....
... *Vaccinium*
(p. 344)

115. Petioles 2–5
mm. long;
leaves mostly
coarsely serrate
(in one species
finely but
sharply serrate)
...... *Spiraea*
(p. 193)

114. Petioles over 5 mm.
long, leaves mostly
over 2 cm. wide.

116. Leaf scars
forming trans-
verse lines;
buds acute;
flowers and
fruit in terminal
clusters ......
.... *Aronia*
(p. 213)

116. Leaf scars
almost round;
buds blunt;
flowers and
fruit axillary.

117. Principal
veins
breaking
up into a
network
before
reaching
the mar-
gin; fruit
red .....
.... *Ilex*
(p. 279)

117. Principal
veins
curving
upward
and run-
ning to
the mar-
gin; fruit
black ...
Rhamnus
(p. 297)

110. Leaves less than twice as long as
broad.

118. Pith triangular or flattened in cross section.
    119. Leaves rhombic or obovate, narrowed to the base . . . . .Betula (p. 100)
    119. Leaves ovate or elliptical, rounded or cordate at the base. . . . . .Alnus (p. 108)
118. Pith round in cross section.
    120. Petioles with a few large glands; foliage and bark with the odor of bitter almonds . . . . .Prunus (p. 246)
    120. Petioles without conspicuous glands; foliage and bark without characteristic odor.
        121. Thorny shrubs . . . . Crataegus (p. 235)
        121. Unarmed shrubs.
            122. Leaves under 5 cm. in width, acute or short acuminate, finely serrate . . . . Amelanchier (p. 224)
            122. Leaves mostly over 5 cm. in width, long acuminate, coarsely doubly serrate . . . .Corylus (p. 95)

95. Leaves lobed, pinnatifid, or dissected.
    123. Leaves pinnatifid or dissected, aromatic.
        124. Leaves linear, once pinnatifid. . . . . .Comptonia (p. 94)

     124. Leaves elliptical in outline, completely dissected into linear lobes...*Artemisia* (p. 393)

   123. Leaves lobed, not aromatic.

     125. Tall, thorny shrubs......*Crataegus* (p. 235)

     125. Shrubs of moderate height, unarmed or prickly.

      126. Stipules or stipular scars present.

       127. Leaves ovate, 3–6 cm. long, petioles stellate pubescent.................... *Physocarpus* (p. 190)

       127. Leaves almost orbicular in outline, 6–15 cm. long, petioles glandular hispid .... *Rubus* (p. 161)

      126. Stipules wanting.

       128. Leaves about twice as long as wide, obscurely lobed, entirely glabrous ....*Spiraea* (p. 193)

       128. Leaves but little longer than wide, distinctly lobed, more or less pubescent or glandular..*Ribes* (p. 144)

68. Leaves all compound.*

  129. Unarmed climbing vines.

    130. Leaves opposite, the petioles twisting about the support..*Clematis* (p. 133)

    130. Leaves alternate.

     131. Vines with tendrils; leaves palmate, mostly with five leaflets ....*Parthenocissus* (p. 304)

     131. Tendrils wanting; leaflets three, the middle one long-stalked ....*Rhus* (p. 273)

  129. Erect or trailing shrubs (the latter armed with prickles).

    132. Leaves opposite.

     133. Leaflets three................*Staphylea* (p. 284)

     133. Leaflets five to nine..........*Sambucus* (p. 369)

    132'. Leaves alternate.

     134. Margin of leaflets entire or slightly crenulate.

      135. Leaves with an even number of leaflets (abruptly pinnate or digitate).......*Caragana* (p. 265)

      135. Leaves with an odd number of leaflets.

       136. Leaflets three.........*Ptelea* (p. 269)

       136. Leaflets five or more, odd pinnate.

        137. Stems spiny or bristly.

         138. Stems with paired spines, not bristly; leaves aromatic.............*Xanthoxylum* (p. 268)

         138. Stems bristly, sometimes also spiny; leaves not aromatic...............*Robinia* (p. 263)

        137. Stems neither spiny nor bristly.

         139. Leaflets over 5 cm. long, glabrous ....*Rhus* (p. 273)

         139. Leaflets under 5 cm. long, pubescent.

* Occasionally simple, deeply lobed leaves occur on the flowering shoots of some species of *Rubus*.

140. Leaflets five to seven....
......*Potentilla* (p. 159)
140. Leaflets eleven to forty-
nine..*Amorpha* (p. 261)
134. Margin of leaflets toothed, lobed, or dissected.
141. Stems spiny, prickly, or bristly.
142. Leaves two to three times compound.....
...................*Aralia* (p. 321)
142. Leaves once compound.
143. Stipules present.
144. Stipules adherent to the petiole,
leaflets mostly five to eleven, pinnate ....*Rosa* (p. 198)
144. Stipules free from the petiole,
leaflets three to five, often palmate ....*Rubus* (p. 161)
143. Stipules wanting, leaflets five, palmate
..........*Acanthopanax* (p. 322)
141. Stem not spiny, prickly, or bristly.
145. Leaflets three.......... *Rhus* (p. 273)
145. Leaflets five to many.
146. Sap milky.........*Rhus* (p. 273)
146. Sap not milky....*Sorbaria* (p. 197)

TREES AND SHRUBS *belong to the major division of the vegetable kingdom called the* Spermatophyta, *which is subdivided according to whether these seed-bearing plants do* (Angiospermae) *or do not* (Gymnospermae) *have closed pistils.*

SUBDIVISION I. GYMNOSPERMAE

Seed-bearing plants without closed pistils, ovules and seeds exposed, or protected by the separate but overlapping scales on which they are borne; pollen grains in nearly all cases entering the micropyle of the ovule and germinating within the developing seed; the body of the seed formed by the female gametophyte, developed previous to the fertilization of the egg and the development of the embryo.

Class I. Ginkgoales*

Stem much branched, woody, the wood without true vessels; leaves simple, fan-shaped, dichotomously veined; seeds wholly naked, fleshy; fertilization by means of free swimming sperms, which are discharged from the pollen tube within the developing seed; embryo with two cotyledons. A class represented among living plants by only the following family.

GINKGO FAMILY, Ginkgoaceae

A family consisting of one genus. Flowers dioecious, the staminate cone-like, consisting of an axis bearing numerous stamens; stamens stalked, furnished with two pendent pollen sacs; pistillate flowers consisting of a naked stalk bearing at its summit a pair of ovules, each surrounded at its base with a collar-like growth; seeds drupe-like, the integument consisting of an outer fleshy coat, a firm stony coat, and a thin inner papery layer.

Ginkgo L., Mant. ed. 2, 313, 1771

This is the only genus of the family; it contains the following species. (*Ginkgo*, the Chinese name of the tree.)

* In the general classification of gymnosperms we follow Pilger in Engler and Prantl, *Die Natürlichen Pflanzenfamilien*, ed. 2, vol. 13. Pilger divides the gymnosperms into seven classes. Of these, three are extinct and are represented only by paleozoic and mesozoic fossils. Besides the classes treated in the body of the text, Pilger recognizes two classes of living gymnosperms, the *Cycadales* and the *Gnetales*. No representatives of either of these classes are found in the Upper Midwest except as hothouse plants.

MAIDENHAIR TREE, GINKGO, *Ginkgo biloba*, L., Mant. ed. 2, 313, 1771 [*Salisburia adiantifolia* Smith 1797]

A deciduous tree reaching in old age a height of 20 m.; trunk straight, extending to the top of the tree; branches long, ascending, or on some trees irregularly spreading, twigs not numerous, covered with many short spurs, or dwarf twigs; bark at first smooth, the epidermis separating as a shredded papery layer, later roughened and seamed longitudinally, gray; leaves borne scattered on the long twigs and in dense clusters on the spur shoots, petioled, glabrous, fan-shaped, usually two-lobed, 3–5 cm. long, 4–7 cm. wide, veins forking repeatedly and running free to the margin; petioles 3–5 cm. long; flowers as described under the family; seeds plum-like, scarlet, ill-smelling, about 2 cm. in diameter. (*Bíloba*, two-lobed, referring to the leaves.)

The Ginkgo tree is the sole survivor of a very ancient and interesting group,

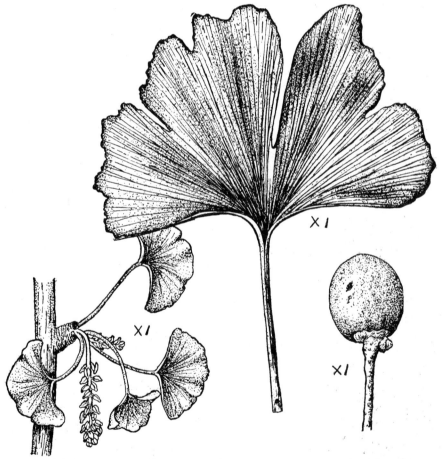

Ginkgo biloba, staminate flowers at the left and mature seed at the right

which in former geological periods occurred abundantly in many parts of the world. It has survived only in China and Japan, and it is doubtful whether even in those countries any truly wild specimens occur.

In our region it is planted to some extent in the upper Mississippi Valley as far north as the forty-fifth parallel, where it is perfectly hardy but rather slow-growing. It is a handsome tree, with very ornamental foliage. The staminate tree is preferable, as the seeds of the pistillate tree have a very offensive odor.

Class II. *Coniferae*

Stem much branched, woody, the wood without true vessels, often with resin canals; leaves mostly needle-like or scale-like and evergreen; seeds either naked or concealed between the scales of a definite strobilus, hard shelled or sometimes fleshy; fertilization by means of a pollen tube, without the formation of swimming sperms; embryo with from two to many cotyledons. A large class, containing the vast majority of living gymnosperms.

YEW FAMILY, TAXACEAE

Trees or shrubs with alternate small evergreen linear leaves (not resinous-aromatic in the genus *Taxus*); flowers dioecious, the staminate consisting of a short axis bearing peltate stamens, each with two to six pollen sacs or sporangia, the pistillate of a single naked ovule borne at the end of a short, scaly pedicel; seed exposed at maturity, furnished with a fleshy outer coat.

The family, as here limited, consists of three genera and twelve species, widely distributed throughout the warmer parts of the North Temperate Zone, with one species in New Caledonia. Only the following genus occurs in the Upper Midwest.

Yew
Taxus L., Sp. Pl. 1040, 1753

Nonresinous trees or shrubs; leaves evergreen, flattened, linear, bitter, borne alternately in a close spiral, but twisted so as to appear two-ranked; flowers in the axils of the leaves of the current year's growth, dioecious or monoecious; staminate flowers solitary, sessile, surrounded at the base by perianth-like bud scales from the midst of which projects a short axis bearing at the summit from four to twelve peltate stamens, each with from four to six pollen sacs; pistillate flowers usually solitary, rarely in pairs, borne on a short peduncle covered with minute, spirally arranged scales, the flower (or flowers) borne in the uppermost axil (or axils), consisting of a short axis bearing three pairs of opposite scales and a terminal, erect, naked ovule; the scales of the flower (but not those of the peduncle) considerably enlarged in fruit; the seed as it ripens becoming surrounded by a cup-like aril, which remains free from the seed, and becomes red and fleshy when ripe.

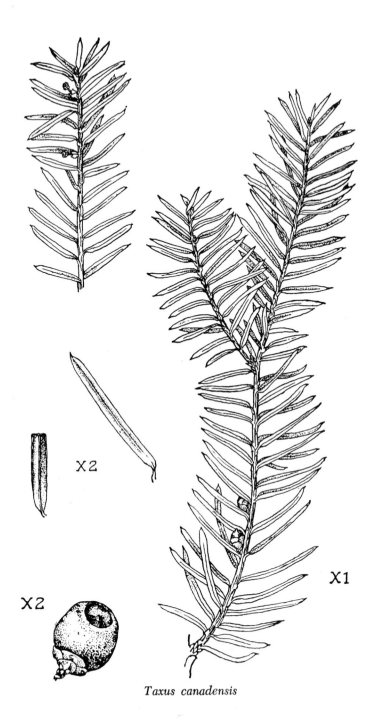

X2

X2

X1

Taxus canadensis

36

Six closely allied species are included in this genus, natives of the North Temperate Zone, sometimes treated as subspecies of a single species. (Latin *táxus*, the yew tree, probably from Greek *toxos*, a bow, referring to the immemorial use of the wood for making bows.)

KEY TO SPECIES OF TAXUS

1. Native straggling shrub; leaves 1–2 mm. wide, yellowish-green...............
....*T. canadensis* (p. 37)
1. Cultivated upright shrub or tree; leaves 2–3 mm. wide, dull green with yellow stripes beneath.......................................*T. cuspidata* (p. 37)

AMERICAN YEW, *Taxus canadensis* Marsh., Arb. Am. 151, 1785 [*T. baccata* var. *minor* Michx. 1796]

A low, straggling shrub about 1 m. high; winter buds scaly; spray very flat; leaves linear, short-petioled, 10–25 mm. long, yellow-green, apex acute, mucronate, margin involute; flowers monoecious or dioecious, borne in the axils of the leaves of the new growth; seed erect about 4 mm. long, somewhat flattened, ellipsoidal with a short, beak-like micropyle, dark brown, finely pitted, the ripe aril coral red, translucent, broader than long. Flowers in May; seeds ripe early in August of second summer. (*Canadénsis*, Canadian.)

The American yew is distributed from Newfoundland to Manitoba, south to Virginia and Iowa. It is common in the region of the coniferous forests and extends somewhat beyond their limits in southeastern Minnesota and adjoining Wisconsin and Iowa.

Alone of our conifers, the foliage of the yew is without any resinous odor or taste. It sometimes is eaten by cattle, and may cause serious poisoning.

JAPANESE YEW, *Taxus cuspidata* Sieb. & Zucc., Flor. Jap. Fam. Nat. 2:108, 1846

In its native habitat, a tree 15 m. high; in cultivation in the Upper Midwest, usually an upright, compact shrub; leaves linear, 2–3 mm. wide, abruptly mucronate, dull green above, marked with two broad yellow bands beneath, or in some forms golden-yellow throughout; spray usually forming a V-shaped trough; seed about 6 mm. long, compressed, slightly angled. (*Cuspidáta*, sharp-pointed, referring to the mucronate leaves.)

This yew is a native of Japan, Korea, and Manchuria. It is occasionally planted as an ornamental evergreen, especially in the vicinity of Minneapolis and St. Paul.

PINE FAMILY, Pinaceae

Trees or rarely shrubs; leaves and cone scales primarily alternate, but sometimes with the foliage leaves clustered in dense fascicles in the axils of scale leaves or at the end of short shoots, foliage leaves linear, needle-like or flattened; flowers monoecious, cone-like, the staminate consisting of an axis that bears numerous, usually scale-like stamens, each with two pollen sacs or sporangia, the pistillate with two distinct kinds of scales, the bracts or sterile scales, and the seed-bearing scales, one of which is borne in the axil of each bract, each seed-bearing scale bearing two inverted seeds on its upper side.

The pine is a very ancient family consisting of about nine genera and two hundred species, natives of almost the entire Northern Hemisphere. It is most abundant in the warm temperate regions, although several species reach the arctic limits of tree growth, and a comparatively small number of species form the great evergreen forests of the cool temperate regions.

KEY TO GENERA OF PINACEAE

1. Foliage leaves all scattered, alternate.
  2. Leaves flat, linear, more or less twisted into two ranks.
    3. Winter buds small, round, resinous; cones upright, with deciduous scales
    . . . . *Abies* (p. 38)
    3. Winter buds scaly, not resinous; cones pendent, with persistent scales.
      4. Leaves about 2 cm. long, their scars scarcely raised; bracts of the cone long, conspicuous. . . . .*Pseudotsuga* (p. 39)
      4. Leaves about 1 cm. long, their scars raised on woody projections (sterigmata); bracts of the cone short, concealed between the seed-bearing scales. . . . .*Tsuga* (p. 41)
  2. Leaves four-sided in section, not at all two-ranked, theirs scars raised on woody projections (sterigmata) . . . .*Picea* (p. 42)
1. Foliage leaves or some of them in fascicles.
  5. Leaves deciduous, some scattered, others in large fascicles. . . . .*Larix* (p. 46)
  5. Leaves evergreen, in fascicles of two to five. . . . .*Pinus* (p. 48)

Fir

Abies Mill., Gard. Dict. abr. ed. 4, 1754

Evergreen trees, sometimes shrubby at high altitudes, trunk straight, running to the top of the tree, branches irregular or whorled, horizontal; leaves needle-like but usually flat and blunt, sessile, scattered, and borne in many rows, but often twisted into an apparently two-ranked arrangement, remaining on the twigs for many years, and when they fall, leaving the bark nearly smooth with round scars; buds usually round and covered with resin; flowers in spring, monoecious, the staminate in the axils of last year's leaves, very small, consisting of an axis bare at the base and covered above with the numerous stamens, stamens with a spur- or knob-like tip, pollen sacs opening transversely, pollen winged as in pine; pistillate cones erect, on the sides of the uppermost branches, the young cone with long and conspicuous bracts, which may later be hidden by the developing seed-bearing scales, cones ripening in the autumn of the first year, at maturity falling to pieces leaving their bare axes standing upon the branches; seeds winged, resinous. (Latin *ábies*, fir tree.)

Firs are trees of the cooler parts of the North Temperate Zone and of the adjacent mountainous parts of the tropics. There are about forty species, over one-half of which occur in the lands bordering the north Pacific. One species occurs in eastern North America, eight in western North America.

BALSAM FIR, *Abies balsamea* (L.) Mill., Gard. Dict. ed. 8, no. 3, 1768

A tree 15–20 m. high with a slender, straight trunk 3–5 dm. in diameter, and short, spreading branches forming a spire-like crown; bark smooth, grayish, covered with numerous blisters containing resin; leaves resinous, very fragrant, flat, blunt, 1–3 cm. long, except on the uppermost branches twisted into an apparently two-ranked arrangement; buds small, globular, covered with a varnish-like resin; young pistillate cones purple, mature cones bluish green, cylindrical, 6–10 cm. long, the bracts usually concealed by the longer seed-bearing scales, ripening in autumn, when the scales fall away leaving the bare axes standing upon the branches. Flowers in April or May; cones ripe in the autumn of the same year. (*Balsámea*, referring to the abundance of balsam in the bark.)

Balsam fir is distributed from Labrador and Newfoundland to Minnesota and Manitoba, south to Virginia and Iowa. It is a common tree of the evergreen forests, not occurring beyond their limits except in a few scattered localities of southeastern Minnesota and northeastern Iowa. In cultivation it is a very beautiful tree for a few years, but soon becomes thin and straggling.

The wood is light brown, soft, and weak, and weighs 24 lbs. It is seldom used except for paper pulp. The oleoresin from the blisters in the bark is "Canada Balsam," much used in optical instruments, microscopic slides, etc., as a transparent cement for glass. The fragrant dry twigs are often used to stuff sofa pillows and similar articles.

WHITE FIR, *Abies concolor* (Gord.) Hoopes, Book Evergr. 220, 1868

A west American tree with stout bluish-green leaves 50–75 mm. long and 2 mm. wide; cones 7–12 cm. long, narrowed at the ends, greenish or purplish before maturity. (*Cóncolor*, of one color.)

The white fir is sometimes planted, but at least in the upper Mississippi Valley it is not hardy; the upper branches are often killed back in severe winters, so that it remains in the form of a low bush. It is sometimes used for clipped hedges.

Douglas Fir
Pseudotsuga Carr., Trait. Conif. ed. 2, 256, 1867

Evergreen trees, trunk straight, running to the top of the tree, branches horizontal, irregularly whorled; leaves needle-like but flat and blunt, soft, sessile or slightly stalked, scattered, borne in many rows, remaining on the tree for

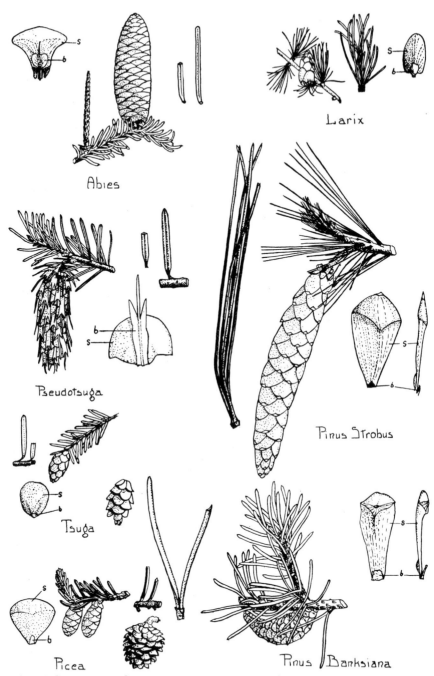

Abies balsamea, Pseudotsuga taxifolia, Tsuga canadensis, Picea mariana, Larix laricina, Pinus Strobus, and *Pinus Banksiana*. (Twigs with cones × 1/2, leaves and cone scales natural size; *b*, bract; *s*, seed-bearing scale.)

40

several years, and when they fall, leaving the bark almost smooth or with slightly raised oval scars; buds scaly, not resinous; flowers in spring, monoecious, the staminate borne in the axils of last year's leaves, consisting of an axis, bare at the base and covered above with the numerous stamens; stamens with a spur-like tip, pollen sacs opening obliquely, pollen grains not winged; pistillate cones terminal or axillary, pendent at maturity, the bracts long, conspicuous, cleft at the summit into three lobes, cones ripening in the autumn of the first year, opening to discharge the seeds and finally falling entire from the tree; seed winged, not resinous. (*Pseudotsúga*, false hemlock, from Gr. *pseudes*, false, Japanese, *tsuga*, hemlock.)

This is a genus of only three species, one a native of southern California, one a native of Japan, and the third widely distributed throughout western North America.

DOUGLAS FIR, *Pseudotsuga taxifolia* (Lamb.) Brit., Trans. N.Y. Acad. Sci. 8:74, 1889 [*P. mucronata* (Raf.) Sudworth 1895; *P. Douglasii* (Lindl.) Carr. 1867]

In the Upper Midwest seldom exceeding 12 m. in height (on the Pacific Coast sometimes 80 m. high), trunk straight, running to the crown of the tree, branches horizontal, bark in young trees grayish, smooth, often with a few resin blisters resembling those of the balsam fir, in older trees becoming rough and brown and in old trees in their native habitat very thick, deeply fissured, and falling off in large scales; buds brown, sharp pointed, not resinous, covered with numerous papery scales; leaves fragrant, flat, blunt, and soft, arranged all about the twigs, or twisted into an apparently two-ranked arrangement; cones oval-cylindrical, pendulous, when ripe woody, 4–8 cm. long. (*Taxifólia*, yew-leaved.)

Douglas fir is native to the forests of the Rocky Mountains and the Pacific Coast region from British Columbia south to Texas, Mexico, and central California. Only trees from the Rocky Mountain region are hardy in our area, where Douglas fir is often planted as an ornamental tree. It is very hardy, but has a tendency to grow thin in foliage. It has proved a successful plant for evergreen hedges, stands clipping well, and will endure dry weather better than most conifers.

In its natural habitat, particularly in the vicinity of the Pacific Coast, it is one of the finest of North American trees, reaching a height of over 200 ft., and a trunk diameter of 15 ft. It is the most valuable timber tree of British Columbia, Washington, and Oregon.

Hemlock
Tsuga Carr., Trait. Conif. 185, 1855

Evergreen trees, trunk straight, reaching to the top of the tree, branches irregular, spreading or often drooping, twigs slender; leaves linear, flat, and blunt, short-petioled, scattered, and borne in many rows but usually twisted

41

into an apparently two-ranked arrangement, remaining on the twigs for two or three years but rapidly falling if the twig is dried; when they fall, leaving the twigs roughened by woody, raised projections (sterigmata), on top of which are the leaf scars; buds scaly, not resinous; flowers in spring, monoecious, the staminate in the axils of last year's leaves, very small, with a bare stalk and an almost globular bunch of stamens, stamens with a spur- or knob-like tip, pollen sacs opening transversely, pollen grains not winged; pistillate cones terminal, drooping, with inconspicuous bracts; cones ripening the first autumn, opening at maturity and discharging the seeds after which the whole cone falls from the trees; seeds winged, slightly resinous. (*Tsúga*, the Japanese name for hemlock.)

Hemlocks are trees of North America and eastern Asia. The genus has seven species; one of which occurs in the eastern United States, and two in northwestern North America. One of the last departs in several respects from the usual characters of the genus, and is more properly segregated into a distinct genus. Only the following species occurs in the Upper Midwest.

HEMLOCK, *Tsuga canadensis* (L.) Carr., Trait. Conif. 189, 1855

A tall tree over 15 m. in height; trunk straight, upright, extending to the summit, branches spreading, nearly horizontal, the leading shoot in young trees usually more or less drooping; twigs slender, leaves flat, 8–13 mm. long, short-petioled, scattered, but twisted so as to appear two-ranked, dark green above, white beneath; pistillate cones small, ovoid, 1.5–2.5 cm. long. (*Canadénsis*, Canadian.)

This hemlock grows in coniferous forests, usually in acid soil containing considerable organic matter, from Nova Scotia to Delaware and southward along the Alleghanies, westward through northern Michigan and Wisconsin, in the latter of which states it is abundant. It barely reaches Minnesota, occurring native only in several scattered sites, mostly as small colonies of a few trees each, in Chisago, Pine, Mille Lacs, Carlton, St. Louis, and Itasca counties. As late as 1918 a grove of nearly forty acres of hemlock, mixed with other forest trees, remained near the village of Paupores in southwestern St. Louis County, but the disastrous fire of that year completely destroyed it.

The hemlock is occasionally planted as an ornamental tree or as an evergreen hedge. Neither the dry autumns nor the prevailing limestone soils of Minnesota suit the hemlock, and it is apt to die out here after a few years. In upper Michigan and Wisconsin it is a valuable timber tree much used for coarse lumber, piles, etc. The wood is light reddish brown, soft, coarse, brittle, and splintering; its weight is 26 lbs. The bark is extensively used in tanning leather.

Spruce
Picea Link, Abh. Akad. Wis. Berlin 1827:179, 1827–30

Trees with straight trunks running to the top of the crown, and abundant, horizontal, drooping or slightly ascending branches; smaller twigs clothed with closely set, evergreen, needle-like leaves arranged in a close spiral; leaves usually four-sided, sharp-pointed, spreading in all directions from the twig, borne upon small woody projections (sterigmata), which render the twigs rough when the leaves fall (spruce and hemlock leaves fall quickly when a twig is dried, fir and Douglas fir leaves are apt to remain attached to the dried twig); buds scaly, not resinous; flowers monoecious, the staminate solitary, lateral, consisting of an axis bearing the numerous overlapping, scale-like stamens, each of which bears two pollen sacs which open longitudinally, pollen grains winged as in pine; pistillate cones usually borne laterally on the twigs, sessile, or with very short peduncles, drooping, ripening the same year, dry and woody or membranous when ripe; the seed-bearing scales entirely concealing the small bracts; seeds winged, not resinous, discharged from the ripe cones, which often remain on the tree for some time after the fall of the seeds and finally fall off entire. (Latin *picea*, spruce or fir tree, from *pix*, pitch.)

This is a genus of about fourteen species of the far northern and the mountainous parts of the Northern Hemisphere. It includes the most boreal conifers in the world. Besides the following there are, in North America, one eastern and two western species.

KEY TO SPECIES OF PICEA

1. Twigs spreading horizontally or ascending; cones less than 8 cm. long.
    2. Leaves 5–20 mm. long, sterigmata less than 1 mm. long; cone scales rounded at the apex, not conspicuously thin-margined.
        3. Leaves dark green, bluntly pointed, pleasantly aromatic when bruised; twigs minutely pubescent. . . . . *P. mariana* (p. 43)
        3. Leaves pale bluish green, sharply pointed, very unpleasant smelling when bruised; twigs glabrous. . . . . *P. glauca* (p. 44)
    2. Leaves 20–30 mm. long, sterigmata 1–2 mm. long; cone scales narrowed or truncate at the apex, conspicuously thin-margined.
        4. Leaves stiff, twigs glabrous. . . . . *P. pungens* (p. 45)
        4. Leaves flexible, twigs pubescent. . . . . *P. Engelmanni* (p. 45)
1. Twigs pendulous, cones 10–20 cm. long. *P. Abies* (p. 46)

BLACK SPRUCE, *Picea mariana* (Mill) B.S.P., Prelim. Cat. N.Y. 71, 1888

Usually a small tree 8–10 m. high, rarely much taller, with a straight trunk rarely over 3 dm. in diameter, and short, mostly drooping branches forming a narrow, spire-like head; bark scaly, dark gray-brown; twigs slender, spreading, minutely pubescent, yellowish-brown when young, becoming darker with age and often nearly black; sterigmata about 0.8 mm. long, standing almost perpendicular to the stem; leaves 5–15 mm. long, quadrangular, slender, mostly bluntly pointed, dark green with glaucous stripes on the upper faces, pleasantly aromatic in odor and taste; cones ovoid, 1.5–3.5 cm. long, borne on sharply recurved stalks, persisting on the branches for many years; cone scales rigid, nearly orbicular, dark brown with paler entire or somewhat erose margins; seeds about 2 mm. long, dark brown, the wing obovate, somewhat oblique, 5–10 mm.

long. (*Mariána*, the Latin adjective derived from *Maria*, said to have a geographical reference in this case to *Terra Mariana*, or Maryland, where, however, this tree does not occur.)

Black spruce usually grows in cold, acid bogs, often accompanied by tamarack, and in thin soil over stony hills. It is mainly confined to the continuous coniferous forest of the region, but has a few outposts in acid bogs nearly as far south as latitude 45° in Minnesota. It is distributed from Labrador and Newfoundland to the valley of the Yukon, south to northern Virginia, central Wisconsin, Minnesota, and northern British Columbia.

As black spruce has little beauty to commend it, it is seldom cultivated. The wood, which is pale yellow or nearly white, is soft and weak; its weight is 28 lbs. It is seldom used for anything except paper pulp. The resinous exudation from the trunk is "spruce gum," and the leaves are boiled to produce the flavor of "spruce beer." A large percentage of the Christmas trees sold in the cities of the Middle Northwest are black spruce.

WHITE SPRUCE, *Picea glauca* (Moench) Voss, Mitt. Deutsch, Dendr. Ges. 16:93, 1908 [*P. canadensis* (Mill.) B.S.P. 1888]

A large tree up to 30 m. high, with a straight trunk 3–6 dm. in diameter and long stout branches forming a broadly conical head; bark scaly, light gray; twigs slender, spreading, glabrous, buff-colored, becoming somewhat darker with age; sterigmata about 0.8 mm. long, standing at an angle of about 45° to the stem. Leaves 8–20 mm. long, slender, quadrangular, sharp-pointed, pale bluish-green, glaucous, having a very unpleasant strong odor when crushed; cones short-cylindrical, 3–5 cm. long, sessile or with short, straight stalks, usually deciduous within six months of the ripening of the seeds; cone scales thin and elastic but firm, dark brown, broadly obovate, usually truncate at the tip, and nearly entire; seeds dark brown, the wing obovate 7–10 mm. long. Flowers in May; cones ripe in autumn of the same year. (*Glaúca*, blue-green.)

White spruce grows chiefly in upland and at least moderately calcareous soils. In Minnesota it is nearly confined to the region of coniferous forests, but straggles southward along the valley of the St. Croix River at least as far as the vicinity of Osceola, Wisconsin, where it is common on the dolomitic bluffs. It is distributed from Newfoundland and Labrador to the vicinity of Bering Sea, reaching the northern limit of tree growth, southward to northern New England, New York, the upper Great Lakes, the Black Hills, and the Rocky Mountains of Alberta and British Columbia, forming extensive forests north of the belt of pines.

White spruce is occasionally planted in the Upper Midwest, as is also its variety *albertiana*, the Black Hills spruce, native to the Black Hills and northern Rocky Mountains, which is characterized by a narrower pyramidal crown and somewhat shorter and thicker cones. It does well in cultivation, but like all northern conifers, is apt to suffer from dry autumns and winters in the southern and western parts of the area. The wood is light-yellow, soft, weak, and straight-grained; its weight is 25 lbs. It is used in eastern Canada for lumber and for paper pulp, for the latter of which purposes it is more extensively employed than any other wood.

COLORADO BLUE SPRUCE, *Picea pungens* Engelm., Gard. Chron. 1:334, 1879

A tree reaching in its native habitat a height of 30 m.; trunk straight, rarely 1 m. in diameter, branches horizontal, stout, rather short, forming in young trees a conical crown, later becoming irregular, branchlets and twigs spreading or ascending; bark scaly, gray, usually tinged with red; twigs stout, yellow-brown, glabrous; sterigmata very prominent, about 1.5 mm. long; leaves 2–3 cm. long, quadrangular, stout, usually curved, very stiff and sharp-pointed, very blue and glaucous, particularly on young trees, unpleasant-smelling when bruised (resembling white spruce); cones sessile or short-stalked, oblong-cylindric, about 7 cm. long; cone scales rhombic, flexible, with thin margins and tip, acute, rounded or truncate at the narrowed apex, mostly erose dentate; seeds brown, 2–3 mm. long, the wing elliptical, about 7 mm. long. (*Púngens*, sharp-pointed, referring to the leaves.)

Colorado blue spruce is native to the Rocky Mountain regions of Colorado, Wyoming, and Utah. It is much planted as an ornamental tree on account of its striking color. Though hardy, it tends with age to become somewhat straggling and to take on a darker green color. Different specimens vary much in the intensity of the blue color, and the best are sometimes propagated by grafting.

ENGELMANN'S SPRUCE, *Picea Engelmanni* (Parry) Engelm., Trans. Acad. Sci. St. Louis 2:212, 1863

A large tree, reaching in its native habitat a height of 40 m.; trunk straight, 1 m. or over in diameter, branches of moderate and nearly equal length, spreading horizontally, branchlets and twigs spreading, forming a nearly cylindrical crown, bark reddish-brown, scaly; twigs stout, light brown, pubescent; sterigmata very prominent, 1–2 mm. long; leaves 2–3 cm. long, soft and flexible, quadrangular, sharp-pointed, pale bluish-green, often very glaucous, unpleasant-smelling when bruised (resembling white spruce); cones oblong-cylindric or ovoid, about 5 cm. long; cone scales rhombic or obovate, conspicuously thin-margined, truncate or acute at the apex, and usually erose-dentate; seeds about 3 mm. long, nearly black, furnished with a large, very oblique thin wing. (*Engelmánni*, named for the botanist George Engelmann.)

This spruce is native to the mountains of western North America from Alberta and Alaska to New Mexico and Oregon. Occasionally planted and entirely hardy, it is nearly as ornamental as Colorado blue spruce and more permanent than that species.

NORWAY SPRUCE, *Picea Abies* (L.) Karst., Deutsche Fl. 325, 1881 [*P. excelsa* (Lam.) Link]

A large tree, reaching in its native habitat a height of 50 m.; trunk straight, 1–2 m. in diameter; branches of moderate length, spreading, branchlets at first horizontal, but soon pendulous, crown broadly conical; bark scaly, reddish-brown; twigs moderately stout, bright yellow-brown, pubescent; sterigmata prominent, about 1 mm. long; leaves 1.5–2.5 cm. long, rather stiff, quadrangular, sharp-pointed, bright green, not unpleasant-smelling; cones cylindrical, 12–15 cm. long; scales thick, firm, broad, and usually with an irregular margin. Flowers in April; cones ripe in autumn of the same year. (*A'bies*, the Latin name of the spruce or fir.)

Norway spruce is a native of Europe, where it grows from the extreme north to the Alpine regions of the Alps and Pyrenees.

More commonly planted for ornament than any other spruce, it is hardy and grows rapidly, but is apt to be injured by hot, dry summers and loses its beauty after thirty or forty years by the dying of the lower branches. The wood is reddish or yellowish, soft, and fine-grained, and is much used in Europe for lumber for floors, boxes, cheap furniture, scaffolds, masts, spars, etc. The oleoresin from this tree, "Burgundy pitch," is used medicinally. The bark is used in tanning leather.

Larch, Tamarack
Larix Mill., Gard. Dict. abr. ed. 4, 1754

Trees with straight, upright trunks extending to the treetops and indistinctly whorled, spreading or ascending branches; leaves needle-like, bright green, turning yellow and falling in autumn, upon the new twigs borne singly in a close spiral, like the leaves of spruce, but upon the older branches and the trunk borne in tassel-like tufts, or fascicles (dwarf shoots), which produce twenty to thirty leaves each year for many years; flowers monoecious, staminate cones solitary, borne without accompanying leaves on the sides of twigs and branches, globose or nearly so, the stamens two-celled, opening longitudinally, pollen wingless; pistillate cones appearing with the leaves in early spring, red or greenish, the ovule-bearing scales shorter than the bract-scales, cones small, ripening and opening the first autumn, but remaining on the tree throughout the winter, the seed-bearing scales in our species concealing the short bracts.

These are our only deciduous conifers. Besides the following two, there are six other species native to western North America, Siberia, and Japan. (*Lárix*, the classical Latin name for the larch.)

KEY TO SPECIES OF LARIX

1. Native tree; leaves 15–30 mm. long; mature cones 10–20 mm. long, cone scales glabrous..*L. laricina* (p. 47)

1. Cultivated tree; leaves 20–40 mm. long; mature cones 20–35 mm. long, cone scales puberulent. . . . .*L. decidua* (p. 47)

TAMARACK, AMERICAN LARCH, *Larix laricina* (Du Roi) Koch, Dendrol. 2:263, 1873 [*L. americana* Michx. 1803]

A tree 12–20 m. high; trunk straight, 3–5 dm. in diameter; branches short, forming a narrow, conical head in young trees and in crowded growth, longer and more irregular in old trees growing in the open; bark rough, scaly, red-brown; leaves triangular in section, 15–30 mm. long, very soft and flexible, light, bright green in summer, turning golden-yellow in autumn; young cones red or greenish; mature cones dull brown, ovoid, 1–2 cm. long, composed of ten to twelve scales; seed-bearing scales very convex, broadly ovate or nearly orbicular, glabrous, much exceeding the small acuminate bracts; seeds brown, 2–3 mm. long, about one-third as long as the broad unilateral wing which is broader at or above the middle. (*Larícina*, larch-like.)

The tamarack is abundant in Minnesota in the region of coniferous forests. It grows chiefly in bogs, along with black spruce, but occasionally is found in drier situations, where it reaches larger size. It is found southward in cold swamps scattered throughout the hardwood region as far south as the Twin Cities and Lake Minnetonka. South of the Minnesota River it is known only from one or two localities in Scott County, from near Faribault, Rice County, and in La Crescent Township, Houston County. It occurs, however, at intermediate points on the Wisconsin side of the Mississippi. It is distributed from Labrador to the Yukon Valley, south to West Virginia, northern Indiana, Minnesota, and northeastern British Columbia.

In cultivation the tamarack grows well in soil much drier than that which it naturally inhabits. It is not, however, so handsome or graceful a tree as the European larch. The wood is light-brown, hard, coarse, resinous, very strong and durable; its weight is 39 lbs. It is much used for fence posts, railway ties, telephone poles, and fuel. In Manitoba, northern Minnesota, and northern Wisconsin it has been much injured and in many places entirely killed by the depredations of a sawfly.

LARCH, *Larix decidua* Mill., Gard. Dict. ed. 8, no. 1, 1768 [*L. europaea* De Candolle 1805; L. Larix (L.) Karsten 1882]

A tree about 12 m. high and 5 dm. in diameter at the base; branches spreading, young twigs somewhat drooping; bark rough and scaly; leaves 2–4 cm. long, bright green, soft and flexible, turning yellow in autumn; young cones scarlet, mature cones yellow-brown, ovoid or oblong, 2.5–4 cm. long; seed-bearing scales broadly ovate, puberulent, about twice as long as the rounded or acuminate bracts; seeds dark brown, 3–4 mm. long, the wing unilateral, broadest towards the base. (*Decídua*, deciduous.)

The larch comes from the mountainous parts of Europe and grows well in

PINE FAMILY

dry soil. It is planted as an ornamental tree and does well in situations too dry for any of the evergreen conifers except the red cedar.

Pine

Pinus L., Sp. Pl. 1000, 1753

Trees or sometimes shrubs with variously branched trunks; foliage leaves evergreen, needle-like, in fascicles of two to five,° the young twigs at first without foliage leaves and clothed only with scattered, spirally arranged scales, the fascicles of foliage leaves appearing in the axils of these scales, each fascicle at first surrounded by a sheath of similar scales, which may later fall away, or may be permanent, the whole fascicle eventually falling away from the branch at the end of several years' time; flowers monoecious, usually on separate branches, the staminate clustered near the ends of the twigs surrounding the base of a shoot of the current season, consisting of an axis bearing numerous overlapping scale-like stamens, each of which bears two pollen sacs that open longitudinally; tip of stamen knob-like, or with a small, scale-like appendage, pollen grains winged, the round grain bearing two air bladders, which are about equal in size to the grain proper; pistillate cones solitary or in small groups, lateral or subterminal, the ovule-bearing scales of the young cones longer than the bracts; cones ripening in two or three years, woody, the seed-bearing scales often much thickened at the outer end, the bracts small and inconspicuous; cones opening at maturity to scatter the seeds, or in some species remaining closed for many years; seeds usually winged, not resinous. (*Pínus*, the classical Latin name of the pine.)

About seventy species of pine occur in the North Temperate Zone and the mountainous parts of the northern tropics, most abundantly in the warm temperate regions. Pines are among the most valuable forest trees for timber and for such various resinous products as turpentine, rosin, pitch, and tar.

The genus *Pinus* contains two subgenera, each with several sections. The various subgenera and sections are recognized by many authors as genera.

KEY TO SPECIES OF PINUS

1. The exposed portions of the cone scales but slightly thickened; stamens nearly crest-less: leaves in fascicles of five, the scaly sheath usually quickly deciduous; wood soft: subgenus *Strobus* (soft pines) . . . .*P. Strobus* (p. 49)
1. The exposed portions of the cone scales much thickened; stamens bearing a crest-like scale; leaves in fascicles of one to five (two in all our species), the scaly sheath usually persistent around the base of the fascicle; wood often hard: subgenus *Pinaster* (hard pines).
    2. Leaves more than 1 dm. long.
        3. Leaves thin, flexible; bark reddish; native. . . . .*P. resinosa* (p. 50)
        3. Leaves thick, stiff; bark gray; cultivated. . . . .*P. nigra* (p. 51)
    2. Leaves less than 1 dm. long.
        4. Trees usually 4–20 m. high.

° In a peculiar species of the southwestern United States there is only one foliage leaf in each fascicle.

48

5. Leaves flexible, blue-green, 2.5–7 cm. long; cones reflexed; cultivated....
....*P. sylvestris* (p. 51)
5. Leaves stiff, yellow-green, 2.5 to 5.5 cm. long; cones pointing forward;
native.....................................*P. Banksiana* (p. 52)
4. Low branching shrub, 1–4 m. high, leaves 4–7 cm. long..*P. montana* (p. 51)

ADDITIONAL KEY TO SPECIES OF PINASTER GROWING IN
THE UPPER MIDWEST, BASED ON LEAF STRUCTURE

Leaves in all our species semicircular or crescentic in cross section, and with two vascular bundles.
1. Resin ducts numerous, close to the surface; strengthening cells epidermal.
  2. Leaves over 1 dm. long; bundles close together.................*P. resinosa*
  2. Leaves less than 1 dm. long; bundles widely separated.
    3. Bundles embedded in sclerenchyma, epidermal cells nearly square *P. sylvestris*
    3. Bundles not surrounded by sclerenchyma, epidermal cells radially elongated
    ....*P. montana*
1. Resin ducts two, in the midst of parenchyma; strengthening cells beneath the epidermis.
  4. Leaves over 1 dm. long...*P. nigra*
  4. Leaves under 5 cm. long....................................*P. Banksiana*

WHITE PINE, *Pinus Strobus* L., Sp. Pl. 1001, 1753

A large forest tree with a straight trunk up to 40 m. high and up to 1 m. in diameter at the base; young trees with regular whorled horizontal branches, the older ones with strong, irregular, ascending branches forming an open irregular crown; the bark of the young tree smooth, greenish-gray, very resinous, becoming very thick, gray, and roughly fissured; leaves in fascicles of five, the needles surrounded at first with numerous scales, which soon fall off, leaving them without a scaly sheath, fascicles usually falling at the end of the second year; leaves slender, soft, 7–10 cm. long, triangular in section, minutely serrate; cones woody, cylindrical, stalked, ripening at the end of the second season, 10–15 cm. long, about 3 cm. wide when open, cone scales woody, thin, dark brown when ripe, the exposed parts glossy; seeds winged, escaping from the ripe cone. Flowers in May; fruit ripe in September of the following year. (*Stróbus*, the Latin name of some tree.)

White pine grows throughout the region of the coniferous forests, chiefly on clayey or loamy soils. It is also found scattered in isolated groves, especially in sheltered ravines or on the bluffs of the Mississippi River and many of its tributaries as far south as northwestern Illinois and southeastern Iowa. In Minnesota it occurs as far west as Spring Valley in western Fillmore County. It is distributed from Newfoundland to Manitoba, south to Pennsylvania, northern Ohio, Illinois, and Iowa, and in the mountains to northern Georgia.

White pine is the most valuable timber tree in our region. The wood is light brown or reddish, soft, fine-grained, and not strong; its weight is 24 lbs. It is used for building construction, siding, doors, sash, and the like. In cultivation it is ornamental and does well in areas where the late summers and autumns are

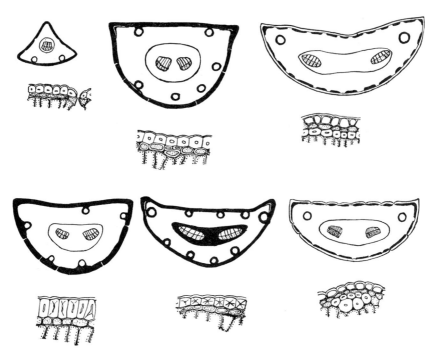

Cross sections of leaves of species of *Pinus*: Above, *P. Strobus*, *P. resinosa*, and *P. nigra*. Below, *P. montana*, *P. sylvestris*, and *P. Banksiana*. (Diagrams × 20, detail of epidermis and the layers immediately beneath it × 150. In the diagrams the sclerenchyma layer is heavily shaded.)

not too dry. It flourishes in the soil of our hardwood regions better than any other pine.

RED PINE, NORWAY PINE, *Pinus resinosa* Ait., Hort. Kew. 3:367, 1789

A forest tree 24–30 m. high, with a straight trunk 6–10 dm. in diameter, which extends to the crown of the tree; branches of young trees nearly horizontal, whorled, in old trees forming a rounded crown; bark reddish-brown, thin, on the older branches and trunk forming broad, flat scales; leaves in pairs, each pair surrounded at the base by a persistent scaly sheath; leaves slender, soft, 8–15 cm. long, semicircular in section, minutely serrate; cones ovoid, about 5 cm. long, and when open nearly as broad, standing straight out from the stem; cone scales woody, thickened at the tips, the exposed part diamond-shaped with a scar in the center; seeds dark, winged, escaping from the ripe cone. Flowers in May; cones ripe the second autumn. (*Resinósa*, resinous, not particularly appropriate to this pine.)

Red pine is common in the northern coniferous forests, where it once formed almost pure stands, chiefly on sandy soils, avoiding calcareous areas; it rarely occurs beyond the limits of the prevailingly evergreen forests. It is distributed from Nova Scotia and central Quebec to eastern Manitoba, and south to Massachusetts, Pennsylvania, Michigan, and Minnesota.

The wood is hard, fine-grained, and pale reddish, with yellow or often nearly white sapwood; its weight is 30 lbs. It is largely used for the construction of bridges and for piles and masts. It is increasingly used for reforestation in the Lake States area.

By an act of the Minnesota Legislature in 1953, the red or Norway pine was designated as the state tree.

SWISS MOUNTAIN PINE, MUGHO PINE, *Pinus montana* Mill., Gard. Dict. ed. 8, no. 5, 1768 [*P. Mughus* Scopoli 1772]

A shrub or small tree, seldom over 3 or 4 m. high, branches flexible, twigs short, bark brown, roughened with small conical projections; leaves in clusters of two, 4–7 cm. long, pointed, thick, dark green, with a basal sheath 5–6 mm. long, dark brown, papery, and with torn edges; cones small, 3–4 cm. long, in groups of two or three, horizontal or oblique, subsessile, persistent; cone scales rounded at the top, furnished with a rhomboid boss, which bears at its depressed center a large, sharp-pointed spine. (*Montána*, of the mountains.)

This pine is a native of the mountains of central and western Europe. In our region it is cultivated as a hardy, ornamental evergreen shrub used for covering rocky slopes or combining with other and larger conifers. Several unimportant varieties are distinguished by the shape of the cones.

SCOTCH PINE, SCOTCH FIR, *Pinus sylvestris* L., Sp. Pl. 1000, 1753

A tree up to 30 m. high, with a straight trunk, but in this area seldom over 15 m. high and often irregular, straggling, and somewhat shrubby; branches irregular, bark red and smooth above, becoming grayish and scaly on the older trunks; leaves in clusters of two, bluish-green, 3–8 cm. long, with a basal sheath 5–8 mm. long, wrinkled transversely and rough; cones small, 5–8 cm. long, yellow-brown, usually in clusters of two or three, nearly sessile, horizontal or bent backward along the branch, cone scales thin, woody, ending in a four-sided boss that in young cones bears a short, weak spine in the middle, which may persist in the mature cone but often disappears. (*Sylvéstris*, relating to the forest.)

Scotch pine is a native of Europe and of western Asia. In our region it is occasionally planted for ornament, but though entirely hardy, it seldom forms anything but a small straggling tree with very little beauty. The wood is reddish-brown, soft, and easily split. It is much used in Europe for building construction, taking the same position there that white pine does in our northeastern states.

AUSTRIAN PINE, *Pinus nigra* Arnold, Reise nach Mariazell 8, 1785 [*P. Laricio* var. *austriaca* Endl. 1847]

A tree up to 25 m. high, with a somewhat irregular trunk and long horizontal branches in whorls, giving the young tree a thick conical form, and the adult a broad, rounded head; bark grayish-brown; leaves in clusters of two, 10–15 cm. long, stiff, dark green, with a basal sheath 12 mm. long, gray, wrinkled; cones small, sessile, reddish, about 5 cm. long, projecting at right angles to the branches, solitary or in groups of two or three, falling after they open, cone scales thickened and with a rounded boss at the end, often with a dull spine arising from the center of the boss. (*Nígra*, black.)

P. *nigra* is a native of southern Europe and Asia Minor; only the northern variety, native to Austria, is hardy here. It is much planted as an ornamental tree, and is successful west and south of the natural range of our native pines.

The wood is soft, resinous, and durable. *P. nigra* with its varieties is the most valuable forest tree of southern Europe. It is used both for lumber and for the production of turpentine.

JACK PINE, *Pinus Banksiana* Lamb., Pinus 1:7, pl. 3, 1803 [*P. divaricata* Gord. 1858]

Usually a small tree 9–12 m. high, but occasionally taller, with a trunk about 3 dm. in diameter, head pyramidal, bark dark brown, irregularly divided into small scales; leaves in pairs, each pair surrounded at the base by a short, persistent, scaly sheath, leaves flat, rigid, 2–5.5 cm. long, minutely serrate; cones about 3 cm. long, curved, conical, sessile, pointing toward the ends of the branches, often failing to open at maturity and persisting on the tree for many years; cone scales woody, thickened at the tips, spineless; seeds blackish, winged. (*Banksiána*, named for Sir Joseph Banks, British naturalist and president of the Royal Society.)

Jack pine grows on sterile, acid soils throughout the region of coniferous forests, often forming nearly pure stands on sandy outwash plains. A single outpost is known in southeastern Minnesota near Rushford, Fillmore County. It is distributed from western Nova Scotia and northern Quebec to the valley of the Mackenzie River, and south to Maine, the southern shore of Lake Michigan, and Minnesota. It is absent everywhere from calcareous areas.

The wood is pale brown, soft, coarse-grained, and weak; its weight is 27 lbs. It is used for firewood and for posts, railway ties, mine timbers, lath, and the like, but it is the least valuable of our native pines. As it has little beauty to commend it, it is seldom cultivated. Occasionally, however, transplanted trees are to be found, mostly around farmhouses in districts where it is easily accessible.

CYPRESS FAMILY, CUPRESSACEAE

Trees or shrubs; leaves and cone scales opposite or in whorls; foliage leaves needle-like or more frequently reduced to small, flattened scales, which adhere to the twigs; flowers monoecious or dioecious, cone-like, the staminate consisting of an axis that bears several pairs (or whorls) of stamens each with from two to forty pollen sacs or sporangia, the pistillate cones without distinct "bracts," each fertile scale bearing from one to forty erect ovules; fruit a dry and more or less woody cone, or fleshy and berry-like.

CYPRESS FAMILY

The family includes about sixteen genera and a hundred and thirty species of cosmopolitan distribution, of which only the following two genera occur in the Upper Midwest.

KEY TO GENERA OF CUPRESSACEAE

1. Cones woody, twigs and spray flattened, leaves scale-like, of two alternating types, seeds winged...*Thuja* (p. 53)
1. Mature cones fleshy, drupe-like, with coalescent scales, twigs and spray not flattened, leaves opposite or in whorls of three, scale-like or needle-like, seeds wingless ....*Juniperus* (p. 54)

White Cedar, Arbor Vitae
Thuja L., Sp. Pl. 1002, 1753

Trees with fibrous bark, fragrant wood, and flat, fragrant spray clothed with the small, overlapping scale-like leaves which adhere to the twigs by their inner faces; leaves opposite, of two kinds in alternating pairs, those on the face of the twig flat, those on the side of the twig doubled over the edge; flowers monoecious, the staminate consisting of an axis bearing two or three pairs of peltate stamens, each with two to four pollen sacs, pistillate with four to six pairs of thin oval scales, the uppermost and lower scales usually sterile, the middle ones each bearing two to four erect ovules; cone small, woody; seeds with lateral wings, borne usually two on each fertile scale. (*Thúja*, the Greek name for some evergreen tree.)

The genus has four species, of which only the following is found in the Upper Midwest. The others occur in northwestern North America, Japan, and China.

WHITE CEDAR, ARBOR VITAE, *Thuja occidentalis* L., Sp. Pl. 1002, 1753

An evergreen tree with straight or forked trunk, 15–20 m. high and 5–10 dm. in diameter, the short horizontal branches forming a narrow conical head; the bark of the branches reddish brown, on old trunks forming loose scales; spray much branched, flat, leaves except on leading shoots about 3 mm. long, scale-like; flowers in spring, cones ripening the same autumn, usually with two pairs of fertile scales; seeds with winged margins, two on each fertile scale. (*Occidentális*, Western, i.e., native of the New World.)

White cedar is common in the northern portions of our region of coniferous forests, growing usually in wet situations, where it often forms dense, pure stands. It is not common in acid bogs. Occasionally it is found in drier ground or on bare rocks; a single outpost of stunted specimens occurs in southeastern Minnesota, on limestone ledges at the summit of Gwinn's Bluff, southeastern Winona County. It is distributed from Prince Edward Island and eastern Quebec to Hudson Bay and the Saskatchewan Valley, and south to Pennsylvania, northern Indiana, and southern Minnesota. It is found also in the mountains of North Carolina, chiefly on calcareous soils.

It is often cultivated as an ornamental tree or shrub and is much used for hedges, as it bears clipping well. In the southern part of the area it often winter-kills badly from lack of moisture following a dry fall. Several forms of this species, distinguished by varying habit of growth and color of foliage, are handled by nurserymen. The wood is light brown, coarse, brittle, weak, but durable; its weight is 20 lbs., the lightest wood of the northeastern states. It is much used for posts, telegraph poles, shingles, and in the manufacture of canoes.

Juniper, Savin

Juniperus L., Sp. Pl. 1038, 1753

Evergreen trees or shrubs with shreddy, fibrous bark and fragrant wood; leaves opposite or in whorls of three, scale-like or needle-like; flowers dioecious or, rarely, monoecious, axillary or terminal, the staminate with several whorls of peltate stamens, each bearing from two to six pollen sacs, pistillate flowers consisting of several pairs (or whorls) of minute, fleshy, coalescent scales, bearing one or two ovules in their axils, fruit fleshy, formed of the concrescent scales, scaly-bracted below, bluish-black with white bloom when ripe (brown in *J. chinensis*); seeds one to twelve, ovoid, wingless and bony. (*Juníperus*, the classical Latin name).

The genus includes about forty species, widely distributed throughout the Northern Hemisphere.

KEY TO SPECIES OF JUNIPERUS

1. Leaves in whorls of three, linear or linear-subulate, free and jointed at the base, without dorsal glands....................*J. communis* var. *depressa* (p. 54)
1. Leaves mostly opposite, sometimes subulate and loose or sometimes scale-like, decurrent, and not jointed at the base, appressed-imbricated and crowded; the scale-like ones usually with a dorsal gland.
    2. Upright shrubs and trees.
        3. Scale-leaves acute; needle-leaves not marked with white stripes above, berry blue, glaucous; native.........................*J. virginiana* (p. 56)
        3. Scale-leaves obtuse, needle-leaves marked above with two white stripes, berry brown; cultivated.........................*J. chinensis* (p. 56)
    2. Prostrate, matted, sometimes trailing shrubs..........*J. horizontalis* (p. 56)

PROSTRATE JUNIPER, *Juniperus communis* L. var. *depressa* Pursh, Fl. Am. Sept. 646, 1814

A depressed shrub with long, prostrate branches turning up at the ends to form a dense mat about 1 m. high; leaves in whorls of three, jointed at the base, spreading, subulate, boat-shaped, very sharp-pointed, marked with a bluish-white stripe on the upper side, 8–15 mm. long, 1–1.5 mm. wide; flowers in the axils of the younger leaves, opening in spring; fruits borne on short, scaly peduncles, blue, spherical, about 10 mm. in diameter, sweet, fleshy, and aromatic, ripening in the autumn of the third year; seeds one to three, with distinct resin vesicles. Blossoms in May; fruit ripe two years from the following August, some-

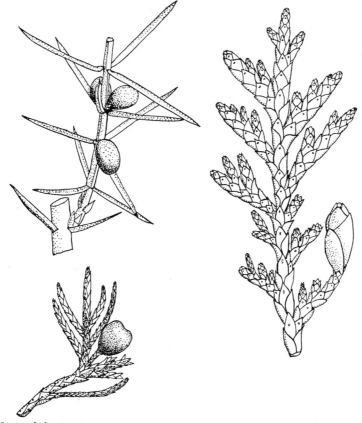

Upper left, *Juniperus communis* var. *depressa*. Lower left, *Juniperus virginiana* (fruiting twig). Right, *Thuja occidentalis*.

times persisting on the plant through the third winter. (*Commúnis*, common; *depréssa*, depressed, low.)

Prostrate juniper occurs in very varied situations (steep bluffs, river bottoms, margins of swamps, etc.) throughout the area except in the southwestern prairie region. It is most abundant in the northern and the southeastern portions. It is distributed from Newfoundland to Alaska, south to Connecticut, Indiana, Minnesota, and in the mountains to Colorado.

J. communis is a polymorphic species, which in one form or another occurs throughout the cooler parts of the north temperate regions. Its varieties differ greatly from one another in habit, and somewhat in leaf form. The typical European form is an upright shrub or small tree with nearly flat leaves, grayish above. It is not known in our area, but one of the European varieties, the Swedish juniper, *J. communis* var. *suecica* Loud. is occasionally planted. It is a narrowly columnar shrub with bluish-green foliage. A few specimens from the northern part of our area approach the boreal and Alpine *J. communis* var. *montana* Ait., which is an entirely prostrate shrub with appressed leaves shorter and broader

55

than in var. *depressa*. No local material has been seen, however, which can be referred clearly to var. *montana*.

The nearly ripe berries of juniper are used medicinally as a diuretic, and are employed in the manufacture of gin.

RED CEDAR, SAVIN, *Juniperus virginiana* L., Sp. Pl. 1039, 1753 [*Sabina virginiana* (L.) Antoine 1857]

In this area a tree rarely over 10 m. high when well grown, with a straight trunk and a broad conical head, often distorted, or even a straggling, irregular, upright shrub; mature twigs covered with scale-like, opposite, triangular leaves, 1–2 mm. long, but on young trees, rapidly growing shoots, or occasionally on whole trees the leaves spreading, awl-shaped, 8 mm. long, opposite or sometimes in whorls of three, decurrent and not jointed at the base; foliage dark green in summer, becoming reddish in winter; fruit globose, borne on a straight, scaly stalk, maturing the first season, dark blue and fleshy and much eaten by birds, which distribute the seeds. Flowers in May; fruit ripe in the autumn of the same year. (*Virginiána*, Virginian, applied at an early date to many American plants.)

Red cedar grows in dry, gravelly, usually calcareous soil, and on rocky ledges, most abundantly on river bluffs southeastward. It is distributed from Nova Scotia to eastern Dakota and south to Georgia and Mississippi.

The wood is red, fine-grained, soft, weak, fragrant, and very durable; its weight is 31 lbs. It is much used for chests, pails, posts, sills of buildings, and lead pencils. The tree seldoms reaches commercial size in the Upper Midwest. It is often planted as a small ornamental tree and does well even in dry situations where other evergreens will not grow. It is sometimes planted to form windbreaks, but this use is objectionable in regions where there are apple orchards as it harbors various species of the fungus *Gymnosporangium*, which produces leaf rust of apple.

Numerous horticultural forms of this species are handled by nurserymen, varying in habit of growth and color of foliage. Some forms are quite glaucous.

CHINESE JUNIPER, *Juniperus chinensis* L., Mant. Pl. 127, 1767 [*Sabina chinensis* Antoine 1857]

A shrub or small tree; scale-leaves appressed, obtuse, juvenile leaves needle-shaped, acute, decurrent, marked above with two white bands; fruit brownish, about 1 cm. in diameter, usually with two or three seeds. (*Chinénsis*, Chinese.)

This juniper is a native of China and Japan. There are numerous horticultural forms. Occasionally it is planted in Minnesota, especially the variety *Pfitzeriana*, which has spreading branches and pendulous twigs with grayish-green foliage.

CREEPING SAVIN, *Juniperus horizontalis* Moench, Meth. Pl. 699, 1794 [*Sabina horizontalis* (Moench) Rydb. 1912; *J. Sabina* var. *procumbens* Pursh 1814]

A prostrate evergreen shrub, often spreading over a considerable area; foliage

Red cedar, *Juniperus virginiana*

57

Landscape, southeastern Minnesota: Creeping savin, *Juniperus horizontalis*, in the foreground. Prostrate juniper, *Juniperus communis* var. *depressa*, near the center.

strong-smelling, leaves bluish-green, scale-like, triangular, or on young, strong-growing shoots, awl-shaped; fruit on a short, recurved, scaly stalk, oval or irregular, dark blue, fleshy, ripening during the second summer. Flowers in May; fruit ripe in midsummer of the following year. (*Horizontális*, horizontal.)

Creeping savin is abundant in the extreme north of our area and less abundant southward in the region of the coniferous forests. Locally it is abundant on exposed sandstone ledges in the southeast corner of Minnesota. It is distributed from Newfoundland to British Columbia, south to New England, New York, the south end of Lake Michigan, southeastern Minnesota, and in the mountains to Colorado. It grows also in Asia.

J. horizontalis has been confused with the savin of Europe, *Sabina officinalis* Garcke (*Juniperus Sabina* L.), which is distinguished by its more erect habit and by blunter, more closely appressed leaves. The twigs of the European species are used medicinally on account of the irritating volatile oil they contain. The American form contains the same oil and has presumably the same medicinal action.

✢ ✢ ✢

SUBDIVISION II. ANGIOSPERMAE

Seed-bearing plants with closed pistils; the ovules and seeds developing within a closed ovary; the pollen grains received by and germinating upon the stigma; the body of the seed (endosperm), not the female gametophyte, developing after fertilization of the egg and during the development of the embryo.

Class I. Monocotyledons

Embryo with one cotyledon, stem with numerous scattered vascular bundles, without secondary growth in thickness by means of cambium; flowers usually trimerous. In this latitude monocotyledons are nearly all herbs with parallel-veined leaves. The class contains several large groups of tropical trees and shrubs such as the palms and bamboos. The only genus of woody monocotyledonous plants occurring in the Upper Midwest belongs to the following family.

LILY FAMILY, LILIACEAE

Herbs or woody plants, sometimes woody vines, with alternate, simple, linear or lanceolate, to ovate or broadly cordate leaves; flowers regular, mostly perfect, rarely imperfect, perianth segments usually six, in two alternating whorls or cycles, mostly similar in form and color; stamens six; carpels three, united; ovary three-celled or one-celled with three parietal placentas, superior; fruit a capsule or a berry. In our flora only the following genus is woody.

Greenbrier
Smilax L., Sp. Pl. 1038, 1753

Woody or herbaceous vines, usually climbing by a pair of tendrils at the base of each petiole; leaves alternate, simple, entire or sometimes lobed, lanceolate to ovate or broadly cordate, net-veined, with three to seven prominent nerves; flowers in umbels on axillary peduncles, dioecious, small, yellowish-green; perianth segments distinct, deciduous; stamens six, filaments inserted on the base of the perianth segments; staminate flowers without a pistil; pistillate flowers usually smaller than the staminate and with one to six abortive stamens, stigmas thick and spreading, ovary three-celled with one or two ovules in each cell; fruit a berry, usually bluish-black, sometimes red or purple. (*Smilax*, the Greek name of a woody climber.)

This is a genus of about two hundred species, widely distributed but most abundant in tropical America, temperate Asia, and the Mediterranean region. Seventeen species occur in the United States. The following is the only woody species occurring as far north as Minnesota.

PRICKLY GREENBRIER, *Smilax hispida* Muhl., in Torr. Fl. N.Y. 2:302, 1843

Stems climbing, the lower and older parts generally thickly beset with long, bristly prickles, the flowering branches mostly naked; leaves membranous, deciduous, ovate, the larger ones heart-shaped, mostly seven-nerved, sharply pointed, or acuminate at the apex, margin usually fringed with minute teeth; peduncles 2–5 cm. long, umbels six- to twenty-flowered, berries bluish-black, 5–6 mm. in diameter. (*Hispida*, referring to the prickly stem.)

Prickly greenbrier grows in woods and thickets throughout southeastern Minnesota and adjoining Wisconsin, Iowa, and southeastern South Dakota. It is infrequent in Minnesota as far north as southern Kanabec County. It is distributed from Connecticut to Ontario, Minnesota, South Dakota and Nebraska, south to Virginia and Texas.

Class II. Dicotyledons

Embryo with two cotyledons; vascular tissue of stem forming a cylinder with distinct central pith, stem increasing in thickness by means of a cambium; flowers usually pentamerous or tetramerous.

WILLOW FAMILY, SALICACEAE

Trees or shrubs with alternate, simple leaves; flowers dioecious, both kinds in catkins, each flower subtended by a bract, without perianth; the staminate with from two to many stamens, the pistillate with a single compound pistil of from two to four carpels; ovary one-celled, placentas parietal; seeds numerous, covered with silky hairs; stigmas two to four, each usually two-lobed.

KEY TO GENERA OF SALICACEAE

1. Buds with several scales, bracts of the catkins fringed, stamens usually numerous
   ....*Populus* (p. 61)
1. Buds with one scale, bracts entire, stamens one to ten, usually two..*Salix* (p. 69)

Poplar
Populus L., Sp. Pl. 1753

Trees with round or angular branches and resinous buds covered with several scales; leaves broad, more or less heart-shaped, long-petioled, stipules minute, fugaceous; flowers appearing before the leaves in spreading or hanging catkins, each borne on a cup-shaped, somewhat oblique disk and subtended by a fimbriate, incised scale; staminate flowers with from eight to sixty stamens, their filaments distinct; pistillate flowers with from two to four united carpels and two- to four-lobed or entire stigmas; ovary one-celled, with two to four parietal placentas; fruit a capsule; seeds hairy. (*Pópulus,* the classical Latin name.)

This genus has about thirty species, widely distributed throughout the northern hemisphere. About twenty species occur in North America.

KEY TO SPECIES OF POPULUS

1. Leaves densely white tomentose beneath, retaining the tomentum in age........
....*P. alba* (p. 62)
1. Leaves not white tomentose when mature, glabrous or sparingly pubescent.
  2. Leaves with rounded or channeled petioles.
    3. Leaves ovate to ovate-lanceolate; petioles and lower surface not hairy.....
....*P. balsamifera* (p. 63)
    3. Leaves broader, cordate; petioles and veins of lower surface pubescent....
....*P. candicans* (p. 64)
  2. Leaves with petioles strongly flattened laterally, especially near the blade.
    4. Leaves broadly ovate to orbicular, rounded or subcordate at the base, short pointed at the apex.
      5. Margin of leaf coarsely undulate dentate......*P. grandidentata* (p. 65)
      5. Margin of leaf finely crenulate all around.......*P. tremuloides* (p. 66)
    4. Leaves deltoid to rhombic-ovate, truncate or broadly cuneate at the base, abruptly acuminate at the apex.
      6. Leaves broadly deltoid, truncate at the base, branches widely spreading, crown broad.............................*P. deltoides* (p. 66)
      6. Leaves rhombic to rhombic-ovate, broadly wedge-shaped or rounded at the base, branches ascending to erect; crown narrower.
        7. Leaves rhombic, nearly as broad or broader than long, 3–7 cm. long, crown very narrow.................*P. nigra* var. *italica* (p. 67)
        7. Leaves rhombic-ovate, longer than broad, 7–14 cm. long, crown pyramidal ....× *P. Eugenei* (p. 68)

SILVER-LEAF POPLAR, *Populus alba* L., Sp. Pl. 1034, 1753

A round-topped tree, 10–25 m. high and 3–10 dm. in diameter; bark on young trees greenish-white or gray, becoming dark brown and furrowed with age; leaf buds downy-pubescent; young twigs white-tomentose, at length becoming glabrous; leaves rhombic-oval or nearly orbicular, sometimes angular, truncate, or subcordate at the base, acute at the apex, 4–10 cm. long, 3–8 cm. wide, densely white-tomentose when young, becoming glabrous and dark green above, remaining white-tomentose below, margin coarsely and irregularly sinuate dentate; petiole nearly round, tomentose, shorter than the blade; staminate catkins 3–6 cm. long, cylindrical, 10–14 mm. in diameter; stamens about eight; pistillate catkins 2.5–5 cm. long, narrowly cylindrical, becoming 5–7 cm. long in fruit; capsule ovoid, 2.5–3 mm. long, short-pedicelled, glabrous; style

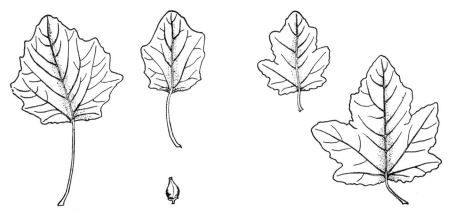

Species of *Populus*: Left, *P. alba*. Right, *P. alba* var. *nivea*.
(Leaves × 1/2, capsule × 2.)

short; stigma with two or three narrow, filiform lobes. Flowers in April; fruit ripe in May. (*Al'ba*, white, referring to the leaves and bark.)

Silver-leaf poplar is a cultivated tree, introduced from Europe. It spreads extensively by the root. The wood is light, soft, weak, and reddish yellow; the sapwood is nearly white.

Populus alba var. *nivea* (Willd.) Wesm., in DC. Prod. 16:324, 1868

The leaves of this form are three- to five-lobed, maple-like, and very white beneath. It is the commonest form in cultivation in this area. (*Nivea*, snowy, referring to the very white leaves.)

BOLLEANA POPLAR, *Populus alba* var. *pyramidalis* Bunge; Al Lehmann Rel. Bot., in Mem. prés à lac. de St. Pét. par div. sav. 7:498, 1851 [*P. alba* var. *Bolleana* (Lauche) Wesm. 1887]

Bolleana poplar is a narrow-topped tree, resembling the Lombardy poplar in habit but having leaves rather deeply three- to five-lobed and white-cottony beneath. (*Pyramidális*, pyramidal, referring to the form of the tree.)

BALSAM POPLAR, TACAMAHAC, *Populus balsamifera* L., Sp. Pl. 1034, 1753* [*P. tacamahacca* Mill. 1768]

A tree 6–30 m. high, with a trunk diameter of 3–15 dm., bark gray or greenish, smooth or more or less furrowed and darker on old trunks; buds large and very resinous, young twigs light brown and lustrous, older twigs gray; leaves ovate-lanceolate to cordate-ovate, gradually tapering, acute or acuminate at the apex, rounded or subcordate at the base, 4–12 cm. long, 3–7 cm. wide, dark green, shining and glabrous above, pale and silvery beneath or often

* There can be no doubt that Linnaeus' original *Populus balsamifera* was a composite species made up in part of this species and in part of the southern form of the cottonwood. The name has been applied consistently for over a century to this species, and there seems to be no good reason for transferring it at this late date to the other portion of Linnaeus' aggregate as has been done recently by several authors. On the other hand, such a change always leads to confusion.

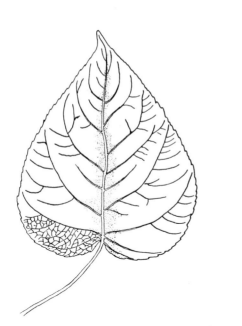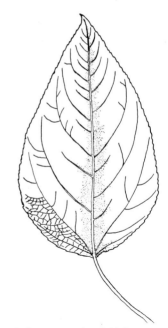

Species of *Populus*: Left, *P. candicans*. Right, *P. balsamifera*. ($\times$ 2/3.)

rusty owing to the resinous secretion, reticulate-veined, glabrous or sometimes puberulent along the veins, margin finely crenate; petiole round, shorter than the blades; stipules linear-lanceolate, early fugaceous; staminate catkins 3–5 cm. long, about 1 cm. in diameter, pistillate catkins 6–8 cm. long, slender, rather loose-flowered, becoming 12–15 cm. long in fruit, the rachis somewhat pubescent; capsule ovoid, glabrous, 7–9 mm. long, short-pedicelled; stigmas broad, irregularly lobed. (*Balsamifera*, balsam-bearing, referring to the resinous buds and leaves.)

Balsam poplar grows generally along streams and in swamps but also in somewhat drier situations. It is common throughout the coniferous forest area of Wisconsin, Minnesota, and Manitoba and is found in scattered places outside the continuous range of the conifers in eastern North and South Dakota and north central Iowa. It is distributed from Labrador to Alaska, south to western New England, Michigan, and Iowa, and in the Rocky Mountains to Colorado.

The wood is light, soft, and weak, and is light brown, with nearly white sapwood. It is used for pulp, boxes, pails, packing cases, etc.

BALM OF GILEAD, *Populus candicans* Ait., Hort. Kew. 3:406, 1789

A large tree 15–25 m. high with an open, irregular crown and a trunk diameter of 3–15 dm.; bark of trunk gray, ridged; buds large, resinous, and very aromatic; young twigs sparingly pubescent, brownish, becoming smooth and lustrous; leaves cordate or broadly ovate, cordate at the base, apex acuminate,

64

8–16 cm. long, 6–12 cm. wide, dark green and glabrous above (sometimes slightly pubescent along the principal veins), pale and often rusty-tinged beneath, pubescent along the veins, margin crenulate, petiole long, rather stout, round, pubescent, stipules lanceolate, early deciduous; staminate catkins 3–6 cm. long, about 1 cm. thick; pistillate catkins 9–15 cm. long, slender, becoming 15–20 cm. long in fruit, rachis pubescent, scales lacerate, long silky-pubescent, 6–8 mm. long; capsule ovoid, acute, glabrous, warty, 6–8 mm. long; pedicel about half as long as capsule, stigmas broad, much lobed. Flowers in April; fruit ripe in May. (*Cándicans*, whitish.)

This species is cultivated in the southern half of Minnesota and adjacent areas and occasionally escapes. Its origin is unknown.

LARGE-TOOTHED ASPEN, *Populus grandidentata* Michx., Fl. Bor. Am. 2:243, 1803

A medium-sized to large tree 10–20 m. high and 2–12 dm. in diameter; bark smooth, grayish, or yellowish-green, becoming furrowed and dark brown on the trunks of old trees; twigs more or less tomentose when young, later becoming smooth and gray or brownish; bud scales tomentose; leaves round ovate, acute or short-acuminate at the apex, rounded or truncate at the base, 5–9 cm. long, 4–7.5 cm. wide, sometimes much larger on vigorous sprouts, densely white-tomentose when young, becoming glabrous on both sides when mature, yellowish-green, slightly paler beneath, margin coarsely undulate-toothed; petioles slender, slightly shorter than the blade, strongly flattened near the blade; stipules very early deciduous; staminate catkins 4–7 cm. long, about 1 cm. in diameter, scales irregularly five to seven cleft, silky-pubescent, stamens six to twelve; pistillate catkins rather dense, 3–5 cm. long, becoming 10–15 cm. long in fruit, scales long-pubescent, capsule conical, about 5–6 mm. long,

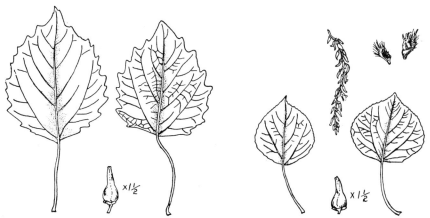

Species of *Populus*: Left, *P. grandidentata*. Right, *P. tremuloides*.
(Leaves × 1/2.)

glabrous, slender-pedicelled, stigmas with two or three slender lobes. Flowers in early May; fruit ripe in late May. (*Grandidentáta*, large-toothed, referring to the leaf margin.)

Large-toothed aspen is common in the rich mixed woods of our area except northeastward. It is distributed from Nova Scotia west to southern Ontario and Minnesota and south to North Carolina and northeastern Missouri.

The wood is weak, soft, and light brown, with thin, white sapwood. It is used for paper pulp, excelsior, and woodenware.

AMERICAN ASPEN, QUAKING ASP, TREMBLING POPLAR, *Populus tremuloides* Michx., Fl. Bor. Am. 2:243, 1803

A straight, slender tree, 6–20 m. high and 2–6 dm. in diameter; bark smooth, greenish-white or gray, becoming furrowed and dark in older trees; twigs smooth, reddish-brown the first year, later turning gray; bud scales smooth and shining; leaves broadly ovate or nearly orbicular, truncate or, more rarely, sub-cordate at the base, abruptly short acuminate at the apex, rounded, 2.5–5 cm. long, 2.3–5 cm. wide, or those of young trees and sprouts considerably larger, at first silky-hairy, especially along the margin, entirely glabrous when mature, bluish or yellowish-green, lower surface generally somewhat paler, margin evenly crenate-serrulate; petioles about as long as the blades, very slender and laterally flattened; staminate catkins 3–6 cm. long, less than 1 cm. thick, scales deeply three to five cleft, long silky-hairy, stamens six to twelve; pistillate catkins 3–6 cm. long, slender, scales deeply three to five cleft into linear segments, silky-hairy, disk very oblique, capsule conical, about 5 mm. long, pedicel short, stigma lobes linear. Flowers in April; fruit ripe in May. (*Tremuloídes*, resembling *P. tremula*, so called from the quivering habit of the leaves.)

This aspen grows in various situations, common throughout the region. It is most abundant in the north, where it frequently occurs in nearly pure stands on logged or burnt- over areas. It is distributed from Labrador to Alaska, south to Pennsylvania, Maryland, and Nebraska, and in the Rocky Mountains to Mexico.

The wood is soft, weak, and light brown, with nearly white sapwood. It is used extensively for paper pulp and excelsior. The bark constitutes the principal food of the beaver.

COTTONWOOD, *Populus deltoides* Marsh., Arb. Am. 106, 1785 [*P. balsamifera* L., Sp. Pl. 1753, in part]

A large tree 15–30 m. high and 4–20 dm. in diameter, bark at first smooth and grayish green, becoming dark gray and prominently ridged on the trunks of older trees; buds large, pointed, bud scales glabrous and very resinous; twigs stout, with prominent leaf scars, smooth, at first yellowish, later turning gray; leaves broadly deltoid, mostly long acuminate at the apex, truncate or broadly wedge-shaped or broadly cordate at the base, 4–10 cm. long, 4–10 cm. wide or sometimes slightly broader than long, at first resinous all over and more or less

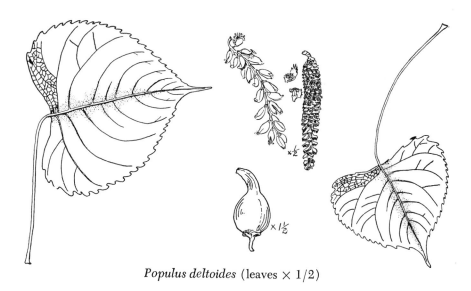

Populus deltoides (leaves × 1/2)

pubescent along the margin, soon glabrous, except for minute puberulence on the margin of the teeth, bright green on both surfaces, margin crenate-serrate, hyaline, thickened; petiole rather stout, about as long as the blade, strongly flattened; staminate catkins 6–12 cm. long or more, 1–1.5 cm. in diameter, scales lacerate-fringed, glabrous, stamens thirty to sixty; pistillate catkins 6–10 cm. long, becoming 10–20 cm. long in fruit, scales glabrous, capsule ovoid, acute, 10–14 mm. long, finely warty, two-valved to four-valved, pedicel 4–8 mm. long; stigmas broad and irregularly lobed. Flowers in April; fruit ripe in early June. (*Deltoídes*, triangular, referring to the leaf.)

Cottonwood grows mostly on bottomlands, river banks, and along lake shores, prevailingly throughout the southern part of our area. It is also very extensively planted as a windbreak and shade tree around farmsteads of the prairie area. It is distributed from southwestern Quebec to Manitoba and North Dakota, south to Florida and Texas.

The wood is light, soft, and brownish, with nearly white sapwood. It warps badly while drying and is difficult to split. It is used for boxes, paper pulp, firewood, and to some extent as lumber.

LOMBARDY POPLAR, *Populus nigra* L. var. *italica* Du Roi, Harbk. Baumz 2:141, 1772

A tall, pyramidal tree 15–25 m. high and 3–8 dm. in diameter, bark at first yellowish, later becoming gray, more or less ridged and dark brown on the trunks of old trees; branches strongly ascending, springing from all parts of the trunk; buds but slightly resinous; twigs slender, glabrous, yellowish, and shining; leaves rhombic-deltoid, cuneate to truncate at the base, short or long acuminate at the apex, 3–7 cm. long, 3–9 cm. wide, the larger ones generally broader than long, dull green above, slightly paler beneath, glabrous when mature, margin rather finely crenate-serrate; petioles flattened, shorter than the

67

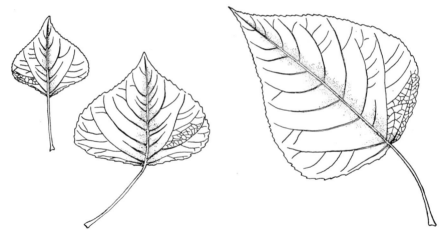

Species of *Populus*: Left, *P. nigra* var. *italica* ($\times 1/2$). Right, $\times$ *P. Eugenei*.

blades; staminate catkins 3–6 cm. long, scales lacerate-fringed, glabrous, stamens six to thirty. All Lombardy poplars are staminate. (*Nigra*, black; *italica*, Italian, on account of its being one of the characteristic trees of some parts of Italy. It is probably a native of Asia.)

Lombardy poplar is extensively planted in many parts of the area, but is rather short-lived. It frequently becomes disfigured through winterkilling of the top and main branches. The wood is soft, weak, and reddish-brown, with thick, nearly white sapwood. It is of little value and very little used.

NORWAY POPLAR, SUDDEN SAWLOG, $\times$ *Populus Eugenei* Simon-Louis Catal. ex Schneider, Ill. Handb. Laubholzk. 1:9, 1904 [*P. deltoides* $\times$ *P. nigra* var. *italica*]

A very rapid-growing, upright tree with ascending branches, 15–25 m. high, 3–8 dm. in diameter; bark yellowish-gray, becoming dark and somewhat ridged toward the base of the trunk, characteristically marked by crescent-shaped dark blotches of earlier leaf-scars, sometimes 1–2 dm. across and visible on the main trunk for many years; buds large and resinous; twigs somewhat angular, yellowish-green, glabrous; leaves rhombic-ovate, long acuminate at the apex, broadly cuneate or rounded at the base, 7–14 cm. long, 5–9 cm. wide, glabrous, thick and leathery in texture, dull green above, slightly paler and with prominent veins beneath, margin crenate-serrate, the serrations prominently gland-tipped and incurved; petioles stout, strongly flattened near the blade, 2.5–5 cm. long. Only staminate trees, the catkins resembling those of the cottonwood. (*Eugénei*, named for the French florist, Eugene Simon.)

This tree is becoming extensively planted throughout the Middle Northwest on account of its vigorous habit and very rapid growth (hence the name "Sudden Sawlog"). Bailey in his *Manual of Cultivated Plants* states that the Norway or Sudden Sawlog poplar of the Minnesota-Dakota region is apparently a form of *P. balsamifera* [*P. deltoides*] or a hybrid from it and that it was brought prominently to notice in 1904, having been distributed from a Norwegian settlement in Minnesota. He states further that it is supposed to be of Siberian origin. According to Schneider (*l.c.*) this hybrid first originated in the garden of Simon-Louis at Plantières near Metz. It is not known whether or not the common form in Minnesota is identical with the European form.

Willow

Salix L., Sp. Pl. 1015, 1753

Trees or shrubs, leaves alternate, simple, pinnately veined; buds with a single scale, not resinous; flowers in catkins with entire, usually hairy scales, dioecious, naked, fragrant, appearing before or with the leaves; staminate flower with from one to ten, usually two stamens, with one or more nectar-bearing glands at the base; pistillate flower with a small gland at the base; ovary one-celled, with two parietal placentas; stigmas two, more or less two-lobed; fruit a capsule; seeds hairy. (*Sálix*, the classical Latin name.)

This is a genus of one hundred and seventy species, widely distributed throughout the North Temperate and Arctic zones. About eighty species occur in North America. Natural hybrids between the species of willows are extremely common, but no attempt is made to describe hybrids in this treatment.

KEY TO SPECIES OF SALIX[*]

1. Catkins borne on short, more or less leafy lateral branchlets; mature capsules glabrous (except sometimes in S. *interior*).
    2. Scales of pistillate catkins yellow, falling before the catkins are ripe; filaments of stamens hairy below.
        3. Stamens mostly three to five, sometimes more, leaf margins serrate or serrulate.
            4. Native trees becoming over 7 m. high; pistillate catkins slender and loose.
                5. Leaves ovate-lanceolate, whitish beneath...S. *amygdaloides* (p. 71)
                5. Leaves narrowly lanceolate, green beneath.........S. *nigra* (p. 72)
            4. Shrubs, pistillate catkins thick, short, and dense.
                6. Leaves green on both surfaces, margins serrate; fruit ripe in early summer.
                    7. Leaves ovate-lanceolate, long-acuminate, shining on both surfaces; capsule conic-ovoid; native..................S. *lucida* (p. 72)
                    7. Leaves ovate or oblong-ovate, somewhat paler beneath, acute or short-acuminate; capsule conic-subulate; cultivated.............
                    ....S. *pentandra* (p. 73)
                6. Leaves glaucous or white beneath, margin finely serrulate; fruit ripe in autumn...............................S. *serissima* (p. 74)
        3. Stamens two.
            8. Native shrub, leaves linear, very distantly toothed....S. *interior* (p. 74)
            8. Commonly cultivated trees, leaves lanceolate, finely to coarsely serrate.
                9. Branchlets very slender and pendent (weeping willow)...........
                ....S. *babylonica* (p. 75)
                9. Branchlets stouter, more or less ascending.

[*] *Salix pellita*, not included in this key, is described on p. 81, after S. *candida*, which it closely resembles in foliage.

10. Branches very brittle at the base; leaves essentially glabrous; capsules long, conic-lanceolate, pedicelled......*S. fragilis* (p. 76)
10. Branches not very brittle; leaves silky when young; capsules, short, ovoid, sessile..........................*S. alba* (p. 76)
2. Scales of pistillate catkins brownish to black (except in *S. Bebbiana*), persistent; stamens two, filaments glabrous, leaves whitish beneath.
11. Low, bog-loving shrub; leaves entire, elliptic to oblanceolate, 3–6 cm. long, very finely reticulate; scales glabrous.....................
...........................*S. pedicellaris* var. *hypoglauca* (p. 77)
11. Taller shrubs of stream and lake margins; leaves serrate, lanceolate to ovate, generally more than 7 cm. long; scales villous.
12. Branchlets red, shining, glabrous; petioles slender, 1–2 cm. long; stipules wanting; blades short-oval to oblong-lanceolate, glaucous and prominently reticulate-veined beneath, slightly glandular-serrulate........
........................*S. pyrifolia* (p. 78)
12. Branchlets brownish or yellowish, dull, the younger pubescent; petioles stoutish, 1 cm. long or less; stipules usually large on vegetative shoots; blades lanceolate, closely serrate or serrulate.
13. Young twigs and bud scales puberulent to pubescent; leaf blades pale or whitish beneath; fruiting catkins up to 5–6 cm. long; capsules 5–7 mm. long.....................*S. rigida* (p. 78)
13. Young twigs and bud scales usually pubescent to villous; blades glaucous beneath; fruiting catkins up to 10 cm. long; capsules 8–10 mm. long.....................*S. eriocephala* (p. 78)
1. Catkins appearing with the leaves, sessile or short-stalked, naked or with a few leafy bracts at the base which do not develop into ordinary foliage leaves; mature capsules pubescent (except in *S. rigida* and *S. eriocephala*).
14. Mature capsules glabrous; leaves closely serrate or serrulate.
15. Young twigs and bud scales puberulent to pubescent; leaf blades pale or whitish beneath; fruiting aments up to 5–6 cm. long; capsules 5–7 mm. long.....................*S. rigida* (p. 78)
15. Young twigs and bud scales usually pubescent to villous; blades glaucous beneath; fruiting aments up to 10 cm. long; capsules 8–10 mm. long......
.....................*S. eriocephala* (p. 78)
14. Mature capsules pubescent; catkins appearing before or with the leaves.
16. Leaves closely serrate, lanceolate, acuminate.......*S. petiolaris* (p. 79)
16. Leaves entire or only remotely and irregularly crenate-serrulate.
17. Low shrubs of bogs or cold, wet places.
18. Leaves narrowly lanceolate or oblanceolate, rugose above.
19. Leaves densely white-woolly beneath...*S. candida* (p. 80)
19. Leaves nearly glabrate beneath........................
.....................*S. candida* var. *denudata* (p. 80)
18. Leaves narrowly to broadly elliptical or ovate.
20. Leaves bright green, very thinly sericeous beneath; capsules sessile.....................*S. planifolia* (p. 81)
20. Leaves gray, rugose, and densely pubescent beneath; capsule long-pedicelled.....................*S. Bebbiana* (p. 82)
17. Tall shrubs or, if low, then in drier places.
21. Leaves elliptical or broadly elliptical to ovate, margins distantly and irregularly crenate-serrate.
22. Leaves rugose and densely pubescent beneath; capsule long-pedicelled; scales yellow...........*S. Bebbiana* (p. 82)
22. Leaves glabrous or thinly pubescent beneath; capsule short-pedicelled; scales black.

23. Branchlets and leaves glabrous.
    24. Leaves short-lanceolate to elliptic or elliptic-oblance-
        olate.....................*S. discolor* (p. 82)
    24. Leaves broadly elliptic to oval or broadly ovate....
        ....*S. discolor* var. *Overi* (p. 83)
23. Branchlets tomentose; leaves thinly pubescent beneath
    ....*S. discolor* var. *latifolia* (p. 83)
21. Leaves narrowly to broadly oblanceolate, pubescent beneath, margins entire, revolute.
    25. Leaves 4–10 cm. long; mature aments 2–4 cm. long.
        26. Leaves narrowly elliptical or oblanceolate............
        ....*S. humilis* (p. 83)
        26. Leaves broadly oblanceolate to obovate..............
        ....*S. humilis* var. *keweenawensis* (p. 83)
    25. Leaves 2–5 cm. long; mature aments 1–2 cm. long........
    ....*S. tristis* (p. 84)

PEACH-LEAVED WILLOW, *Salix amygdaloides* Anderss., Ofv. Handl. Vet.
Akad. 114, 1858

A medium-sized to large tree 12–30 m. high, with a trunk diameter of 2–6
dm.; dark brown, ridged and more or less scaly; leaves lanceolate to ovate-
lanceolate, 6–12 cm. long, 1.5–2.5 cm. wide, narrowed or rounded at the base,
long-acuminate at the apex, finely serrate, at first pubescent, glabrate in age,
dark green above, whitish beneath; petiole slender, 1–3 cm. long; stipules

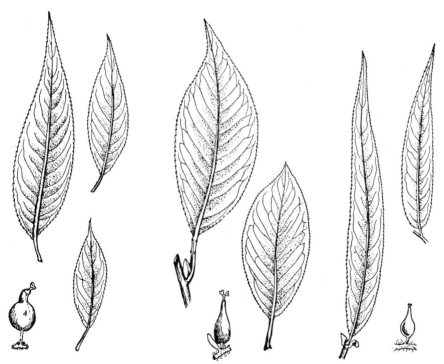

Species of *Salix*: Left, S. *amygdaloides.* Center, S. *pentandra.* Right, S. *nigra.*

71

minute, early deciduous except occasionally on strong, sterile shoots; catkins appearing with the leaves on short, leafy peduncles; staminate catkins 3–7 cm. long, stamens five or more; pistillate catkins 4–10 cm. long, becoming very loose in fruit; scales early deciduous, capsule globose-conical, glabrous, 4–6 mm. long, slender-pedicelled; stigmas nearly sessile, faintly lobed. (*Amygdaloides*, almond-like, referring to the form of leaf.)

This willow is common along streams and in low or moist situations throughout our area except northeastward in Minnesota, where it occurs infrequently as far as southern St. Louis County. It is distributed from western Quebec and Vermont to southern British Columbia, south to New York, Ohio, Missouri, Kansas, and northwestern Oklahoma.

BLACK WILLOW, *Salix nigra* Marsh., Arb. Am. 139, 1785

A tree 10–20 m. high, or sometimes only a shrub; the bark on the trunk thick, rough, and flaky, dark brown to nearly black; young twigs green and generally pubescent or puberulent, becoming dark brown and glabrous with age, brittle at the base; leaves narrowly lanceolate, very long-attenuate from the rounded or narrowed base to the tip, frequently falcate, 6–15 cm. long, 5–18 mm. wide, closely serrulate with incurved teeth, often pubescent when young, green and glabrous above when mature, slightly paler and sometimes pubescent along the veins beneath; petioles 2–6 mm. long, pubescent; stipules either large, semicordate, and pointed, or else small and ovate, persistent or deciduous; catkins appearing with the leaves, on short, leafy shoots; staminate catkins 3–5 cm. long, 6–8 mm. in diameter, stamens three to seven, filaments hairy; pistillate catkins 4–8 cm. long, 5–6 mm. in diameter, generally loose; scales ovate, early deciduous, densely soft-pubescent, capsules ovoid-conical, rounded at the base, glabrous, 3–5 mm. long, pedicels slender, spreading, 1–2 mm. long, style very short, undivided, stigmas unlobed. (*Nigra*, black, referring perhaps to the dark appearance of the foliage in mass.)

Black willow grows along banks of streams and lake shores, infrequently along the eastern border of Minnesota, as far north as Aitkin and southwestern St. Louis counties.

SHINING WILLOW, *Salix lucida* Muhl., Neue Schrift. Ges. Nat. Fr. Berlin 4:239, 1803

A shrub 2–5 m. high; bark smooth or somewhat scaly; twigs yellowish-brown and glossy; leaves ovate-lanceolate, 6–12 cm. long, 2–3.5 cm. wide, rounded at the base, long-acuminate at the apex, finely and evenly serrate, thick, coriaceous, glabrous, green and glossy on both sides or sparingly rusty-pubescent when very young; petioles stout, glandular at the top; stipules commonly persistent, semicordate to reniform; catkins appearing with the leaves, on short, leafy branches; staminate catkins stout, golden-yellow, 2–3 cm. long, stamens about five, filaments pubescent below; pistillate catkins 2–3.5 cm. long, narrower than

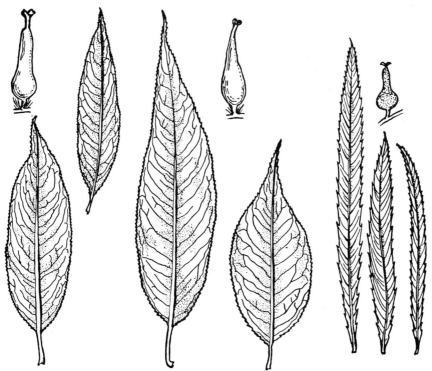

Species of *Salix*: Left, *S. serissima*. Center, *S. lucida*.
Right, *S. interior*. (Leaves × 2/3, capsules × 2.)

the staminate, becoming 3–4 cm. long in fruit; scales prominent, pale, more or
less erose, hairy on the back, deciduous, capsules rounded at the base, long-
beaked, 4.5–6.5 mm. long, pedicels 1–1.5 mm. long, style about 1 mm. long,
stigmas slightly lobed. (*Lúcida*, shining, referring to the shining leaves and
twigs.)

This shrub is common along banks of streams, roadside ditches, and edges
of moist meadows throughout the area as far north as middle Minnesota; it is
less frequent northwestward to Manitoba and North Dakota. It is distributed
from southeastern Labrador to Manitoba, south to New England, Maryland,
Ohio, Illinois, and South Dakota.

BAY-LEAVED WILLOW, LAUREL-LEAVED WILLOW, *Salix pentandra* L., Sp. Pl. 1016, 1753

A shrub or small tree 1.5–10 m. high; the bark of the old trunks gray and furrowed; twigs shining, yellowish-green or reddish-brown, more or less resinous or
gummy when young; leaves elliptic, ovate, or oblong-ovate, 5–12 cm. long, 1.5–4
cm. wide, mostly rounded at the base, acute or acuminate at the apex, finely and
closely glandular serrate; glabrous, bright green, and shining above, slightly
paler beneath, becoming leathery; petiole glandular, 5–15 mm. long; stipules
generally reduced to a pair of glands; catkins appearing with the leaves, on

73

short, leafy branches; staminate catkins 2.5–5 cm. long, 1–1.5 cm. thick, stamens mostly five (sometimes more), filaments pubescent below; pistillate catkins 2–6.5 cm. long, 7–12 mm. thick; scales conspicuous, oblong, pubescent, especially toward the base, deciduous, capsules long-conic, 5–7 mm. long, cordate at the base, straw-color or brown, lustrous, pedicels very short, style two-cleft, stigmas two-lobed. (*Pentándra*, referring to the five-stamened flowers.)

Bay-leaved willow is frequently cultivated on account of the glossy foliage. It is a native of Europe and northern Asia.

AUTUMN WILLOW, *Salix serissima* (Bailey) Fernald, Rhodora, 6:6, 1906

A shrub 2–4 m. high; bark brown and shining; leaves elliptic-lanceolate, 4–8 cm. long, 1–3 cm. wide, narrowed and glandular at the base, somewhat acuminate at the apex, very finely serrulate, dark green and shining above, whitish or glaucous beneath, glabrous, coriaceous when mature; petioles about 1 cm. long; stipules early deciduous; catkins appearing with the leaves, on short, leafy twigs; staminate catkins 2–4 cm. long, stamens five or more; pistillate catkins 2–3.5 cm. long, becoming 3–5 cm. long in fruit; scales pale, hairy, early deciduous, capsule conic-subulate, 7–10 mm. long, brown, becoming straw-colored and indurated at maturity, ripe in late summer; pedicels rather stout, 1–2 mm. long; style short and thick; branches of stigmas scarcely lobed. (*Seríssima*, latest, referring to the late fruiting habit.)

Autumn willow grows in calcareous bogs and swamps, occurring mostly throughout the coniferous forest area of the region, infrequently beyond. It is distributed from Newfoundland to Alberta, and south to northern New Jersey, Ohio, Indiana, Wisconsin, Minnesota, North Dakota, and Colorado.

SANDBAR WILLOW, *Salix interior* Rowlee, Bull. Torr. Bot. Club 27:253, 1900 [*S. fluviatilis* of many authors including Minn. T. & S. 1912, not of Nutt.; *S. longifolia* Muhl. 1803]

A shrub with clustered stems 1.5–4 m. high; bark smooth and gray; twigs reddish-brown and usually glabrous; leaves linear to linear-lanceolate, 5–12 cm. long, 5–12 mm. wide, narrowed to the base, acute at the apex, remotely denticulate, thinly silky-pubescent when young, glabrous in age, green on both sides; petiole very short; stipules mostly lacking; catkins appearing with and after the leaves, mostly in June; staminate catkins clustered at the tips of slender branches, 1.5–3 cm. long, 5–8 mm. wide, stamens two, filaments pubescent at the base; pistillate catkins solitary, at the ends of rather long, leafy shoots, which proliferate from the axils of the upper leaves, 2.5–4 cm. long, very loose-flowered; scales pale, slightly pubescent, very early deciduous, capsules rounded at the base, long-beaked, 4–5 mm. long, somewhat strigose, pedicel up to 1 mm. long, stigmas large, sessile, deeply lobed. (*Intérior*, inland.)

This shrub is common throughout the entire region but most abundant southward. It occurs chiefly on sand bars, sandy shores of lakes, and alluvial flats.

It is distributed from eastern Quebec to Alaska, south to western New England, Delaware, Maryland, Indiana, Arkansas, and Oklahoma.

WEEPING WILLOW, *Salix babylonica* L., Sp. Pl. 1017, 1753

A large tree attaining a height of 20 m. and a trunk diameter of 1.5 m., generally considerably smaller; bark gray and rough; twigs slender, elongated, and drooping, yellowish-green; leaves narrowly lanceolate, 6–15 cm. long, 8–15 mm. wide (those of the catkin-bearing twigs much smaller), narrowed at the base, long-acuminate at the apex, finely and evenly serrate, sparsely pubescent when young, soon becoming glabrous, green above, paler beneath; petioles 3–15 mm. long; stipules narrowly lanceolate, falling early; catkins appearing with the leaves on short, leafy twigs; staminate catkins 1.5–3 cm. long, cylindrical, stamens two; pistillate catkins 1–2 cm. long, less than 5 mm. in diameter, becoming 3–4 cm. long in fruit; scales ovate, acute, somewhat pubescent, early deciduous, capsules ovoid, sessile, 1–1.5 mm. long, stigmas deeply lobed, almost sessile. (*Babylónica*, pertaining to Babylon.)

This willow is a native of Asia. It is cultivated to some extent, but is seldom pure in cultivation. The following hybrid is the weeping willow most commonly planted in the Upper Midwest.

WISCONSIN WEEPING WILLOW, × *Salix pendulina* Wender., Schrift. Nat. Ges. Marburg 2:235, 1831 [*S. babylonica* × *fragilis*; *S. blanda* Anderss.]

Differs from pure *S. babylonica* in the somewhat wider leaves, in having two

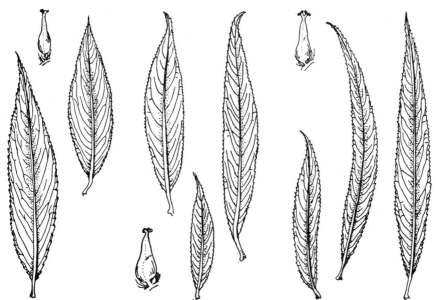

Species of *Salix*: Left, *S. fragilis*. Center, *S. alba*. Right, *S. babylonica*.
(Leaves × 2/3, capsules × 2.)

nectaries or glands instead of one at the base of the pistillate flower, and in the longer pedicel of the capsule. (*Pendulína*, pendulous.)

In the trade this hybrid generally passes as true *S. babylonica*. The "Niobe Weeping Willow" is of doubtful parentage (see note under *S. alba* var. *vitellina*).

CRACK WILLLOW, *Salix fragilis* L., Sp. Pl. 1017, 1753

A medium-sized to tall tree, 10–20 m. high, with a trunk diameter up to 1.5 m.; bark at first brownish and rather smooth, later becoming dark gray and flaky; twigs dull green, very brittle at the base; leaves lanceolate, 7–15 cm. long, 2–2.5 cm. wide, narrowed at the base, long-acuminate at the apex, rather coarsely undulate-serrate, dark green above, somewhat paler beneath, essentially glabrous even when young; petiole 1–1.5 cm. long, slightly glandular; stipules minute and fugaceous; catkins appearing with the leaves on short, leafy twigs; staminate catkins 4–6 cm. long, stamens two; pistillate catkins 4–6 cm. long, narrow, loose-flowered, becoming 6–8 cm. long in fruit; scales deciduous, capsules long-conic, glabrous, 4–5 mm. long, short-pedicelled, stigmas nearly sessile, distinctly two-lobed. (*Frágilis*, fragile, referring to the brittle twigs.)

Crack willow is a European tree. It has been extensively planted and is becoming naturalized, especially throughout the southern half of area. Of all willows it is the most frequently planted. It hybridizes freely with *S. alba*.

WHITE WILLOW, *Salix alba* L., Sp. Pl. 1021, 1753

A medium-sized to large tree, 6–25 m. high, with a trunk-diameter of 4–10 dm.; bark gray, rough; twigs green to olive-brown; leaves oblong-lanceolate to lanceolate, 6–12 cm. long, 1.5–2.5 cm. wide, narrowed at the base, acuminate at the apex, serrulate, green above, much paler beneath, silky-pubescent, in the typical form remaining pubescent even in maturity; petiole 5–10 mm. long, slightly glandular; stipules lanceolate, early deciduous; catkins on short, leafy shoots, appearing with the leaves; staminate catkins 3–4 cm. long, stamens two; pistillate catkins 3.5–6 cm. long, very slender, loose-flowered; scales finally deciduous, capsule ovoid, 3–4 mm. long, glabrous, almost sessile, stigmas nearly sessile, two-lobed. (*Al'ba*, white, referring to the pale hairs.)

This willow is a European tree. It is occasionally planted in the typical form, but more frequently in the following variety.

GOLDEN WILLOW, *Salix alba* L. var. *vitellina* (L.) Ser. Ess. Saule Suisse 83, 1815

Twigs yellow or reddish, mature leaves glabrous, white beneath. A large tree of rapid growth, valuable for windbreaks. (*Vitellína*, like the yolk of eggs, referring to the color of the twigs.)

The form *pendula* of this variety is sometimes planted as a "Weeping Willow" and is probably the "Niobe Weeping Willow" of horticulturists. The long, drooping twigs are more yellow than those of the true weeping willow (*S. babylonica*).

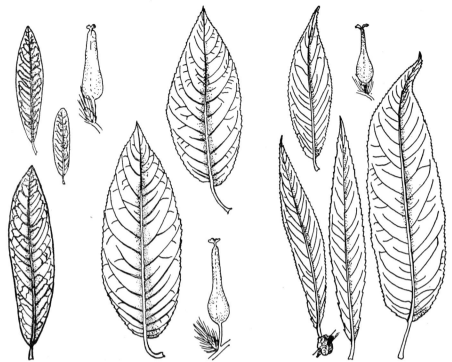

Species of *Salix*: Left, *S. pedicellaris*. Center, *S. pyrifolia*. Right, *S. rigida*. (Leaves × 2/3, capsules × 2.)

BOG WILLOW, *Salix pedicellaris* Pursh var. *hypoglauca* Fernald, Rhodora 11:161, 1909

A low, more or less erect shrub, 3–10 dm. high; bark grayish or light brown on young twigs; leaves obovate-oblong or broadly oblanceolate 1.5–6 cm. long, 6–19 mm. broad, narrowed or rounded at the base, obtuse or subacute at the apex, with entire revolute margin, reticulate-veined and subcoriaceous when mature, glabrous, bright green above, glaucous beneath; petioles 2–5 mm. long, not glandular; stipules deciduous; catkins on leafy peduncles, expanding with the leaves; staminate catkins 1.5–2 cm. long, stamens two; pistillate catkins 1.5–2.5 cm. long, becoming longer in fruit, rather loosely flowered; scales greenish-yellow, persistent, villous towards the apex or glabrate, capsules oblong-conic, obtuse, 4–6 mm. long, reddish, pedicels slender, about twice the length of the scales, style short, about the length of the stigma. (*Pedicelláris*, referring to the distinctly pedicelled capsules; *hypoglaúca*, referring to the glaucous undersurface of the leaf.)

This shrub is common in bogs and wet meadows throughout the northern half of Minnesota and Wisconsin; it is infrequent or rare southward to northern Iowa. It is distributed from Labrador to British Columbia, south to New Jersey, Pennsylvania, northern Illinois, and Iowa.

The true *S. pedicellaris* Pursh differs in having the leaves deep green on both surfaces. Its range lies mainly to the north of the variety described and it probably does not reach the borders of Minnesota.

BALSAM WILLOW, *Salyx pyrifolia* Anderss. Sv. Vet. Akad. Handl. 6:162, 1867 [*S. cordata β balsamifera* Hook. 1839; *S. balsamifera* Barratt ex Hook., as synonym]

A shrub 2–3 m. high, much branched; twigs reddish-brown or dark olive, glabrous and shining; leaves oval to oblong-lanceolate or lanceolate, 2.5–8 cm. long, 1.5–4 cm. wide, rounded or subcordate at the base, acute or short-acuminate at the apex, slightly glandular serrate, very thin at first and pubescent beneath, later becoming firm in texture, dark green above, paler and glaucous beneath and prominently reticulately veined; petiole slender, 8–15 mm. long; stipules minute, early deciduous; catkins on leafy peduncles, staminate catkins 2–3 cm. long, pistillate catkins 3–5 cm. long, becoming lax in fruit, and 6–8 cm. long; scales pubescent, persistent; capsules narrowly conic, long-beaked, 8–10 mm. long, glabrous, pedicels very slender, 2.5–3.5 mm. long, exceeding the scales, style short, stigmas distinctly two-lobed. (*Pyrifólia*, with leaves like a pear tree.)

Balsam willow is infrequent in our region, and is found mostly in spruce-tamarack bogs throughout the coniferous forest area. It is distributed from southern Labrador to Mackenzie and northern British Columbia, southward to New England, northern New York, Michigan and Minnesota.

HEART-LEAVED WILLOW, *Salix rigida* Muhl., Neu. Schrift. Ges. Naturf. Fr. Berlin 4:236, 1803 [*S. cordata* Muhl. 1803]

A shrub 2–4 m. high; twigs grayish-green or brown, sometimes glabrous and shining; mature leaves oblong-lanceolate or narrowly lanceolate, 4–12 cm. long, 1–4 cm. wide, rounded or cordate at the base on vigorous shoots, often narrowed or tapering on flowering shoots, acuminate at the apex, sharply serrulate, glabrous, dark green above, frequently paler beneath; petiole 1–2.5 cm. long; stipules ovate or reniform, somewhat oblique, serrulate, usually large and persistent on strong, sterile shoots; catkins on mostly leafy peduncles (rarely without leaves), the rachis pubescent;staminate catkins 2–3.5 cm. long, stamens two; pistillate catkins slender, 3–4 cm. long, becoming 4–6 cm. long in fruit; scales generally very pubescent, persistent, capsule narrowly ovoid, glabrous, 4–5 mm. long, short-pedicelled, style short, stigmas entire, obscurely lobed. (*Rígida*, stiff.)

Heart-leaved willow is common along banks of streams, lake shores, and moist thickets throughout our area. It is distributed from Newfoundland to Ontario and North Dakota, south to North Carolina, Mississippi, Arkansas, and Kansas.

MISSOURI WILLOW, *Salix eriocephala* Michx., Fl. Bor. Am. 2:225, 1803 [*S. missouriensis* Bebb. 1895]

A shrub or small tree, 3–12 m. high; bark dark-brown or black; one-year-old twigs brownish-gray, pubescent or tomentose; bud scales densely tomentose;

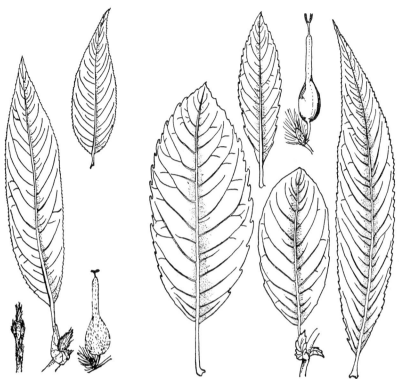

Species of *Salix*: Left, *S. eriocephala.* Right, *S. discolor.*
(Leaves × 2/3, capsules × 2.)

leaves lanceolate to obovate-oblong or oblanceolate, 6–12 cm. long, 1.5–3.5 cm. wide, rounded at the base, more or less abruptly so in the broader leaves, acuminate at the apex, sharply serrate, bright green above, pale and glaucous beneath, more or less pubescent above along the midvein and the lowermost lateral veins, glabrous below except along the lower portion of the midvein; petiole 8–15 mm. long, pubescent; stipules semicordate to semiovate, conspicuous on strong, sterile shoots; catkins mostly with few to several small leaves and a prominent coma of long white hairs at the base; staminate catkins 2–3 cm. long, slender, stamens two; pistillate catkins 2–3 cm. long, becoming 6–8 cm. long in fruit, scales persistent, pilose, capsule narrowly ovoid, 7–8 mm. long, long-beaked, pedicel slender, about twice the length of the scales, style short, stigmas obscurely lobed. (*Eriocéphala*, cottony-headed.)

On low ground this willow is fairly common in southwestern Minnesota and adjoining parts of Iowa, westward to the Missouri River in South and North Dakota. It is distributed from southern Indiana to North Dakota, south to Kentucky and Missouri.

SLENDER WILLOW, *Salix petiolaris* J. E. Smith, Trans. Linn. Soc. 6:122, 1802 [*S. gracilis* Anderss. 1858]

A low, much branched shrub, 1–3 m. high, with slender, dark brown or purplish, glabrous to puberulent twigs; leaves narrowly lanceolate, 3–9 cm. long, 6–12 mm. wide, narrowed or rounded at the base, acuminate at the apex, finely and evenly serrate with a cartilaginous margin, bright green above, paler and somewhat glaucous beneath, silky pubescent when young, usually becoming glabrate and finely reticulate on both sides in age; petiole 6–12 mm. long; stipules minute, deciduous; catkins appearing with or slightly before the leaves, peduncles with few to several bract-like leaves; staminate catkins obovoid, 1.3–1.8 cm. long, stamens two; pistillate catkins cylindrical 1–2 cm. long, becoming 2–3.5 cm. long in fruit, rather loose, scales persistent, pubescent, capsule conic-ovoid, short silky-pubescent, sometimes becoming glabrate, 5–7 mm. long, pedicel slender, 1.5–3 mm. long, stigmas nearly sessile, rather deeply lobed. (*Petioláris*, petioled.)

This shrub grows in moist meadows, swales, and poorly drained areas throughout our area. It is distributed from Quebec to Alberta, south to Massachusetts, New York, Michigan, Iowa, and South Dakota.

HOARY WILLOW, SAGE WILLOW, *Salix candida* Fluegge, Willd. Sp. Pl. 4:708, 1806

A shrub 0.5–2 m. high; young twigs white-tomentose, older twig yellowish- or light-brown; leaves oblong-lanceolate to linear-lanceolate 4–12 cm. long, 5–17 mm. wide, narrowed at the base, acute at the apex or obtuse in some of the lowermost ones, nearly or quite entire with a revolute margin, rather firm in texture, dark green, dull and slightly tomentose or glabrescent above with impressed veins, densely white-tomentose beneath; petiole 3–4 mm. long, tomentose; stipules lanceolate to ovate, about equalling the petiole; catkins with a few bract-like leaves at the base, appearing with the leaves; staminate catkins ovoid, 1–2 cm. long, scales very long-pilose, stamens two, anthers red; pistillate catkins cylindrical, 1–2 cm. long, becoming 2.5–5 cm. long in fruit; scales persistent, pilose, capsule ovoid-conic, densely white-tomentose, 5–7 mm. long, pedicel 0.5 mm. long, style about 1 mm. long, stigmas rather distinctly two-lobed. (*Cándida*, white, referring to the white-tomentose leaves.)

Hoary willow is frequent in calcareous bogs and swamps; it is most abundant in the northern half of our area, less common southward. It is distributed from Newfoundland and Labrador to British Columbia, south to New England, New Jersey, northern Ohio, Illinois, Iowa, the Black Hills of South Dakota, and Colorado.

Salix candida var. *denudata* Anderss., in DC. Prod. 16:278, 1868

Leaves narrower, dark green and glabrate above, sparingly pubescent or glabrate and pale beneath. (*Denudáta*, bare.)

This variety appears to be limited in our area to northeastern Minnesota and northern Wisconsin. It is distributed from Quebec to Minnesota, south to Connecticut, New Jersey and Wisconsin.

Salix pellita Anderss. Sv. Vet. Akad. Handl. 6:139, 1867

A large shrub or small tree, branches olivaceous to reddish, with a bloom; leaves linear-lanceolate to broadly lanceolate, narrowed to the apex, entire or nearly so, thick and firm, green and glabrous above, whitened and silky-velvety beneath or glabrescent; capsule densely white-pubescent. (*Péllita*, clad in skins.)

This willow grows on stream banks and in thickets. It is infrequent in our area, occurring at Grand Portage, Minnesota, and Isle Royale, Michigan. It is distributed from Labrador to northern Ontario, south to northern New England, Michigan, and Minnesota.

The foliage of *S. pellita* resembles that of *S. candida*, but the pubescence of the lower surface of the leaves is silky-velvety instead of white-tomentose. It is a taller-growing shrub.

Salix planifolia Pursh, Fl. Am. Sept. 2:611, 1814

A much branched shrub 1–3 m. high; twigs purplish, glabrous, and sometimes glaucous; leaves elliptic-lanceolate, 2–4 cm. long, 6–15 mm. wide, narrowed at the base, acute or sometimes rounded at the apex, margin remotely and minutely repand-toothed or slightly crenate, upper surface at first somewhat rusty-pubescent, in age becoming glabrous and shining, lower surface much paler, at first white or rusty-sericeous, later generally becoming glabrous and glaucous; petiole 2–4 mm. long; stipules minute, fugaceous; catkins with a few leafy bracts at the base, appearing with the leaves; staminate catkins elliptical, about 1.5 cm. long; pistillate catkins cylindrical 2.5–3.5 cm. long, becoming 3.5–5 cm. long in fruit; scales persistent, silvery-hairy, capsule conical with an ovate base, 4–6.5 mm. long, short white-pubescent, sessile or very short-pedicelled,

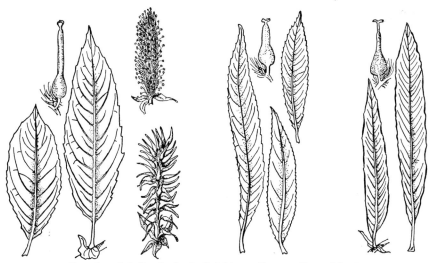

Species of *Salix*: Left, *S. Bebbiana.* Center, *S. petiolaris.*
Right, *S. candida.* (Leaves × 2/3, capsules × 2.)

81

style 1–2 mm. long, stigmas deeply cleft, lobes cylindrical. (*Planifólia*, flat-leaved.)

This shrub grows on the north shore of Lake Superior and has lately also been found in Roseau County, Minnesota. It is distributed from Labrador to Alaska, south in the mountains to northern New England.

BEAKED WILLOW, BEBB'S WILLOW, *Salix Bebbiana* Sarg., Gard. & For. 8:463, 1895 [*S. rostrata* Richards. 1833; not *S. rostrata* Thuill. 1797]

A shrub 2–6 m. high, or sometimes a small tree up to 9 m. high, with one to few stems; young twigs brownish, covered with a gray, crisped puberulence, older twigs brown, often with a reddish tinge; leaves obovate to elliptic-oblance-olate, 3–7 cm. long, 1.5–2.5 cm. wide, narrowed or sometimes slightly rounded at the base, acute to short-acuminate at the apex, margin entire to sparingly crenate-serrate, somewhat revolute, upper surface dull green and finely pubes-cent or puberulent, lower surface grayish-green and pubescent or puberulent with prominent reticulate veins; petiole about 0.5–1 cm. long; stipules semi-cordate, deciduous; catkins sessile, with a few leafy bracts at the base, expanding with or before the leaves; staminate catkins 2–4 cm. long, narrowly cylindrical, very hairy; pistillate catkins 2–4 cm. long becoming 4–8 cm. long in fruit; scales persistent, with a dark-gray pubescence, capsule tapering from a broad oval base into a long, slender beak, pubescent, about 7 mm. long, pedicel slender, 2–4 mm. long, style very short, stigmas entire or deeply parted. (*Bebbiána*, named for M. S. Bebb, a distinguished student of willows.)

This willow is common in moist to dry ground throughout our area. It is distributed from Newfoundland to Alaska, south to New Jersey, Nebraska, Utah, and Arizona. Several varieties have been recognized in different areas of the wide geographical range of this species.

PUSSY WILLOW, GLAUCOUS WILLOW, *Salix discolor* Muhl., Neue Schrift. Ges. Nat. Fr. Berlin 4:234, 1803

A tall shrub or small tree, 2–8 m. high, with a trunk up to 2.5 dm. in diameter; bark dark gray, somewhat scaly; twigs light to dark brown, glabrous or sometimes gray-pubescent; buds large with a glossy scale; leaves elliptic, oblong-lanceolate, or oblanceolate, 5–12 cm. long, 1.5–3 cm. wide, mostly narrowed toward the base, acute at the apex, irregularly crenate-serrate, bright green and glabrous above, pale and glaucous beneath or sometimes pubescent when young; petiole 6–15 mm. long, more or less pubescent; stipules semicordate or oblique lance-olate, usually deciduous; catkins appearing before the leaves in earliest spring; staminate catkins thick-cylindrical, mostly sessile, naked, 2.5–4 cm. long, dense, with copious long, silky hairs; pistillate catkins sessile or with a few small bract-like leaves on the peduncles, cylindrical, 2–4 cm. long, becoming 4–6 cm. long in fruit; scales persistent, long silky-hairy, capsule narrowly conic, 5–6 mm. long, tomentose, pedicels slender, shorter than the scales, styles short, stigmas prominently lobed. (*Discolor*, referring to the contrast in color between the upper and lower surfaces of the leaf.)

Pussy willow is common everywhere along streams, in swamps, and other moist situations. It is distributed from Labrador to Alberta, south to Nova Scotia, New England, Maryland, Kentucky, Missouri, and South Dakota.

Salix discolor var. *Overi* Ball, Rhodora 26:137, 1924

Leaves broadly elliptical to oval or broadly obovate, 4–7 cm. long, 2.5–4.5 cm. wide. (*O'veri*, named for W. H. Over.)

This variety is found in the region of Big Stone Lake, South Dakota, and Minnesota.

Salix discolor var. *latifolia* Anderss., Svenska Vetensk. Akad. Handl. 6,1:84, 1867

This variety differs from the species in the somewhat densely pubescent twigs and bud scales, in the thicker and more lanceolate leaves, usually more or less persistently pubescent beneath, and in the more densely silky-pubescent catkins. (*Latifólia*, broad-leaved.)

Its range is the same as that of the species.

PRAIRIE WILLOW, *Salix humilis* Marsh., Arb. Am. 140, 1785

A shrub with clustered stems 0.5–3 m. high; young twigs hoary with a gray tomentum, older twigs yellowish to brown, more or less puberulent or glabrate; leaves oblong-lanceolate to oblanceolate, 4–10 cm. long, 8–25 mm. broad, mostly narrowed at the base, acute or abruptly short-acuminate at the apex, margin revolute, undulate, entire or with a few minute appressed teeth, upper surface bright green, glabrate except along the midrib, lower surface pale-tomentose with rather prominent reticulate veins; petiole 2–8 mm. long; stipules oblique-lanceolate; catkins appearing before the leaves, naked or with a few small bracts; staminate catkins ovoid-cylindrical, 1–1.5 cm. long; pistillate catkins ovoid 1.5–2 cm. long, becoming 2–4 cm. long in fruit, fruit ripening almost before the foliage appears; scales persistent, with long, silky pubescence, capsule long-conical, 8–9 mm. long, tomentose, pedicel about the length of the scale, style very short, lobes of the stigma not cleft. (*Húmilis*, low, referring to its frequently dwarf habit.)

Prairie willow grows on dry sandy plains, jack-pine barrens, and in dry thickets; it is common eastward but infrequent or rare toward the western part of Minnesota. It is distributed from Newfoundland to Minnesota, south to North Carolina, Kentucky, and Kansas.

Salix humilis var. *keweenawensis* Farwell, Mich. Acad. Sc. Ann. Rep. 6:206, 1904

This variety differs from the species in having broadish-obovate leaves with a satiny or lustrous velvety pubescence. (*Keweenawénsis*, named from its type locality, the Keweenaw Peninsula.)

It grows in northeastern Minnesota and the upper peninsula of Michigan.

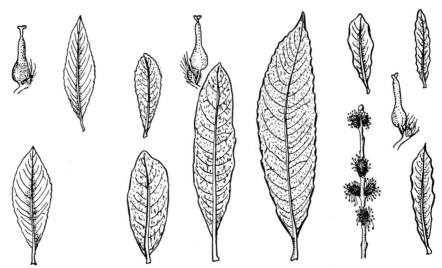

Species of *Salix*: Left, *S. planifolia*. Center, *S. humilis*.
Right, *S. tristis*. (Leaves × 2/3, capsules × 2.)

DWARF GRAY WILLOW, SAGE WILLOW, *Salix tristis* Ait., Hort. Kew. 3:393, 1789

A low shrub with numerous stems, 0.4–1 m. high; young twigs dingy puberulent, older twigs dark yellow-brown and glabrate; leaves crowded, narrowly oblanceolate to linear-lanceolate, 2–5 cm. long, 5–12 mm. wide, narrowed at the base, obtuse or acute at the apex, entire with a revolute margin, green and more or less pubescent above, densely white-tomentose beneath; petiole about 1 mm. long; stipules minute, deciduous; catkins appearing before the leaves; staminate catkins elliptical or almost globular, 0.5–1 cm. long; pistillate catkins short-elliptical, 4–10 mm. long, becoming 15–20 mm. long in fruit; scales persistent, long-hairy, capsule 5–6 mm. long, narrowly conic, with a rounded base and long, slender beak, pedicel about the length of the scale, style about 0.5 mm. long, stigma lobed, deeply cleft or nearly entire. (*Tristis*, sad, from the dark-colored twigs.)

This shrub grows on dry, sandy barrens, plains, slopes, and dunes; it is most common in the eastern part of Minnesota and the sand plain of Wisconsin, infrequent westward to North and South Dakota. It is distributed from New England to North Dakota, south to Virginia and Oklahoma.

WALNUT FAMILY, JUGLANDACEAE

Trees with alternate, pinnately compound leaves, stipules lacking; flowers monoecious, the staminate in catkins, the pistillate solitary or two or three together in a cluster or spike; staminate flowers consisting of from three to many stamens and an irregular perianth, adnate to the bract; pistillate flower mostly with a four-lobed regular perianth (sometimes one to three, or all segments

84

lacking) adherent to the ovary; pistil consisting of two carpels; ovule one, basal; styles two; fruit a kind of drupe with dehiscent or indehiscent exocarp enclosing the bony endocarp (nut shell); nut incompletely two- to four-celled; seed solitary, two- to four-lobed, the cotyledons very much corrugated.

This family includes six genera (of which two occur in our area) and about forty species, mostly of the North Temperate Zone.

KEY TO GENERA OF JUGLANDACEAE

1. Husk indehiscent, nut rugose, pith of twigs chambered.........*Juglans* (p. 85)
1. Husk splitting into segments, nut smooth or angled, pith not chambered..........
....*Carya* (p. 89)

Walnut
Juglans L., Sp. Pl., 997, 1753

Trees with spreading branches; bark fragrant; buds superposed; twigs with dark, chambered pith; leaves compound, odd-pinnate; staminate flowers in drooping, cylindrical catkins, borne on the twigs of the previous year; stamens eight to forty, subtended by a bract and a three- to six-parted perianth; pistillate flowers borne singly or in clusters at the ends of the shoots produced in the spring, perianth mostly four-parted, subtended by the fused bract and bractlets all adnate to the ovary; styles two, short; stigmas two, large and fringed; drupe large, globose or ovoid, the exocarp somewhat fleshy, fibrous, and indehiscent, endocarp bony, rough, or rugose; nut indehiscent or separating into two valves in decaying. (*Júglans*, the classical Latin name of the walnut, from *Jovis glans*, nut of Jupiter.)

This is a genus of about fifteen species, mostly natives of the North Temperate Zone; one occurs in the West Indies and one or two in the Andes of South America.

KEY TO SPECIES OF JUGLANS

1. Bark gray; fruit oblong; twigs and foliage viscid-hairy.........*J. cinerea* (p. 85)
1. Bark dark brown; fruit globose; twigs and foliage not viscid-hairy.*J. nigra* (p. 89)

BUTTERNUT, WHITE WALNUT, *Juglans cinerea* L., Sp. Pl. ed. 2, 1415, 1763

A tree 15–30 m. high, with widespreading branches; bark of trunk divided into ridges, light brown or gray; young twigs glandular-pubescent; leaves with glandular-pubescent petioles 20–50 cm. long, leaflets eleven to seventeen oblong-lanceolate, round or cordate at the base, acuminate at the apex, evenly and somewhat distantly fine-serrate, very pubescent when young, becoming nearly glabrate above, permanently soft-pubescent beneath, 5–12 cm. long, 2–5 cm. wide; staminate flowers in thick catkins, 5–8 cm. long; pistillate flowers in two- to six-flowered spikes, the flowers about 1 cm. long, stigma red, large and fringed, 5–7 mm. long; fruit oblong-ovoid, clammy, obscurely two- to four-ridged, pointed, 4–6 cm. long; nut deeply sculptured and rough with sharp ridges, two-celled at

Staminate and pistillate flowers of *Juglans cinerea*

the base; seed very oily and sweet, edible. Blossoms in April and May; fruit ripe in September and October. (*Cinérea*, ash-colored, referring to the bark.)

Butternut grows in rich woods, on river terraces, and on the lower slopes of hills in the valleys of the Mississippi and St. Croix rivers and the lower reaches of their tributaries, as far north in Minnesota as northern Aitkin County. It is distributed from New Brunswick to the northern peninsula of Michigan, south to Georgia, Arkansas, and Kansas.

The wood is coarse-grained and not strong, light brown, becoming darker with exposure; its weight is 25 lbs. It takes a good polish, and is used in cabinet-making and in the interior finish of houses. The nuts are of excellent quality and will keep for years in good condition; they are rather unpopular because the thick, rugose shell is hard to crack. The green husks of the fruit were once much used for dyeing cloth yellow or orange. Sugar is sometimes made from the sap.

Butternut, *Juglans cinerea*

Juglans nigra

88

WALNUT FAMILY

BLACK WALNUT, *Juglans nigra* L., Sp. Pl. 997, 1753

A large, handsome tree, 20–40 m. high, with a trunk diameter of 4–8 dm.; branches widespreading; bark rough, very dark brown; young twigs glandular-pubescent; leaves with glandular-pubescent petioles 25–50 cm. long; leaflets eleven to seventeen, 4–12 cm. long, 1.5–5 cm. wide, ovate-lanceolate, rounded and often unequal at the base, acuminate at the apex, sharply serrate, sparsely pubescent when young, soon becoming nearly glabrate except along the midrib beneath, lower surface gland-dotted; staminate flowers in stout, puberulous catkins 6–12 cm. long; pistillate flowers in three- to five-flowered spikes, stigmas yellowish-green tinged with red, 1–1.5 cm. long; fruit solitary or in pairs, globose, light yellowish-green, slightly roughened, 4–5 cm. in diameter; nut oval or oblong, slightly flattened, 3–4 cm. in diameter, dark brown, irregularly ridged or corrugated, four-celled at the base, slightly two-celled at the apex; seed oily, strong flavored, edible. Blossoms in May; fruit ripe in October and November. (*Nigra*, black.)

Black walnut is common in rich woods and fertile bottomlands in the southern parts of our area, reaching its northern limit in Minnesota, at Hastings, Dakota County, thence southwestward to Nobles County. It is distributed from western Massachusetts to Minnesota, south to Florida and Texas.

The wood is heavy, hard, strong, rather coarse-grained, rich dark-brown, and very durable, weighing 38 lbs. In many respects it is the most valuable of our native woods. It takes a beautiful finish, and is used in fine furniture and cabinet-making, for the interior finish of houses, for gun stocks, etc. The nuts resemble butternuts in quality, but have a stronger flavor, which some people find unpleasant.

Hickory

Carya Nutt., Gen. 2:221, 1818 [*Hicoria* Raf. 1808]

Trees with compound, odd-pinnate leaves; bark close and smooth, or shaggy; wood very tough and hard; staminate flowers in slender, pendulous catkins, borne in threes on a common peduncle at the base of the shoots of the season, calyx adnate to the bract, two- or three-cleft; pistillate flowers sessile in two- to six-flowered spikes, with a calyx-like involucre, usually four-lobed; styles two or four, short, papillose or fimbriate; fruit subglobose, oblong or obovoid, the husk separating more or less completely into four valves; nut bony, smooth or angled, incompletely two- to four-celled; seed sweet and delicious or very bitter and astringent. (Gr. *cárya*, nut, walnut.)

A genus of about twelve species, mostly natives of eastern North America; one occurs in Mexico, and one in China.

KEY TO SPECIES OF CARYA

1. Bark shaggy; leaves white-tufted along the margin; nut sweet...*C. ovata* (p. 91)
1. Bark not shaggy; mature leaves almost smooth; nut bitter..*C. cordiformis* (p. 91)

89

Black walnut, *Juglans nigra*

SHELLBARK HICKORY, SHAGBARK HICKORY, *Carya ovata* (Mill.) K. Koch, Dendrol. 1:598, 1869 [*Hicoria ovata* (Mill.) Britton 1888]

A large tree 16–30 m. high; bark of trunk shaggy, separating into narrow plates that are sometimes 25 cm. long, light gray, hard and tough; buds large, ovoid, obtuse or somewhat acute, the bud scales pubescent, the inner scales becoming greatly enlarged, petaloid, and very conspicuous when they unfold in the spring; leaves with petioles 15–30 cm. long, glabrous or pubescent; leaflets five, rarely seven, narrowed at the base, acuminate at the apex, serrate, glabrous in age except the points of the serrations, which have tufts of hairs, the three upper leaflets obovate-lanceolate, 12–16 cm. long, 6–8 cm. wide, the lowest pair smaller and oblong-lanceolate; staminate catkins in groups of three, 6–8 cm. long, slender; fruit subglobose or depressed, 4–6 cm. long; nut white, slightly flattened and angled, mucronate-tipped, four-celled at the base, shell hard; seed sweet and edible. Blossoms in May; fruit ripe in September. (*Ováta*, ovate.)

Shagbark hickory grows in rich woods, on bottomlands, and on slopes, reaching the northern limit of its range in central Wisconsin, Wabasha County in southeastern Minnesota, northeastern Iowa, and southeastern Nebraska. It is distributed from southern Maine to Minnesota, south to Florida, Alabama, and Texas.

The wood is light brown in color, close-grained, very hard, strong, flexible, and heavy, weighing 52 lbs. It is the strongest and heaviest of our native woods and is extensively used in the manufacture of axe, fork, and other tool handles, skis, bows, and baskets. The hickory nuts of commerce are obtained mainly from this species, probably the best-flavored of our native nuts.

BITTERNUT, SWAMP HICKORY, *Carya cordiformis* (Wang.) K. Koch, Dendrol. 1:597, 1869 [*Hicoria minima* (Marsh.) Britton 1888]

A rather slender tree 12–25 m. high; bark of trunk smooth or rough, but not peeling off in large, loose plates as in the preceding species; lateral buds obovoid, somewhat acute, terminal buds much elongated, narrow-cylindrical with a conical tip, bud scales resin-dotted, ciliate, not becoming enlarged and petaloid in the spring; leaves 12–25 cm. long, with slender pubescent petioles; leaflets five to nine, lanceolate or oblong-lanceolate, sessile, narrowed or slightly rounded at the base, acuminate at the apex, sharply serrate, puberulent when young, glabrate in age, the three upper leaflets 9–12 cm. long, 2.5–4 cm. wide; staminate catkins in groups of three, slender, 8–12 cm. long; fruit subglobose, narrowly six-ridged, 2.5–4 cm. long, husk thin, irregularly four-valved; nut slightly compressed, short-pointed with a persistent stigma, 1.5–2.5 cm. long, thin-shelled; seed very bitter. (*Cordifórmis*, heart-shaped, not particularly appropriate.)

Butternut is fairly common in rich, moist woods along streams or in drier situations on slopes and rolling uplands, northward to the southern limit of the coniferous forest, and infrequent to the upper Mississippi and tributaries of the

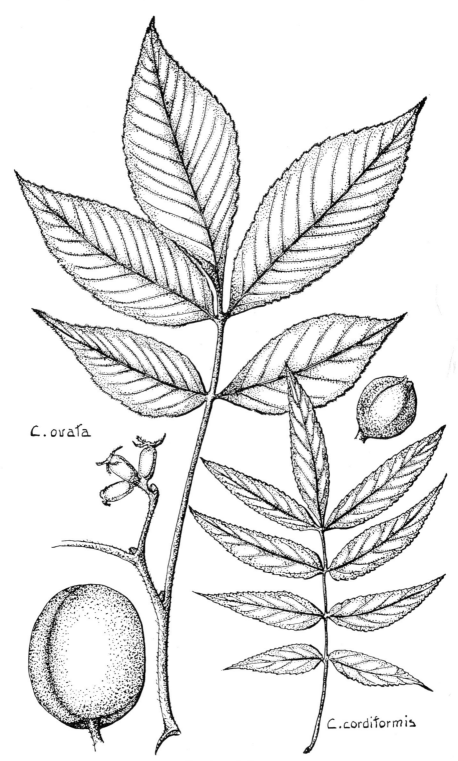

C. ovata

C. cordiformis

Species of *Carya*

92

St. Louis River in Minnesota. It is distributed from New Hampshire to Minnesota, south to Florida and Texas.

The wood is light- to dark-brown, close-grained, very hard, strong and tough, weighing 47 lbs. It is largely used for tool handles, hoops, and fuel.

BAYBERRY FAMILY, Myricaceae

Shrubs or trees, leaves simple, alternate, generally coriaceous, resin-dotted and aromatic; flowers monoecious or dioecious, in short, scaly catkins, solitary in the axil of the bract; calyx and corolla lacking; staminate flower with from two to sixteen stamens; filaments short, free or more or less united, anthers two-celled; pistillate flowers consisting of a solitary one-celled ovary, subtended by from two to eight bracts; ovule one; style short, stigmas two, linear; fruit a drupe-like nut.

This is a family of two genera and about forty species, of wide geographic distribution, most abundant in the subtropics.

KEY TO GENERA OF MYRICACEAE

1. Leaves entire or slightly serrate, without stipules . . . . *Myrica* (p. 93)
1. Leaves deeply pinnatifid or cut, stipulate . . . . *Comptonia* (p. 94)

Myrica L. Sp. Pl. 1024, 1753

Shrubs or small trees; leaves entire, serrate, or dentate, mostly resin-dotted; flowers monoecious or dioecious; staminate catkins oblong or cylindric; stamens four to eight, filaments slightly united below; pistillate catkins ovoid or globular; pistil subtended by from two to four deciduous or persistent bractlets; fruit small, globular or short-cylindric, dry, coated with resinous granules or wax. (*Myrica*, the ancient Greek name of a shrub, perhaps from the fragrance.)

This genus includes thirty-nine species, of wide geographical distribution. Besides the following, three occur in the eastern and southern parts of the United States and two on the Pacific Coast. Only the following species occurs in the Upper Midwest.

SWEET GALE, *Myrica Gale* L., Sp. Pl. 1024, 1753

A branching shrub 0.5–1.5 m. high; branches dark-brown, with pale lenticels; young shoots slightly pubescent; leaves oblanceolate, cuneate at the base, obtuse and dentate at the apex, dark green and glabrous above, pale and pubescent or glabrous beneath, mostly resin-dotted on both sides and aromatic, 3–6 cm. long, 8–18 mm. wide; petioles about 2 mm. long; staminate catkins oblong-cylindrical, 10–15 mm. long, loose-bracted; pistillate catkins ovoid-oblong, about 5 mm. long, stigma very prominent; fruiting catkin 7–10 mm. long; drupe resinous-waxy, enclosed by two thick, persistent bractlets, 2–3 mm. long. Blossoms in May and June, fruit ripe in August. (*Gále*, an aromatic plant.)

Growing in swamps and in shallow water along lakes and stream, sweet gale

Left, *Comptonia peregrina.* Right, *Myrica Gale.*

is frequent in the northern part of our area, especially north of Lake Superior. It is distributed from Labrador to Alaska; south to Nova Scotia, New England, New York, Ontario, northern Wisconsin, Minnesota, and Oregon; and in the mountains to North Carolina and Tennessee. It occurs also in Europe and Asia.

Comptonia L'Her., *ex* Ait., Hort. Kew. 3:334, 1789.

A low, branching shrub; leaves with stipules; flowers in catkins, monoecious or dioecious; staminate catkins cylindric; stamens four to eight in the axils of the bracts; pistillate catkins ovoid or globose, borne below the staminate catkins in monoecious plants; pistil subtended by eight persistent narrow bracts which form a bristly involucre in the ripe fruit; fruit a bony oblong nut. (*Comptónia*, named for Bishop Compton of Oxford.)

This is a monotypic genus of eastern North America.

BIRCH FAMILY

SWEET FERN, *Comptonia peregrina* (L.) Coulter, Mem. Torr. Bot. Club 5:127, 1894 [*Myrica asplenifolia* L. 1753; *C. asplenifolia* (L.) Ait. 1789]

A shrub 3–6 dm. high; leaves linear-lanceolate, regularly and deeply pinnatifid and fern-like, sweet-scented, acute or rounded at the apex, narrowed at the base, glutinous, sparingly pubescent, 6–12 cm. long, 10–15 mm. wide; lobes uniform, rhombic, or nearly semicircular, entire; petiole about 5 mm. long; stipules semicordate, usually deciduous; staminate catkins clustered at the ends of branches, 3–4 cm. long; pistillate catkins becoming bur-like in fruit, about 1 cm. in diameter. Blossoms in April and May; fruit ripe in autumn. (*Peregrína*, foreign, to the original European author.)

Sweet fern grows in dry, acid, sandy soils, and is frequent in jack-pine stands of the coniferous forest area. It is distributed from New Brunswick to Manitoba, south to Virginia, northern Indiana, and northeastern Illinois.

BIRCH FAMILY, Betulaceae

Monoecious or rarely dioecious trees or shrubs with alternate, petioled, simple, pinnately veined, serrate or dentate leaves with deciduous stipules; flowers in catkins or spikes or head-like clusters; staminate flowers one to three, in the axil of each bract, each flower consisting of from two to several stamens, naked or with a two- to four-parted membranous perianth, filaments distinct, sometimes two-forked and with the two anther sacs separate, or undivided and the anther sacs united; pistillate flowers two or three in the axils of each bract, with or without a perianth adnate to the two-celled ovary, carpels two; style deeply two-cleft or divided; ovules one or two in each cell of the ovary; fruit a one-seeded nut or nutlet, subglobose or ovoid, more or less flattened and frequently membranous-winged (samara), subtended or completely enclosed by the more or less enlarged bract and connate bracteoles.

This is a family of six genera and about ninety species, mostly natives of the North Temperate Zone.

KEY TO GENERA OF BETULACEAE

1. Pistillate flowers clustered, not in catkins; fruit a hard-shelled nut, tightly enclosed in a large fringed or beaked involucre......................*Corylus* (p. 96)
1. Pistillate flowers in catkins; fruit a thin-shelled nutlet, with or without wing, subtended by bracts or enclosed in a loose sack.
    2. Pistillate catkins loose and few-flowered; nutlet ovoid, wingless, subtended by or enclosed in an enlarged bract.
        3. Fruiting bract three-lobed, leaf-like, with serrate margin, bark smooth......
        ....*Carpinus* (p. 98)
        3. Fruiting bract closed, sack-like, bark scaly..............*Ostrya* (p. 99)
    2. Pistillate catkins compact, many-flowered; fruit a flattened, generally winged nutlet, subtended by a small, three- to five-lobed bract.
        4. Fruiting bract three-lobed, deciduous with the nutlets....*Betula* (p. 100)
        4. Fruiting bract five-lobed, persistent...................*Alnus* (p. 108)

BIRCH FAMILY

Hazel

Corylus L., Sp. Pl. 998, 1753

Shrubs or small trees with alternate, broad, serrate or slightly lobed or incised leaves; staminate catkins one to three at the ends of twigs of the previous season, expanding long before the leaves, the flowers solitary in the axil of each bract; stamens four, each filament two-cleft or forked and each branch bearing an anther sac (making apparently eight stamens); pistillate flowers several, from scaly buds, terminating early, leafy shoots; ovary inferior, crowned with a small, adherent perianth; stigmas two, long and slender; nut ovoid or subglobose, enclosed in a leafy involucre or husk, consisting of two more or less united and enlarged bracts. (*Córylus*, the classical name of the hazel, perhaps from Gr. *corys*, a helmet, in allusion to the involucre.)

KEY TO SPECIES OF CORYLUS

1. Young twigs hispid-pubescent; involucre consisting of two broad, fringed bracts..
....*C. americana* (p. 96)
1. Young twigs with scattered long hairs, becoming glabrate; involucral bracts united and prolonged into a tubular bristly beak.................*C. cornuta* (p. 96)

HAZELNUT, *Corylus americana* Walt., Fl. Car. 236, 1788

A shrub 1–2.5 m. high; bark gray and smooth; young twigs and petioles hispid-pubescent or glandular-bristly; leaves ovate or broadly oval, obtuse or cordate at the base, acuminate at the apex, serrate all around, sometimes slightly lobed, glabrous or nearly so above, finely tomentose especially along the veins beneath, 6–16 cm. long, 4–12 cm. wide; petioles 5–20 mm. long; staminate catkins 4–8 cm. long; involucre of the nut composed of two leaf-like bracts, free down to the nut, serrate or cut along the margins, finely pubescent and with scattered glandular bristles; nut compressed, light brown and mostly striate, 1–1.5 cm. long; seed edible. Flowers in April and May; fruit ripe in August and September. (*Americána*, American.)

Growing in thickets, pastures, and on hillsides, hazelnut is common and in places abundant throughout the region. It is distributed from Maine to Saskatchewan, south to Georgia, Missouri, and Oklahoma.

BEAKED HAZELNUT, *Corylus cornuta* Marsh., Arb. Am. 37, 1785 [*C. rostrata* Ait. 1789]

A shrub 2–5 m. high; bark gray, with scattered lenticels; young twigs with a few long hairs most abundant toward the base of the year's growth, tending to become glabrate in late summer; leaves ovate or oval, cordate or rounded at the base, acuminate at the apex, sharply and somewhat irregularly serrate or slightly lobed, glabrous above, or with a few scattered hairs, pubescent at least along the veins beneath, 5–13 cm. long, 3.5–8 cm. wide, occasionally larger; petiole about 1 cm. long, puberulent, and with scattered long hairs; involucral

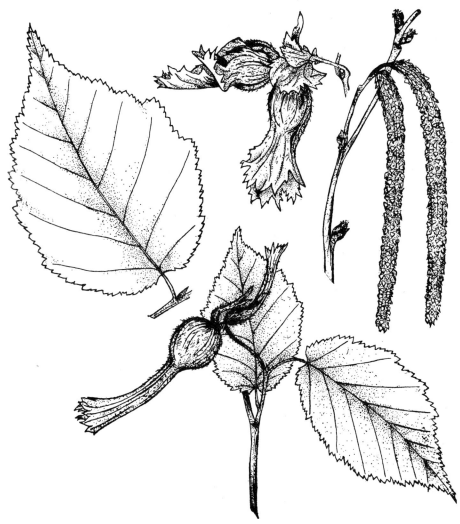

Species of *Corylus*: Above, *C. americana*, leaf, fruiting involucres, and flowering twig. Below, *C. cornuta*.

bracts united into a beak, lacerate at the end, 3–4 cm. long beyond the nut, bristly-hairy; nut ovoid, slightly compressed, and striate, 10–12 mm. long; seed edible. Blossoms in April and May; fruit ripe in August and September. (*Cornúta*, horned.)

Beaked hazelnut grows in woods, thickets, and clearings. It is common northward, especially north of Lake Superior, where the bushes reach a height of 4–5 m., and infrequent or rare southward to southeastern Minnesota, northeastern Iowa, and southeastern Wisconsin. It is distributed from Newfoundland to British Columbia, south to Georgia, Tennessee, Missouri, eastern Kansas, and in Colorado.

Left, *Carpinus caroliniana.* Right, *Ostrya virginiana.*

Hornbeam
Carpinus L., Sp. Pl. 998, 1753

Trees and shrubs with smooth gray bark, stem ridged; leaves with straight veins, ending in the primary teeth; flowers in catkins; staminate catkins from lateral, short branches, cylindric, about 4–6 cm. long, one staminate flower to each bract; stamens three to several; pistillate flowers in short terminal catkins, two flowers to each primary, deciduous bract, each subtended by a secondary bract and two bracteoles, which persist, enlarge, and become a three-lobed wing at maturity; stigmas two, awl-shaped; fruit a nutlet, ovoid, several-nerved, not winged, situated at the base of the secondary bract. (*Carpínus*, the Latin name of the hornbeam.)

This is a genus of about twelve species, natives of the Northern Hemisphere. Only the following species is native to America.

AMERICAN HORNBEAM, "BLUE BEECH," *Carpinus caroliniana* Walt., Fl. Car. 236, 1788

A small tree, 6–10 m. high; stem ridged; bark smooth, gray, sometimes with lighter blotches; leaves ovate to ovate-lanceolate, with the principal veins nearly straight and parallel, rounded at the base, acuminate at the apex, sharply and doubly serrate, glabrous above, pubescent in the axils of the veins beneath, 4–8 cm. long, 2–4 cm. wide; petioles slender, about 1 cm. long; staminate catkins 3–5 cm. long, scales brown, triangular, veiny and pubescent along the margin, anthers hairy at the tips; pistillate catkins terminating leafy shoots, very pubescent, secondary bract in fruit three-lobed and prominently veined, about 25 mm. long; nutlets ovate, veined, 5 mm. long. Flowers in April and May; fruit ripe in August. (*Caroliniána*, from Carolina.)

This tree grows in rich, moist soil, generally along borders of streams and swamps, occurring throughout but more abundantly southward, becoming scattered and infrequent northward to the headwaters of the Mississippi River. It is distributed from New England to Ontario and Minnesota, south to Florida and eastern Texas.

The wood is light brown, close-grained, and very hard and durable; its weight is 45 lbs. It is used for wedges, levers, and fuel.

Ironwood
Ostrya Scop., Fl. Carn. 243, 1772

Small to medium-sized trees; bark brown and furrowed, foliage resembling that of the birch; leaves with slightly bent veins; staminate catkins one to three together, from scaly buds at the tips of the branches of the previous year; flowers solitary in the axil of each bract, stamens two to ten; pistillate catkins solitary, at the ends of short leafy branches of the season, two flowers to each primary bract, each flower subtended by a secondary bract, which enlarges and becomes sack-like in fruit, pistil incompletely two-celled, tipped with two long stigmas, ovules two; nutlet ovoid or oblong, smooth and shiny, at the bottom of an inflated sac, the mature pistillate catkin hop-like. (*Os'trya*, the classical name of this tree.)

This genus includes four species. Besides the following, another occurs in the southwestern part of the United States, one in Europe and Asia, and one in Japan.

HOP HORNBEAM, IRONWOOD, *Ostrya virginiana* (Mill.) Koch, Dendrol. 2:6, 1873

A tree 7–13 m. high and 1–3 dm. in diameter; bark brown, finely furrowed and scaly; twigs of the season pubescent; leaves ovate or oblong-ovate, rounded or slightly cordate at the base, often oblique, acuminate at the apex, sharply

99

Flowering twigs of *Ostrya virginiana*

and mostly doubly serrate, slightly pubescent especially along the veins, 5–11 cm. long, 2.5–5 cm. broad; petioles 3–10 mm. long, pubescent; staminate catkins 2–3 cm. long, bracts triangular, acute, anthers with a tuft of hairs at the apex; the secondary bract of each pistillate flower forming a sack in fruit, 12–14 mm. long, veined, bristly-hairy at the base; nutlets compressed, shining, 5 mm. long, the ripe hop-like catkin drooping or spreading. Blossoms in May; fruit ripe in July and August. (*Virginiána*, from Virginia.)

Ironwood is common throughout our region, on slopes, ridges, and rich woods, often in the shade of oaks, maples, and other large trees. It is distributed from Nova Scotia to Manitoba, eastern North Dakota, the Black Hills of South Dakota, south to Florida, Arkansas, and eastern Texas.

The wood is light brown, close-grained, hard, durable, and heavy, next to shellbark hickory our hardest and heaviest wood (weight 51 lbs.), but limited in usefulness by its small size. It is used for wedges, levers, etc., and for fuel.

Birch
Betula L., Sp. Pl. 982, 1753

Trees or shrubs with serrate or dentate, sometimes lobed leaves; flowers in catkins, the staminate terminal and lateral, formed in the summer and remaining naked during the winter, expanding in the spring with or before the leaves; the pistillate terminating short, usually two-leaved shoots of the season; the staminate flowers usually three in the axil of each shield-shaped scale or bract, subtended by two bractlets, each flower consisting of two two-cleft stamens (each division

100

a half anther) and a perianth of two unequal segments; pistillate flowers two or three to each primary bract, subtended by two bractlets, without a perianth; ovary two-celled, stigmas two, elongated, mostly persistent; fruit a lenticular winged nutlet or samara; scales of the fruiting catkins three-lobed, deciduous with the nutlets. (*Bétula*, Latin name of the birch.)

A genus of about forty species, natives of the Arctic and North Temperate zones; several of the species hybridize in nature.

KEY TO SPECIES OF BETULA

1. Trees with white or nearly white outer bark.
   2. Leaves serrate, doubly serrate, or obscurely lobed, but not deeply divided or cut; twigs not long-pendulous.
      3. Bark of trunk not furrowed; leaves ovate to cordate; middle lobe of fruiting bract twice as long as the lateral lobes. Native.
         4. Leaves ovate, rounded or truncate at the base; fruiting catkins 1.5–4.5 cm. long; bracts 4–6 mm. long.....................*B. papyrifera* (p. 101)
         4. Leaves cordate; fruiting catkins 5–7 cm. long; bracts 6.5–8.5 mm. long...
         ....*B. cordifolia* (p. 102)
      3. Bark dark-furrowed toward the base of the trunk; leaves rhombic or triangular; middle lobe of fruiting bract triangular, scarcely longer than the spreading or reflexed lateral lobes. Cultivated...................*B. pendula* (p. 103)
   2. Leaves deeply cut and lobed, twigs very slender and drooping...............
   ....*B. pendula* f. *dalecarlica* (p. 104)
1. Trees or shrubs with gray, yellowish, or reddish-brown bark.
   5. Trees, bark peeling in thin layers at least on upper trunk and branches.
      6. Outer bark yellowish or gray, inner bark with flavor of wintergreen; fruiting catkins sessile or nearly so; bracts ciliate-margined.......*B. lutea* (p. 104)
      6. Outer bark greenish-brown or reddish, inner bark without wintergreen flavor; fruiting catkins peduncled; bracts tomentose...........*B. nigra* (p. 105)
   5. Shrubs or small trees, bark not peeling, grayish to reddish-brown.
      7. Slender shrubs 0.5–3 m. high; leaves obovate to suborbicular, petioles 3–5 mm. long.......................*B. pumila* var. *glandulifera* (p. 106)
      7. Tall shrubs or small trees 4–8 m. high; leaves ovate, rhombic-ovate or elliptic, petioles 7–14 mm. long.
         8. Inner bark without wintergreen flavor; fruiting catkins 6–7 mm. in diameter; wings of samara as wide or wider than the nutlet.............
         ....× *B. Sandbergi* (p. 106)
         8. Inner bark with wintergreen flavor; fruiting catkins 10–12 mm. in diameter; wings of the samara narrower than the nutlet....................
         ....× *B. Purpusii* (p. 107)

PAPER BIRCH, CANOE BIRCH, *Betula papyrifera* Marsh., Arb. Am. 19, 1785 [*B. alba* var. *papyrifera* (Marsh.) Spach 1841]

A large tree, reaching a maximum height of 25 m. and a trunk diameter of 2–5 dm.; bark white (except on young trees, where it is reddish-brown) and peeling off in papery layers; twigs slender with pale lenticels; leaves ovate, 4–8 cm. long, 3–5 cm. wide, with from six to eight pairs of lateral veins, abruptly cuneate, rounded, truncate or subcordate at the base, acute or acuminate at the apex, doubly and often irregularly serrate or somewhat lobed, dark green and glabrous

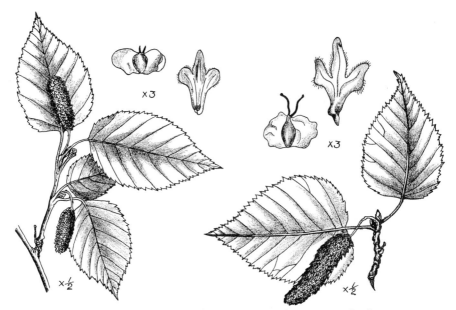

Species of *Betula*: Left, *B. papyrifera*. Right, *B. cordifolia*.

above, pubescent along the veins beneath and glandular or resin-dotted; staminate catkins 5–10 cm. long; pistillate catkins slender, erect, at the ends of short, leafy shoots, 2–3 cm. long; fruiting catkin drooping, 3–5 cm. long, 7–10 mm. in diameter; fruiting bracts three-lobed, about 4 mm. long, puberulent, the middle lobe narrowly ovate, longer than the rounded, slightly ascending lateral lobes; samara 3.5–4.5 mm. wide; nutlet elliptic, narrower than the wings of the samara. Blossoms in April and May; fruit ripe in August and September. (*Papyrifera*. paper-bearing.)

This birch grows on wooded slopes and along borders of streams, lakes, and swamps. It is common and in places abundant throughout the forested area, less frequent westward to eastern North and South Dakota and southward to north central Iowa. It is distributed from Newfoundland and Labrador to Hudson Bay and Alaska, south to New England, New York, Pennsylvania, Indiana, eastern Nebraska, and Wyoming.

The wood is light brown, close-grained, strong and tough, weighing 37 lbs. It is used for making spools, shoe lasts, and pegs, and for wood pulp and fuel. The Indians use the wood for making snow-shoe frames, sledges, and paddles; the bark in making canoes, receptacles for gathering maple sap, drinking cups, and for covering tepees; the sap sometimes as a drink and boiled down as a syrup.

HEART-LEAVED BIRCH, *Betula cordifolia* Regel, Nouv. Mem. Soc. Nat. Mousc. 13:86, 1860

A large tree, 20–25 m. high, of erect growth, with a trunk diameter up to 8 dm.; bark smooth, peeling in papery layers, flesh-colored on the outside, pale orange in the deeper layers; buds ovoid, reddish-brown, 5–6 mm. long; young twigs brownish-yellow, glabrous, abundantly glandular-dotted; older twigs reddish-brown, conspicuously marked by numerous pale lenticels; leaves broadly ovate, 5–9 cm. long, 4–7.5 cm. wide, with from six to nine pairs of lateral veins, cordate at the base, acuminate at the apex, margin doubly or somewhat irregularly serrate, dull green and glabrous above, or with a few hairs along the veins, paler beneath and pilose along the veins, both surfaces with small resinous dots; petiole rather stout, 1–2.5 cm. long, sparingly villous or glabrate; staminate catkins from terminal buds, usually in pairs; pistillate catkins on short, one- to three-leaved shoots from short lateral spurs, in fruit becoming 5–7 cm. long, and 8–12 mm. in diameter; peduncles 1.5–2.5 cm. long; fruiting bracts, 6.5–8.5 mm. long, deeply three-lobed, the middle lobe much longer than the strongly ascending lateral lobes, margins of the lobes ciliate; samara about 5 mm. wide, the elliptical nutlet narrower than the wings, persistent styles fully 2 mm. long. (*Cordifólia*, referring to the heart-shaped leaves.)

Heart-leaved birch is a large and handsome tree, common north of Lake Superior west to St. Louis County in Minnesota. It has also been reported from Manitoba and several scattered localities in Wisconsin, of which the southerly ones are of doubtful authenticity. It is distributed from Labrador and Newfoundland to northern New England, westward to Minnesota; it also occurs in Mt. Mitchell, North Carolina.

EUROPEAN WHITE BIRCH, *Betula pendula* Roth, Tent. Fl. Germ. 1:405, 1788 [*B. verrucosa* Ehrh. 1791; *B. alba* L. 1753, in part]

A small to medium-sized tree, 6–12 m. high; bark white, peeling slightly into papery layers except at the base, where it is more or less rough and furrowed and dark gray in color; branches slender and more or less drooping; young twigs reddish and glandular-dotted, older twigs gray to dark brown; leaves rhombic-ovate, 4–8 cm. long, 3.5–5.5 cm. wide, broadly wedge-shaped or truncate at the base (on vigorous shoots subcordate at the base and often larger), acuminate at the apex, doubly serrate to somewhat lobed, at first sparsely pubescent and glutinous, soon becoming entirely glabrous, bright green above, somewhat paler beneath, more or less gland-dotted on both surfaces; petioles slender, 2–3 cm. long; staminate catkins 3–6 cm. long; pistillate catkins on short, lateral, bifoliate shoots, in fruit 2–3.5 cm. long and 7–10 mm. in diameter, pointing toward the tip of the branch on which they are borne; peduncles 10–18 mm. long; fruiting bracts three-lobed, 5–7 mm. long, the middle lobe triangular, shorter than the spreading or somewhat recurved, rounded lateral lobes; samaras 5–6 mm. wide; nutlet narrowly elliptic, narrower than the wings. Blossoms in April or May; fruit ripe in September or October. (*Péndula*, referring to the somewhat drooping twigs.)

This birch, introduced from Europe, is sometimes planted as a park tree, passing under the name of *Betula alba* L. It is less frequently planted than the following horticultural variety.

BIRCH FAMILY

CUT-LEAF WEEPING BIRCH, *Betula pendula* f. *dalecarlica* (L. f.) Schneid., Ill. Handb. Laubh. 1:112, 1904 [*B. laciniata* Wahlenb. 1824]

A medium-sized tree with long, slender, drooping branches and deeply lobed or cut leaves; leaves narrowly ovate in outline, 4–7 cm. long, 2–5 cm. wide, with usually three or four pairs of long-attenuate pointed lobes, narrowed at the base, long-acuminate at the apex, sharply and irregularly serrate, glabrous and glandular-dotted on both surfaces, dark green above, somewhat paler beneath; petioles very slender, 2–3.5 cm. long; fruiting catkins 3–4 cm. long and about 1 cm. in diameter, borne on drooping peduncles (*Dalecárlica*, named from the province Dalecarlia of Sweden, where the form occurs spontaneously.)

The horticultural form known as forma *gracilis* is a cross between this form and Young's weeping birch (*B. pendula* f. *Youngi* Schneider). It has even longer and more drooping branches. It passes under the horticultural names *B. elegans laciniata* and *B. alba laciniata gracilis pendula*, but like many minor horticultural forms is probably best called by its vernacular name, the cut-leaf weeping birch.

YELLOW BIRCH, *Betula lutea* Michx. f., Arb. Am. 2:152, 1812

A large tree sometimes attaining a height of 25–30 m. and a trunk diameter of 1 m.; the bark of the trunk gray or yellowish-gray, peeling freely into thin papery layers and producing a ragged appearance of the main stem and lower branches; twigs gray or brownish, dotted with light-colored lenticels; inner bark aromatic, with the flavor of wintergreen; leaves ovate to oblong-ovate, 5–11 cm. long, 3–7 cm. wide, rounded or subcordate and mostly unequal at the base, acuminate at the apex, sharply doubly serrate, dark green and dull above, paler beneath and pubescent along the veins; petioles 1–1.5 cm. long, pubescent; staminate catkins 2–4 together, 4–8 cm. long; pistillate catkins sessile, about 1 cm. long; fruiting catkins oblong-ovate to subglobose, 1.5–2.5 cm. long, 1.2–1.6 cm. in diameter; fruiting bracts deeply three-lobed, 6–8 mm. long, ciliate on the margins, middle lobe oblong, longer than the ovate-oblong, ascending lateral lobes; nutlet elliptic, wider than the wings of the samara. Flowers in May; fruit ripe in August and September. (*Lútea*, yellow, referring to the bark.)

Growing in rich, moist woods, yellow birch is most common in the eastern and northeastern parts of the area, less frequent southward to central Iowa and northward to northwestern Minnesota and Manitoba. In the coniferous forest area it occurs mostly in boggy places with tamarack or black ash. It is distributed from Quebec to Ontario and Manitoba, south to Delaware, Maryland, West Virginia, northern Indiana, Illinois, and Iowa.

The yellow birch is one of the most valuable timber trees of eastern North America. The wood is light brown, close-grained, hard, and heavy, taking a beautiful polish; its weight is 40 lbs. It is largely used in the manufacture of furniture, inside finish, and for fuel. Most imitation mahogany is made from this wood.

104

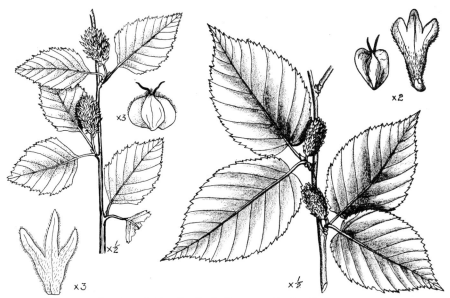

Species of *Betula*: Left, *B. nigra*. Right, *B. lutea*.

RED BIRCH, RIVER BIRCH, *Betula nigra* L., Sp. Pl. 982, 1753

A tall, usually slender tree, sometimes attaining a height of 30 m.; the bark at the base of old trunks dark brown, deeply furrowed, higher up on the main stem and on the larger branches lustrous reddish-brown and peeling more or less freely; twigs reddish; young twigs pubescent; leaves triangular-ovate, 3.5–8 cm. long, 2.5–6 cm. wide, broadly wedge-shaped or truncate at the base, obtuse or acute at the apex, irregularly serrate or somewhat pinnately lobed, dark green and glabrous above when mature, paler and glabrous or somewhat tomentose beneath; petioles 8–15 mm. long; staminate catkins 2–3 together, 6–10 cm. long; pistillate catkins oblong-cylindric, 1–1.5 cm. long, about 4 mm. in diameter; fruiting catkins oblong-ovoid, stalked, spreading, 1.5–2.5 cm. long, 11–14 mm. in diameter; fruiting bracts deeply three-lobed, 6–8 mm. long, tomentose, the lateral lobes ascending and nearly as long as the middle lobe; samaras 6–7 mm. wide; nutlet twice as wide as the wings of the samara. Blossoms in April and May; fruit ripe in autumn. (*Nígra*, black.)

Red birch grows along the bottomlands of streams and rivers. It is common along the Mississippi River as far north as Wabasha County, Minnesota, less frequent north to the confluence of the St. Croix River in Minnesota and to Chippewa County in Wisconsin; it has been reported, but is of doubtful occurrence, at Mankato, Minnesota. It is distributed on the Atlantic and Gulf coastal plain from Massachusetts to Florida and Texas and up the Mississippi River and its tributaries to Indiana, Wisconsin, Minnesota, and Kansas.

The wood is light brown, close-grained, hard, and strong, weighing 36 lbs. It is used in the manufacture of furniture and for staves and fuel.

105

LOW BIRCH, DWARF BIRCH, *Betula pumila* var. *glandulifera* Regel, Bull. Soc. Nat. Mousc. 38:410, 1865

A shrub 0.5–3 m. high, with erect or ascending stems and slender branches; bark dark gray to reddish-brown or dark brown, with numerous light-colored lenticels; young twigs more or less abundantly gland-dotted, at first finely puberulent or sparingly pubescent but at length glabrate; leaves obovate or elliptic to suborbicular, 1–3 cm. long, 8–20 mm. wide (occasionally larger on vigorous vegetative shoots), usually acute or sometimes rounded at the apex, narrowly to broadly cuneate at the base, serrate or crenate-serrate, gland-dotted on both surfaces and glutinous when young, at first somewhat pubescent along the veins but generally becoming quite glabrous with age, finely reticulate-veined; petioles 2–5 mm. long; staminate catkins erect, about 1 cm. long; pistillate catkins 5–8 mm. long, borne on very short, naked or one- or two-leaved lateral shoots; fruiting catkins oblong-cylindrical 8–20 mm. long, 6–8 mm. in diameter; fruiting bracts 3–3.5 mm. long, lateral lobes ascending, generally shorter than the middle lobe, sparingly ciliate along the margins; samaras nearly orbicular, the wings narrower than the nutlet. (*Púmila*, dwarf, referring to the low stature; *glandulifera*, gland-bearing, referring to the gland-dotted leaves and young twigs.)

Dwarf birch is common in acid meadows, swamps, and tamarack bogs throughout the northern part of the region; it is less frequent to rare and local southward, to northeastern Iowa, southern Wisconsin, and northern Illinois. It is distributed from western Quebec to British Columbia, south to northern New York, Indiana, Illinois, Iowa, and southeastern North Dakota.

The true dwarf birch, *B. pumila*, of the northeastern United States, eastern Canada, Labrador, and Newfoundland, is represented in the Great Lakes region by the above-described variety. Occasional pubescent forms of dwarf birch occurring in this region closely simulate true *B. pumila*, but in all cases they appear to be segregates of the following hybrid.

SANDBERG BIRCH, × *Betula Sandbergi* Britton, Bull. Torr. Bot. Club 31:166, 1904 [*B. papyrifera* × *pumila* var. *glandulifera*]

A shrub or sometimes a shrub-like tree, 2–10 m. high; bark dark brown, not separating into layers; young branches rusty-pubescent, in late summer or fall mostly shedding the hairs and remaining merely puberulent and showing scattered resiniferous dots and lenticels, older twigs at first grayish, later becoming reddish-brown through exfoliation of the epidermal layers; leaves ovate, rhombic-ovate or rarely elliptical to obovate, with four or five pairs of veins, cuneate or sometimes rounded at the base, acute or rounded at the apex, 2.5–5.5 cm. long, 1.5–3.5 cm. wide (on sterile shoots usually more broadly ovate and larger), serrate, the serrations somewhat crenate and occasionally uneven, thick and firm in texture, dull green, glabrous and finely reticulate-veined above, the reticulations conspicuous in dried specimens, paler beneath and pubescent, especially

106

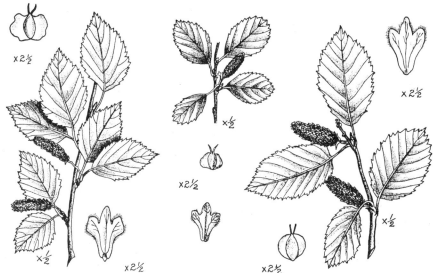

Species of *Betula*: Left, *B. Sandbergi*. Center, *B. pumila* var. *glandulifera*. Right, *B. Purpusii*.

along the veins, at length becoming nearly or quite glabrous, dotted with fine resinous glands; petioles 7–13 mm. long; staminate catkins borne singly or in pairs at the ends of the branches, 3–5 cm. long, 5 mm. thick; pistillate catkins 10–14 mm. long, 1.5–2 mm. thick, stalked; fruiting catkins cylindrical, erect, 2–2.5 cm. long, 5–7 mm. in diameter, their peduncles about 1 cm. long; bracts 4 mm. long, about 3.6 mm. wide, the lateral lobes spreading, shorter than the tapering middle lobe, puberulent on the back and finely ciliate-pubescent along the margins of the lobes; samara 3.2–3.5 mm. wide, nutlet 1.3 mm. wide, mostly slightly narrower than the wing. (*Sandbérgi*, named for J. H. Sandberg, who made extensive collections of Minnesota plants.)

This birch is infrequent in tamarack and spruce bogs or other moist habitats, mostly within the coniferous forest area of the region but occasionally beyond, in all cases, however, associated with the parent species. It is distributed from Wisconsin to eastern North Dakota and Manitoba, and has also been reported from Saskatchewan and Montana. This hybrid is fertile to a limited degree, and its progeny segregates into forms more or less resembling one or the other parent. Some of these segregates apparently occur in nature in the vicinity of the Twin Cities, and occasionally they very closely simulate typical *B. pumila*.

PURPUS BIRCH, × *Betula Purpusii* Schneid., Ill. Handb. Laubh. 1:102, 1904 [*B. lutea* × *pumila* var. *glandulifera*]

A shrub or shrub-like tree 3–6 m. high, with grayish-brown bark not separating into layers, inner bark with wintergreen flavor; young twigs puberulent or thinly pubescent, with a few small resin glands, one- to three-year-old twigs gray, changing to grayish-brown on older branches; spur shoots numerous with closely

107

crowded leaf scars; leaves ovate to oblong-ovate or elliptical, rarely obovate, with five to seven pairs of veins, broadly cuneate or rounded to subcordate at the base, acute at the apex, 2.5–6 cm. long, 1.5–3.5 cm. wide, dull green and gla-brous above, much lighter and at first pubescent along the veins beneath, soon becoming nearly or quite glabrous, often glandular-dotted, mostly unevenly and sharply serrate to crenate-serrate, thick and firm in texture; petioles stout, 7–14 mm. long, with a few scattered hairs; staminate catkins borne singly or in pairs at the ends of the branches, 3–5 cm. long in anthesis, about 5 mm. in diameter; pistillate catkins erect, sessile or nearly so, about 10 mm. long, 2–2.3 mm. thick; fruiting catkins oblong-ovoid, 1.5–2.8 cm. long, 10–12 mm. in diameter, erect, peduncles 3–8 mm. long; bracts 5.4–7 mm. long, 4.3–5.5 mm. wide, ciliate-pu-bescent along the margins of the lobes, lateral lobes broad and only slightly spreading, middle lobe blunt-triangular; samara ovate to slightly obovate, 2.5–3 mm. wide, nutlet 1.6–1.8 mm. wide, about twice as wide as the wing. (*Purpúsii*, named for J. A. Purpus of the Darmstadt botanical garden.)

Purpus birch grows in tamarack swamps, but is comparatively rare. Its gen-eral range is unknown. The original specimens came from "Clark's Lake," Michi-gan.

Alder

Alnus Hill, Brit. Herb. 510, 1756

Shrubs or trees with dentate or serrate leaves and few-scaled buds; flowers in catkins, appearing the preceding season and expanding before or with the leaves; staminate flowers three in the axil of each bract, subtended by four bract-lets, each flower with a perianth of four parts, stamens four; pistillate flowers two in the axil of each bract, two small bractlets subtending each flower, perianth lacking, ovary two-celled, styles two; in fruit the bracts becoming woody and five-toothed or pointed and together forming a cone-like structure; nutlet flat-tened, with or without wings. (*Al'nus*, the Latin name of the alder.)

A genus of about fourteen species, natives of the Northern Hemisphere and the Andes. In addition to the following, some six or seven species occur in North America.

KEY TO SPECIES OF ALNUS

1. Leaves finely serrate, resinous beneath when young; nutlets with a membranous wing. . . . .*A. crispa* (p. 108)
1. Leaves coarsely serrate, not resinous, nutlet acute-margined, wingless. . . . .*A. rugosa* var. *americana* (p. 110)

GREEN ALDER, MOUNTAIN ALDER, *Alnus crispa* (Ait.) Pursh, Fl. Am. Sept. 2:623, 1814

A shrub 0.6–3 m. high, bark gray or brownish; young shoots brownish, more or less pubescent and glutinous; leaves ovate or oval, rounded at the base, obtuse or acute at the apex, finely, sharply, and often irregularly serrulate or incised-

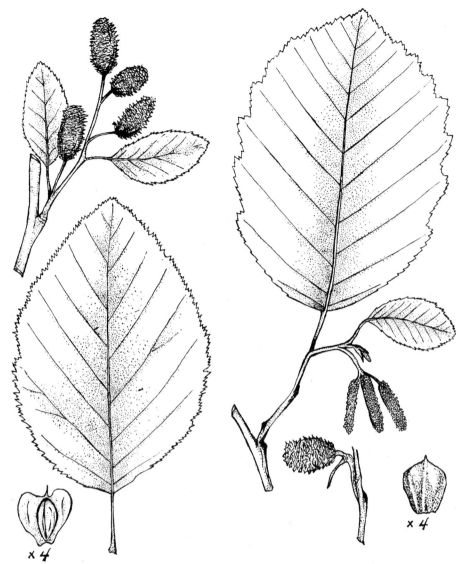

Species of *Alnus*: Left, *A. crispa*. Right, *A. rugosa* var. *americana*.

serrate, dark green and glabrous above, lighter green and usually pubescent beneath along the veins (young foliage glutinous and more or less pubescent), 4–8 cm. long, 3.5–5 cm. wide; petioles 8–10 mm. long; catkins expanding with the leaves, the staminate two or three together, slender, 6–10 cm. long, the pistillate in a loose raceme; fruiting catkin 15–18 mm. long, 7–9 mm. thick, the persistent scales firm and woody, irregularly five-lobed, about 4 mm. long; samara 2–2.5 mm. wide, nutlet ovoid, slightly broader than the wing. Flowers in May and June; fruit ripe in September. (*Crispa*, curled, referring to the margin of the leaves.)

109

Green alder grows on cool shores and banks, and is common in the Lake Superior region and northwestward to Manitoba. It is distributed from Labrador to Alaska, south to the mountains of New England, northern New York, Michigan, Wisconsin, Minnesota, Manitoba, and Alberta, and also in the mountains of Virginia and North Carolina.

SPECKLED ALDER, HOARY ALDER, *Alnus rugosa* var. *americana* (Regel) Fernald Rhodora 47:350, 1945 [*A. incana* (L) Tuckerm. 1794]

A tall shrub or occasionally a small tree, 2–8 m. high, stems erect or ascending; bark dark brown; young twigs reddish-brown; leaves oval or ovate, rounded or narrowed at the base, obtuse or acute at the apex, serrate or dentate, with serrulate teeth, dark green and glabrous above, paler and glaucous beneath and pubescent at least along the veins, 5–9 cm. long, 4–6 cm. wide; petioles 1.5–2 cm. long; staminate catkins three or four in a short raceme, 6–10 cm. long, in winter purplish-brown; pistillate catkins exposed through the winter, three or four together, borne below the staminate, expanding before the leaves; fruiting catkin 1–1.5 cm. long, 6–10 mm. thick, scales woody and five-toothed, about 4 mm. long; samara orbicular or slightly ovoid, without wings but with thin margins. Flowers in April; fruit ripe in autumn. (*Rugósa*, wrinkled; *americana*, American.)

Speckled alder grows in moist habitats, usually along shores of lakes or banks of streams. It is common throughout our area as far south as latitude 45°, infrequent southward to northeastern Iowa and southern Wisconsin. It is distributed from Labrador to Saskatchewan, south to New England, the mountains of Pennsylvania and West Virginia, westward to northern Indiana and northeastern Iowa.

BEECH FAMILY, Fagaceae

Trees or shrubs, with alternate, simple, often deeply lobed or cleft leaves; flowers small, monoecious; the staminate in pendulous or erect catkins, the pistillate solitary or several together, subtended by an involucre of united bracts which becomes a bur or cup in fruit; staminate flowers with from four to seven sepals; no petals; stamens four to seven, sometimes eight to fourteen; pistillate flowers with a four- to six-lobed calyx, adnate to the ovary; no petals; ovary inferior three- to six-celled; styles as many as the cells of the ovary; ovules one or two in each cell; fruit a one-seeded nut.

This family includes about four hundred species of temperate and tropical regions. Only the following genus is native to our region.*

* The beech *Fagus grandiflora* Ehrh. occurs in eastern Wisconsin and in the upper peninsula of Michigan. It has been reported in Minnesota, but to date there is no evidence of its occurrence within the state. It is a large tree with very smooth, light-gray bark, and thin but firm, unlobed, distantly toothed leaves. The staminate flowers are in stalked globular clusters appearing with the leaves; the fruit consists of from two to four three-cornered nuts surrounded by a bur-like involucre.

A few specimens of the chestnut *Castanea dentata* Borkh. have been planted in the ex-

BEECH FAMILY
Oak
Quercus L., Sp. Pl. 994, 1753

Trees or sometimes shrubs; leaves deciduous, withering persistent or (in some species of warm climates) evergreen, alternate, five-ranked, simple, pinnately veined, variously shaped, often lobed, furnished with small deciduous stipules; buds covered with numerous scales; flowers monoecious, apetalous, in all our species appearing with the leaves in spring, the staminate in catkins, clustered from scaly buds of the past year's growth and also from the lower nodes of the new growth; sepals four to seven, no petals; stamens four to twelve; no pistil; the pistillate solitary or in small clusters, in the axils of the leaves of the new growth; sepals six, united; no petals; no stamens; pistil three-parted; ovary inferior, nearly three-celled; ovules usually six; stigmas three; each pistillate flower surrounded by a cup-like involucre of many small, concrescent scales; fruit (acorn) a nut surrounded at the base by a cup-like involucre; seed solitary, without endosperm, the large embryo with thick, elliptical cotyledons which remain within the nut during germination. (*Quércus*, the classical Latin name of the oak.)

This is a genus of about three hundred species, native to the warm parts of the North Temperate Zone and of the adjacent tropical mountains. About fifty species occur in the United States, twenty-two of them in the eastern half of the country. Many oaks are valuable for their hard, strong wood, the astringent bark of several species is used in tanning leather, and the outer bark of two species from southwestern Europe and northern Africa furnishes the cork of commerce.

In cultivation oaks are raised from seed. After cutting they renew themselves by the growth of shoots from the stumps.

KEY TO SPECIES OF QUERCUS

1. Leaves acutely lobed, the lobes bristle-pointed; acorns ripening the second autumn. BLACK OAKS.
   2. Leaves dull green, their lobes cut about halfway to the midrib.
      3. Acorn cup cup-shaped, covering about one third of the acorn. . . . . *Q. borealis* (p. 112)
      3. Acorn cup saucer-shaped, covering only the base of the acorn. . . . .*Q. borealis* var. *maxima* (p. 113)
   2. Leaves glossy, their lobes cut about three-fourths of the way to the midrib; acorn cup covering one-third to one-half the acorn.
      4. Scales of acorn cup appressed, glabrous or somewhat puberulent, leaves thin but firm.

treme southeastern corner of Minnesota. It is a tree with scaly bark, and elliptic-lanceolate, strongly toothed leaves. The catkins (wholly staminate, or with a few pistillate flowers near the base) are produced in midsummer, and are very conspicuous, 15–20 cm. long, golden-yellow at anthesis; the fruit consists of several large, flattened ovate nuts surrounded by a bur-like involucre about 5 cm. in diameter; the seeds are very sweet and edible, particularly when roasted.

111

5. Acorn nearly round, scales of cup acute; autumn foliage scarlet; staminate catkins 8–10 cm. long..........................*Q. coccinea* (p. 114)
5. Acorn usually elongated, scales of cup obtuse or truncate; autumn foliage brown; staminate catkins about 4 cm. long......*Q. ellipsoidalis* (p. 115)
   4. Scales of acorn cup loose, silky-pubescent; leaves coriaceous, thick........
   ....*Q. velutina* (p. 116)
1. Leaves with rounded lobes or merely crenate-dentate, lobes and teeth not bristle-tipped; acorns ripening the first autumn. WHITE OAKS.
   6. Leaves deeply round-lobed.
      7. Leaves dull, glabrous; acorn cup not fringed.............*Q. alba* (p. 117)
      7. Leaves glossy above, hairy below; acorn cup fringed.
         8. Acorn cup 2.5–5 cm. in dm................*Q. macrocarpa* (p. 118)
         8. Acorn cup 1–2 cm. in dm......*Q. macrocarpa* var. *olivaeformis* (p. 120)
   6. Leaves shallowly lobed; acorn cup fringed, peduncled.. × *Q. Schuettii* (p. 121)
   6. Leaves crenate or crenate-dentate, not lobed.
      9. Tree, leaves broadly rhombic-obovate, rounded or obtuse, acorns long peduncled.......................................*Q. bicolor* (p. 122)
      9. Shrub or small tree, leaves oblanceolate, acute, acorns short peduncled.....
      ....*Q. Muehlenbergii* (p. 122)

NORTHERN RED OAK, *Quercus borealis* Michx. f., N.A. Sylv. 1:98, 1817
[*Q. rubra* var. *ambigua* (Michx. f.) Fernald 1908]

A large tree, 12–24 m. high, 3–10 dm. in diameter, trunk straight, limbs spreading, not gnarled; bark of limbs and small trunks smooth, gray, of large trunks fissured, with broad, flat-topped ridges, grayish-brown; buds thick, pointed at the top, narrowed at the base, 5 mm. long, 3 mm. wide, glabrous except at the top; leaves 10–18 cm. long, 7–16 cm. wide, widest about the middle, lobed about halfway to the midrib into several broad, triangular, acute, bristle-pointed lobes, each lobe having usually two or three narrow, bristle-tipped teeth near its outer end, apex of leaf acute, bristle-pointed, base rounded or broadly wedge-shaped, upper surface dull dark green, glabrous, lower surface paler, glabrous or with small tufts of brownish hairs in the axils of the large veins; petioles 2–4 cm. long; young leaves pink and covered with light down, soon glabrate and changing to a deep bronze color, which is maintained until they are nearly full grown; autumn coloration red; flowers opening when the leaves are about half-grown; staminate catkins slender, 4–10 cm. long, flowers scattered, often short-pedicelled, about 3 mm. in diameter; acorns ripening the second year, solitary or in pairs, sessile or borne on stalks 5 mm. long or less; acorn ovoid or cylindric, pale brown, lustrous, more or less downy toward the ends, 1.5–2.5 cm. long, 1–2 cm. wide, seed very astringent; cup cup-shaped, covering about one-third of the acorn, the scales closely appressed, small, ovate, acute, dark brown with a darker margin, puberulent. (*Boreális*, northern.)

This oak is common in upland woods and on hillsides throughout the forested parts of the region, even to extreme northeastern Minnesota; it is less common southward than its variety *maxima*. It is distributed from Quebec to Ontario and Minnesota, south to New England, northwestern Pennsylvania,

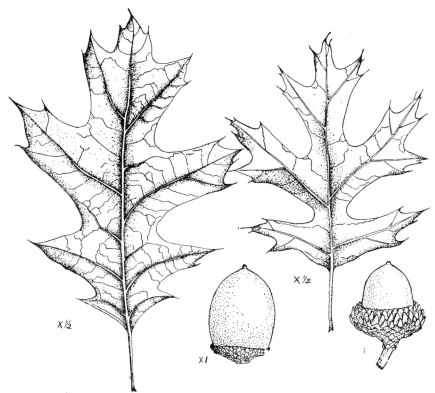

X½

X½

X1

Species of *Quercus*: Left, *Q. borealis* var. *maxima*. Right, *Q. velutina*.

Michigan, Wisconsin, and northern Iowa, and also in the mountains of North Carolina.

COMMON RED OAK, *Quercus borealis* var. *maxima* (Marsh.) Ashe, Proc. Soc. Am. Forest. 11:90, 1916 [*Q. rubra* β L. 1753; *Q. rubra* Du Roi and all later authors, not L.]

A somewhat larger tree (in the eastern states occasionally 45 m. high), differing from the species in having a larger, broad-based acorn 2–3 cm. long, 1.5–2 cm. wide, and a very flat, saucer-shaped cup that covers only the base of the acorn. (*Máxima*, largest.)

This variety grows throughout the area of mixed hardwood forests, most abundantly southward, and is one of the dominant trees on the rich calcareous clays of the "Big Woods" of central Minnesota. It is distributed from New Brunswick, southern Quebec, to Wisconsin and Minnesota, south to Georgia, Oklahoma, and Nebraska.

The wood is light reddish-brown, hard, strong, and coarse; its weight is 41 lbs. It is used for construction and finish of houses, cheap furniture, and for fuel. On account of its coarse grain and liability to crack in drying, the wood of this species and of others of the black oak class is much less valuable than that of the white oaks.

113

The common red oak is cultivated as an ornamental tree both in this country and in Europe. It makes a more rapid growth than most of the oaks, frequently having a second growing season in July, when the bronze-colored new leaves make a beautiful contrast to the deep green of the mature foliage. The red oak and other species of the black oak class have comparatively shallow and fibrous roots. They are, therefore, easily transplanted, but are also easily injured by grading operations, the trampling of cattle, and similar disturbances of the surface soil. This often leads to the erroneous impression that they will not thrive in cultivation.

SCARLET OAK, *Quercus coccinea* Muenchh., Hausv. 254, 1770

A tree 10–20 m. high, 3–6 dm. in diameter, occasionally larger; bark rather smooth, divided by shallow fissures into irregular ridges and plates, dark brown or grayish, inner bark reddish; buds oval, acute, 3–5 mm. long, 1.5–3 mm. wide, slightly hairy towards the top; leaves thin and firm 8–12 cm. long, 7–11 cm. wide, widest about the middle, deeply cut into about seven lobes, the lobes mostly two- to four-toothed, all the ultimate divisions long bristle-pointed; apex acute, bristle-pointed, base truncate or very broadly wedge-shaped, upper surface bright green, very glossy, glabrous, lower surface somewhat paler, less glossy, glabrous except sometimes with small tufts of hair in the axils of the large veins; petioles 2.5–4 cm. long; young leaves bright red, loosely pubescent above, silvery-tomentose beneath, soon becoming green and glabrate; autumn coloration bright scar-

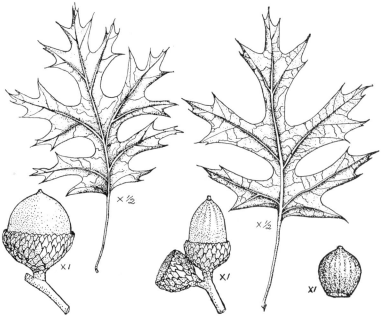

Species of *Quercus*: Left, *Q. coccinea*. Right, *Q. ellipsoidalis*.

let; flowers opening when the leaves are about half-grown, staminate catkins slender, glabrous or somewhat pubescent, 8–10 cm. long, flowers scattered, about 2.5 mm. in diameter, the stamens much longer than the sepals, pistillate flowers mostly on peduncles about 1 cm. long, stigmas about 1 mm. long; acorns ripening the second year, solitary or in pairs, usually peduncled; acorn oval, hemispheric, or slightly elongated, 1.5–1.8 cm. long, about 1.3 cm. wide, light reddish-brown, often slightly downy, seed pale yellow, bitter; cup turbinate, about 1.8 cm. wide, narrowed at the base, covering one-half to one-third of the acorn, its scales closely appressed, thin or somewhat thickened, deltoid lanceolate, acute, light reddish-brown, glabrous or slightly puberulent. (*Coccinea*, scarlet, referring to the autumn foliage.)

Growing on light, dry, sandy and usually acid soils, scarlet oak is infrequent northwestward to southern Wisconsin and probably southeastern Minnesota. It is often confused with *Q. ellipsoidalis* or possible hybrids between the latter and *Q. borealis*. It is distributed from Maine to Minnesota (?), south to Georgia, Arkansas, and Oklahoma.

Scarlet oak is easily grown from seed and transplanted, and is a useful ornamental tree on account of its beautiful autumn foliage. The wood is reddish-brown, hard, strong, and coarse, weighing 42 lbs. It is little used except for fuel.

NORTHERN PIN OAK, HILL'S OAK, "BLACK OAK," *Quercus ellipsoidalis* E. J. Hill, Bot. Gaz. 27:204, 1899

A tree 10–20 m. high, 3–6 dm. in diameter, or often low and almost shrub-like; bark at first smooth, later roughened and divided by shallow fissures into large plates, dark brown or blackish, branches dark gray, inner bark light yellow; buds rounded or pointed 1–3 mm. long, 0.75–1.5 mm. wide; nearly glabrous; leaves thin and firm, 7–14 cm. long, 7–12 cm. wide, widest at or above the middle, deeply cut into about five lobes, the lobes again lobulate or deeply cut or toothed, the ultimate divisions all acute and bristle-pointed; apex acute, bristle-pointed, base truncate or very broadly wedge-shaped, upper surface bright green, glossy, glabrous, lower surface somewhat paler, less glossy, glabrous except usually with small tufts of hairs in the axils of the large veins; petioles 2.5–4 cm. long; young leaves with but a trace of red, pubescent above, silvery-tomentose below, half-grown leaves very pale, rather tardily glabrate; autumn coloration brown, sometimes with blotches of purplish-red, leaves persisting throughout the winter; flowers opening when the leaves are about half-grown; staminate catkins pubescent 3.5–4.5 cm. long, flowers rather crowded, about 2.5 mm. in diameter, the stamens about the length of the sepals; pistillate flowers short-peduncled; stigmas about 2 mm. long; acorns ripening the second season, solitary or in pairs, borne on peduncles 1 cm. or less in length; acorn ellipsoidal or nearly globose, 1.3–2 cm. long, about 1 cm. wide, light brown, usually striped with darker lines, slightly downy or glabrous; seed bitter; cup turbinate, narrowed at the base, about 1.4 cm. wide, covering one-third to one-half of the acorn, its scales closely appressed, thin, ovate, obtuse or truncate, slightly pubescent. (*Ellipsoidális*, ellipsoidal, referring to the shape of the acorns.)

Northern pin oak is common and in places abundant on acid, sandy soils throughout the wooded districts of the region except northeastward; it is infrequent in the groves of the prairie districts and apparently does not reach the western border of Minnesota. It is distributed from southern Michigan to Manitoba, south to northern Indiana and northern Iowa. This is the common "black oak" of east central Minnesota and adjoining Wisconsin, where it covers large areas of sterile, sandy soil with a copse-like growth. The wood is light brown, strong, coarse, and heavy, and is used mostly for fuel.

Quercus palustris Muenchh., the true pin oak, is rarely planted in our area. It has leaves somewhat resembling those of *Q. coccinea* but tending to be longer and narrower, with wider, square-bottomed sinuses between the lobes. The acorn resembles a miniature red-oak acorn a trifle over 1 cm. in diameter. It is native from Massachusetts to Michigan and southward.

BLACK OAK, *Quercus velutina* Lam., Encycl. Meth. Bot. 1:721, 1783

A large tree 12–24 m. high, 6 dm.–1.2 m. in diameter (occasionally much larger in the Ohio Valley); bark dark brown or nearly black, ridged, scaly, inner bark orange; buds angled, rounded, or obtusely pointed, 3–10 mm. long, 2–6 mm. wide, hoary-tomentose; leaves thick, coriaceous, 8–17 cm. long, 10–15 cm. wide, variable in shape, but usually widest about the middle, deeply divided into five or seven lobes, the lobes again lobulate or more or less deeply toothed, all the ultimate divisions very acute and bristle-pointed; apex of leaf acute, bristle-pointed, base truncate or very broadly wedge-shaped, upper surface dark green and glossy, glabrate, lower surface yellowish or brownish, more or less pubescent with axillary tufts of brown hairs, rarely nearly glabrate; petioles 3.5–6 cm. long; young leaves crimson, pubescent above, silvery-tomentose below; when half-grown, golden-green and still conspicuously pubescent; autumn coloration brown, dark orange, or dull red, the leaves persisting far into the winter; flowers opening when the leaves are half-grown, staminate catkins 8–18 cm. long, hairy; flowers about 4 mm. in diameter, reddish-brown, the stamens apiculate, about half again as long as the sepals; acorns ripening the second year, solitary or in pairs, sessile or short-stalked, ovoid-oblong to hemispheric, 1.2–1.8 cm. long, 1.1–1.7 cm. wide, dark brown, covered with whitish down; cup turbinate about 2 cm. broad, covering one-third to one-half of the acorn, scales large, loose, thin, light brown, covered with a satiny pubescence, the tips of the upper scales free and spreading. (*Velútina*, velvety, referring probably to the acorn cups.)

Black oak grows in dry woods, often with shellbark hickory and mostly on noncalcareous soils, reaching its northern limit of distribution in the Mississippi

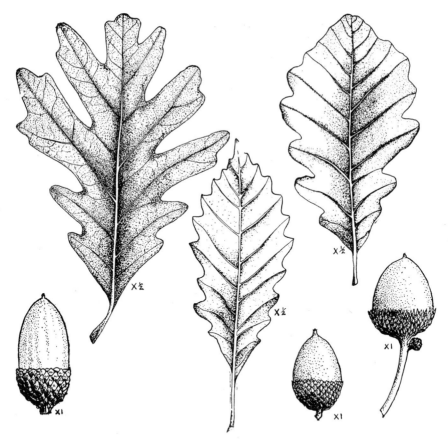

Species of *Quercus*: Left, *Q. alba*. Center, *Q. Muehlenbergii*. Right, *Q. bicolor*.

River Valley in the region of Lake Pepin. It is distributed from Maine to Minnesota, south to northern Florida and eastern Texas.

The wood is reddish-brown, hard, strong, and coarse; its weight is 44 lbs. It is little used, except for fuel. The bark is used for tanning, as a yellow dye, and medicinally as an astringent.

WHITE OAK, *Quercus alba* L., Sp. Pl. 996, 1753

A large tree 15–20 m. high, 1–1.5 m. in diameter (in the Ohio Valley sometimes 30 m. high, and 2–3.5 m. in diameter); bark pale gray, scaly but not deeply fissured; buds ovate, blunt, slightly hairy, about 3 mm. long; leaves crowded toward the ends of the twigs, 7–16 cm. long, 3.5–12 cm. wide, widest about the middle, rather uniformly lobed halfway to the midrib or deeper into about seven rounded, oblique lobes, the middle lobes largest and sometimes slightly lobulate, the depth of the lobing and the width of the lobes varying greatly in different individuals; apex of leaf rounded, base wedge-shaped, upper surface light dull green, glabrous, lower surface pale, veiny, glabrous; young leaves bright red above, pale below and soft-pubescent, when half-grown silvery-white; autumn

117

coloration purple-red, the leaves persisting far into the winter; petioles 1–2 cm. long; flowers opening when the leaves are about half-grown; staminate catkins 7–8 cm. long, very slender, flowers scattered about 2.5 mm. in diameter, yellow; pistillate flowers in clusters of two or three on a peduncle about 5 mm. long, or nearly sessile, bright red; acorns ripening the first season, sessile or on slender peduncles 1–3 cm. long; acorn oblong-ovoid 2.2–3 cm. long, 1.4–2 cm. wide, pale brown, glossy; seed sweet and edible; acorn cup finely downy, covering one-fourth to one-third of the acorn, its scales firm and broad, the lower ones much thickened, the upper thin, not forming a fringe. (*Al'ba*, white, referring to the pale leaves and bark.)

White oak occurs on heavy, well-drained, mostly acid soils. It is common and in places abundant throughout the wooded districts of our area as far north in the Mississippi and St. Croix River valleys as latitude 45°, less frequent and scattered to Morrison County, Minnesota, and Burnet County, Wisconsin. On the calcareous soils of the "Big Woods" of Minnesota it is absent except at a few stations along their eastern margin. It is distributed from Maine to Minnesota, south to Florida and Texas.

White oak can be grown from seed, the acorns germinating within a few weeks of their ripening and producing a long tap-root before winter. Oaks of the white-oak group are very deep rooted and difficult to transplant after they pass the seedling stage; on the other hand, they are far less sensitive to disturbance of the surface soils than are the black oaks. Despite their slow growth they are such fine and permanent trees that they should be planted wherever the soil is suitable. In calcareous soils planting is completely useless.

The wood of white oak is light brown, hard, and durable, weighing 46 lbs. It is one of our most useful woods for heavy construction, ship-building, railway ties, the interior finish of houses, and furniture, and is also much used for fuel. The "white oak" lumber of commerce is obtained indiscriminately from this and the two following species. The bark is astringent and is used for tanning and in medicine.

Hybrids apparently occur occasionally between this species and *Q. macrocarpa* var. *olivaeformis*. They have the leaf form of *Q. alba*, but with more or less stellate pubescence on the lower side of the leaves. So far as has been noted in this area, they are sterile. They are quite infrequent, as the parents are seldom found growing in close proximity to one another, and in ordinary seasons they bloom about a week apart. Whether or not this is the form described from Vermont and Pennsylvania as × *Q. Bebbiana* is unknown at present.

BUR OAK, *Quercus macrocarpa* Michx., Hist. Chênes no. 2, 1801

A large tree, 10–25 m. high, 3 dm.–1.5 m. in diameter (in the Ohio Valley sometimes twice this size), or under unfavorable situations stunted and sometimes barely 2 m. high, branches very strong and gnarled, producing in open-

118

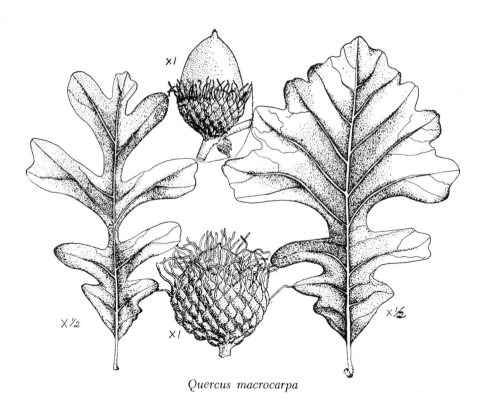

Quercus macrocarpa

grown trees an irregular and widely spreading crown, in dense forests often with a tall, straight trunk and short branches; bark dark grayish-brown, rough, heavily ridged and fissured, the twigs and smaller branches often with prominent corky wings; buds rounded, pubescent, about 2–3 mm. long; leaves crowded at the extremities of the twigs, thick and firm, 7–18 cm. long, 4–6 cm. wide, very variable in shape, irregularly round-lobed, usually most deeply lobed about the middle, broadest and much less deeply lobed above the middle, on some trees very slightly lobed, on others cut almost to the midrib; apex of leaf rounded, base wedge-shaped, upper surface glossy dark-green, glabrous or slightly pubescent, lower surface paler, sometimes silvery-white, tomentose with stellate pubescence; young leaves pale golden-green, densely woolly-pubescent; autumn coloration dull yellowish-brown; flowers opening when the leaves are about one-fourth-grown; staminate catkins 6–15 cm. long, pubescent; flowers green, about 1.5 mm. in diameter; pistillate flowers usually in pairs, sessile or short-peduncled, reddish; acorns ripening the same autumn, solitary or in pairs, sessile or peduncled, very variable in size and form, in typical *Q. macrocarpa* 1.8–5 cm. long, 1.5–3.5 cm. wide, ellipsoidal or broad-ovoid, with rounded, obtuse, or usually depressed apex; seed somewhat bitter; acorn cup thick, 2.5–5 cm. in diameter, hoary-tomentose, often nearly covering the nut, its scales tuberculate thickened, appressed, but those near the rim furnished with long, slender awns forming a conspicuous, matted fringe-like border. (*Macrocárpa*, large-fruited.)

119

Staminate and pistillate flowers of *Quercus macrocarpa*

The typical large-fruited form occurs sparingly on bottomlands and rich woods only in the southeastern part of Minnesota. It is distributed through North Carolina, Arkansas, Texas and northward, the exact northern limits of the typical form being somewhat doubtful.

NORTHERN BUR OAK, *Quercus macrocarpa* var. *olivaeformis* (Michx. f.) Gray, Man. Bot. ed. 2, 404, 1856 [*Q. olivaeformis* Michx. f. 1812]

Acorns 1–1.5 cm. long; acorn cup thin, less than 2 cm. in diameter, the fringe at its border sometimes sparse; staminate catkins 2–6 cm. long, the anthers nearly sessile. (*Olivaefórmis*, olive-shaped, relating to the shape of the acorns.)

This common northern variety of the bur oak seems to be quite sharply separated from the large-fruited southern form. Its most distinguishing peculiarities are its relatively small acorn and much thinner and smaller acorn cup. Even when the acorns themselves are of nearly the same size, the whole fruit of the northern form is only about half as large as that of the southern. It is here identified somewhat doubtfully with Michaux's *Q. olivaeformis*, which appears to be a rather extreme form of the northern variety. The acorn figured by Michaux is of the northern type, though rather unusually long and narrow. However, it

120

can be very closely matched on occasional trees. The very deeply and narrowly lobed leaves described and figured by Michaux are characteristic of a rather small minority of individuals in Minnesota, the great majority having leaves very similar to the typical large-fruited form. It seems questionable how much importance can be attributed to this character, particularly in a species with such variable foliage. Quite probably it represents an extreme case of individual variation. No correlation has been found to exist between leaf form and fruit characters, nor does the deeply lobed form seem to have any peculiar geographical range, but occurs more or less throughout the range of the species.

The common Upper Midwest tree has twigs greenish-gray in color, becoming nearly glabrate by the end of the first season, and usually developing corky ridges when three or four years old, but occasionally becoming corky the first season, and on other trees remaining smooth for many years and simulating *Q. alba*. In a small number of trees the twigs are pale orange, resembling the typical form. The buds are smaller than in typical *Q. macrocarpa*, about 2 mm. long, with several buds crowded together at the end of the twig. The leaves are stellate-pubescent beneath but usually less tomentose than in the typical form, and rarely much whitened; their autumn coloration is a peculiarly dead gray-brown, and they are the first of all oak leaves to fall. The varieties of this species need intensive study.

This oak is common in rich to sandy and acid soils throughout except north of Lake Superior; on the poorer soils and along the edges of the prairies it forms groves and thickets in which the trees are much reduced in size and often scrubby. It is distributed from Nova Scotia to Manitoba and Montana, south to New York, Indiana and Iowa.

Northern bur oak can be grown from the acorns, which germinate very freely. Its slow growth during its early years in our climate and the difficulty of transplanting saplings of any considerable size have prevented it from being planted to any great extent. It was naturally the most abundant tree in the vicinity of Minneapolis, and care should be taken to raise young trees to take the place of the old native specimens when they die, as it is one of our finest ornamental trees.

The wood is light brown, hard, very strong, tough, and durable; its weight is 46.5 lbs. It is somewhat stronger than white oak, has the same uses as the latter, and is not distinguished from it commercially. It is one of our most valuable timber trees.

$\times$ *Quercus Schuettii* Trel., Am. Phil. Soc. 59:51, 1917 [*Q. bicolor* $\times$ *macrocarpa* (var. *olivaeformis?*)]

Leaves intermediate between the two species, shallowly lobed, acorns peduncled, the cup but slightly fringed. (*Schuéttii*, named for J. H. Schuette of Green Bay, Wisconsin.)

This hybrid appears to be fairly common in certain places in the vicinity of the Twin Cities, where both parents occur. Sometimes it approaches more closely to one species, sometimes to the other. Nothing is known further of its distribution in the area. It was originally described from Brown County, Wisconsin, and occurs also in the vicinity of Montreal, and Rochester, New York.

SWAMP WHITE OAK, *Quercus bicolor* Willd., Neue Schrift. Ges. Nat. Fr. Berlin 3:396, 1801 [*Q. platinoides* Sudworth 1892]

A tree 10–20 m. high, 6 dm.–1 m. in diameter (sometimes considerably larger in New York, Ohio, and other parts of the East); the bark of the trunk grayish-brown, ridged and furrowed, the bark of the twigs ragged and irregularly peeling; buds rounded, 2 mm. long, nearly smooth; leaves often crowded at the extremities of the twigs, rhombic-ovate in outline, broadest a little above the middle, 7–18 cm. long, 3.5–11.5 cm. wide, coarsely crenate-dentate, or with shallow, somewhat acute lobes, leaves of exposed branches thick, dark green above, densely white-tomentose below with short, stellate hairs, leaves of lower shaded branches much thinner, pale green on both sides, sparingly pubescent below; young leaves bronze-green, silvery-pubescent beneath; autumn coloration rich golden-brown, the leaves rather tardily deciduous; flowers opening when the leaves are about one-third grown; staminate catkins about 6 cm. long, slender, flowers scattered, about 2.5 mm. in diameter; pistillate flowers in few-flowered, long-peduncled clusters; acorns ripening the first season, solitary, paired, or in clusters of three, borne on slender peduncles, 3–7 cm. long; acorn 2–3 cm. long, 1.5–2 cm. wide, light brown, slightly downy above; cup cup-shaped, one-third to one-half as long as the acorn, pubescent, its lower scales thickened, upper ones loose and some of them often with thread-like tips forming a fringe about the acorn, but never so prominently as in bur oak. (*Bicolor*, two-colored, referring to the dark green and white of the leaves.)

This oak grows in moist soil, bottomlands, and swamps. It is rather sparsely distributed over southern Wisconsin, northeastern Iowa, and southeastern Minnesota, and is infrequent to rare northward to Wood and Buffalo counties in Wisconsin and Ramsey County in Minnesota. It is distributed from Maine to Minnesota, south to Georgia, Arkansas, and Oklahoma.

The wood is light brown, hard, strong, tough, and durable, weighing 47.5 lbs. It has the same uses and properties as white oak and bur oak and is not distinguished from them commercially.

CHESTNUT OAK, *Quercus Muehlenbergii* Engelm., Trans. Acad. St. Louis 3:391, 1878

A shrub or small tree, 2–5 m. high, up to 1 dm. in diameter; bark light brown, scaly; buds rounded, slightly hairy, 2–3 mm. long; leaves oblanceolate, broadest above the middle, 4–12 cm. long, 2–5 cm. wide, sharply and coarsely toothed, apex acuminate, base wedge-shaped, upper side light green and glossy, with a few scattered stellate hairs, lower side pale, densely hairy; petioles 0.5–2 cm.

long; staminate catkins about 4 cm. long; pistillate flowers sessile or short-peduncled; acorns ripening the first season, sessile or borne on peduncles about 1 cm. long, elliptical, 1.5–2 cm. long, 1–1.5 cm. wide, light brown, downy toward the top; cups pubescent, about one-third as long as the acorn, the basal scales thickened and prominent. (*Muehlenbérgii*, named for G. H. E. Muhlenberg.)

Chestnut oak grows on dry calcareous bluffs and slopes. It is infrequent to rare southward in our area, reaching its northwestern limit in extreme southeastern Minnesota. It is distributed from Vermont and New York to southern Wisconsin and Minnesota, and south to northern Florida and Texas.

ELM FAMILY, Ulmaceae

Trees or shrubs with simple, alternate leaves; flowers perfect or monoecious or polygamous, clustered or the pistillate solitary; sepals three to nine, often united; no petals, stamens as many as the sepals and opposite them; carpels two, styles or sessile stigmas two; ovary mostly one-celled, superior; ovule one, pendulous; fruit a samara, drupe, or nut.

This family includes thirteen genera and about a hundred and forty species, widely distributed in temperate and tropical regions.

KEY TO GENERA OF ULMACEAE

1. Leaves pinnate with numerous, subequal lateral veins; flowers appearing before the leaves; fruit a winged samara.........................*Ulmus* (p. 123)
1. Leaves usually three-nerved from the base, flowers borne on the new growth with the leaves, fruit a drupe.................................*Celtis* (p. 128)

Elm
Ulmus L., Sp. Pl. 225, 1753

Trees, leaves alternate in two ranks, simple, mostly doubly serrate, pinnately veined with a large number of rather uniform lateral veins leaving the midrib at a wide angle, short-petioled, usually oblique at the base; stipules early deciduous; flowers in clusters, small, appearing before the leaves from special buds; calyx campanulate, usually somewhat oblique, consisting of from four to nine united sepals, petals wanting, stamens four to nine, opposite the sepals; carpels two, united, ovary one- or two-celled, styles two, divergent, stigmatic along the inner edge; fruit a one-seeded round or elliptical samara. (*Ul'mus*, the classical Latin name for the elm.)

This genus includes twenty-six species of the North Temperate Zone and the mountains of tropical Asia.

KEY TO SPECIES OF ULMUS BASED ON FLOWERS AND FRUIT

1. Pedicels much longer than the flowers; margin of samara ciliate.
   2. Flowers in racemes; samara large, its surface pubescent..*U. Thomasii* (p. 124)
   2. Flowers in umbel-like clusters; samara small, its surface smooth.............
   ....*U. americana* (p. 125)

123

1. Pedicels short, flowers in dense clusters; wing and margin of samara smooth.
   3. Bud scales conspicuously brown-hairy; nutlet pubescent with rusty-brown hairs
   . . . . *U. rubra* (p. 126)
   3. Bud scales nearly glabrous except along the ciliated margin; samara wholly glabrous.
      4. Buds nearly spherical, bud scales entirely glabrous except the ciliated margins; nutlet in the center of the samara. *U. pumila* (p. 127)
      4. Buds pointed, bud scales obscurely pubescent; nutlet above the center of the samara. . . . . *U. procera* (p. 127)

KEY TO SPECIES OF ULMUS IN SUMMER CONDITION

1. Upper surface of leaf very rough.
   2. Leaves folded along the midrib; inner bark mucilaginous. . . . . *U. rubra*
   2. Leaves flat; inner bark astringent. . . . . *U. americana*
1. Upper surface of leaf nearly or quite smooth.
   3. Leaves small, the largest not over 7 cm. long, nearly equal at the base. . *U. pumila*
   3. Leaves larger, distinctly unequal at the base.
      4. Twigs with prominent corky ridges; native tree. . . . . *U. Thomasii*
      4. Twigs without corky ridges.
         5. Young twigs nearly glabrous; under surface of leaves practically glabrous except for tufts of hairs in the axils of the veins; cultivated European tree. . . . . *U. procera*
         5. Young twigs pubescent; under surface of leaves with numerous, scattered short hairs; native tree, very frequently planted. . . . . *U. americana*

CORK ELM, ROCK ELM, *Ulmus Thomasii* Sarg., Silva N. Am. 14:102, 1902 [*U. racemosa* Thomas 1831]

A large tree with a somewhat cylindrical or conical top, 12–20 m. high and 5–10 dm. in diameter; the bark of the trunk dark-gray and ridged, the bark of the small branches frequently winged with heavy, corky ridges; young twigs somewhat pubescent; buds short-cylindrical, bud scales ciliate along the margin, surface sparsely pubescent; leaves elliptical or somewhat obovate, unequal, rounded, or more or less cordate on one or both sides, apex acute or short-acuminate, 5–13 cm. long, 4–7 cm. wide, nearly or quite glabrous above, short-pubescent beneath, doubly serrate; petiole short; stipules deciduous; flowers in loose racemes, appearing before the leaves; pedicels 4–7 mm. long; calyx broadly turbinate or campanulate, somewhat oblique, 3.5–4.5 mm. long; sepals oblong, free for about 1 mm.; samara obovate, 16–22 mm. long, strongly ciliate and with a short, white pubescence covering the faces, beaks short, crossed, nutlet above the center of the samara. (*Thomásii*, named for its discoverer, David Thomas.)

Cork elm is common in rich bottomland woods. It is sometimes found on slopes and river cliffs in southeastern Minnesota and the adjacent areas of Wisconsin and Iowa, and is less frequent to rare northward to the headwaters of the Mississippi River. It is distributed from Quebec to Minnesota, south to New Jersey, Kentucky, and Nebraska.

The wood is reddish-brown, hard, strong, and compact, even heavier and tougher than white elm, and the most valuable elm wood.

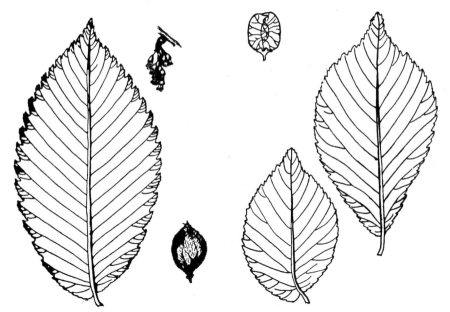

Species of *Ulmus*: Left, *U. Thomasii*. Right, *U. procera*.
(Leaves and fruits × 2/3.)

AMERICAN ELM, WHITE ELM, COMMON ELM, *Ulmus americana* L.,
Sp. Pl. 226, 1753

A large tree, when growing in the open usually with ascending, wide-spreading branches and more or less drooping branchlets, 12–25 m. high and 5–20 dm. in diameter, often attaining much greater size in the eastern and southeastern parts of the United States; the bark of the trunk gray and flaky; twigs and branches not corky, young twigs pubescent; buds pointed, bud scales ciliate along the margin, surface sparsely short-pubescent; leaves ovate to elliptical, base very unequal, one side usually cordate, the other side rounded or contracted, apex long-acuminate, 7–16 cm. long, 4.5–9 cm. wide, upper surface nearly glabrous or moderately rough-pubescent, lower surface sparsely pubescent, chiefly along the veins, margin doubly serrate; petiole short; stipules early deciduous; flowers in umbel-like clusters, appearing in early spring before the leaves, pedicels 5–10 mm. long, filiform; calyx turbinate, oblique, 2.5–3 mm. long, sepals blunt, united nearly to the summit; samara elliptical, 9–12 mm. long with two prominent converging beaks, margin densely white-ciliate, surface glabrous, strongly veined. (*Americána*, American.)

This elm is common in various habitats, but most abundant on the bottomlands of streams and rivers throughout the region. It is distributed from Newfoundland to Manitoba, south to Florida and Texas. It is the most extensively planted ornamental tree of the Upper Midwest region. The wood is rather coarse-grained, hard, tough, strong, and difficult to split.

125

ELM FAMILY

SLIPPERY ELM, RED ELM, *Ulmus rubra* Muhl., Trans. Am. Phil. Soc. 3:165 1793 [*U. fulva* Michx. 1803]

A large tree, with the main branches frequently extending out at right angles to the trunk, 12–20 m. high, 5–10 dm. in diameter; the bark of the trunk gray, rough, the inner bark very mucilaginous; twigs and branches not corky, young twigs rough, pubescent; buds rounded, inner bud scales rusty-pubescent, becoming very prominent when the buds unfold in the spring; leaves ovate or elliptical, strongly folded along the midrib, base rounded, somewhat unequal, sometimes slightly cordate on one side, apex acuminate, 6–14 cm. long, 4–7 cm. wide, very scabrous above, scabrous-pubescent along the veins beneath, margin doubly serrate; petiole short; stipules deciduous; flowers in glomerule-like clusters, appearing before the leaves; pedicels about 2 mm. long; calyx turbinate, very oblique, about 3 mm. long; sepals truncate, united nearly to the summit; samara orbicular or elliptical, 12–20 mm. long, whole samara glabrous except for a tuft of short, brownish hairs covering the nutlet, beaks obsolete, nutlet central. (*Rúbra*, red, referring to the buds.)

Slippery elm grows in rich soil, often along river banks and lake shores. It is common throughout the southern parts of the area, less frequent northward to the valley of the Red River of the North. It is distributed from Quebec to North Dakota, south to northern Florida and Texas. The wood is reddish-brown, hard, and strong. The inner bark is mucilaginous when chewed and is used in medicine as a demulcent.

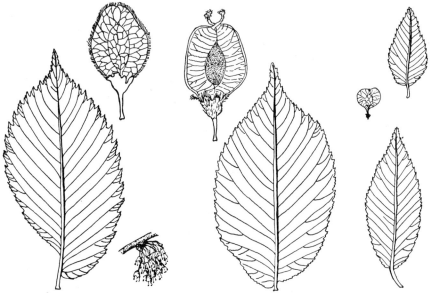

Species of *Ulmus*: Left, *U. americana*. Center, *U. rubra*. Right, *U. pumila*.
(Leaves × 2/3, fruit ×2.)

126

ELM FAMILY

SIBERIAN ELM, *Ulmus pumila* L., Sp. Pl. 226, 1753

A small tree, 5–10 m. high, 1–2 dm. in diameter; the bark of the trunk dark-gray, fissured, branches not at all corky, twigs slender, glabrous; leaf buds small, ovate, rounded at the top, flower buds much larger, globose, bud scales with ciliate margins, otherwise smooth and glossy; leaves elliptical or ovate to slightly obovate, base slightly unequal, rounded, acute at the apex, 3–7 cm. long, 1.5–4 cm. wide, almost completely glabrous, margin doubly serrate; petiole short; stipules deciduous; flowers in glomerule-like clusters, appearing before the leaves, pedicels less than 1 mm. long; calyx narrowly campanulate, scarcely oblique, 3–3.5 mm. long; sepals somewhat spatulate, truncate and ciliate at the apex, free for about 1.5 mm.; samara nearly orbicular, about 1.5 cm. long, glabrous; beaks crossed; nutlet central (*Púmila,* dwarf.)

This elm is a native of eastern Siberia, northern China, and Turkestan. Passing in the trade as "Chinese Elm," it has been planted extensively throughout the Upper Midwest as a windbreak around farmsteads and in shelter belts and as a shade tree along boulevards and in parks. Some of the plantings have proved successful while many others have not, apparently because of a lack of winter hardiness. That the seeds were derived from climatically different areas of the wide geographical range of the species may explain this difference.

The true Chinese Elm, *U. parvifolia* of north and central China, Korea, and Japan, is not cultivated in the Upper Midwest. In its native area it is a fall-blooming tree.

ENGLISH ELM, *Ulmus procera* Salisb., Prodr. Stirp. Chap. Allert. 391, 1796 [*U. campestris* L. 1753; *U. glabra* Mill. 1768]

A large tree with spreading branches and an oval head, under favorable conditions reaching somewhat larger size than the white elm; the bark of the trunk gray, corky, deeply fissured into rectangular flakes; branches not corky in the form usually planted in America; twigs mostly glabrous, glossy, brown; buds ovate, the inner bud scales ciliate along the margin, the surface with a few scattered hairs, the outer nearly or quite glabrous; leaves rhombic-obovate, sometimes nearly elliptical, apex acute or acuminate, base narrowed and somewhat unequal, 5–10 cm. long, 3.5–6 cm. wide, slightly scabrous above, practically glabrate beneath except for tufts of white hairs in the axils of the veins, margin doubly serrate (less sharply and deeply so than in the white elm); petiole short; stipules deciduous; flowers in glomerule-like clusters, appearing before the leaves; pedicels less than 1 mm. long; calyx narrowly obconic, scarcely oblique, 2–3 mm. long; sepals oblong, free for about 1 mm.; samara elliptical, orbicular or obcordate, 10–16 mm. long, smooth throughout; beaks crossed; nutlet somewhat above the center of the samara. (*Prócera,* tall.)

This European tree is much planted in the eastern United States and occasionally in Minnesota.

ELM FAMILY

Hackberry
Celtis L., Sp. Pl. 1043, 1753

Trees or shrubs; leaves simple, alternate, three- to five-nerved or in some species pinnately veined; flowers greenish, borne in the axils of the leaves of the season, polygamous or monoecious, the staminate clustered, the pistillate mostly solitary; sepals four to six, free or somewhat united; no petals; stamens four to six opposite the sepals; ovary one-celled; stigmas two, long and pointed, recurved or divergent; fruit an ovoid or globose drupe. (*Céltis*, an ancient name used by Pliny for an African species of lotus.)

This genus includes about sixty species (of which only the following occur in our area); they are natives of the North Temperate and tropical regions.

KEY TO SPECIES OF CELTIS

1. Leaves smooth or nearly so above....................*C. occidentalis* (p. 128)
1. Leaves very rough above..............*C. occidentalis* var. *crassifolia* (p. 129)

HACKBERRY, *Celtis occidentalis* L., Sp. Pl. 1044, 1753

A tree 10–16 m. high, 3–6 dm. in diameter, with a somewhat cylindric to rounded head; the bark of the trunk grayish-brown, much roughened with prominent, short, corky ridges; twigs slender, somewhat zigzag, brownish, shining, glabrous or sometimes slightly pubescent, knotty with prominent bud bases; buds pointed, prominent, bud scales pubescent and ciliate; leaves ovate to

Species of *Celtis*: Left, *C. occidentalis*. Right, *C. occidentalis* var. *crassifolia*.
(Leaves × 2/3, flowers × 2.)

rhombic-ovate, base unequal, usually narrowed or sometimes rounded, apex long-acuminate, 6–12 cm. long, 4–7 cm. wide, midrib prominent, the lateral veins five to fifteen, the basal ones prominent, often giving the leaf a three-nerved appearance, glabrous above, slightly pubescent along the veins beneath, margin serrate in the middle portion, about the lower one-third entire; petiole pubescent, about 1 cm. long; stipules falling as the leaves unfold; flowers appearing with the leaves, the lower staminate, arising in clusters from naked nodes, the upper perfect and solitary in the axils of the foliage leaves; sepals free, about 2 mm. long; drupe globose, dark purple to nearly black (rarely orange), with a thin, sweet, edible flesh. (*Occidentális*, Western, contrasted by Linnaeus to the two Old World species that he describes.)

Hackberry grows on wooded slopes, rich bottomlands, and along lake shores throughout the region, but is neither common nor anywhere abundant. It is distributed from New England to Manitoba and Idaho, south to northern Florida, Tennessee, Arkansas, and Oklahoma.

It is frequently planted as a street tree, but is somewhat undesirable as it is almost always afflicted with insect galls, which produce unsightly bunches of short twigs, looking like dilapidated birds' nests. It is very sensitive to late spring frosts. The wood is light yellow, coarse, and weak.

Celtis occidentalis L. var. *crassifolia* (Lam.) Gray, Man. Bot. ed. 2, 357, 1856 [*C. crassifolia* Lam. 1797]

A larger tree than the species, in Minnesota sometimes reaching a height of 25 m. and a trunk diameter of 9 dm.; twigs pubescent; leaves with base unequal, usually cordate, apex acuminate, ovate to ovate-lanceolate, 9–15 cm. long, 4–8 cm. wide, upper surface scabrous-pubescent, lower surface hirsute-pubescent, margin serrate almost to the base, the serrations sharper and coarser than in the species. (*Crassifólia*, thick-leaved.)

This variety occurs in similar habitats to those of the species and probably throughout most of the same range, except northward, where it is infrequent or rare. Most of the collections of the variety in Minnesota are from the southern half of the state. It is distributed from New Jersey to South Dakota, south to South Carolina and Colorado. It may possibly be a distinct species.

MULBERRY FAMILY, Moraceae

Trees or shrubs with milky sap, simple, alternate leaves; flowers monoecious or dioecious, in catkin-like or head-like clusters; sepals four or five somewhat united; no petals; stamens four or five, opposite the sepals; carpels two, styles one or two; ovary superior, mostly one-celled; ovule one, pendulous; fruit mostly aggregate, the calyx lobes persistent and becoming fleshy.

The mulberry family includes about fifty-five genera and a thousand species, mostly tropical. Only the following genus occurs in the Upper Midwest.

MULBERRY FAMILY

Mulberry

Morus L., Sp. Pl. 986, 1753

Trees or shrubs with milky sap; leaves alternate, simple, often lobed, three-nerved; stipules early deciduous; flowers in axillary catkin-like clusters, the pistillate clusters ripening into a succulent aggregate fruit; staminate flowers with four sepals, stamens four; pistillate flowers with four sepals, somewhat united below; ovary one-celled, stigmas two, spreading; true fruit an achene which is surrounded by the fleshy persistent calyx. (*Mórus*, the classical Latin name of the mulberry.)

This is a genus of about ten species of the Northern Hemisphere, of which two are found in our region.

KEY TO SPECIES OF MORUS

1. Leaves rough above, pubescent beneath; fruit purple. Native tree............... ....*M. rubra* (p. 130)
1. Leaves glabrous or nearly so; fruit white or pink. Cultivated tree..*M. alba* (p. 130)

RED MULBERRY, Morus rubra L., Sp. Pl. 986, 1753

A small tree or a shrub, in Minnesota rarely exceeding 6 m. in height, 1–5 dm. in diameter, in the southern states sometimes much larger; trunk short, dividing into several spreading branches; the bark of the trunk dark brown, irregularly flaky; twigs rather slender, at first green, finely puberulent, later becoming glabrous and brown or gray; buds conspicuous, ovoid, blunt, bud scales slightly ciliate and puberulent; leaves broadly ovate, occasional leaves deeply and irregularly three- to five-lobed, prominently three-nerved, more or less cordate or truncate at the base, apex long-acuminate, 7–19 cm. long, 6–13 cm. wide, upper surface slightly scabrous, lower surface pubescent, margin rather coarsely serrate; petiole about 2 cm. long; stipules linear-lanceolate, about 1.5 cm. long, deciduous about the time the leaf attains full size; staminate flowers in cylindrical, drooping catkin-like clusters, 3–4 cm. long, peduncle about 1 cm. long; pistillate clusters spreading, oval-cylindrical, about 1 cm. long, peduncle 0.5–1 cm. long; fruit reddish-black, 2.5–4 cm. long, 8–10 mm. in diameter, edible. (*Rúbra*, red, in reference to the fruit.)

The red mulberry is infrequent in the Upper Midwest, occuring chiefly in rich woods in the southern parts of the area; it is occasional in the Mississippi River Valley as far north as Hennepin County, Minnesota. It is distributed from Vermont to southern Ontario, Minnesota, and South Dakota, south to Florida and Texas.

The wood is yellow, light, soft, and weak, but durable in contact with the soil and hence frequently used for fence posts.

WHITE MULBERRY, Morus alba L., Sp. Pl. 986, 1753

A small tree rarely over 6 m. in height, 1–5 dm. in diameter, with gnarled,

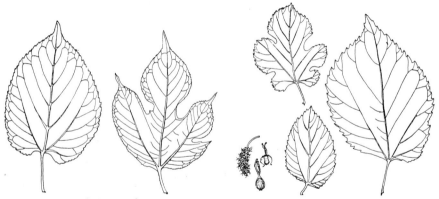

Species of *Morus*: Left, *M. rubra*. Right, *M. alba*.
(Leaves × 2/5, spike × 1/2, flowers × 1.)

irregular branches; the bark of the trunk yellowish-brown, with irregular sinuous ridges; twigs slender, puberulent when young, soon becoming smooth, light yellowish-gray; buds very broadly ovoid, short-pointed, bud scales obscurely ciliate, otherwise glabrous; leaves broadly ovate, often more or less three-lobed, prominently three-nerved, acute or acuminate at the apex, mostly cordate at the base, 5–12 cm. long, 3–8 cm. wide, upper surface minutely papillate, otherwise glabrous, lower surface glabrous except for a few hairs along the main veins, margin coarsely and rather bluntly serrate; petiole 2–3 cm. long; stipules very early deciduous; staminate spikes spreading or somewhat drooping, about 1.5 cm. long; peduncles very slender, 0.5 cm. long; pistillate spikes elliptic to globose, about 1 cm. long, peduncles 1 cm. long; fruit oblong to elliptic, about 1.5 cm. long, edible but insipid. (*Al'ba*, white, referring to the fruit.)

White mulberry is occasionally planted throughout the southern half of this area. It is not entirely hardy, the twigs often killing back during severe winters. It was introduced from Asia and occasionally escapes from cultivation. It is grown for feeding silk worms.

BIRTHWORT FAMILY, Aristolochiaceae

Herbs or woody plants, the latter mostly twining vines, with alternate, petioled leaves, for the most part cordate and entire; flowers perfect, mostly apetalous and epigynous; calyx of three sepals more or less completely united, often strongly zygomorphic; petals wanting (rarely three, rudimentary); stamens six to thirty-six, more or less fused with the pistil, appearing either as free stamens borne on the top of the ovary, or completely united with the style to form a column, anther-bearing below, and stigma-bearing at the summit; pistil compound, consisting of from four to six carpels; ovary mostly inferior (rarely partially superior) four- to six-celled; styles more or less completely united; stigmas free; fruit a capsule with from several to many seeds.

A family of five genera and about two hundred species of tropical and tem-

131

perate regions is most abundant in South America. The following is the only woody genus occurring in temperate North America.

Birthwort
Aristolochia L., Sp. Pl. 960, 1753

Perennial herbs or woody climbers often of large size, with alternate, petioled, heart-shaped or lobed, palmately veined leaves; flowers medium-sized to large, often unpleasantly scented; calyx tubular, variously bent, often with an expanded limb; petals wanting; stamens usually six, united with the style; carpels four to six, ovary inferior. (*Aristolóchia*, the Greek name of an herb used in obstetrics, from *aristos*, best, and *locheia*, birth.)

This is a genus of about a hundred and sixty species, of wide distribution. The following is the only woody species found in the northern United States.

DUTCHMAN'S PIPE, *Aristolochia durior* Hill, Twenty-five New Pl. 9, 1773 [*A. macrophylla* Lam. 1783; *A. Sipho* L'Her. 1784]

A tall, twining **vine**, with main stems up to 3 cm. in diameter; twigs slender, green, glabrous; **leaves** broadly reniform or orbicular, 15–25 cm. in diameter, palmately veined, apex rounded or short-acuminate, base deeply cordate, margin entire, upper surface deep green, glabrous, lower surface grayish-green, pubescent when young, becoming glabrate, petioles about 10 cm. long; flowers solitary, or two or three from the same axil; calyx tube sharply bent, yellowish-green, veiny, about 3 cm. long, the limb three-lobed, purple-brown, spreading, about 2 cm. in diameter; anthers six, arranged in pairs; stigma three-lobed; capsule oblong-cylindric 5–8 cm. long, about 2 cm. in diameter. (*Dúrior*, tougher.)

Dutchman's pipe grows in rich woods and on the banks of streams in southwestern Pennsylvania and West Virginia, and south in the uplands to Georgia and Alabama. It is frequently planted as an ornamental vine on porches and trellises and entirely hardy in the Upper Midwest as far north as latitude 45°.

BUTTERCUP FAMILY, Ranunculaceae

Herbs or sometimes woody plants, with acrid, usually colorless sap; leaves alternate (opposite in *Clematis*), simple or compound, petioles dilated at the base, sometimes with stipule-like appendages; flowers hypogynous, regular or irregular, polypetalous or apetalous, with sepals often colored like petals; stamens numerous (or rarely few); pistils many, or rarely solitary, one-celled; ovules many, anatropous; fruit a cluster of achenes or follicles, a single follicle, a berry, or in one genus a capsule.

This is a family of about thirty-five genera and twelve hundred species, distributed mostly throughout the temperate and frigid zones. It is well represented in our flora, but only the following genus is woody.

BUTTERCUP FAMILY

Virgin's Bower
Clematis L., Sp. Pl. 543, 1753

Climbing vines or erect or ascending perennial herbs, sometimes woody; climbing by bending or twining of the leaf stalks; leaves opposite, pinnately compound, lobed or in some species entire; flowers solitary or in panicles; sepals four or rarely five, petaloid; petals none, or as many as the sepals; pistils many; styles long-plumose, silky, or naked, persistent; fruit a cluster of achenes. (Greek *clématis*, a climbing plant.)

This genus includes over a hundred species of wide geographical distribution. The greatest number of species occur in the temperate regions. Besides the following, some twenty others occur in the southern and western parts of North America. In addition to the following woody species, several herbaceous species are commonly cultivated in the Upper Midwest.

KEY TO SPECIES OF CLEMATIS

1. Flowers large, solitary on the old branches; sepals purple...*C. verticillaris* (p. 133)
1. Flowers smaller, numerous, on the year's growth; sepals white.
   2. Leaflets toothed; flowering in summer...............*C. virginiana* (p. 133)
   2. Leaflets entire; flowering in autumn.................*C. paniculata* (p. 134)

PURPLE VIRGIN'S BOWER, *Clematis verticillaris* DC., Syst. 1:166, 1818 [*Atragene americana* Sims 1806]

A trailing or climbing vine with smooth, angular stems and large nodes; leaves trifoliolate, leaflets ovate, rounded or cordate at the base, acute at the apex, coarsely and evenly serrate, thin, glabrous, 3–6 cm. long, 1.5–3 cm. wide; petioles 2–3 cm. long; flowers axillary, purple, 5–7 cm. broad when expanded; sepals 3–4.5 cm. long, thin and prominently veined, silky-hairy along the margin; petals spatulate, 1.2–1.8 cm. long, persistent; styles persistent, becoming plumose and 5–6 cm. long in fruit. Blossoms in May and June; fruits in July and August. (*Verticilláris*, in a whorl, possibly in allusion to the climbing habit.)

Purple virgin's bower grows on rocky slopes and open woods. It is infrequent in our area and occurs mostly throughout the eastern part. It is distributed from Quebec to southeastern Manitoba, south to New England, Maryland, West Virginia, Wisconsin, and northeastern Iowa.

VIRGINIA VIRGIN'S BOWER, *Clematis virginiana* L., Amoen. Acad. 4:275, 1759

A long vine, climbing freely over shrubs and fences; stems furrowed; leaves opposite, trifoliolate; petioles straight and deflexed, or bent and acting as tendrils; leaflets ovate, rounded or cordate at the base, acute or acuminate at the apex, coarsely toothed or sometimes slightly three-lobed, bright green and glabrous above, paler and sometimes slightly pubescent beneath, 4–9 cm. long, 2–6 cm. broad; flowers in leafy panicles, white, 15–20 mm. broad; styles persis-

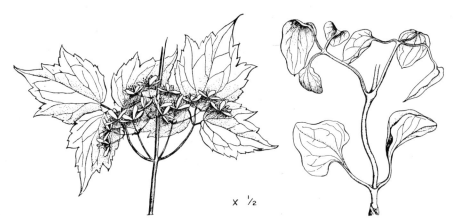

Species of *Clematis*: Left, *C. virginiana*. Right, *C. paniculata*.

tent, becoming 4–5 cm. long in fruit, and forming whitish, feathery plumes on the achenes. Flowers in June and July; fruits in August and September. (*Virginiána*, Virginian.)

Clematis virginiana grows in woods and thickets and on river banks and bottomlands throughout the wooded areas. It is distributed from Nova Scotia to Manitoba, south to Georgia, Alabama, Louisiana, and eastern Kansas.

CLEMATIS, *Clematis paniculata* Thunb., Trans. Lin. Soc. 2:337, 1794

A vigorous climbing vine, climbing over bushes, fences, and trellises; leaves three- to five-foliolate, the first pair of leaves of a shoot usually entire and cordate; leaflets ovate, rounded or mostly cordate at the base, acuminate at the apex, glabrous on both sides, young leaves with blotches of white along the veins, 2.5–5 cm. long, 1.8–3 cm. wide, the widened bases of the petioles connate; flowers in axillary and terminal panicles, white, fragrant, 2.5–3 cm. broad; fruit with persistent, plumose styles. Flowers and fruits in autumn (September–October). (*Paniculáta*, in a panicle.)

A native of Japan, this clematis is extensively cultivated as an arbor and trellis plant.

BARBERRY FAMILY, Berberidaceae

Shrubs or herbs with alternate or basal, simple or compound leaves, with or without stipules; flowers in racemes or solitary; sepals and petals imbricated in the bud, each mostly in two whorls of three (occasionally two or four in the whorl); stamens as many as the petals and in front of them or more numerous; anthers usually opening by two valves; carpel one; styles short; ovules two to many; fruit a berry or capsule.

The family includes about ten genera and over two hundred species, mainly of the North Temperate Zone.

The following genus is represented in our area by two cultivated species, one of which has become naturalized.

134

BARBERRY FAMILY

Barberry

Berberis L., Sp. Pl. 330, 1753

Shrubs with yellow wood and inner bark, usually spiny; leaves mostly in fascicles, simple or compound; flowers yellow, in drooping racemes or singly from each fascicle of leaves; sepals six, oblong, with from two to six acutish, sepal-like bracts on the outside; petals six, obovate, with two glands at the base; stamens six, with sensitive filaments closing up around the style when touched; anthers opening by valves; pistil one, stigma shield-shaped; fruit a one-seeded to few-seeded berry. (*Bérberis*, the Latin form of the Arabic name.)

This is a genus of about a hundred and sixty species, natives of North America, Europe, northern Asia, and South America. About twelve species occur in North America, of which our region has the following two.

KEY TO SPECIES OF BERBERIS

1. Leaves serrate; flowers and fruits in racemes. . . . .*B. vulgaris* (p. 135)
   2. Leaves entire; flowers mostly one to each leaf-cluster. . .*B. Thunbergii* (p. 135)

COMMON BARBERRY, *Berberis vulgaris* L., Sp. Pl. 330, 1753

A spiny shrub, 2–3 m. high, with arching branches, glabrous throughout; leaves alternate or fascicled, obovate or spatulate, obtuse at the apex, cuneate at the base, bristly serrate, glabrous on both sides, prominently reticulate-veined beneath, 2.5–7 cm. long, 0.8–2 cm. wide, a simple or more frequently a triple prolonged spine (modified leaf) below each fascicle; racemes pendulous, terminating the short shoots bearing the leaves, 4–8 cm. long, many-flowered; flowers yellow, about 8 mm. broad, ill-smelling; petals entire; fruit an oblong berry, scarlet when ripe, acid, persistent through the winter. Blossoms in April and May; fruit ripe in autumn. (*Vulgáris*, common.)

A native of Europe, common barberry was formerly much planted as an ornamental shrub and hedge plant and naturalized in many parts of the country. But it has proved to be the alternate host of the fungus that causes black stem rust of wheat. For this reason it has been outlawed, and should be destroyed wherever found.

Several forms have been developed through cultivation, among which the following has been the most commonly planted.

Berberis vulgaris f. *atropurpurea* Regel, in Gartenfl. 9:278, 1860

This form has purple-colored leaves. Otherwise it is like the species, and equally objectionable.

JAPANESE BARBERRY, *Berberis Thunbergii* DC., Syst. 2:9, 1821

A low, very dense shrub, 0.5–1 m. high; branches spreading and slightly curved; twigs brown, grooved; leaves in dense fascicles, spatulate, rounded or sometimes mucronate-tipped at the apex, glabrous throughout, glaucescent be-

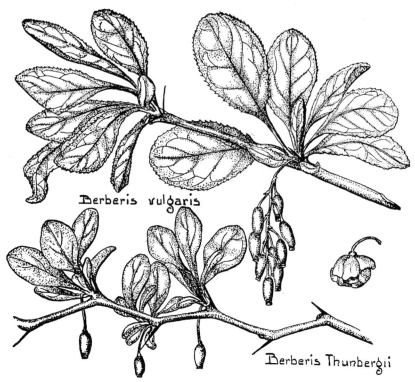

Species of *Berberis*

neath, entire, 5–40 mm. long, 2–10 mm. wide, fascicle subtended by a simple spine; flowers one to three (mostly one) terminating the short shoots, yellow with pinkish bracts, 6–8 mm. broad; pedicels 8–10 mm. long; fruit elliptic or ovoid, bright red when ripe, about 8 mm. long. Blossoms in early May; fruit ripe in August. (*Thunbérgii*, named for the botanist Thunberg.)

A native of Japan, this barberry is planted extensively as an ornamental shrub on account of its dense, spreading growth, its dark-red berries, and the handsome autumn coloring of the foliage. It is especially well adapted for borders of walks and drives and is perfectly hardy in our climate. It does not act as a host for wheat rust, and is entirely unobjectionable.

MOONSEED FAMILY, Menispermaceae

Climbing or twining, woody or herbaceous vines; leaves alternate, palmate or peltate, entire or lobed, stipules lacking; flowers in panicles, racemes, or cymes, small, dioecious; sepals four to twelve; petals six, in two whorls of three each, sometimes fewer or none, imbricated in the bud; stamens about the same number as petals; carpels from three to many (mostly six), ovule one; fruit a drupe, ovary often curving in development into a fruit, causing the seed to be bent into a crescent.

136

This family of fifty-five genera and about two hundred and sixty species, chiefly of tropical regions, is represented in our flora by the following genus only.

Moonseed

Menispermum L., Sp. Pl. 340, 1753

Climbing vines with large, peltate or cordate, lobed or entire, alternate leaves; flowers in panicles, small, dioecious; sepals four to eight, in two series or whorls; petals six to eight, shorter than the sepals; stamens twelve to twenty-four; pistils in the fertile flowers two to four, on a raised receptacle; staminodia usually present; stigma broad and flat; fruit a flattened drupe; seed bent into a crescent, hence the name. (*Menispérmum*, moonseed, from Greek *mene*, the moon, *sperma*, seed.)

This is a genus of two species, one of them occurring in North America, the other in eastern Asia.

MOONSEED, *Menispermum canadense* L., Sp. Pl. 340, 1753

A vine climbing over bushes or fences, 2–4 m. in length; stems slightly pubescent, twining; leaves on long, slender petioles, cordate and entire or variously three- to seven-lobed or angled, mostly peltate near the margin, glabrate above, pubescent beneath, 6–17 cm. long, 7–29 cm. broad; flowers in loose panicles, greenish-white; drupe oblong, bluish-black; seed crescent-shaped. Blossoms in June; the drupes, ripening in September, are black with a bloom and look like frost-grapes. (*Canadénse*, Canadian.)

Moonseed grows in woods and thickets and along stream banks rather commonly throughout the area. It is distributed from western Quebec and western

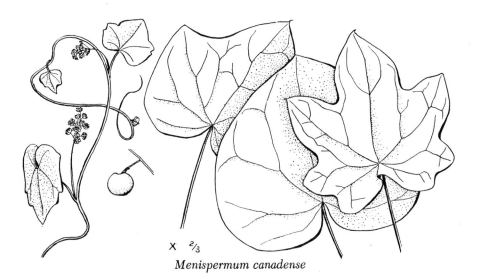

X ²⁄₃

Menispermum canadense

137

New England to the Red River Valley in Manitoba, south to Georgia, Alabama, Arkansas, and Oklahoma.

"The long, slender, bitter, yellow root is used by the Sioux as medicine, being called *Pejuta zizi*; and from this came the name Pejuta zizi or Yellow Medicine River" (T. M. Young).

MAGNOLIA FAMILY, Magnoliaceae

Trees or shrubs; leaves alternate, entire or lobed, marked with transparent dots; leaf buds covered with membranous stipules; bark bitter and aromatic; flowers large and solitary; sepals and petals colored alike, arranged in threes, mostly imbricated in the bud, hypogynous and deciduous; stamens numerous, large, anthers adnate; carpels many, on an elongated or cone-shaped receptacle, free or cohering with each other and in the fruit forming a sort of fleshy strobilus; seeds one or two in each carpel.

This is a family of about ten genera and a hundred species, of wide geographic distribution. The following genus is represented by one cultivated species in our area.

Magnolia
Magnolia L., Sp. Pl. 535, 1753

Trees or shrubs with large, usually thick, entire leaves; leaf buds covered with sheathing stipules; flowers large, fragrant, borne singly at the ends of branches, appearing before or with the leaves; sepals three, petal-like; petals six to nine, in whorls of three; stamens imbricated, with short filaments and large anthers; carpels on a cone-shaped receptacle, cohering and forming at maturity an aggregate, cone-like fruit with dry or fleshy follicles that dehisce and let out by slender threads one or two, usually red seeds. Flowers in June. (*Magnólia*, named for the French botanist, Magnol.)

This genus includes about thirty species, natives of eastern North America, southern Mexico, and eastern and southern Asia. Several Asiatic species with large white flowers, which open before the leaves appear, are favorite ornamental trees. The following species, planted to some extent in the Upper Midwest, is the only one that endures our climate.

CUCUMBER TREE, *Magnolia acuminata* L., Sp. Pl. 536, 1753

A tree about 15–20 m. high, attaining a maximum height farther south of 30 m.; leaf buds silvery-gray and silky-pubescent; leaves oblong or ovate, acuminate at the apex, pinnately veined, margin entire, glabrous above, more or less pubescent beneath, 13–24 cm. long, 7–13 cm. wide; flowers somewhat narrowly campanulate, greenish-yellow, glaucous, orange-colored within, 4–7 cm. long; fruit cone about 4–7 cm. long. (*Acumináta*, pointed, in reference to the leaf.)

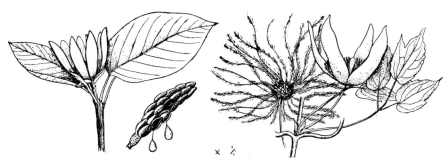

x ½

Left, *Magnolia acuminata.* Right, *Clematis verticillaris.*

The cucumber tree grows in rich woods in western New York and southern Ontario west to southern Illinois, and south, chiefly in the uplands, to Georgia, Alabama, and Arkansas. It is occasionally planted in the Upper Midwest and apparently is hardy as far north as the Twin Cities in Minnesota.

SAXIFRAGE FAMILY, SAXIFRAGACEAE

Herbs or shrubs, mostly with alternate, rarely opposite leaves, without true stipules (often with stipule-like sheaths); flowers mostly perfect, rarely polygamo-dioecious, regular or infrequently irregular, hypogynous, perigynous, or epigynous, solitary or in inflorescences of various kinds, sepals four or five borne on a more or less developed hypanthium; petals four or five, rarely wanting; stamens mostly eight to ten (less frequently four or five). or numerous; carpels mostly two, rarely three to five, more or less united or nearly free; ovary two-celled (rarely three- to five-celled) or frequently one-celled with two mostly parietal placentae; seeds numerous, small, sometimes more or less winged, with copious endosperm.

This family of about fifty-five genera and six hundred and fifty species is widely distributed, but most abundant in the North Temperate Zone and in the Andes, rare in the tropics.

KEY TO GENERA OF SAXIFRAGACEAE

1. Leaves opposite or whorled, not lobed; stamens more than five.
    2. Stamens more than ten, flowers white and showy, leaves opposite . . . .
    . . . .*Philadelphus* (p. 139)
    2. Stamens eight to ten, flowers greenish, outer ones often sterile, leaves mostly in
    whorls of three . . . .*Hydrangea* (p. 142)
1. Leaves alternate, lobed; stamens four to five . . . .*Ribes* (p. 144)

Syringa, Mock Orange
Philadelphus L., Sp. Pl. 470, 1753

Shrubs with opposite, simple, toothed, or entire leaves; flowers large, white or cream-colored, terminal or axillary, in cymes, racemes, or solitary; hypanthium top-shaped adnate to the lower two-thirds of the ovary; sepals four or five,

139

rounded or obovate; petals four or five; stamens twenty to forty; styles free or united below, ovary three- to five-celled; fruit a three- to five-celled capsule; seeds numerous. (*Philadélphus*, from Greek *philadelphon*, a sweet-flowering shrub.)

This genus includes about fifty species, natives of North America, Asia, and Central Europe. In addition to the following, six other species occur in the southern and western parts of North America.

KEY TO SPECIES OF PHILADELPHUS

1. Flowers in racemose clusters of from five to nine, odorous.
   2. Shrub up to 3–4 m. high; leaves remotely serrate, pubescent beneath. . . . . *P. coronarius* (p. 140)
   2. Shrubs 1–2 m. high; leaves nearly entire, glabrous beneath. . . . . × *P. Lemoinei* (p. 141)
1. Flowers solitary or in short clusters of three or rarely five, nearly scentless, leaves remotely denticulate. . . . .*P. grandiflorus* (p. 141)

MOCK ORANGE, GARDEN SYRINGA, *Philadelphus coronarius* L., Sp. Pl. 470, 1753

A shrub 2–4 m. high, with grayish, somewhat shredded bark; young twigs reddish- or yellowish-brown, glabrous or with a few sparse hairs, peeling during the second season with papery layers; leaves ovate or elliptic, 4–7 cm. long, 2–5 cm. wide, base rounded or narrowed, apex acuminate, margin remotely serrate with from seven to ten very small teeth on each side, upper surface dull dark-green, glabrous, lower surface paler, rough-pubescent at least along the veins, petiole about 5 mm. long, pubescent; flowers in raceme-like clusters with a terminal flower and from two to four pairs of lateral flowers; pedicels pubescent, about 5 mm. long; flowers cream-colored, very fragrant, 3–4 cm. broad; hypanthium nearly glabrous; sepals lanceolate, 5–6 mm. long, somewhat pubescent within; petals elliptic, 12–16 mm. long, 8–12 mm. wide; stamens 5–6 mm. long, the anthers yellow; styles a little shorter than the stamens, united at the base or sometimes for nearly half their length; fruit a top-shaped capsule 7–10 mm long. Blossoms in June; fruit ripe in August and September. (*Coronárius*, garland-like.)

A native of Europe, mock orange is much cultivated as an ornamental shrub and is entirely hardy in the Upper Midwest. As it comes up freely from seed in gardens, it is likely to be found growing spontaneously in our area as it does in some other parts of the United States.

There are a number of cultivated forms of this species. One with golden-yellow leaves (*P. coronarius* var. *aureus*) is frequently planted. There are also a number of garden hybrids of this with other species, and where two species are grown in proximity natural hybrids are likely to appear. The most planted of the hybrids is the following.

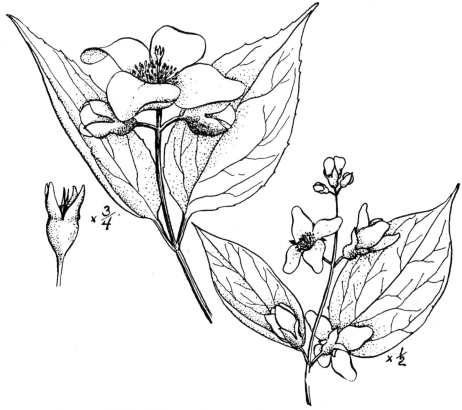

Species of *Philadelphus*: Left, *P. grandiflorus*. Right, *P. coronarius*.

$\times$ *Philadelphus Lemoinei* Lemoine, Cat. 1887 [*P. coronarius* $\times$ *microphyllus*]

A shrub about 2 m. high, the leaves smaller than in *P. coronarius* and nearly or quite entire; pedicels glabrous, hypanthium and sepals pale, glabrous; styles often much shorter than the stamens and united to above the middle. (*Lemoinei*, named for the originator, the French florist Lemoine.)

There are a series of garden forms, some of them with double flowers.

LARGE-FLOWERED SYRINGA, *Philadelphus grandiflorus* Willd., Enum. Pl. Hort. Berol. 511, 1809

A shrub 2–3 m. high, with grayish, somewhat shredded bark; twigs dark reddish-brown, glabrous, exfoliating the second or third year; leaves ovate to ovate-lanceolate 6–10 cm. long, 3–6 cm. wide, base narrowed or somewhat rounded, apex acuminate, margin denticulate with six to eight remote teeth, upper surface dull dark-green, glabrous, lower surface somewhat paler, glabrous except for a little pubescence in the axils of the veins; petioles 6–8 mm. long, glabrous; flowers solitary or in three-flowered cymes at the end of branchlets, rarely with additional flowers in the axils of the uppermost leaves; pedicels glabrous; flowers pure white, scentless, 3–5 cm. broad; hypanthium glabrous; sepals lance-

141

olate, about 1 cm. long, glabrous without, tomentose within; petals broadly ovate, 1.5–2 cm. long; stamens about 1 cm. long; styles rather exceeding the stamens, united nearly to the summit; fruit a top-shaped capsule, 9–12 mm. long. Flowers in May or early June, about ten days before *P. coronarius*; fruit ripe in August. (*Grandiflórus*, large-flowered.)

Large-flowered syringa is a native of the southern Appalachian Mountains. It is frequently planted as an ornamental shrub and is entirely hardy.

Hydrangea
Hydrangea L., Sp. Pl. 397, 1753

Shrubs with opposite or whorled, simple leaves; flowers white or tinged with pink, in terminal, compound cymes, the marginal ones usually sterile and consisting of a large, membranous, flat, colored calyx, fertile flowers small, hypanthium hemispherical, adnate to the ovary, sepals four or five, petals four or five, ovate, stamens eight to ten, ovary two- to four-celled, styles two to four, distinct; fruit a many-ribbed, many-seeded capsule, opening between the styles.

This genus includes about thirty-five species, natives of eastern North America, eastern Asia and the Himalayas, and South America. Three of them occur in the southeastern states. The following are cultivated in this region. (*Hydrángea*, from Greek *hydrangeion*, a water vessel, referring to the shape of the capsule.)

KEY TO SPECIES OF HYDRANGEA

1. Leaves opposite, broadly ovate, mostly cordate at base, flower cluster nearly flat-topped..*H. arborescens* (p. 142)
1. Leaves mostly in threes, ovate-lanceolate, flower cluster pyramidal.............. ....*H. paniculata* (p. 143)

Hydrangea arborescens L., Sp. Pl. 397, 1753

A shrub 1–3 m. high (in our climate seldom over 1.5 m.), young twigs pubescent; leaves opposite, broadly ovate to nearly orbicular, rounded or cordate at the base, acute or rounded at the apex, coarsely serrate, glabrate above or with a few scattered rough hairs along the main veins, somewhat pubescent along the veins below, 6–12 cm. long, 4–8 cm. wide; petioles 1–2 cm. long; cyme compound, flattened, 5–25 cm. broad, sterile marginal flowers few or quite numerous (in the cultivated forms often constituting nearly the whole flower cluster), white and showy, becoming green in old age; fruit a two-beaked capsule. (*Arboréscens*, tree-like.)

This species grows from southern New York to Florida, west to Iowa and Missouri. It is not native to the Upper Midwest. The following variety is frequently cultivated.

HILLS OF SNOW, *Hydrangea arborescens* L. f. *grandiflora* Rehder, Mitt. D. D. G. 16:71, 1907

Almost all the flowers sterile, leaves cordate at the base.

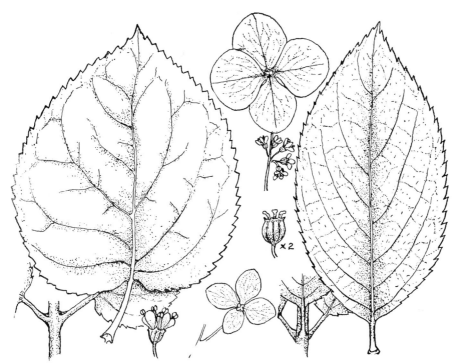

Species of *Hydrangea*: Left, *H. arborescens*. Right
H. paniculata. ($\times$ 4/5)

This is an excellent ornamental shrub. Though in the latitude of Minneapolis it is not quite hardy, killing back in severe winters to about the level of the snow. However, as it blossoms on the new growth, this winterkilling is not injurious, though it prevents the shrub from reaching its maximum size here. (*Grandiflóra*, large-flowered.)

Hydrangea paniculata Sieb., Nov. Act. Leop. 691, 1829

A shrub or small tree 1–9 m. high; leaves opposite or mostly in whorls of three, elliptic or ovate, narrowed at the base, acuminate at the apex, serrate, pubescent with stiff, scattered hairs above, more densely and finely pubescent on the veins beneath, 5–12 cm. long, 4–6 cm. wide; petioles less than 1 cm. long; cymes terminal, 9–30 cm. long, flowers whitish, the sterile ones later changing to purplish, styles three; fruit a three-beaked capsule about 4 mm. long. (*Paniculáta*, in a panicle.)

A native of Japan, the typical form is seldom seen in our area. The following variety is perfectly hardy and is the one commonly grown here.

Hydrangea paniculata var. *grandiflora* Sieb., Ill. Gartenz 1866:81, 1866

Almost all the flowers sterile, the panicles very large and showy. Commonly known to gardeners as "Peegee." Blossoms in August and September. (*Grandiflóra*, large-flowered.)

143

SAXIFRAGE FAMILY

Currant, Gooseberry
Ribes L., Sp. Pl. 200, 1753

Shrubs with alternate, often fascicled, usually lobed, petioled leaves; stems frequently spiny; flowers racemose or subsolitary, borne with the leaves or from separate lateral buds, perfect or rarely polygamo-dioecious, regular, epigynous; hypanthium saucer-shaped, campanulate, or tubular; sepals five, petals five small, stamens five, alternate with the petals, carpels two, ovary inferior or half-inferior, one-celled, with numerous ovules borne on two mostly parietal placentae; styles free or united, stigmas two, rarely one; fruit a berry. (*Ribes*, the Arabic name.)

This is a genus of about a hundred and twenty species of the North Temperate Zone and the Andes, most abundant in western North America and eastern Asia.

KEY TO SPECIES OF RIBES

1. Flowers in racemes; pedicel jointed at the base of the flower; stems smooth except in *Ribes lacustre*. CURRANTS.
    2. Stems very prickly; hypanthium saucer-shaped..........*R. lacustre* (p. 145)
    2. Stems smooth.
        3. Hypanthium campanulate to saucer-shaped or nearly obsolete.
            4. Hypanthium saucer-shaped or nearly obsolete; leaves without yellow resinous glands on the lower surface.
                5. Racemes compact; bracts longer than the pedicels, with very glandular margins.................................*R. alpinum* (p. 146)
                5. Racemes lax; pedicels much exceeding the bracts.
                    6. Pedicels and ovaries covered with stalked glands..............
                    ....*R. glandulosum* (p. 146)
                    6. Pedicels and ovaries without stalked glands.
                        7. Flowers purplish; low, creeping, or ascending shrub.........
                        ....*R. triste* (p. 147)
                        7. Flowers greenish-yellow; erect shrub.....*R. sativum* (p. 148)
            4. Hypanthium campanulate or crateriform; leaves with yellow, resinous dots on the lower surface.
                8. Hypanthium campanulate, 2.5–5 mm. high; flowers greenish-yellow; flowering racemes drooping.
                    9. Bracts 5–8 mm. long, exceeding the pedicels....................
                    .... *R. americanum* (p. 149)
                    9. Bracts less than 3 mm. long, much shorter than the pedicels.......
                    .... *R. nigrum* (p. 149)
                8. Hypanthium crateriform, about 1 mm. high; flowers white; flowering racemes erect........................*R. hudsonianum* (p. 150)
        3. Hypanthium long-tubular; flowers bright yellow, fragrant..............
        ....*R. odoratum* (p. 151)
1. Peduncles one- to four-flowered, borne at the summit of short, leafy shoots; pedicel not jointed at the base of the flower; stems more or less prickly. GOOSEBERRIES, genus *Grossularia* of many authors.
    10. Ovary bristly, fruit prickly; styles united to the summit. .*R. Cynosbati* (p. 151)
    10. Ovary glabrous, pubescent, or with stalked glands; styles free above the middle.
        11. Stamens and styles long-exserted (about 1 cm.); flowers greenish-white...
        ....*R. missouriense* (p. 152)
        11. Stamens and styles little or not at all exserted; flowers greenish or purplish.

144

Species of Ribes: Left, *R. odoratum*. Right, *R. lacustre*.

12. Stamens about equaling the petals........*R. oxyacanthoides* (p. 153)
12. Stamens twice as long as the petals.
    13. Hypanthium broadly campanulate, pubescent; ovary pubescent, often glandular....................*R. Grossularia* (p. 153)
    13. Hypanthium narrowly campanulate, glabrous or with a few scattered hairs; ovary glabrous, rarely sparingly pubescent or with stalked glands.......................*R. hirtellum* (p. 155)

SWAMP BLACK CURRANT, *Ribes lacustre* (Pers.) Poir, in Lam., Encycl. Meth. Bot. Suppl. 2:56, 1812

A low shrub 4–6 dm. high, stems and branches yellowish-brown covered with bristly prickles and somewhat longer, slender spines at the nodes; leaves thin, nearly glabrous, but with scattered hairs on both surfaces and finely ciliate margin, pentagonal in outline, 2.5–7 cm. long and about as broad, cordate at the base, mostly deeply five-lobed, the lobes acutish, with rounded, incised teeth; petioles about as long as the blades or slightly shorter, pubescent with spreading gland-tipped hairs; racemes drooping, 2–5 cm. long, rather few-flowered, the peduncle and pedicels puberulent and glandular-bristly, flowers greenish or purplish, about 7 mm. in diameter, hypanthium saucer-shaped, sepals blunt, about twice as long as the petals, stamens very short, styles about 1.5 mm. long, united for about one-third of their length, ovary densely covered with gland-tipped bristles, berry reddish-black, 6–10 mm. in diameter, glandular-bristly. Blossoms in late June; fruit ripe in August. (*Lacústre*, of the lake.)

Swamp black currant grows in cool woods and swamps of the coniferous forest area, most commonly northward. It is distributed from Newfoundland and Labrador to Alaska, south to western Massachusetts, New York, the mountains of Tennessee, northern Ohio, Michigan, Wisconsin, Colorado, Utah, and California.

The bruised twigs and berries of this species have a skunk-like odor.

MOUNTAIN CURRANT, *Ribes alpinum* L., Sp. Pl. 200, 1753

A dense, spreading shrub 1–2 m. high, young twigs yellowish-gray, the stem after the exfoliation of the epidermis becoming blackish-gray; leaves rather firm, puberulent along the veins and with scattered hairs and sessile or stalked black glands especially on the upper surface and a sparsely ciliate margin, broadly ovate to rhombic in outline, 2–5 cm. long, 1.5–4.5 cm. wide, mostly three-lobed, lobes triangular, irregularly toothed, teeth usually rather rounded, base generally rounded, varying to cordate or narrowed; petioles about one-half of the length of the blades, pubescent with scattered gland-tipped hairs; racemes from the base of leafy shoots, erect, compact, 1.5–4 cm. long, peduncles and pedicels glandular, bracts conspicuous, the lower ones exceeding the flowers, their margins glandular; flowers polygamo-dioecious, greenish-yellow, about 5 mm. in diameter, hypanthium saucer-shaped in the staminate flowers, nearly obsolete in the pistillate flowers, sepals oblong, nearly four times as long as the broadly cuneate petals, stamens about as long as the petals, styles very short, nearly separate, ovary pyriform, glabrous. Fruit red, persistent, large. Blossoms in April or early May. (*Alpínum*, alpine.)

A native of Europe, mountain currant is cultivated as an ornamental shrub, chiefly valuable on account of the brilliant fruit.

SKUNK CURRANT, *Ribes glandulosum* Grauer, Weber Pl. Min. Cog. Dec. 2, 1784 [*R. prostratum* L'Her. 1785]

A low shrub with decumbent or spreading, unarmed branches, young twigs yellowish-brown, becoming gray the second year, blackish with age; foliage ill-smelling, leaves thin, essentially glabrous, sometimes with scattered hairs on one or both surfaces, and with sparsely ciliate margin, orbicular or reniform in outline, 3.5–6 cm. long, 5–8 cm. wide, deeply cordate at the base, deeply five-lobed, lobes acute, somewhat rhombic, slightly narrowed toward the base, irregularly and coarsely doubly serrate, the teeth generally rounded and callus-tipped; petioles about as long as the blades, the dilated bases usually glandular ciliate; racemes ascending, 3–6 cm. long, loosely several-flowered, peduncles and pedicels puberulent and with numerous stalked glands, bracts shorter than the pedicels, glandular; flowers yellowish-green or somewhat purplish, short-campanulate, about 4 mm. in diameter; hypanthium deeply saucer-shaped, less than 1 mm. high, sepals oblong, about twice as long as the petals, glabrous, stamens about as long as the petals, anther sacs in contact with each other, styles erect,

146

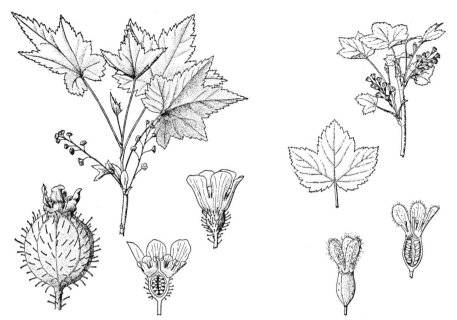

Species of *Ribes*: Left, *R. glandulosum*. Right, *R. hudsonianum*.

free nearly to the base, ovary densely glandular-bristly, berry dark red, glandular-bristly, 6–7 mm. in diameter, unpleasantly flavored. Blossoms in May and June; fruit ripe in July. (*Glandulósum*, glandular.)

Skunk currant is common in swamps throughout the coniferous forest, most abundant northeastward. It is distributed from Newfoundland and Labrador to Mackenzie and northeastern British Columbia, south to northeastern Minnesota, and in the mountains of North Carolina.

SWAMP RED CURRANT, *Ribes triste* Pall., Nova Acta Petrop. 10:378, 1797

A low, unarmed, straggling, or reclining shrub, the branches often rooting freely, young twigs yellowish-brown, second-year twigs with exfoliating epidermis, becoming blackish-gray; leaves thin, nearly or quite glabrous above, pale and pubescent beneath, with sparsely ciliate margin, pentagonal in outline with nearly parallel sides, 5–10 cm. long, and about as broad, cordate or truncate at the base, usually conspicuously decurrent on the petiole, mostly three-lobed, lobes broadly triangular, doubly crenate-serrate, teeth conspicuously callus-tipped; petioles mostly shorter than the blades, more or less pubescent and minutely glandular; racemes drooping, usually naked, 3–4 cm. long, several-flowered, peduncles and pedicels puberulent and glandular, bracts very small; flowers purplish, 4–5 mm. in diameter, flat, hypanthium nearly obsolete, sepals broadly wedge-shaped, very obtuse, petals about one-third the length of the sepals, wedge-shaped, stamens about the length of the petals, anther sacs in contact with each other, styles very short, free almost to the base, ovary glabrous, berry bright red, glabrous, 4–7 mm. in diameter, acid. Blossoms in May

147

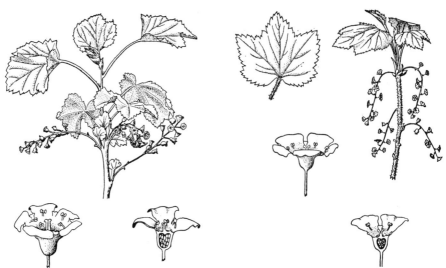

Species of *Ribes*: Left, *R. sativum*. Right, *R. triste*.

while the leaves are unfolding; fruit ripe in late June and July. (*Triste*, sad, probably referring to the dark color of the flowers.)

This currant grows in cool woods and swamps, mostly within the coniferous forest area. It is distributed from Newfoundland to Alaska, south to New Jersey, Michigan, South Dakota, and Oregon. It is also found in Asia.

RED CURRANT, *Ribes sativum* (Reichenb.) Syme, Engl. Bot. 4;42, 1865 [*R. vulgare* Lam. 1789]

An erect, unarmed shrub 1–2 m. high, young twigs greenish-yellow, second-year twigs gray, becoming dark brown with age, without much exfoliation of the outer epidermis; leaves rather firm, nearly glabrous above, or with a few scattered hairs, strigose-pubescent beneath, especially along the veins, ciliate on the margin, suborbicular to pentagonal in outline, the sides diverging upward, 4–7 cm. long, 4.5–9 cm. wide, cordate to subcordate at the base, scarcely decurrent on the petiole, three- to five-lobed, lobes ovate-triangular, irregularly crenate-dentate, teeth at maturity very blunt, glandular-mucronate; petioles about the length of the blades, puberulent, slightly glandular, their dilated bases strongly glandular-ciliate; racemes drooping, 3–10 cm. long, several- to many-flowered, peduncles puberulent and slightly glandular, pedicels essentially glabrous, bracts much shorter than the pedicels, truncate at the apex; flowers greenish, flat, about 5 mm. in diameter, hypanthium obsolete, disc five-lobed, sepals broadly wedge-shaped, petals truncate at the apex, about one-third as long as the sepals, stamens slightly longer than the petals, inflexed, anther sacs widely separated by the broad connective, styles united at the base, divergent at the top, ovary glabrous, berry bright red or whitish, 8–12 mm. in diameter, pleasantly acid. Blossoms in May; berries ripe in late June and July. (*Sativum*, planted.)

148

This shrub is cultivated throughout the area, occasionally escaping, generally to swamps. It is probably a native of western Europe.

WILD BLACK CURRANT, *Ribes americanum* Mill., Gard. Dict. ed. 8, no. 4, 1768 [*R. floridum* L'Her. 1785]

An erect, unarmed shrub 1–1.5 m. high, young twigs pale yellowish-green, becoming brownish-gray and later dark brown, more or less angled; leaves thin, glabrous above, pubescent beneath, especially along the veins, ciliate along the margin, dotted on the back with yellow resinous glands, broadly ovate, orbicular or reniform in outline, 4–7 cm. long, 4–9 cm. wide, cordate or truncate at the base, rather deeply three- to five-lobed, lobes triangular, ovate or somewhat rhombic, rather acute, coarsely doubly serrate, teeth moderately acute; petioles slightly shorter than the blades, puberulent, often glandular-dotted, dilated and fimbriate towards the base, the fimbriae puberulent; racemes axillary or terminal on short, leafy shoots, drooping, 4–8 cm. long, several-flowered, peduncles and pedicels downy, bracts longer than the pedicels, linear-lanceolate, persistent, flowers greenish-white, 8–10 mm. in diameter; hypanthium campanulate, pubescent on the outside, 3–5 mm. long, sepals obovate, rounded at the apex, spreading, nearly as long as the hypanthium, slightly pubescent on the outside, petals oblong, erect, three-fourths as long as the sepals, stamens shorter than the petals, styles united almost to the summit, 6–7 mm. long, ovary elongated, only half-inferior, puberulent or nearly glabrous; berry black, smooth, 6–10 mm. in diameter, edible. Blossoms in May or early June; fruit ripe in July. (*Americánum*, American.)

This shrub is common in woods and thickets throughout the Upper Midwest. It is distributed from Nova Scotia west to Alberta, south to Virginia, Nebraska, and Wyoming; it occurs also in New Mexico.

BLACK CURRANT, *Ribes nigrum* L., Sp. Pl. 201, 1753

An upright shrub 1–2 m. high, unarmed, young twigs greenish-gray, second-year twigs yellowish-gray, becoming blackish with age, foliage ill-smelling,

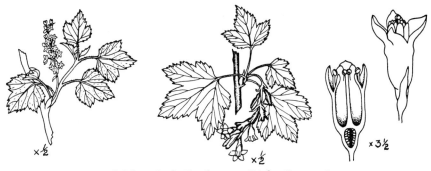

Species of *Ribes*: Left, *R. alpinum*. Right, *R. americanum*.

149

leaves thin, somewhat rugose, at first puberulent, becoming nearly glabrate with age, with a few resinous glands especially on the lower surface, ciliate along the margin, orbicular to reniform in outline, 2–6 cm. long, 3–8 cm. wide, mostly deeply cordate at the base, three- to five-lobed, lobes triangular or broadly ovate, coarsely doubly serrate, the teeth sharp or more or less rounded, gland-tipped; petioles mostly longer than the blades, puberulent and sparsely gland-dotted, fimbriate toward the expanded base, fimbriae puberulent; racemes from the base of leafy shoots, somewhat drooping, 4–6 cm. long, rather few-flowered, peduncles and pedicels puberulent, bracts much shorter than the pedicels; flowers greenish-white, campanulate, 7–12 mm. in diameter, hypanthium broadly campanulate, about 3 mm. high, puberulent and gland-dotted, sepals oblong, reflexed, about 5 mm. long, puberulent, petals about half as long as the sepals, broadly ovate, denticulate at the apex, stamens about as long as the petals, styles united nearly to the summit, stigma two-lobed, ovary only half-inferior, the lower part turbinate, glandular-dotted; berry black, dotted with resinous glands, 6–10 mm. in diameter. Blossoms in late May; fruit ripe in late July. (*Nigrum*, black, referring to the black fruit.)

Black currant has been sparingly cultivated, and escapes into swamps. It is a native of Europe and western Asia.

Ribes hudsonianum Richards., Bot. App. Frankl. Journ. ed. 2, 6, 1823

A more or less erect, unarmed shrub, 5–10 dm. high, young twigs yellowish-brown, densely puberulent, one-year-old twigs light gray, exfoliating with age and becoming reddish-black, foliage ill-scented; leaves rather firm and rugose, nearly glabrate above, densely pubescent and gland-dotted beneath, ciliate on the margin, suborbicular to reniform in outline, 4–7 cm. long, 5–9 cm. wide, deeply cordate at the base, three- to five-lobed, the lobes broadly triangular to somewhat rhombic, coarsely and doubly crenate-serrate, teeth (in mature leaves) rounded and callus-tipped; petioles about three-fourths the length of the blades, densely puberulent and dotted with resinous glands, the dilated base fimbriate; racemes erect, borne from the base of leafy shoots, 2–4 cm. long, several-flowered, peduncles and pedicels puberulent, bracts narrowly lanceolate, much shorter than the pedicels; flowers white, turbinate, about 5 mm. in diameter, hypanthium crateriform, about 1 mm. high, sepals oblong-lanceolate, slightly spreading, about 3 mm. long, sepals and hypanthium densely pubescent, petals about one-half as long as the sepals, narrowly cuneate, truncate at the apex, stamens about as long as the petals, styles conical, united for about three-fourths of their length, stigmas slightly divergent, ovary about three-fourths inferior, the lower part obconical and gland-dotted; berry black, glabrous, 5–10 mm. in diameter. Blossoms in May and early June; fruit ripe in July and August. (*Hudsoniánum*, referring to Hudson Bay.)

This species is locally common in cool swamps as far south as the headwaters of the Mississippi River and the north shore of Lake Superior. It is distributed from Hudson Bay to central Alaska, south to Ontario, Minnesota, and eastern British Columbia.

GOLDEN CURRANT, FLOWERING CURRANT, *Ribes odoratum* Wendl., in Bartl. & Wendl., Beitr. 2:15, 1825 [*R. aureum* of many authors (including Minn. T. & S. 1912), not *R. aureum* Pursh]

An upright or straggling, unarmed shrub 1–2 mm. high, twigs yellow-brown, one-year-old twigs brownish-gray, becoming blackish-gray and rough with age; leaves firm in texture, at first pubescent with scattered hairs on both surfaces, and with abundant resinous, glandular dots, soon glabrate, ciliate on the margin, broadly wedge-shaped to orbicular in outline, 2.5–5 cm. long, 2.5–6 cm. wide, cuneate or truncate at the base, deeply three- to five-lobed, lobes oblong or somewhat rhombic, tending to be three-lobulate, nearly entire, or with a few coarse crenate-dentate teeth; petioles very slender, mostly longer than the blades, pubescent; racemes spreading, borne on the ends of leafy twigs, about 3 cm. long, rather few-flowered, peduncles strongly pubescent, pedicels puberulent, bracts foliaceous, persistent, the upper ones elliptical; flowers golden-yellow, salver-form, very fragrant, with the odor of cloves, about 1.5 cm. in diameter and 1.5 cm. long, hypanthium long-tubular 10–13 mm. long, 2.5 mm. in diameter, sepals spreading, obovate, rounded at the apex, petals erect, oblong, usually tinged with crimson, about 3 mm. long, stamens slightly shorter than the petals, fused with them at the base, styles united to the apex, stigma one, obscurely two-lobed, slightly exserted, ovary glabrous; fruit black, about 8 mm. in diameter. Flowers in May; fruit nearly black, ripe in July. (*Odorátum*, scented.)

Much planted as an ornamental shrub, golden currant occasionally escapes in the southern parts of the area. It is a native of the Great Plains from North Dakota to Texas. The far western *Ribes aureum* Pursh is a distinct species.

PRICKLY GOOSEBERRY, *Ribes Cynosbati* L., Sp. Pl. 202, 1753 [*Grossularia Cynosbati* (L.) Mill. 1768]

An erect or spreading, spiny shrub 0.5–1.5 m. high, twigs and branches more or less prickly and with one to three spines at each node, young twigs pubescent and generally brownish, one-year-old twigs greenish-gray, becoming dark gray with age; leaves rather thin, finely pubescent above, densely and velvety-pubescent beneath with some of the hairs gland-tipped, nearly orbicular in outline, 3–5 cm. long, 3.5–5.5 cm. wide, cordate to truncate at the base, three- to five-lobed, the lobes oblong to rhombic, irregularly crenate-dentate, the teeth rounded and callus-tipped; petioles slender, mostly shorter than the blades, pubescent with both simple and gland-tipped hairs; peduncles one- to three-flowered, pubescent like the petioles, pedicels 5–12 mm. long, pubescent, bracts small, ovate; flowers greenish-white, campanulate to urceolate, 5–7 mm. in diameter, hypanthium greenish, broad-cylindrical 3–5 mm. long, glabrous on the

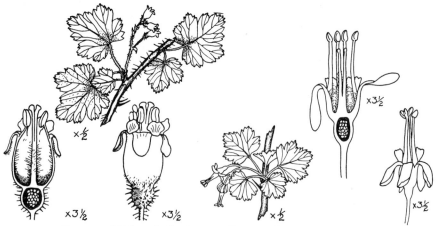

Species of *Ribes*: Left, *R. Cynosbati*. Right, *R. missouriense*.

outside or with a few spreading hairs, pubescent within, sepals oblong to obovate, about 3 mm. long, spreading to reflexed at anthesis, petals obovate, one-fourth to one-third as long as the sepals, somewhat spreading at anthesis, stamens three-fourths as long as the sepals, inserted below the summit of the hypanthium, styles united nearly to the summit but easily separable in the distal portion, hairy toward the base, stigmas two, ovary half-elliptical, pubescent or glabrous, more or less prickly, the prickles at first gland-tipped; berry prickly, 8–15 mm. in diameter, reddish-purple when mature. Blossoms in May to early June; fruit ripe in July and August. (*Cynósbati*, Greek, dog brier.)

Prickly gooseberry is common in woods and thickets throughout our area. It is distributed from New Brunswick to Manitoba and North Dakota, south to North Carolina, Alabama, and Missouri.

MISSOURI GOOSEBERRY, *Ribes missouriense* Nutt., *ex* Torr. & Gray 1:548, 1840. [*R. gracile* of various authors, not of Michaux; *Grossularia missouriensis* (Nutt.) Coville & Britton 1908]

A more or less upright shrub 1–2 m. high, armed with from one to three stout nodal spines and sometimes weakly prickly, young twigs slender, greenish-yellow, one-year-old twigs gray, soon exfoliating and becoming blackish; leaves mostly on short shoots, rather firm and rugose, sparingly pubescent or glabrate above, strongly pubescent with rather stiff hairs beneath, nearly orbicular in outline, 2–4 cm. long, 2–4 cm. wide, cuneate or truncate at the base, mostly three-lobed, lobes oblong or rhombic, coarsely and irregularly incised crenate-dentate, the teeth obscurely callus-tipped; petioles generally shorter than the blades, pubescent and more or less fimbriate toward the base; peduncles mostly longer than the petioles, two- or three-flowered, slightly puberulent and with a few glandular hairs, pedicels slender, 5–8 mm. long, pubescent or glabrate, bracts broadly ovate, about 2 mm. long, glandular-ciliate; flowers greenish-white, hypanthium cylindrical, 2–2.5 mm. long and about 1.5 mm. in diam-

152

eter, glabrous or pubescent, sepals linear-oblong, about 7 mm. long, reflexed at anthesis; petals spatulate, 2–3 mm. long, slightly erose, erect, stamens long-exserted, about 10 mm. long, styles 12 mm. long, united halfway to the summit, stigmas small, capitate; ovary subcylindrical, glabrous; berry globose, 8–15 mm. in diameter, nearly black when ripe. Blossoms in April and May; fruit ripe in July and August. (*Missouriénse*, Missouri, the original collection being from that state.)

This gooseberry grows in woods and thickets and on rocky hillsides; in many places in our area it is abundant. It is distributed from Connecticut to Minnesota and North Dakota, south to Tennessee, Arkansas, and Kansas, and is rare eastward.

NORTHERN GOOSEBERRY, *Ribes oxyacanthoides* L., Sp. Pl. 201, 1753 [*Grossularia oxyacanthoides* (L.) Mill. 1768]

A low, more or less prickly shrub, with from one to three light-colored nodal spines; young twigs puberulent, greenish-yellow, one-year-old twigs yellowish-gray, in age becoming dark reddish-brown; leaves rather thin, usually rugose when mature, sparsely rough-pubescent, usually with some glandular hairs on the lower surface, obscurely ciliate on the margin; suborbicular in outline, 2–4 cm. long and about as wide, slightly cordate, truncate or broadly cuneate at the base, incisely three- to five-lobed, lobes rhombic, rather irregularly crenate-dentate; petioles usually shorter than the blades, puberulent and with scattered glandular hairs, somewhat fimbriate, the fimbriae often gland-tipped and sparsely pubescent; peduncles very short, scarcely exserted from the bud scales, pubescent, mostly one- or two-flowered, pedicels 2–3 mm. long; bracts broadly ovate, clasping, glandular-hairy; flowers greenish, about 7–8 mm. long, hypanthium broadly cylindrical, about 3 mm. long and about 2.5 mm. in diameter, glabrous, sepals oblong, 3–4 mm. long, reflexed at anthesis, petals spatulate, about 3 mm. long, stamens about as long or slightly shorter than the petals, styles exserted, approximate, united for a little more than half their length, hairy, ovary ellipsoid, typically glabrous, about three-fourths inferior; berry globose, about 1 cm. in diameter. Blossoms in May and early June; fruit ripe in August. (*Oxyacanthoídes*, with sharp spines.)

This gooseberry grows in swamps and on low ground, and is confined to the region of the coniferous forest. It is distributed from Hudson Bay to Yukon and British Columbia, south to northern Michigan, Minnesota, North Dakota, and Montana.

GARDEN GOOSEBERRY, *Ribes Grossularia* L., Sp. Pl. 201, 1753 [*Grossularia reclinata* (L.) Mill. 1768]

A shrub 6–10 dm. high with ascending or reclining stems, nodal spines one to three, rather stout, sometimes with a few scattered prickles, young twigs yellowish-gray, puberulent, one-year-old twigs gray, glabrate, becoming somewhat

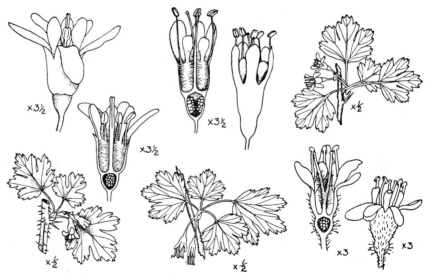

Species of *Ribes*: Left, *R. oxyacanthoides*. Center,
R. hirtellum. Right, *R. Grossularia*.

darker with age; leaves rather firm in texture, more or less pubescent on both
sides, suborbicular in outline, 2–4 cm. long, 2–4 cm. wide, mostly cordate or
truncate at the base, rarely somewhat cuneate, deeply three- to five-lobed, lobes
rhombic to somewhat wedge-shaped, deeply and irregularly crenate-dentate,
teeth obtuse, not mucronate-tipped; petioles mostly as long or longer than the
blades, pubescent, sometimes with a few gland-tipped hairs; peduncles one- to
two-flowered, less than 1 cm. long, pubescent, pedicels shorter than the peduncles, strongly pubescent and glandular, bracts very short, pubescent; flowers
greenish to purplish, 8–10 mm. in diameter; hypanthium broadly campanulate,
about 3 mm. long and 4–5 mm. in diameter, pubescent, sepals greenish, oblong
to obovate, about 5 mm. long, usually pubescent, reflexed at anthesis, petals
whitish, obovate or cuneate with rounded apex, one-third to one-half the length
of the sepals, stamens twice as long as the petals, styles united for about one-
third of their length, approximate, hairy below, ovary wholly inferior, pubescent,
and with stalked glands; berry mostly globose, 1–2 cm. in diameter, pale green
to dark purple when ripe, more or less pubescent, and with stalked glands.
Blossoms in late April or early May; fruit ripe in June. (*Grossulária*, like a small
unripe fig.)

Garden gooseberry is cultivated throughout the region; it is a native of
Europe.

Ribes Grossularia var. *Uva-crispa* (L.) Sm., Engl. Fl. 2:333, 1824 [*R. Uva-crispa*
L. 1753]

Differs from the species in having the ovary and fruit pubescent but not
glandular, fruit small and yellowish. (*U'va-críspa*, curly grape or berry.)

154

A native of Europe, this variety is somewhat more northern in range than the type.

Ribes hirtellum Michx., Fl. Bor. Am. 1:111, 1803 [*Grossularia hirtella* (Michx.) Spach 1838]

A low, armed or unarmed shrub 6–12 dm. high, prickles weak, bristle-like or more frequently wanting, nodal spines one to three at a node, slender, short, frequently wholly wanting, young twigs yellowish-brown, nearly or quite glabrous, one-year-old twigs pale gray, becoming dark reddish-brown with age; leaves thin, essentially glabrous above, sparsely pubescent beneath, strongly ciliate on the margin, obovate-orbicular to reniform-orbicular in outline, 2–3.5 cm. long, 2–4 cm. wide, cuneate, truncate or slightly cordate at the base, incisely mostly five-lobed, lobes oblong to rhombic, irregularly crenate-dentate, teeth acute to very blunt, minutely callus-apiculate; petioles puberulent, slightly fimbriate, mostly shorter than the blades; peduncles one- to three-flowered, about 5 mm. long, glabrous, pedicels about as long as the peduncles, bracts obovate; flowers greenish, about 7 mm. long, hypanthium narrowly campanulate, about 3.5 mm. long, 2–2.5 mm. in diameter, glabrous outside, pubescent within, sepals oblong, about the length of the hypanthium, slightly spreading at anthesis, petals obovate, about half as long as the sepals, stamens as long as the sepals or slightly longer, exserted, styles united for about one-third of their length, hairy, divergent, ovary nearly globular, wholly inferior, glabrous, or with stalked glands; berry globose, purple or black when ripe, 8–10 mm. in diameter. Blossoms in May and June; fruit ripe in late July. (*Hirtéllum*, slightly hirsute.)

This species grows in swamps and moist woods. It is common throughout the coniferous region, infrequent beyond it as far south in Minnesota as latitude 45°. It is distributed from southern Labrador to eastern Manitoba, south to Nova Scotia, New England, Pennsylvania, northern Ohio, Indiana, Illinois, and Minnesota.

R. hirtellum is the source of some of our cultivated gooseberries, both directly through a process of selection and through hybridization with *R. Grossularia*.

WITCHHAZEL FAMILY, HAMAMELIDACEAE

Shrubs or trees with alternate simple leaves and deciduous stipules; flowers in heads or spikes, often polygamous or monoecious; calyx adhering to the base of the pistil, four- or five-parted or lobed; petals four to many or none, long and narrow; stamens four to many, distinct; pistil compound; carpels two, united at the base; fruit a two-beaked, two-celled, woody capsule, opening at the summit, with from one to several bony seeds in each cell.

The family includes about thirteen genera and fifty species, natives of North America, Asia, and South Africa. Only the following genus occurs in our area.

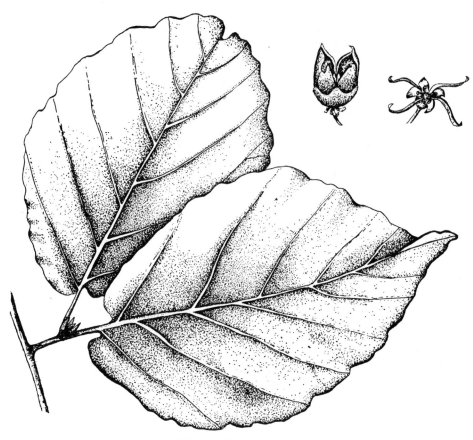

Hamamelis virginiana

Witchhazel
Hamamelis L., Sp. Pl. 124, 1753

Tall shrubs or small trees, with alternate, toothed, straight-veined leaves; flowers in small axillary clusters, bright yellow, surrounded by a scale-like three-leaved involucre, appearing in late summer or autumn; calyx four-parted, persistent, adnate to the base of the ovary; petals four, narrow strap-shaped; stamens eight, short, the four opposite the petals imperfect and scale-like; pistil two-celled; styles two, short; fruit a woody capsule, opening by two valves at the top. (*Hamamélis*, Greek name for some tree.)

This is a genus of three species, one native to eastern North America, the others to Japan.

WITCHHAZEL, *Hamamelis virginiana* L., Sp. Pl. 124, 1753

A branching shrub 2–4 m. high; twigs with slightly scurfy or smooth bark, leaves short-petioled, obovate or oval, 6–15 cm. long, 4–10 cm. wide; wavy-toothed and stellate-pubescent at least when young; flowers appearing in autumn when the leaves are falling and while the previous fruit remains; seeds mature the summer after the flowering. (*Virginiána*, Virginian.)

Witch hazel grows in low, rich soil or on the rocky banks of streams. It is infrequent in southeastern Minnesota and northeastern Iowa, more common and widely distributed in Wisconsin, occurring as far north as Polk, Barron, Oconto, and Marinette counties. It is distributed from southern Quebec to western Wisconsin, south to New England, northern Georgia, Tennessee, and Missouri.

The bark and leaves are astringent and are used in the form of extracts and decoctions, but are not known to have any essential properties. The forked branches were formerly much used as divining rods for locating sources of underground water.

PLANE TREE FAMILY, Platanaceae

Trees with deciduous bark and alternate, simple, palmately lobed leaves; petioles hollow at the base and concealing the axillary bud; flowers in spherical monoecious heads, the flowers in a head so crowded together that the limits of the individual flowers are difficult to determine; anthers of staminate head nearly sessile, consisting of two pollen sacs and an enlarged peltate connective; pistillate heads consisting of simple pistils, intermixed with staminodes; in both heads there occur very minute scales, which have been variously interpreted*; fruit a dense globular head of club-shaped nutlets each with a tuft of hairs at the base.

The family contains only the following genus. Its relation to other families is somewhat doubtful.

Sycamore, Plane Tree
Platanus L., Sp. Pl. 999, 1753

Characters of the family.

This is a genus of eight species, mostly natives of the southwestern United States and Mexico; the following one occurs in the eastern United States, and one occurs in southwestern Asia. (*Platánus*, the classical name of the Asiatic plane tree.)

SYCAMORE, BUTTONWOOD, *Platanus occidentalis* L., Sp. Pl. 999, 1753

A large tree, reaching in the Ohio Valley a height of 40 m.; bark deciduous, greenish-white when newly exposed, gradually becoming yellowish-brown, the trunk in consequence commonly mottled; leaves alternate, rhombic-reniform in

---

*The best interpretation seems to be that the staminate flower consists of a group of three or four stamens surrounded by minute scales, which constitute a perianth, and the pistillate flower of from six to eight free carpels surrounded by a ring of staminodes and that again by a perianth; some authors distinguish "sepals" and "petals" among the scales; others regard each carpel as constituting a "flower," and consider the scales as bracts.

outline, 10–20 cm. long, 15–30 cm. wide, strongly three-nerved, deeply lobed, the lobes triangular to ovate, acuminate, base truncate or cordate, margin entire except for a few coarse teeth or secondary lobes, surface very woolly when young, soon becoming glabrous above, and nearly glabrous except along the veins beneath; heads of fruit about 3.5 cm. in diameter, borne on drooping peduncles nearly 1 dm. long. (*Occidentális*, Western, i.e., belonging to the New World.)

Sycamore is native to eastern North America from southern Maine to southern Ontario and central Iowa, south to Florida, Mississippi, and Texas. Early reports of this tree from southeastern Minnesota seem to be in error; at any rate, there is no evidence at present of its occurrence there. It is occasionally planted and is entirely hardy at least as far north as Minneapolis.

ROSE FAMILY, Rosaceae

Herbs, shrubs, or trees, unarmed, prickly, spiny, or thorny; leaves alternate,* simple or compound, usually stipulate, the stipules often early deciduous; flowers perfect or polygamo-dioecious, regular; the receptacle or hypanthium varying from slightly concave to cup-shaped or deeply urn-shaped, lined with a glandular disk; sepals four or five (an epicalyx of five bracts, alternating with the sepals, sometimes present); petals four or five, rarely lacking; stamens generally numerous in whorls or cycles of five or ten, inserted along the edge of the disk; carpels one to many, free or united below into a two- to ten-celled compound ovary; styles as many as carpels, terminal or lateral; ovules one or two or several; fruit various — achenes, follicles, pome, hip, drupe, or an aggregation of drupelets.

This is a large family of cosmopolitan distribution, but mainly of the North Temperate regions. Wide differences of opinion exist in regard to the taxonomic unity of the family. Accordingly it is either divided into subfamilies or split up into a number of separate families. Differences also affect conceptions of genera and species, the number in these classifications varying, as a result, between very wide limits. In a broader sense the family embraces about ninety genera and two thousand species.

KEY TO GENERA OF ROSACEAE

1. Leaves compound.
    2. Carpels numerous (more than five), free; fruit achenes, drupelets, or nutlets.
        3. Flowers yellow, fruit ripening into dry, hairy achenes; unarmed shrub.....
        ....*Potentilla* (p. 159)
        3. Flowers white or pink, fruit drupelets or nutlets enclosed in a fleshy hip; spiny or prickly shrubs.
            4. Pistils on a raised or conical receptacle, fruit an aggregate of drupelets...
            ....*Rubus* (p. 161)

* Rarely opposite.

158

4. Pistils in a fleshy urn-shaped receptacle, which encloses the nutlets.....
....*Rosa* (p. 198)
2. Carpels few (five or less); free or united with one another and with the receptacle; fruit follicles or a pome.
   5. Flowers in flat corymbs; fruit a pome..................*Sorbus* (p. 215)
   5. Flowers in ample panicles; fruit follicles..............*Sorbaria* (p. 197)
1. Leaves simple.
   6. Leaves opposite; sepals foliaceous, about 1 cm. broad....*Rhodotypos* (p. 190)
   6. Leaves alternate; sepals smaller, not foliaceous.
      7. Carpels more than one (three to five or many).
         8. Pistils on a conical receptacle; fruit an aggregation of drupelets........
....*Rubus* (p. 161)
         8. Carpels in a concave or hollow receptacle, free or united with it and with one another.
            9. Flowers perigynous; fruit dry, two to five follicles.
               10. Follicles inflated, splitting on both sides, seeds shiny...........
....*Physocarpus* (p. 190)
               10. Follicles not inflated, splitting on one side, seeds dull...........
....*Spiraea* (p. 193)
            9. Flowers epigynous; fruit a fleshy pome.
               11. Carpels cartilaginous or leathery when mature imbedded in the receptacle.
                  12. Cavities of the compound ovary as many as styles.
                     13. Ovules and seeds one or two in each cavity.
                        14. Trees; flowers in cymes..........*Malus* (p. 219)
                        14. Low shrubs; flowers in compound cymes..........
....*Aronia* (p. 213)
                     13. Ovules and seeds numerous in each cavity............
....*Chaenomeles* (p. 213)
                  12. Cavities of the ovary becoming twice as many as the styles...
....*Amelanchier* (p. 224)
               11. Carpels hard and bony when ripe; distinct or cohering in fruit.
                  15. Fertile ovule one in each carpel; leaves mostly lobed and doubly serrate; thorny trees or shrubs...................
....*Crataegus* (p. 235)
                  15. Fertile ovules two in each carpel, stones two-seeded, thornless shrubs ....*Cotoneaster* (p. 245)
      7. Carpel one, fruit a drupe.........................*Prunus* (p. 246)

Cinquefoil, Fivefinger
Potentilla L., Sp. Pl. 495, 1753

Herbs, or rarely shrubs; leaves alternate, compound and stipulate; flowers mostly yellow, cymose or solitary; hypanthium flat or hemispheric; sepals five, persistent, with five bracts alternating with them; petals five, obovate or orbicular; stamens mostly numerous; carpels many, on a dry, usually hairy receptacle; fruit a collection of achenes. (*Potentilla*, from Latin *potens*, powerful, with a diminutive suffix, referring to the medical properties.)

This genus includes about a hundred and fifty species, nearly all of them natives of the North Temperate Zone. Some twenty-four species occur in eastern North America and about thirty others in the western and northwestern parts of

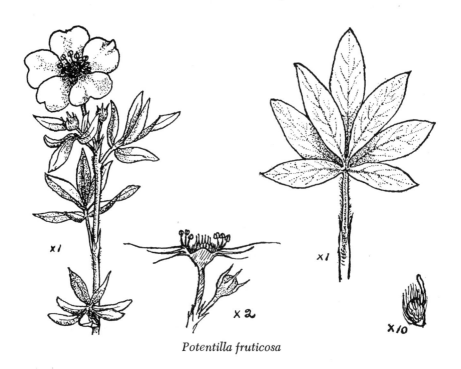

Potentilla fruticosa

the continent. The great majority of the species are herbaceous; the following one is strictly shrubby.

SHRUBBY CINQUEFOIL, *Potentilla fruticosa* L., Sp. Pl. 495, 1753 [*Dasiphora fruticosa* Rydb. 1898]

Stem more or less erect, shrubby, 2–10 dm. high, much branched; bark reddish-brown, becoming much shredded; leaves pinnate, 1–3 cm. long; petiole pubescent, about 1 cm. long; stipules conspicuous, lanceolate, papery, about as long as the petiole; leaflets mostly five, crowded, 10–17 mm. long, 2–4 mm. wide, oblong-lanceolate, sparsely hairy above, silky-pubescent below, entire with revolute margins; flowers in few-flowered cymes at the ends of the branches, about 2 cm. in diameter, petals bright yellow, orbicular; carpels densely pubescent; achenes long, hairy. Flowers and fruits from June to September. (*Fruticósa*, shrubby.)

Shrubby cinquefoil is frequent in rocky situations and open meadows along the north shore of Lake Superior and in scattered localities southward and westward. It is distributed from Labrador to Alaska, south to New Jersey, Pennsylvania, the southern end of Lake Michigan, northern Iowa, Arizona, and California. It is found also in Europe and Asia.

It is a somewhat polymorphic, circumboreal species. Several geographic varieties and horticultural forms are in cultivation, varying in the form and pubescence of the leaflets and in the size and color (deep yellow to pure white) of the flowers. Much of our native material belongs to the following variety.

160

Potentilla fruticosa var. *tenuifolia* (Willd.) Lehm., Monog. 31, 1820

A plant somewhat more dwarf than the species; leaves more densely silky-pubescent, leaflets linear-lanceolate, about 2 mm. wide. (*Tenuifólia*, narrow-leaved.)

The distribution in the Upper Midwest is similar to that of the species, but apparently the plant is more common southward. It occurs in a marl bog about fifteen miles south of Minneapolis. Its range is North America and eastern Asia.

Bramble, Blackberry, Raspberry
Rubus L., Sp. Pl. 492, 1753

Shrubs with erect to procumbent or trailing, vine-like stems, frequently prickly; with alternate, simple, lobed, or three- to seven-foliolate leaves; flowers white (sometimes pink or purple); hypanthium saucer-shaped; sepals five, persistent; petals five, deciduous; stamens numerous; carpels usually many, borne on a spongy or succulent receptacle, ripening into drupelets and forming an aggregate fruit, edible. (*Rúbus*, bramble, akin to *ruber*, red.)

Most of the shrubby species have biennial canes, and the leaves produced on the first year's canes, or primocanes, are often quite different from those borne on the lateral flowering shoots of the second year's growth. Both types of shoots should be studied by anyone attempting to identify the species.

The genus is of wide geographical distribution but most abundant in the North Temperate Zone. According to L. H. Bailey, the foremost student of the genus in this country, it comprises over seven hundred species.

KEY TO SPECIES OF RUBUS[*]

1. All of the leaves simple, palmately lobed..............*R. parviflorus* (p. 164)
1. Some or all of the leaves compound.
  2. Plants low, unarmed, woody only at the base.
    3. Stems erect, 3–12 cm. high, without runners, petals pink..*R. acaulis* (p. 164)
    3. Flowering stems ascending, 1–4 dm. high, runners long and trailing, petals white......................................*R. pubescens* (p. 166)
  2. Plants with woody biennial canes, more or less armed with prickles or bristles.
    4. Ripe fruit falling off whole from the dry receptacle; leaves white-tomentose beneath. RASPBERRIES
      5. Stems erect or ascending, armed with straight needle-like prickles or bristles; fruit red.
        6. Calyx and pedicels without stalked glands, finely pubescent.
          7. Cultivated plant, leaves thick and firm, terminal leaflet three-fourths

[*] In the present treatment of *Rubus* several of the species described by Bailey for the Upper Midwest have not been included because of lack of material for study. Only those species of common occurrence in our flora and available in adequate collections are dealt with. See Bailey, Gentes Herbarum, vols. 5 and 7, addendum 1.

Since the preparation of the manuscript, a station for the Cloudberry, *Rubus Chamaemorus* L., has been discovered at Basswood Lake, Lake County, Minnesota. With the exception of a few stations recorded for northern New England and Montauk Point, Long Island, this is the first known occurrence of the species south of the international boundary.

or more as broad as long, blunt to short-acute at the apex.........
....................................*R. idaeus* (p. 166)
7. Native plant, leaves thin, terminal leaflet less than three-fourths as broad as long, taper pointed.............................
............rare forms of *R. strigosus* var. *canadensis* (p. 168)
6. Calyx and pedicels hispid with stalked glands.
8. Stems, peduncles, and pedicels without fine pubescence..........
.... *R. strigosus* (p. 167)
8. Stems, peduncles, and pedicels finely pubescent...............
......................*R. strigosus* var. *canadensis* (p. 168)
5. Stems arching or recurving and rooting at the tips, armed with strong, hooked prickles; fruit black or red.
9. Pedicels and calyx without stalked glands; fruit becoming black.....
....................................*R. occidentalis* (p. 169)
9. Pedicels and calyx with stalked glands, fruit dark-red.............
....................................× *R. neglectus* (p. 171)
4. Ripe fruit not separating from the fleshy receptacle; leaves green beneath, more or less pubescent but not white-tomentose. BLACKBERRIES, DEWBERRIES
10. Canes erect or high-arching, 1.5–3 m. high; flowers in racemiform or corymbiform clusters, two to four times as long as wide.
11. Canes generally tall, armed with strong, broad-based, straight or slightly curved prickles; leaves velvety-pubescent beneath.
12. Primary inflorescence an elongated raceme, with numerous stalked glands on rachis and pedicels. *R. allegheniensis* (p. 171)
12. Primary inflorescence shorter and relatively broader, corymbiform, usually broadest above the middle, without stalked glands
............................*R. pensilvanicus* (p. 171)
11. Canes mostly lower, with or without a few straight prickles; leaves glabrous beneath.....................*R. canadensis* (p. 172)
10. Canes mostly less than 1.2 m. high, ascending to recurving or low-arching to prostrate and trailing, frequently tip-rooting; flowers in few-flowered (ascendate), short-racemiform, to many-flowered, corymbose inflorescences.
13. Primocanes ascending to more or less arching, 3–6 dm. high; floricanes depressed or prostrate and trailing, generally tip-rooting; prickles mostly less than twenty-five per dm., small but firm, 1.5–2.5 mm. long, recurved or hooked and claw-like, with slightly enlarged bases.
14. Floricanes long-trailing and tip-rooting; flowers one to five, in ascendate inflorescences, the pedicels of the lowermost flowers elongated-ascending; leaves glabrous to somewhat pilose along the veins beneath.
15. Leaves of primocanes three- to five-foliolate, thin, terminal leaflet ovate, abruptly tapered to the apex, sharply serrate, sparsely pubescent beneath; petioles with a few, weak, hooked prickles.................*R. flagellaris* (p. 174)
15. Leaves of primocanes five-foliolate, firm in texture, terminal leaflet ovate-acuminate, more gradually tapered, coarsely serrate-dentate, nearly or quite glabrous; petioles with short, firm, hooked prickles..............*R. multifer* (p. 175)
14. Floricanes low-arching to depressed and more or less short-trailing, sometimes tip-rooting; flowers four to nine, in short-racemiform or racemose-corymbose inflorescences, the pedicels

relatively short and more or less spreading; leaves pilose to velvety-pubescent beneath.

    16. Terminal leaflet of primocane leaves round-cordate, almost as broad as long, velvety-pubescent beneath; flowers four or five, in close clusters, mostly over-topped by the broadly ovate floral leaves..............*R. folioflorus* (p. 176)

    16. Terminal leaflet of primocane leaves elliptic, rounded at the base, thinly pilose on the lower surface; flowers five to nine, in more open racemose-corymbose clusters, not overtopped by the elliptic floral leaves.......*R. Rosendahlii* (p. 179)

13. Primocanes erect or ascending, 6–12 dm. high, or low-arching, 3–6 dm. high; floricanes oblique or recurving to depressed and tip-trailing; prickles twenty to forty per dm. of cane, 3–4.5 mm. long, straight, more or less declined to somewhat recurved but not short and claw-like.

    17. Primocanes erect or ascending, 6–12 dm. high; floricanes oblique to recurving, with from twenty to forty slender, straight, or slightly bent prickles per dm.; margins of primocane leaves coarsely and sharply doubly serrate; simple leaves of flower clusters elliptic to lanceolate, their margins cut-toothed.

        18. Leaves glabrous above, sparsely pilose, mainly along the veins beneath; flowers in three- to six-flowered, leafy clusters.........................*R. acridens* (p. 179)

        18. Leaves lightly pilose above, velvety-pubescent beneath; flowers in four- to nine-flowered clusters................
.............................*R. recurvans* (p. 181)

    17. Primocanes moderate- to low-arching, often tending to trail toward the tips, 3–6 dm. high; floricanes usually becoming somewhat depressed late in the season and occasionally tip-rooting; prickles thirty to ninety per dm.; margins of primocane leaflets sharply but not deeply serrate-dentate.

        19. Primocanes mostly stout (4–10 mm. thick), usually angled, armed with from thirty to ninety strong, subulate, straight, or slightly curved prickles per dm., 3.5–5.5 mm. long, with broadened bases; terminal leaflet of primocane leaves prevailingly ovate, broadly rounded to subcordate or cordate at the base. Vigorous, leafy, mounding plants.

            20. Terminal leaflet elliptic-ovate to ovate, rounded to subcordate at the base, more or less pilose beneath along the principal veins, prickles thirty to sixty per dm.....
.....................*R. minnesotanus* (p. 181)

            20. Terminal leaflet broadly ovate, cordate at the base, thin and somewhat plicate, glabrous or nearly so beneath; prickles sixty to ninety per dm...*R. latifoliolus* (p. 183)

        19. Primocanes mostly slender (2–4 mm. thick), terete or sometimes obscurely angled, armed with from eighty to five hundred acicular prickles and bristles per dm. (sometimes fewer in *R. vermontanus* and *R. semisetosus*), prickles mostly declined, straight or more or less recurved, without broadened bases; terminal leaflet of primocane leaves prevailingly elliptic, with narrowly rounded to cuneate base. Small, low-arching to nearly prostrate, needle-prickled brambles, neither very leafy nor mounding.

            21. Prickles and bristles a hundred and fifty to five hundred

per dm. of primocanes, with numerous intermixed gland-
tipped bristles and hairs . . . . . . *R. Groutianus* (p. 186)
    21. Prickles and bristles up to ninety per dm. but sometimes
fewer, without intermixed gland-tipped bristles and
hairs on the primocanes.
        22. Leaves mostly thin, glabrous, or slightly pilose along
the veins beneath, not strongly side-ribbed below
nor impressed-veined above, a very variable species
. . . . *R. vermontanus* (p. 186)
        22. Leaves firm, coriaceous, impressed-veined above,
velvety-pubescent and strongly side-ribbed beneath
. . . . *R. semisetosus* (p. 189)

THIMBLEBERRY, SALMONBERRY, *Rubus parviflorus* Nutt., Gen. 1:308,
1818

An upright shrub 1–2 m. high, young shoots glandular-hispid but not prickly,
older twigs with gray, shreddy bark; leaves simple, reniform to nearly orbicular
in outline, 7–20 cm. long and about as broad, three- to five-lobed, mostly palmately five-nerved, lobes broadly triangular, acute, dentate, the teeth mucronate, upper surface sparsely pubescent to glabrate, lower surface pubescent at
least along the veins, petioles glandular-hispid, about half as long as the blades;
stipules lanceolate, slightly adnate, glandular; inflorescence cymose, three- to
twelve-flowered; flowers 3–5 cm. in diameter; sepals broadly ovate, abruptly
long-caudate-acuminate, 1.5–2.5 cm. long, densely glandular on the back, puberulent toward the margins, densely white-tomentose within; petals white,
broadly oval, 15–30 mm. long; fruit convex, light red, 15–20 mm. wide, drupelets
cohering, separating from the receptacle, furnished with a hairy crest. Blossoms
in June and July; fruit ripe in August and September. (*Parviflórus*, small-
flowered, a most inapplicable name.)

Thimbleberry is common in rocky woods and thickets in northeastern Minnesota and northern Wisconsin, especially along the Superior shore. It is distributed
from Bruce Peninsula, Ontario, to Minnesota, from Alberta to southern Alaska,
south to the mountains of Mexico, Arizona, and California; it occurs also in
the Black Hills of South Dakota.

It is a polymorphic species, very variable in the degree of pubescence and
glandularity — characters that have been utilized for differentiating several varieties and numerous forms.

NAGOONBERRY, KNESHENEKA, ARCTIC RASPBERRY, *Rubus acaulis*
Michx., Fl. Bor. Am. 1:298, 1803 [*R. arcticus* L. var. *grandiflorus* Ledeb. 1844]

A low, unarmed, nearly herbaceous perennial, rhizomes and bases of the
stems slightly woody, stem 3–12 cm. high, more or less finely pubescent with
prominent scale leaves at the base; leaves three-foliolate, sparingly appressed-
pubescent on both sides, leaflets crenate-serrate, often entire toward the base,
terminal leaflet rhombic to obovate, 2–3 cm. long, its petiolule about 2 mm. long,

Thimbleberry, *Rubus parviflorus*

lateral leaflets somewhat smaller, broadly obovate, petiolules about 1 mm. long; stipules narrowly spatulate to lanceolate, about 5 mm. long; flowers usually solitary, terminal pedicel 2–5 cm. long; sepals narrowly lanceolate, acuminate, 8–10 mm. long, reflexed in anthesis; petals rose-colored, spatulate to obovate, with distinct claws, 9–13 mm. long; stamens numerous, filaments dilated, clavate, incurved; drupelets many; fruit similar to that of *R. pubescens*, edible. (*Acaúlis*, stemless.)

This species grows in peat bogs and moist woods. It is fairly common in extreme northern Minnesota and adjacent parts of Manitoba and Ontario, infrequent southward in Minnesota to southwestern St. Louis County. It is distributed from Labrador to Alaska, south to Quebec, northern Minnesota, Saskatchewan, and in the mountains to Colorado.

DWARF RASPBERRY, *Rubus pubescens* Raf., Med. Repos. 3:333, 1811 [*R. triflorus* Richards. 1823]

A low, unarmed, nearly herbaceous perennial, slightly woody at the base, flowering stems erect, 1–4 dm. high, sterile shoots trailing, 0.5–2 m. long, both erect and trailing stems finely and sparsely pubescent; leaves three-foliolate (rarely five-foliolate), sparingly pubescent on both sides, leaflets sharply and usually doubly serrate, petioles slender 3–8 cm. long, sparingly pubescent; stipules generally very prominent, obovate to lanceolate, 5–20 mm. long; terminal leaflet rhombic-ovate, 3–10 cm. long, petiolule about 5 mm. long or less, lateral leaflets subsessile, obliquely ovate, often more or less two-lobed; flowers erect, solitary or in two- to four-flowered cymes, pedicels puberulent, and sparingly glandular, 2–5 cm. long, slender; sepals ovate to broadly lanceolate, obtuse to acuminate, pubescent and glandular, 4–5 mm. long, reflexed in anthesis; petals white, erect, elliptic or oblanceolate, about as long as the sepals, short-clawed; hypanthium deeply concave; stamens numerous, filaments broad, linear to near the top, then somewhat hastate with subulate tip; styles much shorter than the stamens; fruit globose, dark red, the drupelets not separating from the torus, edible. Blossoms in May and June; fruit ripe in July and August. (*Pubéscens*, pubescent, not particularly applicable.)

Dwarf raspberry is common in spruce and tamarack bogs throughout the coniferous forest area, less frequent in moist deciduous woods southward to southern Wisconsin and northeastern Iowa. It is distributed from Labrador to northern British Columbia, south to New Jersey, northern Indiana, northern Iowa, South Dakota, and Colorado.

EUROPEAN RASPBERRY, *Rubus idaeus* L., Sp. Pl. 492, 1753

A shrub closely resembling *R. strigosus* but differing in lack of glandular bristles; young canes finely tomentose, becoming glabrate, sparingly armed with bristles or weak prickles; leaves of the first-year canes mostly five-foliolate, those of the second-year twigs three-foliolate, petioles, rachis, and midveins finely pubescent and with a few scattered prickles; peduncles and pedicels finely pubescent and generally bearing few to many hooked prickles; sepals ovate-lanceolate, long-acuminate, tomentose, often with a few hooked prickles; petals dull-white, elliptic, shorter than the sepals, stamens erect, not incurved; hypanthium broad and easily seen in the open flower; styles stouter than in *R. strigosus*; fruit red, sweet, drupelets tomentose. Blossoms in June; fruit ripe in July and August. (*Idaéus*, Greek, of the woods.)

A native of Europe, this raspberry is the parent of many of our cultivated raspberries. It escapes in the states adjacent to Minnesota and probably also

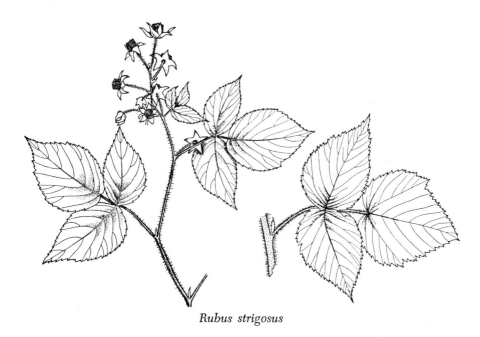

Rubus strigosus

in Minnesota. Forms occurring native in the northern part of the area with similar pubescence have the floral characters of R. *strigosus* and are referable to varieties of that species.

AMERICAN RED RASPBERRY, *Rubus strigosus* Michx., Fl. Bor. Am. 1:297, 1803

A branching shrub 1–2 m. high, stems biennial, usually brownish or reddish, frequently glaucous, young twigs bristly, the bristles mostly gland-tipped, sometimes with scattered, hooked prickles, typically without puberulence or villous pubescence; leaves of the primocanes three- to five-foliolate, those of the floricanes three-foliolate, petioles and rachis often bristly and mostly glandular, petioles 4–7 cm. long, terminal leaflet mostly ovate, sometimes three-lobed, 5–10 cm. long, 3–7 cm. wide, rounded to cordate at the base, acuminate at the apex, petiolule of terminal leaflet 0.5–3 cm. long, lateral leaflets essentially sessile, obliquely ovate, rounded or somewhat narrowed at the base, somewhat smaller than the terminal leaflets, all leaflets dark green and sparingly pubescent or soon glabrate above, white-tomentose beneath, sometimes with bristly prickles along the veins; inflorescence cymose, three-flowered to several-flowered, terminal and also often from the axils of the upper leaves, peduncles and pedicels glandular-bristly; sepals lanceolate, long-acuminate, glandular and hispid, puberulent without, white-tomentose within; petals dull-white, elliptic, erect, 5–6 mm. long, shorter than the sepals; stamens curved inward, concealing the narrow hypanthium; styles very slender; fruit hemispheric, light red, separating from the torus, slightly acid; drupelets, compared with the cultivated raspberry, relatively few and, when ripe, large and loosely cohering; stone of drupe-

167

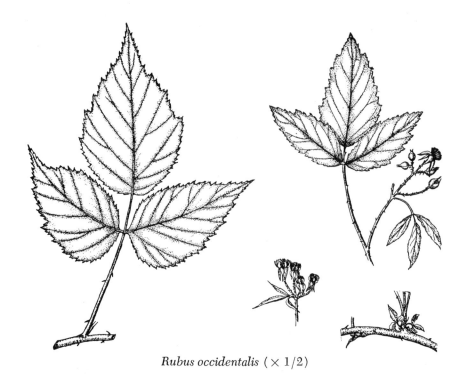

Rubus occidentalis ($\times\,1/2$)

let reticulate, not keeled on the back. Blossoms in June; fruit ripe in July and August. (*Strigósus*, beset with stiff straight hairs.)

American red raspberry is common in woods and thickets throughout the wooded parts of the Upper Midwest. It is distributed from Labrador to British Columbia, south to New Jersey, the mountains of North Carolina, Indiana, Nebraska, and in the Rocky Mountains to New Mexico. It occurs also in eastern Asia.

The species varies considerably in pubescence and other minor characters and has been segregated into a number of poorly defined species. It has also been frequently united with the European *R. idaeus* as a subspecies or variety. The following seems to be a fairly distinguishable geographical variety.

R. strigosus Michx. var. *canadensis* (Richards.) House, N.Y. State Mus. Bull. 243:50, 1923 [*R. idaeus* var. *canadensis* Richards. 1823; *Batidaea subarctica* Greene 1906; *Batidaea itascica* Greene 1906]

Stems, peduncles, and pedicels puberulent or finely pilose as well as bristly-glandular. (*Canadénsis*, Canadian.)

This variety grows throughout the area, but more commonly northward, where it appears to be the commonest form. It is distributed from Labrador to Alaska.

Occasional specimens occur with very few or no glandular bristles (*R. itascica*). Their pubescence then is almost identical with that of *R. idaeus*. The leaf and floral characters, however, agree with the American rather than with the European species.

BLACK RASPBERRY, THIMBLEBERRY, *Rubus occidentalis* L., Sp. Pl. 493, 1753

A shrub with biennial, arching stems, often rooting at the tips, 1–3 m. long, usually purplish-brown and glaucous, glabrous, armed with stiff, hooked prickles 3–5 mm. long, flowering twigs green; leaves three-foliolate (rarely palmately five-foliolate), dark green and glabrate above, slightly puberulent along the veins, white-tomentose beneath, sharply and doubly serrate with mucronate teeth; petioles 3–8 cm. long, sparingly prickly, more or less pubescent; stipules linear to subulate; terminal leaflet ovate, rounded to cordate at the base, long-acuminate at the apex, the petiolule 1–3 cm. long, lateral leaflets obliquely ovate, sometimes two-lobed, their petiolules 1–2 mm. long; inflorescence cymose, corymb-like, three- to ten-flowered, peduncles and pedicels more or less puberulent and prickly; sepals ovate-lanceolate, long-acuminate, tomentose on both surfaces, 7–8 mm. long, reflexed at anthesis; petals white, elliptic, much shorter than the sepals, fugaceous; stamens somewhat incurved, styles very numerous, filiform, exceeding the stamens; unripe fruit bright red, becoming at length black with a bloom, hemispherical, edible; drupelets very many, tomentose, cohering and separating from the torus. Blossoms in late May and June; fruit ripe in July and August. (*Occidentális*, Western, i.e., native of the New World.)

Rubus allegheniensis ($\times$ 2/5)

169

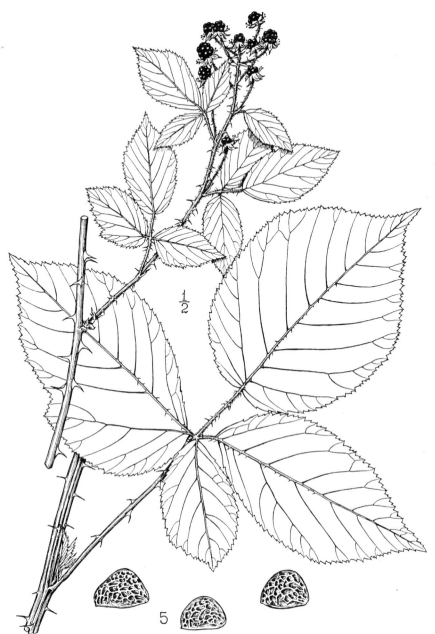

$\frac{1}{2}$

5

Rubus pensilvanicus. (Courtesy of L. H. Bailey.)

Black raspberry is common in rocky woods, thickets, and along fence rows throughout the southern part of the area, frequently cultivated and freely escaping, also possibly native, most common in the deciduous forest area. It ranges from New Brunswick south to the mountains of Georgia; its native western distribution is very uncertain as it was early planted and escapes freely.

170

× *Rubus neglectus* Peck, Rep. Reg. N.Y. 22:53, 1869 [*R. occidentalis* × *strigosus*]

Resembling *R. occidentalis*, but the leaves of the young shoots sometimes pinnately five-foliolate as in *R. strigosus* and the peduncles and petioles more or less glandular-hispid; fruit dark red, with the flavor of the red raspberry. (*Negléctus*, neglected, i.e., unrecognized.)

This hybrid is fairly common in the southeastern part of the area, where the two parents abound.

HIGH-BUSH BLACKBERRY, *Rubus allegheniensis* Porter, *ex* Bailey, Sketch Evol. Nat. Fr. 381, 1898 [*R. nigrobaccus* L. H. Bailey 1898]

A shrub with erect or high arching canes 1–3 m. high, usually armed with broad-based straight or curved prickles, young primocanes often ridged or angled and pubescent with simple hairs and stalked glands; primocane leaves mostly five-foliolate (sometimes three- or seven-foliolate), their petioles pubescent and generally stipitate-glandular, with or without prickles, leaflets elliptic-ovate to broadly ovate, rounded, subcordate to cordate at the base, abruptly acuminate at the apex, margin sharply and rather finely doubly serrate, velvety-pubescent beneath, somewhat pilose above when young, terminal leaflet 8–20 cm. long, 5–12 cm. wide, the lateral leaflets somewhat smaller and on shorter petiolules; floricane leaves three-foliolate, elliptic to oblong-ovate, short-pointed or sometimes obtuse at the apex, the lower pair mostly somewhat oblique at the base; inflorescence racemiform, 8–25 cm. long, leafy-bracted below, peduncles and pedicels pubescent and stipitate-glandular, often somewhat prickly; flowers 2–3 cm. across, sepals ovate, abruptly cuspidate-acuminate, 6–8 mm. long, more or less pubescent and slightly glandular-hispid without, tomentose within; petals ovate to oblong-elliptic; fruit globose to thimble-shaped, 1–2 cm. long, black, sweet, drupelets numerous, small, glabrous. Blossoms in late May and June; fruit ripe in August. Occasionally belated flowers occur on novirames in July and August. (*Alleghениénsis*, of the Alleghenies.)

High-bush blackberry grows in thickets, clearings, and borders of woods. It is common throughout the hardwood forest areas of the region, less frequent in the coniferous forest northward to the headwaters of the Mississippi River, rare or lacking in the northeast. It is distributed from Nova Scotia to Minnesota, south to North Carolina and Arkansas.

TALL BLACKBERRY, *Rubus pensilvanicus* Poir., in Lam., Encycl. Meth. Bot. 4:246, 1804[*]

A shrub with erect or ascending or somewhat arching canes, 1–2 m. high, armed with scattered, broad-based straight prickles, primocanes strongly angled,

[*] In the first edition of this book this bramble was mistakenly referred to *Rubus argutus*, a species of the eastern and southeastern United States that does not range farther northwestward than southern Illinois.

glabrous and without stalked glands; primocanes usually somewhat ridged, reddish-brown or purplish; primocane leaves mostly five-foliolate, their petioles and petiolules pubescent to glabrate, usually armed with a few hooked prickles; terminal leaflet oblong-ovate to broadly ovate, rounded, subcordate, or cordate at the base, abruptly long-acuminate at the apex, 8–14 cm. long, 4–5 cm. wide, lateral leaflets similar but smaller, margins conspicuously doubly serrate, the teeth sharp and long-pointed; upper surface of leaves sparsely pilose, lower surface soft or velvety-pubescent, in late season pubescence sometimes confined to the veins; floricane leaves three-foliolate, elliptic to narrowly ovate or obovate, narrowed at the base, acute at the apex, or sometimes abruptly tapered to a short point; margin sharply and often irregularly serrate or cut-toothed; racemes corymbiform 6–13 cm. long, 3–8 cm. broad, usually about half as broad as long; peduncles densely villous; pedicels elongated, spreading, pilose and mostly unarmed, subtended by stipule-like bracts, except for the lowermost one to three, which are subtended by foliaceous bracts; flowers 2–3 cm. in diameter, showy; sepals 5–6 mm. long, with abruptly acuminate prominent tips; petals oblong-ovate, 8–11 mm. long; fruit subglobose to thick ellipsoid, 1–2 cm. long, juicy and of good quality. Blossoms in June; fruit ripe in August. (*Pensilvánicus,* Pennsylvanian.)

Tall blackberry is fairly common in woods and thickets and along roadsides. In Minnesota it is found mostly in the hardwood areas from the southeastern corner thence northward to Ottertail County, Itasca Park, and southern St. Louis County. It is distributed from Newfoundland to southern Ontario, Minnesota, south to Virginia, Alabama, Arkansas and Oklahoma.

SMOOTH BLACKBERRY, *Rubus canadensis* L., Sp. Pl. 494, 1753

Canes erect or high-arching, 1–2 m. high (in our range apparently not exceeding 1 m. in height), more or less angled, smooth and without prickles or sometimes with remote, weak, straight prickles; primocanes reddish-brown or purplish; primocane leaves mostly five-foliolate, occasionally three- or seven-foliolate, glabrous on both surfaces or sometimes thinly pubescent beneath on the prominent rusty veins; petiolule smooth or with one to three small, hooked prickles, the three upper leaflets on elongate petiolules, the two lowermost sessile or nearly so and somewhat reflexed; terminal leaflet 8–15 cm. long, 5–7 cm. broad, ovate to narrow-ovate to oblong-ovate, rounded to cordate at the base, the apex long-acuminate to almost caudate; the lateral leaflets relatively narrower; margins coarsely and unevenly serrate, the teeth sharp and long-pointed; inflorescence racemiform, 5–13 cm. long, 3–6 cm. wide, bearing from six to twenty flowers on ascending to divaricate pedicels, the lowermost one to three flowers subtended by foliaceous bracts, the upper bracts stipuliform, rachis and pedicels pilose; flowers 2–3 cm. broad; petals obtuse 1–1.5 cm. long; sepals ovate, generally prolonged into acuminate tips, puberulent or sparsely pilose without, to-

Rubus canadensis. (Courtesy of L. H. Bailey.)

mentose within; fruit globose to oblong. Blossoms in June; fruit ripe in August. (*Canadénsis*, Canadian.)

This blackberry grows in clearings, on the edges of forests, and along roadsides; it is apparently confined to the northeastern part of the area, the only collections from Minnesota in the University herbarium being from St. Louis

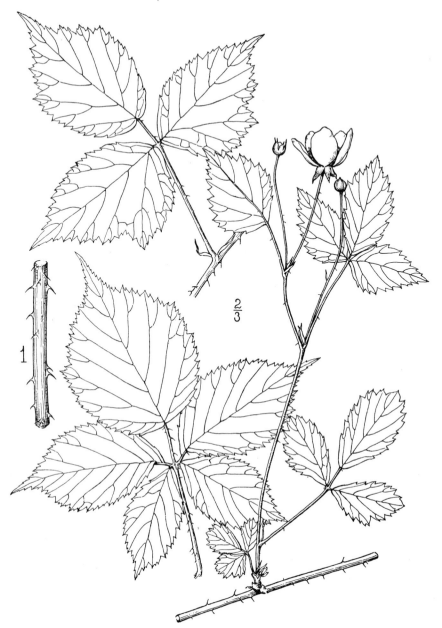

Rubus flagellaris. (Courtesy of L. H. Bailey.)

County. It is distributed from Newfoundland to western Ontario and Minnesota, south to New England, Pennsylvania, Georgia, and Tennessee.

COMMON EASTERN DEWBERRY, *Rubus flagellaris* Willd., Enum. Pl. Hort. Berol. 549, 1809 [*R. procumbens* Muhl. *apud* authors]

A prostrate shrub with slender, terete trailing canes 2–4 m. long, armed with

174

scattered, sharp, recurved, broad-based prickles 1–2 mm. long; primocanes at first short-ascending, soon becoming prostrate; primocane leaves three- to five-foliolate, essentially glabrous on the upper surface, more or less pilose along the veins beneath; petioles thinly pilose, unarmed or with a few small, hooked prickles; stipules linear-lanceolate, 5–12 mm. long; terminal leaflet 5–8 cm. long, 4–5 cm. broad, ovate, broadly rounded to subcordate at the base, tapering abruptly to an acute point; margins mostly prominently doubly and sharply serrate; lateral leaflet often somewhat asymmetrical; floricane leaves three-foliolate, leaflets elliptic to rhombic or obovate, usually broadest at or above the middle, narrowed to the base and abruptly acute to sometimes rounded at the apex, glabrous or nearly so on the upper surface, more or less pilose, mostly along the veins beneath; flowering shoots numerous, erect, 5–25 cm. high, bearing from two to eight flowers in ascendate inflorescences; pedicels slender, the lowermost elongated, sometimes up to 5–6 cm. long, more or less pilose, occasionally with one to three weak, hooked prickles; sepals ovate, apiculate, puberulent to thinly pilose on the outer surface, tomentose within; petals oblong to elliptic-oval or obovate, 9–12 mm. long, 4–8 mm. broad; fruit globose to short-oblong, usually of good flavor. Blossoms in late May and June; fruit ripe in August. (*Flagelláris*, whip-like, referring to the long, slender floricanes.)

Common eastern dewberry grows in fields, on banks, along roadsides and borders of thickets, chiefly on acid soils. It is common in the southeastern, eastern, and central parts of Minnesota as far north as Pine County and north to Becker County.

The species is highly variable and widely distributed, from New Brunswick and southwestern Quebec to southern Ontario and Minnesota, south to Georgia, Tennessee, Arkansas, and Oklahoma.

Rubus multifer Bailey, Gent. Herb. 5:262, 1943

A prostrate shrub with terete, trailing canes up to 3 m. long and frequently tip-rooting, glabrous but armed with slender, hooked prickles 1–2 mm. long, primocanes angled, at first short-ascending but soon recurving and becoming prostrate and trailing; primocane leaves three- to five-foliolate, firm, glabrous on the upper surface, thinly pubescent on the veins beneath, or nearly or quite glabrous with advance of the season; margins coarsely serrate or dentate; petioles 4–7 cm. long, usually armed with several short, hooked prickles; stipules conspicuous, linear-lanceolate, 10–14 mm. long, usually borne 2–4 mm. above the base of the petiole; terminal leaflet broadly ovate, rounded to subcordate at the base, gradually short-acuminate at the apex, 6–8 cm. long, 5–7 cm. broad; lateral leaflets narrower, elliptic-ovate, narrowed to the base; flowering shoots numerous, erect, 8–16 cm. high; leaves three-foliolate, leaflets ovate to slightly obovate, narrowed to the base, acute to acuminate or rarely blunt at the apex, all coarsely and irregularly serrate-dentate; flowers 2–3 cm. in diameter, in from

175

two to eight flowered cymes, at first close together but pedicels elongating and becoming ascendate; petals elliptic-obovate, 10–15 mm. long; sepals elliptic-oblong, 5–6 mm. rounded and apiculate at the apex, thinly pilose on the outer surface; fruit hemispheric to ovoid, of inferior quality. Blossoms in late May and June; fruit ripe in July and August. (*Múltifer*, fruitful.)

This dewberry occurs mostly on acid, sandy soils, and is found in eastern Minnesota and western Wisconsin.

It is closely related to *R. flagellaris*, but differs in the slightly stouter canes, with fewer prickles, and in the firmer, more coarsely serrate-dentate, nearly glabrous leaflets of the primocane leaves; furthermore the petioles of the primocane leaves are usually provided with more hooked prickles.

Rubus folioflorus Bailey, Gent. Herb. 5:376, 1943

A low-arching to trailing shrub with woody, terete, stoutish canes up to 12 dm. long; primocanes armed with from ten to twenty prickles per dm., the prickles strong, basally thickened, straight, declined, or slightly recurved; primocane leaves three- to five-foliolate; petioles stout, 4–9 cm. long, more or less armed with hooked prickles; stipules prominent, lanceolate to linear, 8–15 mm. long, inserted on the petiole above its base; terminal leaflet broadly ovate 6–12 cm. long, 5–11 cm. broad, cordate at the base, abruptly acuminate at the apex, in the five-foliolate leaves the intermediate and lowermost pairs of leaflets less broadly ovate and with subcordate or rounded to narrowed bases; lateral leaflets

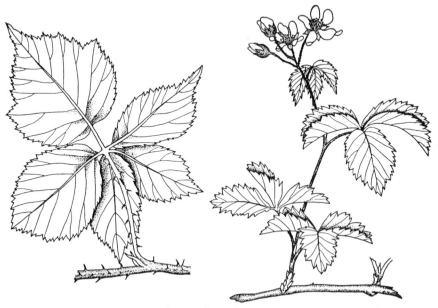

Rubus multifer (× 1/2)

176

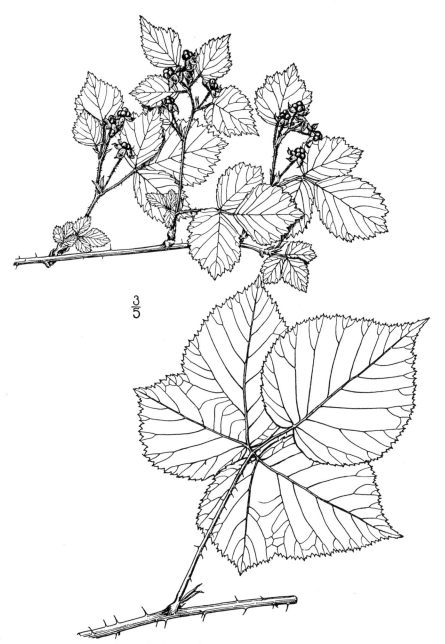

$\frac{3}{5}$

Rubus folioflorus. (Courtesy of L. H. Bailey.)

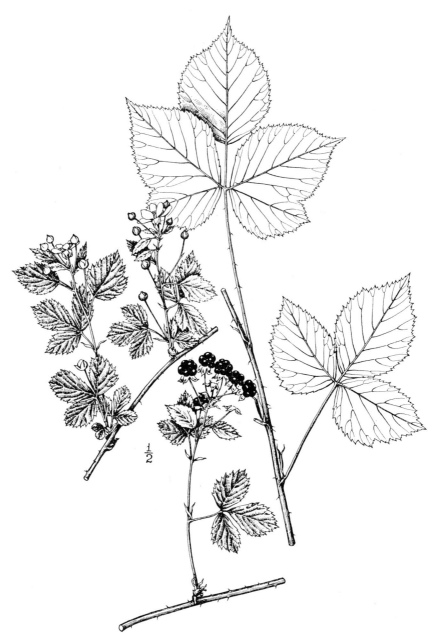

Rubus Rosendahlii. (Courtesy of L. H. Bailey.)

of the trifoliolate leaves strongly asymmetrical, broader than long and often more or less lobulate; the upper surface of the leaves glabrous and lustrous, the lower surface velvety-pubescent; margins unevenly and closely serrate; the leaves of the floricanes trifoliolate, with ovate to elliptic leaflets, rounded to narrowed at the base and serrate-dentate margins or some leaves simple and more or less

178

three-lobed; flowering shoots erect, 7–12 cm. high; inflorescence short-racemi-form, four- to six-flowered; flowers subtended by conspicuous, broadly ovate foliaceous bracts, rounded or subcordate at the base and irregularly serrate-dentate margins, sometimes the lowermost flower long-pedicelled; flowers 1.5–2 cm. broad; sepals ovate-oblong, 5–6 mm. long, with apiculate to caudate tips, strongly pilose on the outer surface; fruit small, drupelets few. Blossoms in June; fruit ripe in late July and August. (*Folioflórus*, with leaves and flowers, alluding to the prominent foliaceous bracts of the flower clusters.)

This shrub is infrequent in sandy soils along lake shores and in thickets, and has hitherto been reported only from Ramsey, Anoka, and Washington counties, Minnesota.

Rubus Rosendahlii Bailey, Gent. Herb. 7:Fasc. 3, 284, 1947

A small, slender, weakly armed shrub with ascending primocanes 4–5 dm. high and low-arching to depressed and trailing, frequently tip-rooting floricanes; prickles usually less than twenty per dm. of stem, somewhat recurved, mostly less than 2 mm. long; primocane leaves three-foliolate, rarely four- to five-foliolate, petioles slender, 3–8 cm. long, usually with a few small, hooked prickles; terminal leaflet elliptic-ovate, 4–6 cm. long, 3–4 cm. broad, rounded at the base, apex short-acuminate; upper surface glabrous, lower surface spar-ingly pilose along the veins; margins sharply serrate; lateral leaflets ovate and more or less oblique at the base or often unequally bilobed; floricane leaflets small, the terminal one cuneate at the base and short-acute to obtuse at the apex; flowers six to twelve; in racemose-corymbose inflorescences, the lowermost on slender, elongated pedicels in the axils of three-foliolate leaves, the inter-mediate and uppermost ones subtended by foliaceous to stipulaceous bracts; corolla 1.5–2 cm. across; sepals ovate, short-apiculate, puberulent without, to-mentose within; fruit hemispheric, 6–9 mm. in diameter, drupelets few. Blossoms in June; fruit ripe in late July and August. (*Rosendahlii*, named for the discov-erer.)

This bramble is known only from the type locality at Snail Lake, Ramsey County, Minnesota.

Rubus acridens Bailey, Gent. Herb. 5:480, 1944

A medium-sized bramble up to 1 m., more often 5–8 dm.; primocanes erect or ascending, faintly angled and armed with few to many weak, straight, usually slightly declined prickles 2–3 mm. long; floricanes oblique to arching, terete, with few, scattered, short, straight prickles, sometimes nearly or quite unarmed; primocane leaves three- to five-foliolate, thin, pubescent to glabrous above, more or less pilose beneath, especially on the veins; margins coarsely and very sharply doubly serrate; stipules narrowly lanceolate to subulate, 8–15 mm. long; terminal leaflet ovate, rounded to subcordate at the base, acute to acuminate at the apex, 8–12 cm. long, 5–6 cm. broad; lateral leaflets elliptic-ovate to slightly obovate,

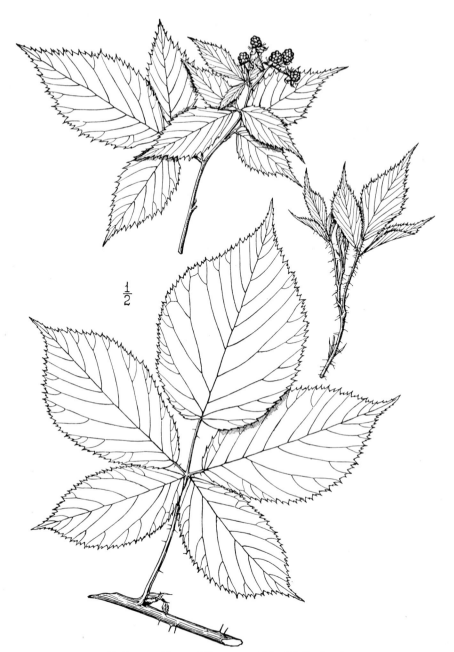

Rubus acridens. (Courtesy of L. H. Bailey.)

narrowed to the base, the lowermost pair often asymmetrical or bilobed; floricane leaves three-foliolate, leaflets elliptic-ovate, to rhombic-ovate, acute, the
paired leaflets often oblique at the base and sessile or nearly so; flowers 1.5–2.5
cm. broad, borne in four- to seven-flowered, corymbose, leafy clusters, the foliaceous bracts elliptic to lanceolate, with sharply dentate, sometimes jagged mar-

180

gins, occasionally the uppermost flowers subtended by stipulaceous bracts; sepals ovate with caudate tips, minutely pilose on the outer surface, densely tomentose within; fruit globose, small, mostly less than 1 cm. in diameter. Blossoms from the middle of June until early July; fruit ripe in August. (*Ac'ridens*, sharply dentate, referring to the sharp teeth of the floral leaves.)

This species occurs in the forested areas of Minnesota from the southeast corner northwestward and northward to the headwaters of the Mississippi River and St. Louis County. It is most common in the northern part of its range.

Rubus recurvans Blanchard, Rhodora 6:224, 1904

A shrub with ascending or somewhat arching primocanes, less than 1 m. high and strongly recurving to almost prostrate, occasionally tip-rooting; primocanes usually armed with from four to six slender, straight prickles to 2 cm. of stem; primocane leaves three- to five-foliolate, sparingly pubescent to glabrate on the upper surface, velvety-pubescent beneath, becoming less dense with advance of the season; petioles usually armed with a few hooked prickles; stipules subulate; terminal leaflet ovate, rounded to subcordate at the base with long-acuminate apex, 8–10 cm. long, 4–6 cm. broad; lateral leaflets elliptic-ovate, mostly rounded at the base and acute to short-acuminate at the apex, all the leaflets acutely and irregularly serrate-dentate or cut-toothed and jagged; floricane leaves three-foliolate, elliptic-ovate to lanceolate or narrowly obovate, tapered about equally to the base and apex; margins deeply and sharply serrate-dentate; flowering shoots numerous, 6–15 cm. high; flowers five to twelve, in corymbiform or short racemiform clusters, sometimes equaled or overtopped by foliaceous bracts, or the uppermost flowers subtended by stipulaceous bracts and standing above the foliage; flowers 1.5–2 cm. broad; petals narrowly obovate 8–11 mm. long; sepals lance-ovate, usually with elongated or caudate tips, minutely pilose to nearly glabrous on the outer surface; fruit ovoid 7–10 mm. in diameter, slightly longer than broad, drupelets relatively few. Blossoms in June; fruit ripe in August. (*Recúrvans*, recurving, referring to the low, arching canes which often tend to trail toward the tips.)

This shrub appears to be largely confined to the northeastern part of the region. It is distributed from southeastern Quebec to Minnesota, south to Nova Scotia, New England, Virginia, Illinois, and Missouri.

Occasional specimens bear a superficial resemblance to *R. acridens* in their sharply serrate-dentate leaves, but they can be distinguished from that species by the more numerous and more floriferous inflorescences and the denser and velvety pubescence of the under side of the leaves.

Rubus minnesotanus Bailey, Gent. Herb. 5:Fasc. 5, 328, 1943

A leafy, vigorous, rather strongly armed shrub with ascending primocanes 3–5 dm. high, floricanes prostrate and trailing, 1–2 m. long and 2–5 mm. thick, often tip-rooting; prickles strong, mostly about twenty per dm. of cane (occasionally

Rubus recurvans. (Courtesy of L. H. Bailey.)

up to fifty or more) 2–4 mm. long, nearly straight and declined to more or less recurved, most of them with enlarged, laterally flattened bases; primocane leaves three- to five-foliolate, petioles 4–8 cm. long, pubescent, and armed with several hooked prickles; terminal leaflet ovate, 6–10 cm. long, 4–8 cm. broad, rounded, subcordate to cordate at the base, apex abruptly acuminate; lateral leaflets elliptic-ovate, the lowermost pair usually narrowed to the base; the upper surface of the leaves glabrous or nearly so, more or less pilose beneath, especially on the veins; margins sharply doubly serrate; floricane leaves simple or three-foliolate, the simple ones ovate with subcordate base and cut-toothed or jagged or lobulate margins, the leaflets of the three-foliolate leaves narrowly ovate to elliptic, mostly narrowed to the base and less deeply serrate; inflorescence racemose-corymbiform, four- to nine-flowered, the lowermost one or two flowers usually in the axils of three-foliolate leaves, the others subtended by and either equaled or overtopped by large, ovate foliaceous bracts with subcordate to rounded or narrowed bases and acuminate tips; pedicels ascending, 1–4 cm. long, often bearing a few prickles; flowers 2.5–3 cm. broad; sepals ovate-oblong, 5–7 mm. long, subulate-tipped, minutely pubescent on the back; petals mostly oblong 10–13 mm. long; fruit nearly globular, about 1 cm. in diameter. Blossoms in June; fruit ripe in late July and August. (*Minnesotánus*, of Minnesota.)

This shrub is common in the southeastern and middle eastern parts of Minnesota, and is found northwestward to the region of Leech Lake, less frequently north to Lake Kabetogama. It also occurs over a considerable area of western Wisconsin.

Rubus latifoliolus Bailey, Gent. Herb. 5: Fasc. 9, 778, 1945

A very leafy, vigorous, strongly armed bramble with arching primocanes 5–6 dm. high and 1 m. or more long; prickles 2.5–5 mm. long, straight and more or less declined to slightly recurved, somewhat flattened laterally and with bases enlarged in the longitudinal axis of the cane; primocane leaves ample, three- to five-foliolate; petioles and petiolules with numerous hooked prickles; leaflets broadly ovate, plicate, the terminal one 8–12 cm. long, 6–9 cm. broad, cordate at the base, apex acuminate; lateral leaflets less broadly ovate and with rounded to subcordate bases; upper surface glabrous, lower surface sparsely pilose along the veins, midribs prominent and prickly; margins doubly serrate, serrations not deep; floricane leaves trifoliolate or simple, terminal leaflets obovate with cuneate base, lateral leaflets ovate, somewhat oblique at the base, simple leaves ovate, rounded at the base, short acuminate at the apex, margins sharply serrate-dentate; inflorescence racemose, the four or five flowers borne on somewhat elongated, prickly pedicels in the axils of the relatively large, foliaceous bracts which overtop the flowers; sepals oblong ovate, 6–7 mm. long, caudate-tipped; fruit hemispheric to short-oblong, about 1 cm. in diameter. Blossoms in the latter part of June; fruit ripe in August. (*Latifoliósus*, with broad leaflets.)

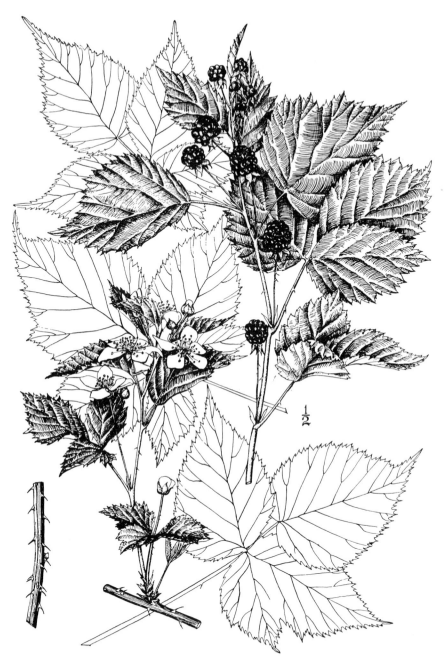

Rubus minnesotanus. (Courtesy of L. H. Bailey.)

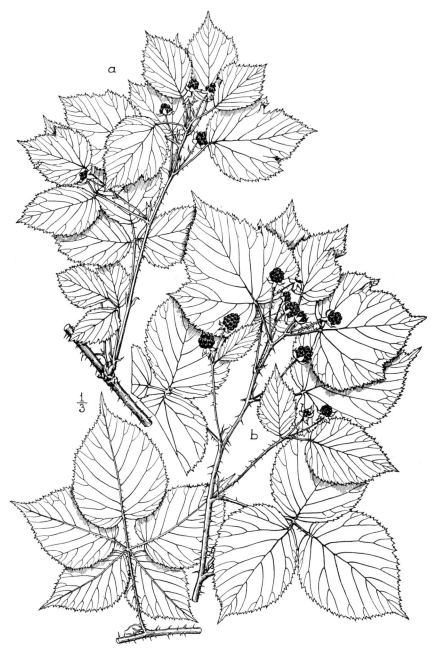

Rubus latifoliolus. (Courtesy of L. H. Bailey.)

This bramble has so far been recorded only from Ramsey and Anoka counties in Minnesota.

The species is well marked by the broad, thin, plicate, nearly glabrous leaflets, the very prickly canes, petioles and petiolules, and the few-flowered inflorescences with relatively large floral leaves.

Rubus Groutianus Blanchard, Am. Bot. 10:108, 1906 [*R. setosus* var. *Groutianus* Bailey 1925; *R. setosus* of authors, not Bigel., Bailey 1935; *R. nigricans* of authors, not Rydb.]

A sprawling shrub with ascending primocanes up to 4 dm. high, floricanes low-recurving to prostrate and trailing, sometimes tip-rooting; canes terete, thickly beset with from a hundred and fifty to five hundred acicular prickles per dm., intermixed with stalked, glandular bristles and hairs, prickles straight or more often recurved; primocane leaves three- to five-foliolate, firm, dark green and glabrous above, paler beneath and somewhat pilose along the prominent midrib and lateral veins, leaflets elliptic, narrowed to the more or less rounded base, acute to short-acuminate at the apex, margins sharply serrate, terminal leaflet 5–7 cm. long, 3–4 cm. broad, the leaflets of the lower leaves usually somewhat broader than those of the upper ones; flowers six to ten, in corymbiform inflorescences; bracts prominent; pedicels somewhat spreading, tomentose and with numerous gland-tipped hairs and occasional weak, acicular prickles; sepals oblong-ovate, 3.5–4 mm. long, tomentose and glandular hairy; petals oblong, with a narrow claw; fruit subglobose, 8–12 mm. in diameter, with few drupelets. Blossoms in June and early July; fruit ripe in August. (*Groutiánus*, named for the Grout family.)

This shrub occurs in sandy and peaty acid soils, along the borders of ponds, swales, and roadside ditches. It is common in Minnesota in Anoka and Ramsey counties and infrequent northward to Cass County. It is distributed from Nova Scotia, New Brunswick, and New England westward through northern New York, Ontario, Wisconsin, and Minnesota.

Rubus vermontanus Blanchard, Am. Bot. 7:3, 1904

An erect to depressed bramble 2–8 dm. high, in habit resembling *R. Groutianus* but with canes that have fewer acicular prickles and no interspersed glandular hairs and setae, the number of prickles varying from forty or less to a hundred and twenty-five per dm.; primocane leaves three- to five-foliolate, mostly the latter, leaflets elliptic to rhombic, narrowed to the base, sometimes more or less abruptly so, or even truncate or subcordate, acute to acuminate at the apex, margins finely to somewhat coarsely sharply serrate, thinnish, bright green and glabrous above, paler beneath and not strongly side-ribbed, glabrous or only sparsely pilose along the veins, terminal leaflet up to 10 cm. long, usually less, short-stalked, the lateral leaflets sessile or subsessile; inflorescence varying from a simple raceme to a forking corymb, eight- to twelve-flowered; lower bracts foliaceous, the

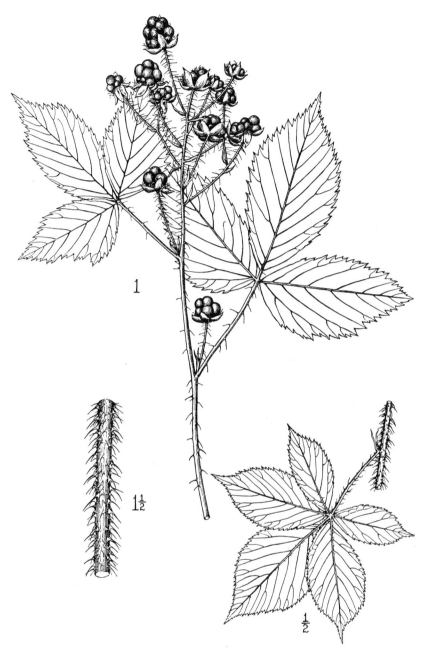

Rubus Groutianus. (Courtesy of L. H. Bailey.)

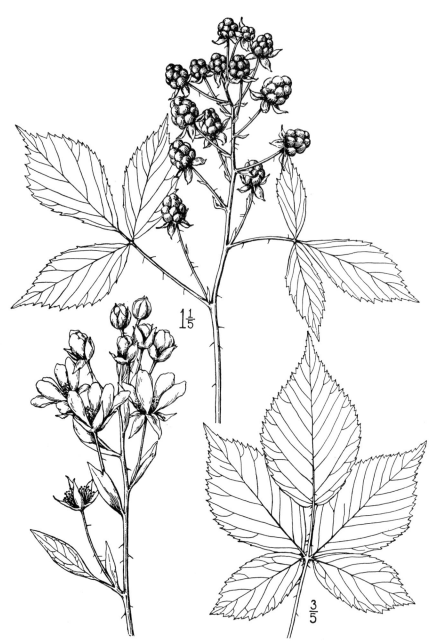

Rubus vermontanus. (Courtesy of L. H. Bailey.)

upper reduced and stipule-like; pedicels mostly unarmed but often with a few gland-tipped setae; sepals oblong-triangular, 5–7 mm. long, mostly apiculate, tomentulose and often with glandular hairs; petals 1–1.5 cm. long, obovate; fruit globose to short-oblong, about 1 cm. in diameter. Blossoms in late June to the middle of July; fruit ripe in August. (*Vermontánus*, of Vermont.)

This bramble is largely confined to sandy and acid soils, but is sometimes found in moist, rocky situations. It is common in Minnesota from Ramsey and Anoka counties northwestward to Cass County and north to St. Louis, Lake, and Cook counties, and also in adjacent parts of Wisconsin. It is distributed from Newfoundland to Ontario, Pennsylvania, Michigan, Wisconsin, and Minnesota.

It is deemed preferable in a work of this kind to treat *R. vermontanus* as a polymorphic species rather than attempt to assign its variants within our area to *R. superioris, R. spectatus, R. uniformis, R. regionalis*, and possibly other segregates in the western part of the geographical range of the species.

Rubus semisetosus Blanchard, Rhodora 9:8, 1907

A low shrub, in habit and stature closely similar to *R. Groutianus* and *R. vermontanus*, but differing mainly in the dull, coriaceous foliage and more ample inflorescences; primocanes with up to ninety acicular prickles per dm. but often fewer, and without intermixed gland-tipped hairs or bristles; primocane leaves three- to five-foliolate, leaflets elliptic to sometimes slightly obovate, tapered below to the narrowly rounded or cuneate base, pointed at the apex and with sharply serrate-dentate margins, coriaceous in texture, dull, grayish-green and with deeply impressed veins above, strongly side-ribbed and velvety-pubescent beneath; floricane leaflets elliptic to oblong-lanceolate, with cuneate base and acute apex, the two lowermost leaflets frequently side-lobed and asymmetrical; inflorescence mostly short-racemiform, six- to fifteen-flowered, with from one to three trifoliolate or simple lanceolate floral leaves below and stipulaceous bracts above; pedicels more or less spreading, tomentulose, with or without gland-tipped hairs and slender prickles; flowers showy, 2.5 cm. across; sepals triangular-ovate, tomentose and usually glandiferous; petals narrowly obovate, with a narrow claw; fruit short-oblong to nearly globose, 8–10 mm. in diameter. Blossoms in late June to the middle of July; fruit ripe in August. (*Semisetósus*, half-bristly.)

This short shrub grows in sandy, mostly acid soils, along the edges of thickets and borders of bogs. The only collections to date from our area are from northern Ramsey County in Minnesota, but the shrub is probably of wider distribution northward. It has previously been reported from New England. The local material matches very closely collections from Connecticut.[*]

[*] *R. Groutianus, R. vermontanus*, and *R. semisetosus*, three members of the *Setosi* group, occur in similar habitats and not infrequently grow together at the same site. There is therefore the possibility and likelihood of hybridization among them, and this is indicated by the occurrence of intermediate or bridging forms which cannot be assigned with any degree of certainty to one or another of the three species.

ROSE FAMILY

Jetbead

Rhodotypos Sieb. & Zucc., Flor. Jap. 1:187, 1835

A genus of a single known species, native to Japan. (*Rhodotýpos*, rose type, from the resemblance of the flowers to a small single rose.)

Rhodotypos scandens (Thunb.) Mak., in Bot. Mag. Tokyo 27:126, 1913 [*Rhodotypos kerrioides* Sieb. & Zucc. 1835]

A somewhat spreading, loosely branched, unarmed shrub, 1–2.5 m. high; young twigs olive-green, becoming brownish toward the end of the season, second-year twigs reddish-brown; leaves opposite, simple, ovate, 4–10 cm. long, 2–6 cm. wide, mostly rounded at the base, acuminate at the apex, sharply and doubly serrate, bright green on both sides, glabrous above, pubescent beneath, or glabrate in age; petioles very short; stipules subulate, caducous; flowers borne singly at the ends of leafy shoots, white, 2.5–4 cm. in diameter; sepals four, large, ovate, sharply serrate or toothed; petals four, nearly orbicular; stamens numerous, much shorter than the spreading petals; carpels two to six, enclosed in the short, urn-shaped receptacle; fruit consisting of several nearly black, dryish, shining drupelets, surrounded by the large persistent sepals, persisting until late in the autumn. Flowers in June, and frequently for a second time in August. (*Scándens*, climbing.)

This species is occasionally planted, but is not sufficiently winter hardy to make a successful ornamental shrub.

Ninebark

Physocarpus Maxim., Acta Hort. Petrop. 6:219, 1879

Branching shrubs with shreddy bark and alternate, simple, palmately lobed, stipulate leaves; flowers white or pinkish, numerous, in umbel-like corymbs; hypanthium broadly campanulate; sepals five, valvate; petals five, imbricate; stamens twenty to forty, in two or three cycles, inserted along the edge of the disk; carpels one to five, more or less connate at the base; styles terminal; stigma capitate; fruit, one to five inflated follicles, splitting halfway to the base along both sutures. (*Physocárpus*, bladder fruit.)

A genus of about five species and several varieties, natives of North America and northeastern Asia, of which the following occur in this area.

KEY TO SPECIES OF PHYSOCARPUS

1. Leaves becoming nearly glabrous beneath, follicles glabrous. .*P. opulifolius* (p. 190)
1. Leaves mostly stellate pubescent beneath, follicles stellate pubescent. . . . .
. . . .*P. opulifolius* var. *intermedius* (p. 192)

COMMON NINEBARK, *Physocarpus opulifolius* (L.) Maxim., Acta Hort. Petrop. 6:219, 1879 [*Spiraea opulifolia* L. 1753; *Opulaster opulifolius* Kuntze 1891]

A shrub 1–3 m. high, with arching or recurved branches; young twigs yellow-

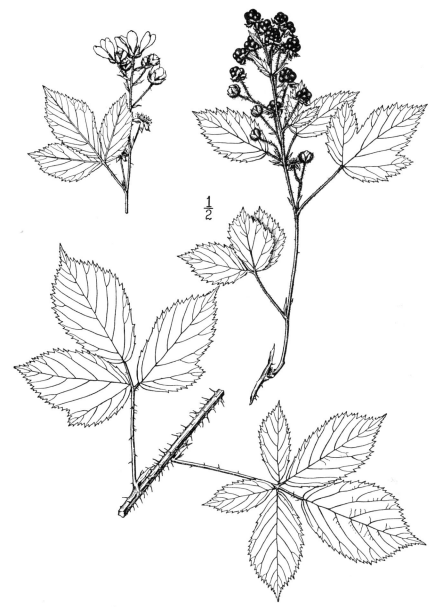

Rubus semisetosus. (Courtesy of L. H. Bailey.)

ish-green, soon turning brownish, slightly angled, glabrous or nearly so; older twigs and branches grayish-brown, the bark fissured and peeling off in strips and layers; leaves mostly ovate in outline, and more or less distinctly three-lobed, 3–7 cm. long, often larger on sterile shoots, subcordate, truncate, rounded, or narrowed at the base, mostly acute at the apex, the margin irregularly crenate-dentate, dark green above, paler beneath, glabrous or somewhat pubescent in the axils of the veins; petioles slender, 1–2 cm. long; stipules caducous; peduncle

191

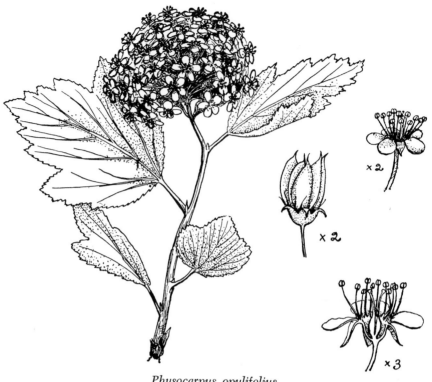

Physocarpus opulifolius

and pedicels glabrous or the latter more or less pubescent; flowers white, about 9–12 mm. in diameter; follicles three to five, glabrous, shining, much exceeding the calyx and conspicuous when ripe. Blossoms in June and July. (*Opulifólius*, leaves as in **Viburnum Opulus**.)

Common ninebark grows on shores, rocky banks, and in thickets. It is distributed from Quebec to Hudson Bay, westward to Wisconsin and northeastern Minnesota, south to South Carolina, Tennessee, and northern Illinois. It is common in our area only in the vicinity of Lake Superior.

A form with yellow leaves (f. *luteus*), known as Golden Ninebark, is cultivated to some extent in the Upper Midwest.

Physocarpus opulifolius var. *intermedius* (Rydb.) Robinson, Rhodora 10:32, 1908

Resembles the species in habit and inflorescence, but differs in the frequently narrower leaves, which are mostly more or less stellate-pubescent beneath, and in the duller, permanently stellate-pubescent follicles. (*Intermédius*, intermediate.)

This variety grows along streams, on rocky hillsides, and along the edges of woods and thickets. It is common in the deciduous forest area of southeastern Minnesota and the adjacent parts of Wisconsin and Iowa. It is distributed from

192

western New York to Minnesota and South Dakota, south to Indiana, Illinois, Arkansas, and Colorado.

Spirea
Spiraea L., Sp. Pl. 480, 1753

Shrubs with alternate, simple, sometimes pinnately lobed leaves without stipules; flowers small, white, pink or reddish, in umbel-like racemes, corymbs or panicles; hypanthium campanulate or cup-shaped, bearing a disk; sepals five, persistent; petals five; stamens twenty to fifty, distinct, inserted with the petals along the edge of the disk; carpels generally five, superior, distinct; ovules two to many; fruit composed of several follicles. (*Spiraéa*, probably from the Greek *speira*, meaning wreath.)

This is a genus of about seventy-five species of the North Temperate Zone, only two of which are native to our area. Many species are cultivated as ornamental shrubs, and among these several are of garden origin.

KEY TO SPECIES OF SPIRAEA

1. Flowers pure white, in sessile umbels or simple corymbs.
  2. Flowers borne on old wood, in sessile leafless umbels, not on new leafy shoots (sometimes a few small leaves at the base of the clusters), leaves pinnately veined.
    3. Leaves ovate or ovate-oblong, pubescent at least when young............ .... *S. prunifolia* (p. 193)
    3. Leaves narrowly lanceolate to oblanceolate, glabrous.
      4. Leaves narrowly lanceolate, flowers 6–8 mm. in diameter, two or three in each cluster................................*S. Thunbergii* (p. 194)
      4. Leaves oblanceolate, flowers 8–11 mm. in diameter, two to five in each cluster.................................... × *S. arguta* (p. 194)
  2. Flowers in many-flowered corymbs, terminating short, leafy shoots of the season, leaves palmately three- to five-veined........... × *S. Van-Houttei* (p. 194)
1. Flowers pink or white, sometimes with a slight tinge of pink, in compound inflorescences (peduncle branched).
  5. Flowers in corymbs or rounded clusters.
    6. Branches terete, pubescent at least when young, flowers pink............ .... *S. japonica* (p. 195)
    6. Branches angled, nearly or quite glabrous, flowers pink to whitish......... .... × *S. Bumalda* (p. 195)
  5. Flowers in panicles.
    7. Leaves nearly or quite glabrous, oblong to oblanceolate, flowers white..... ....*S. alba* (p. 196)
    7. Leaves pubescent or tomentose beneath.
      8. Leaves grayish or whitish beneath; fruit glabrous. × *S. Billiardii* (p. 196)
      8. Leaves tawny beneath; fruit pubescent when young, becoming glabrate ....*S. tomentosa* var. *rosea* (p. 197)

BRIDAL WREATH, *Spiraea prunifolia* Sieb. & Zucc., Flor. Jap. 1:131, 1840

A shrub 1–2 m. high, with slender, more or less erect branches; young twigs slightly pubescent, becoming glabrous; leaves ovate to oblong, 2.5–5 cm. long. 1–2 cm. broad, narrowed toward the base, rounded or acutish at the apex, finely serrate except at the base, glabrous or nearly so above, pubescent beneath; petioles about 6 mm. long; flowers in two- to seven-flowered sessile umbels, appearing before the leaves, white, 10–12 mm. in diameter; pedicels slender, 1–2 cm. long; sepals ovate, obtuse, about 1.5 mm. long; petals pure white, broadly obovate or nearly orbicular, 5 mm. long, exceeding the stamens; follicles glabrous. (*Prunifólia*, with leaves like a plum tree.)

The double-flowered form of this species is the one most common in cultivation. The stems are subject to killing-back in the winter, as a result of which the shrub remains low. It is a native of China and Japan.

Spiraea Thunbergii Sieb., *ex.* Blume, Fl. Nederl. Ind. 1115, 1826

A low shrub 5–12 dm. high, with numerous slender, arching branches, reddish-brown, at first more or less pubescent, in age becoming glabrous and the outer bark shreddy; leaves linear-lanceolate, 2–4 cm. long, 2–8 mm. wide, glabrate, gradually narrowed toward both ends, sharply serrate, petioles 1–3 mm. long; flowers in sessile umbels, appearing just before the leaves, two or three in each cluster, white, 6–8 mm. in diameter; sepals ovate-triangular; petals obovate, more than twice as long as the stamens; pedicels slender, glabrous, 5–10 mm. long; follicles projecting prominently when ripe. Blossoms in April and early May. (*Thunbérgii*, named for the Swedish botanist, Thunberg.)

This shrub is a native of China and Japan. The tips of the branches generally kill back in winter; as the branches are thus left naked except for the prominent, unopened buds, the appearance of the shrub is somewhat disfigured. The following hybrid, derived in part from this species, is frequently cultivated in the Upper Midwest.

× *Spiraea arguta* Zabel, Deut. Gartenz. 3:494, 1884 [*S. Thunbergii* × *multiflora*]

A low shrub of similar habit to that of the preceding species, but more robust; leaves oblanceolate, 1.5–3 cm. long, 5–10 mm. broad, narrowed toward the base, acute at the apex, serrate above the middle, glabrous on both sides; flowers in numerous, two- to five-flowered umbels, white, 8–11 mm. in diameter, pedicels 12–15 mm. long. (*Argúta*, bright.)

The ends of the branches of this hybrid kill back during winter as in the first of the parent species.

BRIDAL WREATH, × *Spiraea Van-Houttei* (Briot) Zabel, Deut. Gartenz. 3:496, 1884 [*S. cantoniensis* × *trilobata*]

A shrub 1–2 m. high with arching branches; the bark on young branches smooth, yellowish-brown, on older parts gray and somewhat shreddy; leaves rhombic ovate, cut-serrate or obscurely lobed, narrowed at the base, dark green above, pale bluish-green beneath, 1.5–4 cm. long; flowers in numerous, many-flowered umbels, white, 5–7 mm. broad; sepals upright or spreading in fruit; petals twice as long as the stamens. Flowers in May and June. (*Van Hoúttei*, named for Louis Van Houtte, a Belgian horticulturist.)

Species of *Spiraea*: Left, × *S. arguta*. Right, × *S. Van-Houttei*. (× 2/3)

Bridal wreath is very extensively cultivated as an ornamental shrub. A very handsome, early-flowering spirea of garden origin, it is a hybrid between *S. cantoniensis* and *S. triloba*. It is quite hardy and endures our winter climate without injury.

JAPANESE SPIREA, *Spiraea japonica* L. f., Suppl. 262, 1781

An upright shrub, 8–15 dm. high; young branches more or less tomentose, one-year-old twigs reddish-brown, glabrous or remaining more or less pubescent; leaves oval, narrowly ovate to oblong-lanceolate, 4–11 cm. long, 1.5–4 cm. wide, narrowed at the base, acute or acuminate at the apex, doubly and sharply serrate, the serrations extending almost to the base, bright green above, bluish or grayish-green beneath, sparsely pubescent on both surfaces or glabrous; petioles 2–7 mm. long; inflorescence terminal, on elongated shoots of the season, consisting of several aggregated corymbs, rather loose; flowers pink, 4–6 dm. in diameter; hypanthium and sepals pubescent; petals broadly obovate or nearly orbicular; stamens very prominent; sepals spreading or reflexed in fruit; follicles erect or nearly so, glabrous. Flowers in July or August; fruit ripe in September and October. (*Japónica*, Japanese.)

This species varies considerably in the color of the flowers, the size of the leaves, and the degree of pubescence. It is a native of China and Japan.

× *Spiraea Bumalda* Burvenich, Rev. Hort. Belg. 17:12, 1891 [*S. japonica* × *albiflora*]

A more or less erect shrub, about 5 dm. high; bark brown, striped; young shoots with small ridges running from the base of the petiole; leaves ovate-lanceolate, sharply and mostly doubly serrate, narrowed towards the base, acute at the apex, dark green above, paler beneath, glabrous on both sides, 2–8 cm. long, 1.2–2 cm. wide; flowers numerous, in corymbs, whitish to pink; follicles diverging when ripe. Flowers in July and August. (*Bumálda*, a generic name, coming originally from J. A. Bumalda, an Italian botanist of the seventeenth century.)

This is a shrub of garden origin, a hybrid between S. *japonica* and S. *albiflora*. Numerous forms are cultivated, among which the most commonly planted within the state is the horticultural variety, Anthony Waterer, a low, compact shrub, flowers pink-purple, very numerous in compound cymes. Most of the branches kill back almost to the ground in the winter, but the plant renews itself very rapidly from the basal parts and bears the flowers on the season's growth. The variety *Froebelii* is similar in habit and foliage, but has flowers of deeper and better color.

Spiraea alba DuRoi, Harbk. Baumz. 2:430, 1772 [S. *salicifolia* of Am. authors (including Minn. T. & S. 1912), not S. *salicifolia* L., which is Asiatic]

An erect shrub 5–12 dm. high; twigs round or somewhat angled, reddish- or yellowish-brown, glabrous or nearly so, old stems with grayish, somewhat exfoliating outer bark; leaves from broadly to narrowly oblanceolate or narrowly oblong, 3–6 cm. long, 7–15 mm. broad, narrowed at the base, mostly acute at the apex, sharply and fine serrate, glabrous on both sides or sparingly pubescent along the midvein beneath; petiole 2–6 mm. long, often somewhat tomentose on the margins; inflorescence a terminal panicle, somewhat leafy at the base, axis, peduncles, and pedicels more or less puberulent or tomentose; flowers numerous, white, 6–7 mm. in diameter; hypanthium turbinate, puberulent to glabrous or nearly so; sepals about as long as the hypanthium, becoming erect or incurved in fruit; petals nearly orbicular, with short claw; stamens very numerous, exceeding the petals; pedicels 2–5 mm. long; follicles glabrous. Blossoms from the latter part of June until August. (*Al'ba*, white, referring to the flowers.)

This shrub grows on low ground and is common throughout the region. It is distributed from New York to Saskatchewan, south to North Carolina and Missouri.

Occasional forms occur which approach the eastern S. *latifolia* in the broader (up to 2.5 cm.) leaves, with coarser, sometimes double, serrations; but in the pubescence as well as the form of the inflorescence they agree more closely with S. *alba*.*

× **Spiraea Billiardii** Herincq, L'Hort. Franc. 3, 1855 [S. *Douglasii* × *salicifolia*]

A shrub 1–2 m. high, with erect, nearly simple, brownish-pubescent branches;

* A form with pink petals, S. *alba* f. *rosea* Moore, Rhodora 52:57, 1950, occurs occasionally.

leaves oblong to oblong-lanceolate, 5–8 cm. long, narrowed toward the base, and tapering, generally acute, at the apex, sharply and more or less doubly serrate, glabrous above, at first sparsely grayish-tomentose beneath, becoming nearly or quite glabrous with age; petioles 4–5 mm. long; inflorescence a narrow, elongated panicle, densely flowered, pubescent throughout, flowers pink, 5–6 mm. in diameter; hypanthium and sepals pubescent; petals nearly orbicular; stamens much exserted; follicles glabrous. (*Billiárdii*, named for the French florist in whose garden it originated.)

This hybrid resembles very closely others in which S. *Douglasii* figures as one of the parents, and it is doubtful whether the form handled by the horticulturists as the above combination actually is what it purports to be. As yet it is cultivated only to a limited extent within the area.

HARDHACK, STEEPLEBUSH, *Spiraea tomentosa* L. var. *rosea* (Raf.) Fernald, Rhodora 14:188, 1912

An erect shrub 3–12 dm. high, stems covered with a tawny or rusty tomentum, at length becoming glabrate and reddish-brown; leaves ovate to oblong or ovate-lanceolate, 2–6 cm. long, 1–2.5 cm. wide, narrowed or somewhat rounded at the base, usually acute at the apex, coarsely crenate-serrate, dark green and and slightly puberulent above, densely pale-tomentose beneath or, more frequently, tawny or rusty, the veins prominent; petiole 2–3 mm. long; inflorescence paniculate, 1–2 dm. long, terminating in a long, slender point, somewhat branched below, the lower branches slightly compound, tomentose throughout; flowers pink, purplish, or rarely white, crowded, short-pedicelled; hypanthium hemispherical, tomentose, sepals triangular, reflexed, petals broadly ovate or suborbicular, about 1.5 mm. long, follicles about 2.5 mm. long, short-tomentose, soon becoming glabrate. (*Tomentósa*, tomentose, referring to the woolly pubescence of the leaves and stem; *rósea*, rosy, referring to the color of the flowers.)

Hardhack is frequent, especially in low, acid soil, in the northeastern part of the area, and as far south as the forty-fifth parallel. It is distributed from New York to Minnesota, south in the mountains to South Carolina.

All Upper Midwest specimens of this species appear to belong to the variety *rosea*. The typical species, found in the eastern part of the United States, has a more freely branched and more crowded inflorescence, with the individual flowers so closely packed that their pedicels cannot be seen, and densely lanate follicles, which are very tardily glabrate. Despite the name there is no color difference between the species and its variety.

Sorbaria A. Br., in Aschers., Fl. Brandenb. 177, 1864

Woody or semi-woody plants; leaves deciduous, alternate, compound, odd-pinnate with conspicuous stipules; flowers white, perfect, small, and numerous in terminal panicles; hypanthium hemispheric; sepals five, imbricate, early-re-

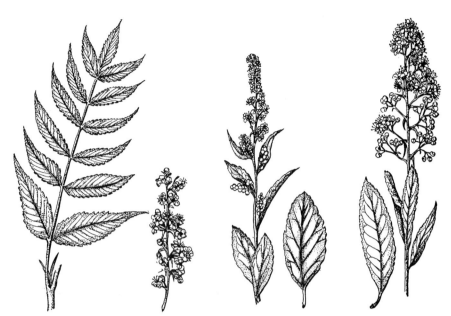

Left, *Sorbaria sorbifolia*. Center, *Spiraea tomtentosa* var. *rosea* (× 1/2). Right, *Spiraea alba*.

flexed; petals five, imbricate, spreading; stamens numerous, borne on the margin of the disk; carpels five, opposite the sepals, connate below; styles terminal or nearly so; ovules several; follicles thin, dehiscent along both sutures; seeds few. (*Sorbária*, resembling *Sorbus* in foliage.)

This is a genus of about eight species, natives of northern and eastern Asia. The following species is cultivated in the Upper Midwest.

Sorbaria sorbifolia (L.) A. Br., in Aschers., Fl. Brandenb. 177, 1864 [*Spiraea sorbifolia* L. 1753; *Basilima sorbifolia* Raf. 1836]

An erect, soft-woody shrub, 1–2 m. high, spreading freely by suckers; young twigs more or less pubescent; leaves 1–4 dm. long, leaflets thirteen to twenty-three, lanceolate, narrowed at the base, long-acuminate at the apex, sharply serrate, often stellate-pubescent beneath when young; panicles terminal, 15–30 cm. long; flowers white, with yellowish or reddish center, 7–8 mm. in diameter; hypanthium glabrous; sepals ovate; petals obovate, clawed, about 3 mm. long; stamens numerous and conspicuous; follicles glabrous. Flowers in May and June. (*Sorbifólia*, with leaves like *Sorbus*.)

This species is a native of Asia from the Ural region to Japan. It is frequently cultivated, spreading freely by underground shoots, and occasionally escapes.

Rose

Rosa L., Sp. 491, 1753

Bushes, sometimes with very long canes which take on a semiclimbing or vine-like habit; stems usually armed with prickles, often with a pair of unusually large ones just below each node (infrastipular prickles); buds scaly; leaves deciduous or in warm climates sometimes evergreen, pinnately compound with from three to eleven leaflets (simple in one Asiatic species), stipules persistent, large, mostly adherent to the petiole with short, free auricles at the top; flowers perfect, hypanthium deeply cup-shaped, sepals five, petals five (numerous in many cultivated forms), stamens many, pistils many, the ovaries free, becoming achenes in fruit, the styles sometimes united, sepals, petals, and stamens borne on the upper edge of the hypanthium, ovaries borne on its inner surface completely concealed by the cup; fruit a "hip" formed by the fleshy hypanthium containing the numerous bony achenes; seed solitary, with endosperm. (*Rósa*, the classical Latin name.)

Rosa is a very large genus of the Northern Hemisphere. The limits of the species are exceedingly difficult to define, owing to the variability of the species themselves and the hybridizing of different species whenever they occur together. These two characteristics have served as a foundation for the great and ever increasing number of cultivated forms of roses. Our native roses need further study, especially in the living state. In collecting roses for study it is well to have all parts of the plant — flowering branches, fruit, and young, non-flowering shoots. Roses that have been cut down at or before the usual flowering time often flower late in the season on new, rapidly grown shoots, which differ greatly in appearance from the normal type of the species.

KEY TO SPECIES OF ROSA

1. Upright shrubs; styles free, scarcely exserted from the mouth of the hypanthium.
    2. Native species and introduced species that have become established; flowers pink (rarely nearly white) with five petals.
        3. Infrastipular prickles well developed, with or without other prickles.
            4. Leaflets mostly five (rarely seven); stems greenish, mostly armed with bristles as well as slender prickles; sepals about 2 cm. long, soon reflexed and deciduous............................*R. carolina* (p. 200)
            4. Leaflets seven to nine; stems red-purple, bristly only at the base; prickles with a conspicuously enlarged pale base; sepals about 1.5 cm. long, erect and persistent in fruit.
                5. Leaflets puberulent, prickles slender about 5 mm. long............
                .... *R. Macounii* (p. 201)
                5. Leaflets glabrous, prickles stouter, about 10 mm. long............
                ....*R. Woodsii* (p. 201)
        3. Definite infrastipular prickles wanting, prickles needle- or bristle-like with scarcely enlarged bases.
            6. Leaflets mostly five, their serrations coarse and spreading; whole plant very prickly; flowers mostly solitary [*R. acicularis*].
                7. Hip elongated; serration of leaflets mostly simple................
                ....*R. acicularis* (typical) (p. 202)
                7. Hip spherical.
                    8. Leaflets doubly serrate...*R. acicularis* var. *Bourgeauiana* (p. 203)
                    8. Serration of leaflets mostly simple........................
                    ....*R. acicularis* var. *rotunda* (p. 203)

199

6. Leaflets seven to eleven, their serrations fine and ascending; flowers mostly in corymbs.
  9. Shrub mostly about 1 m. high; twigs red-purple, unarmed or sparingly armed; corymbs few-flowered, borne on the old wood; leaflets mostly seven [*R. blanda*].
    10. Leaflets simply serrate, rachis of leaf not glandular.
      11. Leaflets pubescent...........*R. blanda* (typical) (p. 203)
      11. Leaflets glabrous..........*R. blanda* var. *glabra* (p. 205)
    10. Leaflets doubly serrate....*R. blanda* var. *acicularioides* (p. 205)
  9. Plant mostly 3–4 dm. high; twigs green (sometimes tinged with red on one side), mostly densely bristly-prickly; corymbs often many-flowered, borne on young shoots as well as on the old growth; leaflets mostly nine to eleven [*R. arkansana*].
    12. Leaflets glabrous.............*R. arkansana* (typical) (p. 205)
    12. Leaflets pubescent.
      13. Hip globular...........*R. arkansana* var. *suffulta* (p. 206)
      13. Hip top-shaped.........*R. arkansana* var. *Bushii* (p. 207)
2. Cultivated species, occasionally persisting in the vicinity of old gardens; flowers of various colors, petals often numerous.
  14. Leaflets 2–5 cm. long.
    15. Leaflets downy beneath, not glandular or very slightly so.
      16. Twigs red with hooked infrastipular prickles; leaflets thin; flowers pink.............................*R. cinnamomea* (p. 207)
      16. Twigs grayish-brown, without infrastipular prickles; leaflets thick and rugose; flowers red or white.............*R. rugosa* (p. 207)
    15. Leaflets nearly or quite glabrous beneath, more or less glandular, thick and firm (no infrastipular prickles).
      17. Stipules not fimbriate, flowers large.
        18. Prickles slender; leaflets obtuse, rugose....*R. gallica* (p. 208)
        18. Prickles stout, hooked; leaflets usually acute...............
        ....*R. centifolia* (p. 208)
      17. Stipules fimbriate, flowers about 2 cm. in diameter.............
      ....*R. multiflora* (p. 212)
  14. Leaflets 1–2 cm. long.
    19. Foliage glandular, fragrant.
      20. Stems green, with stout infrastipular prickles, flowers pink.......
      .... *R. Eglanteria* (p. 210)
      20. Stems brown, without infrastipular prickles; flowers yellow......
      ....*R. foetida* (p. 210)
    19. Foliage glabrous, not scented; stems brown.
      21. Stems erect, densely bristly-prickly; flowers mostly white........
      ....*R. spinosissima* (p. 211)
      21. Stems arching, with scattered prickles; flowers yellow...........
      ....*R. Hugonis* (p. 211)
1. Shrubs with long, vine-like canes requiring support; styles united to form an exserted column, cultivated.
  22. Stipules nearly entire, leaflets three to five.............*R. setigera* (p. 211)
  22. Stipules fimbriate, leaflets mostly nine...............*R. multiflora* (p. 212)

Rosa carolina L., Sp. Pl. 492, 1753 [*R. humilis* Marsh. 1785]

A low shrub with greenish stems, 3–10 dm. high; young growth very bristly and armed with straight, slender infrastipular prickles 5–8 mm. long, branches with infrastipular prickles or unarmed; leaves with five or rarely seven leaflets;

leaflets elliptic or lance-elliptic, rarely obovate, apex acute or rarely obtuse, base wedge-shaped, margin sharply serrate with ascending teeth, upper surface glabrous, lower surface paler, glabrate or pubescent along the veins, midrib prominent, the other veins rather obscure, upper leaflets 1–3 cm. long, lower somewhat smaller, third pair when present much reduced; petiole and rachis glabrous or sparingly pubescent; stipules very narrow, nearly glabrous, entire or with a few glandular teeth; flowers mostly solitary, pedicel and hypanthium usually glandular-hispid, sepals mostly with narrow lateral lobes, 1.5–2 cm. long, mostly very glandular-hispid on the outside, tomentose within; petals pink, flower about 5 cm. wide; calyx reflexed after anthesis and soon deciduous; hip globose or somewhat flattened, red; achenes dark brown, slender, about 4.5 mm. long, attached mainly to the bottom of the hypanthium. (*Carolína*, Carolinian.)

Roses of this group with infrastipular prickles, deciduous calyx, and achenes borne in the bottom of the hypanthium are abundant in eastern North America, chiefly in regions of acid soil. This representative of the group is apparently very rare in the Upper Midwest, barely reaching the eastern border of Minnesota. It is distributed from Nova Scotia and New England, west to Wisconsin, Minnesota, and Nebraska, south to Texas and Florida.

Rosa Macounii Greene, Pittonia 4:10, 1899 [*R. Woodsii* of Minn. T. & S. 1912, not *R. Woodsii* Lindl.]

Stems 2–20 dm. high; young woody twigs glossy reddish-brown; prickles slender, straight or slightly bent at the base, 2–9 mm. long with a conspicuously enlarged base, infrastipular prickles well developed, often the only ones present on flowering branches, young shoots from the rhizome often with numerous other prickles, some of them as large as the infrastipular ones; leaves with five to nine leaflets; leaflets elliptical or obovate with petiolules 1–2.5 mm. long, thin, apex rounded, base rounded or somewhat wedge-shaped, margin sharply and simply serrate except at the base, upper surface dull green, glabrous, lower surface whitish, puberulent with a few longer hairs, the midrib and principal veins somewhat prominent beneath; upper leaflets 1–3 cm. long, 6–18 mm. wide, lower leaflets somewhat smaller; petiole and rachis finely woolly-pubescent and often bearing a few slender prickles; stipules entire or slightly glandular-serrate, the pair about 4–7 mm., wide, veiny, slightly woolly-pubescent beneath; flowering shoots borne on old wood, flowers solitary or in clusters of from two to eight, lower bracts leafy, upper much reduced, lanceolate; pedicel and hypanthium glabrous; sepals slightly broadened at the tip, simple, or the outer ones slightly lobed, about 1.5 cm. long, slightly pubescent and often a little glandular on the outside, finely cobwebby within; petals pink, flowers about 3 cm. wide; calyx persistent in the fruit, erect or somewhat spreading; hip globose or nearly so, red, about 8 mm. in diameter, wall thin; achenes about 4 mm. long, light brown, borne on the bottom and sides of the hypanthium. (*Macoúnii*, named for the Canadian botanist John Macoun.)

This rose is common in the western part of the Minnesota Valley and along the western border of the state. It is distributed from Minnesota to British Columbia, south to Nebraska, Texas, and Oregon.

True *Rosa Woodsii* Lindl. differs from *R. Macounii* in having much stouter spines, smaller glabrous leaflets, and smaller flowers and fruit. It is a western species reaching its eastern limits in the Dakotas. A colony of this species has long been established along the tracks of the Belt Line Railway in the vicinity of Minneapolis, but it shows little or no tendency to spread. Collections from this colony are the only Minnesota specimens of this species in the University herbarium.

PRICKLY WILD ROSE, *Rosa acicularis* Lindl. Ros. Monog. 44, 1820 [*R. Sayi* Schwein. 1824]

A shrub 3–10 dm. high; stems greenish or somewhat reddish, thickly beset with slender, straight prickles 3–6 mm. long, those by the nodes often longer and stouter than the others, but scarcely forming definite infrastipular spines; leaves with from five to seven leaflets, leaflets elliptical or ovate, short-stalked (about 1 mm.) or often entirely sessile, thin, apex commonly acute, sometimes rounded, base wedge-shaped or, more often, rounded or cordate, margin rather coarsely serrate, the teeth pointed outward, convex on both sides, simple or, more frequently, glandular-serrulate, upper surface dull, glabrous, lower surface paler, somewhat silky and usually more or less resinous glandular; upper leaflets 2–5 cm. long, 1.5–2.5 cm. broad, lower leaflets one-third to two-thirds as large; petiole and rachis glandular, with or without long, silky hairs; stipules simple, usually widely dilated, a pair of stipules often 1.5 cm. broad, occasionally narrow, thin, veiny, glandular, and sometimes also woolly-pubescent, the margin roughened by glands but usually otherwise entire; flowering shoots borne on the old wood, mostly less than 1 dm. long, flowers solitary or rarely in clusters of two or three; pedicel and hypanthium glabrous or rarely glandular; sepals usually simple, somewhat broadened at the tip, 2–3 cm. long, glandular on the outside and sometimes finely pubescent within; petals bright pink, flower 5–7 cm. wide; calyx persistent in fruit, sepals erect; hip elongated, tapering at the base, or nearly globular, about 1.5 cm. in diameter, red and translucent; achenes thick, very light-colored, about 4 mm. long, borne at the base and on the sides of the hypanthium. Flowers in May and June, somewhat earlier than *R. blanda.* (*Aciculáris,* furnished with needles, referring to the many needle-like prickles.)

Prickly wild rose is a polymorphic, circumboreal species originally described from Siberia. The typical form has elongated pyriform hips and leaflets with nearly simple serration. The amount of resinous glandular granulation on the under side of the leaflets varies considerably, but is usually less abundant than in var. *Bourgeauiana,* and it is sometimes practically wanting. There seems to be no good reason for distinguishing the forms with resinous glandular leaflets as a variety (var. *Sayiana* Erlanson), for they occur throughout the range of the species, in Siberia as well as in America, and in this character a completely graded series connects the eglandular forms with the strongly glandular type seen in var. *Bourgeauiana*.

This species is common chiefly in the region of the evergreen forests. It is distributed from Anticosti to Alaska, south to Vermont, the region of the Great Lakes, and Colorado; it occurs also in Asia and Europe. In Siberia it is found growing within three hundred miles of the Arctic Ocean.

Forms apparently intermediate between this rose and *R. arkansana* occur in the northern Red River Valley. They are very possibly of hybrid origin.

Several American varieties of this species have been described, of which the following are known to occur in our flora.

Rosa acicularis Lindl. var. *Bourgeauiana* Crepin, Bull. Soc. Bot. Belg. 15:29, 1867 [*R. Bourgeauiana* Crepin 1876]

Fruit globular, leaflets soft-pubescent and rather strongly resinous-glandular beneath, doubly serrate with minute glandular serrulations.

This variety has the same range as the species, and in the Upper Midwest is apparently more abundant, at least northward. It is distributed from Ontario to Mackenzie, south to Michigan, Minnesota, and in the mountains to Colorado.

Rosa acicularis Lindl. var. *rotunda* Erlanson, Papers Mich. Acad. of Sci. Arts & Let. 5:84, 1925

Fruit globular as in var. *Bourgeauiana*, but with leaflets of typical *R. acicularis*. (*Rotúnda*, round.)

In the Upper Midwest this variety has the same range as the species. Its general range is undetermined; it was originally described from Michigan.

SMOOTH WILD ROSE, *Rosa blanda* Ait., Hort. Kew 2:202, 1789

A much branched shrub 2–12 dm. high, spreading widely by creeping rhizomes; woody twigs usually dark purplish-red, first year's shoots from the rhizome usually covered with many weak bristle-like prickles, shoots on the old wood with a few scattered prickles or often entirely glabrous; leaves with from five to seven leaflets, very rarely with more; leaflets ovate to lanceolate, usually with stalks about 1 mm. long, apex rounded, obtuse, or acute, base wedge-shaped, margin sharply and usually simply serrate down to the middle or a little lower, upper surface dull green, somewhat puberulent or nearly glabrous, lower surface finely pubescent, rarely glabrous, the midrib prominent and ridged, the principal veins distinct but scarcely ridged; upper leaflets 2–4 cm. long, 1–2 cm. wide, lower leaflets one-half or two-thirds as large; petiole and rachis with fine, woolly pubescence, very rarely glandular; stipules simple, entire or with the free auricles finely serrate, thin, veiny, usually glabrous except along the margin, wide-expanded, especially those of the upper leaves, the pair

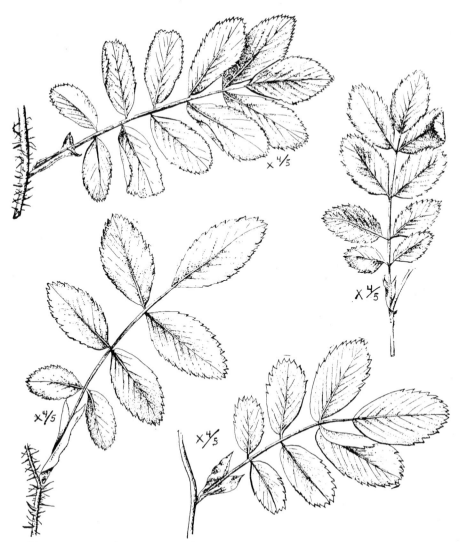

Native species of *Rosa*: Upper left, *R. arkansana*. Upper right, *R. Macounii*.
Lower left, *R. acicularis*. Lower right, *R. blanda*.

often 1 cm. wide; flowering shoots borne on the old wood, flowers solitary or in loose clusters of two to eight, bracts of the inflorescence leaf-like, or with the blade reduced or lacking and the stipules forming broad, round-ovate bracts; pedicel of flower and hypanthium glabrous, sepals usually simple, slightly broadened at the tip, 1.5–2 cm. long, glandular on the outside or rarely glabrous, finely woolly-pubescent within; petals bright pink or sometimes pale, flower 3.5 cm. broad; calyx persistent, in fruit more or less erect; fruit scarlet, opaque, round or somewhat elongated; achenes slender, about 4 mm. long, light brown. (*Blánda*, smooth.)

This is a species that grows in copses, on the edges of woods, and on prairies throughout the area, most abundantly in the region of the hardwood forests. It is distributed from Anticosti to Manitoba, south to Pennsylvania and Missouri.

In latitude 45° N. *R. blanda* blooms in late May and June, the earliest of the wild roses; northward it is preceded somewhat by *R. acicularis*.

Several varieties of this rose occur in the Upper Midwest. The typical form has pubescent leaflets, with simple serration, and very few prickles except on young shoots from the rhizome. Forms with more prickles on the branches have been described as var. *hispida* Farwell and var. *subgeminata* Schuette, the latter with prickles tending to occur more or less in pairs at the nodes. The following have sometimes been considered species.

Rosa blanda Ait. var. *glabra* Crepin, Bull. Soc. Belg. 15:33, 1876 [*R. subblanda* Rydb.]

Leaflets and stipules glabrous on both sides, rachis and petiole glabrous or with a few scattered hairs. (*Glábra*, glabrous.)

All the specimens seen have been from the southern part of the range. It is distributed from New Hampshire to Manitoba, south to Michigan and Iowa.

Some plants agreeing otherwise with this variety have the hypanthium with scattered prickles, some of them gland-tipped. It has been suggested that these may be hybrids with *R. carolina*, but their distribution in Minnesota does not indicate this, as the latter rose barely enters the eastern border of the state, and the variety *glabra* occurs as far west as the upper Minnesota Valley.

Rosa blanda Ait. var. *acicularioides* (Schuette) Butters, in Trees & Shrubs of Minn. 184, 1928 [*R. acicularioides* Schuette, Proc. Am. Assoc. Adv. Sci. 46:279, 1898]

Stipules, petiole, and rachis puberulent and glandular, leaflets glandular, doubly serrate, pubescent but scarcely at all glandular beneath; stem relatively prickly. (*Acicularioídes*, resembling *R. acicularis*.)

In Minnesota, this variety occurs chiefly in the Minnesota Valley, particularly in the eastern part within thirty miles of Minneapolis, where it is quite abundant. It is distributed through Michigan, Wisconsin, and Minnesota.

While the glandular rachis and double serration of the leaflets are somewhat suggestive of *R. acicularis*, the distribution of this rose in Minnesota indicates that it has no connection with that species. It is certainly very closely allied to *R. blanda*, and seems best regarded as a variety of that species.

PRAIRIE WILD ROSE, *Rosa arkansana* Porter, Porter & Coulter, Syn. Fl. Colo. 38, 1874 [*R. polyanthema* Lunnell]

A low shrub about 3–5 dm. high, rarely taller, sometimes almost herbaceous from the widespreading woody rhizome; woody twigs reddish-green, rarely dull purplish-red, twigs usually covered with fine bristle-like prickles about 3 mm. long, the prickles sometimes larger in the vicinity of the nodes but not forming distinct pairs of infrastipular prickles; leaves with from seven to eleven, mostly nine, leaflets; leaflets broadly obovate or oblanceolate, with stalks about 1 mm. long, or sessile, thick, apex occasionally rounded but usually broadly or acutely wedge-shaped, base rounded or wedge-shaped, margin sharply and usually simply serrate down to the middle or a little below, upper surface dull green, nearly glabrous, lower surface scarcely paler, finely woolly-pubescent, rarely nearly or quite glabrous, the midrib and principal veins prominently ridged; upper leaflets 2–4 cm. long, 1.2–2.5 cm. wide, lower leaflets smaller; petiole and rachis with fine, woolly pubescence, sometimes with a few stalked glands or nonglandular prickles; stipules simple, entire or serrate, rather narrow, the pair of stipules rarely exceeding 8 mm. in breadth, widest in the region of the sharply acute auricles, thick, finely woolly-pubescent or nearly glabrous, usually glandular along the margin and frequently also on the lower side, veins obscure except for a prominent vein in each auricle; flowering shoots borne on the old wood or often arising directly from the rhizome, flowers usually in dense corymbs of from three to ten (sometimes as many as thirty), bracts of the inflorescence lanceolate, acute; pedicel and hypanthium glabrous; sepals usually simple, more or less broadened at the tip, 2–2.5 cm. long, glabrous or glandular-pubescent on the outside, densely fine-woolly-pubescent within; petals bright pink, often of a salmon tone, rarely nearly white; flower 4–6 cm. wide; calyx persistent in the fruit, reflexed after anthesis, but finally more or less ascending; hip round or somewhat elongated, scarlet, opaque; achenes stout, light brown, about 5 mm. long, borne on the bottom and lower sides of the hypanthium. (*Arkansána*, Arkansan, the species being originally described from the valley of the Arkansas River in Colorado.)

Typical *Rosa arkansana* has the leaves entirely glabrous or with slightly pubescent petiole, rachis, and veins. It is far less common in our flora than the following variety, being most abundant in the southeastern part of the area. *R. polyanthema* Lunnell, described as differing in its tall habit, appears to have no taxonomic standing, even as a variety. Lunnell's specimens appear to be merely extraordinarily vigorous examples of typical *R. arkansana*.

This species is distributed from Wisconsin and North Dakota south to Kansas and Colorado.

Rosa arkansana Porter var. *suffulta* (Greene) Cockerell, Bull. Torr. Bot. Club 27:88, 1900 [*R. pratincola* Greene; *R. suffulta* Greene]

Petioles, rachis, and lower side of the leaflets finely woolly-pubescent. (*Suffúlta*, supported beneath.)

This variety is very abundant throughout the prairie regions, less common in the wooded districts, and wanting in the northeast corner of Minnesota. It is distributed from Illinois to Alberta, south to Texas and New Mexico.

This is the common wild rose of the prairies, blooming about two weeks later than *R. blanda,* about June 15 in latitude 45° N., and continuing to bloom throughout much of the summer. In unprotected situations it often kills nearly or quite to the ground during the winter, but this does not interfere with its free blooming the following summer.

Rosa arkansana Porter var. *Bushii* (Rydberg) Butters, in Trees & Shrubs of Minn. 185, 1928 [*R. Bushii* Rydb. 1919]

Differs from *R. arkansana* var. *suffulta* chiefly in the shape of the hip, which is pyriform with an acute base. Specimens with this form of hips occur in southeastern Minnesota. (*Búshii,* named for B. F. Bush, of Courtney, Missouri.)

The original description of this rose calls for a branched plant about 1 m. high. As above noted, habit in roses depends so much on conditions of growth that it is a very unsafe criterion of species.

CINNAMON ROSE, *Rosa cinnamomea* L., Sp. Pl. 491, 1753

A tall bush, 2 m. in height; stems reddish, armed with somewhat hooked, broad-based, infrastipular prickles about 5 mm. in length, often with other smaller scattering prickles; leaves with from five to seven leaflets; leaflets narrowly elliptical, finely, sharply, and simply serrate almost to the base, dull green and puberulent above, paler and soft-pubescent below; upper leaflets 2–3.5 cm. long, 1.2–1.8 cm. wide, rachis and petiole soft-pubescent and sometimes slightly glandular, stipules narrow or more or less widely dilated on flowering twigs, the pair sometimes 12 mm. wide, veiny, more or less pubescent and glandular; flowering shoots borne on the old wood, flowers usually solitary, fragrant; pedicel and hypanthium nearly glabrous; sepals up to 3 cm. long, woolly-pubescent, enlarged at the tips, the outer usually with prominent lateral lobes; petals dull pink, flower about 4 cm. wide; sepals persistent and erect in the fruit; hips elongated, tapering upward, 12–15 mm. long, red. (*Cinnamómea,* cinnamon-like, probably from the fragrance of the flowers.)

This native of northern Europe and northwestern Asia is closely related to our common wild roses. The double-flowered form, *R. cinnamomea* var. *foecundissima* Koch., which has flat, very double, pink flowers, is often planted in old-fashioned gardens. It is perfectly hardy and sometimes persists for some time without cultivation and spreads by suckers.

Rosa rugosa Thunb., Flor. Jap. 213, 1784

A shrub 6 dm. to 2 m. high; stems stout, grayish-brown or black, pubescent, armed with many crowded bristles and strong, pubescent, needle-like prickles, infrastipular prickles not obvious; leaves with from five to nine leaflets; leaflets elliptical or ovate-lanceolate, finely blunt-serrate or crenate to the base, thick and firm, rugose, glossy and dark green above, paler and soft-pubescent beneath, apex rounded or pointed, base cordate or rounded; upper leaflets 2.5–4 cm. long, 1.5–2.75 cm. wide, lower ones somewhat smaller, petioles soft-pubescent and prickly, stipules dilated, finely crenate, the pair often 15 mm. wide; flowers in small clusters borne on all the shoots throughout the season; pedicels pubescent or prickly, hypanthium glabrous; sepals pubescent, pointed, usually simple, 1.5–2 cm. long; petals deep rose or white; flower 6–8 cm. wide; sepals persistent in the fruit, hip globular, scarlet, 2 cm. or more in diameter. (*Rugósa*, rugose, referring to the leaves.)

This is a very variable rose, a native of Japan, Siberia, and eastern Europe, and belongs to the same group as our common wild roses. The forms from Russia and Siberia are perfectly hardy in our climate without protection in winter. It is much planted in shrubberies and hedges and is valuable on account of its fine foliage, large flowers borne throughout the summer, and handsome scarlet fruit. Double-flowered forms are in cultivation and also several hybrids of this species with various garden roses. They are not all as hardy as the original species.

FRENCH ROSE, *Rosa gallica* L., Sp. Pl. 492, 1753

A low bush with stems 1 m. or less high, prickles unequal, scattered, slender, straight; leaves with from three to seven leaflets, leaflets thick, somewhat rugose, simply serrate, dull green and smooth above, paler, glabrous or somewhat pubescent beneath, tip usually rounded, base rounded; upper leaflets 1.5–4 cm. long, 1–3 cm. wide; petiole hairy and somewhat glandular; stipules somewhat dilated, thin; flowers solitary or in small clusters; pedicel glandular, hypanthium somewhat prickly; sepals 2–3 cm. long, glandular, the outer ones with lateral lobes; petals red or pinkish; flower 5 cm. or more wide; sepals inflexed and finally deciduous in fruit, hip dark red, almost globose. (*Gállica*, French.)

This native of southwestern Europe has been established in the eastern United States. It is the parent of many garden varieties, some of which, like the pale pink "blush rose," are the only large-flowered garden roses that are truly hardy in the Upper Midwest. They bloom about June 15 in the latitude of Minneapolis.

CABBAGE ROSE, *Rosa centifolia* L., Sp. Pl. 491, 1753

A bush 5–15 dm. high; stems green, prickles unequal, stout, hooked; leaves with from five to seven leaflets; leaflets thick, sharply serrate, nearly glabrous on both faces, tip usually pointed, base rounded; upper leaflets 4–5 cm. long, 2.5–3 cm. wide; petiole glandular; stipules somewhat dilated, glandular; flowers solitary or in small clusters, fragrant; pedicel glandular, hypanthium glabrous or somewhat prickly; sepals 2.5 cm. long, glandular, the tips expanded and leafy with many lateral lobes; petals very numerous, pink; flower 8 cm. wide; fruit seldom formed, subglobose, orange red. (*Centifólia*, hundred-leaved.)

The cabbage rose is a double pink rose of ancient and unknown origin, sometimes regarded as a variety of *Rosa gallica* L., sometimes as a distinct species. The type and the moss varieties of various colors are often grown as garden

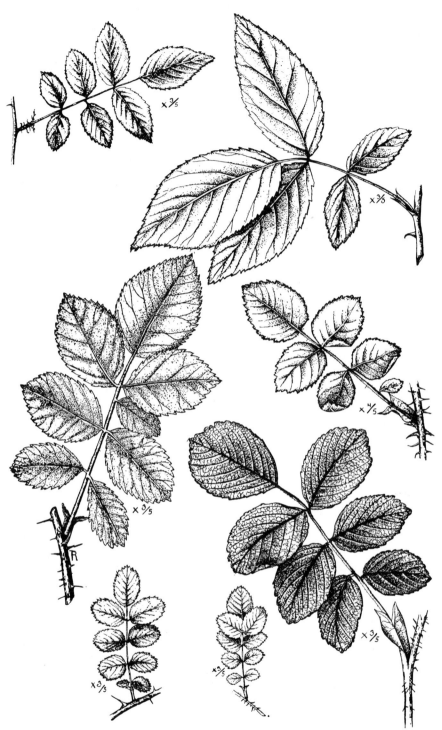

Cultivated species of *Rosa*: Left, top to bottom, *R. multiflora*, *R. gallica*, and *R. foetida*. Right, top to bottom, *R. setigera*, *R. Eglanteria*, *R. rugosa*, and *R. spinosissima*.

209

roses in Minnesota, but are not quite hardy without protection. During severe winters the canes often kill back to the level of the snow unless covered with straw.

MOSS ROSE, *Rosa centifolia* L. f. *muscosa* Seringe, Mus. Helv. 1:18, 1818

Whole plant more prickly and glandular than the species. The glandular pubescence is particularly noticeable on the pedicels, receptacles, and large sepals. (*Muscósa*, mossy.)

SWEET BRIER, *Rosa Eglanteria* L. Sp. Pl. 491, 1753 [*R. rubiginosa* L. 1771]

A shrub 6 dm. to 2 m. high; stems greenish or brown, armed with stout, hooked infrastipular prickles, 6–12 mm. long, often also with scattering prickles; leaves with from five to seven leaflets, fragrant; leaflets broadly elliptical or obovate, sharply doubly serrate almost to the base, bright green, finely pubescent on the upper side, slightly paler and densely glandular-pubescent below, tip broadly wedge-shaped or rounded, base usually rounded; upper leaflets 1–2 cm. long, 8–18 mm. wide, lower about one-half as large, rachis and petiole soft-pubescent, glandular and prickly, stipules widely dilated, veiny, glandular along the margin and on the under side; flowering shoots borne on the old wood, flowers solitary or in few-flowered clusters, mostly with leafy bracts; pedicel and often hypanthium prickly and glandular; sepals 1.5–2 cm. long, very glandular, the outer ones with well-developed lateral lobes; petals pink, flower 2–3.5 cm. in diameter; sepals deciduous in the fruit, hip obovate, scarlet, about 12–15 mm. in diameter. (*Eglantéria*, Latinization of the old English and French name.)

Sweet brier is a native of Europe, widely naturalized in the eastern United States and on the Pacific Coast. It is occasionally planted for its fragrant foliage. It is hardy without protection in the vicinity of Minneapolis, but the longer canes are apt to kill back, and it seldom flowers.

AUSTRIAN BRIER, *Rosa foetida* Herm., Dis. Bot Med. Ros. 18, 1762 [*R. Eglanteria* of authors (L. 1753, in part)]

A shrub 6–12 dm. high; stems dark reddish-brown, armed with very numerous straight, strong, needle-like prickles, the longest about 1 cm. long; leaves with from five to seven leaflets, fragrant; leaflets oblong, doubly serrate, glabrous above, hairy and somewhat glandular beneath, tip usually broadly wedge-shaped, base rounded or wedge-shaped; upper leaflets about 1.5 cm. long, 1 cm. wide; petiole hairy and prickly; stipules glandular, small, narrow, with acute triangular auricles; flowering shoots borne on the old wood, flowers usually solitary; pedicel glabrous or prickly, hypanthium glabrous or hispid; sepals entire, glandular-pubescent; petals golden-yellow or coppery, flower 4–5 cm. wide; fruit globose, nearly black. (*Foétida*, fetid, the fragrance being rather unpleasant.)

This rose is a native of eastern Europe and western Asia. It is seldom cultivated in our area except in the var. *Harisonii*, "Harison yellow rose, a semi-double form originated in New York City about a century ago. It is probably a hybrid of this and the following species. It is the only yellow rose commonly grown in Minnesota, is perfectly hardy without protection, and blooms about June 1 in the latitude of Minneapolis. It ripens a large amount of seed, and it would not be surprising to find it growing spontaneously in the vicinity of old gardens.

There are many recent hybrids of *R. foetida*, several of them very fine garden roses. They are of varying degrees of hardiness depending upon their other parentage.

SCOTCH ROSE, *Rosa spinosissima* L., Sp. Pl. 491, 1753 [*R. pimpinellifolia* L. 1759]

A shrub 6–10 dm. high; branches grayish, armed with numerous bristles and strong, needle-like prickles; leaves with from seven to eleven leaflets; leaflets broadly elliptical, doubly or simply sharply serrate, glabrous and bright green above, similar or slightly glandular beneath, 8–18 mm. long, 5–15 mm. wide; stipules very small; flowering shoots borne on the old wood, flowers solitary, very fragrant; pedicel smooth or somewhat glandular; sepals entire, glabrous; petals white or, in some forms, yellowish or pinkish, flower 3–4 cm. across; sepals persistent and erect in the fruit; hip globular, black. (*Spinosíssima*, most spiny.)

This rose is a native of northern Eurasia, from Iceland to China. In the Upper Midwest it is cultivated chiefly in a semidouble, white-flowered form. It is perfectly hardy, blooming in late May and early June.

Rosa Hugonis Hemsl., Bot. Mag. 131:t. 8004, 1905

A shrub with arching canes 1–2 m. long, armed with stout prickles, the young growth also bristly; leaves with from five to eleven small leaflets, leaflets obovate or elliptical, 1.5–2 cm. long, obtuse at the apex, mostly rounded at the base, finely serrate, glabrous; stipules very narrow; flowers solitary on lateral shoots, 5–7 cm. in diameter, the pedicels glabrous; sepals acute, glabrous without; petals yellow; fruit spherical, scarlet, becoming very dark. (*Hugónis*, named in honor of its discoverer, Father Hugh.)

This species, recently introduced from western China, appears to be entirely hardy in Minnesota and bids fair to become a popular ornamental shrub.

PRAIRIE ROSE, *Rosa setigera* Michx., Fl. Bor. Am. 1:295, 1803

A vine with canes 2–6 m. long, armed with stout, hooked, infrastipular prickles 6–8 mm. long and about the same width at the base; leaves with three large leaflets, often with an additional much smaller basal pair; leaflets ovate, sharply doubly serrate to the base, glabrous, glossy, dark green above, paler and glabrous or soft-pubescent beneath, tip acute, base rounded; upper leaflets 4–7 cm. long, 2.5–4 cm. wide; petiole and rachis prickly, glandular, stipules narrow with sharply acute auricles, the pair only about 3 mm. wide, entire except for a row of small glands along the margin; flowers borne in many-flowered corymbs with narrow lanceolate bracts; pedicel, hypanthium, and calyx glandular; sepals 1–1.7 cm. long, the outer ones usually with narrow linear lateral lobes; petals deep pink, changing to nearly white; styles long, cohering in a projecting column; flowers 3–5 cm. wide, nearly scentless; calyx deciduous after flowering, fruit globular, about 1 cm. in diameter, achenes pale, angular about 4 mm. long. (*Setígera*, prickle-bearing.)

Prairie rose is a native of the eastern United States, from the Gulf states north to Nebraska, Wisconsin, and southern Ontario; it is not native to Minnesota. It is cultivated occasionally in its typical form and in the double-flowered form "Prairie Queen." The canes winterkill in the vicinity of Minneapolis unless laid on the ground and given a light protection of straw. It flowers in July.

RAMBLER ROSE, *Rosa multiflora* Thunb. var. *cathayensis* Rehder & Wilson, Plantae Wilsonianae 2:304, 1915

A vine with canes up to 3 m. in length, armed with stout, curved, infrastipular prickles about 5 mm. long; leaves with from seven to nine leaflets; leaflets lanceolate, simple and sharply serrate, bright green and glabrous above, paler and soft-pubescent beneath, tip acute, wedge-shaped, base wedge-shaped; upper leaflets 2.5–3 cm. long, about 1.5 wide; rachis and petiole prickly and soft-pubescent; stipules narrow, glandular, conspicuously and strongly fringed; flowers in many-flowered corymbs with lanceolate, fringed bracts; pedicel glandular, hypanthium nearly or quite glabrous; sepals 5–7 mm. long, glandular, the outer with narrow lateral lobes; petals pink or rose-colored; styles long and cohering in a column, flowers about 2 cm. wide, nearly scentless; sepals deciduous in the fruit, fruit globose about 5 mm. in diameter, achenes pale, angular, about 3.5 mm. long. (*Multiflóra*, many flowered.)

Typical *R. multiflora* Thunb., a native of Japan, has white, fragrant flowers. *R. multiflora* var. *cathayensis*, possibly a distinct species, from China, has flowers pink or rose-colored and nearly scentless. The latter is frequently cultivated in Minnesota in the semidouble form known as "Crimson Rambler." The canes are not reliably hardy in Minnesota unless laid on the ground and covered with straw. A dwarf form of this rose is also commonly cultivated ("Baby Rambler").

GARDEN ROSES

The large-flowered garden roses are mainly varieties of *R. gallica*, *R. centifolia*, and *R. damascena* (the damask rose of southwestern Asia), and hybrids of these with other species. Two very important stocks are the everblooming but tender *R. chinensis* Jacq. (Bengal rose) and *R. odorata* Sweet (tea rose), native of China, the parents of most of our hothouse roses. Many of the garden roses have most complicated pedigrees, the above-mentioned species being crossed and recrossed with one another, and with yet other species.

The hardiest garden roses are the varieties of *R. gallica* and *R. centifolia*, but they flower but once a year. Next in hardiness come the so-called "hybrid perpetual" roses. Their pedigree is probably (*R. gallica* × *R. chinensis*) × *damascena*, etc., but without any strain of *R. odorata*. They have very abundant blooms in June and continue to give occasional flowers throughout the season. They are reliably hardy in our region if well covered with straw and thatched with tar paper or some similar material to keep the straw from becoming damp and mouldy. The "hybrid tea" roses, which have as a basis *R. gallica* × *R. chinensis* × *R. odorata*, are the most continuous bloomers, but many of them are not reliably hardy, even when well covered.

The so-called hardy climbing roses are nearly all hybrids of *R. multiflora* var. *cathayensis*, *R. setigera*, or *R. wichuraiana*. None of them are reliably hardy in this area unless they are laid on the ground and well covered with straw.

Chaenomeles Lindl., Trans. Linn. Soc. 13:97, 1822

Thorny shrubs, with conspicuous flowers appearing mostly before the leaves; leaves simple, with conspicuous persistent stipules; flowers nearly sessile, single or in small clusters, from lateral winter-buds; hypanthium and calyx colored, sepals five, deciduous in the fruit; petals five; stamens many; carpels five, the ovaries united and buried in the hypanthium; styles united at the base; fruit a closed pome, with five many-seeded locules.

This is a genus of two or three species of eastern Asia. It is closely related to *Cydonia*, the common quince, which, however, has solitary flowers borne on leafy shoots, sepals persistent in the fruit, styles free to the base, and the pome open at the center. The following species is cultivated in the Upper Midwest.

JAPANESE QUINCE, *Chaenomeles japonica* (Thunb.) Lindl., *ex* Spach, Hist. Nat. Veg. 2:159, 1834 [*C. Maulei* (Mast.) C. K. Schneider 1906; *Pyrus japonica* Thunb. 1784; *Cydonia japonica* Pers. 1806]

A small, more or less spiny shrub, 1–2 m. high; leaves ovate, serrate, glossy above, 3.5–7.5 cm. long; flowers on the old twigs in two- to six-flowered clusters, appearing before or with the leaves, typically scarlet-red, 3.5–5 cm. wide, sometimes only staminate; fruit globular or ovoid, 3.5–5 cm. in diameter, yellowish-green, fragrant. Flowers in April and May. (*Japónica*, Japanese.)

This quince is a native of Japan. It is used as an ornamental shrub in parks and gardens and is adapted for borders or shrubberies and low ornamental hedges.

Chokeberry
Aronia Pers., Syn. Pl. 2:39, 1807

Low, deciduous, thornless shrubs, with alternate, simple, finely crenate-serrate leaves, glandular along the midrib on the upper side; stipules small and caducous; flowers in compound cymes, white or tinted with rose, appearing with the leaves; hypanthium low, urn-shaped; sepals five, persistent on the top of the fruit; petals five, spreading; stamens many; carpels usually five, styles as many, united at the base; fruit a small, globose, berry-like pome, with as many cells as styles, red, purplish, or black. (*Arónia*, formed from Aria, the beam tree.)

This is a North American genus consisting of two or three species scarcely separable from *Sorbus*. This and the two following genera are frequently united with the genus *Pyrus*, the pear.

KEY TO SPECIES OF ARONIA

1. Leaves persistently gray-tomentose beneath, pedicels, hypanthium, and sepals tomentose, fruit red...............................*A. arbutifolia* (p. 214)
1. Leaves glabrous from the first or pubescent only when young, pedicels, hypanthium, and sepals glabrous or only loosely pubescent, fruit black.............
....*A. melanocarpa* (p. 214)

RED CHOKEBERRY, *Aronia arbutifolia* (L.) Pers., Syn. Pl. 2:39, 1806

A branching shrub, mostly 1–2 m. high; young twigs gray-tomentose, older twigs glabrous, gray to reddish-brown; leaves elliptical to narrowly obovate or oblanceolate, 4–8 cm. long, 1.5–4 cm. wide, gradually narrowed at the base, acute or short-acuminate at the apex, finely crenate-serrate, the teeth with dark, incurved, mucronate tips, dark green and glabrous or glabrate above, usually with dark, hair-like glands along the midvein, persistently gray-tomentose beneath; petiole 4–10 mm. long; cymes compound, peduncles and pedicels gray-canescent; flowers white or pinkish, 8–12 mm. in diameter; hypanthium and sepals densely tomentose; petals obovate, 4–5 mm. long, spreading; stamens nearly erect, slightly shorter than the petals; pedicels 5–8 mm. long, becoming somewhat longer in fruit; fruit globose, 6–8 mm. in diameter, red (*Arbutifólia*, having leaves like *Arbutus*.)

Red chokeberry grows in low woods, thickets, swamps, and damp pine barrens. It is distributed from Nova Scotia, New England, southern Ontario, Michigan, and Missouri, south to Florida and eastern Texas. It is not native to the Upper Midwest, but is occasionally planted. Its astringent fruit makes excellent jelly. The foliage turns red in autumn.

BLACK CHOKEBERRY, *Aronia melanocarpa* (Michx.) Ell., Sketch Bot. S. Carol. 1:556, 1821 [*A. nigra* (Willd.) Britton, 1894; Minn. T. & S. 1912]

A branching shrub 1–1.5 m. high; bark smooth, brown to grayish; leaves obovate to oblanceolate or sometimes elliptic, 2–7 cm. long, 1–2.7 cm. wide, narrowed at the base, acute or abruptly short-acuminate to mucronate at the apex, finely crenate-serrate, the teeth incurved, mucronate-tipped, dark green and somewhat shining above, glabrous but with dark, hair-like glands along the midrib, paler beneath, more or less tomentose-pubescent when young, be-

Aronia melanocarpa

coming quite glabrous with age; petiole 3–6 mm. long; inflorescence seven- to fifteen-flowered; pedicels and peduncles more or less loosely pubescent or nearly glabrous, becoming entirely glabrous with age; flowers white, 10–12 mm. in diameter; hypanthium loosely pubescent or glabrous; sepals ovate to triangular, more or less woolly along the inner margins; petals ovate, 4–5 mm. long; stamens shorter than the petals; pedicels 5–12 mm. long; fruit globose 6–8 mm. in diameter, black or purplish. (*Melanocárpa*, dark-fruited.)

Black chokeberry grows in swamps and on low ground or sometimes in drier thickets and clearings or on bluffs and cliffs. It is common in the coniferous forest area, infrequent southward to southeastern Minnesota and adjacent Wisconsin. It is distributed from Newfoundland to northwestern Ontario and Minnesota, south to New England, South Carolina and Tennessee.

The species varies considerably in the degree of pubescence of the inflorescence, hypanthium, and sepals, but generally it becomes nearly or quite glabrous before the fruit is mature.

Mountain Ash
Sorbus L., Sp. Pl. 477, 1753

Deciduous small trees or tall shrubs with large winter buds; leaves alternate, simple or more often odd-pinnately compound, sharply and sometimes doubly serrate; stipules deciduous; flowers white, numerous, showy, in terminal compound cymes; hypanthium urn-shaped; sepals five, usually persistent on the fruit; petals five, broad, with a short claw, spreading; stamens fifteen to twenty; carpels two to five, inferior to half-inferior; styles two to five (usually three), free or connate at the base; ovules two in each cell; fruit a two- to five-celled berry-like pome, four- to ten-seeded. (*Sórbus*, the classical Latin name.)

This genus includes about a hundred species, natives of the North Temperate Zone.

KEY TO SPECIES OF SORBUS

1. Leaves regularly pinnately compound.
  2. Leaflets lanceolate, glabrous; flowers about 6 mm. in diameter; fruit 4–5 mm. in diameter..*S. americana* (p. 216)

2. Leaflets oblong to oblong-lanceolate, more or less pubescent; flowers and fruits larger.
   3. Leaflets short-acuminate, sparsely pubescent beneath. Northern native tree. .
   . . . . .S. *decora* (p. 216)
   3. Leaflets merely acute, persistently tomentose beneath. Cultivated, occasionally spontaneous. . . . . .S. *Aucuparia* (p. 218)
1. Leaves irregularly pinnately lobed, sometimes with a few leaflets at the base. . . . .
. . . . × S. *thuringiaca* (p. 219)

Sorbus americana Marsh., Arb. Am. 145, 1785

A shrub or small tree 4–9 m. high, with a spreading crown; bark smooth, gray, with irregular, plate-like scales; buds elongate-conical, 1–1.8 cm. long, gummy; young twigs glabrous or slightly pubescent, reddish-brown, marked by numerous whitish, elongate-elliptical lenticels; leaves with from six to eight pairs of leaflets; leaflets lanceolate to oblong-lanceolate, 5–8 cm. long, 1–2.3 cm. wide, mostly rounded at the base, generally slightly inequilateral, acuminate or taper-pointed at the apex, sharply serrate nearly to the base with slightly appressed, sharp-pointed teeth, frequently faintly doubly serrate, bright green above, paler beneath, at first sparingly pubescent but usually becoming entirely glabrous with age; rachis green or red, usually with several glands and with a few long hairs at the base of the leaflets, otherwise nearly glabrous in age; inflorescence 6–12 cm. in diameter, pedicels and peduncles essentially glabrous; flowers about 6 mm. in diameter; hypanthium broadly obconical; sepals broadly triangular, slightly glandular along the margin, glabrous; petals nearly orbicular; stamens fifteen to twenty, considerably shorter than the petals; fruit 4–5 mm. in diameter, bright red. Blossoms in July; fruit ripe in late August. (*Americána,* American.)

This mountain ash is common through the coniferous forest region, most abundant northeastward. It is distributed from Labrador to Manitoba, south to northwestern New England, the Great Lakes region, and in the mountains to North Carolina.

Sorbus decora (Sarg.) Schneid., Bull. Herb. Boiss. II, 6:313, 1906 [S. *subvestita* Greene, 1900; S. *sambucifolia* of many authors (including Minn. T. & S. 1912), *not Pyrus sambucifolia* C. & S.]

A small to medium-sized tree, 6–12 m. high; bark dark gray; buds narrowly conical, scales reddish-brown, the two or three outer ones glabrous, the inner brownish-tomentose; young twigs at first grayish-tomentose, soon becoming glabrate and reddish-brown, with scattered elliptical lenticels; leaves with mostly six to seven pairs of leaflets (rarely five or eight); lateral leaflets oblong to elliptic-oblong, 5–6 cm. long, 1.8–2.5 cm. wide, the lowermost pair occasionally much smaller, base inequilateral, rounded or somewhat narrowed, apex short-acuminate; terminal leaflet often broadly elliptic to obovate, generally very abruptly acuminate; margin sharply and mostly simply serrate from about the middle (rarely almost to the base), upper surface dull

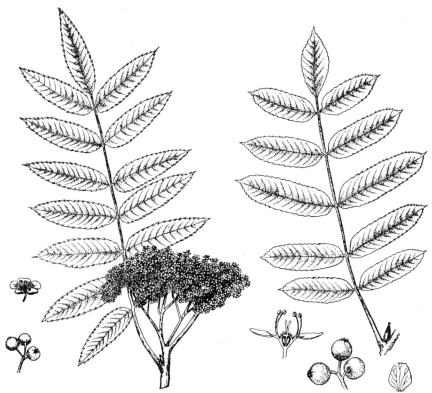

Species of *Sorbus*: Left, *S. americana*. Right, *S. decora*.
(Leaves × 1/2, fruits × 2/3.)

green and glabrous, lower surface much paler, minutely papillose and more or less persistently pubescent, especially along the midrib; rachis slightly pubescent throughout, with resinous glands and long hairs at the base of the leaflets; inflorescence rather dense, 8–15 cm. in diameter, loosely pubescent throughout; flowers about 1 cm. in diameter; hypanthium pubescent, broadly obconic at the base, its free portion saucer-shaped; sepals broadly triangular, sparingly ciliate and with a few glandular teeth; petals ovate to elliptic, spreading; stamens slightly shorter than the petals; styles three or four, about 2 mm. long; top of the ovary woolly-pubescent; fruit vermilion red, 8–10 mm. in diameter. (*Decóra*, handsome, referring to the showy, vermilion fruit.)

Growing in woods, on rocky slopes, and along shores, mountain ash is common along the north shore of Lake Superior, less frequent westward to northern Ontario and southeastern Manitoba. It is distributed from Greenland and Labrador to Manitoba, south to Nova Scotia, western Massachusetts, New York, northern Ohio, Indiana and Wisconsin.

This handsome tree forms a conspicuous element of the forest along the north shore of Lake Superior especially in the autumn, on account of its bright red fruit.

217

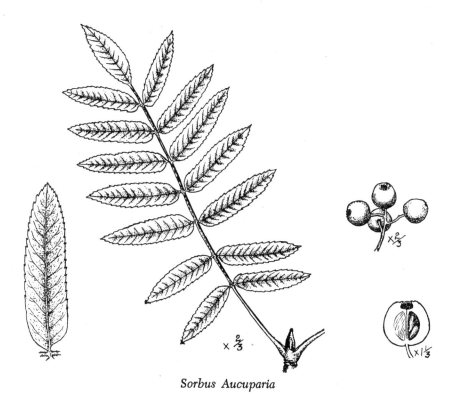

Sorbus Aucuparia

This species was long confused with the Asiatic S. *sambucifolia* (C. & S.) Roemer, which is entirely distinct; it has been treated more recently as conspecific with one or more shrubby species of the Rocky Mountain region — S. *dumosa* Greene and S. *scopulina* Greene.* Our plant appears to be amply distinct from the western species. In the region of Lake Superior it is a considerably larger tree than S. *americana*.

MOUNTAIN ASH, ROWAN TREE, *Sorbus Aucuparia* L., Sp. Pl. 477, 1753

A small tree, 6–10 m. high; bark grayish, smooth; buds conical, 10–12 mm. long, vinous red, more or less white-tomentose; young twigs more or less white-pubescent, generally becoming glabrous, dull gray, or reddish-brown; leaflets mostly six or seven pairs (rarely four to eight), oblong to elliptic-lanceolate, 4–6 cm. long, 1–1.8 cm. wide, rounded and somewhat inequilateral at the base, mostly acute at the apex, rather coarsely and mostly simply serrate almost to the base, dull green above, more or less pubescent, at least when young, much paler beneath and permanently white-tomentose; rachis white tomentose, glandular and pubescent at the base of the leaflets; inflorescence large, 10–18 cm. in diameter; peduncles and pedicels hoary-pubescent; flowers 8–9 mm. in diameter; hypanthium flatly obconical, pubescent; sepals ovate-triangular, scarcely glandu-

* The name S. *sitchensis*, which has often been used for the plant of the northern Rocky Mountains, belongs to an entirely distinct species of the Pacific Coast and far western mountains.

lar along the margin; petals nearly orbicular, slightly pubescent toward the base on the upper side; stamens about as long as the petals; styles three or four, slender, about 1.5 mm. long; fruit about 9 mm. in diameter, scarlet. Blossoms in May and June; fruit ripe in August. (*Aucupária*, bird-catching.)

A frequently planted tree, this mountain ash is becoming naturalized. It is a native of Europe.

OAK-LEAVED MOUNTAIN ASH, × *Sorbus thuringiaca* (Ilsa) Fritsch, Kerner Fl. Exsicc. Austr. Hung. No. 2443, 1896 [× *S. semipinnata* (Roth) Hedlund 1901; *S. Aucuparia* × *aria*]

This hybrid between the European mountain ash and the simple-leaved European species, *S. aria*, is sometimes planted. It has leaves with a few decurrent leaflets at the base, followed by a deeply lobed middle portion, and a nearly unlobed apical region. In pubescence it closely resembles *S. Aucuparia*. The flowers are larger than in that species, with a much deeper hypanthium, and longer and narrower sepals. (*Thuringíaca*, from Thuringia, a region of Germany.)

Several forms of this hybrid are described by European botanists. In this country they generally pass under the name *S. quercifolia*.

Apple
Malus Mill., Gard. Dict. abr. ed. 4, 1754

Trees or shrubs, sometimes with more or less thorn-like spurs; leaves alternate, simple but sometimes more or less deeply lobed, serrate or dentate; stipules small, early deciduous; flowers in corymbs or umbel-like clusters, white or pink, showy, appearing with or before the leaves; hypanthium campanulate or urn-shaped; sepals five; petals five, obovate; stamens fifteen to twenty or more; carpels two to five, imbedded in the hypanthium, their inner portions becoming cartilaginous in fruit; styles as many as carpels, more or less united at the base; ovary two- to five-celled; ovules two in each cell; fruit a pome. (*Málus*, classical Latin name for the apple tree.)

This genus of the North Temperate Zone embraces about fifteen species, seven of which are native to North America. It is frequently united with the closely related genus *Pyrus*, the pear, from which it differs chiefly in its cartilaginous carpels, and in the absence of grit cells in the flesh of the pome.

KEY TO SPECIES OF MALUS

1. Lower surface of the leaves and outer surface of the sepals persistently tomentose; sepals persistent in the fruit.
   2. Leaves closely crenate-serrate, abruptly short-acuminate; sepals reflexed......
   ....*M. pumila* (p. 220)
   2. Leaves, obtuse or short-acute, irregularly toothed, notched, or lobed; calyx lobes erect or spreading.
      3. Some of the leaves more or less prominently notched or lobed toward the

base; sepals mostly erect; fruiting pedicels slender, generally over 2.5 cm.
long, fruit green.
1. Lower surface of leaves glabrous or pubescent when young, mostly glabrate with
  age, hypanthium and outer surface of sepals glabrous or somewhat pubescent but
  not densely and persistently tomentose.
  5. Leaves with crenate-serrulate or with incurved callus-serrulate margins, rarely
    entire.
    6. Flowers white, pedicels and hypanthium glabrous, sepals connate at the base,
     forming a short tube, young foliage, pedicels, and calyx bright green.
    6. Flowers rose-red to purple-red, pedicels and hypanthium more or less pubes-
     cent, sepals free to the base, young foliage, pedicels, and calyx purplish.

APPLE, *Malus pumila* Mill., Gard. Dict. ed. 8, no. 3, 1768 [*Pyrus Malus* L. 1753, in part; *Malus Malus* Britton; *M. sylvestris* of authors (including Minn. T. & S. 1912), not of Miller]

A round-topped tree with spreading branches, sometimes attaining a height of 8 m.; the bark of the trunk rough and dark gray; young twigs pubescent, becoming glabrous and dark brown the second year; leaves broadly elliptical, oblong-ovate, or broadly ovate, 5–10 cm. long, 4–6 cm. wide, mostly rounded or subcordate at the base, sometimes abruptly narrowed, acute or short-acuminate at the apex, somewhat irregularly crenate-serrate, becoming glabrate and more or less glossy above, paler beneath and persistently tomentose; petiole 2–5 cm. long, tomentose; flowers in umbel-like corymbs, appearing with, or just before the leaves, white, pink or rose, 3.5–5 cm. in diameter; pedicels stout, densely tomentose, 1–2.5 cm. long; hypanthium campanulate, tomentose; sepals lanceolate, densely tomentose on both surfaces, reflexed in anthesis; styles mostly glabrous; fruit variable in size and shape, mostly globular to oblate, depressed at both ends, calyx persistent. Flowers in May; fruit ripe from August to October. (*Púmila*, small.)

The apple is a common fruit tree, much cultivated, and occasionally escaping from cultivation. A native of Europe and western Asia, it has been cultivated since ancient times. Numerous horticultural races and varieties have been developed within this species, and some as a result of hybridization with other species. Only the hardiest of these varieties can be generally grown in the Upper Midwest. This species has been confused with *M. sylvestris*, the wild crab of

Species of *Malus*: Left, *M. baccata*. Center, *M. pumila*. Right, *M. ioensis*.

western Europe. The two species are generally regarded as distinct by competent European botanists.

WILD CRAB, IOWA CRAB, *Malus ioensis* (Wood) Britton, in Britt. & Brown, Ill. Fl. ed. 1, 2:235, 1897 [*Pyrus coronaria* var. *ioensis* Wood 1860; *P. ioensis* Carruth 1877]

A small tree, 5–9 m. high, spurs frequently thorn-like, young twigs gray-tomentose, in the second year generally becoming glabrous and purplish-brown through exfoliation of the gray epidermal layers; leaves ovate to oblong, 3–6.5 cm. long, 1.5–4 cm. wide, irregularly crenate-serrate and frequently more or less pinnately lobed, especially toward the base, rounded or narrowed at the base, obtuse or wide-acute at the apex, dark green and sparsely pubescent or glabrate above, much paler and tomentose beneath; petiole 1–2 cm. long, tomentose; flowers rose-tinted in two- to four-flowered corymbs; pedicels slender, tomentose, 2–3 cm. long; hypanthium turbinate, densely tomentose; sepals about as long as the hypanthium, narrowly lanceolate, tomentose, mostly erect or slightly spreading; fruit short-oblong or subglobose, on pedicels 2.5 cm. long, dull green and with a greasy feeling, about 2.5 cm. long; sepals persistent. Flowers in late May and early June; fruit ripe in September and October. (*Ioénsis*, named from the original locality, Iowa.)

Along edges of woods and thickets, wild crab is common in the southeastern part of the area as far as the Minnesota River Valley; it is rare and local northward to Elk River, Minnesota. It is distributed from Wisconsin and Minnesota south to Kansas and Oklahoma.

BECHTEL'S DOUBLE-FLOWERING CRAB, *Malus ioensis* f. *plena* Rehder, Mitt. Deutsch. Dendr. Ges. 23:262, 1914

A form with double flowers, 4–7 cm. in diameter; grading from pink to white in color; hypanthium generally larger and pedicels stouter and longer than in the

ROSE FAMILY

species (sometimes up to 7 cm. long); styles frequently eight to twelve, in leaf and other vegetative characters identical with the species.

This crab is a handsome small tree, entirely hardy and very desirable as an ornamental — a spontaneous variation, originally discovered in the wild state in Illinois.

SOULARD'S CRAB, × *Malus Soulardi* (Bailey) Britton, in Britt. & Brown, Ill. Fl. ed. 1, 2:235, 1897 [*M. ioensis × pumila*]

A natural hybrid between the two preceding species and resembling them in general habit; leaves ovate, elliptic or obovate, obtuse or truncate at the base, acute or rounded at the apex, irregularly crenate-dentate, or slightly lobed, densely tomentose beneath; flowers in rather dense corymbs, somewhat tinted; sepals spreading, tomentose, fruiting pedicels stout, less than 2.5 cm. long; fruit yellow, 4–7 cm. in diameter. (*Soulárdi*, named for James G. Soulard of Galena, Illinois.)

This tree is infrequent in southeastern Minnesota, more common southward to Texas.

HALL CRAB, *Malus Halliana* Koehne f. ˙*Parkmanii* (Temple) Rehder, Plantae Wilsonianae 2:286, 1915 [*Pyrus Halliana* Voss 1896]

A shrub or small tree 2.5–3.5 m. high, with somewhat open crown; young twigs brownish-red, soon becoming glabrous; leaves long-ovate or oblong, 5–7 cm. long, 2.5–4.5 cm. wide, narrowed at the base, acute or acuminate at the apex, at first sparsely pubescent, but soon entirely glabrous, margin very closely crenate-serrate or sometimes entire, firm in texture, dark green and glossy above, paler beneath, petiole and midrib purplish; flowers deep rose, 2.5–3.5 cm. in diameter, double; calyx purple, sepals erect, triangular-ovate, pubescent on the inside; pedicels purple, about 3 cm. long. (*Parkmánii*, named for Francis Parkman, the historian, who early grew the double-flowered form.)

Schneider (Laubh. 1:720) is inclined to regard *M. Halliana* as a horticultural form of Japanese origin (perhaps a mutation) to be maintained provisionally as a species until further light on its origin is obtained.

SIBERIAN CRAB, *Malus baccata* (L.) Borkh., Handb. Forstb. 2:1280, 1803 [*Pyrus baccata* L. 1767]

A small, wide-topped tree 6–10 m. high, with spreading or ascending branches; young twigs generally glabrous from the first, one-year-old twigs purplish-brown; leaves elliptic or ovate to ovate-lanceolate, 3–8 cm. long, 1.5–4 cm. wide, narrowed or somewhat rounded at the base, acuminate at the apex, closely crenate-serrate, rather thin, upper surface at first somewhat pubescent, especially along the midrib and veins, soon becoming entirely glabrous and shining olive-green, somewhat paler beneath and glabrous when mature; petiole slender, 2–3 cm. long; flowers appearing with the leaves, white, 2.5–3.5 cm.

wide, on green pedicels 5–7 cm. long; pedicels, hypanthium, and sepals at first sparingly pubescent, soon becoming glabrous, or sometimes glabrous from the beginning; fruit globose, about 1 cm. in diameter or occasionally larger, yellow or red, on long, slender pedicels; sepals deciduous. Blossoms in May. (*Baccáta*, having berries.)

This crab is a native of Siberia, Manchuria, and northern China and the Himalaya region. It is extensively grown as an ornamental tree.

PLUM-LEAF CRAB, *Malus prunifolia* (Willd.) Borkh., Handb. Forstb. 2:1278, 1803 [*Pyrus prunifolia* Willd. 1794]

A small tree with a rounded crown and spreading or somewhat ascending branches; young twigs pubescent, reddish-brown, leaves oval to obovate 4–8 cm. long, narrowed toward the base, acute or short-acuminate at the apex, crenate-serrate, at first pubescent, soon becoming glabrous on both sides except along the midvein, firm in texture and shining above; flowers numerous, white, 2.5–3.5 cm. wide, on pubescent pedicels; fruit ovoid, 3–4 cm. long, 2.5–3.5 cm. in diameter, slightly depressed at the base, narrowed toward the apex, with protruding, persistent calyx, yellowish or bright red when ripe. (*Prunifólia*, plum-leaved.)

Plum-leaf crab is a native of China and probably of hybrid origin. A form of this species imported by Professor N. E. Hansen from Siberia in 1897 and known as the *Dolgo Crab* is being cultivated to a considerable extent in the middle Northwest both for ornamental purposes and for its fruit. It is said to be blight resistant and perfectly hardy far north in Canada.

FLOWERING CRAB, *Malus floribunda*, Sieb., *ex* Van Houtte, Fl. d. Serr. 15:161, 1864 [*Pyrus pulcherrima* Aschers. & Graebn. Syn. 6:71, 1906]

A shrub or sometimes a small tree up to 7 m. high, sometimes thorny; branches slender and often somewhat drooping, young twigs pubescent but soon becoming glabrous; leaves conduplicate in the bud, ovate to narrowly elliptic or oblong, 3–7 cm. long, 1.5–3 cm. wide, narrowed or rounded at the base, acuminate at the apex, margin sharply and simply or occasionally doubly serrate, upper surface dull green and glabrous, at first pubescent beneath but soon becoming glabrous, firm in texture; petiole up to 2.5 cm. long; flowers numerous, appearing with the leaves, rose or rose red, usually fading to white, 2.5–3 cm. wide, on pubescent pedicels 2.5–3 cm. long; hypanthium and outer surface of sepals sparingly pubescent or glabrous, sepals oblong-lanceolate, longer than the hypanthium, densely tomentose within, not long persistent; styles usually four, longer than the stamens; fruit subglobose, slightly depressed at the ends, 8–12 mm. in diameter, red or yellow. (*Floribúnda*, many-flowered.)

This crab is frequently planted. It was introduced from Japan and is presumed to be of Chinese origin. It is sometimes regarded as a hybrid between *M. baccata* and *M. Toringo*.

HOPA CRAB, *Malus baccata* (L.) Borkh. × *M. pumila* var. *Niedzwetzkyana* Schneid., Ill. Handb. Laubh. 1:716, 1906

A profusely flowering crab of hybrid origin, bearing dense clusters of rose-purple flowers; veins and petioles of the leaves, pedicels of the flowers, and inner bark and wood of the twigs tinged with red; flowers 2.5–3.5 cm. wide, mature fruit red, 1–2 cm. in diameter.

The Hopa, one of N. E. Hansen's introductions, is the showiest of our ornamental crabs. It is extensively planted and has proved entirely hardy in the Upper Midwest.

Juneberry, Serviceberry, Saskatoon
Amelanchier Medic., Phil. Bot. 1:55, 1789

Unarmed shrubs and small trees with alternate, simple, pinnately veined, serrate or dentate leaves, with small, early-deciduous stipules; flowers white, in racemes or rarely solitary; hypanthium campanulate or saucer-shaped, adnate below to the ovary; sepals five, persistent in the fruit; petals five, ovate to oblong or rarely linear; stamens numerous; petals and stamens inserted in the throat of the hypanthium; carpels three to five, more or less united, ovary inferior or half-inferior, three- to five-celled with each cell nearly divided by a false partition, styles three to five; united at the base and sometimes almost to the summit, pubescent below, stigmas three to five; fruit a small berry-like pome, six- to ten-celled, six- to ten-seeded, generally sweet and edible. (*Amelánchier*, the Savoy name of the medlar.)

This is a genus of at least twenty-five closely related species, natives of the North Temperate Zone.

KEY TO SPECIES OF AMELANCHIER

1. Flowers racemose, leaves rounded or subcordate at the base, conduplicate in the bud, summit of ovary rounded.
    2. Leaves entire or with a few obscure teeth near the tip, most of the veins anastomosing before reaching the margin.
        3. Leaves narrowly to broadly ovate, short-acuminate or mucronate at the apex, racemes 3–5 cm. long, sparsely pubescent at flowering time, soon glabrate... ....*A. mucronata* (p. 226)
        3. Leaves elliptic to oblong, rounded or merely apiculate at the apex, racemes 2–2.5 cm. long, densely tomentose at flowering time, tardily glabrate....... ....*A. humilis* var. *exserrata* (p. 228)
    2. Leaves serrate-dentate to finely serrate, at least in the upper third, principal veins running branched or unbranched into the teeth.
        4. Leaves coarsely toothed (three to five teeth per cm.), main lateral veins conspicuous, regularly spaced and parallel, mostly without shorter intermediate ones.
            5. Stoloniferous, mostly low shrubs, forming colonies, racemes erect, 1.5–4 cm. long, densely tomentose at flowering time, hypanthium shallowly cup-shaped, 3–4 mm. in diameter, petals not over 10 mm. long.
                6. Leaves broadly elliptic to broadly obovate or quadrangular to nearly

orbicular, abruptly rounded, truncate or retuse at the apex; shrub mostly
of the prairie region.......................*A. alnifolia* (p. 227)
6. Leaves oblong, oblong-ovate to ovate, broadly acute or obtuse at the
apex, shrub mostly of the forested areas........*A. humilis* (p. 227)
5. Straggling shrubs or small trees, not stoloniferous and not forming colonies,
racemes nodding or drooping, 4–7.5 cm. long, sometimes silky-pubescent
at flowering time but soon glabrate, hypanthium saucer-shaped, 4–7.5 mm.
in diameter, petals 11–18 mm. long.
7. Straggling or arching shrub, 1–3 m. high, leaves oval to oval-oblong,
rarely suborbicular, upper veins straight, parallel and running to the
apex of the teeth without branching, petals narrowly spatulate, hypanthium 4–5 mm. in diameter...............*A. sanguinea* (p. 228)
7. Shrub or small tree, 3–7 m. high, leaves elliptic to oval-oblong or sometimes obovate, veins curving upward and generally forking near the
margin, their branches running into the teeth, petals obovate, hypanthium 5–7.5 mm. in diameter.............*A. huronensis* (p. 229)
4. Leaves finely toothed or serrate (5–12 per cm.), main lateral veins not prominent, somewhat irregularly and unequally spaced, usually with shorter intermediate ones.
8. Low stoloniferous shrub, forming clumps or small colonies, leaves oval,
oblong-oval or elliptic-oval, rarely suborbicular, rounded or obtuse at the
apex, occasionally mucronate.................*A. stolonifera* (p. 229)
8. Tall shrubs or small trees, not stoloniferous or forming colonies (sometimes
fastigiate), leaves ovate, elliptic-ovate to slightly obovate or elliptic to oblong, apex acute to more or less acuminate or apiculate.
9. Top of the ovary tomentose.
10. Leaves elliptic, elliptic-ovate to elliptic-obovate, gradually tapered
to an acute or acuminate apex, racemes erect or ascending, relatively few-flowered, rachis silky-pubescent at flowering time, sepals
of maturing fruit spreading to irregularly reflexed..............
..................................*A. intermedia* (p. 231)
10. Leaves ovate to slightly obovate or oblong, abruptly tapered to a
short-acuminate or apiculate apex, racemes more or less drooping or
pendent, loosely flowered, flowering rachis glabrous, sepals in maturing fruit reflexed from the base.
11. Mature leaves broadly ovate to broadly elliptic, mostly about
three-fourths as broad as long, serrations fine (five to seven
per cm.), sinuses between the teeth rounded. Southeastern
Minnesota north to Anoka County......*A. interior* (p. 231)
11. Leaves prevailingly oblong and generally nearly twice as long
as broad, serration sharp (four or five per cm.), sinuses between
the teeth acute. Northeastern Minnesota..................
.... *A. Wiegandii* (p. 232)
9. Top of the ovary glabrous.
12. Leaves densely tomentose, usually small and folded at flowering
time, mature blades ovate to slightly obovate, acuminate, petioles
and lower surface remaining more or less pubescent, racemes usually ascending to nodding...............*A. arborea* (p. 233)
12. Leaves glabrous at unfolding or with a few silky hairs, mostly
bronze-purple at flowering time, mature blades elliptic, ovate,
ovate-oblong to somewhat obovate, acute to acuminate, glabrous,
racemes pendulous.....................*A. laevis* (p. 233)
1. Flowers solitary or in clusters of two or three, leaves cuneate at the base, imbricate
in the bud, summit of the ovary conical..............*A. Bartramiana* (p. 234)

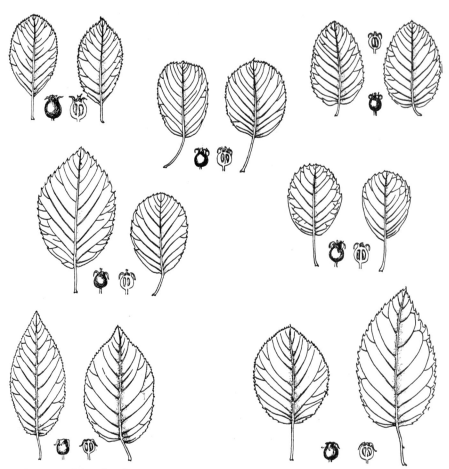

Species of *Amelanchier*: Top, left to right, *A. Bartramiana*, *A. stolonifera*, and *A. humilis*. Center, left to right, *A. sanguinea* and *A. alnifolia*. Bottom, left to right, *A. arborea* and *A. laevis*.

Amelanchier mucronata Nielsen, Am. Midland Naturalist 22:172, 1939

A low, stoloniferous shrub, up to 1 m. high, leaves at first densely yellow-green-tomentose, unfolded and nearly glabrate at flowering time, mature blades mostly broadly ovate to elliptic-ovate, rarely elliptic-obovate, 3.5 cm. long, 2.5–3 cm. broad, rounded or rarely subcordate at the base, short-acuminate or mucronate at the apex, margin entire or with a few obscure serrations near the apex, primary veins mostly from nine to eleven pairs, freely branching near the margin and many of them not entering the teeth; petiole slender, 2–2.5 cm. long; racemes strict, dense, 3–5 cm. long, flowering rachis with a sparse yellowish-green pubescence, soon glabrate; lowermost pedicel 10–14 mm. long (dead pedicels often persisting until the following season); sepals acute, narrowly triangular 3.5–5 mm. long, soon recurving, petals elliptic to broadly oblong, 8–9 mm. long; hypanthium saucer-shaped, 4–5 mm. in diameter; summit of ovary densely woolly; fruit globose, somewhat constricted above. Blossoms about the middle of June; fruit ripe in late August. (*Mucronáta*, tipped with a mucro, referring to the abruptly pointed leaves.)

The only collections of this species seen are from the extreme northeastern part of Minnesota. Its general distribution is still unknown.

SASKATOON, *Amelanchier alnifolia* Nutt., Journ. Phil. Acad. 7:22, 1834 [*A. florida* (Lindl.) Wiegand 1912 and in Trees & Shrubs of Minn. 1928]

A stoloniferous colonial shrub 1–3 (7) m. high, terminal overwintering buds 7–8 mm. long, dull chestnut-brown; leaves mostly unfolded at flowering time, yellowish-tomentose beneath, soon glabrate, sometimes retaining a sparse pubescence on the petiole and lower midrib, blades broadly elliptic to quadrate-rotund, sometimes broadly obovate, 2.5–5 cm. long, 2.5–4 cm. broad, rounded or truncate or often somewhat retuse at the apex, mostly rounded at the base, margin serrate-dentate, mostly above the middle, with from two to five teeth per cm.; veins eight to ten pairs, prominent, curving upward and often forking, they or their forks entering the teeth; racemes erect, few-flowered, 1.5–3 cm. long in anthesis, flowering rachis silky-pubescent, glabrate with age, lowermost pedicel 5–11 mm. long; sepals triangular, 2.5–3 mm. long and nearly as broad, their tips recurving; petals obovate to spatulate, 6–7.5 mm. long; hypanthium shallowly cup-shaped, 3.5–4 mm. in diameter; summit of the ovary tomentose; mature fruit globose to obpyriform, purplish-blue when ripe, sweet and juicy. Blossoms from the middle of May to early June; fruit ripe in July and August. (*Alnifólia*, alder-leaved.)

This shrub grows along forest margins and on stream and river banks. It occurs mostly throughout the prairie parts of the Upper Midwest and occasionally in the bordering forested areas. It is widely distributed in the plains area from Nebraska to the Canadian provinces and westward to the foothills of the Rocky Mountains.

LOW JUNEBERRY, *Amelanchier humilis* Wiegand, Rhodora 14:141, 1912 [*A. spicata* of Am. authors, in part]

An upright, rather stiff, stoloniferous shrub forming colonies, 0.3–6 m. high, overwintering buds 4–9 mm. long, dull or somewhat vernicose; leaves partly or fully unfolded at flowering time, densely white- to grayish-green-tomentose beneath, at length glabrate or with sparsely pubescent petioles; mature blades elliptic, oblong, ovate or somewhat obovate, 2–4 cm. broad, 2.5–5 cm. long, broadly subacute to rounded at the apex, rounded or subcordate at the base; margin coarsely serrate-dentate to below the middle, occasionally nearly entire, four or five (six) teeth per cm. separated by acute sinuses; primary lateral veins seven to thirteen pairs, usually forking before reaching the margin and entering the teeth; racemes erect, 2–5 cm. long, densely silky-tomentose, lowermost pedicel 9–13 mm. long; sepals triangular, about as long as broad or sometimes nearly twice as long, reflexed from the middle after anthesis; petals oblong-obovate, 7–10 mm. long; hypanthium shallowly cup-shaped, 3–4 (5) mm. in diameter; top of the ovary tomentose; fruit globose or thick-ellipsoid, black, glaucous, sweet and juicy. (*Humilis*, low, referring to the habit of growth.)

Low Juneberry grows chiefly on rocky banks, sandy shores, and in other dry situations. It is common throughout most of the area except in the extreme northeast and the unforested prairie parts. It is distributed from Quebec to western Ontario, south to Pennsylvania, Ohio, Michigan, Wisconsin, and Minnesota.

The species is highly variable and in the Upper Midwest Nielsen has recognized the following varieties.

KEY TO VARIETIES OF AMELANCHIER HUMILIS

1. Leaves typically oblong, sometimes ovate.
    2. Racemes generally 4–5 cm. long (occasionally shorter); flowers large, hypanthium 4–5 mm. in diameter; leaves usually coarsely dentate-serrate above the middle, 4–5 teeth per cm. occasionally entire; buds glabrous. Common in the deciduous forest...var. *humilis*
    2. Racemes 2.5–3 cm. long, flowers small; hypanthium 3–3.5 mm. in diameter; leaves entire or with a few teeth near the apex, about six teeth per cm.; bud scales with prominent hairs on the outer surface. On quartzite rocks in southwestern Minnesota...var. *exserrata*
1. Leaves typically elliptic, sometimes ovate or obovate.
    3. Veins conspicuous and running into the coarse serrations; racemes mostly 2–3.5 (5) cm. long, loose; hypanthium 3.5–4 mm. in diameter; sepals acute and somewhat longer than wide (about 3 mm. long). Typically of the prairie region.....
    ....var. *campestris*
    3. Veins generally forking and less prominent near the margin; racemes mostly 2–2.5 (3) cm. long, very compact; hypanthium about 3 mm. in diameter; sepals blunt, about as long as wide (about 2–2.5 mm long). Typically of forested regions...var. *compacta*

ROUNDLEAF SERVICEBERRY, *Amelanchier sanguinea* (Pursh) DC., Prod. 2:633, 1825 [*A. rotundifolia* Roemer 1847; *A. spicata* Koehne 1893]

A straggling or arching shrub 1–3 m. high, the solitary or few slender trunks with red or reddish-brown young branchlets, overwintering buds narrowly ovate, acute, reddish-brown, 6–7 mm. long; leaves nearly or fully unfolded at flowering time, at first pale-yellowish-tomentose beneath, soon glabrescent but often retaining a sparse pubescence on the midrib beneath and on the petiole; mature blades elliptic-oblong to suborbicular, rounded or subcordate at the base, blunt to rounded or subacute at the apex, 2.5–4 cm. broad, 3–6 cm. long; margin coarsely serrate-dentate nearly to the base, the teeth sharp and spreading, four or five (six) per cm. with generally open sinuses, veins eleven to thirteen pairs, rather close together, conspicuous, the upper ones straight and running unbranched into the teeth; racemes loose, soon arching or nodding, 4–7 cm. long, flowering rachis pubescent but soon glabrate, lowermost pedicel 10–20 mm. long; sepals ovate-lanceolate, acute, 3–4 mm. long, soon recurving from the middle; petals narrowly spatulate to linear, 11–15 mm. long; hypanthium saucer-

shaped, 4–6 mm. in diameter, spreading after the petals fall; summit of the
ovary densely tomentose; fruit globose, dark purple to black at maturity. Blossoms about the middle of May in southeastern Minnesota and nearly a month
later in the northeast; fruit ripe in July and August. (*Sanguínea*, blood-red, referring to the red branchlets.)

This shrub grows in open woods and on rocky slopes and stream banks. It
appears to be of infrequent occurrence and limited in our area mostly to southeastern Minnesota, northeastern Iowa, and adjacent Wisconsin. It is distributed
from Quebec to Ontario, south to New England, New York, the mountains of
North Carolina, and to northern Ohio westward to northeastern Iowa.

Amelanchier huronensis Wiegand, Rhodora 22:150, 1920

A fastigiate shrub or small tree, 3–7 m. high, overwintering buds 5–8 mm.
long, dark purple or reddish-brown and mostly somewhat varnished; leaves
mostly unfolded at flowering time, floccose-pubescent to glabrescent on the lower
surface but soon glabrate (occasionally retaining tomentum until fruits are nearly
full-grown); mature blades broadly oblong or elliptic to suborbicular or sometimes obovate, 3.5–5.5 cm. broad, 4–7 cm. long, rounded or subcordate at the
base, rounded or occasionally blunt to subacute at the apex, coarsely serrate-
dentate to near the base, teeth rounded, three or four per cm.; veins eleven or
twelve pairs, prominent, curving upward and most of them forking before entering the teeth; racemes loose, many-flowered, 4–7 cm. long, flowering rachis
floccose-pubescent, glabrate or nearly so with age; lowermost pedicel 1.2–3 cm.
long; sepals narrow, acute, 3–5.5 mm. long, widely spreading at anthesis but
later strongly recurved from the middle; petals narrowly obovate to oblanceolate, 1.2–1.8 cm. long; hypanthium broadly saucer-shaped, 5–7 mm. in diameter; summit of the ovary tomentose; fruit subglobose, 5–8 mm. in diameter,
dark purple, sweet and juicy when ripe. Blossoms in May and early June; fruit
ripe in August. (*Huronénsis*, of Lake Huron, referring to the region where the
species was first recognized as distinct.)

This species is common on calcareous drift and on basic rock outcrops
throughout the northern parts of Minnesota and Wisconsin. It occurs along the
Great Lakes from Marsitoulin District westward through northern Michigan,
Wisconsin, and Minnesota.

The species is readily distinguished by its loose racemes, large hypanthium,
long, narrow sepals, and by the coarse, rounded teeth of the leaves.

Amelanchier stolonifera Wiegand, Rhodora 14:144, 1912

A stiff, upright shrub 0.3–1.5 m. high, forming patches; overwintering buds
5–7 mm. long, dull reddish-brown; unfolding leaves about half-grown at flowering time, green or sometimes bronze in color when young, nearly glabrous above,
densely white-tomentose beneath, soon glabrate; mature blades dull green above,
elliptic to oblong or suborbicular, 2–5 cm. long, 2–3.5 cm. broad; rounded or

Species of *Amelanchier*: Top, left to right, *A. huronensis* and *A. mucronata*. Center, *A. interior*. Bottom, left to right, *A. Wiegandii* and *A. intermedia*.

obtuse at the apex, sometimes mucronate, base rounded, rarely subcordate or broadly cuneate; margin sharply serrate above the lower third with (five) six to eight teeth per cm.; primary veins mostly seven to nine pairs, usually curving upward and becoming indistinct near the margin; racemes erect, somewhat dense 1.5–4 cm. long, rachis and pedicels pubescent during anthesis, glabrate with age, lowermost pedicel 7–15 mm. long; sepals triangular-lanceolate 2.5–3 mm. long, soon reflexed from near the middle, the margins becoming revolute; petals oblong or narrowly obovate, 7–9 mm. long; hypanthium saucer-shaped, 3–4 mm. in diameter; summit of the ovary densely tomentose; fruit globose or slightly elongate, black and juicy when ripe. Blossoms about June 15; fruit ripe in late August. (*Stolonifera*, stoloniferous, referring to the habit of growth.)

This species occurs on acid rock outcrops and open sandy areas in the northeastern corner of Minnesota. It is distributed from Newfoundland west to Thunder Bay District, Ontario, and south to New England, Long Island, Virginia, and northern Michigan and Minnesota.

Amelanchier intermedia Spach, Nat. d. Veg. Phan. 2:85, 1834

A tall, generally fastigiate or alder-like shrub, overwintering buds ovate, 7–11 mm. long, reddish-brown; leaves unfolding at flowering time, at first often reddish or somewhat bronze in color, their early deciduous stipules conspicuously pinkish, lower surface of the young leaves flavescent, tomentose, soon glabrate; mature blades elliptic, elliptic-ovate to elliptic-oblong (rarely slightly obovate), 3–5 cm. long, 1.5–3 cm. broad, rounded or subcordate at the base, acute to short-acuminate or sometimes nearly cuspidate at the apex; margin finely serrate with five to seven teeth per cm.; primary veins seven to twelve pairs, freely anastomosing near the margin and often with shorter intermediate ones; racemes erect or ascending, rather compact and few-flowered, 2–5 cm. long, flowering rachis thinly silky-pubescent, soon glabrate, lowermost pedicel 10–15 mm. long; sepals 2–3 mm. long, somewhat spreading to irregularly recurved; petals oblong-cuneate, 7–11 mm. long; hypanthium cup-shaped, about 3 mm. in diameter; summit of ovary more or less tomentose; fruit globose, not constricted above, dark purple, sweet and juicy when ripe. Blossoms from about the middle to late May; fruit mature in August. (*Intermédia*, intermediate, presumably occupying an intermediate position between two other species.)

This shrub is common in the forested part of the area, particularly along the margins of bogs and marshes north of the forty-fifth parallel, less frequent in southeastern Minnesota and adjacent Wisconsin. It is distributed from Newfoundland to Minnesota, south to Nova Scotia, New England, Virginia, and the uplands of North Carolina, and westward to Michigan, Wisconsin, and southern Minnesota.

INLAND SERVICEBERRY, *Amelanchier interior* Nielsen, Am. Midland Naturalist 22:185, 1939

A straggling shrub or small tree up to 11 m. high; overwintering buds narrowly ovate, acute to acuminate and sometimes curved, 6–13 mm. long, reddish-brown; leaves unfolding at flowering time, rather sparsely gray-tomentose beneath, soon glabrate; mature blades broadly ovate to elliptic, 3–5 cm. broad, 4–7 cm. long, rounded or subcordate at the base, apex abruptly short-acuminate, sometimes apiculate; margin finely serrate with five or six (seven) teeth per cm., the teeth somewhat mucronate-tipped and with rounded sinuses between them; primary veins eight to ten pairs, with occasional shorter intermediate ones, anastomosing near the margin; racemes loose, nodding, glabrous, 3–6 (7) cm. long, lowermost pedicel 20–32 mm. long, or sometimes up to 45 mm. long; sepals narrowly triangular, 2–2.5 mm. broad, 3.5–5 mm. long, tomentose above at anthesis, becoming glabrous and reflexed after the petals fall; petals obovate, 15 mm. long; hypanthium broadly cup-shaped, generally about 5 mm. in diameter; summit of the ovary tomentose; fruit globose, 6–8 mm. in diameter, not constricted above. Blossoms in May; fruit mature in July. (*Intérior*, inland.)

Inland serviceberry grows on hillsides and along stream banks in the southeastern part of Minnesota as far north as Washington and Anoka counties. It is distributed from southwestern Wisconsin across northern Iowa and southern Minnesota to eastern South Dakota.

At flowering time *A. interior* has often been confused with either *A. intermedia* or *A. arborea* (*A. canadensis*), and when fully mature, with *A. laevis*. From *A. intermedia* it differs in its drooping, many-flowered, glabrous racemes and in its less tomentose and early glabrate leaves; from *A. arborea* similarly in its glabrous, longer racemes and especially in having the summit of the ovary tomentose instead of glabrous. In the latter respect it also differs from *A. laevis*. The mature leaves of *A. interior* are relatively shorter than those of *A. laevis*, having eight to ten pairs of lateral veins as contrasted with twelve to seventeen for the latter.

A. interior usually grows to greater size than any of the other species of *Amelanchier* in the Upper Midwest, often attaining a height of 11–12 m. and a trunk diameter of 12–14 cm.

Amelanchier Wiegandii Nielsen, Am. Midland Naturalist 22:180, 1939

An arching shrub 3–5 m. high, sometimes up to 8 m.; overwintering buds ovate, 8–10 mm. long, reddish-brown to dark purple; leaves unfolded at flowering time, bronze in color, at first pubescent but nearly or quite glabrate at full anthesis; mature blades oblong to slightly obovate or sometimes narrowly elliptic, 2–3 cm. broad, 3.5–6 cm. long, generally nearly twice as long as broad, rounded or subcordate at the base, short-acuminate or apiculate at the apex; margin serrate nearly to the base, with four or five very sharp teeth per cm., sinuses between the teeth acute; primary veins eight to eleven pairs, often with intermediate ones toward the apex, ascending and branching freely near the margin, the branches running into the teeth; racemes loose, 5.5–7.5 cm. long, generally eight- to nine-flowered, occasionally six- to twelve-flowered, drooping, glabrous from the beginning; lowermost pedicel 1.5–4 cm. long at flowering time; sepals acute, 3.5–5 mm. long, sharply reflexed from the base after anthesis; petals linear to narrowly obovate, 11–15 mm. long; hypanthium broadly cup-shaped, 4–5 mm. in diameter; summit of the ovary densely tomentose, sometimes glabrate or nearly so at maturity; fruit globose, somewhat truncate above, 7–8 mm. in diameter; dark purple when ripe, sweet and juicy. Blossoms about the middle of June; fruit mature in August. (*Wiegándii*, named for K. M. Wiegand, long-time and accurate student of the genus.)

This species grows on rocky slopes, banks of streams, and in coarse sands.

It appears limited in Minnesota and Wisconsin to the shores and vicinity of Lake Superior. It is distributed from Newfoundland to Ontario, south to Nova Scotia, New England, New York, northern Michigan, Wisconsin, and Minnesota.

In our area *A. Wiegandii* is usually a medium-sized to tall shrub, but in the eastern part of its range it often attains tree size, with a height up to 11 m. and a trunk diameter of 12–14 cm. In autumn the foliage turns purplish-red.

DOWNY SERVICEBERRY, *Amelanchier arborea* (Michx. f.) Fernald, Rhodora, 43:563, 1941 [*A. canadensis* (L.) Medic. 1793; *A. canadensis* var. *Botryapium* Torr. & Gray 1840]

A fastigiate shrub or small tree up to 10 m. high; overwintering buds broadly ovate, 6–13 mm. long, greenish-yellow or cinnamon-brown; expanding leaves green above, densely white-tomentose beneath, small and folded at flowering time; mature blades ovate to slightly obovate, cordate to subcordate at the base, mostly acuminate at the apex, 2.2–5 cm. broad, 4–8 cm. long, usually retaining some of the pubescence beneath and on the petioles; margin sharply and often doubly serrate nearly to the base; teeth six to ten per cm., with acute and deep sinuses between them; primary veins mostly eleven to seventeen pairs, these anastomosing and becoming indistinct toward the margins, often with short intermediate veins; racemes short, moderately dense, ascending to nodding, 3–5 cm. long; flowers medium-sized and often fully opened before the leaves have emerged from the bud; lowermost pedicel 8–17 mm. long; sepals broadly oblong-triangular, 2–3 mm. long; soon strongly reflexed from the base; petals linear or narrowly oblong, 10–14 mm. long; hypanthium cup-shaped, 2.5–3 (3.5) mm. in diameter; summit of the ovary glabrous; fruit globose, reddish-purple, dry and insipid. Blossoms in May; fruit mature in late June and early July. (*Arbórea*, tree-like.)

Downy serviceberry occurs mostly in rich woods, thickets, and on hillsides. It is infrequent in the southeastern and northeastern corners of Minnesota and apparently absent from the intervening area; it is more common in the regions to the east and south. It is distributed from northern Florida to Louisiana and Oklahoma and northward to Maine, New Brunswick, southwestern Quebec, southern Ontario, northern Michigan, and Minnesota.

JUNEBERRY, *Amelanchier laevis* Wiegand, Rhodora 14:154, 1912

An irregularly branching, fastigiate shrub or small tree up to 13 m. high (seldom over 7 m. in Minnesota); overwintering buds ovate, acute, 9–17 mm. long, scales greenish-brown or greenish-yellow; leaves about half-grown at flowering time, usually purple-bronze or reddish, rarely green, glabrous from the first or with a few silky hairs; mature blades dark green above, glaucescent beneath, elliptic, ovate, ovate-oblong or slightly obovate, 2.5–4 cm. broad, 4–6 cm. long, rounded or subcordate at the base, apex short-acuminate; margin sharply serrate nearly to the base, the sharp, callous-tipped teeth 6–8 per cm. with

Species of *Amelanchier*: Left, *A. Bartramiana*. Center, *A. humilis.*
Right, *A. laevis* (× 1/2).

mostly rounded sinuses; primary veins twelve to seventeen pairs, often with
short intermediate ones, unequally spaced, curving upward and anastomosing
near the margin; racemes few- to many-flowered, drooping, glabrous or nearly
so at flowering time, 3–7 cm. long; lower pedicel 15–33 mm. long; sepals triangular-lanceolate to subulate, 2.7–4 mm. long, soon abruptly reflexed from the base;
petals oblong-linear, 10–18 mm. long; hypanthium cup-shaped, 2.5–5 mm. in
diameter; summit of the ovary glabrous; fruit globose, 6–8 mm. in diameter,
often somewhat broader than long, dark purple to blackish when ripe, sweet
and juicy. Blossoms in the southern part of the area in April and early May,
northward up to early June; fruit ripe in June and July. (*Laévis*, smooth.)

This shrub is common on the edges of woods, on moist hillsides, and in ravines, particularly throughout the deciduous forest areas. It is less frequent
northeastward in the coniferous forest. It is distributed from Newfoundland to
Minnesota, south to Pennsylvania and Kansas, and southward, mostly in the
mountains, to Georgia and Alabama.

Amelanchier Bartramiana (Tausch) Roemer, Syn. Rosif. 3:145, 1847

A slender shrub 0.5–2.5 m. high, stems several together, fastigiate; leaves
imbricated in the bud, flat and not folded on expanding, glabrous except for
the slightly silky petiole; blades elliptic, elliptic-oblong or elliptic-oval, sometimes somewhat obovate, 1.5–3 cm. broad, 3–5 cm. long, tapering or cuneate at
the base, rounded to acute at the apex; petiole stout, 2–7 mm. long; margin
sharply and often doubly serrate to below the middle or nearly to the base;
teeth usually abruptly acuminate from a broad base, 6–12 per cm.; primary veins
twelve to seventeen pairs, irregularly spaced and with short, intermediate ones,
anastomosing and indistinct toward the margin; flowers solitary or two or three
(rarely four) together, appearing when the leaves are about half grown; pedi-

234

cels glabrous, 10–25 mm. long; sepals triangular-subulate, loosely spreading, 3–4 mm. long, more or less persistently tomentose above; petals oblong-oval, broadest at the middle, 6–8 mm. long; hypanthium cup-shaped, 3–6 mm. in diameter, ovary densely tomentose, conically tapering to the pubescent style bases; fruit 10–13 mm. long, somewhat longer than thick, purplish-black, sweet and juicy when ripe. Blossoms about June 15; fruit ripe in August. (*Bartramiána*, named for the early American botanist William Bartram.)

This species grows in peaty or boggy thickets, on the borders of bogs, and on damp uplands. It is common in northern Wisconsin and northeastern Minnesota as far west as eastern Carlton and Itasca counties. It is distributed from Labrador to the Thunder Bay district of Ontario, south to Newfoundland, Nova Scotia, the mountains of New England, northeastern Pennsylvania, northern Michigan, Wisconsin, and Minnesota.

Hawthorn, Thorn Apple
Crataegus L., Sp. Pl. 475, 1753

Thorny shrubs or small trees with alternate, simple, frequently lobed leaves; buds small, obtuse to hemispherical, with imbricated scales; flowers in corymbs, appearing with or after the leaves, usually white; hypanthium cup-shaped or campanulate, adnate to the carpels, sometimes with a free margin; epigynous disk covering the top of the ovary; sepals five; petals five, spreading, nearly orbicular, inserted on the margin of the disk; stamens five to twenty-five, in one to three cycles; filaments broad at the base, subulate; anthers oblong, white, yellow, or red; carpels one to five, ovaries imbedded in the hypanthium but scarcely united; styles one to five, free, persistent; stigmas terminal; fertile ovules one in each carpel; fruit a pome, the carpels forming one-seeded stones or nutlets. (*Crataégus*, classical Greek name for the hawthorn.)

Crataegus is a large genus, widely distributed throughout the North Temperate Zone and in the tablelands of Mexico and the Andes.

The genus offers great taxonomic difficulties, and it is impossible at present to say how many species it includes. About a thousand have been described from the United States alone, but it appears probable that many of these are hybrids or segregates of subspecific rank. No critical work has as yet been done on the *Crataegi* of the Upper Midwest, and for that reason it has been thought advisable to adhere to the broader concept of species in this work.

For identification of species of *Crataegus*, and especially for their critical study, it is necessary to have material both in the flowering and ripe-fruiting condition. Furthermore the color of the anthers is an important character and should always be noted. In our area the various species blossom from the middle of May until about June 10, and the fruit ripens from the latter part of August through September.

KEY TO SPECIES OF CRATAEGUS

1. Leaves deeply incised, with one to three pairs of oblong lateral lobes; carpel and style one; flowers pink. Cultivated shrubs..............*C. monogyna* (p. 237)
1. Leaves with three to six pairs of more or less shallow triangular or rounded lobes or nearly unlobed or with merely serrate margins; carpels and styles two to five; flowers white. Native shrubs or trees (except for *C. Crus-Galli*).
   2. Leaves of flowering branchlets prevailingly broadest above the middle, obovate, rounded or short-acute at the apex, mostly narrowly cuneate at the base.
      3. Ripe fruit purplish-black, sepals with marginal glands; thorns 1–3 cm. long or sometimes lacking. Northeastern Minnesota......*C. Douglasii* (p. 237)
      3. Ripe fruit red or orange-red, sepals mostly without marginal glands, thorns more than 3 cm. long. Not confined to northeastern Minnesota.
         4. Leaves shining, glabrous, not impressed-veined above. Cultivated......
         ....*C. Crus-Galli* (p. 238)
         4. Leaves pubescent beneath, impressed-veined above. Native shrub or tree....................................*C. punctata* (p. 238)
   2. Leaves of flowering branchlets broadest at or below the middle, elliptic, rhombic, oblong-ovate to broadly ovate, deltoid, or sometimes suborbicular, mostly broadly cuneate to truncate or rounded to subcordate at the base.
      5. Leaves prevailingly broadest at the middle, elliptic, rhombic, oval, or sometimes suborbicular.
         6. Mature leaves deeply impressed-veined above, mostly with shallow lobing or often only serrate-dentate; sepals glandular-pectinate or glandular serrate, nutlets with pits on the inner faces.
            7. Sepals glandular-pectinate, fruit glabrous, nutlets deeply pitted.
               8. Leaves glabrate above, pubescent especially along the veins beneath; stamens ten; filaments short and thick; fruit subglobose, mostly over 1 cm. in diameter, succulent when ripe.*C. succulenta* (p. 239)
               8. Leaves strigose above, becoming scabrate, tomentose beneath, stamens mostly twenty, strongly exserted: filaments slender; fruit ellipsoid or pyriform, mostly less than 1 cm. in diameter, with thin, sweet flesh.......................*C. Calpodendron* (p. 240)
            7. Sepals glandular-serrate, fruit pubescent at the ends; nutlets with shallow pits..............................*C. pertomentosa* (p. 241)
         6. Mature leaves only slightly impressed-veined above, prominently lobed; sepals gland-margined or sometimes glandular-serrate; nutlets without pits on the inner faces.
            9. Leaves mostly broadly elliptic to suborbicular, with three to five pairs of spreading, short-triangular lobes, broadly acute at the apex, glabrous or nearly so on both surfaces. Common and widely distributed.......
            ....*C. chrysocarpa* (p. 241)
            9. Leaves elliptic, incisely lobed with four or five acuminate lobes, narrowly acute to acuminate at the apex, more or less strigose-pubescent on both surfaces. Frequent northeast........*C. Brunetiana* (p. 242)
      5. Leaves broadest below the middle, prevailingly ovate, sometimes deltoid, broadly cuneate to truncate, rounded or subcordate at the base.
         10. Leaves tomentose beneath; corymbs tomentose, mature fruit more or less pubescent.
            11. Mature leaves thick and coriaceous; with four or five pairs of short triangular lobes, teeth short and blunt; nutlets with shallow pits. Southwestern.....................*C. pertomentosa* (p. 241)
            11. Mature leaves thin and membranaceous, with five or six sharply triangular pairs of lobes. Often deeply lobed toward the base, teeth

236

sharp and acuminate; nutlets without pits. Southern . . . .
. . . . *C. mollis* (p. 243)
10. Leaves glabrous beneath or sparingly villous along the veins; corymbs
glabrous or somewhat villous; mature fruit glabrous and often glaucous.
12. Leaves bright green, thin, not impressed-veined above; teeth sharp,
acuminate-tipped, corymbs glabrous.
13. Average leaves 7–8 cm. long, with mostly five pairs of broad,
triangular lateral lobes; fruit 10–18 mm. in diameter, flesh soft.
. . . . *C. macrosperma* (p. 244)
13. Average leaves 4–5 cm. long, deeply indented with four or five
pairs of acute, spreading lateral lobes; fruit 6–9 mm. in diameter,
flesh firm . . . . *C. macrosperma* var. *roanensis* (p. 245)
12. Leaves yellow-green, firm and somewhat impressed-veined above and
coriaceous when mature; teeth bluntish; corymbs loosely villous;
tardily glabrate . . . . *C. chrysocarpa* (p. 241)

ENGLISH HAWTHORN, *Crataegus monogyna* Jacq., Fl. Aust. 3:50, 1775

A shrub or tree with ascending branches, with numerous thorns mostly about
1 cm. long, frequently with thorn-like, short spurs up to 5 cm. long; young twigs
reddish and glabrous, eventually becoming grayish-black or dark reddish-brown;
leaves ovate, 2–5 cm. long, 1–6 cm. wide, deeply three- to seven-lobed, the lobes
entire or with a few teeth toward the ends, leaves cuneate to truncate at the base,
slightly pubescent along the veins when young, becoming glabrate and dark
green above, somewhat paler beneath; petiole slender, 1–2 cm. long, slightly
wing-margined above, glabrous; corymbs glabrous, many-flowered; flowers white
or pink, about 14 mm. in diameter; hypanthium obconic, glabrous or villous;
sepals narrowly triangular, entire, obtuse or acute, strongly reflexed in anthesis;
stamens about twenty, filaments very slender; style one, surrounded at the base
by a ring of white hairs; fruit elliptic to subglobose, red, about 6 mm. in diameter; nutlet one, ovoid, somewhat ridged. (*Monógyna*, one woman, referring to
the single carpel.)

English hawthorn is occasionally planted as an ornamental shrub. It is a
native of Europe, North Africa, and western Asia. Double-flowered forms are
sometimes planted.

This species has been frequently confused with *Crataegus oxyacantha* L.,
which differs in its less lobed leaves with finely serrate margins and in having
two styles and nutlets. So far as known, *C. oxyacantha* is not planted in the Upper
Midwest.

BLACK HAWTHORN, DOUGLAS THORN-APPLE, *Crataegus Douglasii* Lindl., Bot. Reg. 21, 1835

A shrub or small tree, 4–12 m. high; young branchlets reddish-brown, glabrous, usually dotted with numerous light-colored lenticels, older twigs brownish-gray, scaly bark; thorns stout, short, mostly less than 3 cm. long, dark
reddish-brown to nearly black, sometimes lacking; leaves obovate, sometimes
oval or elliptic, 3–7 cm. long, 2–5 cm. broad, serrate except toward the cuneate

base, usually indented above the middle or near the apex with two to four pairs of shallow-rounded or acute-lateral lobes, upper surface thinly pubescent with appressed hairs, firm, dark green, and lustrous at maturity, lower surface paler, glabrous or nearly so; flowers 10–13 mm. broad, mostly five to twelve in glabrous corymbs; sepals linear-lanceolate above the broadened base, glandular serrate; petals broadly obovate to suborbicular, 5–6 mm. long; stamens ten or fewer; anthers white or pink; fruit broadly ellipsoid to subglobose, 8–10 mm. in diameter, dark wine-colored or black when ripe, flesh thick, succulent; nutlets three to five, somewhat ridged on the back and pitted on the inner faces. (*Douglásii*, named for the botanical explorer David Douglas.)

This species is a western one, occurring infrequently in Cook and Lake counties, Minnesota.

COCKSPUR THORN, NEWCASTLE THORN, *Crataegus Crus-Galli*, L., Sp. Pl. 476, 1753

A small tree, sometimes up to 8 m. high; the bark of the trunk dark brown, scaly; young twigs glabrous, yellowish-brown, becoming glossy, older twigs grayish-brown; spines straight or slightly curved, chestnut-brown to ashy-gray, 3–10 cm. long; leaves mostly obovate varying to oblanceolate and elliptic, 2.5–10 cm. long, 1–3 cm. wide, finely serrate above the middle with appressed, usually gland-tipped teeth, gradually narrowed to the base, rounded or more or less acute at the apex, dark green and shining above, paler and dull beneath, glabrous, coriaceous; petiole 5–10 mm. long, wing-margined at least above; corymbs glabrous, many-flowered; flowers about 1.5–2 cm. in diameter; sepals narrowly lanceolate, entire, glandular-serrate or laciniate-toothed; stamens ten to twenty, anthers rose-colored; styles usually two; fruit ellipsoid-ovoid to subglobose, about 1 cm. in diameter, greenish to red, flesh hard and dry; nutlets usually two, rounded at the ends, inner surface flat, ridged on the back. (*Crus-Gálli*, cockspur, in reference to the long thorns.)

Cockspur thorn is distributed from northern New York to southern Michigan and eastern Kansas, south to Georgia. It is occasionally planted in Minnesota.

WHITE THORN, *Crataegus punctata* Jacq., Hort. Vind. 1:10, pl. 28, 1770

A flat-topped tree up to 9 m. high, usually with horizontal or slightly ascending branches; the bark of the trunk rough, dark gray or brown; young twigs brownish, with gray pubescence, becoming glabrate and ashy- or silvery-gray the second year; spines usually few, slender, straight or slightly curved, gray, 3–10 cm. long; leaves obovate to rhombic-obovate, 4–8 cm. long, 2–4 cm. wide, sharply and doubly serrate above the middle and usually more or less incisely lobed, gradually narrowed toward the base, rounded to short-acuminate at the apex, upper surface gray-green, impressed-veined, at first sparsely pubescent, becoming glabrate, lower surface somewhat paler and persistently villous, especially along the veins; petiole 6–15 mm. long, margined above, pubescent; cor-

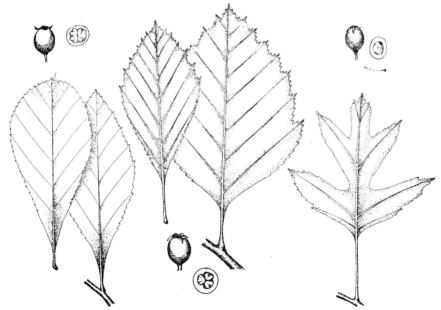

Species of *Crataegus*: Left, *C. Crus-Galli*. Center,
C. punctata. Right, *C. monogyna*.

ymbs villous, many-flowered; flowers 12–18 mm. in diameter; hypanthium narrowly obconic; sepals linear-lanceolate, with rather open sinuses between them,
mostly entire or minutely glandular-serrate, villous on both surfaces; stamens
twenty, anthers yellowish or pink; disk deeply concave; styles three or four;
fruit short-oblong, truncate at the ends, dull red or bright yellow, light-dotted;
nutlets three or four, smooth on the inner faces, only slightly ridged on the
back, 5–6 mm. long. (*Punctáta*, dotted, referring to the fruit.)

White thorn grows in thickets, clearings, and pastures. It is common throughout the hardwood forest area of the Upper Midwest, less frequent northward
into the borders of the coniferous forest. It is distributed from New England
west to Ontario and Minnesota, south to West Virginia, Kentucky, and central
Iowa.

FLESHY HAWTHORN, *Crataegus succulenta* Schrader, in Link, Handb. 3:78,
1831 [*C. macracantha* Lodd. 1838]

A small tree, sometimes 10 m. high, with ascending branches; the bark of the
trunk reddish-brown, scaly; young twigs glabrous, yellowish-green, becoming
orange-brown and lustrous, in the second year becoming dark gray; spines numerous, straight or slightly curved, bright chestnut-brown, shining, 4–8 cm. long;
leaves broadly rhombic-ovate to obovate, 4–8 cm. long, 3–7 cm. wide, rather
coarsely and doubly serrate, the teeth spreading; leaves with from four to six
short, acute or obtuse, often obscure, lobes above the middle, the lower half of
the leave unlobed, simply serrate to entire, gradually narrowed from about the

239

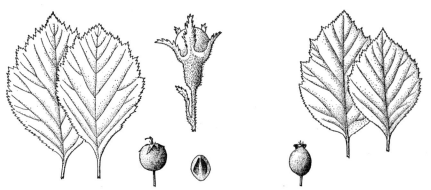

Species of *Crataegus*: Left, *C. succulenta*. Right, *C. Calpodendron*.

middle, acute at the apex, coriaceous, dark shining-green above, with strongly impressed veins, sparsely pubescent or glabrate, much paler beneath and pubescent especially along the veins, the pubescence forming a fringe of short, stiff hairs on each side of the principal veins; petiole stout, 1–2 cm. long, winged above; corymbs sparingly villous, many-flowered; flowers about 16–20 mm. in diameter; hypanthium campanulate, usually strongly villous; sepals lanceolate, acuminate, glandular-laciniate, villous; stamens ten to twenty, anthers pink or sometimes yellow; disk prominent; styles two or three, surrounded at the base by a ring of pale hairs; fruit subglobose, 7–15 mm. in diameter, dark red, sparsely villous and pale-dotted, pulp soft; nutlets two or three, prominently ridged on the back, deeply pitted on the ventral surfaces, 6–8 mm. long. (*Succulénta*, referring to the soft character of the fruit.)

This hawthorn is common in thickets, in pastures, and along the edges of woods throughout the middle Northwest. It is distributed from New England and New York to Minnesota and Manitoba, south to North Carolina, Missouri, Nebraska and Colorado.

PEAR THORN, *Crataegus Calpodendron* (Ehrh.) Medic., Gesch. Bot. 83, 1793 [*C. tomentosa* of authors (including Minn. T. & S. 1912), not of L.]

A shrub or small tree up to 6 m. high with ascending or spreading branches; bark smooth and pale gray to furrowed and dark brown; young twigs greenish, more or less tomentose, becoming orange-brown in the fall of the first year, later turning gray; spines usually few, nearly straight, 3–5 cm. long, generally ashy-gray in color; leaves ovate, rhombic-ovate, to elliptic, 4–8 cm. long, 2.5–6 cm. wide, unlobed or often with several short lobes above the middle, gradually narrowed to the base or somewhat rounded, acute, acuminate, or sometimes rounded at the apex, sharply and irregularly doubly serrate, the teeth rather spreading, membranous to subcoriaceous, upper surface bright green with slightly impressed veins, sparingly pubescent, usually tending to become scabrous, lower surface paler, persistently somewhat woolly-pubescent, especially on the veins; petiole stout, about 1 cm. long, wing-margined almost to the base;

240

corymbs white-tomentose, many-flowered; flowers about 15 mm. in diameter; hypanthium narrowly obconic, tomentose; sepals narrowly lanceolate, glandular-laciniate, tomentose; stamens about twenty, filaments slender and strongly exserted, anthers small, pink; disk concave; styles two or three, slightly hairy at the base; fruit pyriform or ellipsoid, about 1 cm. long, orange-red or red, very persistent, its flesh glutinous; nutlets two or three, short and broad, deeply pitted on the ventral faces, about 5 mm. long. (*Calpodéndron*, derivation of name obscure.)

Pear thorn is infrequent in southeastern Minnesota, more common southward in adjacent Wisconsin and Iowa. It is distributed from southern Ontario and New York to Minnesota, south to Georgia, eastern Texas, Arkansas, and Nebraska.

PRAIRIE THORN, *Crataegus pertomentosa* Ashe, Journ. E. Mitch. Soc. 16:70, 1900

A small tree with nearly horizontal branches and a flattened crown; spines numerous, slightly curved, 2.5–8 cm. long; young twigs tomentose, becoming yellow-brown and glabrate by the end of the first season, older twigs brownish-gray; leaves broadly ovate to obovate or oblong, 4–8 cm. long, 3.5–7.5 cm. wide, finely and doubly serrate, with short and wide, minutely gland-tipped teeth; leaves with four or five pairs of short, acute lobes, abruptly narrowed or almost truncate at the base, mostly acute at the apex, sparingly villous or glabrate above, tomentose beneath, especially along the veins, vivid dark-green, subcoriaceous; petiole 2–3 cm. long, slightly winged above; corymbs many-flowered, tomentose; flowers 18–20 mm. in diameter; sepals lanceolate, deeply glandular-serrate; stamens ten to fifteen; styles two to four; disk deeply concave; top of the ovary tomentose; fruit depressed, globose, 8–12 mm. in diameter, hard, red, villous; nutlets two to four, thick, with shallow pits on the ventral faces, slightly grooved on the back, about 7 mm. long. (*Pertomentósa*, very tomentose.)

Prairie thorn grows in thickets, in pastures, and on rock outcrops. It is infrequent in southwestern Minnesota and adjacent parts of South Dakota and Iowa, and ranges south to Illinois, Missouri, and eastern Kansas.

FIREBERRY THORN, ROUND-LEAVED THORN, *Crataegus chrysocarpa* Ashe, Bull. N.C. Exp. Sta. 175:110, 1900 [*C. rotundifolia* Borckh. 1798]

A round-topped shrub or tree, sometimes up to 7 m. high; the bark of the trunk reddish-brown, scaly; spines numerous, deep chestnut-brown, spotted with gray, slender, and more or less curved, 3–6 cm. long; young twigs yellowish-green, more or less villous, becoming reddish-brown by autumn and tending to become completely glabrate, marked by numerous nearly white lenticels; older twigs ashy-gray or grayish-brown; leaves elliptic or obovate, sometimes nearly orbicular, 3–6 cm. long, 2.5–5 cm. wide, finely and sharply doubly serrate, with nearly straight, gland-tipped teeth; leaves divided from slightly below the

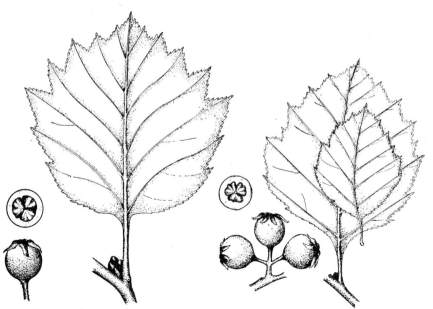

Species of *Crataegus*: Left, *C. pertomentosa*. Right, *C. chrysocarpa*.

middle into four or five pairs of short, acute lobes, the lower lobes most prominent, cuneate at the base, rarely rounded, wide-acute at the apex, thin, subcoriaceous, dark yellow-green and somewhat shining above with scarcely impressed veins, glabrous or slightly pubescent, somewhat paler beneath and glabrous, or villous especially along the veins; petiole 1.5–2.5 cm. long, slender, winged above, glandular and pubescent or glabrous; corymbs more or less villous, many-flowered; flowers 15–20 mm. in diameter; hypanthium narrowly campanulate, villous or glabrous; sepals narrowly lanceolate, glandular-margined, more or less villous on the inside, strongly reflexed at anthesis; stamens mostly ten, anthers small, pale yellow; disk flat; styles three or four, surrounded at the base by a conspicuous tuft of hairs; fruit subglobose to elliptical, dark crimson, 7–10 mm. in diameter, sepals persistent; nutlets three or four, rounded at the ends with a sharp keel on the ventral edge, about 6 mm. long. (*Chrysocárpa*, golden-fruited, fruit generally red, rarely yellow.)

This is a polymorphic species, widely distributed and common throughout the Upper Midwest, most frequent northward. It ranges from Newfoundland and New England to Manitoba and Saskatchewan, south to Pennsylvania, Wisconsin, Colorado, and New Mexico.

Crataegus Brunetiana Sarg., Rhodora 5:164, 1903 [*C. columbiana* var. *Brunetiana* (Sarg.) Eggl. 1908]

A shrub 2–3 m. high; young branchlets at first tomentose, soon glabrate, reddish-brown, with light-colored lenticels, the bark of the older twigs gray; thorns usually numerous, 4–6 cm. long, slender, shining, reddish-brown, on older twigs grayish; leaves rhombic to broadly elliptic, rarely subrotund, 3.5–6 cm. long, 2–4.5 cm. broad, cuneate at the base, acute to short-acuminate at the apex, sharply incised, with four or five pairs of acute to acuminate-tipped, irregularly serrate lobes; sparingly strigose-pubescent on both surfaces, glossy above, dull and paler beneath, usually becoming nearly glabrate and turning brown late in the season; petioles slender, 1.5–2.5 cm. long: corymbs six- to twelve-flowered, pedicels and hypanthium, strigose-villous; flowers 14–18 mm. long, sepals glandular-serrate, sharply reflexed at anthesis; petals broadly ovate to suborbicular, 6–8 mm. long, margin often minutely crenulate; stamens eight to ten; filaments slender; styles two to four; fruit ellipsoid to subglobose, 8–12 mm. long, coral-red and usually sparsely pubescent even when mature; flesh glutinous; nutlets three or four, not pitted on the inner faces.(*Brunetiána*, named for Abbé Louis Ovide Brunet.)

This hawthorn grows in thickets, on rocky banks, and along streams. It is frequent in the Lake Superior region, especially in Cook, Lake, and St. Louis counties, Minnesota. It is distributed from Newfoundland to Ontario, south to Nova Scotia, Maine, and Minnesota.

The species varies considerably in the depth of lobing of the leaves and in the degree of sharpness of the serrations. Minnesota collections previously referred to *C. columbiana* var. *Piperi* Britton belong to this species. The latter is a far western shrub.

DOWNY HAWTHORN,*Crataegus mollis* (T. & G.) Scheele, Linnaea 21:569, 1848

A tree sometimes up to 12 m. high, with spreading branches forming a broad-topped crown; spines few, mostly on the young growth, blackish-brown, shining, nearly straight, 4–6 cm. long; young twigs yellowish-green and villous, towards autumn turning dark yellow-brown and more or less glabrate, with numerous pale and conspicuous lenticels, in age becoming gray with a yellowish tinge; leaves broadly ovate, 6–10 cm. long, 5–10 cm. wide, coarsely and generally doubly serrate, the teeth spreading, often broad at the base and acuminate; leaves with four or five pairs of short or moderately deep lobes, the basal lobes usually longer than the others, truncate to cordate at the base, mostly acute at the apex, dark yellow-green above with slightly impressed veins, at first pubescent with short, pale hairs, later becoming scabrate, somewhat paler below and persistently tomentose, particularly along the veins; petioles 2–5 cm. long, stout, terete, tomentose, and with a few stalked glands; corymbs tomentose, four- to fifteen-flowered; flowers 2–2.5 cm. in diameter; hypanthium narrowly campanulate to obconic, tomentose; sepals with triangular base and acuminate tips, coarsely glandular-serrate, with bright-red glands, tomentose on both sides; stamens twenty, anthers pale yellow; disk somewhat concave; styles four or five, surrounded at the base by a ring of stiff hairs; fruit ellipsoid to subglobose,

1.5–2.5 cm. in diameter (calyx very conspicuous on the half-grown fruit, usually deciduous before it is ripe), scarlet, flesh thick, yellow; nutlets four or five, thin, rounded and obscurely ridged on the back, about 6 mm. long. (*Móllis*, soft, referring to the pubescence.)

Downy hawthorn grows on bottomlands, hillsides, and the borders of woods. It is common throughout the Upper Midwest as far north as the forty-fifth parallel. It is distributed from southern Ontario to Minnesota and eastern South Dakota, south to Alabama, Arkansas, and Oklahoma.

LARGE-SEED HAWTHORN, *Crataegus macrosperma* Ashe, Journ. E. Mitch. Soc. 16:73, 1900

A shrub or small tree up to 7 m. high, with ascending branches; spines numerous, curved, 2–5 cm. long, dark chestnut-brown, soon becoming gray; young twigs bronze-green, glabrous, by the end of the first season dull reddish-brown, with fairly well marked lenticels, very soon turning gray or grayish-brown; leaves elliptic-ovate to broadly ovate, 4–9 cm. long, 3–8 cm. wide, sharply doubly serrate, the teeth very spreading and acuminate; leaves with four to six pairs of short, broad, and often obscure acuminate lobes, broadly cuneate, rounded, truncate, or subcordate at the base, acute to short-acuminate at the apex, membranous, the veins not impressed, bronze-green and sparingly pubescent above when young, becoming dark yellow-green and slightly scabrate in age, much paler, subglaucous, and glabrous beneath; petiole slender, 1–4 cm. long, scarcely winged, glandular; corymbs very loose, five- to fifteen-flowered, glabrous or slightly villous; flowers 1.4–2 cm. in diameter; hypanthium narrowly campanulate, mostly sparingly villous; sepals mostly longer than the hypanthium, linear from a triangular base, entire or with one or two irregular, gland-tipped teeth, glabrous on the outside, sparingly pubescent on the inside; stamens five to twenty (usually five to ten), anthers small, pink; disk somewhat concave; styles two to four, surrounded at the base by a small tuft of hairs; fruit ellipsoid or

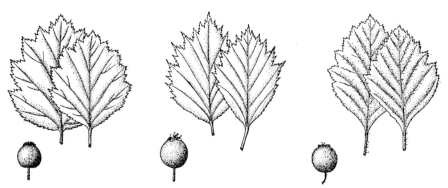

Species of *Crataegus*: Left, *C. macrosperma*. Center, *C. macrosperma* var. *roanensis*. Right, *C. Brunetiana*.

244

pyriform, scarlet to crimson, often glaucous, 10–18 mm. in diameter, flesh soft
when ripe, calyx persistent; nutlets two to four, thick, ridged on the back, flattened or with a short keel on the ventral surface, 7–8 mm. long. (*Macrospérma*,
large-seeded, referring to the nutlets.)

This hawthorn grows in woods and thickets, usually on rocky ground. It
occurs mainly in the hardwood forests of the region, and is common in the southeast, infrequent northward in Minnesota to Pine County in the east and to
Hubbard County in the northwest. It is distributed from New England to the
mountains of North Carolina and Tennessee, west to Minnesota and Illinois.

Crataegus macrosperma var. *roanensis* (Ashe) Palmer, Brittonia 5:486, 1946

This variety differs from the species in the smaller, more deeply indented
leaves, which have four or five pairs of acute, spreading, lateral lobes, often
acuminate but not reflexed at the tips. The fruit is 6–9 mm. in diameter, the
flesh firm.

The variety occurs in the range of the species, but in Minnesota somewhat
more frequently northward.

Cotoneaster

Cotoneaster Medic., Gesch. Bot. 85, 1793

Shrubs, sometimes becoming tree-like, evergreen or deciduous, hardly ever
thorny; leaves alternate, simple, entire, stipulate, short-petioled, mostly small
and numerous; flowers white or pink, solitary or numerous, in cymose clusters
terminating short, lateral, leafy shoots, appearing after the leaves are out; hypanthium campanulate, united with the ovary; sepals five, small, persistent on the
fruit; petals five; stamens about twenty; ovary inferior; fruit black or red, small,
generally long persistent; stones two to five. (*Cotonéaster*, Latin, quince-like, in
reference to the leaves of some species.)

This genus embraces about forty species of the temperate regions of the
Old World; they are most numerous in eastern Asia. The following species appears to be the only one so far cultivated to any extent in the state.

Cotoneaster lucida Schlecht., Linnaea 27:541, 1854

An upright, bushy shrub, 1–2 m. high; young twigs strigose-pubescent, becoming reddish-brown and glabrate toward the end of the season, during the
second year the outer epidermis exfoliating as a silvery-gray layer, exposing the
reddish-brown bark; older twigs dark brown or grayish-black; leaves thick and
firm in texture, elliptic or ovate, 2–5 cm. long, 10–28 mm. wide, mostly narrowed
at the base, broadly to narrowly acute at the apex, frequently mucronate, entire,
dark green and shining above, at first pubescent but later becoming glabrous,
paler beneath and pubescent; petiole 2–5 mm. long, pubescent; inflorescence
terminating short, leafy, lateral shoots, two- to four-flowered, the peduncle

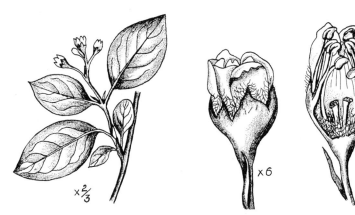

Cotoneaster lucida

strigose-pubescent; flowers pink; hypanthium broadly campanulate, sparsely pubescent; sepals triangular, erect or slightly spreading, tomentose along the margins and at the tips; petals obovate, crenulate-margined; stamens about twenty, shorter than the petals; fruit oblong, black when ripe, about 1 cm. long; stones two or three, pubescent at the summit and marked with a transverse band. Blossoms in June; fruit ripe in autumn and long persistent. (*Lúcida*, shining, referring to the glossy foliage.)

A native of the Altai Mountains and the Lake Baikal region of central Asia, this shrub has been in cultivation for a long time. It is frequently planted as an ornamental and is entirely hardy in our climate. It appears to be confused with the true Pekin Cotoneaster — *C. acutifolia* Turcz. or *C. acutifolia* var. *pekinensis* Koehne, which it closely resembles in habit as well as in foliage and flowers, but which, according to C. K. Schneider (Handb. Laubh. 1:751), is rather infrequent in cultivation.

Plum, Cherry
Prunus L., Sp. Pl. 473, 1753

Trees or shrubs, sometimes spiny; leaves alternate, simple, mostly serrate, and often bearing glands along the petiole or at the base of the blade, stipules small and early deciduous; flowers sometimes solitary but mostly in umbel-like clusters or racemes, white or pink; hypanthium campanulate or obconic; sepals five; petals five, spreading; stamens fifteen to thirty, distinct, inserted with the petals on the hypanthium; pistil normally one, simple, superior in the bottom of the hypanthium, style one, stigma capitate; ovules two; fruit a drupe; stone globose or oval and flattened, smooth or somewhat roughened, usually one-seeded. (*Prúnus*, the classical Latin name for the plum.)

This genus embraces about a hundred and fifty species, mostly of temperate climates of the Northern Hemisphere. In North America there are about thirty native species, some of which are of importance in horticulture.

ROSE FAMILY

1. Flowers single (i.e., petals normally five). CHERRIES AND PLUMS.
   2. Trees or large shrubs; leaves broad or, if narrow, serrate almost to the base.
      3. Flowers in racemes, terminating short, leafy shoots. CHOKECHERRIES.
         4. Small trees or large shrubs; bark smooth; leaves elliptic or oval to obovate; principal lateral veins beneath prominent; only basal part of hypanthium persisting as a collar in fruit.
            5. Racemes loose-flowered, pendulous or spreading; petals about twice as long as stamens; hypanthium hairy within; stone strongly corrugated...................................*P. Padus* (p. 248)
            5. Racemes dense-flowered, ascending or horizontal; petals about as long as stamens; hypanthium smooth or nearly so within; stone smooth..... ....*P. virginiana* (p. 248)
         4. Medium-sized to large tree; bark rough; leaves oblong to oblong-lanceolate; principal lateral veins beneath not raised; entire hypanthium persistent in fruit...................................*P. serotina* (p. 250)
      3. Flowers in umbel-like clusters, appearing from clustered buds, with or before the leaves.
         6. Branches usually thorny or armed; fruit subglobose or sulcate, usually borne singly. PLUMS.
            7. Foliage purple; small tree; cultivated............................ ....*P. cerasifera* var. *atropurpurea* (p. 250)
            7. Foliage green; native trees.
               8. Teeth of leaves gland-tipped; calyx lobes glandular; stone much flattened...............................*P. nigra* (p. 251)
               8. Teeth of leaves acute, bristle-tipped; calyx lobes not glandular; stone round............................. *P. americana* (p. 251)
         6. Branches not thorny or armed; fruit globose, not sulcate, usually in clusters. CHERRIES.
            9. Flowers in corymbs; petals 4–6 mm. long; fruit 3–6 mm. in diameter; native tree or shrub....................*P. pensylvanica* (p. 251)
            9. Flowers in umbels; petals 8–12 mm. long; fruit 8–25 mm. in diameter; cultivated.
               10. Trees 4–8 m. high, fruit red, 8–15 mm. in diameter............ ....*P. Cerasus* (p. 252)
               10 Shrubs or shrub-like trees 1–2.5 m. high; fruit dark red or nearly black, 2–2.5 cm. in diameter.
                  11. Flowers numerous, fruit black or nearly so, in dense, numerous clusters along the slender branches... × *P. zumbra* (p. 252)
                  11. Flowers less numerous; fruit dark red, not densely crowded on the branches................× *P. Knudsoni* (p. 252)
   2. Dwarf shrubs (3–15 dm. high); leaves relatively narrow, not serrate at the cuneate base. SAND CHERRIES.
      12. Leaves usually narrowly oblanceolate-spatulate and acute; flowering branches generally wand-like.....................*P. pumila* (p. 254)
      12. Leaves oblong-spatulate to oval or somewhat obovate.
         13. Petioles 5–10 mm. long; leaves 3–6 cm. long, obtuse or sometimes acute at the apex; fruit 10–14 mm. in diameter; branches erect or ascending ....*P. susquehanae* (p. 254)
         13. Petioles 5–6 mm. long; leaves 3–4.5 cm. long, acute or rarely obtuse at the apex, thick and firm; fruit about 15–18 mm. in diameter; branches irregularly spreading........................*P. Besseyi* (p. 256)
1. Flowers double (i.e., with numerous petals). FLOWERING ALMONDS AND FLOWERING PLUMS.

14. Leaves obovate, abruptly acuminate, sharply serrate.
  15. Leaves densely tomentose beneath..............*P. tomentosa* (p. 256)
  15. Leaves sparingly pubescent on both sides, often tending to be three-lobed
    at the apex....................................*P. triloba* (p. 257)
14. Leaves oblong-lanceolate, blunt or acutish at the apex, crenate-serrate, the
  serrations glandular-serrulate....................*P. glandulosa* (p. 257)

EUROPEAN BIRD CHERRY, *Prunus Padus* L., Sp. Pl. 473, 1753

A small tree 5–10 m. high; bark dull dark-gray, inner bark yellow with disagreeable odor; leaves elliptic or oval to oblong-ovate or obovate, 6–10 cm. long, 3–6 cm. wide, slightly obliquely rounded or subcordate at the base, acute to short-acuminate at the apex, finely and sharply serrate, dark green and glabrous above, somewhat bluish-green and glabrous beneath or sometimes with tufts of rusty pubescence in the axils of the principal veins; petiole 10–15 mm. long, usually with two prominent glands near the base of the blade; racemes rather loose-flowered, 7–15 cm. long, spreading or drooping; flowers white, 13–16 mm. in diameter; hypanthium short campanulate, woolly-pubescent within, only its base remaining as a collar at the base of the ripe fruit; sepals ovate, about half as long as the hypanthium, prominently glandular-serrate; petals obovate, about twice as long as the stamens; pedicels 6–10 mm. long, sometimes up to 20 mm.; fruit 6–8 mm. in diameter, black when ripe, bitter; stone prominently corrugated. Blossoms in May. (*Pádus*, the ancient Greek name for this species of cherry.)

This native of Europe and Asia is ornamental and is occasionally planted.

CHOKECHERRY, *Prunus virginiana* L., Sp. Pl. 473, 1753

A tall shrub or small tree, 1–4 m. high with grayish-brown bark, the inner layers of which have a strong, disagreeable odor, lenticels numerous, light-colored; leaves oval, oblong, or obovate, 4–8 cm. long, 2–4.5 cm. wide, acute or short-acuminate at the apex, rounded or sometimes narrowed at the base, sharply and finely serrate, dark green and glabrous above, somewhat paler beneath, glabrous or slightly pubescent along the veins; the lateral nerves prominent, the reticulate veins appearing dark against the paler background, becoming impressed in drying; petiole 1–1.5 cm. long, with from one to several glands; racemes erect or spreading, dense-flowered, 5–12 cm. long; flowers white, strong-scented, 8–10 mm. broad; hypanthium short-campanulate, nearly glabrous within, only its base remaining as a small collar at the base of the fruit; sepals ovate, glandular-serrate; petals obovate, slightly exceeding the stamens; stamens about thirty; pedicels 4–6 mm. long; fruit dark red or nearly black, 8–10 mm. in diameter, very astringent; stone globose, smooth. Blossoms in May; fruit ripe in July and August. (*Virginiána*, Virginian.)

Chokecherry grows in thickets, on shores, and on the borders of woods; it is common throughout the region. It is distributed from Newfoundland to Saskatchewan, south to New England, North Carolina, Tennessee, Missouri, and Kansas. Several varieties occur farther west.

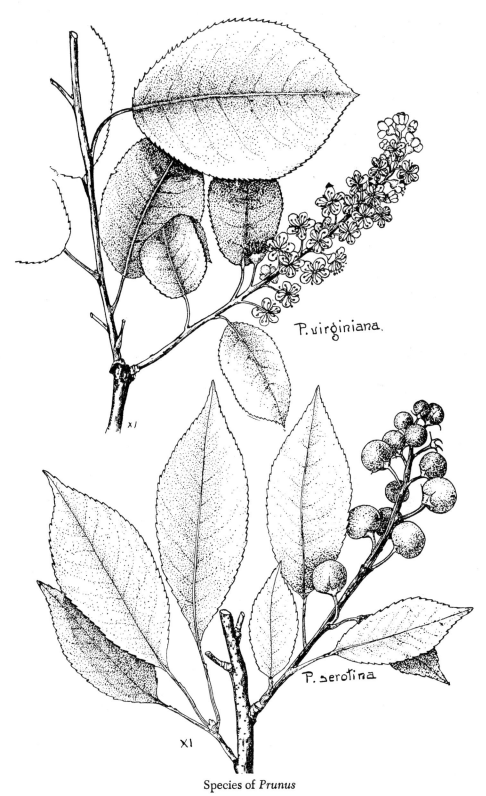

P. virginiana.

P. serotina

Species of *Prunus*

249

WILD BLACK CHERRY, CABINET CHERRY, RUM CHERRY, *Prunus serotina* Erhr., Beitr. 3:20, 1788

A medium-sized to large tree, 12–25 m. high and 2–6 dm. in diameter (in more southern latitudes reaching much greater dimensions); the bark of the trunk dark brown, very rough, and peeling off in flakes, the bark of the young branches and twigs reddish-brown, the inner layers fragrant; lenticels numerous; leaves narrowly ovate to elliptic-lanceolate, 4–12 cm. long, 2.5–3.5 cm. wide, mostly narrowed at the base, long-acuminate at the apex, serrate with appressed callous teeth, of firm texture, glabrous and shining above, glabrous or sparingly pubescent along the veins beneath, the lateral veins not prominent, the reticulate veins not appearing darker against the background, becoming more or less raised in drying; petiole 10–18 mm. long with from two to four glands; racemes spreading or erect, 8–15 cm. long; flowers numerous, white, 8–10 mm. broad; pedicels 8–10 mm. long; hypanthium short campanulate, nearly glabrous within, persisting at the base of the fruit; sepals oblong to triangular, separated by broad sinuses, more or less glandular-serrate, persistent; petals obovate, about 4 mm. long; stamens twenty, about as long as the petals; fruit black, globose, 7–10 mm. in diameter, dark purple to black, edible but somewhat astringent; stone smooth. Blossoms in May and early June; fruit ripe in August and September. (*Serótina*, autumnal, referring to the late ripening of the fruit.)

This cherry is common in the hardwood forests of the region, infrequent northeastward, and absent north of Lake Superior. It is distributed from Nova Scotia and southern Quebec to Minnesota and North Dakota, south to Florida and Texas.

The wood is bright red-brown, close-grained and hard, weighing 36 lbs. It takes a beautiful finish and is extensively used in cabinet-making — with the exception of black walnut, probably the finest of our native woods.

Prunus cerasifera var. *atropurpúrea* Jäger, in Jäger & Biessn., Ziergeh. ed. 2, 262, 1884 [*P. Pissardii* Car. Rev. Hort. 1881]

A large shrub or small tree, generally somewhat thorny, with slender branches and ovate, reddish-purple leaves; flowers borne singly, appearing with the leaves, about 2 cm. in diameter, pink; fruit dark wine-red. (*Cerasífera*, cherry-bearing; *atropurpúrea*, dark purple.)

This small tree was introduced to France by M. Pissart, gardener to the Shah of Persia. It is occasionally cultivated in this country as an ornamental tree on account of its attractive foliage. It does not grow very satisfactorily in Minnesota, but a form with similarly colored leaves, a cross between the variety and the Omaha Plum (*P. americana* × *triflora*), developed at the State Fruit Breeding Farm at Zumbra Heights and known as the Newport Plum, has proved entirely hardy for the general region. It is a tree with deep reddish-purple foliage, which retains its color throughout the season; the fruit is small to medium-sized, but of poor quality.

CANADA PLUM, WILD PLUM, *Prunus nigra* Ait., Hort. Kew 2:165, 1789

A shrub or small tree, 2–7 m. high, armed with thorns; bark brownish-gray, exfoliating in plates; leaves oval to broadly ovate, 7–13 cm. long, 3–7 cm. wide; obtuse or slightly cordate at the base, long-acuminate at the apex, crenate-serrate, the teeth usually gland-tipped, pubescent when young, petiole 1–1.5 cm. long with one or two red glands near the base; flowers in lateral umbels, opening before the leaves, 2.5–3 cm. broad, very fragrant; calyx lobes glandular-serrate, glabrous within; petals white, pinkish-tinged toward the base, broadly obovate, 1.2–1.4 cm. long; stamens pinkish-tinged; fruit orange-pink or yellow, subglobose or compressed ovoid, with little or no bloom, 2.5 cm. long; stone oval, compressed or flattened. Blossoms in May; fruit ripe in August. (*Nígra*, black.)

Canada plum grows in thickets, on stream banks, and on the borders of woods. It is not common, but occurs scattered in most of the forested areas south as far as latitude 44° N. and occasionally farther southeastward. It is distributed from Quebec to Manitoba, south to New England, Virginia, northern Ohio, Indiana, and Iowa.

The fruit is delicious and rather firm-fleshed. It is used for making jellies and preserves.

WILD PLUM, *Prunus americana* Marsh., Arb. Am. 111, 1785

A shrub or a small tree, 3–10 m. high; branches more or less thorny; bark thick and rough, dark brownish-gray, exfoliating in irregular plates; leaves ovate or obovate, rounded at the base, long-acuminate at the apex, sharply and doubly serrate, the teeth bristle-tipped, not glandular, pubescent when young, glabrous or nearly so when mature, 4–10 cm. long, 2–5 cm. wide; petiole with or without glands, about 1 cm. long; flowers in sessile, lateral umbels, opening before the leaves, white, 1.5–2.5 cm. broad, very fragrant; pedicels 1.5–2.5 cm. long; calyx lobes entire, hairy on the inner surface; petals narrowly obovate, about 1 cm. long; fruit subglobose, red or yellow, 1.5–2 cm. in diameter, bloom light or none; stone but little flattened, slightly rugose. Flowers in April and May; fruit ripe in August and September. (*Americána*, American.)

Wild plum is common in thickets, along roadsides and riverbanks, and in similar places throughout the region. It is distributed from Connecticut to Montana, south to Florida, New Mexico, and northern Mexico.

The fruit has a tough, astringent skin, and a pleasantly flavored, subacid, juicy flesh. It is frequently eaten raw, and is much used for making jellies and preserves. This and the preceding species are the source of nearly all the cultivated plums grown in Minnesota, in some cases directly, by selection, in others by hybridization with other species.

PIN CHERRY, WILD RED CHERRY, *Prunus pensylvanica* L. f., Suppl. 252, 1781

A tall shrub or a small tree, 5–10 m. high; bark light reddish-brown, bitter and aromatic, on the trunk separating horizontally into broad, papery plates; leaves oblong-lanceolate, 4–8 cm. long, 1–3 cm. wide, rounded at the base, acute or acuminate at the apex, finely and sharply serrate, with unequal serrations, shining, green and glabrous on both sides, petiole 1-2 cm. long; flowers numerous, in umbel-like clusters, white, appearing with the leaves, 1–1.2 cm. broad; sepals 2 mm. long, glabrous; petals ovate, 5 mm. long; pedicels 1.5–2.5 cm. long; fruit globose, light red, 4–6 mm. in diameter, without bloom, its flesh thin and sour; stone globular. Flowers in April and May; fruit ripe in August. (*Pensylvánica*, named from the original locality.)

Pin cherry grows in woods, thickets, and clearings. It is common throughout the Upper Midwest, especially northward, infrequent to rare in the southwest. It is distributed from Labrador to British Columbia, south to New England, Virginia, the mountains of North Carolina, Tennessee, Illinois, Iowa, and South Dakota.

The fruit is sometimes used domestically and in the preparation of medicine. The light-brown wood is soft, light, and close-grained; it weighs 31 lbs.

SOUR, PIE, or MORELLO CHERRY, *Prunus Cerasus* L., Sp. Pl. 474, 1753

A small tree, 2–4 m. high with a round crown; bark gray; leaves ovate to obovate, 4–8 cm. long, 2–5 cm. wide; rounded at the base, abruptly short-pointed at the apex, serrate, firm in texture and more or less glossy above; flowers in small clusters, from lateral buds appearing mostly before the leaves, large, 3–4 cm. broad; petals 1.2–1.5 cm. long; fruit depressed, globose, 8–15 mm. in diameter. Flowers in May; fruit ripe in July. (*Cerásus*, Greek for cherry tree, from the town Cerasus in Pontus, where the cherry is native.)

This cherry is commonly cultivated in the southeastern part of the area. It was introduced from southern Europe and is probably a native of Asia Minor.

ZUMBRA CHERRY, × *Prunus zumbra* Rosend. & Butters, Trees & Shrubs of Minn. 227, 1928 [*P. avium* × (*pensylvanica* × *pumila*)?]

A low-growing tree of vigorous growth; leaves ovate, narrowed toward the base, acute at the apex, serrate, the serratures rather widely spaced, somewhat rugose and shining above; flowers in many-flowered umbels along the slender branches of the previous season; fruit subglobose, in very dense clusters, 2–2.5 cm. in diameter, nearly black when ripe, flesh firm, greenish, sometimes tinged with red when fully mature, of good quality and with somewhat the flavor of the sweet cherry. (*Zumbra*, named from the place of origin.)

The parentage of this hybrid is not entirely certain. It was developed at the State Fruit Breeding Farm at Zumbra Heights, Minnesota.

COMPASS CHERRY, × *Prunus Knudsoni* Rosend. & Butters, Trees & Shrubs of Minn. 227, 1928 [*P. hortulana* var. *Mineri* × *pumila* Ann. Rep. Minn. State Hort. Soc. 24:132, 1896]

A small tree, 2–4 m. high; leaves oblong or oblong-oval, 5–9 cm. long, 2.5–4

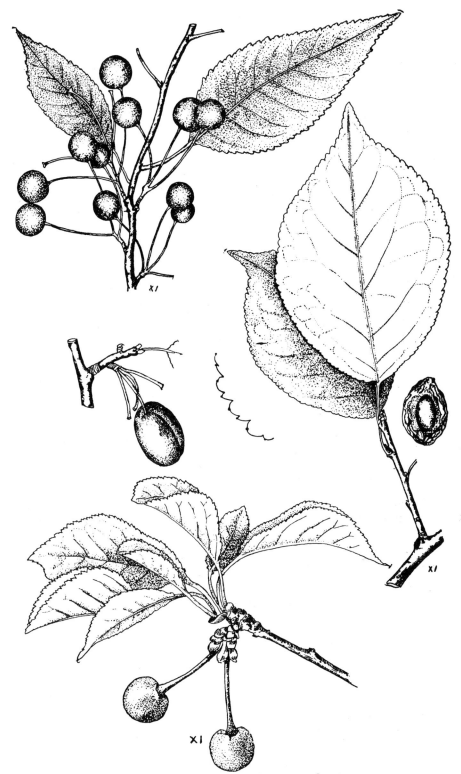

Species of *Prunus*: Top, left, *P. pensylvanica.*
Center, *P. nigra.* Bottom, *P. Cerasus.*

cm. wide, narrowed or rounded toward the base, acute or short-acuminate at the apex, serrate, with rounded or glandular teeth, dark green and glabrous above, paler and sparingly pubescent beneath; flowers appearing mostly before the leaves, about 2 cm. in diameter; pedicels 5–8 mm. long; hypanthium campanulate, sepals oblong, about as long as the tube, glandular; fruit dark red, 2–2.5 cm. in diameter; stone oval. Blossoms in May; fruit ripe in early August. (*Knúdsoni*, named for H. Knudson, a Minnesota horticulturist.)

This hybrid is frequently cultivated, though the fruit is of little value. It was originated by H. Knudson as a cross between the Miner plum and a sand cherry, reported to be *P. Besseyi*, but more probably *P. pumila*, as it was obtained from eastern Minnesota.

SAND CHERRY, *Prunus pumila* L., Mant. 75, 1767

A shrub with a willow-like habit of growth, 5–15 dm. high, the stems generally unbranched, erect and wand-like or sometimes branching near the base and ascending but never prostrate; young twigs angled, reddish-brown, dotted with small, lighter-colored lenticels; the bark of the stems and the twigs of the previous season gray but turning dark brown with age; leaves oblanceolate to obovate or narrowly elliptic, 3–7 cm. long, 1–2.5 cm. wide, more or less acute at the apex, gradually narrowed to the base, serrate from below the middle, the serrations of the young leaves appressed and obscure but becoming much more prominent with age and on the leaves which appear later in the season, bright green above, somewhat paler beneath and with prominent veins, glabrous throughout; petiole 6–12 mm. long; stipules subulate, 4–7 mm. long, conspicuously fimbriate; flowers in fascicles of two to four, appearing with the leaves, 10–15 mm. in diameter, sepals oblong, 2–2.3 mm. long, serrulate-margined; pedicels 10–14 mm. long, slender, fruit globose, 10–15 mm. long, nearly black when ripe, usually astringent and of poor quality; stone ovoid, more or less pointed at the apex, slightly grooved on either side of the ventral ridge. Blossoms from about the middle of May until early June; fruit ripe in July and August. (*Púmila*, dwarf, referring to the low stature.)

This cherry is common on sandy lake shores, outwash plains, dunes, and jack pine barrens, in Wisconsin and Minnesota. It is distributed from Ontario south to the St. Lawrence Basin from New York to Minnesota.

APPALACHIAN CHERRY, *Prunus susquehanae* Willd. Enum. Pl. Hort. Berol. 519, 1809 [*P. cuneata* Raf. 1820]

A low shrub, 3–12 dm. high, with ascending or erect stems, often considerably branched and bushy; young twigs glabrous, at first reddish-brown, becoming gray with age, lenticels generally numerous but small and obscure; leaves elliptic to narrowly obovate or oblanceolate, 3–6 cm. long, 8–22 mm. wide, obtuse or sometimes acute at the apex, gradually narrowed toward the base, usually serrate above the middle but the teeth mostly obscure and with incurved points,

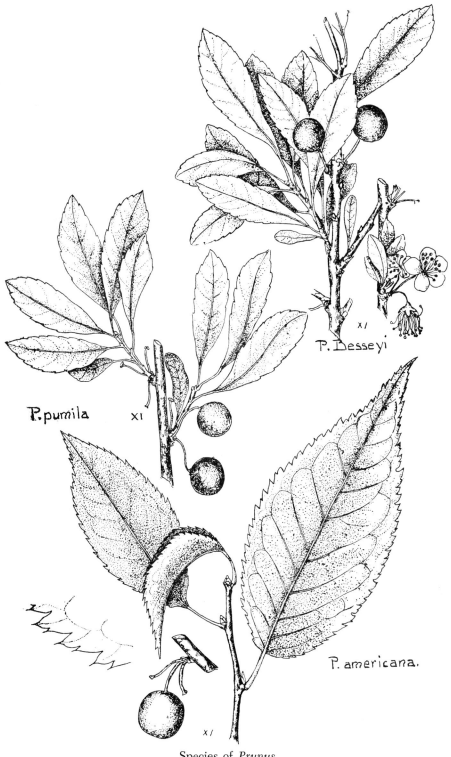

P. Desseyi

X I

P. pumila

X I

P. americana.

Species of *Prunus*

255

green and glabrous above, pale and glaucous beneath; petioles 5–10 mm. long; stipules subulate 4–5 mm. long, with fimbriate margins, deciduous; flowers mostly in fascicles of three, appearing with or shortly after the leaves, 10–12 mm. in diameter; sepals ovate-oblong, 1.5–2 mm. long, with serrulate margins; pedicels very slender, 6–10 mm. long; fruit nearly black, subglobose, 10–14 mm. long; pedicels slender, 6–12 mm. long; stone oblong-ovate, somewhat pointed at the apex, 7–9 mm. long, 5–6 mm. in diameter. Blossoms in May; fruit ripe in July and August. (*Susquehánae*, referring to the original locality on the banks of the Susquehanna River.)

This cherry grows in sandy, wet to dry habitats, often on rocky bluffs and hillsides, mostly in the eastern part of the area. It is distributed from Maine and southwestern Quebec to southeastern Manitoba, south to Long Island, Virginia, Illinois, and Minnesota.

This species differs from *P. pumila* in the less wand-like habit of growth, in the relatively shorter and broader, more acutely toothed and coriaceous leaves, and in the larger fruit, up to 1.8 cm. in diameter.

WESTERN SAND CHERRY, *Prunus Besseyi* Bailey, Bull. Cornell Exp. Sta. 70:261, 1804*

A low, bushy shrub 3–12 dm. high, the branches diffuse, spreading or more or less prostrate, not strict; bark grayish; leaves oval-elliptic or oblong-obovate, rarely narrower and oblanceolate, 3–3.5 cm. long, 9–12 mm. broad, acute or rarely obtuse at the apex, cuneate at the base, serrate from below the middle, thick and somewhat rugose, glabrous on both surfaces; petiole 5–6 mm. long; flowers in fascicles of three or four, appearing with or before the leaves, 10–12 mm. in diameter; pedicels and calyx glabrous, pedicels 6–7 mm. long; fruit globose or somewhat oblong, nearly black when ripe or sometimes yellowish, 15–18 mm. long, about as long as the stout pedicel; stone nearly globose to somewhat ovoid, 7.5–10 mm. long, mostly obtuse at the apex. (*Bésseyi*, named for Professor C. E. Bessey.)

This shrub grows on sandy hills, open plains, and rocky slopes and shores, in western Minnesota and the adjacent parts of South and North Dakota and Manitoba. It is distributed from Manitoba to Minnesota and southwestward to Nebraska, Kansas, and Wyoming.

NANKIN CHERRY, *Prunus tomentosa* Thunb., Flor. Jap. 203, 1784

A compact, bushy-topped shrub, not over 1.5 m. high in cultivation; twigs of the first and second year more or less densely yellowish-gray-pubescent, slightly angled, later becoming brown with gradually exfoliating outer bark;

* The three species of sand cherries are poorly defined and in Minnesota, at least, they seem to grade into each other almost imperceptibly. It is therefore nearly impossible to distinguish them by the characters that are generally given to differentiate species, and it might be better to regard *P. pumila* as a single, somewhat polymorphic species, tending towards *P. susquehanae* in the eastern and *P. Besseyi* in the southwestern parts of the region.

leaves crowded, broadly oval to obovate, 3–7 cm. long, 2–4 cm. wide, abruptly acuminate at the apex, narrowed toward the base, rather coarsely serrate, dull green, rugose and more or less pubescent above, densely yellowish-gray-tomentose beneath; petiole 5–7 mm. long, stipules twice as long as the petiole; flowers appearing shortly before the leaves, mostly one or two or else clustered on spurs, nearly sessile, 12-18 mm. in diameter; hypanthium narrowly campanulate, red; sepals erect or somewhat spreading; petals white or tinted (numerous in some forms); fruit globular, light red, slightly pubescent. Blossoms in May; fruit ripe in July. (*Tomentósa*, tomentose or woolly-pubescent.)

This cherry is a native of China and Manchuria. The form most frequently cultivated in the Upper Midwest is the one with double flowers.

FLOWERING PLUM, *Prunus triloba* Lindl., Gard. Chron. 268, 1857

An erect shrub, 1–3 m. high, with spreading or ascending branches; bark brownish; young shoots reddish, puberulous or glabrous; leaves obovate, 3–6 cm. long, 2–4 cm. wide; cuneate at the base, three-lobed and abruptly pointed at the apex, sometimes merely obtuse or acute, coarsely and doubly serrate, rough with a few bristly hairs and impressed-veined on the upper surface, prominently veined and with scattered hairs beneath; petiole 1–1.5 cm. long, pubescent along the upper side; flowers solitary, appearing before the leaves, 3–4 cm. broad, petals numerous, light pink; pistil hairy; the fruit usually does not set from the double flowers; from fertile flowers the fruit is small, red, and shining when ripe. Flowers in May. (*Triloba*, three-lobed, in reference to the leaf.)

This shrub is a native of China. The commonly cultivated form is the one with double flowers (f. *plena* Dipp.). It is entirely hardy in our climate, but is not as free-flowering as the following species.

FLOWERING CHERRY, FLOWERING ALMOND, *Prunus glandulosa* Thunb., Flor. Jap. 202, 1784 [*P. japonica* of various authors, including Minn. T. & S. 1912, not Thunb.]

A shrub 8–12 dm. high; branches erect or ascending, reddish, especially on the upper side, glabrous; leaves oblong-lanceolate or lanceolate, 4–8 cm. long, 1–3 cm. wide, narrowed or slightly rounded at the base, tapering above, but usually blunt at the apex, crenate-serrate, the serrations glandular-serrulate, glabrous above, pubescent on the veins beneath, the veins and reticulations prominent beneath; petioles 3–4 mm. long, pubescent; stipules lance-linear, generally remotely glandular-serrate, 5–6 mm. long; flowers appearing just before or with the leaves, single or in clusters of two or three, blush pink or sometimes paler, 2–3 cm. in diameter; petals very numerous, stamens few or lacking, the double flowers usually producing no fruit (when formed, the ripe fruit is globular or short oblong, about 12 mm. in diameter, red, smooth and shining). Blossoms in April or early May. (*Glandulósa*, glandular, probably referring to the glandular serrations of the leaf.)

Species of *Prunus*: Left *P. glandulosa*. Right, *P. triloba*.

Flowering almond is a native of central and northern China and Japan. The form in cultivation in the Upper Midwest is the one with double flowers (f. *sinensis* Koehne). It is a handsome ornamental shrub and is reasonably hardy, but does best with a slight covering during the winter.

PULSE OR PEA FAMILY, Leguminosae

Herbs, shrubs, vines, or trees; leaves alternate, mostly compound, with stipules; flowers perfect, monoecious, dioecious, or polygamous, in spikes, heads, racemes, or panicles, apopetalous, hypogynous, or perigynous and regular or irregular; sepals three to five, more or less united; petals five, rarely fewer; stamens ten, more or less united by their filaments or distinct; pistil one, simple, from one- to many-seeded, becoming a pod or legume in fruit. The typical flower of this family — e.g., the pea — has the sepals united into an irregular cup; the petals of three forms, an upper odd petal (standard), two lateral, spreading petals (the wings), and two lower ones (the keel), more or less united and enclosing the stamens and pistil; nine of the stamens united by their filaments into a group, the tenth stamen free.

This immense family numbers fully twelve thousand species, widely distributed from the tropics to the frigid zones.

KEY TO GENERA OF LEGUMINOSAE

1. Flowers regular or nearly so, imperfect, monoecious or dioecious. Large trees.
   2. Leaflets ovate, acuminate at the apex, margin entire; calyx tube elongated; stamens ten . . . .*Gymnocladus* (p. 259)

258

2. Leaflets oblong-lanceolate, rounded at the apex, margin crenulate-serrate; calyx tube short; stamens three to five........................*Gleditsia* (p. 261)
1. Flowers irregular, papilionaceous (sometimes with only one petal), perfect. Trees or shrubs.
   3. Flowers numerous, in spikes or racemes, not yellow.
      4. Flowers small, in dense spikes, one petaled; pods less than 2 cm. long......
      ....*Amorpha* (p. 261)
      4. Flowers large, in drooping racemes; pods over 2 cm. long..*Robinia* (p. 263)
   3. Flowers solitary or in few-flowered racemes, yellow........*Caragana* (p. 265)

Kentucky Coffee-Tree
Gymnocladus Lam., Encycl. Meth. Bot. 1:733, 1783

Trees with rough bark and stout branchlets; leaves large and bipinnate; flowers showy, in terminal racemes, monoecious or dioecious; calyx tubular, five-lobed, lobes narrow; petals five, oblong, equal, inserted at the top of the calyx tube; stamens ten, distinct, short; pistil rudimentary or lacking in the staminate flowers, sessile and many-ovuled in the pistillate and polygamous ones; fruit an oblong pod, flat, hard, pulpy inside; seeds numerous. (*Gymnócladus,* Greek *gymnos,* naked, *clados,* branch, in allusion to the stout, naked branches.)

This is a monotypic genus of eastern North America.

KENTUCKY COFFEE-TREE, *Gymnocladus dioica* (L.) K. Koch, Dendrol. 1:5, 1869

A tree attaining a height of 15–30 m. and a trunk diameter of 1.5–8 dm.; bark gray; deep-fissured and roughened by persistent scales; buds small, in hairy cavities, two in the axil of each leaf, one above the other, the lower sterile; leaves large, 6–9 dm. long, bipinnate, the pinnae with seven to fifteen leaflets each, leaflets stalked, ovate, 2–10 cm. long, 2–6 cm. wide, rounded at the base, acute or acuminate at the apex, sometimes pubescent on the veins beneath; racemes many-flowered, 10–18 cm. long; flowers 15–18 mm. long; calyx tube

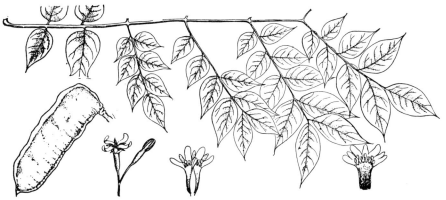

Gymnocladus dioica. (Leaf and pod × 1/3, flowers nearly natural size.)

Gleditsia triacanthos. (Leaves × 2/3, staminate and pistillate flowers × 4.)

campanulate, 1 cm. long; pod 12–25 cm. long, 4–5 cm. wide. Flowers in June. (*Dioíca*, dioecious.)

Kentucky coffee-tree grows in rich soil, mostly on river bottoms. It is common in the south, infrequent northward in the Mississippi River Valley to St. Paul and in the valley of the Minnesota River west to New Ulm. It is distributed from New York to South Dakota, south to Tennessee, Missouri, and Arkansas.

The wood is heavy but not very hard, strong and coarse-grained and very durable in contact with the soil. It is light brown and takes a good polish; its weight is 48 lbs. Though not very ornamental, it is often planted as a park tree.

Honey Locust
Gleditsia L., Sp. Pl. 1056, 1753

Thorny trees (sometimes unarmed) with evenly, once or twice pinnate leaves; thorns branched or simple, situated above the axils of the leaves, often very large; flowers small, greenish, in axillary spikes; calyx short, three- to five-cleft; petals equal, the two lower sometimes united; stamens three to ten, distinct; pistil rudimentary or none in the staminate flowers, in the pistillate ones elongated or ovoid; ovules two to many; pods flat, nearly straight at first, twisted at maturity, pulpy between the seeds. (*Gledítsia*, named for J. G. Gleditsch, a German botanist who lived at the same time as Linnaeus.)

This is a genus of five species, natives of eastern North America and Asia. Besides the following, one other species occurs in the southeastern United States.

HONEY LOCUST, *Gleditsia triacanthos*, L., Sp. Pl. 1056, 1753

A tree attaining a height of 15–20 m. within our range and a trunk diameter of 15–40 cm.; bark dark brown, fissured; thorns large and numerous, simple or branched; branches slender, spreading or somewhat pendulous, with numerous lenticels; buds minute, several together and superposed, upper ones with scurfy scales, the others hidden by the base of the petiole; leaves one- or two-pinnate, 10–20 cm. long; leaflets short-stalked, oblong-lanceolate, somewhat crenulate, 2–3 cm. long, 6–10 mm. wide; inflorescence 5–10 cm. long, the staminate more slender than the pistillate; calyx obconic; pods 15–45 cm. long, bent or twisted, pulp sweetish, edible. (*Triacánthos*, three-spined.)

Honey locust grows in rich woods. As a native tree it occurs infrequently southward, barely reaching the southeastern border of Minnesota, but it is often planted and entirely hardy in the region of the Twin Cities. It is distributed from western New York to South Dakota, south to Florida and Texas.

The wood is red or light reddish-brown in color, coarse-grained, hard, strong, and durable in contact with the soil; its weight is 42 lbs. It is used for fence posts, rails, hubs of wheels, and the like. It is frequently planted as a park tree.

Gleditsia triacanthos f. *inermis* (L.) Zabel, in Biessn. *et al.*, Handb. Laubh. 255, 1903

This form of the species is almost or quite thornless. It is occasionally cultivated in the Upper Midwest. (*Inérmis*, unarmed, referring to the lack of thorns.)

False Indigo
Amorpha L., Sp. Pl. 713, 1753

Branching shrubs with odd-pinnate, compound leaves; leaflets marked with minute dots or glands; flowers violet or purple, in dense terminal spikes; calyx

Species of *Amorpha*: Left, *A. canescens.* Center, *A. nana.* Right, *A. fruticosa.*

teeth five, nearly equal; only one petal, the standard, present, wrapped around the stamens and style; stamens ten, united at the base; pistil two-celled; fruit an oblong pod, exceeding the calyx, one- or two-seeded, tardily splitting. (*Amórpha*, Greek *amorphos*, without form, referring to the absence of four of the petals.)

This genus includes about fifteen species, natives of North America and Mexico.

KEY TO SPECIES OF AMORPHA

1. Tall shrub, 1–3 m. high; leaflets 2–5 cm. long . . . .*A. fruticosa* (p. 262)
1. Low shrubs, 3–14 dm. high; leaflets 6–12 mm. long.
    2. Densely silky-hairy all over, 3–14 dm. high . . . .*A. canescens* (p. 263)
    2. Smooth or nearly so throughout, 3 dm. high or less . . . .*A. nana* (p. 263)

FALSE INDIGO, *Amorpha fruticosa* L., Sp. Pl. 713, 1753

A shrub 1–3 m. high; leaves 15–30 cm. long; leaflets nine to twenty-five, short-stalked, oblong or broadly elliptic, rounded and mucronate at the tip, rounded or slightly narrowed at the base, 2–3.5 cm. long, 1.2 cm. wide; spikes 7–15 cm.

long, clustered or solitary; flowers very numerous, purple, 7–10 mm. long; stamens exserted, with bright-orange anthers; pod 5–10 mm. long with numerous dark glands, thick-stalked. (*Fruticósa*, shrubby.)

False indigo grows along river banks, lake shores, and in rich thickets. It is common throughout our region northward to the borders of the coniferous forest. It is a widely distributed species with numerous geographic varieties, and ranges from Pennsylvania to Manitoba and Saskatchewan, south to Florida, Louisiana, Texas, and Arizona.

LEAD PLANT, SHOESTRING, *Amorpha canescens* Pursh, Fl. Am. Sept. 2:467, 1814

A bushy shrub, 3–14 dm. high, densely white-canescent all over; stems longitudinally ridged or furrowed; leaves 5–10 cm. long, leaflets twenty-one to forty-nine, crowded, oblong-elliptic, short-stalked, rounded at the base, obtuse or acutish and mucronate at the apex, less hairy on the upper than on the lower side, 8–14 mm. long, 4–9 mm. wide; spikes densely clustered at the summit of the stems, 5–18 cm. long; flowers deep purple; stamens orange-yellow; pods one-seeded, slightly exceeding the calyx in length. Blossoms in June and July. (*Canéscens*, hoary.)

Growing on exposed hillsides, sandy prairies, gravelly moraines, and dunes, this shrub is common throughout the Upper Midwest except northeastward in the coniferous forest area. It is distributed from Michigan to Saskatchewan, south to Indiana, Illinois, Arkansas, Texas, and New Mexico.

FRAGRANT FALSE INDIGO, *Amorpha nana* Nutt., in Fraser, Cat. 1813 [*A. microphylla* Pursh 1814]

A low, bushy shrub, 2–3 dm. high; branches glabrous or nearly so throughout; leaves 3–8 cm. long; leaflets thirteen to nineteen, oval or oblong, rounded at the base, blunt and mucronate at the tip, glabrous or nearly so, with glistening glands or dots, rather firm in texture; spikes usually only one to a branch, 4–7 cm. long; flowers fragrant, dark purple; pods one-seeded, gland-dotted, about 3 mm. long. (*Nána*, dwarf.)

Fragrant false indigo, which is common in the prairies of western Minnesota, ranges from Manitoba and Saskatchewan south to Iowa and Kansas. It blossoms in May, bearing dense spikes of dark-purple, very fragrant flowers, a handsome element of the prairie flora.

Locust

Robinia L., Sp. Pl. 722, 1753

Small to medium-sized trees or shrubs with rough and furrowed bark and spiny stipules or, in the shrubby form, bristly; leaves alternate, compound, odd-pinnate; leaflets oblong or ovate, short-stalked; flowers showy, white or deep-rose color, in hanging axillary racemes; calyx five-toothed, the two upper teeth

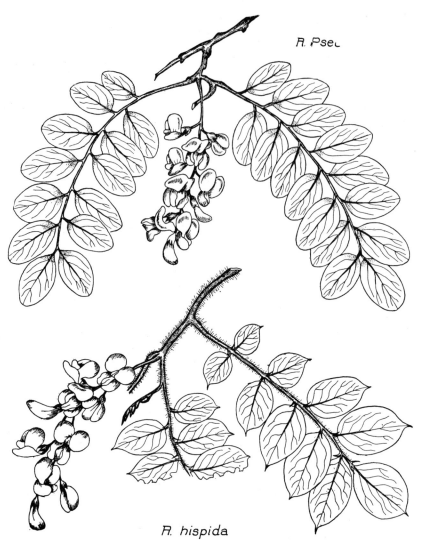

R. PseL

R. hispida

Species of *Robinia* (× 1/2)

slightly united; upper petal or standard rounded, reflexed, wings oblong, curved, blunt; stamens diadelphous; pistil stalked; ovules numerous; fruit a flat, linear pod, several-seeded. (*Robinia*, named for John and Vespasian Robin, the latter being the first who cultivated the locust tree in Europe.)

This genus includes eight species, natives of the southern United States and Mexico, of which two are cultivated in our area.

KEY TO SPECIES OF ROBINIA

1. A tree, with glabrous twigs, petioles, and pods; flowers white. . . . .*R. Pseudo-Acacia* (p. 265)
1. A shrub, with bristly twigs, petioles, and pods; flowers pink or purple. . . . .*R. hispida* (p. 265)

COMMON LOCUST, FALSE ACACIA, *Robinia Pseudo-Acacia* L., Sp. Pl. 722, 1753

A tree 6–20 m. high with a trunk diameter of 2–4 dm.; bark nearly black, rough and deeply furrowed; twigs glabrous, with spines in pairs (stipules); leaves 12–25 cm. long; leaflets eleven to fifteen, ovate to oblong, 2–6 cm. long, 1–3 cm. wide, glabrous, margin entire, petiolules short; racemes slender, 9–20 cm. long, loose; flowers white, fragrant, about 2 cm. long; pod smooth, 6–12 cm. long, flat, brown. Flowers in late May or June. (*Pseúdo-Acácia*, false acacia.)

Common locust is found along the mountains from Pennsylvania to Georgia and in the Ozark Mountains of Missouri, also in Arkansas and Oklahoma. It is extensively planted as an ornamental tree and is becoming more or less naturalized, often spreading by means of underground stems and forming thickets of small trees. It is perfectly hardy in the Upper Midwest, but suffers greatly from the attacks of borers, and as a result is usually short-lived.

The wood is brown or light green in color, close-grained, very hard and heavy, and very durable in contact with the soil; its weight is about 45 lbs. It is used to some extent for fence posts.

ROSE ACACIA, BRISTLY LOCUST, *Robinia hispida* L., Mant. 1:101, 1767

A much branched shrub, 1–3 m. high; branches, twigs, and petioles bristly; leaves 10–20 cm. long; leaflets nine to fifteen, ovate or orbicular, 2–5 cm. long, 2–3.5 cm. wide, rounded at the base, blunt at the apex and mucronate-tipped, glabrous above, pubescent on the veins beneath; racemes drooping, 6–10 cm. long; flowers large, of a deep-rose color or purple, not fragrant, 2–3 cm. long; pod linear, bristly hispid, constricted between the seeds, 4–6 cm. long, brown. Flowers in June; fruit ripe in September. (*Hispida*, prickly.)

Rose acacia is a native of the mountains from Virginia to eastern Tennessee and Georgia. It is cultivated to some extent as an ornamental shrub, and reasonably hardy in the vicinity of the Twin Cities, though it sometimes kills back almost to the ground in severe winters.

Pea Tree
Caragana Lam., Encycl. Meth. Bot. 1:615, 1783

Branching shrubs or small trees, with alternate, compound, even-pinnate, often fascicled leaves; stipules sometimes spiny and persistent; flowers yellow, in few-flowered, umbel-like clusters or solitary, borne on short, lateral spurs; calyx tubular, the two upper sepals smaller; standard with reflexed sides and long-clawed; wings oblique, elongated; keel short, blunt; pistil nearly sessile; ovules many; style straight or slightly bent; fruit a sessile, linear, at length cylindrical pod, about 2–5 cm. long, pointed; seeds oblong or nearly spherical. (*Caragána*, Tartar name of the original species.)

This is a genus of twenty species, distributed from southern Russia to China.

KEY TO SPECIES OF CARAGANA

1. Low shrub with arching branches; leaves sessile, mostly in fascicles, usually subtended by three spines; leaflets oblanceolate or linear........*C. pygmaea* (p. 266)
1. Erect shrubs or small trees, 2–7 m. high; unarmed or with a pair of stipular spines
   at each node; leaves petioled; leaflets elliptic, oblong or obovate.
   2. Leaves digitately compound; leaflets four, obovate; unarmed shrub..........
      ....*C. frutex* (p. 267)
   2. Leaves pinnately compound; leaflets eight to twelve, mostly elliptic; often with
      a pair of stipular spines at the nodes................*C. arborescens* (p. 267)

DWARF RUSSIAN PEA TREE, *Caragana pygmaea* (L.) DC., Prod. 2:268, 1825

A low, spiny shrub with slender, arching branches; the bark on the older twigs dark gray and more or less shreddy; young twigs reddish-brown, angled, more or less pubescent; leaves sessile, mostly in fascicles, generally subtended by three spines, formed from the persistent stipules and bristle-tipped rachis of the primary leaf of the node; leaflets four, having the appearance of distinct leaves, oblanceolate or linear, 10–14 mm. long, 1–2 mm. wide, mucronate at the apex or sometimes blunt, sparingly pubescent or glabrous; flowers solitary in the leaf fascicles, bright yellow, 15–20 mm. long; calyx tubular-campanulate, pubescent or nearly glabrous, about 6 mm. long, the lobes triangular, with pubescent margins and mostly mucronate-tipped; pedicels pubescent, 5–10 mm. long, jointed at the middle; pod 2–2.5 cm. long, reddish-brown, silky-pubescent or

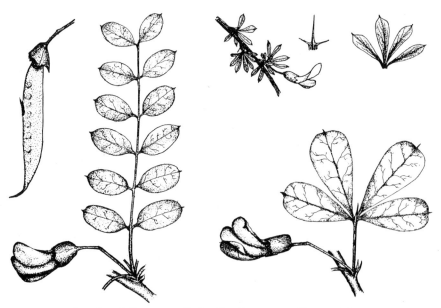

Species of *Caragana*: Left, *C. arborescens.* Upper right,
C. pygmaea. Lower right, *C. frutex.*

nearly glabrous. Blossoms in May and June. (*Pygmáea*, dwarf, referring to the low stature.)

A native of central Asia, this dwarf is sometimes planted as an ornamental shrub.

SHRUBBY PEA TREE, *Caragana frutex* (L.) K. Koch, Dendr. 1:48, 1869 [*C. frutescens* (L.) DC. 1825]

An unarmed shrub, 2–3 m. high, with long, erect branches; bark gray or brownish, more or less shreddy; young twigs greenish-yellow, glabrous; leaves short-petioled, with four leaflets digitately arranged; rachis bristle-tipped; leaflets obovate 1–2.5 cm. long, 5–10 mm. wide, narrowed toward the base, rounded or emarginate at the apex and generally mucronate, bright green, glabrous on both sides; petioles 3–10 mm. long; stipules subulate, not hardening into spines; flowers solitary, bright yellow, about 2 cm. long; pedicels slender, 1.5–2.5 cm. long, jointed above the middle; calyx narrowly campanulate, about 5 mm. long, glabrous, somewhat gibbous at the base, the lobes broadly triangular, with pubescent margins and mucronate-tipped; pods about 3 mm. long. (*Frutex*, shrubby.)

This shrub occurs from southern and southeastern Russia to northern China. It is not so frequent in cultivation as the Siberian pea tree.

SIBERIAN PEA TREE, *Caragana arborescens* Lam., Encycl. Meth. Bot. 1:615, 1785

An upright, branching shrub or small tree up to 6 m. high; the bark of the stem and branches gray; young twigs yellowish-green, somewhat angled and sparingly pubescent; leaves 4–10 cm. long, with eight to twelve pairs of leaflets; rachis bristle-tipped; leaflets elliptic to obovate, 1–3 cm. long, 6–15 mm. wide, rounded or narrowed at the base, rounded or acute at the apex and generally mucronate, at first more or less pubescent on both sides, later becoming quite glabrous or remaining pubescent mainly along the veins beneath; petiolules about 1 mm. long; stipules linear, generally spine-tipped and developing into a pair of stiff spines; flowers yellow, 1.5–2 cm. long, borne on slender, pubescent pedicels 2–5 cm. long, usually several from each bud of the previous season's wood; calyx tubular-campanulate, obscurely five-toothed, with hairy margin; pods 3–5 cm. long, sharply pointed, brown and glabrous, their pedicels 3–6 cm. long and jointed a short distance below the persistent calyx. Blossoms in May and June. (*Arboréscens*, tree-like.)

A native of Siberia and Manchuria, this pea tree is frequently cultivated and is entirely hardy. Several varieties are in cultivation. The following is the most likely to be met with.

Caragana arborescens f. *pendula* Zabel, in Biessn. *et. al.*, Handb. Laubh. 274, 1903

Tall-growing, with strongly pendulous branches. (*Péndula*, drooping.)

267

RUE FAMILY, Rutaceae

Trees or shrubs, rarely herbs, with heavy-scented foliage dotted with translucent oil glands, and alternate or opposite, mostly compound leaves; flowers perfect or unisexual; sepals three to five or none, often more or less united; petals three to five, free or rarely united; stamens as many as the petals and alternating with them, or twice as many as the petals, rarely numerous; carpels one to five, rarely numerous, free or more or less united to form a compound pistil; ovary superior; ovules one to many in each cell; receptacle growing out between the base of the stamens and the carpels to form an annular disk; fruit variable.

This family embraces about a hundred and ten genera and nearly a thousand species, most abundant in the Southern Hemisphere. The citrus fruits belong to this family.

KEY TO GENERA OF RUTACEAE

1. Leaves pinnately compound; twigs with stipular spines....*Xanthoxylum* (p. 268)
1. Leaves trifoliolate; twigs not spiny.........................*Ptelea* (p. 269)

Prickly Ash
Xanthoxylum L., Sp. Pl. 270, 1753

Trees or shrub with alternate, pinnately compound leaves; twigs with stipular spines; flowers small, in cymose clusters, either axillary or terminal, dioecious or polygamous, greenish or yellowish, small; sepals three to five or none; petals three to five, imbricated; staminate flowers with three to five stamens alternating with the petals; pistillate flowers rarely with some stamens and one to five distinct stalked pistils, each with two ovules; fruit dehiscent, fleshy, two-valved, one- to two-seeded. (*Xanthóxylum*, Greek *xanthos*, yellow, *xylon*, wood.)

There are about fifteen species in this genus, natives of east Asia and North America. Only one species occurs in our native flora.

PRICKLY ASH, *Xanthoxylum americanum* Mill., Gard. Dict. ed. 8, no. 2, 1768

A prickly shrub 2–4 m. high, often forming dense thickets; leaves alternate, odd-pinnate, with seven to eleven leaflets; rachis often with a few sharp prickles; leaflets 2–8 cm. long, 1–5 cm. wide, ovate, sessile, pinnately veined, apex rounded, narrowed, or minutely retuse, base rounded or narrowed, at first sparingly hirsute on both sides, in age becoming nearly glabrous above but remaining hirsute beneath, rather thick and dotted with translucent oil glands, margin obscurely crenulate; flowers in small, cymose, axillary clusters, appearing before or with the leaves, greenish, dioecious; calyx lacking; fruit reddish-brown when mature; seeds black, shining, about 3.5 mm. long. (*Americánum*, American.)

Prickly ash is frequent along the edges of woodlands throughout the area except in the northeast. It is distributed from Quebec to North Dakota, south to Virginia and Oklahoma.

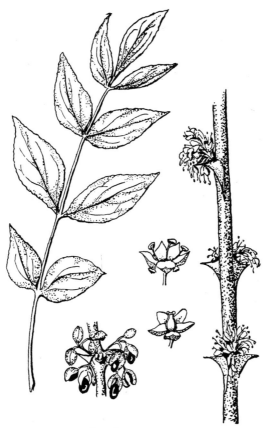

Xanthoxylum americanum

The foliage and fruit are filled with a pleasantly aromatic oil, but are disagreeably pungent to the taste.

Hop Tree
Ptelea L., Sp. Pl. 118, 1753

Shrubs or small trees without prickles and alternate three- to five- foliolate leaves; flowers greenish-white, polygamous, in paniculate clusters;sepals four or five, slightly united below; petals four or five, much longer than the calyx, imbricated; stamens four or five, alternate with the petals; filaments hairy at the base, in the pistillate flower reduced to staminodes with small, wrinkled anthers; carpels two or three, united, inserted on a gynophore; pistil in the staminate flowers linear, sterile and with reduced stigma; ovary in the pistillate flower compressed, two-celled and two-winged, rarely three-celled and three-winged; each cell with two ovules; style short; stigma capitate, two-lobed; fruit a broadly two-winged (rarely three-winged) samara, two- (rarely three-) celled, each cell with one seed. (*Ptélea*, Greek name for the elm so called from the similarity in the fruits.)

269

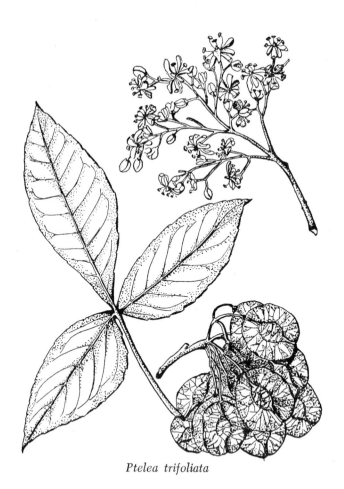

Ptelea trifoliata

Of the three North American species in this genus, only the following is found in the Upper Midwest.

HOP TREE, *Ptelea trifoliata* L., Sp. Pl. 118, 1753

A small tree or large shrub up to 6 m. high and with a trunk diameter of 5–15 cm.; the bark of the trunk dark reddish-brown, smooth except for small irregular lines of exfoliolating cork; twigs glabrous, soon becoming dark red-brown; leaves trifoliolate, with petioles 3–12 cm. long; stipules wanting; leaflets nearly sessile, the middle leaflet obovate or lance-ovate, base long-attenuate, apex acute or acuminate, 5–15 cm. long, 2.5–9 cm. wide, the lateral leaflets somewhat smaller, inequilateral elliptic-ovate, the base much more abruptly narrowed than in the middle leaflet, sometimes rounded, apex mostly acute, the surface of the leaflets pubescent when young, usually becoming nearly or quite glabrous before they are full-grown, dark green and glossy above, paler beneath, margins crenulate; foliage marked with small, rounded, translucent oil glands; flowers small, greenish, appearing after the leaves, in terminal compound clusters; samaras nearly orbicular, 2–3 cm. in diameter, glabrous, veiny, mostly two-seeded,

270

borne on slender pedicels, 1–2 cm. long. (*Trifoliáta*, three-leaved, referring to the trifoliolate leaves.)

This tree grows in alluvial thickets, on rocky slopes, and in gravelly places. It is occasionally planted in the Upper Midwest and sometimes escapes and becomes established. It is distributed from Quebec and New York to southern Ontario and Nebraska, south to Florida, Alabama, Louisiana, and Texas.

The foliage and fruit have a strong, disagreeable odor when crushed. The bark and fruit are bitter. The wood is hard, close-grained, and bright yellow.

CROWBERRY FAMILY, Empetraceae

Low, evergreen, heath-like shrubs; leaves small, narrow, sessile, channeled on the lower side; flowers small, dioecious or monoecious, rarely polygamous or perfect, axillary or in terminal heads; sepals two or three or none; staminate flowers with two to four stamens, filaments slender, sometimes with a rudimentary pistil; pistillate flowers with from two- to several-celled ovary, styles two to several; fruit a berry-like drupe containing from two to several one-seeded nutlets.

This is a family of three genera and five species. The family is probably an apetalous offshoot from the *Ericaceae*.

Crowberry
Empetrum L., Sp. Pl. 1022, 1753

Low, spreading, freely branching shrubs with the aspect of heaths; flowers dioecious or monoecious, rarely perfect, purplish, scattered and solitary in the axils of the leaves, scaly-bracted, inconspicuous; calyx of three somewhat petal-like, spreading sepals; stamens three, exserted; styles short, stigma six- to nine-lobed; fruit a berry-like drupe, black or red, with from six to nine seed-like nutlets. (*Empétrum*, Greek, upon a rock.)

A genus of four species of the arctic and boreal regions and of Patagonia, southern Chile, and some of the antarctic islands.

KEY TO SPECIES OF EMPETRUM

1. Branchlets minutely glandular or thinly pilose with viscid, crinkly hairs, sometimes glabrous; mature leaves divergent, soon reflexed, glabrous or pulverulent, ripe fruit black or dark purple. . . . .*E. nigrum* (p. 271)
1. Branchlets tomentulose, not glandular, leaves ascending to divergent, more or less arachnoid pubescent on the margins; fruit red or purplish. . . . .
. . . .*E. atropurpureum* (p. 272)

BLACK CROWBERRY, *Empetrum nigrum* L., Sp. Pl. 1022, 1753

Procumbent, heath-like, much branched shrub, branchlets glandular puberulent or thinly pilose with viscid, sordid hairs, sometimes glabrous; leaves crowded, divergent, soon reflexed, linear-oblong to narrowly elliptical, thick, obtuse at the apex, 3–7 mm. long, 1–1.5 mm. wide, glabrous or glandular-pulverulent; fruit black, or dark purple, 4–8 mm. in diameter, seeds 1.5–3 mm. long. (*Nígrum,* black, referring to the color of the fruit.)

This species grows mostly in peaty soil but also on moist ledges, gravelly ridges, and moraines. It is infrequent on the islands off Pigeon Point, Minnesota; Thunder Bay District, Ontario; and the Keweenaw Peninsula, Michigan. It is distributed from Greenland to Alaska, south to the coast of Maine, the mountains of New England, northern New York, Michigan and Minnesota, southern Alberta and northern California. It occurs also in northern Eurasia.

Typical *P. nigrum* is apparently less common in our area than the following species.

PURPLE CROWBERRY, *Empetrum atropurpureum* Fern. & Wieg., Rhodora 15:214, 1913

A low, trailing, or creeping shrub, young branchlets more or less white-tomentose and eglandular; leaves linear-oblong, 4–6.5 mm. long, at first closely crowded and ascending, later loosely divaricate, sometimes becoming more or less reflexed with age, young leaves thinly arachnoid pubescent, mostly along the margins and at the tip; drupes 5–9 mm. in diameter, red to purplish-black when mature; seeds 2–2.4 mm. long. (*Atropurpúreum,* dark purple.)

This shrub grows mostly on moist ledges and in crevices of rocks. It is fairly common on the rocky islands of the Pigeon Point area, including Isle Royale. In the eighth edition of Gray's Manual the general distribution of the species is given as the south coast of Labrador Peninsula to Lake Mistassini, Quebec, south to Magdalen Island, Prince Edward Island, the south coast of Nova Scotia, and the mountains of northern New England. While most of the material from the Lake Superior region does not have branchlets as "white-tomentose" as some of the specimens from the above cited range, it nevertheless belongs with the *E. atropurpureum* segregate.

SUMAC FAMILY, ANACARDIACEAE

Trees or shrubs with acrid, resinous or milky sap; leaves alternate, rarely opposite, simple or compound; flowers small, regular, perfect or polygamous; calyx three- to five-cleft; petals three to seven, imbricated in the bud, sometimes lacking; stamens as many or twice as many as the petals, inserted along the edge of a rounded disk; ovary one- to five-celled; styles one to three; ovule one in each cavity; fruit mostly a small drupe; seed coat crustaceous or bony.

This family includes about sixty genera and five hundred species, most abundant in warm and tropical regions, a few extending into the Temperate Zone.

KEY TO GENERA OF ANACARDIACEAE

1. Leaves compound; fruit clusters with numerous fruits and no elongated, plumose, sterile pedicels . . . .*Rhus* (p. 273)

SUMAC FAMILY

1. Leaves simple; fruit clusters a mass of elongated, plumose, sterile pedicels with a few scattered fruits...................................*Cotinus* (p. 278)

Sumac

Rhus L., Sp. Pl. 265, 1753

Shrubs or trees with alternate, compound or simple leaves; stipules none; flowers in axillary or terminal panicles, greenish-white or yellow, small, polygamous; calyx five-cleft or five-parted; petals five, spreading; stamens five, inserted between the lobes of the disk; ovary one-celled, ovule solitary, styles three; fruit a kind of drupe, small, one-seeded. (*Rhús*, Greek *rhous*, sumac.)

This is a genus of about a hundred and twenty species, natives of warm and temperate regions. The greatest number of species occur in South Africa. In addition to the following, about twelve others occur in the eastern, southern and western parts of the United States.

KEY TO SPECIES OF RHUS

1. Leaves pinnate (in cut-leaf forms bipinnatifid or bipinnate), leaflets more than three; flowers in dense terminal or loose axillary panicles.
    2. Leaflets serrate to deeply dissected or compound; fruit with crimson hairs; stone smooth.
        3. Twigs and petioles villous-hirsute.
            4. Leaflets serrate.............................*R. typhina* (p. 273)
            4. Leaflets deeply dissected or compound (cut-leaf)...................
            ....*R. typhina* f. *dissecta* (p. 275)
        3. Twigs and petioles glabrous.
            5. Leaflets serrate.............................*R. glabra* (p. 275)
            5. Leaflets deeply dissected or compound (cut-leaf)...................
            ....*R. glabra* f. *laciniata* (p. 275)
    2. Leaflets entire; fruit grayish-white; stone striate..........*R. Vernix* (p. 275)
1. Leaves trifoliolate, flowers in small, clustered panicles.
    6. Terminal leaflet long-stalked; flowers greenish, in loose clusters, appearing after the leaves.
        7. Stems strongly woody, bushy and much branched, trailing, leaning or high-climbing and then with aerial, clinging roots; leaves scattered along the branches.......................................*R. radicans* (p. 276)
        7. Stems woody for only 0.5–0.6 dm. above the subterranean, stoloniferous base, simple or sparingly branched; leaves at the summit of stems and branches..
        ....*R. radicans* var. *Rydbergii* (p. 277)
    6. Terminal leaflet sessile; flowers yellow, in dense clusters, appearing before or with the opening of the leaves......................*R. aromatica* (p. 277)

STAGHORN SUMAC, *Rhus typhina* L., Amoen. Acad. 4:311, 1760 [*R. hirta* Sudw. 1892]

A shrub or sometimes a small tree reaching a height of 10 m., more commonly 3–4 m.; bark smooth and gray; twigs densely velvety-hairy; leaves odd-pinnate; petioles pubescent, 15–30 cm. long; leaflets eleven to thirty-one, oblong-lanceolate, 4–14 cm. long, 1.5–4.5 cm. broad, rounded at the base, acuminate at the apex, sharply and sometimes coarsely serrate, dark green and nearly glabrous

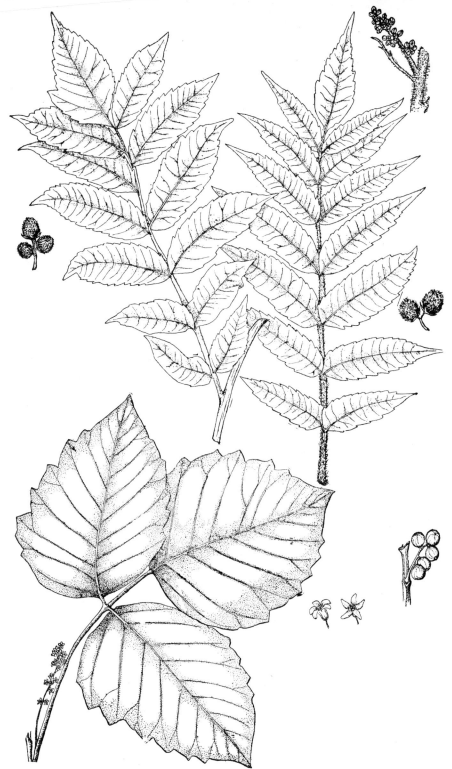

Species of *Rhus*: Upper left, *R. glabra.* Upper right, *R. typhina.*
Bottom, *R. radicans* (× 2/3).

above, paler and pubescent beneath, sessile; panicles terminal, dense-flowered, 9–12 cm. long; flowers yellowish-green, polygamous, 5–6 mm. broad; drupe globose, about 4 mm. in diameter, thickly covered with bright-crimson, straight hairs. Blossoms in June; fruit persists into the winter. (*Typhína*, smoky.)

Staghorn sumac grows in dry, rocky, or gravelly soil, often at the base of bluffs. It is common southward in the hardwood forest area, infrequent northward in Minnesota to the region of Duluth. It is distributed from eastern Quebec to Minnesota, south to North Carolina, Kentucky, Illinois, and Iowa.

The wood is soft, greenish-yellow, and takes a satiny finish. The bark is rich in tannin.

CUT-LEAF SUMAC, *Rhus typhina* f. *dissecta* Rehder, Rhodora 9:115, 1907

Leaves bipinnatifid to bipinnate. (*Disssécta*, dissected.)

This form is frequently planted as an ornamental shrub.

SCARLET SUMAC, UPLAND SUMAC, *Rhus glabra*, L., Sp. Pl. 265, 1753

A shrub or very rarely a small tree, 0.5–6 m. high; bark smooth and grayish; twigs glabrous and somewhat glaucous; petioles often purplish, glabrous; leaflets eleven to thirty-one, oblong-lanceolate, rounded and slightly oblique at the base, acuminate at the apex, sharply serrate, dark green and often shining above, paler beneath, glabrous throughout, 4–10 cm. long, 1.5–3 cm. wide; panicles many-flowered, about 8–10 cm. long, puberulent when young; flowers small, greenish, about 5 mm. broad; drupe globose, 3–4 mm. in diameter, covered with short, reddish, acid hairs. Blossoms in June and July. (*Glábra*, smooth.)

This species, like the preceding, often has the whole or part of the inflorescence transformed into clusters of contorted small leaves.

Growing in dry soil or rocky hillsides, gravelly moraines, and sandy tracts, scarlet sumac is common throughout the Upper Midwest. It is distributed from central Maine to British Columbia, south to Florida, Texas, and Arizona.

The leaves are sometimes used for tanning.

Rhus glabra f. *laciniata* (Carr.) Robinson, Rhodora 10:35, 1908

Leaves that are laciniately bipinnatifid to bipinnate. (*Laciniáta*, torn, referring to the deeply cut margin of the leaflets.)

This form is planted as an ornamental shrub.

POISON SUMAC, POISON OAK, *Rhus Vernix* L., Sp. Pl. 265, 1753

A shrub or small tree, sometimes reaching a height of 8 m., more commonly 2–4 m. high; bark gray; twigs greenish; leaves petioled, pinnate, 15–36 cm. long; leaflets 7–13, obovate or oval, or the lowermost ovate, narrowed or rounded at the base, acute or acuminate at the apex, entire, green on both sides, glabrous or slightly puberulent, 4–14 cm. long, 1.5–6 cm. wide; panicles axillary, numerous, long-peduncled, 10–17 cm. long; flowers green, very small, about 2 mm. broad; fruit yellowish-green, smooth and shining, about 4 mm. in diameter.

Rhus vernix ($\times$ 1/2)

Blossoms in May and June; fruit ripe in August and September; the large panicles of yellowish-green, dry drupes persist into the winter. (*Vérnix*, varnish.)

Poison sumac grows in swamps and tamarack bogs. Its occurrence in Minnesota is largely confined to Hennepin, Ramsey, Anoka, and Chisago counties. It
is distributed from western Maine to southern Ontario and eastern Minnesota,
south to Florida, Mississippi, and Louisiana.

This species is said to be much more poisonous than poison ivy and should
be avoided.

POISON IVY, *Rhus radicans* L. Sp. Pl. 266, 1753

A suberect, scrambling, or trailing shrub, or high climbing by aerial roots;
stems strongly woody, sometimes attaining a diameter of 3–6 cm.; leaves trifoliolate, firm to subcoriaceous, dark green, shining and mostly glabrous above,
paler and pilose to bristly-pubescent mainly along the veins beneath, rarely
glabrous; terminal leaflets longer-stalked than the lateral ones, 5–12 cm. long,
narrowly to broadly ovate, rounded or broadly cuneate at the base, gradually
tapered to the acute or short-acuminate apex; margin mostly entire or sometimes sparingly and coarsely dentate or sinuate; lateral leaflets usually somewhat
smaller and more or less inequilateral at the base; flowers polygamodioecious,
yellowish-green, in small axillary panicles, 3–10 cm. long; those bearing staminate flowers more ample than the ones with pistillate; pistillate flowers with

abortive stamens not exceeding the pistils; fruit subglobose, with shallow longitudinal grooves, dun-colored to yellowish-white, shining, 5–6 mm. in diameter, usually persisting through the winter. Blossoms in late June. (*Rádicans*, rooting, from the aerial roots.)

Poison ivy grows in thickets, open woods, along fence rows, and on walls. The trailing or climbing form is not common in the area. In Minnesota it occurs mainly in the southeastern corner and only infrequently as far north as Morrison County. It is distributed from Quebec and Nova Scotia to Florida and west to Minnesota, Nebraska, and Arkansas.

Rhus radicans var. *Rydbergii* (Small) Rehder, in Journ. Arnold Arb. 20:416, 1939

A low, erect, or suberect shrub, 2–6 dm. high, from creeping, underground, stoloniferous bases, simple or sparingly branched and without aerial roots; leaves trifoliolate, approximate on erect petioles at the summit of the stems and branches; leaflets 5–14 cm. long, 4–10 cm. broad, rhombic or broadly ovate to suborbicular, rounded at the base, mostly abruptly acuminate at the apex or sometimes short-acute or blunt, their margins entire, undulate or irregularly and coarsely few-toothed, membranaceous to subcoriaceous, shining and mostly glabrous above, more or less bristly-pubescent along the veins beneath; flowers and fruits as in the typical variety. (*Rydbérgii*, named for Dr. P. A. Rydberg.)

This shrub, which grows in thickets and woods and along fence rows and roadsides, is common and in many places abundant throughout the Upper Midwest. It is distributed from Quebec to British Columbia, south to New England, the mountains of Virginia, Illinois, Kansas, New Mexico, and Arizona.

The plant is very poisonous to the touch and causes serious inflammation of the skin. The irritation is caused by an oleoresin found in all parts of the plant and secreted by the leaves and the bark. While some persons are much less sensitive to the poison than others, no one should handle the plants carelessly because of assumed immunity.

SWEET-SCENTED SUMAC, *Rhus aromatica* Ait., Hort. Kew 1:367, 1789 [*R. canadensis* Marsh. 1785]

A shrub 1–2.5 m. high with ascending or spreading branches; young twigs more or less pubescent, older twigs glabrous, brown or reddish-brown and dotted with small round lenticels; leaves trifoliolate, with petioles 1–3 cm. long; terminal leaflet rhombic-ovate, rarely obovate, 3.5–7.5 cm. long, 2.5–4.5 cm. wide, narrowed at the base, acute at the apex, sessile or slightly stalked; lateral leaflets somewhat smaller, sessile, rounded and generally inequilateral at the base, short-acute or rounded at the apex, all crenate or crenate-dentate, pubescent on both sides, especially when young, bristly-hairy along the margin, becoming glabrate with age; flowers yellow, appearing before the leaves in clustered spikes 1–1.5 cm. long (the inflorescence catkin-like before flowering); bracts dark reddish-brown, with bristly-ciliate margins; sepals ovate, scale-like, about 1 mm. long; petals elliptic or ovate, 2–2.5 mm. long; stamens included; drupe globose, red, pubescent, 6–8 mm. in diameter. (*Aromática*, fragrant.)

This sumac grows on dry, rocky banks from Vermont to Illinois, south to Florida, Louisiana, and Kansas. The reports in various floras of the occurrence of this species in Minnesota have not been verified by authentic collections so far as this writer has been able to ascertain. It is occasionally planted as an ornamental shrub.

Smoke Tree
Cotinus Adans., Fam. 2:345, 1763

Shrubs or small trees with alternate, petioled, ovate, elliptical or obovate, entire, simple leaves; flowers in large, terminal panicles, polygamous, yellowish; calyx five-cleft; sepals lance-ovate, imbricated; petals five, oblong, about twice as long as the sepals; stamens five, shorter than the petals; ovary superior, with three short lateral styles; stigmas small; fruit an obliquely ovoid drupe, somewhat compressed, one-seeded; the fruiting panicles with few fruits and the numerous pedicels of the sterile flowers much elongated and plumose. (*Cotínus*, Greek name for the wild olive.)

Of the two species of this genus, one occurs in the southeastern United States, the other in southern Europe and Asia.

SMOKE TREE, *Cotinus coggygria* Scop., Fl. Carn. ed. 2, 1:220, 1772

A shrub up to 5 m. high; leaves elliptic to obovate, 3–8 cm. long, rounded or slightly notched at the apex, and either rounded or somewhat narrowed at the base, margin entire, glabrous on both surfaces; petiole mostly 1–1.5 cm. long; fruiting panicles dull purple, very conspicuous, appearing like clouds of smoke, whence the common name of the plant. (*Coggýgria*, name unexplained.)

Smoke tree is occasionally planted as an ornamental shrub on account of its conspicuous fruiting panicles. It is moderately hardy in the latitude of the Twin Cities.

HOLLY FAMILY, Aquifoliaceae

Trees or shrubs with watery sap; leaves simple, alternate, petioled, often leathery in texture; flowers in axillary clusters or borne singly, small, regular, white or greenish, mostly polygamo-dioecious; calyx three- to six-parted, generally persistent; petals four to six or sometimes more, separate or slightly united at the base, deciduous; stamens hypogynous, as many as the petals or more; anthers cordate; disk lacking; ovary superior, three- to several-celled; style short or none; ovules one or two in each cavity of the ovary; fruit a small berry-like drupe enclosing several nutlets.

This family of five genera includes nearly three hundred species of temperate and tropical regions.

Holly
Ilex, L., Sp. Pl. 125, 1753

Shrubs or trees; leaves alternate, entire or dentate or spiny-toothed, sometimes leathery; stipules minute; flowers axillary, cymose or solitary, perfect or
polygamous; calyx small, four- to six-toothed; petals four to six, separate or
united only at the base, oval or obovate, spreading; stamens as many as the petals
and attached to their base; fruit a berry-like drupe containing four to six nutlets.
(*I'lex*, classical Latin name of the holly oak.)

This genus embraces about two hundred and eighty species, mostly natives
of America, some of the Old World. In addition to the following, about twelve
species occur in the eastern and southeastern parts of the United States.

VIRGINIA WINTERBERRY, BLACK ALDER, *Ilex verticillata* (L.) Gray,
Man. Bot. ed. 2, 264, 1856

A shrub 1–6 m. high, with a smooth, grayish bark; twigs glabrous or slightly
pubescent; leaves oval, obovate, or oblong-lanceolate, 4–11 cm. long, 1.5–4 cm.

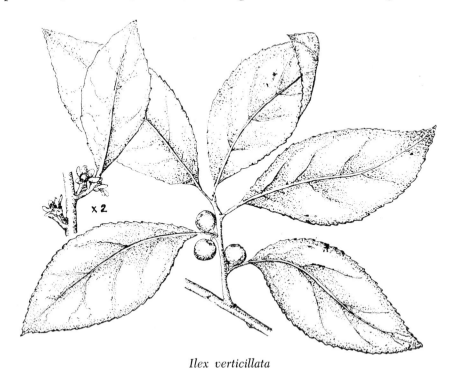

Ilex verticillata

279

wide, acute at the base, acute or acuminate at the apex, serrate, dark green and nearly glabrous above, pubescent at least on the veins beneath; petioles 8–12 mm. long; flowers mostly crowded; pedicels about 3 mm. long; sepals ciliate on the margins; petals spreading or reflexed; fruit a bright-red drupe, 6–7 mm. in diameter. Blossoms in June; fruit ripe in September. (*Verticillàta*, in whorls.)

This shrub is common in swamps and damp thickets northward, infrequent southward to southeastern Minnesota and adjacent parts of Wisconsin and Iowa. It is distributed from Newfoundland to Minnesota, south to Georgia and Missouri.

Mountain Holly
Nemopanthus Raf., Journ. Phys. 89:96, 1819

A much-branched shrub with ash-gray bark and alternate, deciduous, mostly entire leaves; flowers greenish-yellow, on long, slender, axillary pedicels, polygamo-dioecious; sepals four or five, subulate, minute and generally early deciduous; petals four or five, oblong-linear, spreading, distinct; stamens four or five; filaments slender; anthers ovoid; ovary three- to five-celled, with one ovule in each cell; stigmas three to five, sessile; fruit a subglobose drupe with from three to five bony nutlets. (*Nemopánthus*, said to mean a flower with a filiform peduncle.)

This is a monotypic genus of eastern North America.

MOUNTAIN HOLLY, *Nemopanthus mucronata* (L.) Trelease, Trans. Acad. St. Louis 5:349, 1898

A shrub 1.5–4 m. high with ash-colored bark; buds short and broadly conical; young twigs dark reddish-brown, glabrous, generally with many small, light-colored lenticels; leaves elliptic to elliptic-oblong or sometimes ovate, 2–5 cm.

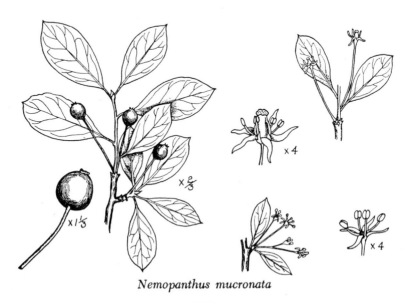

Nemopanthus mucronata

long, 1–2.5 cm. wide, rounded or narrowed at the base, rounded and mucronate at the apex or occasionally acute, entire or with a few minute teeth, glabrous on both sides, somewhat paler beneath; petioles 5-12 mm. long; both staminate and pistillate flowers solitary in the axils of the leaves or the staminate sometimes two to four together; pedicels very slender, 1–3 cm. long; drupe red, 6–8 mm. long; nutlets slightly ridged. Blossoms in May; fruit ripe in August and September. (*Mucronáta*, referring to the mucronate-tipped leaves.)

Growing in damp woods, thickets, and swamps, mountain holly occurs mostly in the coniferous forest area; it is infrequent to rare southeastward to northern Illinois. It is distributed from Newfoundland to Minnesota, south to New England, the uplands of Virginia, Ohio, Indiana, and Illinois.

BITTERSWEET FAMILY, CELASTRACEAE

Shrubs or twining, woody vines with simple, alternate or opposite leaves; flowers small, regular, in cymes or racemes; sepals four or five, more or less united; petals four or five, stamens four or five, alternate with the petals, borne on a fleshy disk, which fills the bottom of the calyx; ovary three- to five-celled; fruit fleshy, dehiscent; seeds arilled, remaining on till late in the winter.

This family of about forty-five genera and four hundred and thirty species is widely distributed in warm and temperate regions.

KEY TO GENERA OF CELASTRACEAE

1. Shrub with opposite leaves; flowers in cymes; fruit lobed....*Euonymus* (p. 281)
1. Twining vine; leaves alternate; flowers in racemes..........*Celastrus* (p. 283)

Spindle Tree
Euonymus L., Sp. Pl. 197, 1753

Shrubs with opposite, simple, petioled, serrate leaves; branchlets four-sided; cymes axillary, several-flowered, 4–6 cm. long, borne on the season's growth; flowers flat, 7–10 mm. wide; sepals four or five, united at the base; petals four or five, rounded, spreading, about 3 mm. long; stamens four or five, usually borne on the top of a flat disk which adheres to the calyx; ovary three- to five-celled; fruit three- to five-lobed, loculicidal; seeds one to three in each cell. (*Euónymus*, classical name for the spindle tree, often spelled *Evonymus*.)

This is a genus of seventy species, of the North Temperate Zone. Besides the first of the following described species, two occur in eastern North America and two in California.

KEY TO SPECIES OF EUONYMUS

1. Twigs with two to four broad, corky wings, fruit divided nearly to the base.....
   ....*E. alatus* (p. 283)
1. Twigs without broad, corky wings, four-angled, fruit deeply lobed.
   2. Petals dark purplish-brown, anthers sessile, aril scarlet; leaves elliptical, more or less pubescent over whole lower surface........*E. atropurpureus* (p. 282)

2. Petals yellowish-green, anthers with distinct filaments, aril orange; leaves ovate-lanceolate, glabrous or hispid-pubescent along the veins only..............
....*E. europaeus* (p. 283)

BURNING BUSH, WAHOO, *Euonymus atropurpureus* Jacq., Hort. Vind. 2:5, 1772

A shrub or small tree 2–7 m. high, with grayish-green bark; twigs green, glabrous, and generally obtusely four-angled; leaves thin, elliptic, 5–13 cm. long, 3–6.5 mm. wide, narrowed or rarely rounded at the base, acuminate at the apex, crenate-serrulate, mostly glabrous above, pubescent beneath with short, stiff hairs, the pubescence generally most pronounced along the veins; petioles 8–18 m. long, glabrous or pubescent; flowers purplish-brown, 6–8 mm. in diameter, in five- to fifteen-flowered diachasial cymes; peduncles slender, 1.5–4 cm. long; sepals semicircular, about 1 mm. long; petals brownish-purple, broadly ovate, 2–2.5 mm. long; stamens borne on a prominent four-sided disk; filaments very short, the anthers appearing nearly sessile; style short, conical; capsule pink when ripe, deeply three- to four-lobed, the lobes bluntly wedge-shaped; aril

Left, *Euonymus atropurpureus.* Right, *Celastrus scandens.*

scarlet; seeds brown, narrowly elliptical, 6–7 mm. long. Blossoms in June; fruit ripe in September, often persisting until early winter. (*Atropurpúreus*, dark purple, referring to the flower.)

Burning bush grows in rich woods and thickets throughout the deciduous forest area as far northwestward in Minnesota as Clay County. It is distributed from Ontario to southeastern North Dakota, south to Virginia, Alabama, Tennessee, Arkansas, and Oklahoma.

EUROPEAN SPINDLE TREE, *Euonymus europaeus* L., Sp. Pl. 197, 1753

A bushy shrub or small tree, sometimes up to 6 m. high, with grayish bark; twigs greenish or grayish-green, terete or obtusely four-angled; leaves of firm texture, ovate-lanceolate, 5-7 cm. long (sometimes longer), 1.5–3.5 cm. wide, narrowed at the base, acute to acuminate at the apex, glabrous above or sometimes short-bristly-pubescent along the veins, glabrous or pubescent along the veins beneath, margin crenate-serrulate, often somewhat revolute; petioles 4–10 mm. long; flowers greenish-yellow, mostly in three- to five-flowered cymes; peduncles rather stout, 1.5–3 cm. long; sepals semicircular; petals ovate, about 3 mm. long; stamens borne on the disk, the filaments about twice as long as the anthers; style enlarged at the base, the cylindrical upper part about 1 mm. long; capsule mostly rose-red, 12–14 mm. in diameter, three- to four-lobed, the lobes rounded; aril orange; seeds white, ovate, flattened, about 5.5 m. long. Blossoms in May or June; fruit ripe in September. (*Europaéus*, European.)

A native of Europe and western Asia, this species is occasionally planted as an ornamental shrub on account of the showy fruit. Several varieties are recognized, based on form and size of leaves and color and size of fruit.

WINGED SPINDLE TREE, *Euonymus alatus* (Thunb.) Sieb., Verh. Batav. 12:49, 1830

A shrub with stiff, spreading branches, usually with two or four broad, corky wings, leaves short-stalked, elliptic to obovate, finely and sharply serrate, dark green; flowers yellowish; fruit one to four purplish pods; seeds brown, with orange-red aril.

The winged spindle tree is showy in the fall, with brightly colored fruits and crimson or scarlet leaves. It is cultivated to some extent as an ornamental in the Upper Midwest and is hardy in our climate.

Shrubby Bittersweet
Celastrus L., Sp. Pl. 196, 1753

Shrubs, mostly climbing; leaves alternate, thin, deciduous; flowers in terminal or axillary racemes, or paniculate, inconspicuous, dioecious or polygamo-dioecious; calyx five-lobed; petals five, inserted below or along the margin of the disk; stamens in the staminate flowers five, in the sinuses of the disk; ovary two- to four-lobed and two- to four-celled; two ovules in each cell; capsule two- to four-celled, dehiscent into as many valves, one or two seeds in each cell, each with a scarlet aril. (*Celástrus*, Greek name of some evergreen.)

This genus embraces about thirty species, one of which occurs in North America. The others are found in Asia, Australia, and Madagascar.

SHRUBBY or CLIMBING BITTERSWEET, *Celastrus scandens* L., Sp. Pl. 196, 1753

A twining, woody vine, climbing up trees to a height of 8–10 m., sometimes trailing on the ground; bark gray or brownish, smooth; leaves alternate, appearing two-ranked by the twisting of the stem, ovate to obovate, or ovate-lanceolate, 5–10 cm. long, 3–5 cm. wide, narrowed or rounded at the base, acuminate at the apex, crenulate-serrate, thin, glabrous on both sides; petioles 1–2 cm. long; flowers in terminal racemes or panicles, yellowish–green, 8–9 mm. broad; sepals short, triangular; petals 3–4 mm. long, crenulate; fruit a yellow, globular capsule, about 1 cm. in diameter; seeds with a scarlet aril. Blossoms in June; fruit ripe in September and persisting through the winter. (*Scándens*, climbing.)

This vine is common in thickets, on river banks, and in woods throughout the deciduous forest area; it is less frequent northeastward. It is distributed from southern Quebec to southern Manitoba, south to New England, Georgia, Alabama, Louisiana, and Oklahoma.

Bittersweet is often planted as a climber near trellises, porches, and similar places. Sometimes it is troublesome among young trees as it encircles and strangles them.

BLADDERNUT FAMILY, Staphyleaceae

Shrubs or trees with mostly opposite, odd-pinnate or three-foliolate leaves with stipules; flowers perfect, in terminal or axillary clusters; sepals five; petals five; stamens five, alternate with the petals, inserted along the edge of the conspicuous disk; fruit a bladdery capsule (in our species); seeds solitary or few in each cavity of the ovary.

This is a small family of five genera and about twenty species, widely distributed.

Bladdernut

Staphylea L., Sp. Pl. 270, 1753

Shrubs with opposite, three-foliolate, pinnate leaves; flowers whitish, in drooping terminal racemes or panicles; calyx deeply five-parted, the lobes erect; petals five, erect, spatulate; pistil consisting of from three to several carpels; styles slightly cohering; fruit a three-lobed, inflated capsule, dehiscent at the summit; seeds hard and globose. (*Staphyléa*, Greek *staphyle*, cluster.)

This genus includes about eight species of the North Temperate Zone, two of which are native to North America.

284

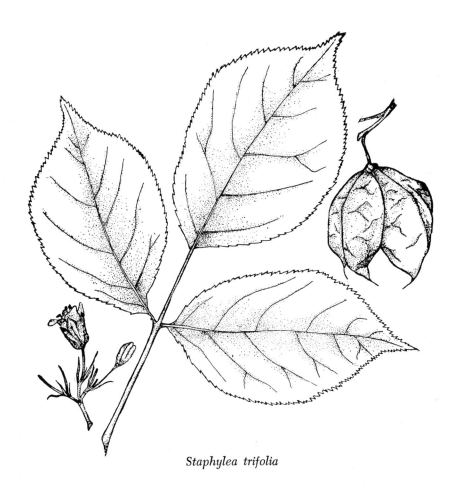

Staphylea trifolia

AMERICAN BLADDERNUT, *Staphylea trifolia* L., Sp. Pl. 270, 1753

A shrub 1–3 m. high, with grayish bark; branches greenish and striped; leaves long-petioled, trifoliolate; leaflets ovate to obovate, 4–10 cm. long, 2–6 cm. wide, the terminal leaflet slightly larger than the lateral ones, narrowed at the base, acuminate at the apex, finely serrate, smooth above, pubescent at least along the veins beneath; racemes 3–6 cm. long, flowers 8–10 mm. long; fruit an inflated capsule 2–3 cm. in diameter. Blossoms in May; fruit ripe in August. (*Trifólia*, three-leaved, in reference to the three leaflets of the compound leaf.)

Bladdernut is common in moist thickets, in ravines, and on the wooded slopes of the hardwood forests of southeastern Minnesota and the adjacent parts of Wisconsin and Iowa; it is infrequent northward in the valley of the St. Croix River to Chisago County, Minnesota. It ranges from southwestern Quebec to Minnesota, south to Massachusetts, Georgia, Alabama, Arkansas, and Oklahoma.

MAPLE FAMILY, ACERACEAE

Trees or shrubs with watery, often sugary sap; leaves opposite, simple or palmately lobed or more rarely palmately or pinnately three- to fifteen-foliolate;

285

flowers in axillary or terminal cymes, clusters or racemes, polygamous or dioecious, regular; calyx mostly four- or five-parted, petals four or five or none; disk
thick, round or lobed, sometimes wanting; stamens four to twelve, mostly eight;
ovary two-celled, two-lobed; styles two, from between the lobes; fruit two long-
winged samaras united at the base, each one-seeded; cotyledons rolled up in
the seed.

The family consists of two genera, *Acer* and *Dipteronia*. The latter differs
from *Acer* in that the samara is winged all around.

Maple
Acer L., Sp. Pl. 1055, 1753

Samaras winged on one side only, otherwise as in the family description.
(*A'cer*, the classical Latin name for the maple.)

This is a genus of about a hundred and fifteen species, natives of the North
Temperate Zone.

KEY TO SPECIES OF ACER

1. Leaves simple; flowers polygamous.
    2. Flowers appearing much before the leaves in dense clusters from separate buds;
    fruits borne in leafless clusters on the older twigs.
        3. Flowers sessile or short-stalked; petals lacking; middle lobe of leaf rhombic,
        narrowed at the base........................*A. saccharinum* (p. 287)
        3. Flowers on long pedicels; petals present; middle lobe of leaf triangular,
        broadest at the base...........................*A. rubrum* (p. 287)
    2. Flowers appearing with or after the leaves; clusters of fruit borne on leafy shoots
    of the season's growth.
        4. Leaves pinnately veined, unlobed or obscurely and irregularly pinnately
        lobed...*A. tataricum* (p. 289)
        4. Leaves palmately veined, palmately three- to seven-lobed.
            5. Leaves with serrate margins; flowers appearing after the leaves; samaras
            2–2.5 cm. long, their wings close together and only slightly divergent.
                6. Leaves almost as wide as long, middle lobe triangular, flowers in slen-
                der, upright racemes. Native...............*A. spicatum* (p. 289)
                6. Leaves much longer than wide, middle lobe oblong to lanceolate,
                elongated; flowers in corymbs. Introduced.......*A. ginnala* (p. 289)
            5. Leaves with coarsely dentate, undulate-dentate, or entire margins; flowers
            appearing with the leaves; samaras mostly 3–5 cm. long, wings moder-
            ately to widely spreading.
                7. Flowers in sessile umbel-like corymbs, drooping; pedicels hairy; petals
                absent; samaras about 3 cm. long, their wings moderately spreading.
                    8. Leaves with deep lobing, pale and nearly glabrous beneath; sinus
                    at the base open or shallow; petioles glabrous...................
                    ....*A. saccharum* (p. 291)
                    8. Leaves with shallow lobing, sinus at the base closed; green and pu-
                    bescent along the veins beneath; petioles pubescent.............
                    .... *A. nigrum* (p. 291)
                7. Flowers in terminal corymbs; petals present; pedicels glabrous; samaras
                4–5 cm. long, their wings nearly horizontally spreading............
                ....*A. platanoides* (p. 293)
1. Leaves compound; flowers dioecious....................*A. Negundo* (p. 293)

MAPLE FAMILY

SOFT MAPLE, SILVER MAPLE, *Acer saccharinum* L., Sp. Pl. 1055, 1753

A large tree attaining a height of 33 m. and a trunk diameter of 10–14 dm., usually branched into three or four secondary stems; bark furrowed, the surface separating into scales, reddish-brown, the bark of the secondary stems and large branches smooth and gray; leaves deeply five-lobed, with narrow sinuses, 7–16 cm. long, 6–14 cm. wide, truncate or slightly heart-shaped at the base, lobes remotely and irregularly serrate, upper surface green and glabrous, lower surface silvery-white and more or less pubescent at least when young; petioles 5–12 cm. long; flowers yellowish-red, in nearly sessile, lateral clusters, appearing many days before the leaves, the staminate and pistillate in separate clusters, sometimes on the same tree, sometimes on different ones; calyx slightly five-lobed; petals lacking; stamens five to seven, exceeding the calyx in the staminate flowers; samaras spreading, pubescent when young, about 5 cm. long, wings 12–14 mm. wide. Blossoms in March and April; fruit ripe in June. (*Saccharínum*, sugary.)

Soft maple is common southward on river banks and bottomlands, infrequent and scattered northward in Minnesota to the upper Mississippi and southern St. Louis County. It is distributed from New Brunswick to Ontario to Minnesota and South Dakota, south to Florida and Oklahoma.

Soft maple is very extensively planted as a shade and ornamental tree. The wood is light brown, close-grained, strong and hard, weighing 33 lbs. It is easily worked and is used for furniture and floors. Some sugar is made from the sap.

Among the more commonly cultivated forms of this species is the cut-leaf maple, *A. saccharinum* var. *laciniatum* Pax, 1901, more familiarly known in the trade as *A. dasycarpum* var. *Weiri* Schwerin., distinguished by pendulous branches and deeply cleft leaves with dissected lobes.

RED MAPLE, SWAMP MAPLE, *Acer rubrum* L., Sp. Pl. 1055, 1753

A medium-sized, slender tree, 6–20 m. high, with a trunk diameter of 1–4 dm.; the bark of the stem gray, separating into flaky ridges; twigs dark red and lustrous; leaves sharply three- to five-lobed, 5–12 cm. long, 6–12 cm. wide, cordate or truncate at the base, lobes acuminate, irregularly serrate or toothed, green and glabrous above, paler and tomentose at least along the veins beneath; petioles 3–8 cm. long; flowers monoecious or dioecious, crimson or yellowish, in lateral sessile clusters, appearing long before the leaves; petals present, linear-oblong; stamens three to seven, in the pistillate flowers much reduced; fruits on drooping pedicels, glabrous; samaras slightly spreading, about 3 cm. long, 8–9 mm. wide. Blossoms in March and April; fruit ripe in June. (*Rúbrum*, red.)

Growing in swamps and moist woods, red maple is common throughout the northern part of the area, less frequent southward to southeastern Minnesota and adjacent Wisconsin. It is distributed from Newfoundland and Quebec west to Manitoba, south to Florida and Texas.

287

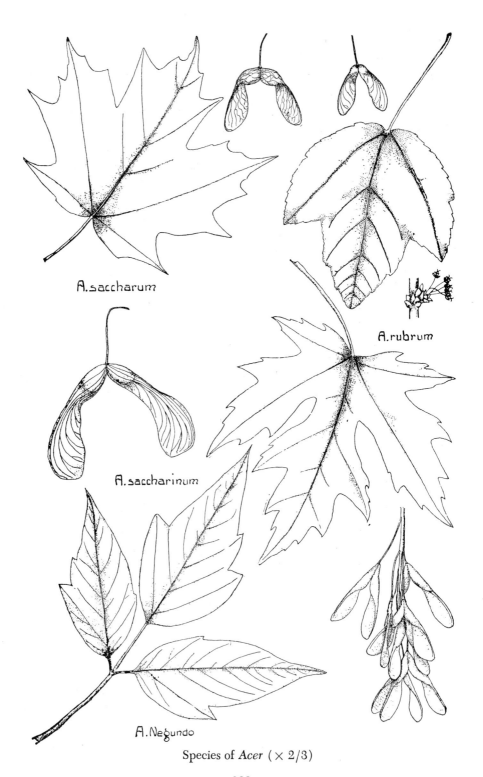

A.saccharum

A.rubrum

A.saccharinum

A.Negundo

Species of *Acer* (× 2/3)

The wood is light brown in color, close-grained, heavy but not strong, weighing 39 lbs. It is used in the manufacture of furniture. The bark is sometimes used in dyeing.

TARTARIAN MAPLE, *Acer tataricum* L., Sp. Pl. 1054, 1753

A small tree, 6–8 m. high; leaves ovate, 5–8 cm. long, 3–5 cm. wide, slightly cordate at the base, acute or acuminate at the apex, doubly and irregularly serrate or sometimes obscurely lobed, glabrous above, sometimes pubescent along the veins beneath; panicles narrow, erect or ascending, 6–8 cm. long; flowers whitish, 6–7 mm. broad; samaras slightly spreading, 3.5–4.5 cm. long, wings 10–12 mm. wide. Blossoms in May; fruit ripe in August and September. (*Tatáricum*, of Tartary.)

The Tartarian maple is frequently cultivated as an ornamental tree and is perfectly hardy. It is a native of southeastern Europe.

MOUNTAIN MAPLE, *Acer spicatum* Lam., Encycl. Meth. Bot. 2:381, 1786

A shrub 2–4 m. high, very rarely a small tree; bark green or greenish; leaves mostly three- (rarely five-) lobed, 6–12 cm. long, 5–10 cm. wide, coarsely serrate, cordate at the base, lobes acute or taper-pointed, glabrate above, pubescent beneath; petioles 3–10 cm. long; inflorescence a raceme or narrow panicle, 7–10 cm. long; flowers greenish-yellow, 6–8 mm. broad; samaras 2–2.5 cm. long, wings slightly divergent, 7–8 mm. wide. Blossoms in May and June; fruit ripe in August and September. (*Spicátum*, in spikes.)

Mountain maple grows in moist, cool, often rocky woods. It is common throughout the northern parts of the region, infrequent to rare southeastward to northeastern Iowa and southern Wisconsin. It is distributed from Newfoundland to Manitoba and Saskatchewan, south to New England, New Jersey, the uplands of Georgia and Tennessee, Ohio, Michigan, and Iowa.

The wood is soft, light reddish-brown, and weighs 33 lbs.

SIBERIAN MAPLE, *Acer ginnala* Maxim., Bull. Phys. Math. Acad. Petersb. 15:126, 1857

A graceful, small tree or shrub up to 6 m. high; young twigs slender, yellowish-brown, somewhat angled, glabrous; leaves much longer than wide, 3–8 cm. long, mostly three-lobed, rarely five-lobed, rounded or truncate at the base, acuminate at the apex, middle lobe oblong or sometimes narrowed at the base and ovate-oblong, lateral lobes spreading and much shorter than the middle lobe, triangular or sometimes lanceolate, margin sharply and irregularly serrate, bright green and glabrous above, sparingly pubescent beneath, becoming nearly or quite glabrous with age, turning a brilliant red in autumn; petioles slender, 3–4 cm. long; flowers in terminal corymbs, yellowish-white; sepals and petals oblong; style elongated; samaras about 2.5 cm. long, with slightly divergent wings. Flowers in May and June; fruit ripe in July and August. (*Ginnála*, the vernacular name for the plant where it occurs native.)

Mountain maple, *Acer spicatum*

This maple is occasionally planted and is apparently entirely hardy in our climate. It is a native of northeastern Asia and Japan.

SUGAR MAPLE, HARD MAPLE, *Acer saccharum* Marsh., Arb. Am. 4, 1785

A large, handsome tree, attaining a height of 30–40 m. and a trunk diameter of 6–12 dm.; the bark of the trunk furrowed and rough, grayish-brown, separating into scales, the bark of the branches and young trees smooth and pale gray, sometimes with whitish blotches; leaves three- to five-lobed, 5–16 cm. long, 6–20 cm. broad, cordate, truncate or cuneate at the base, with rounded sinuses and pointed, sparingly sinuate-toothed lobes, glabrous and dark green above, brighter beneath and slightly hairy in the axils of the veins; petioles 4–10 cm. long; flowers in umbellate, drooping clusters, from terminal leaf-bearing and lateral leafless buds; pedicels long and very slender, hairy; calyx campanulate, greenish-yellow; sepals hairy at the apex, about 4 mm. long; petals none; stamens in the staminate flowers twice as long as the calyx, in the pistillate flower shorter than the calyx; samaras slightly spreading, 2.5–3.5 cm. long, wings 8 mm. wide. Blossoms in April and May; fruit ripe in July and August. (*Sacchárum*, sugar.)

Sugar maple grows in rich, mostly hilly woods. It is common throughout the forested parts of the Upper Midwest, except far northwestward, where it is infrequent. It is distributed from southern Newfoundland southward along the mountains to northern Georgia and western Florida, westward to Lake of the Woods, eastern Nebraska, eastern Kansas, and Texas.

This maple is often planted as a shade tree. The wood is heavy and close-grained, hard, tough, and takes a good polish. It has a high fuel value and is much used as firewood. Forms with the grain curled or contorted are known as "curled" or "birdseye maple" and are much valued in cabinet-making. The sap is the main source of "maple sugar." The Chippewa Indians of the northern part of Minnesota still make considerable sugar from the sap.

BLACK SUGAR MAPLE, *Acer nigrum* Michx. f., Hist. Arb. Am. 2:238, 1812

A tree nearly as large as *A. saccharum*, with bark somewhat darker; leaves green and scarcely paler beneath, usually pubescent on the under side and along the petiole, but not always so, lobes wider and usually shorter than in *A. saccharum*, not toothed, sinus at the base commonly closed, making the leaf appear peltate; stipules often conspicuous; in all other respects like the sugar maple. Blossoms in May. (*Nígrum*, black.)

Black sugar maple grows in rich, calcareous, or alluvial woods. It occurs mostly on stream and river bottoms in the southern parts of the area, where it seems quite distinct; northward it appears to grade into the preceding species. It is distributed from southwestern Quebec and New Hampshire west to Minne-

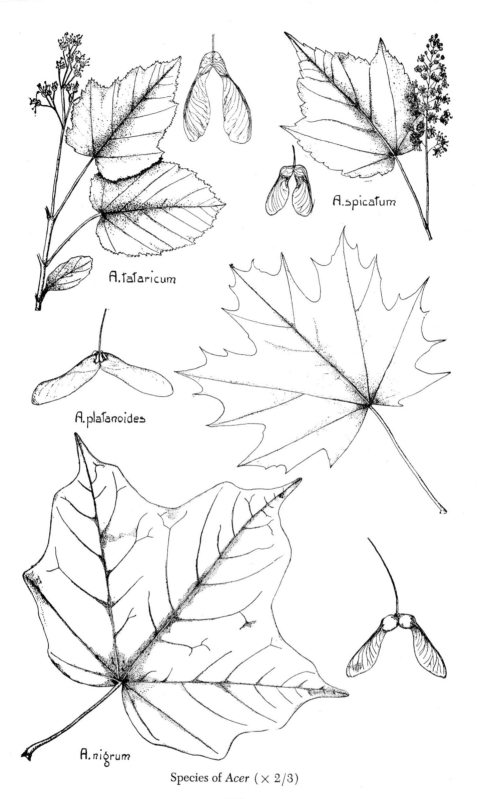

A.spicatum

A.tataricum

A.platanoides

A.nigrum

Species of *Acer* (× 2/3)

sota and South Dakota, south to Georgia, Alabama, Louisiana, and eastern Kansas.

The wood is essentially the same as that of the sugar maple, and the sap is used in the same way.

NORWAY MAPLE, *Acer platanoides* L., Sp. Pl. 1055, 1753

A large tree with spreading branches, sometimes attaining a height of 32 m.; leaves five- (rarely seven-) lobed, 8–20 cm. wide, 7–15 cm. long, slightly cordate at the base, lobes coarsely toothed and acute-pointed, glabrous above, pubescent in the angles of the veins beneath; petioles 8–10 cm. long; inflorescence a corymb, appearing with the leaves, 6–7 cm. broad, glabrous; flowers yellowish-green, 10–12 mm. broad; samaras widely spreading, 3–5 cm. long, wings 8–10 mm. wide. Blossoms in May; fruit ripe in autumn. (*Platanoídes*, like the plane tree.)

Norway maple is grown in parks and along boulevards and sometimes escapes from cultivation in the East. It is a native of middle Europe and Asia Minor.

Several garden forms are recognized, among which the following are frequently planted in our region: f. *globosum*, having a globose head; f. *Reitenbachi*, greenish-red when unfolding, turning dark blood-red in late summer; f. *Schwedleri*, leaves bright red when young, later turning to dark green.

BOX ELDER, *Acer Negundo* L., Sp. Pl. 1056, 1753

A tree 12–20 m. high, usually dividing into a number of stout, spreading branches; the bark on the trunk dark gray or brown, deeply divided into broad, rounded ridges; leaves three- to five-foliolate, with slender petioles, leaflets ovate or oval, 4–10 cm. long, 2–7 cm. broad, rounded or wedge-shaped at the base, acute or acuminate at the apex, coarsely and irregularly serrate, sometimes three-lobed, glabrous or slightly pubescent, bright green above, paler beneath; flowers dioecious, appearing with the leaves, the staminate borne in umbel-like clusters from nonleafy shoots, the pistillate in terminal racemes on leafy shoots, small, greenish, the staminate on long, hairy pedicels; fruit in racemes; samaras slightly spreading, wings 4–5 cm. long, 10–14 mm. wide, greenish-yellow, falling in autumn or persisting into the winter. Blossoms in April; fruit ripe in autumn. (*Negúndo*, of uncertain derivation.)

Along banks of streams and lakes and along fences, edges of thickets, and similar places, box elder is common throughout the area, especially southward and westward, less frequent northeastward. It is distributed from Vermont to Minnesota, south to Florida, Louisiana, and Texas. It is extensively planted as a shade tree and windbreak, especially in the midwestern prairie regions. It reproduces very easily from seed. The wood is creamy-white in color, close-grained, light, soft, and not strong. It is used for fence posts, firewood, and to a small extent for the manufacture of furniture. The sap is used in some localities for making maple sugar.

Acer Negundo L. var. *violaceum* (Kirsch.) Jäger, in Jäger & Biessn., Ziergeh. ed. 2, 6, 1884.

Differs from the species in having the young branches pale- or bluish-violet, covered with a glaucous bloom; winter buds slightly larger than in the species; leaves three- to seven-foliolate, leaflets somewhat thicker and lanceolate to oblong-ovate or obovate, often entire or irregularly dentate or lobed, pubescent along the veins beneath and with conspicuous tufts of hairs in the axils of the veins. (*Violáceum*, purplish, referring to the color of the twigs.)

This variety occurs with the species but is not common. It is distributed from Michigan to Montana, south to Missouri, Kansas, and Colorado.

Acer Negundo var. *interius* (Britton) Sarg., Bot. Gaz. 67:239, 1919

Young branches covered with a close, pale, and short pubescence; leaves tri-foliolate, the petiole and rachis as well as the petiolules short-pubescent; leaflets ovate to obovate, coarsely serrate, the terminal one more or less distinctly three-lobed, generally villous-pubescent along the veins beneath. (*Intérius*, relating to the inner part of the country.)

This variety is infrequent westward in our area. It is distributed from Mani-toba to Montana, south to Missouri, Oklahoma, New Mexico, and Arizona.

SOAPBERRY FAMILY, Sapindaceae

Trees or shrubs, rarely herbaceous plants, with watery sap; leaves alternate, or more rarely opposite, pinnately or palmately compound, without stipules; flowers polygamo-dioecious, regular or more commonly irregular; calyx-lobes four or five, imbricated; petals three to five; disk fleshy; stamens five to ten, often eight, rarely more numerous, usually inserted within the disk; ovary two- to four-celled; ovules one or more in each cavity; fruit various.

This family includes about a hundred and twenty-seven genera and nearly eleven hundred species, chiefly confined to tropical regions, a few subtropical and temperate. One genus is planted in this area.

Horse Chestnut, Buckeye
Aesculus L., Sp. Pl. 344, 1753

Trees or shrubs with opposite, digitately compound leaves; leaflets serrate and straight-veined; flowers in a terminal panicle, often polygamous, most of them with imperfect pistils; calyx tubular, five-lobed, often gibbous at the base; petals four or five, unequal; stamens six to eight (mostly seven), unequal in length; ovary three-celled; style one; ovules two in each cavity of the ovary; fruit a leathery capsule, three-valved, three-seeded, or frequently only one-seeded; seeds very large with thick, shining coat and a large scar; cotyledons very thick and fleshy. (*Aésculus*, Latin name of some oak or mast-bearing tree.)

This genus includes about sixteen species, natives of America and Asia.

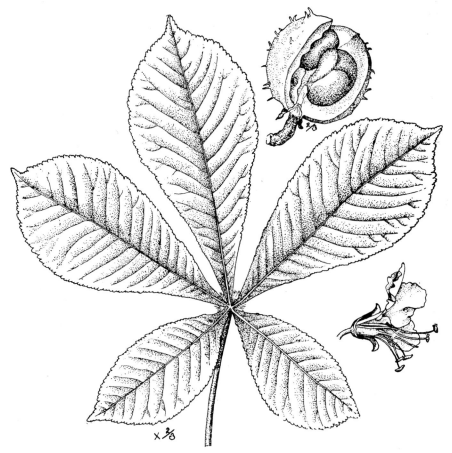

Aesculus Hippocastanum

KEY TO SPECIES OF AESCULUS

1. Flowers white, spotted with yellow and purple; leaflets abruptly acuminate.......
....*Ae. Hippocastanum* (p. 295)
1. Flowers yellow; leaves acuminate; bark fetid..............*Ae. glabra* (p. 296)

HORSE CHESTNUT, *Aesculus Hippocastanum* L., Sp. Pl. 344, 1753

A medium-sized to large tree, 10–20 m. high; bark brown, fissured into irregular, plate-like scales; leaves long-petioled; leaflets five to seven (sometimes three), obovate, sessile, 8–20 cm. long, 2.5–6 cm. wide, narrowed toward the base, abruptly acuminate at the apex, irregularly crenate-serrate, pubescent when young, glabrate when mature; flowers numerous in large panicles, white, blotched with yellow, showy, 12–15 mm. long; stamens exserted; fruit globose, covered with spines; seeds with a large, conspicuous scar. Blossoms in May and June; fruit ripe in August and September. (*Hippocástanum*, horse chestnut.)

This species is cultivated to a slight extent in parks and yards, especially in the southeastern part of the area. It was introduced from Asia via Europe. It is

295

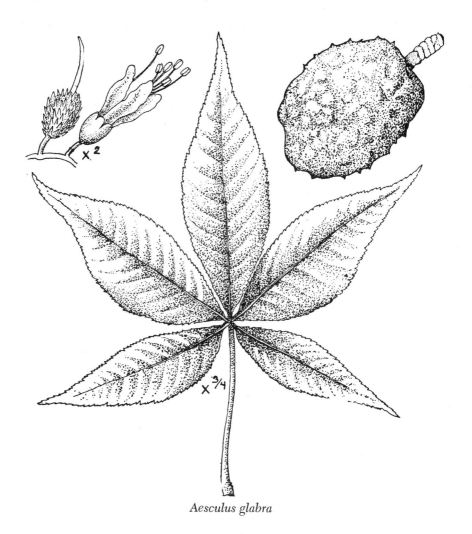

Aesculus glabra

grown very extensively farther south and east and is occasionally found escaped from cultivation.

The wood is whitish, slightly tinged with yellow, light, soft, and very close-grained.

OHIO BUCKEYE, FETID BUCKEYE, *Aesculus glabra* Willd., Enum. Pl. Hort. Berol. 405, 1809

A tree reaching a maximum height of about 16 m.; the bark of the trunk dark and furrowed, exhaling a fetid odor; leaves opposite, long-petioled; leaflets five to seven, oval, oblong or lanceolate, 8–15 cm. long, 2.5–6 cm. wide, narrowed at the base, acuminate at the apex, finely and sharply serrate, glabrous above, pubescent in the axils of the veins beneath; inflorescence a terminal panicle, 10–15 cm. long, about 5 cm. in diameter; flowers numerous, pale yellow, about 15 mm. long; calyx campanulate; petals four, slightly unequal; stamens curved, exserted; fruit 2.5–3.5 cm. in diameter, very prickly when young, becoming smoothish at maturity. Blossoms in April and May; fruit ripe in August and September. (*Glábra*, smooth.)

This tree is frequently planted in our area. It is distributed in woods from the Alleghenies of Pennsylvania west to Michigan, south to Alabama, Nebraska, and Oklahoma.

The wood is soft and white, the sapwood slightly darker, weighing 28 lbs. The timber is used for artificial limbs and for several kinds of woodenware articles.

BUCKTHORN FAMILY, Rhamnaceae

Erect or climbing shrubs or small trees, often thorny; leaves mostly alternate, simple, stipulate, often prominently three- to five-nerved; flowers in axillary or terminal cymes or racemes, small and regular, perfect or polygamous; calyx tube obconic or cylindric; sepals four or five, small; petals four or five, inserted on the calyx tube or lacking; stamens four or five, in front of the petals; disk fleshy; ovary free from or immersed in the disk, three- to five- (mostly three-) celled, one ovule in each cell; fruit a drupe or capsule, mostly three-celled; seeds solitary in each cell.

This family embraces about fifty genera and six hundred species, natives of warm and temperate regions.

KEY TO GENERA OF RHAMNACEAE

1. Calyx and disk free from the ovary; fruit a drupe. . . . .*Rhamnus* (p. 297)
1. Calyx and disk adherent to base of ovary; fruit a dry capsule. .*Ceanothus* (p. 299)

Buckthorn

Rhamnus L., Sp. Pl. 193, 1753

Shrubs or small trees with alternate or sometimes opposite, simple, pinnately veined leaves; flowers in axillary racemes, panicles or cymes, perfect or polygamous, greenish; calyx tube campanulate, lined with a disk, four- or five-toothed; petals four or five, small, short-clawed, notched at the end and wrapped around stamens, or sometimes lacking; disk free from the ovary; stamens four or five, in front of the petals, short; ovary three- or four-celled; style three- or four-cleft; fruit a berry-like drupe, oblong or globose, containing three or four nutlet-like seeds. (*Rhámnus*, Greek *rhamnos*, buckthorn.)

This is a genus of about seventy-five species, natives of temperate and warm regions. Five of these occur in the eastern and six in the western parts of North America. The species of this genus, and particularly the European ones, are the alternate hosts for the oat rust, *Puccinea coronata*. It is therefore inadvisable to plant oats in the vicinity of buckthorn hedges, and where oats are an important crop, the planting of buckthorn should be discouraged.

KEY TO SPECIES OF RHAMNUS

1. Leaves crenate-serrate; flowers dioecious or polygamous, nutlets grooved on the back.
   2. Leaves with 5–7 pairs of veins; sepals and stamens 4, petals wanting; low native shrub . . . .*R. alnifolia* (p. 298)
   2. Leaves with 3–4 pairs of veins; sepals, petals and stamens 4; introduced shrub or small tree . . . .*R. cathartica* (p. 299)
1. Leaves with entire or faintly crenulate margins; flowers perfect; nutlets smooth on the back . . . .*R. Frangula* (p. 299)

DWARF ALDER, *Rhamnus alnifolia* L'Her., Sert. Angl. 3, 1788

A small shrub 3–6 dm. high, thornless; bark gray or dark on the old branches; young twigs puberulent; leaves alternate, ovate to elliptic 4–10 cm. long, 2–5 cm. wide, rounded or narrowed at the base, acute or obtuse at the apex, crenate-serrate, glabrous above, puberulent along the veins beneath, veins nearly straight, in four to six pairs; petioles 4–10 mm. long; flowers one to three in the axils of the leaves and appearing with them, green, small, 2–3 mm. broad, mostly dioecious; sepals five, about 1 mm. long; petals lacking; pedicels slender, 4–5 mm. long; fruit a black, ovoid or globose drupe, about 6 mm. in diameter; nutlets three. Blossoms in May. (*Alnifólia*, leaves as in *Alnus*, the alder.)

Dwarf alder grows mostly in swamps, low woods, and meadows. It is common throughout the northern parts of the Upper Midwest as far south as the forty-fifth parallel, infrequent farther south. It is distributed from Newfoundland to British Columbia, south to New Jersey, Pennsylvania, Illinois, Nebraska, Wyoming, and California.

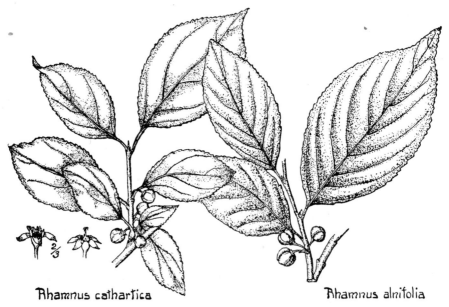

Rhamnus cathartica   Rhamnus alnifolia

Species of *Rhamnus*

BUCKTHORN FAMILY

BUCKTHORN, *Rhamnus cathartica* L., Sp. Pl. 193, 1753

A shrub or small tree 2–6 m. high; bark brown; twigs often ending in stout thorns; leaves alternate or sometimes opposite, ovate or elliptic, 3–6 cm. long, 1.5–3 cm. wide, rounded or narrowed at the base, obtuse or acuminate at the apex, minutely serrate, glabrous; petioles 1–2 cm. long; flowers clustered in the axils of the leaves, dioecious, greenish, about 4 mm. broad; sepals four, spreading or reflex, lanceolate, 2 mm. long; petals four, minute, erect, about the same length as the stamens; pedicels 5–8 mm. long, slender; fruit a globose drupe about 8 mm. in diameter, with three or four grooved nutlets. Flowers in May and June, fruit ripe in August and September. The leaves remain green and are retained on the shrubs until very late in the autumn. (*Cathártica*, purgative.)

This shrub is frequently planted for hedges. It was introduced from Europe and is a native of that continent and Asia.

ALDER BUCKTHORN, *Rhamnus Frangula* L., Sp. Pl. 193, 1753

A shrub or small tree up to 7 m. high; young twigs grayish-brown, somewhat puberulent; older twigs brown or grayish, generally dotted with numerous light-colored lenticels; leaves alternate, thin, elliptic to obovate, 3.5–6.5 cm. long, 2–4.5 cm. wide with from five to eight pairs of veins, rounded or narrowed at the base, acute or short-acuminate at the apex, bright green and glabrous above, somewhat paler and finely pubescent along the veins beneath, becoming nearly or quite glabrous with age, margin entire or sometimes faintly crenulate; petioles 1–2 cm. long; flowers greenish, axillary, in few-flowered umbels or sometimes solitary; hypanthium short-campanulate; sepals five, narrowly ovate, acute, mostly erect; petals obovate, emarginate; pedicels 5–10 mm. long; fruit a sub-globose drupe, about 8 mm. in diameter, purplish-black when ripe; nutlets three, compressed, not grooved on the back. Blossoms in May and June; fruit ripe in July and August. (*Frángula*, Latin name of this plant in the Middle Ages.)

Alder buckthorn is occasionally planted as an ornamental shrub. It is a native of Europe and western Asia, and has been naturalized in New York, New Jersey, and Long Island.

Redroot
Ceanothus L., Sp. Pl. 195, 1753

Low bushes or shrubs with alternate, simple, petioled leaves; flowers white, blue, or yellow, in small umbel-like clusters forming dense panicles or corymbs at the summit of naked flower branches; calyx tube top-shaped, sepals five, incurved; petals five, hooded and spreading, with slender claw, longer than the calyx lobes, attached under the disk; stamens five; filaments elongated; ovary sunk in the disk, three-celled; styles three, short; fruit a dry capsule, three-lobed, splitting lengthwise at maturity into three nutlets. (*Ceanóthus*, ancient Greek name for some plant.)

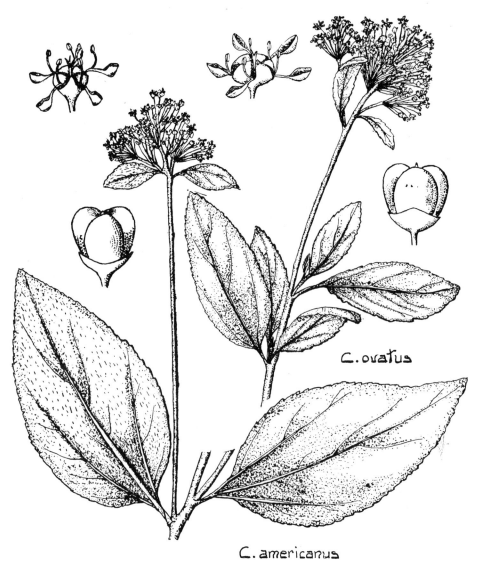

C. ovatus

C. americanus

Species of *Ceanothus*

Of the thirty-five species of this genus, natives of North America and Mexico, only the two following occur within our range.

KEY TO SPECIES OF CEANOTHUS

1. Leaves ovate or ovate-oblong, pubescent...............*C. americanus* (p. 300)
1. Leaves oblong or narrowly oval, or elliptic-lanceolate, nearly smooth............
....*C. ovatus* (p. 301)

NEW JERSEY TEA, *Ceanothus americanus* L., Sp. Pl. 195, 1753

Branching shrub, 3–9 dm. high, with several branches from a deep-reddish root, branches grayish to reddish-brown, more or less downy-pubescent above, nearly or quite glabrous below; leaves ovate or ovate-oblong, with three principal nerves, 3–10 cm. long, 2.5–5.5 cm. broad, mostly obtuse or cordate at the base, acute at the apex, finely serrate, pubescent on both sides, especially along the veins; petioles 6–12 mm. long; peduncles several, axillary and terminal, naked or with one or two leaves just below the flowers, 10–15 cm. long; flowers very numerous, in dense umbel-like clusters, white, small, about 2 mm. broad; pedicels 7–8 mm. long; petals long and narrowly clawed; fruit globose, depressed, faintly three-lobed, splitting into three valves. Blossoms in June and July. (*Americánus*, American.)

In dry, open woods and on gravelly or rocky banks and moraines, this small shrub is common throughout the Upper Midwest except northeastward. It is distributed from central Maine to Ontario and Manitoba, south to Florida and Texas.

The shrub has a thick, gnarled root, often 15–20 cm. thick. The leaves were used for tea during the American Revolution.

SMALLER REDROOT, *Ceanothus ovatus* Desf., Hist. Arb. 2:381, 1809

A shrub 3–6 dm. high, much branched, nearly glabrous throughout; leaves narrowly oval or elliptic-lanceolate, 2–5 cm. long, 1–2.5 cm. wide, narrowed or rounded at the base, obtuse at the apex, finely and sharply glandular-serrate, glabrous or slightly pubescent along the principal veins; petioles about 5 mm. long; peduncles short, nearly always terminal; flowers in dense, umbel-like clusters, white, about 5 mm. broad; pedicels 10–15 mm. long; fruit globose, slightly flattened at the top, faintly three-lobed. Blossoms in June. (*Ovátus*, ovate, referring to the shape of the leaf.)

This shrub grows on rocky slopes and on sandy prairies and plains. It occurs throughout the area, but is less common than *C. americanus*, and is often associated with jack pine. It is distributed from western Maine and western Quebec to Manitoba, south to Georgia, Alabama, Arkansas, and Texas.

Ceanothus ovatus var. *pubescens* T. & G., S. Wats. Bibl. Index 1:166, 1878

Branchlets and lower surface of leaves permanently sordid-villous, fruit subglobose, slightly three-lobed. (*Pubéscens*, hairy.)

This variety is infrequent southward in our region.

GRAPE FAMILY, VITACEAE

Climbing or erect shrubs with watery, acid juice; leaves alternate, simple, palmately veined or lobed, or compound; tendrils and flower clusters opposite the leaves; flowers in panicles, racemes, or cymes, small, regular, greenish, perfect or polygamo-dioecious; calyx entire or four- to five-lobed; petals four or five, separate or coherent, valvate, often falling off when the flowers open; stamens four or five, opposite the petals; filaments short; disk present or some-

GRAPE FAMILY

times lacking; ovary two-celled, generally immersed in the disk; ovules one or two in each cavity; fruit a two-celled berry; seeds usually four, seed-coats bony.

This family of about ten genera and six hundred species is widely distributed, but the greater number of species occur in the tropical regions.

KEY TO GENERA OF VITACEAE

1. Hypogynous disk present; petals deciduous as they open.........*Vitis* (p. 302)
1. Hypogynous disk lacking; petals not deciduous as they open.................
....*Parthenocissus* (p. 302)

Grape
Vitis L., Sp Pl. 202, 1753

Climbing or trailing, woody vines, rarely shrubby, mostly with tendrils; leaves simple (in our species), usually palmately lobed or dentate; flowers in a compound thyrse, very fragrant, mostly dioecious or polygamo-dioecious; calyx very short, usually with a nearly entire border or none at all; petals five, separating only at the base, and falling without expanding; hypogynous disk of five nectar-bearing glands, alternate with the stamens; fruit a globose or ovoid berry, few-seeded and pulpy, seeds with a beak-like base. (*Vitis*, the classical Latin name of the vine.)

This genus includes about forty species, natives of warm and temperate regions. In addition to the following, some other species occur in the southern and western parts of the United States.

KEY TO SPECIES OF VITIS

1. Lower surface of the leaves velvety tomentose; berries 14–18 mm. in diameter. Cultivated ....*V. labrusca* (p. 302)
1. Lower surface of the leaf nearly glabrous, or pubescent along the veins and in their axils, not tomentose all over; berries 8–12 mm. in diameter. Native.
  2. Leaves green beneath, bristly gray-pubescent along the veins or nearly glabrous in age; margins sharply dentate......................*V. riparia* (p. 303)
  2. Leaves whitened or glaucous beneath, rusty flocculent-pubescent along the veins; margin crenate-dentate........................*V. argentifolia* (p. 304)

NORTHERN FOX GRAPE, *Vitis labrusca* L., Sp. Pl. 203, 1753

Climbing or trailing vines, often ascending tall trees; stems sometimes becoming 6–12 cm. in diameter; bark loose and separating into strips; twigs rusty pubescent, especially when young; leaves opposite the tendrils, cordate, dentate or deeply lobed, with rounded sinuses, 4–12 cm. long, 5–14 cm. wide, upper surface glabrous or nearly so when mature, tawny or rusty-pubescent beneath; petioles 5–10 cm. long, rusty pubescent; fertile flowers in compact panicles, 6–10 cm. long; staminate inflorescence looser; flowers yellowish-green, fragrant; berries black or brownish-purple, with a bloom, 10–15 mm. in diameter, borne in compact bunches, strongly musky. Flowers in May or early June; fruit ripe in September. (*Labrúsca*, the wild grapevine.)

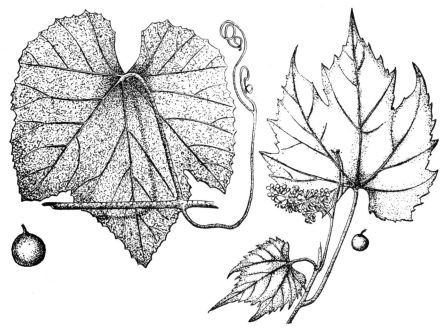

Species of *Vitis*: Left, *V. labrusca*. Right, *V. riparia*.

Northern fox grape occurs in moist or dry thickets, from New England to the Allegheny Mountains, south to Georgia; it occurs also in northwestern Indiana.

This species has given rise, through cultivation, to the Isabella, Catawba, Concord, and other varieties of grapes. The *labrusca* grapes have long been cultivated in the southern half of our region, but are not entirely hardy, requiring protection in winter.

The *Beta* grape, a cross between *V. labrusca* and *V. riparia* with possibly some admixture of *V. aestivalis*, is being increasingly cultivated in the Northwest. The foliage in general resembles that of *V. riparia*; the berries are intermediate in size. It is entirely hardy.

RIVER BANK or FROST GRAPE, *Vitis riparia* Michx., Fl. Bor. Am. 2:231, 1803 [*Vitis vulpina* L. 1753]

Climbing or trailing vine, ascending high into tall trees; stems 2–10 cm. in diameter, with loose, fissured bark; leaves alternate, the upper ones opposite tendrils or inflorescences, 6–20 cm. long, 5–15 cm. broad, cordate, mostly lobed, with broad sinuses, coarsely toothed, glabrous or with scattered hairs along the veins beneath; petioles 5–10 cm. long; inflorescences paniculate, rather loose, 8–12 cm. long; flowers small, greenish, very fragrant; fruit a bluish-black berry, with bloom, 6–10 mm. in diameter, very juicy and sour. Blossoms in May and June; fruit ripe from September to November. (*Ripária*, of river banks.)

On river banks and in rich woods and thickets, this grape is common through-

303

out the area. It is distributed from Quebec to Manitoba and Montana, south to New England, West Virginia, Tennessee, Missouri, Texas, and New Mexico.

The wild grape vine is sometimes grown as a climber on porches, pergolas, and similar structures. The fruit is used in making wine and preserves.

Vitis riparia var. *syrticola* (Fern & Wieg.) Fernald, Rhodora 41:431, 1939

Differs from the species in having the petioles and under surface of the leaves, especially along the veins, densely pilose. Sometimes producing tendrils or inflorescences from several successive nodes. (*Syrticola*, dweller on sand dunes.)

The variety appears to be limited in its occurrence in Minnesota to Houston and Winona counties.

BLUE or WINTER GRAPE, *Vitis argentifolia* Munson, Proc. Soc. Prom. Agric. Sci. 59, 1887 [*V. bicolor* Le Conte 1853]

A high-climbing or trailing vine with cinnamon-colored bark and long, intermittent tendrils; young branches terete, reddish-brown, glabrous or nearly so; leaves nearly orbicular in outline, deeply cordate at the base, 10–25 cm. long and nearly as wide, more or less deeply three- to five-lobed, the lobes broadly triangular with open, shallow sinuses between them or sometimes ovate or irregular with deep, rounded sinuses, their tips acute or acuminate, rarely blunt, margin crenate-dentate, leaves bright green and glabrous above, glaucous or whitened beneath (the bloom sometimes disappearing toward the end of the season), with rusty, flocculent pubescence in the axils of the principal veins and cobwebby along the smaller reticulate veins; petioles rather stout, glabrous, 8–15 cm. long; inflorescence compact; berries bluish-black, with a bloom, 8–10 mm. in diameter, sour; seeds about 4 mm. long. Blossoms in late May or early June; fruit ripe in September and October. (*Argentifólia*, silvery-leaved.)

This grape is infrequent in dry woods and thickets southward, and is known to occur in Minnesota only as far north as Wabasha County. It is distributed from New Hampshire to Michigan, Wisconsin, and Minnesota, south to Virginia, Alabama, Tennessee, Missouri, and Kansas.

Virginia Creeper, Woodbine
Parthenocissus Planch., in A. & C. de Candolle, Mon. Phan. 5:447, 1887

Climbing or trailing, woody vines with alternate, digitately compound or simple, lobed leaves; tendrils tipped with adhesive expansions or disks, or sometimes only coiling; inflorescence a compound cyme or panicle, flowers perfect or polygamo-dioecious; calyx slightly five-lobed; petals thick and concave, expanding before dropping off, disk obsolete or wanting in our species; stamens five; ovary two-celled; ovules two in each cavity; fruit a globose, one- to four-seeded berry, flesh thin, inedible. (*Parthenocissus*, Greek *parthenos*, virgin, *cisso*, ivy.)

304

This is a genus of about ten species, natives of eastern North America and Asia.

KEY TO SPECIES OF PARTHENOCISSUS

1. Leaves simple and three-lobed, sometimes three-foliolate. .*P. tricuspidata* (p. 305)
1. Leaves all palmately compound, five- to seven-foliolate (rarely three-foliolate).
   2. Tendrils with from five to twelve branches, mostly with adhesive disks; leaflets dull green above; cymes forming a terminal panicle. . .*P. quinquefolia* (p. 306)
   2. Tendrils with from two to five branches, mostly without adhesive disks; leaflets lustrous above; cymes dichotomous. . . . .*P. inserta* (p. 308)

BOSTON IVY, *Parthenocissus tricuspidata* (Sieb. & Zucc.) Planch., in A. & C. de Candolle, Mon. Phan. 5:452, 1887

A high-climbing vine, very closely appressed when growing on walls; young shoots, and foliage pinkish, with scattered granules of wax; tendrils short and much branched, adhesive disks large and numerous; leaves mostly simple, three-lobed and palmately veined, more rarely three-foliolate, very coarsely toothed, the teeth mucronate-tipped and bristly ciliate, both surfaces with a few scattered, short, stiff hairs; the simple leaves cordate at the base, acute at the apex, 5–9 cm. long, 5–8 cm. wide; leaflets of the compound leaves 5–7 cm. long, the two lateral ones oblique at the base; petiole stout, 4–8 cm. long; flowers in short-stalked racemes; fruit a blue-black berry. (*Tricuspidáta*, three-toothed.)

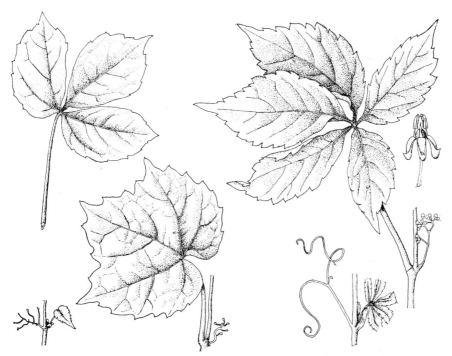

Species of *Parthenocissus*: Left, *P. tricuspidata*. Right, *P. inserta*.

This species is not reliably hardy in the Upper Midwest, but is able to endure our winters if grown in fairly well protected situations. It is very extensively cultivated in the eastern states. It is a native of China and Japan.

VIRGINIA CREEPER, WOODBINE, *Parthenocissus quinquefolia* (L.) Planch., in A. & C. de Candolle, Mon. Phan. 5:448, 1887 [*Ampelopsis quinquefolia* Michx. 1803; *Psedera quinquefolia* Greene 1906]

A high-climbing or trailing, woody vine; stem sometimes 3–6 cm. in diameter; tendrils opposite the leaves, five- to twelve-branched, mostly ending in adhesive disks; leaves petioled, five- to seven-foliolate, leaflets stalked, oval-elliptic or oblong-lanceolate, 4–12 cm. long, 2–6 cm. wide, coarsely serrate, dull green above, much paler or glaucescent beneath, glabrous throughout; inflorescence paniculate, 6–12 cm. long, rather loose, its main branches unequal; flowers small, greenish, about 6 mm. broad; calyx forming a shallow cup; petals spreading or reflexed, about 2.5 mm. long; stamens erect, slightly shorter than the petals; fruit a blue-black berry, not very fleshy, 6–7 mm. in diameter. Blossoms in June; fruit ripe in September. (*Quinquefólia*, five-leaved.)

In woods, in thickets, and on rocky banks, Virginia creeper as a native plant occurs infrequently southward in our area, but is extensively planted as a climber on porches, trellises, and walls. It is called *Parthenocissus* or *Ampelopsis Engelmanni* by horticulturists. It is distributed from southern Maine and southwestern Quebec to southeastern Minnesota, south to Florida, Texas, and Mexico.

Parthenocissus quinquefolia

Woodbine, *Parthenocissus quinquefolia*, on elm trees
in Houston County, Minnesota

307

LINDEN FAMILY

The native material appears to belong to the variety *P. quinquefolia* var. *hirsuta* (Pursh) Planch., characterized by pubescent foliage. A form with numerous aerial roots has been described as var. *Saint-Paulii* Rehder. The latter is known to occur as far north as the Twin Cities.

Parthenocissus inserta (Kerner) Fritsch, Exkursionfl. Oester. ed. 3, 321, 1922 [*P. vitacea* Hitchcock 1894]

A high-climbing or trailing vine; tendrils with from two to five long, twining branches, these only very rarely ending in adhesive disks, no aerial rootlets; leaves petioled, digitately compound; leaflets five to seven, ovate to ovate-lanceolate, 4–13 cm. long, 2–8 cm. wide, cuneate or slightly rounded at the base, acute at the apex, coarsely dentate, deep green, thin, somewhat shining above, scarcely paler beneath, glabrous or slightly pubescent; petioles 5–10 mm. long; inflorescences regularly dichotomous, flat-topped, peduncles 4–8 cm. long, the first branches nearly equal; flowers greenish, about 5 mm. in diameter; calyx entire, shallow; petals spreading or reflexed; fruit obovoid, bluish-black, 6–10 mm. in diameter, somewhat fleshy, at least more so than in the preceding. Blossoms in June. (*Insérta*, inserted.)

In woods, in thickets, and on banks, this species is common throughout the area of the deciduous forest, less frequent in the region of the coniferous forest. It is distributed from Quebec to Manitoba and Montana, south to New England, Pennsylvania, Illinois, Missouri, Kansas, Arizona, and California.

This vine is planted to some extent. Its leaves turn a brilliant scarlet in the fall.

LINDEN FAMILY, Tiliaceae

Trees or shrubs, rarely herbs, mostly with alternate, simple leaves, and deciduous stipules; flowers cymose or paniculate; sepals five, rarely three or four, valvate, deciduous; petals five, rarely three, four, or none, mostly imbricated; stamens many, generally united at the base into five to ten groups; anthers two-celled; carpels two to many, united into a compound pistil; ovary two- to many-celled, style one; stigma capitate or with as many lobes as there are carpels; fruit two- to many-celled, a capsule or nut-like.

This is a family of thirty-five genera and about three hundred fifty species. All the genera except the following are natives of the tropics or of the warm temperate regions. The inner bark of all *Tiliaceae* is very fibrous. The commercial fiber, jute, is derived from the genus *Corchorus*.

Basswood, Linden
Tilia L., Sp. Pl. 514, 1753

Trees with alternate, serrate, cordate leaves; flowers in drooping cymes; peduncle subtended by a broad membranaceous bract with which it is more or

308

less fused; sepals five; petals five; stamens many, free or united into five groups opposite the petals, either all fertile or with one petal-like staminode in each group; ovary five-celled, with the carpels opposite the sepals; ovules two in each cell, ascending; style simple, with a five-lobed stigma, fruit nut-like, one- to few-seeded, globose or pyriform, cotyledons lobed. (*Tília*, the classical Latin name for the linden.)

This genus includes about twenty species, natives of the North Temperate Zone.

KEY TO SPECIES OF TILIA

1. Petioles and leaves glabrous except for tufts of hairs in the axils of the veins beneath, rarely a few scattered hairs along the veins; cymes several- to many-flowered.
   2. Leaves 6–15 cm. long, green on both sides, flowers with a petal-like staminode in front of each petal.......................................*T. americana* (p. 309)
   2. Leaves mostly under 6 cm. long, pale or bluish underneath; flowers without staminodes ....*T. cordata* (p. 311)
1. Petioles and leaves pubescent, especially along the veins beneath; cymes mostly three-flowered ....*T. platyphyllos* (p. 311)

BASSWOOD, AMERICAN LINDEN, *Tilia americana* L., Sp. Pl. 514, 1753

A large tree attaining a maximum height in this area of about 25 m. and a trunk diameter of 1 m., with narrow, pyramidal head, frequently growing in clusters of two or more trees; the bark of the trunk dark gray with deep longitudinal furrows; branches and young trunks remaining smooth and light gray; twigs somewhat zigzag, rather slender, bright red or greenish, smooth and shining; buds elliptical, plump, bud scales glabrous except for ciliation along the margin; leaves broadly ovate, unequally cordate at the base, acuminate at the apex, 6–16 cm. long, 5–13 cm. wide (on stump sprouts sometimes attaining a length of 40 cm.), palmately veined, the main veins, connected with numerous parallel cross veins, dark green and glabrous above, somewhat paler beneath and glabrous except for small tufts of hairs in the axils of the main veins, rarely with a few scattered hairs along the main veins, sharply serrate, serrations terminating in awn-like appendages; petiole about half as long as the blade; stipules oblong, prominent on the young growth but soon deciduous; flowers appearing in midsummer in pendulous cymose clusters from the axils of foliage leaves, each cluster subtended by a membranaceous bract, to which the peduncle is fused for about half its length; bracts spatulate, 7–10 cm. long, very veiny, stalk of the bract very short; flowers very fragrant, 12–15 mm. in diameter; stamens about sixty, much shorter than the petals; style long exserted; fruit gray, covered with short stellate pubescence, without ridges, about 4–5 mm. in diameter. (*Americána*, American.)

Basswood is common in rich woods throughout the Upper Midwest. It is distributed from southern Quebec to Manitoba and North Dakota, south to New England, Alabama, Tennessee, Arkansas, and Texas.

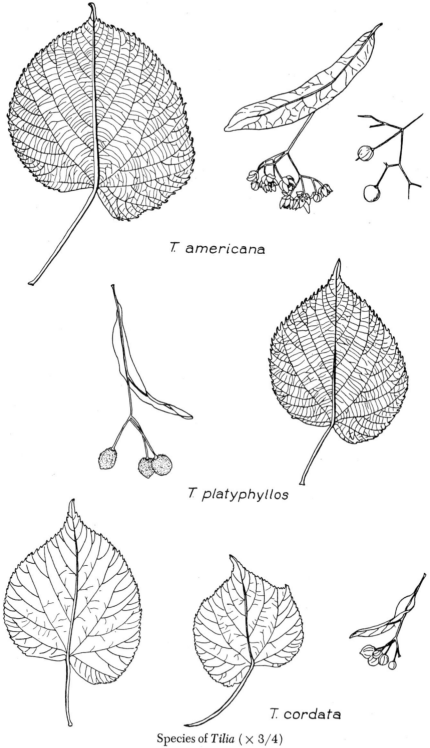

T. americana

T. platyphyllos

T. cordata

Species of *Tilia* (× 3/4)

The wood is white, soft, light, and weak. It is used for cabinet work, boxes, excelsior, pulp, and the like. The inner bark is very tough and fibrous and is used for mats and cordage.

WINTER LINDEN, SMALL-LEAVED LINDEN, *Tilia cordata* Mill., Gard. Dict. ed. 8, no. 1, 1768

A tree attaining a height of about 25 m., with an oblong to spreading crown; twigs glabrous, reddish-brown; buds elliptical, bud scales glabrous or sparsely pubescent and ciliate along the margin, marked with minute, glistening crystals; leaves nearly orbicular, 3.5–8 cm. long, 4–7.5 cm. wide, apex acuminate, base cordate, slightly unequal, palmately veined, the smaller veins forming an irregular network without conspicuous parallel cross-veins, upper surface dark green, glabrous, lower surface much paler and bluish, glabrous except for tufts of rusty hair in the axils of the principal veins, margin sharply serrate; petiole about three-fourths the length of the blade, glabrous; flowers in nearly upright cymes, bract oblanceolate to oblong, narrowed at the base, prominently stalked, stalk 0.6–20 mm. long; flowers about 1 cm. in diameter; stamens about thirty, longer than the petals; staminodes lacking; fruit elliptical to oval, thin-shelled, without ribs, covered with rusty, spreading hairs, about 5 mm. long and 4 mm. in diameter. Blossoms about two weeks later than the other European linden. (*Cordáta*, heart-shaped, referring to the leaf.)

This species is a European tree. It is occasionally planted in the Upper Midwest.

LARGE-LEAVED LINDEN, SUMMER LINDEN, *Tilia platyphyllos* Scop., Fl. Carn. 373, 1772

A medium-sized to large tree with a wide to oval crown; twigs pubescent, becoming smooth and reddish-brown; buds broadly ovoid, plump, bud scales sparsely hirsute or nearly glabrous except at the tips, marked with minute, glistening crystals; leaves broadly ovate to nearly orbicular, 6–10 cm. long, 5–9.5 cm. wide, abruptly acuminate at the apex, base obliquely cordate, palmately veined, the principal veins connected by numerous parallel cross-veins; young foliage gray-white-pubescent, mature leaves nearly or quite glabrous above, hirsute below, especially along the veins, margin sharply serrate; petiole about half as long as the blade, hirsute; cymes mostly three-flowered, rarely up to nine-flowered; bract oblong, narrowed or unequally truncate at the base, its stalk 0.5–1.5 cm. long; flowers about 1.5 cm. in diameter; stamens about thirty, exserted; staminodes lacking; ovary white-pubescent, conspicuous; fruit pear-shaped or oblong, more or less strongly four- or five-ribbed, with an abundant felt-like pubescence. Blossoms about three weeks earlier than the native basswood. (*Platyphýllos*, Greek, broad-leaved.)

A native of Europe, this linden is occasionally cultivated.

311

TAMARISK FAMILY

TAMARISK FAMILY, TAMARICACEAE

Trees or shrubs with alternate, mostly scale-like leaves without stipules; flowers perfect; sepals four or five; petals four or five, separate; stamens four or five (alternate with the petals) or ten or many, with extrorse anthers; carpels three to five, united; ovary superior, one-celled, with three to five parietal or almost basal placentas; stigmas three to five; fruit a three- to five-valved capsule, mostly with numerous hairy seeds; embryo straight, endosperm present or absent.

This family of Old World plants includes four genera and about a hundred species, chiefly of the Mediterranean and central Asiatic regions.

Tamarisk

Tamarix L., Sp. Pl. 270, 1753

Deciduous or sometimes evergreen shrubs or trees with scale-like leaves; flowers small, in panicles, either terminating the growth of the season or on short, lateral, leafless shoots; sepals four or five; petals four or five, imbricated, pink or whitish, usually withering persistent; stamens as many or twice as many as the petals, apiculate, free or united at the base; hypogynous disk more or less evident; carpels three or four; placentas nearly basal; styles three or four, more or less united, short or nearly obsolete; stigmas three or four; fruit a capsule; seeds small, bearing a tuft of hairs. (*Támarix*, the classical Latin name.)

This genus of about seventy-five species belongs to the warmer parts of the Old World, chiefly the Mediterranean and central Asiatic regions. Some of them are very characteristic plants of the Asiatic steppes and deserts. The following species are occasionally cultivated in the Upper Midwest. All are low to medium-sized shrubs in our climate. In all, the flowers have five sepals, five petals, and five stamens. None of them are reliably hardy, but in the latitude of Minneapolis they may be grown in sheltered situations. Even though sometimes they have to be cut back nearly to the ground after a severe winter, they form ornamental plants during the following summer.

KEY TO SPECIES OF TAMARIX

1. Leaves finely pubescent. . . . .*T. hispida* (p. 312)
1. Leaves glabrous.
    2. Petals deciduous; stamens inserted on the ring-like disk, the filaments enlarged at the base. . . . .*T. gallica* (p. 313)
    2. Petals persistent; stamens inserted between the lobes of the deeply lobed disk, the filaments not enlarged at the base.
        3. Bracts and leaves ovate-lanceolate; disk ten-lobed. . . .*T. pentandra* (p. 313)
        3. Bracts and leaves subulate; disk five-lobed. . . . .*T. odessana* (p. 314)

Tamarix hispida Willd., Abh. Akad. Berlin 1812–13, 77, 1816

A shrub about 1.5 m. high; branches upright, downy when young; leaves

Tamarix gallica

widened at the base, finely pubescent; flowers in terminal panicles of dense spike-like racemes, pink; petals deciduous; stamens inserted between the lobes of the five-lobed disk, the filaments somewhat enlarged at the base. (*Híspida*, hispid.)

This shrub is a native of the Caspian region.

Tamarix gallica L., Sp. Pl. 270, 1753

A shrub or small tree, 2–6 m. high, with slender, spreading, feathery branches; leaves rhombic-ovate, broadly clasping at the base, glabrous; flowers in panicled racemes, white or pinkish; petals deciduous; stamens inserted on the ring-like disk, the filaments enlarged at the base. (*Gállica*, French.)

This species ranges native from western Europe to the Himalayas.

Tamarix pentandra Pall., Flor. Ross. 2:72, 1788

A shrub or small tree up to 5 m. high; twigs purple, glabrous; leaves ovate-lanceolate, acute, glabrous; flowers in large panicles of dense racemes, pink; petals persistent; stamens inserted between the lobes of the ten-lobed disk, the filaments not enlarged at the base. (*Pentándra*, having five stamens.)

313

This tamarisk is a native of southeastern Europe and central Asia. Its horticultural variety *amurensis*, the Amur tamarisk, is probably the hardiest tamarisk in Minnesota.

Tamarix odessana Stev., *ex* Bunge, Tent. Gen. Tamaric. 47, 1852

A shrub about 2 m. high, with slender, upright branches; leaves subulate, decurrent, glabrous; flowers in a large, loose panicle of slender racemes, pink; petals persistent; stamens inserted between the lobes of the five-lobed disk, the filaments not enlarged at the base. (*Odessána*, from Odessa in southern Russia.)

This shrub is a native of the Caspian region.

ROCK-ROSE FAMILY, Cistaceae

Low shrubs or herbs, with alternate or opposite, simple, sometimes subulate or scale-like leaves; flowers in racemose or paniculate clusters or solitary, regular and generally perfect; sepals five, the two outer much smaller and bract-like, sometimes only three; petals three or five, convolute in the bud, sometimes wanting; stamens many, free, hypogynous; filaments slender; ovary one-celled with parietal placentas or incompletely three-celled to ten-celled with widely intruding placentas; ovules few to many, orthotropous; style simple or none; stigma entire or three-lobed; fruit a capsule, dehiscent by valves; seeds few to many, with small embryo and starchy or fleshy endosperm.

This is a family of about eight genera and a hundred and seventy species, mostly natives of the Northern Hemisphere. The following genus is represented in our area by a single species.

Hudsonia L., Mant. 1:11, 1767

Low, tufted, diffusely branched, heath-like shrubs, with small, awl-shaped or scale-like, alternate, persistent leaves; flowers yellow, numerous, crowded along the upper part of the branches; sepals three, similar; petals five, obovate or oblong, larger than the sepals; stamens many; style slender; stigma minute; ovary one-celled, placentas three, parietal, each with two ovules; capsule one-celled, three-valved, included in the calyx; seeds one or two at the base of each placenta. (*Hudsónia*, named for the English botanist, Wm. Hudson.) This genus includes three species, natives of eastern North America.

Hudsonia tomentosa Nutt., Gen. 2:5, 1818

A densely tufted, much branched, and matted shrub, 1–3 dm. high, hoary-pubescent throughout; branches very numerous, ascending; leaves densely imbricated and appressed, oblong to lance-oblong, about 2 mm. long, densely pubescent; flowers numerous, bright yellow, sessile or short-pedicelled, about 6 mm. in diameter at anthesis; sepals three, oblong, blunt and notched at the apex, slightly shorter than the petals; petals oblong or narrowly obovate; stamens ten to thirty, shorter than the petals; capsule ovoid, included in the persistent calyx. Blossoms in June; fruit ripe in July and August. (*Tomentósa*, tomentose.)

Growing on dunes, sandy lake-shores, sand blowouts, and outcrops of St. Peter sandstone, this species is infrequent in scattered places in the Upper Midwest. It is distributed from Quebec to northern Alberta, south to southwestern Maine, North Carolina, southern Ontario, northern Indiana and Illinois, Minnesota, North Dakota, and Saskatchewan.

Hudsonia tomentosa var. *intermedia* Peck, Rep. N.Y. State Mus. 45:86, 1893

Differs from the species in having more awl-shaped leaves, generally less densely crowded, and in the more obviously pedicelled flowers. (*Intermédia*, intermediate.)

Growing in similar habitats, this variety occurs infrequently in most of the geographical range of the species.

LEATHERWOOD FAMILY, Thymelaeaceae

Shrubs or trees with very tough, acrid inner bark; leaves alternate, simple and entire; flowers in racemes or capitate clusters or borne singly, regular and mostly perfect; calyx tubular, colored, and corolla-like, petals none (in our genera); stamens usually twice as many as the calyx lobes or fewer, inserted on the calyx tube and longer than its lobes; ovary one-celled; ovule one, style short or elongated; fruit a berry-like drupe.

This family of about thirty-seven genera and four hundred and sixty species is widely distributed, occurring most abundantly in Australia and South Africa. The following genus is represented in our area by a single native species.

Leatherwood, Moosewood
Dirca L., Sp. Pl. 358, 1753

Branching shrubs with tough, fibrous inner bark; branchlets jointed; leaves alternate, thin, short-petioled; flowers two to four in a cluster, appearing before the leaves, subtended by an involucre of hairy bud scales; calyx corolla-like, tubular funnel-shaped, obscurely four-lobed; petals lacking; stamens inserted on the calyx tube about the middle, twice as many as the lobes, the alternate ones longer; filaments very slender; disk lacking; ovary nearly sessile, one-celled; style filiform, long-exserted; fruit a red, oval-oblong drupe. (*Dírca*, perhaps from the name of a fountain in Thebes.)

This is a genus of two species, one found in the eastern United States, the other in California.

LEATHERWOOD, *Dirca palustris* L., Sp. Pl. 358, 1753

A branching shrub, 0.5–2 m. high; the bark on the stem brownish-gray, twigs

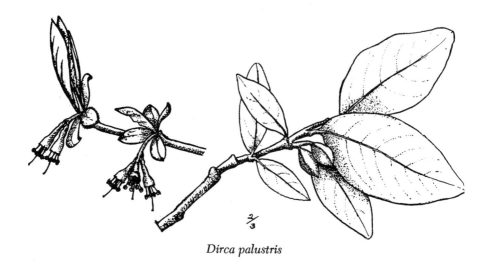

Dirca palustris

yellowish-green, jointed; wood white and brittle; inner bark unusually tough; bud scales hairy, becoming very large when the flowers and leaves unfold; leaves alternate, oval or oblong, 3–8 cm. long, 1.5–5 cm. wide, rounded at the base, blunt at the apex, entire, pubescent when young, glabrous in age; petioles about 2 mm. long; flowers appearing in clusters of two to five before the leaves, nearly sessile, the yellowish calyx about 1 cm. long; drupe oval-oblong, red, 10–12 mm. long. Blossoms in April and May; fruit ripe in August. (*Palústris,* pertaining to marshes.)

Leatherwood grows in rich deciduous or mixed woods. It is common in the northern parts of the region, infrequent southward in the Mississippi Valley to southeastern Minnesota, northeastern Iowa, and adjacent parts of Wisconsin. It is distributed from New Brunswick to Ontario and Minnesota, south to northern Florida and Louisiana.

The bark of this shrub was used by the Indians for making thongs. It produces violent vomiting if taken internally and is an irritant to the skin if applied externally.

OLEASTER FAMILY, ELAEAGNACEAE

Shrubs or trees, mostly silvery-scaly or stellate-pubescent; leaves entire, opposite or alternate; flowers in clusters or, rarely, solitary in the axils of the leaves or at the nodes of twigs of the preceding season; calyx of the perfect or pistillate flowers urn-shaped, four-lobed or -cleft, upper part deciduous; stamens four or eight, those of the perfect flowers inserted on the throat of the calyx; filaments short; disk round or lobed; ovary one-celled; ovule one, erect; style slender; fruit drupe-like, the lower part of the calyx becoming fleshy and enclosing the achene.

This family includes about twenty species, of temperate and tropical regions.

316

OLEASTER FAMILY

KEY TO GENERA OF ELAEAGNACEAE

1. Flowers perfect; stamens four; leaves alternate............*Elaeagnus* (p. 317)
1. Flowers dioecious; stamens eight; leaves opposite..........*Shepherdia* (p. 319)

Elaeagnus L., Sp. Pl. 121, 1753

Shrubs or trees with silvery-scaly branches and foliage; leaves simple, alternate, and petioled; flowers borne singly or in clusters of two to four in the axils of the leaves, short-stalked, perfect, or staminate and pistillate; calyx tubular, slightly constricted just above the ovary, campanulate and four-lobed, deciduous; stamens four, inserted on the upper part of the calyx tube; fruit drupe-like, fleshy or mealy, enclosing ellipsoid achene. (*Elaeágnus*, Greek *elaea*, olive, *agnos*, chaste tree.)

This genus includes about twelve species, natives of Europe, Asia, North America, and Australia, of which two (one native and one cultivated) are found in our region.

KEY TO SPECIES OF ELAEAGNUS

1. Twigs with brown scales, thornless. Native shrub.........*E. commutata* (p. 317)
1. Twigs without brown scales, often thorny. Cultivated tree.*E. angustifolia* (p. 317)

SILVERBERRY,*Elaeagnus commutata* Bernh., Allgem. Thür. Gartenz. 2:137, 1843 [*E. argentea* Pursh 1814]

A much branched, unarmed shrub, 1–4 m. high, stoloniferous; branches covered with ferruginous scales, becoming silvery; leaves oblong-ovate or oval-lanceolate, 3–7 cm. long, 1–3.5 cm. wide, rounded at the base, blunt or acute at the apex, densely silvery-scurfy on both sides; petiole 3–5 mm. long; flowers fragrant, silvery on the outside, yellow on the inside, 10–14 mm. long; lobes of the calyx triangular, about 3 mm. long; fruit 1 cm. long, the achene eight-striate. Blossoms in May; fruit ripe in July and August. (*Commutáta*, changeable.)

Growing on dry calcareous soils, silverberry occurs in northwestern Minnesota and adjacent parts of North Dakota and Manitoba. It is distributed from Quebec to Alaska, south to Minnesota and Utah, and in the Black Hills of South Dakota.

RUSSIAN OLIVE, *Elaeagnus angustifolia* L., Sp. Pl. 121, 1753

A tall shrub or more often a small tree, sometimes attaining a height of 10–16 m., often spiny; the bark on last year's twigs smooth and olive-colored; young shoots silvery-gray and densely covered with stellate hairs; leaves alternate, entire, ovate-lanceolate to lanceolate, 2.5–8 cm. long, 1–1.5 cm. wide, slightly narrowed at the base, obtuse or acutish at the apex, grayish-green with scattered peltate-stellate hairs on the upper surface, silvery-gray beneath; petiole about 1 cm. long; flowers axillary, solitary or in groups of two or three, very fragrant; calyx tubular-campanulate, about 1 cm. long, 8–9 mm. broad, four-lobed, silvery-gray on the outside, lemon-colored within, petals lacking; sta-

317

Species of *Elaeagnus*: Above (left and right), *E. angustifolia*.
Below, *E. commutata*.

318

mens very short, inserted near the throat of the calyx; pedicels 2–3 mm. long; fruit oblong-ovoid. Blossoms in June; fruit ripe in September. (*Angustifólia*, narrow-leafed.)

This tree, a native of Europe and Asia, is entirely hardy in our climate and is extensively planted as an ornamental shrub or tree on account of the silvery-gray foliage and fragrant flowers.

Buffalo Berry
Shepherdia Nutt., Gen. 2:240, 1818

Shrubs or small trees, twigs brown- or silvery-scurfy or stellate-pubescent; leaves opposite, petioled; flowers small, dioecious or sometimes polygamous, in fascicles or short spikes, at the nodes of the shoots of the preceding season or axillary; calyx of pistillate flowers urn-shaped, four-lobed, enclosing the ovary and becoming berry-like in fruit; disk eight-lobed; calyx of staminate flower four-parted, valvate in bud, stamens eight; disk many-lobed; style slender; stigma one-sided; fruit berry-like, the fleshy calyx enclosing an achene or nutlet. (*Shephérdia*, named for John Shepherd, an English botanist.)

Of the three known species of this genus, two occur in the Upper Midwest; the other is western.

KEY TO SPECIES OF SHEPHERDIA

1. Leaves ovate or oval, green above, silvery beneath; thornless shrub............
.... *S. canadensis* (p. 319)
1. Leaves oblong, silvery on both sides; mostly thorny shrub....*S. argentea* (p. 320)

CANADIAN BUFFALO BERRY, *Shepherdia canadensis* (L.) Nutt., Gen. 2:240, 1818 [*Lepargyraea canadensis* (L.) Greene 1890]

A spreading shrub 1–3 m. high, thornless; bark gray, young shoots brown scurfy; leaves ovate or oval, 2–6 cm. long, 1–2.5 cm. wide, rounded at the base, blunt at the apex, green and nearly smooth above, silvery beneath but with rusty scales, petiole 4–6 mm. long; flowers in short spikes at the nodes of the twigs, the flower buds formed in the summer with the leaves, expanding before or with the leaves next spring, perianth yellowish, about 5 mm. in diameter when expanded; fruit a yellowish berry, very bitter and nauseous, about 4–6 mm. long. Blossoms from April to June; fruit ripe in July and August. (*Canadénsis*, Canadian.)

This shrub grows on calcareous rocks and banks and sandy shores. It is fairly common in northern Minnesota and the adjacent parts of Manitoba and Ontario, less frequent in northern and eastern Wisconsin and North Dakota. It is distributed from Newfoundland to Alaska, south to central Maine, Vermont, western New York, northern Indiana, Illinois, and Minnesota; it occurs also in the Black Hills of South Dakota and in the Rocky Mountains to Colorado and New Mexico.

Species of *Shepherdia*: Left, *S. argentea*. Right, *S. canadensis*.
(Twigs about 3/4 natural size.)

BUFFALO BERRY, *Shepherdia argentea* Nutt., Gen. 2:241, 1818 [*Lepargyraea argentea* Greene 1890]

Shrubs or small trees 1–6 m. high, more or less thorny, with gray bark and brown- or silvery-scurfy twigs; leaves opposite, oblong-lanceolate or oblong, 2.5–5 cm. long, 6–15 mm. wide, rounded at the base, obtuse at the apex, densely silvery-scurfy on both sides; petiole 5–10 mm. long; flowers in clusters at the nodes of the twigs, yellowish; fruit ovoid, red, acid, and edible, 4–6 mm. long. Blossoms in May and June; fruit ripe in August and September. (*Argéntea*, silvery.)

Growing along streams, in coulees, and on hillsides, this species is rather infrequent in western Minnesota and the adjacent parts of Manitoba, North and South Dakota, and Iowa; it is more common westward. It is distributed from Manitoba to Alberta, south to Iowa, Kansas, Colorado, and New Mexico.

Buffalo berry is planted to some extent as an ornamental shrub. The acid, edible fruit is used for jelly-making.

GINSENG FAMILY, Araliaceae

Herbs, shrubs, and trees, sometimes climbing by means of aerial roots; stems frequently prickly or spiny; leaves alternate or rarely opposite, simple or palmately or pinnately compound; flowers perfect, polygamous, or dioecious, regular, usually small, greenish or whitish, commonly in umbels or umbellate heads; calyx small, entire or toothed, sometimes obsolete; petals mostly five, valvate or slightly imbricate, sometimes cohering at the apex and falling as a cap; stamens as many as petals and alternate with them, inserted on an epigynous disk; ovary inferior, one- to many-celled; styles free or connate; ovule solitary in each cell and pendulous from the apex, anatropous; fruit a berry or a drupe; seeds with abundant endosperm and small embryo.

This is a family of over fifty genera and about six hundred and sixty species, widely distributed in tropical and temperate regions.

KEY TO GENERA OF ARALIACEAE[*]

1. Leaves pinnately compound; petals imbricate..............*Aralia* (p. 321)
1. Leaves palmately compound; petals valvate...........*Acanthopanax* (p. 322)

Aralia L., Sp. Pl. 273, 1753

Aromatic herbs, shrubs, and small trees, frequently with spiny stems; leaves deciduous, once to thrice pinnately compound; leaflets serrate; flowers on jointed pedicels, in panicled umbels, often very numerous and showy; calyx lobes five, minute or sometimes wanting; petals five, imbricate; stamens five; ovary inferior, usually five-celled, capped with a more or less flattened disk; styles mostly five, distinct or connate only at the base; fruit a few-seeded berry or a drupe-like body, crowned by the persistent styles, frequently becoming dry. (*Arália*, der ivation obscure, perhaps a vernacular name.)

This genus of about forty species is most abundant in the tropics and sub-tropics. Besides the following, two herbaceous species are very abundant in the wooded parts of the Upper Midwest.

KEY TO SPECIES OF ARALIA

1. Stems slender, less than 1 m. high; prickles slender, bristlelike; leaves less than 3 dm. long. Native undershrub........................*A. hispida* (p. 321)
1. Stems very stout, 1–15 m. high; prickles stout; leaves 3–8 dm. long. Cultivated.
   2. Inflorescence with elongated main axis; leaflets closely serrate..............
    ....*A. chinensis* (p. 322)
   2. Inflorescence with short main axis and subumbellate, spreading secondary axes; leaflets more coarsely and remotely serrate..............*A. elata* (p. 322)

BRISTLY SARSAPARILLA, *Aralia hispida* Vent., Jard. Cels. pl. 41, 1800

A nearly herbaceous plant 5–10 dm. high; stems simple, rather slender, woody at the base and occasionally for 2–3 dm. above the base, armed with numerous weak, bristle-like prickles; leaves twice-pinnate, 1–3 dm. long; leaf-lets mostly sessile, lanceolate to lance-ovate, 2.5–5 cm. long, rounded or nar-rowed at the base, acute to acuminate at the apex, margin sharply and irregularly serrate, dark green above, pale beneath, glabrous, or somewhat bristly on the veins beneath; petioles of lower leaves 4–10 cm. long, the upper leaves nearly sessile, the petioles and rachises of the leaves more or less bristly-prickly; flowers in umbels about 2 cm. in diameter, the lower umbels solitary, long-peduncled, the upper three to ten forming a loose, irregular cyme; flowers white, about 2

[*] The Devil's-Club, *Oplopanax horridus* (Sm.) Miq., a coarse, prickly shrub of north-western America, occurs infrequently on Isle Royale in Lake Superior and in the Thunder Bay District of Ontario.

mm. in diameter, more or less monoecious; fruit purple-black, 6–8 mm. in diameter. Blossoms in June; fruit ripe in August. (*Híspida*, bristly.)

Bristly sarsaparilla grows in sandy and open woods and on outcrops of granitic rocks. It is common northeastward, mainly in the area of the coniferous forests. It is distributed from Newfoundland and southern Labrador to Manitoba, south to New England, West Virginia, northern Indiana, Illinois, and Minnesota.

CHINESE ANGELICA, *Aralia chinensis* L., Sp. Pl. 273, 1753

A sparingly branched, upright shrub (in warmer climates attaining the dimensions of a small tree up to 15 m. in height), with more or less prickly stems and branches; leaves 3–8 dm. long, usually thrice-pinnate toward the base, twice-pinnate in the middle and once-pinnate toward the end; leaflets sessile or nearly so, broadly ovate to oblong-ovate, 7–15 cm. long, rounded or narrowed at the base, acuminate at the apex, margin coarsely serrate, dark green above, usually pubescent beneath; petiole 1.5–2.5 dm. long, both the petiole and rachises unarmed; umbels numerous, in large compound panicles; flowers whitish, 6–7 mm. in diameter; styles distinct, disk depressed; fruit ovoid, angled, black. Blossoms after midsummer. (*Chinénsis*, Chinese.)

A native of eastern Asia, this shrub is occasionally planted but is not entirely hardy, new stems being formed from the root each year.

JAPANESE ANGELICA TREE, *Aralia elata* (Miq.) Seem., Journ. Bot. 6:134, 1868 [*A. chinensis* var. *manchurica* Rehder 1900]

A shrub or tree up to 15 m. high; stems usually prickly; leaves 4–8 dm. long, bipinnate, leaflets ovate or elliptic-ovate to narrowly ovate, 6–12 cm. long, apex acuminate, margin serrate with broad teeth or remotely serrulate, dark green above, glaucescent beneath, slightly pubescent along the veins when young; flowers white, in a broad corymbose inflorescence, with a short main axis and several subumbellate spreading branches. (*Eláta*, tall.)

A native of Japan and China, this species is hardier in our climate than the preceding one and therefore more often planted.

Acanthopanax Miq., Ann. Mus Lugd. Bat. 1:10, 1863

Deciduous, smooth or prickly shrubs or trees with palmately lobed or compound, alternate leaves; flowers perfect or polygamo-dioecious, in umbels that frequently are arranged in compound panicles; sepals minute or nearly obsolete; petals five, rarely four, valvate; stamens the same number as petals; carpels two to five; ovary two- to five-celled; styles two to five, more or less united; fruit a berry, somewhat flattened or nearly globose, pericarp thin, endocarp hard or chartaceous; seeds two to five. (*Acanthópanax*, spiny *Panax*.)

This is a genus of about eighteen species, of the eastern Asiatic region. One species is cultivated in our area.

DOGWOOD FAMILY

Acanthopanax Sieboldianus Mak., Bot. Mag. Tokyo 12:10, 1898 [*A. pentaphyllus* March. 1881]

A shrub 1.5–3 m. high, with arching branches and slender, compressed, straight prickles below the petioles; leaves palmately five- to seven-foliolate, on petioles about 10 cm. long; leaflets ovate-oblong to obovate-lanceolate, 2.5–7.5 cm. long, narrowed at the base, acute at the apex, crenate-serrate, green and glabrous on both sides or sometimes slightly spiny along the midrib beneath; petiole pubescent or spiny; umbels peduncled, borne on last year's wood; flowers greenish-white; sepals minute; petals oblong-ovate, reflexed; styles connate; pedicels pubescent at the base, 7–15 mm. long; fruit globose, 5–7 mm. in diameter. Flowers in June; fruit ripe in October. (*Sieboldiánus*, named for Siebold.)

This graceful shrub, a native of Japan, has been in cultivation for a long time and is occasionally planted in the Upper Midwest.

DOGWOOD FAMILY, Cornaceae

Shrubs or small trees, rarely herbs; leaves simple, opposite, verticillate or alternate, usually entire; flowers perfect, polygamous or dioecious, in cymes or heads; calyx four- to five-parted or toothed, adnate to the top of the ovary; petals four or five, valvate or imbricated, inserted at the edge of the cushion-shaped disk; stamens as many as the petals and alternating with them, or more numerous; ovary inferior, one- to four-celled; style one; ovule one in each cell; fruit a one- to four-celled, one- to four-seeded drupe.

Only two genera of the family occur in North America, one of which is represented in our flora.

Dogwood
Cornus L., Sp. Pl. 117, 1753

Shrubs or trees (occasionally herbs); leaves simple, mostly entire, opposite or sometimes alternate; flowers small, white or greenish, in cymes or heads (when in heads subtended by large, white, petal-like bracts in our species); calyx tube campanulate, four-toothed; petals four, spreading; stamens four; ovary two-celled, one ovule in each cell; stigma truncate or capitate; fruit an ovoid or globular drupe; stone two-celled and two-seeded. (Named from *córnus*, horn, alluding to the hardness of the wood.)

To this genus belong about thirty-five species, natives of the North Temperate Zone, Mexico, and Peru. In addition to the following, eleven others occur in North America.

KEY TO SPECIES OF CORNUS

1. Flowers in small umbel-like inflorescences subtended by an involucre of four yellowish bracts, appearing before the leaves from stalked buds of the previous season..*C. mas* (p. 324)

DOGWOOD FAMILY

1. Flowers in compound cymes, terminating leafy shoots of the season; involucre wanting.
    2. Leaves alternate, crowded towards the ends of the twigs . . . .
    . . . . C. alternifolia (p. 325)
    2. Leaves strictly opposite.
        3. Young growth rusty-pubescent; sepals 1–1.5 mm. long; style clavate . . . .
        . . . . .C. obliqua (p. 325)
        3. Young growth not rusty-pubescent; sepals 0.7 mm. long or less; style cylindrical.
            4. Leaves round-ovate; twigs yellowish-green; stems warty . . . .
            . . . . .C. rugosa (p. 326)
            4. Leaves ovate to elliptical or lanceolate, at least twice as long as broad; stems not warty.
                5. Twigs gray; inflorescence pyramidal, about as high as broad; flower buds long-ellipsoidal . . . . .C. racemosa (p. 328)
                5. Twigs red or red-purple, rarely yellowish; inflorescence flattened, broader than long; flower buds oval or oval-conic.
                    6. Pubescence appressed throughout.
                        7. Plants stoloniferous; sepals about as long as the disk; fruit and stone mostly broader than long; style somewhat enlarged at the top but constricted just below the stigma . . . .
                        . . . . C. stolonifera (p. 328)
                        7. Plant not stoloniferous; sepals shorter than the disk; fruit and stone mostly longer than broad; style not constricted just below the stigma . . . . .C. alba (p. 329)
                    6. Pubescence of the inflorescence and lower surface of the leaves spreading, more or less woolly . . . . .C. Baileyi (p. 331)

CORNELIAN CHERRY, Cornus mas L., Sp. Pl. 117, 1753

A shrub 2–5 m. high, with slender branches; young twigs grayish-green, finely appressed pubescent, older twigs yellowish- to reddish-brown, sometimes streaked with darker lines; leaves elliptic to elliptic-ovate, 4–11 cm. long, 2–5 cm. wide, with three or four pairs of veins, narrowed or sometimes rounded at the base, acuminate or acute at the apex, scantily appressed-pubescent above, often somewhat scabrous, lower surface with appressed hairs and also more or less woolly pubescence, particularly in the axils of the veins; petiole 5–10 mm. long, appressed-pubescent; flower buds appearing the previous season, spherical, rusty-pubescent, stalked, with a scaly peduncle about 5 mm. long, the inflorescence enclosed by four valvate bud scales; flowers appearing in early spring before the unfolding of the leaves; inflorescence umbel-like, subtended by an involucre formed from the four bud scales; involucral leaves yellowish, about 5 mm. long; flowers on slender, hairy pedicels about 8 mm. long; sepals minute; petals yellow, lanceolate, about 2 mm. long; fruit elliptical, about 1 cm. long, scarlet when ripe; stone ellipsoid, not ribbed. Blossoms in April and May; fruit ripe in September and October. (Mas, the male.)

This native of central and southern Europe and Asia Minor is cultivated in our area, especially the form with variegated leaves, f. aureo-elegantissima.

The flowering dogwood, C. florida, has been reported from southeastern

324

Minnesota, but there is no authentic evidence of its occurrence there. It has inflorescences similar to those of *C. mas*, but with four large, white, petal-like involucral bracts.

ALTERNATE-LEAVED DOGWOOD, PAGODA DOGWOOD, *Cornus alternifolia* L. f., Suppl. 125, 1781

A shrub or small tree, 2.5–8 m. high, with more or less whorled horizontal branches; bark smooth, dark or brownish on the main stem and streaked with white; young twigs yellowish-green, glabrous, older twigs yellowish-green to brownish; leaves alternate, clustered at the ends of the branches, elliptic-ovate to elliptic-oblong, 5–9 cm. long, 3–6 cm. wide, mostly narrowed at the base, acuminate at the apex, upper surface dark green with impressed veins, at first appressed pubescent, becoming nearly or quite glabrous with age, glaucous beneath, nonpapillate, pubescent with scattered appressed hairs and spreading hairs along the veins; petiole slender, 1–7 cm. long; inflorescence cymose-paniculate, somewhat convex, 3–6 cm. broad; peduncle stout, 2–4 cm. long, glabrous, its branches more or less pubescent; pedicels slender, 2–5 mm. long, appressed-pubescent; flower buds elliptic or obovoid; flowers white; sepals minute or nearly obsolete; petals ovate-oblong, about 3 mm. long, reflexed at anthesis; stamens somewhat exceeding the petals; style cylindrical; stigma capitate; disk inconspicuous; ovary elliptical, densely silky-appressed-pubescent; fruit globose, deep blue when ripe, 6–8 mm. in diameter, stone obovoid, slightly flattened and ridged and with a depression at the apex. Blossoms in May; fruit ripe in August. (*Alternifólia*, alternate-leaved.)

This shrub grows in woods, in thickets, and on rocky slopes, and is common in deciduous and mixed woods throughout the Upper Midwest except far northward to southern Manitoba and northwestern Ontario, where it occurs infrequently. It is distributed from Newfoundland to Minnesota and Manitoba, south to New England, Georgia, Alabama, and Missouri.

Pagoda dogwood, with its horizontal, platform-like stories (or spray) of branches and its dark-green, shining foliage, is a handsome shrub. It lends itself well to ornamental planting.

Cornus obliqua Raf., Western Review 1:228, 1819 [*C. Purpusii* Koehne 1899]

A shrub 1–2.5 m. high with dark to reddish-brown branches; young twigs greenish-gray to yellowish, densely rusty-pubescent; older twigs dark purplish-brown, tardily glabrate; leaves elliptic-ovate to elliptic-lanceolate, 5–8 cm. long, 1.5–4 cm. wide, narrowed or rounded at the base, abruptly and often long-acuminate at the apex, upper surface dark yellow-green, and finely and sparsely appressed-pubescent, lower surface paler yellowish-green, densely minutely papillate, finely appressed-pubescent with more or less spreading pubescence along the veins and occasionally over the entire surface, the pubescence rusty only on immature leaves; petiole about 1 cm. long or less, loose-pubescent; inflorescence a nearly flat cyme, 3–5 cm. in diameter, its branches spreading-pubescent; flower buds long-conic; flowers 8–9 mm. in diameter, white; sepals triangular-lanceolate, 1–1.5 mm. long; petals lanceolate, acute; stamens about as long as the petals; style stout, clavate, longitudinally furrowed; stigma capitate; disk reddish-brown; ovary obovoid, silky-white-puberulent, sometimes also with more or less spreading pubescence; fruit dull-blue, globose; stone broader than long, slightly flattened, oblique, irregularly and obtusely ribbed, about 5 mm. broad. Blossoms in June; fruit ripe in August. (*Oblíqua*, oblique, probably referring to the stone.)

Growing in swamps, in damp thickets, and on river bottoms, this shrub is fairly common in the southern parts of the area, infrequent and occasional northward in the Mississippi Valley to Morrison County, Minnesota. It is distributed from New Brunswick to Minnesota, south to New England, New Jersey, West Virginia, Kentucky, Arkansas, and Oklahoma.

This species can be readily distinguished from all our other dogwoods by its rusty young shoots, relatively large sepals, and stout, clavate style. In *Minnesota Trees and Shrubs* (1912) it was confused with the eastern and Alleghenian *C. amomum*, from which it appears to be satisfactorily distinguished by its papillate leaves, sparser and more appressed pubescence, which is rusty only on immature leaves and shoots, and by differences in the stone.

ROUND-LEAVED DOGWOOD, *Cornus rugosa* Lam., Encycl. Meth. Bot. 2:115, 1786 [*C. circinata* L'Her. 1788]

A shrub 1–3 m. high with yellowish-green to grayish, more or less warty stems and branches; young twigs greenish, sparsely pubescent, with mostly spreading hairs; leaves broadly ovate to nearly orbicular, 6–14 cm. long, 4–10 cm. wide, with from six to eight pairs of nerves, rounded or rarely subcordate or narrowed at the base, acuminate at the apex, dark green, finely appressed-pubescent and slightly hispid above, lower surface paler, bluish, and uniformly crisped-pubescent; petiole 1.5–2 cm. long, appressed-pubescent; inflorescence flat-topped, 4–7 cm. broad; peduncle and branches of the inflorescence rough-pubescent; flower buds ovoid; flowers white, about 6–8 mm. in diameter; sepals minute or nearly obsolete; petals oblong-lanceolate, acute or rounded at the apex, reflexed at anthesis; stamens considerably exceeding the petals; style cylindrical, appressed-pubescent; stigma flat-capitate; disk pubescent; ovary ellipsoid, appressed-puberulent; fruit globose, puberulent, white, 5–6 mm. in diameter; stone globose, bluntly ridged, about 3 mm. in diameter. Blossoms in June; fruit ripe in August. (*Rugósa*, rugose, probably referring to the leaves.)

This dogwood grows in woods, in copses, and on rocky wooded slopes throughout the forested areas of the Upper Midwest. It is distributed from Quebec to Manitoba, south to New England, West Virginia, Ohio, Indiana, Illinois, and northeastern Iowa.

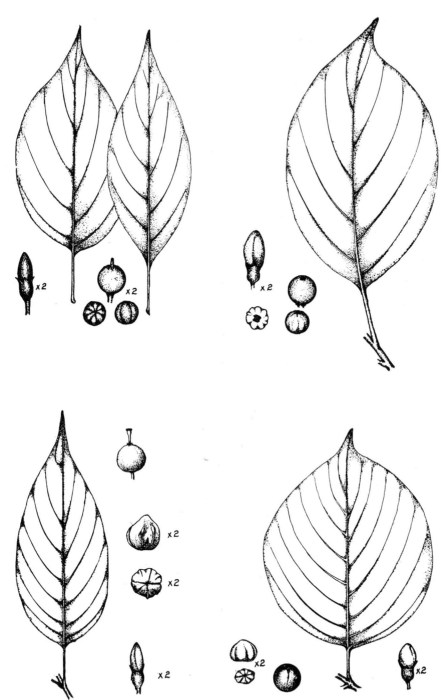

Species of *Cornus* (showing leaf, flower, bud, fruit, and stone):
Upper left, *C. racemosa*. Upper right, *C. alternifolia*. Lower left,
C. obliqua. Lower right, *C. rugosa*.

327

PANICLED DOGWOOD, *Cornus racemosa* Lam., Encycl. Meth. Bot. 2:116, 1786 [*C. candidissima* Marsh. 1785; *C. paniculata* L'Her. 1788]

A much branched shrub, usually 1.2–2 m. high, with ash-gray stems and branches; young twigs brownish, nearly or quite glabrous; leaves lanceolate to narrowly ovate, 4–8 cm. long, 2–4 cm. wide, narrowed at the base, mostly long-acuminate at the apex, with mostly four pairs of veins, margin often slightly crenulate; upper surface green and finely appressed-pubescent, lower surface somewhat paler, minutely papillate and appressed-pubescent; petiole slender, about 1 cm. long, nearly glabrous; inflorescence a cymose panicle, somewhat longer than broad; peduncle nearly glabrous, its branches minutely appressed-puberulent; flower buds long-ellipsoidal; flowers white, about 6 mm. in diameter; sepals triangular, minute; petals lanceolate to linear-lanceolate, acute, spreading at anthesis; stamens slightly exceeding the petals; style cylindrical, sparingly pubescent; stigma capitate; disk small; ovary conspicuously silvery-appressed-puberulent; fruiting pedicels bright red; fruit white, globose, 5–6 mm. in diameter; stone obovoid, somewhat flattened, about 4 mm. wide, nearly smooth. (*Racemósa*, racemose.)

Growing mostly in dry woods, copses, and open habitats, this shrub is common throughout the region except north of Lake Superior. It is distributed from central Maine to Ontario, Minnesota, and Manitoba, south to Delaware, West Virginia, Kentucky, Missouri, and Oklahoma.

Cornus racemosa f. *Nielseni* Moore, Rhodora 52:58, 1950

The form differs from the species in having the leaves variegated with yellow. It occurs infrequently in our area.

RED-OSIER DOGWOOD, *Cornus stolonifera* Michx., Fl. Bor. Am. 1:92, 1803

A shrub 1–3 m. high, stems ascending, often prostrate and rooting at the base, frequently forming extensive clumps; the bark of the stems and branches purplish-red, especially vivid in winter, rarely yellowish; young twigs green, becoming red before the close of the season, more or less finely appressed-pubescent; leaves ovate to ovate-lanceolate, 5–15 cm. long, 2–6 cm. wide, with from five to seven pairs of lateral veins, narrowed or rarely rounded at the base, acuminate at the apex, upper surface bright green, sparsely and finely appressed-pubescent, lower surface paler, bluish, papillate, appressed-pubescent, sometimes with a few spreading hairs along the veins; petiole rather stout, 1–3 cm. long, often tinged with red, scantily pubescent; inflorescence slightly convex, 3–4 cm. in diameter; peduncle and branches pubescent; flower buds ovoid; flowers white, about 8 mm. in diameter; sepals narrowly triangular, about 0.5 mm. long; petals oblong-lanceolate, 3–4 mm. long, acute or obtuse, somewhat reflexed at anthesis; stamens slightly longer than the petals; anthers 1–1.2 mm. long; style slightly expanded at the summit but constricted below the disk-shaped stigma; disk very conspicuous; ovary somewhat whitened and appressed-

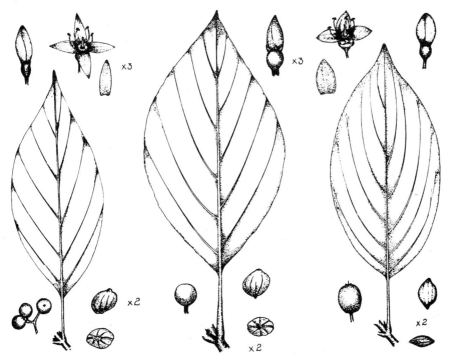

Species of *Cornus*: Left, *C. stolonifera*. Center, *C. Baileyi*. Right, *C. alba*.

pubescent; fruit slightly depressed-globose, 6–7 mm. in diameter, white or lead-colored, rarely bluish; stone usually broader than long, somewhat flattened and asymmetrical, striate. Begins to blossom in May and continues intermittently through the season. (*Stolonifera*, referring to the stoloniferous habit.)

Red-osier dogwood grows in low, moist thickets, in swamps, and on lake shores. It is common throughout the Upper Midwest except north of Lake Superior, where it is largely replaced by *C. Baileyi*. It is distributed from Labrador to the Yukon, south to New England, the District of Columbia, West Virginia, Ohio, Illinois, Iowa, Nebraska, and New Mexico.

From the bark of this dogwood the Indians prepared the "kinnikinnik" which they used for smoking.

This and the two following species are separated by very minor characters. They are regarded by Wangerin (*Pflanzenreich* 456a) as subspecies of a single collective species (*C. alba*). Further study is needed, particularly in the field, to determine the status of these forms.

SIBERIAN DOGWOOD, *Cornus alba* L., Mant. 1:40, 1767 [*C. tatarica* Mill. 1768]

A shrub with mostly upright branches, 1–3 m. high, not stoloniferous; twigs and branches bright red, especially during the winter season, young twigs greenish, becoming red by the end of the season, appressed-pubescent; leaves

329

Siberian dogwood, *Cornus alba*

elliptic-ovate or slightly obovate, with five or six pairs of veins, 6–11 cm. long, 2–6 cm. wide, narrowed or somewhat rounded at the base, mostly short-acuminate at the apex, yellowish-green above and finely appressed-pubescent, somewhat paler beneath, appressed-pubescent and often with a few spreading hairs along the veins, inconspicuously papillate, midvein somewhat rusty in appearance; petioles stout, sparsely pubescent, 1–2 cm. long; inflorescence flat, 4–7 cm. wide; peduncle and branches appressed-pubescent; flower buds short-ovoid; flowers white, 7–8 mm. in diameter; sepals almost obsolete; petals ovate, about 3 mm. long, spreading or somewhat reflexed; stamens much longer than the petals; style somewhat enlarged at the apex, stigma broad and capitate; disk very prominent; ovary appressed-pubescent; fruit somewhat elliptical, white; stone mostly longer than broad, very oblique, usually acute at the base and striate. (*Al'ba,* white.)

A native of European Russia and northern Asia, this dogwood is frequently planted.

The west American species segregated from *C. stolonifera* as *C. instolonea* A. Nelson appears not to be separable from the Old World *C. alba* L. by any reliable characters. It seems at most to be only a geographical variety of this species. It occurs in the Dakotas and apparently enters the western portion of Minnesota.

Cornus Baileyi Coulter & Evans, Bot. Gaz. 15:37, 1890

An erect shrub 1–4 m. high, not stoloniferous; the bark of the stems and branches purplish-red, especially vivid in winter; young twigs with a tinge of purple almost from the first, more or less loose-pubescent; leaves ovate to obovate, 3–10 cm. long, 2–6 cm. wide, with from five to seven pairs of lateral veins, rounded or sometimes narrowed at the base, mostly short-acuminate at the apex, upper surface dull green, rugose, with depressed veins, somewhat pubescent with appressed or more or less spreading hairs, lower surface paler, bluish, papillate, more or less woolly-pubescent with long, spreading hairs; petiole 0.5–1.5 cm. (rarely 2 cm) long, finely pubescent; inflorescence slightly convex, 2–4 cm. in diameter; peduncle and branches of the inflorescence spreading-pubescent; flower buds short-ovoid; flowers white, about 6 mm. in diameter; sepals narrowly triangular, often with a subulate tip, 0.3–1 mm. long, very pubescent, sometimes fimbriate; petals ovate to oblong, spreading at anthesis; stamens somewhat exceeding the petals; anthers 1.3–1.5 mm. long; style cylindrical, the disk-shaped stigma wider than the style; disk prominent, closely surrounding the style; the pubescence of the ovary spreading or bristly, occasionally somewhat appressed; fruit white, nearly spherical; stone somewhat oblique, about as long as broad or slightly elongated, somewhat flattened, faintly furrowed. Begins to blossom in May in the south and in June or July in the north, continuing throughout the summer. (*Baileyi,* named for L. H. Bailey.)

This species grows in swamps and moist, rocky places, chiefly in the region of the coniferous forests. It is infrequent southward to latitude 45° N. It is distributed in the region of the Great Lakes from western New York to Minnesota and Manitoba.

C. Baileyi is almost indistinguishable from *C. pubescens* Nutt. of the Pacific Coast. Certain Minnesota specimens are fully as pubescent as any from the West. The stone in the western species is usually more strongly ribbed than in *C. Baileyi,* but occasionally western specimens have stones that are indistinguishable from our material. Until further study can be made of this problem it is deemed better to retain *C. Baileyi* as the name for the Minnesota plant.

SHINLEAF FAMILY

WHITE ALDER FAMILY, Clethraceae

Shrubs or trees; leaves alternate, simple, stipules none; flowers perfect, fragrant, in terminal racemes or panicles; calyx deeply five-lobed, the lobes imbricate, persistent around the fruit; corolla of five free, imbricate petals; stamens ten to twelve, hypogynous, free; filaments hairy or glabrous; anthers inflexed in the bud, sagittate, opening by apical pores; disk lacking; ovary superior, hairy, three-angled or three-lobed, three-celled; style one, three-lobed at the apex, ovules numerous on axile placentas; fruit a capsule, subglobose or three-lobed, loculicidally three-valved; seeds numerous, compressed or trigonous, often winged.

The family includes but a single genus with about thirty species, widely distributed in subtropical and tropical Asia, Madeira, southeastern United States, Central America, and tropical South America.

Clethra L., Sp. Pl. 396, 1753

Characters of the family. (*Cléthra*, the ancient Greek name for the alder.)

SWEET PEPPER BUSH, WHITE ALDER, *Clethra alnifolia* L., Sp. Pl. 396, 1753

A shrub 1–3 m. high with brown or grayish bark; young twigs brownish, stellate-puberulent; leaves wedge-obovate, 3.5–7 cm. long, 1.5–3.5 cm. wide, sometimes larger, gradually narrowed toward the base, acute or short-acuminate at the apex, margin sharply serrate above the middle, mostly entire toward the base, green and glabrous or nearly so on both sides; petioles 3–12 mm. long, puberulent; flowers numerous, in erect racemes, white and fragrant, about 8 mm. across, pedicels and calyx stellate-canescent; sepals ovate-oblong, about 3 mm. long; petals oblong, about twice as long as the sepals; stamens erect, slightly exceeding the petals, filaments glabrous; style longer than the stamens, three-lobed at the apex; capsule subglobose, about 3 mm. in diameter, loculicidal. Blossoms in July and August. (*Alnifólia*, leaves like the alder.)

White alder grows in swamps and wet woods or sometimes in drier situations. It is a native of the eastern United States from Maine to Mississippi, mostly near the coast.

It is occasionally planted in Minnesota as an ornamental shrub.

SHINLEAF FAMILY, Pyrolaceae

Herbaceous or sometimes suffruticose plants from the slender rootstocks, with evergreen, alternate basal or scattered leaves, sometimes saprophytes or root parasites without chlorophyll; flowers perfect, regular, terminal and solitary or in corymbs or racemes; sepals five, occasionally lacking in parasitic genera; petals five, rarely four, usually free, stamens ten; anthers opening by apical pores which, when mature, usually become inverted and appear basal; ovary superior, five-celled; fruit a many-seeded capsule; seeds with a loose, translucent cellular coat.

This family embraces about forty species of the temperate and boreal regions of the Northern Hemisphere. It is represented in our native flora by a single suffruticose and several herbaceous species.

Chimaphila Pursh, Fl. Am. Sept. 279, 300, 1814

Low, semiherbaceous undershrubs; stems upright from a woody, creeping rootstock; leaves evergreen, leathery; flowers small in a terminal cluster; sepals five, persistent in the fruit; petals five, separate; stamens ten, the anthers opening by pores which are basal in the bud but become inverted in the flower; pistil five-parted; ovary globular, five-celled, superior; style very short; stigma disk-shaped;

Pipsissewa, *Chimaphila umbellata* var. *cisatlantica.*

333

fruit a loculicidal capsule splitting from the top downward; seeds dust-like, very minute. (*Chimáphila*, winter-loving, referring to its evergreen habit.)

The genus includes six species of the Northern Hemisphere. Two besides that described occur in the United States, one eastern, the other far western.

PIPSISSEWA, *Chimaphila umbellata* (L.) Nutt. var. *cisatlantica* Blake, Rhodora 19:241, 1917

A low, semiherbaceous shrub, stems 1–3 dm. high; leaves alternate but crowded toward the top of each year's growth, leathery, evergreen, narrowly wedge-shaped, sharply serrate, dark green and glossy above, paler beneath, 2–6 cm. long, 0.8–2 cm. wide; petioles 3–6 mm. long, tip broadly wedge-shaped, base narrowly wedge-shaped; flowers in a two- to eight-flowered corymb; peduncles bare, 6–10 cm. high; bracts very small, soon deciduous; pedicels about 1 cm. long; flowers bell-shaped; sepals very small, depressed, triangular or oval, mostly broader than long, united; petals round, pink, 6–8 mm. long; stamens purplish. (*Umbelláta*, having umbels; *cisatlántica*, on this side of the Atlantic.)

Pipsissewa occurs in dry, sandy, and acid soils. It is common in the coniferous forest area, infrequent to rare southward and then mostly in white oak forests. It is distributed from Quebec to western Ontario and Minnesota, south to New England, Georgia, Ohio, Michigan, and Illinois.

The eastern *C. maculata* (L.) Pursh, with lanceolate, spotted leaves, is reported from eastern and central Minnesota. There are no specimens in the University herbarium, and it probably does not reach the state.

HEATH FAMILY, Ericaceae

Shrubs or rarely herbs or trees, often evergreen; sepals four or five, free or more or less united; petals four or five, rarely free, usually united more or less completely; stamens usually eight or ten, but sometimes the same in number as the petals, inserted with the petals and free from them; anthers often appendaged, usually opening by pores; disk often present between the stamens and the pistil; ovary superior or inferior, three- to ten-celled; style one; stigma one; fruit a capsule, either septicidal or loculicidal, a berry, or a drupe with a compound stone; seeds small.

This large family embraces about ninety genera and fourteen hundred species, several tribes of which are often segregated as families, notably those with inferior ovary as *Vacciniaceae*.

KEY TO GENERA OF ERICACEAE [*]

1. Ovary superior.
    2. Corolla composed of separate petals; leaves very woolly beneath . . . .
    . . . . *Ledum* (p. 335)

[*] The Lapland Rosebay, *R. laponicum* (L.), of the genus *Rhododendron* (not included in this key), occurs at the Dells of the Wisconsin River. It is the only known station for this arctic and subarctic shrub in the United States west of the Adirondack Mountains.

2. Corolla composed of plainly united petals; leaves not woolly beneath.
   3. Leaves deciduous; corolla bell-shaped..............*Menziesia* (p. 336)
   3. Leaves evergreen.
      4. Corolla with a flat or spreading limb; stamens awnless.
         5. Corolla wheel-shaped; stamens opening by pores....*Kalmia* (p. 337)
         5. Corolla salver-shaped, very fragrant; stamen opening by slits.......
          ....*Epigaea* (p. 337)
      4. Corolla bell-shaped or jug-shaped.
         6. Anthers awnless ....*Chamaedaphne* (p. 338)
         6. Anthers awned.
           7. Leaves not aromatic; fruit a capsule........*Andromeda* (p. 339)
           7. Fruit fleshy.
              8. Leaves aromatic; sepals plainly united at the base, calyx tube
                becoming fleshy in fruit................*Gaultheria* (p. 340)
              8. Leaves not aromatic; sepals imbricated and little connected; fruit
                a drupe.........................*Arctostaphylos* (p. 341)
1. Ovary more or less inferior; fruit fleshy.
   9. Ovary half inferior; foliage aromatic, evergreen.
      10. Berry red, here might be sought fruiting specimens of................
      ....*Gaultheria* (p. 340)
      10. Berry white; anthers awnless, opening by slits........*Chiogenes* (p. 343)
   9. Ovary wholly inferior; foliage not aromatic.
      11. Ovary with ten ovules; fruit drupe-like.............*Gaylussacia* (p. 343)
      11. Ovary with many ovules; fruit a many-seeded berry.................
      ....*Vaccinium* (p. 344)

Ledum L., Sp. Pl. 391, 1753

Erect, evergreen shrubs; leaves alternate, resinous, entire; buds scaly; flowers in dense, terminal clusters; sepals five, very small, united; petals five, free; stamens five to ten, exserted; anthers opening by terminal pores; pistil five-parted; ovary superior; style thread-like; stigma small, capitate; fruit a septicidal five-celled capsule, splitting up from the base. (*Lédum*, Greek name of an oriental shrub.)

All three species of this genus occur in northern North America; one occurs also in northern Europe and Asia.

LABRADOR TEA, *Ledum groenlandicum* Oeder, Fl. Dan. pl. 567, 1771

A shrub 3–10 dm. high; stems slender, brittle; bark gray; young twigs brown, woolly; leaves evergreen, lanceolate, 2–8 cm. long, 5–16 mm. wide, entire, the edges rolled backward; tip rounded, base rounded-wedge-shaped; upper surface green and finely rugose, the midrib depressed and finely hairy, other veins scarcely evident; lower surface completely covered with long, tawny wool; petiole about 2 mm. long; flowers white, borne in a terminal, umbel-like corymb, enclosed during the previous winter in a large, scaly, terminal bud; axis of the cluster and pedicels hairy and glandular; pedicels thread-like, 1.5–2 cm. long; calyx minute, five-toothed; petals narrowly ovate, about 5 mm. long; stamens five to seven; capsule slender, pointed, about 5 mm. long, the style persistent; seeds thread-like. Blossoms usually in June. (*Groenlándicum*, of Greenland.)

Left, *Ledum groenlandicum*. Right, *Kalmia polifolia*.

Labrador tea grows in peaty soils. It is common in the bogs of the coniferous forests, extending very little beyond their limits. It is distributed from Greenland and Labrador to Alaska, south to Nova Scotia, New England, New Jersey, Pennsylvania, Michigan, Wisconsin, Alberta, and Washington.

The leaves are said to have been used as tea by the Indians.

Menziesia J. E. Smith, Icon. Ined. 3, pl. 56, 1791

Shrubs; leaves thin, entire, deciduous; buds very scaly; flowers small, in terminal clusters, opening.with the leaves; calyx small, of four united sepals; corolla bell-shaped, of four united petals; stamens eight, included; anthers appendaged, opening by terminal pores; pistil compound, four-parted; style thread-like; stigma four-lobed; fruit a four-celled capsule, septicidal, many-seeded. (*Menziésia*, named for Archibald Menzies.)

This small genus includes about seven species native to North America and Japan.

Menziesia glabella A. Gray, Syn. Fl. 2:39, 1878

Bark grayish-brown, shreddy; leaves obovate, 3–7 cm. long, 1–3 cm. wide, petioled, entire, light green above, pale and glaucous below, finely and sparsely rough-hairy, tips obtusely wedge-shaped, very slightly bristle-tipped, base narrowly wedge-shaped; flowers in a terminal sessile umbel; pedicels thread-like, about 3 cm. long, flowers about 7 mm. long; calyx barely lobed, ciliate; corolla brownish; seeds thread-like; foliage with a skunk-like odor. Flowers in May. (*Glabélla*, somewhat smooth.)

This species occurs from British Columbia to Oregon and Montana. It has

336

been reported from Minnesota Point, Duluth. It possibly occurs in the north-eastern corner of Minnesota, but there are no specimens in the herbarium of the University.

American Laurel
Kalmia L., Sp. Pl. 391, 1753

Erect shrubs, sometimes very dwarf; leaves entire, leathery, evergreen; buds naked; sepals five, united at the base; corolla flat, wheel-shaped, of five united petals furnished with ten small pouches in which the anthers are situated in the bud and in the newly opened flower; stamens ten; anthers without append-ages, opening by terminal pores; pistil five-parted; ovary superior; style thread-like; stigma slightly enlarged; fruit a five-celled capsule, septicidal, many-seeded; seeds small, round. (*Kálmia*, named for Peter Kalm, a pupil of Linnaeus.)

This genus includes six species native to North America and Cuba. Only the following species reaches as far west as Minnesota.

SWAMP LAUREL, *Kalmia polifolia* Wang., Beob. Ges. Naturf. Freunde Berlin 2:130, 1788 [*K. glauca* Ait. 1789]

A low shrub, 1–6 dm. high; twigs with ridges running down from the bases of the leaves; leaves opposite, sessile, ovate, lanceolate or linear, 1–3 cm. long, 2–10 mm. wide, evergreen, leathery, dark green and glossy above, white beneath, margins entire and rolled backward, midrib prominent beneath, tip blunt-pointed, base tapering; flowers in terminal umbel-like clusters; pedicels thread-like, erect, about 15 cm. long; sepals ovate, persistent; corolla pink-purple, about 1.5 cm. across; capsule globose, about 5 mm. in diameter. Flowers from mid-May to July. (*Polifólia*, smooth-leaved.)

This laurel grows in bogs and muskegs. It is confined to the region of the coniferous forests and is common only toward the northern parts of the area. It is distributed from Labrador to Alaska, south to New England, northern New Jersey, Pennsylvania, Michigan, Minnesota, Idaho, and Oregon.

Epigaea L., Sp. Pl. 395, 1753

Prostrate, semiherbaceous undershrubs; leaves evergreen, alternate, or crowded and nearly opposite; flowers in terminal clusters from scaly buds; sepals five, large, persistent; petals five, united to form a salver-shaped corolla; stamens ten, not exserted; ovary five-lobed, five-celled; style columnar; stigma five-lobed; fruit a fleshy capsule, finally loculicidal; seeds oval. (*Epigaéa*, Greek, upon the ground.)

Of the two species of this genus, one is Japanese, the other is that described.

TRAILING ARBUTUS, *Epigaea repens* L., Sp. Pl. 395, 1753

Leaves petioled, elliptical, 3–6 cm. long, 2–4 cm. wide, rough-hairy, tip round, base round or heart-shaped; flowers pink, very fragrant; sepals lanceo-

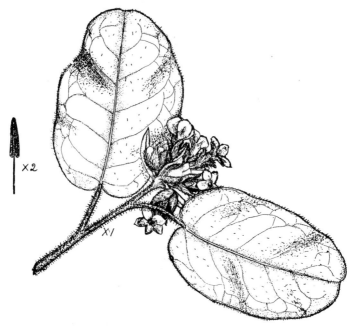

Epigaea repens

late, about 7 mm. long; corolla 1 cm. across, corolla tube about 1 cm. long. Blossoms in earliest spring. (*Répens*, creeping.)

Trailing arbutus grows in sandy or gravelly, acid soils, mostly within the coniferous forest area of the Upper Midwest, and is frequent in stands of jack pine. It is distributed from Labrador to Saskatchewan, south to New England, Pennsylvania, North Carolina, Tennessee, Michigan, Wisconsin, and Minnesota.

Chamaedaphne Moench, Meth. 457, 1794

An erect shrub, branches slender, stiff; buds scaly; leaves alternate petioled, leathery, scurfy, evergreen; flowers in leafy racemes, with two small bractlets just below the calyx; sepals five, separate; corolla cylindric, of five united petals; stamens ten, included in the corolla; anthers not awned, the sacs elongated above into long tubes with terminal pores; pistil of five united carpels; ovary superior, five-celled; style straight; stigma unlobed; fruit a globose capsule surrounded by the persistent calyx, loculicidal, the inner layer of the pericarp separating from the outer layer and splitting into ten valves; seeds small, numerous. (*Chamaedáphne*, Greek, *chamae*, upon the ground, *daphne*, a kind of shrub.)

LEATHER LEAF, *Chamaedaphne caliculata* var. *angustifolia* (Ait.) Rehder, in Bailey, Cycl. Am. Hort. 1:287, 1900

An evergreen shrub 3–10 dm. high; leaves oblong, with scurfy, scale-like hairs, apex pointed, base rounded, 0.5–4 cm. long, 2–15 mm. wide, those of the

338

inflorescence smallest; flowers white, about 5 mm. long. Blossoms in April and May. (*Caliculáta*, cup-like; *angustifólia*, narrow-leaved.)

This shrub grows in peaty swales, in bogs, and on the margins of ponds. It is very abundant in the region of the coniferous forests, where it covers acres of muskeg with a nearly pure growth, less frequent in some of the outlying tamarack bogs of east central Minnesota and adjacent Wisconsin. It is distributed from Newfoundland to Alaska, south to Georgia, Ohio, northern Indiana, Illinois, Wisconsin, northern Iowa, Alberta, and British Columbia.

Chamaedaphne caliculata var. *angustifolia*

Andromeda L., Sp. Pl. 393, 1753

Small, upright shrubs; buds very small, scaly; leaves evergreen, alternate; flowers in terminal clusters; sepals five, pointed, united at the base; petals five, almost completely united to form a jug-shaped corolla; stamens ten, included; anthers awned, opening by terminal pores; ovary five-celled, superior; style short, straight, columnar; stigma terminal, unlobed; fruit a subglobose capsule, loculicidal, many-seeded, seeds small, flat, oval. (*Andrómeda*, a mythological name.)

This is a genus of two closely related species, one arctic, the other of northeastern North America, with which are often included the twelve species of *Pieris* of eastern Asia and eastern North America. Only the following species is known in Minnesota.

BOG ROSEMARY, *Andromeda glaucophylla* Link, Enum. Hort. Berol. 1:394, 1821

A shrub 0.5–4 dm. high, from a creeping base; the bark of young shoots brown, of older shoots gray; leaves linear, 2–5 cm. long, 2–5 mm. wide, leathery, nearly sessile, margins rolled back, dark green above, white and finely hairy beneath, tip acute, base wedge-shaped, midrib prominent; flowers in small, terminal umbel-like clusters, white, about 4 mm. long; pedicels 3–5 mm. long, curved, glaucous; capsule depressed, globular, indented on top. Blossoms in June. (*Glaucophýlla*, glaucous-leaved.)

This shrub is common in bogs and along the margins of ponds throughout the region of the continuous coniferous forest, infrequent southward in outlying tamarack bogs. It is distributed from Labrador to eastern Manitoba, south to New Jersey, Pennsylvania, West Virginia, Ohio, Indiana, Wisconsin, and Minnesota.

Gaultheria L., Sp. Pl. 395, 1753

Shrubs, stems creeping or erect; leaves leathery, evergreen, usually alternate; flowers solitary or clustered; sepals five, more or less united, the calyx surrounded by a few small, scale-like bracts; corolla narrowly bell-shaped, composed of five united petals; stamens ten, included in the corolla; filaments somewhat thickened; anthers opening by terminal pores, awned; ovary superior, five-lobed, five-celled; style somewhat thick, straight; stigma entire; fruit a more or less fleshy capsule, surrounded by the thick and fleshy calyx; seeds minute. (*Gaulthéria*, named for Dr. Hugues Gaultier, a court physician in Quebec in the eighteenth century.)

To this genus belong about a hundred species of wide geographical distribution, most abundant in the cooler parts of the Southern Hemisphere, especially in the Andes. Three species occur in western North America, one in Japan, ten in southeastern Asia. Only the following species occurs in our area.

WINTERGREEN, CHECKERBERRY, *Gaultheria procumbens* L., Sp. Pl. 395, 1753

A low, creeping, almost herbaceous aromatic shrub, about 1 dm. high; leaves petioled, evergreen, alternate, crowded near the tops of the branches, smooth, upper sides dark glossy-green, lower sides paler, margins obscurely serrate with bristle-tipped teeth, tip rounded or obtusely wedge-shaped, base wedge-shaped, 2–5 cm. long, 1–2.5 cm. wide; flowers white or pale pink, axillary, solitary; peduncles about 5 mm. long; bracteoles two or three, close under the calyx; calyx wheel-shaped, five-pointed; corolla jug-shaped, 5–8 mm. long, the tips of the petals triangular; anthers with four terminal awns; fruit scarlet, round, 5–10 mm. in diameter, composed chiefly of the fleshy calyx, surrounding a nearly dry capsule, style persistent. Flowers in August; fruit ripening the following summer. (*Procúmbens*, creeping.)

Wintergreen grows mostly in sandy and gravelly soil. It is common and in places abundant as an undershrub in dry evergreen woods, less frequent southward in mixed jack-pine and oak woods. It is distributed from Newfoundland to Manitoba, south to New England, Georgia, Alabama, Wisconsin, and Minnesota.

Left, *Andromeda glaucophylla.* Center, *Arctostaphylos Uva-ursi.*
Right, *Gaultheria procumbens.*

All parts of the plant, but especially the leaves and fruit, contain the fragrant oil of wintergreen; commercially, however, this oil is most frequently obtained from the twigs of the black birch (*Betula lenta*). It is also made synthetically.

Bearberry
Arctostaphylos Adans., Fam. Pl. 2:165, 1763

Shrubs or small trees; leaves alternate, petioled, leathery, evergreen; flowers in terminal clusters; sepals four or five; corolla bell-shaped or jug-shaped, of four or five united petals; stamens eight or ten, included in the corolla; anthers awned on the back, opening by terminal pores; pistil four- or five-parted; ovary superior, four- or five-celled or eight- or ten-celled with one ovule in each cavity; style slender, stigma terminal; fruit a drupe, with from four to ten coherent stones, the calyx persisting unchanged in the fruit. (*Arctostáphylos*, Greek, bearberry, from *arctos*, a bear, and *staphyle*, a grape.)

About twenty species are included in this genus. The following occurs in all the northern parts of the Northern Hemisphere, the others in western North America, where they are commonly called "Manzanita."

BEARBERRY, *Arctostaphylos Uva-ursi* (L.) Spreng., Syst. 2:287, 1825

A trailing shrub, the branches often a meter or more long, but rising scarcely 1 dm. from the ground; bark gray and scaly, becoming finally smooth and red-brown; leaves alternate, petioled, leathery, evergreen, dark green, glossy, and finely reticulate above, rough and for a time hairy beneath and on the margins, tip round or bluntly angled, base narrowly wedge-shaped, margin entire, leaves 1–1.5 cm. long, 5–7 mm. wide, petioles about 2 mm. long; flowers in small terminal clusters, peduncles about 2 mm. long, recurved, flowers pale pink, corolla narrowly jug-shaped, about 4–7 mm. long; drupe globose, 5–10 mm. in diameter, scarlet, rather dry and scarcely edible, the stone composed usually of five coherent nutlets. (*U'va-úrsi*, bearberry.)

This is a polymorphic, circumboreal species. Three varieties may be recognized in our flora, distinguished most readily by their pubescence.

KEY TO VARIETIES OF ARCTOSTAPHYLOS UVA-URSI

1. Pubescence without stalked, glandular hairs.
    2. Young twigs puberulent and viscid, the puberulence soon disappearing.......
    .... typical *A. Uva-ursi*
    2. Young twigs not viscid, persistently canescent tomentulose...............
    ....*A. Uva-ursi* var. *coactilis*
1. Pubescence with stalked, glandular hairs...........*A. Uva-ursi* var. *adenotricha*

Typical *Arctostaphylos Uva-ursi* (L.) Spreng.

Twigs and petioles minutely puberulent and viscid, the puberulence soon disappearing; leaves thicker and firmer than in the following varieties, glabrous except the margins, which are often minutely tomentulose, upper surface very glossy, rugose veiny, apex of leaf mostly rounded, corolla ovoid, or broad conical, about 5–6 mm. long, 3–4 mm. wide. Blossoms in May and June.

This species grows on nearly pure sand and granitic rocks in the northeastern parts of the area. It is occasional on the outcrops of St. Peter sandstone in southeastern Minnesota. It is distributed from Greenland to Alaska, south to Newfoundland, Quebec, northern Indiana, Minnesota, the Black Hills, New Mexico, and Washington.

Arctostaphylos Uva-ursi var. *coactilis* Fernald & Macbride, Rhodora 16:212, 1914

Twigs and petioles finely and permanently tomentulose, not viscid; leaves slightly pubescent at the base and along the midrib, margin distinctly tomentulose, veining often obscure on the upper side, apex mostly blunt-angled; bud scales dark brown, glabrous except on the margin; flowers as in the typical form. (*Coáctilis*, felted.)

This variety grows on sandy soils and exposed rocks, mostly in the region of the coniferous forests, also at a few stations in southeastern Minnesota. It is distributed from Newfoundland to Manitoba, south to New England, the mountains of Virginia, Indiana, northern Illinois and Minnesota. It is reported to occur in the western mountains from the Yukon to Colorado and California; it seems, however, to the author that much of all the western material will have to be excluded from this variety.

Arctostaphylos Uva-ursi var. *adenotricha* Fernald & Macbride, Rhodora 16:213, 1914

Twigs and petioles viscid-villous, the pubescence intermixed with stout gland-tipped hairs (often black); leaves dark green, rather dull, somewhat thinner than in the typical form, upper surface puberulent toward the base, lower surface persistently puberulent, margin distinctly tomentulose, apex rounded; bud scales conspicuous, pale; flowers usually very small, 3–3.5 mm. long by 2–3 mm. wide. (*Adenotrícha*, glandular-haired.)

This variety is less common than the preceding and is mainly confined to the northern parts of the Upper Midwest, more frequent westward, where it extends beyond the forested area into the Red River Valley. Its distribution suggests that it is more calciphile than the other varieties. It is distributed from Quebec to British Columbia, south to northern Minnesota, North Dakota, and Montana.

Chiogenes Salisb., Trans. Hort. Soc. Lond. 2:94, 1815

Creeping, semiherbaceous, evergreen, aromatic shrubs; leaves small, thin, leathery, alternate; flowers solitary, axillary, furnished with two bractlets close under the calyx; sepals four, united, and fused with the lower part of the ovary; corolla bell-shaped, composed of four united petals; stamens eight, included in the corolla; anthers not awned, opening by short slits; pistil of four united carpels; ovary partly inferior, four-celled; style straight, short; stigma terminal; fruit a fleshy berry, the ovary becoming entirely inferior; seeds numerous, small. (*Chiógenes*, Greek, *chion*, snow, *genes*, born, in allusion to the white berries.)

This is a monotypic genus.

CREEPING SNOWBERRY, *Chiogenes hispidula* (L.) T. & G., in Torr., Fl. N.Y. 1:450, 1843

Stems and lower sides and margins of leaves brown, strigose; leaves elliptical, 5–9 mm. long, 4–7 mm. wide, finely rugose above, leaf margin revolute, apex obtuse with a short, projecting point, base wedge-shaped; petiole 1 mm. long; flowers about 4 mm. long; berry white, about 8 mm. in diameter. Blossoms in May. (*Hispídula*, somewhat bristly.)

Creeping snowberry grows in moist and mossy habitats. It is common throughout the coniferous forest area and infrequent southward in the outlying tamarack bogs. It is distributed from Labrador and Newfoundland to British Columbia, south to New England, in the uplands to North Carolina, Michigan, Wisconsin, Minnesota, and Idaho.

The ripe, white fruit of this species has the flavor of wintergreen.

Gaylussacia H. B. K., Nov. Gen. 3:257, 1819

Shrubs; leaves alternate; flowers in racemes; sepals five, united at the base and fused with the ovary; corolla urn-shaped or bell-shaped, composed of five fused petals; stamens ten, usually included in the corolla; anthers without awns, prolonged upward into two tubes and opening by apical pores; pistil of five united carpels; ovary inferior, ten-celled through the development of false parti-

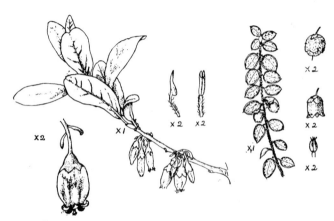

Left, *Gaylussacia baccata*. Right, *Chiogenes hispidula*.

tions, each cell with one ovule; style straight, thread-like; stigma terminal, scarcely lobed; fruit a berry-like drupe with ten stones, which are more or less solidly grown together. (*Gaylussácia*, named for the chemist Gay-Lussac.)

This genus includes about forty species, all American and for the most part South American. About five occur in eastern North America.

HUCKLEBERRY, *Gaylussacia baccata* (Wang.) K. Koch, Dendrol. 2:93, 1872 [*G. resinosa* (Ait.) T. & G. 1843]

A branching shrub, 3 dm.–1 m. high; stems stiff, gray, young twigs hairy; leaves alternate, ovate or ovate-lanceolate, 2–4 cm. long, 1–1.7 cm. wide, tough and somewhat leathery, resin-dotted, smooth except for slight hairiness on the margin and along the larger veins, green on both sides, somewhat pale below, margin entire, tip acute or rounded, base wedge-shaped; petiole about 1 mm. long; flowers in small lateral racemes from scaly winter buds; peduncles and pedicels resinous-dotted; pedicels about 6 mm. long; calyx tube hemispherical, free tips of sepals broadly triangular; corolla tubular bell-shaped, five-sided, reddish, 3–4 mm. long, about 2 mm. wide; stamens included; filaments short, hairy; fruit black, about 6 mm. in diameter, edible. Flowers in May and June; fruit ripe in late summer. (*Baccáta*, having berries.)

Huckleberry grows in dry or moist woods, thickets, and clearings. It is common in acid, sandy soils in Wisconsin, barely entering the borders of southeastern Minnesota and eastern Iowa. It is distributed from Newfoundland to Saskatchewan, south to New England, Georgia, and Louisiana.

Blueberry, Cranberry
Vaccinium L., Sp. Pl. 349, 1753

Shrubs, sometimes semiherbaceous; leaves alternate, deciduous or evergreen, in the latter case leathery; flowers solitary in the axils of the leaves or in terminal or lateral racemes; sepals five (or four), united at the base and fused with the ovary; corolla of five (or four) united petals, variously shaped; stamens ten (or eight), anthers with or without awns, prolonged upward into two tubes and opening by apical pores; pistil of five (or four) united carpels, ovary inferior five- (or four-) celled, or by false partitions ten- (or eight-) celled, each cell with several ovules; style straight; stigma small; fruit a many-seeded berry. (*Vaccinium*, classical Latin name for the blueberry.)

This genus of over a hundred species is distributed throughout the boreal regions and thence southward into the warm temperate regions and the mountainous parts of the tropics. Several of the subgenera are often regarded as genera.

KEY TO SECTIONS OF GENUS VACCINIUM

1. Leaves deciduous; corolla cylindrical, bell-shaped, jug-shaped, or globular.
    2. Anthers awned; berry four- or five-celled.....................*Eu-vaccinium*
    2. Anthers not awned; berry eight- or ten-celled.................*Cyanococcus*
1. Leaves leathery and evergreen.
    3. Corolla bell-shaped, petals plainly united......................*Vitis-Idaea*
    3. Corolla consisting of reflexed, nearly separate petals.............*Oxycoccus*

KEY TO SPECIES

Section *Eu-vaccinium* — Bilberries

Free limb of calyx collar-like, often with scarcely any lobes; corolla bell-shaped, or globular; stamens included, anthers awned; berry four- or five-celled, blue, black, or red; leaves deciduous.
    1. Parts of the flower mostly in fours; leaves entire, thick.....................
    ....*V. uliginosum* var. *alpinum* (p. 345)
    1. Parts of the flower in fives; leaves serrate, thin........*V. caespitosum* (p. 346)

Section *Cyanococcus* — Blueberries

Free limb of calyx deeply lobed; corolla bell-shaped to cylindrical; stamens included, anthers not awned; berry more or less completely ten-celled (rarely eight-celled), blue, black, or sometimes whitish; leaves deciduous.
    1. Leaves finely serrate, nearly smooth; twigs warty, nearly glabrous...........
    .... *V. angustifolium* (p. 347)
    1. Leaves entire; twigs and leaves densely hairy........*V. myrtilloides* (p. 349)

Section *Vitis-Idaea* — Mountain Cranberry

Free limb of calyx deeply lobed; corolla bell-shaped; stamens included, anthers not awned; berry four-celled, red; leaves evergreen....*V. Vitis-Idaea* var. *minus* (p. 350)

Section *Oxycoccus* — Cranberries

Free limb of calyx deeply lobed; corolla reflexed, deeply cleft or of almost or quite separate petals; stamens exserted, not awned, berry four-celled, red; our species prostrate evergreen shrubs with very small leaves.
    1. Leaves ovate, acute; fruit less than 1 cm. in diameter....*V. Oxycoccos* (p. 350)
    1. Leaves elliptical, obtuse; fruit more than 1 cm. in diameter................
    ....*V. macrocarpon* (p. 351)

ALPINE BILBERRY, *Vaccinium uliginosum* var. *alpinum* Bigel., Fl. Bost. ed. 2, 153, 1824

A low, much branched bush; stems upright, 8–60 cm. high, 1–3 mm. in

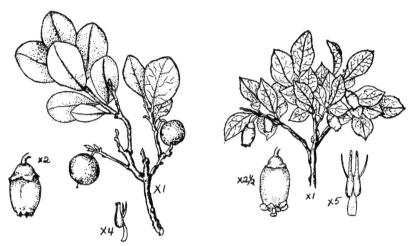

Species of *Vaccinium*: Left, *V. uliginosum* var. *alpinum*.
Right, *V. caespitosum*.

diameter, stiff, smooth, round, dark purplish-gray after shedding of the thin, whitish epidermis; leaves deciduous, somewhat thick and firm, obovate or nearly round, veiny, 9–15 mm. long, 2.5–10 mm. wide, sometimes nearly double this size in the far north, upper side dull green, smooth; lower side paler, slightly hairy; margin slightly revolute, entire; apex rounded, indented, or broadly wedge-shaped; base wedge-shaped; petioles 1 mm. long or wanting; flowers solitary or in groups of two to four from special, scaly winter buds; sepals four (rarely five), their free tips broadly triangular and very obtuse; corolla globular bell-shaped, pink, composed of four (rarely five) petals, which are fused about two-thirds of their length; stamens eight (rarely ten), included, filaments smooth, anthers each bearing two long awns on the back, the sacs tapering upward into short tubes with terminal pores; style shorter than the corolla; berry four-celled (rarely five-celled), bluish-black with a bloom, sweet and edible. Blossoms in July. (*Uliginósum*, marshy, i.e., growing in moist places; *alpínum*, Alpine.)

This bush, which grows on moorland heaths and rocks, is limited in its occurrence in this region to the extreme northeastern corner of Minnesota along the shore of Lake Superior. It is distributed from Newfoundland to northern New England, New York, Michigan, and Minnesota.

DWARF BILBERRY, *Vaccinium caespitosum* Michx., Fl. Bor. Am. 1:234, 1803

A dwarf, tufted shrub; stems upright, branched, 5–30 cm. high, 0.5–3 mm. in diameter, stiff, round, finely pubescent, grayish-brown; leaves deciduous, thin, obovate, or spatulate, veiny, smooth and green on both sides, margin finely serrate, tip rounded or abruptly wedge-shaped, base narrowly wedge-shaped, 10–20 mm. long, 3–10 mm. wide, rarely considerably larger; petioles 1 mm. long or wanting; flowers solitary from the axils of the lower leaves of the new

346

growth, drooping; pedicels 2–3 mm. long; sepals five, almost completely united, their upper portion forming a free, collar-like projection, which is very slightly and obtusely five-lobed; corolla bright pink or red, jug-shaped, about 5 mm. long, composed of five petals, which are united almost to the tip; stamens ten, included in the corolla, filaments smooth, anthers each bearing two long awns on the back, their sacs tapering upward into rather long tubes with terminal pores; style straight, about as long as the corolla; berry five-celled, blue-black with a bloom, sweet and edible. Blossoms in May and June; fruit ripe in August. (*Caespitósum*, sod-like.)

In sandy and gravelly soils, dwarf bilberry is locally abundant in the region of the coniferous forests, especially under jack pine. It is distributed from Labrador to Alaska, south to northern New England, New York, Wisconsin, and Minnesota, and occurs also in the mountains to Colorado and California.

BLUEBERRY, *Vaccinium angustifolium* Ait., Hort. Kew 2:11, 1789 [*V. pensylvanicum* Lam. 1783]

A low, upright shrub; stems 2–6 dm. high, twigs green, warty, glabrous except for two narrow, puberulent lines running down from each node; leaves deciduous, thin, lanceolate, 1.5–3.5 cm. long, 0.5–1.5 cm. wide; apex acute; base wedge-shaped; margin finely serrulate, the teeth bristle-tipped; upper surface glabrous except for minute puberulence along the midrib; lower surface glabrous, or with a few hairs on the midrib; petioles about 1 mm. long; flowers in terminal or lateral racemes or panicles from scaly winter buds, appearing with or rarely before the leaves; bracts broadly oval, reddish; pedicels about 1 mm. long; sepals five, united, thin, the free portion somewhat acute, about 1 mm. long; corolla narrowly campanulate, jug-shaped or nearly spherical, white or pale pink, 4–5 mm. long, consisting of five petals united almost to their tips; stamens ten, included in the corolla, filaments slightly hairy, usually a little shorter than the anthers, anthers without awns, the sacs prolonged upward into narrow tubes with terminal pores; style straight, slightly exserted; berry ten-celled, blue with a bloom, sweet and edible. Blossoms in May and early June; fruit ripe in July to September. (*Angustifólium*, narrow-leaved.)

Blueberry grows in the sandy, acid soil of dry, open woods and clearings and on rocks and barrens. It is common and in many places abundant throughout the region of the coniferous forests, less frequent southward in sandy habitats to southeastern Minnesota and adjacent Wisconsin. The species, including several varieties, is distributed from Labrador and eastern Quebec to Saskatchewan, south to New England, Delaware, West Virginia, Ohio, northern Indiana, Illinois, and northeastern Iowa.

This species is the most abundant blueberry of the Upper Midwest, as well as the best in quality and the earliest to ripen. In addition to the typical form, two varieties occur within the area.

Blueberry, *Vaccinium angustifolium*

Vaccinium angustifolium var. *nigrum* (Wood) Dole, Fl. Verm. ed. 3, 210, 1937 [*V. pensylvanicum* var. *nigrum* Wood 1873]

Differs from the species in having black berries with but little bloom; leaves usually somewhat thicker than in the type and glaucous beneath. (*Nigrum,* black.)

This variety grows in similar habitats and has the same general range as the typical form, but it is much less common.

Vaccinium angustifolium var. *hypolasium* Fernald, Rhodora 51:104, 1949 [*V. pensylvanicum* var. *myrtilloides* (Michx.) Fernald 1908]

Lower surface of leaves strongly pubescent along the midrib and sometimes on the other veins as well, petioles and twigs more pubescent than in the type. The extreme forms are as pubescent as *V. myrtilloides,* from which they may be distinguished by the serrated leaf margins and sweeter berries. It seems probable

·that some of the forms classified here are hybrids between *V. angustifolium* and *V. myrtilloides*. (*Hypolásium*, hairy beneath.)

Of infrequent and scattered occurence, this variety is found mostly northeastward in the area; it is rare southward in Minnesota to Winona County. It is distributed from Newfoundland to Hudson Bay, south to Massachusetts, in the uplands of Virginia, and west to Michigan, Wisconsin, and Minnesota.

SOUR-TOP BILBERRY, VELVET-LEAF BILBERRY, *Vaccinium myrtilloides* Michx., Fl. Bor. Am. 1:234, 1803 [*V. canadense* Kalm 1823]

A low, upright shrub; stems 2–6 dm. high, greenish-brown, finely warty and densely woolly-pubescent; leaves deciduous, thin, lanceolate or ovate, bright green, hairy below and along the veins above; margin entire, apex acute to rounded, base broadly wedge-shaped or rounded; leaves 15–35 mm. long, 7–15 mm. wide; petioles about 1 mm. long; flowers in terminal or lateral, few-flowered racemes from scaly winter buds, opening with the leaves; bracts lanceolate, early deciduous; pedicels 2–5 mm. long; sepals five, their free tips triangular, acute, about 1.5 mm. long; corolla of five petals, united nearly to the tips, white, streaked with pink, narrow bell-shaped, or somewhat constricted at the throat, about 4 mm. long, free tips of the petals about 1 mm. long, not spreading; stamens ten, included in the corolla, filaments hairy, about as long as the anthers, anthers without awns, the sacs prolonged upward into tubes with terminal pores; style

Species of *Vaccinium*: Left, *V. angustifolium*. Right, *V. myrtilloides*.

not exserted; berry ten-celled, blue with a bloom, edible, but rather sour. Blossoms in May and June; fruit ripe in August and September. (*Myrtilloídes*, like *V. myrtillus.*)

This variety grows in moist woods, bogs, and clearings, and on moist ledges and in crevices of rocks. It occurs mostly within the coniferous forest area, but is less common than *V. angustifolium*. It is distributed from Newfoundland and Quebec to British Columbia, south to western New England, Pennsylvania, the mountains of Virginia, Ohio, Michigan, Illinois, and northeastern Iowa.

The fruit of this variety is much less desirable than that of *V. angustifolium*.

MOUNTAIN CRANBERRY, *Vaccinium Vitis-Idaea* L. var. *minus* Lodd., Bot Cab. 11, pl. 1023, 1825

A dwarf, matted shrub; stems creeping, upright branches stiff, 2–15 cm. high, about 1 mm. in diameter; leaves evergreen, leathery, broad-elliptical; upper side dark green, glossy, lower pale and with more or less black, bristly dots; margin entire or finely crenate, revolute; apex rounded or indented, base wedge-shaped; leaves 5–18 mm. long, 3–9 mm. wide; petioles about 2 mm. long; flowers in terminal racemes from scaly winter buds; bracts thin, ovate, about 3 mm. long, green or reddish; pedicels about 2 mm. long, furnished with two bractlets resembling the bracts; sepals four, their free tips triangular, acute, glandular along the margin, about 1 mm. long; corolla pink, bell-shaped, about 5 mm. long, composed of four petals united about half their length; stamens eight, included, filaments hairy, short, anthers without awns, their sacs elongated upward into tubes with terminal pores; style curved, slightly exserted; berry dark red, four-celled, acid and scarcely edible unless cooked. Flowers in June and July; fruit ripe in late autumn but overwintering and best-tasting in early spring. (*Vitis-Idaéa*, grape of Mount Ida; *minus*, smaller.)

Mountain cranberry is locally abundant in sphagnum bogs in the far northern parts of Minnesota and the adjacent parts of Ontario and Manitoba; it is less common on granitic ledges along Lake Superior. It ranges from the subarctic regions of America, south to Newfoundland, New England, the Lake Superior region of Ontario, northern Minnesota, Manitoba, Saskatchewan, Alberta, and British Columbia. The larger typical form occurs in northern Europe.

The berries, known in the vernacular in Germany as *Preisselbeere*, in Scandinavia as *Lingon baer* and *Tyttebaer*, are much used in northern Europe for making preserves and relishes. They sometimes appear in our markets, but are mostly shipped in from Newfoundland and Norway.

SMALL CRANBERRY, *Vaccinium Oxycoccos* L., Sp. Pl. 351, 1753 [*Oxycoccus palustris* Pers. 1805; *Oxycoccus Oxycoccus* MacMillan 1892]

A creeping, prostrate shrub; stems very slender, about 0.5 mm. in diameter; leaves leathery, evergreen, ovate-lanceolate, 4–12 mm. long, 2.5–3.5 mm. wide; upper side dark green, glossy, under side nearly white; margin with a few small

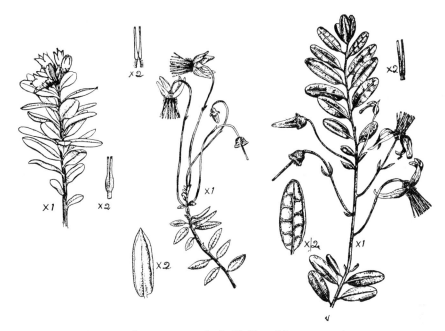

Species of *Vaccinium*: Left, *V. Vitis-Idaea* var. *minus*.
Center, *V. Oxycoccos*. Right, *V. macrocarpon*.

teeth, strongly revolute; apex wedge-shaped, acute; base truncate or slightly heart-shaped; petioles slender, about 1.5 mm. long; flowers in small terminal racemes of one to five, the axis of the raceme usually very short (2–5 mm.), but occasionally prolonged upward into a leafy shoot and then the flower-bearing part often 1 cm. long; bracts about 1.5 mm. long, broadly elliptical, obtuse; pedicels thread-like, red, 2–4 cm. long, bearing two minute, reddish bractlets; sepals four, their free tips broadly triangular, obtuse; petals four, lanceolate, 5–8 mm. long, separate almost to the base, spreading or reflexed, pink; stamens eight, exserted, filaments hairy, anthers without awns, the anther sacs prolonged upward into long tubes with terminal pores; style straight, slightly longer than the stamens; fruit red, less than 1 cm. in diameter, sour and nearly inedible when raw, pleasant when cooked. Blossoms in June; fruit ripe in late fall. (*Oxycóccos*, sour berry.)

This cranberry grows in sphagnum bogs, muskegs, and wet, acid soil generally. It is common throughout the coniferous forest areas, less frequent southward in outlying tamarack bogs. It is distributed from Labrador to Alaska, south to New England, New Jersey, Pennsylvania, upland to Virginia, West Virginia, Michigan, Wisconsin, Minnesota, Manitoba, Alberta, and Washington.

LARGE CRANBERRY, *Vaccinium macrocarpon* Ait., Hort. Kew 2:13, 1789 [*Oxycoccus macrocarpus* Pers. 1805]

A creeping, prostrate shrub; stems slender, often a meter long, about 1–1.5

mm. in diameter, flowering branches more or less erect; leaves leathery, ever-green, elliptical, 6–15 mm. long, 2.5–5 mm. wide; upper side dark green, glossy, under side paler, glaucous; margin entire, slightly revolute; apex rounded, base rounded; petioles slender, about 1.5 mm. long; flowers in raceme-like clusters of from one to ten, the axis of the raceme 1–3 cm. long and prolonged upward into a leafy shoot; bracts 2–4 mm. long, ovate; pedicels thread-like, red, 2–4 cm. long, bearing two small, green, leaf-like bractlets above the middle; sepals four, their free tips broadly triangular, obtuse; petals four, lanceolate, 6–10 mm. long, separate almost to the base, spreading or reflexed, pink; stamens eight, exserted, filaments hairy, very short, anthers without awns, the anther sacs prolonged up-ward into long tubes with terminal pores; style straight, slightly longer than the stamens; fruit red, 1–2 cm. in diameter, sour and nearly inedible when raw, pleasant when cooked. Flowers in June; fruit ripe in the fall and overwintering. (*Macrocárpon*, large-fruited.)

Growing in open bogs, in swamps, and on wet shores, this species is less com-mon than the preceding in the coniferous area and is distributed farther south-ward to southeastern Minnesota, southern Wisconsin, and northern Illinois. Its range is Newfoundland to Manitoba, south to New England, Long Island, North Carolina, West Virginia, Indiana, and Illinois.

The common cranberry of commerce is extensively cultivated in Wisconsin but very little in Minnesota.

OLIVE FAMILY, Oleaceae

Trees or shrubs with simple or pinnately compound, opposite leaves; flowers perfect, polygamous, dioecious or monoecious; sepals four, more or less united, or wanting; corolla regular, of four (rarely five or six) united or nearly free petals, or wanting; stamens two, inserted on the corolla tube or hypogynous; carpels two, united; style one, stigmas two, ovary two-celled, with two (rarely four to eight) ovules in each cell; fruit a capsule, berry, drupe, or samara, one-to few-seeded.

This is a family of twenty-one genera and about four hundred species, mostly of the warm temperate regions and the Old World tropics.

KEY TO GENERA OF OLEACEAE

1. Large trees with odd-pinnate leaves; flowers apetalous; fruit a samara. . . . .
. . . .*Fraxinus* (p. 353)
1. Shrubs or small trees with simple (rarely trifoliolate) leaves; flowers with a con-spicuous corolla.
  2. Petals linear, barely united at the very base. . . . .*Chionanthus* (p. 356)
  2. Petals united to about the middle or higher.
    3. Corolla salver-shaped or funnel-shaped, white or yellowish-white to purple
. . . .*Syringa* (p. 357)
    3. Corolla campanulate, yellow . . . .*Forsythia* (p. 362)

OLIVE FAMILY

Ash

Fraxinus L., Sp. Pl. 1057, 1753

Trees with opposite, odd-pinnate leaves (rarely simple in some exotic species); flowers small, in clusters, dioecious or polygamous, appearing before or with the leaves from separate winter buds; calyx of four united sepals or irregularly lobed or entire or lacking; petals four, more or less united at the base, or lacking (in all our species); stamens two (rarely three or four); ovary two-celled with two ovules in each cell; stigma two-cleft; fruit an elongated one-seeded samara. (*Fráxinus*, the classical Latin name of the ash tree.)

About sixty species of the North Temperate Zone are included in this genus.

KEY TO SPECIES OF FRAXINUS [*]

1. Lateral leaflets more or less stalked; calyx present; body of samara terete; bark ridged.
  2. Body of samara elliptical, wing terminal; leaves pale beneath..............
  ....*F. americana* (p. 353)
  2. Body of samara long cylindrical, wing extending down the sides; leaves green on both sides.
    3. Twigs and rachis of leaves pubescent...........*F. pensylvanica* (p. 354)
    3. Twigs and rachis of leaves glabrous................................
    ....*F. pensylvanica* var. *subintegerrima* (p. 355)
1. Lateral leaflets sessile, calyx wanting; body of samara flattened; bark flaky, without deep ridges..*F. nigra* (p. 355)

WHITE ASH, *Fraxinus americana* L., Sp. Pl. 1057, 1753

A large tree reaching a maximum height of 40 m. and a trunk diameter of nearly 2 m.; the bark of the trunk grayish-brown, deeply furrowed; twigs somewhat flattened at the nodes, glabrous, grayish or greenish-brown, often covered with a bloom; lateral buds nearly spherical or broadly ovate, terminal buds larger, conical, usually with a pair of lateral buds at the same level; bud scales brown, scurfy, those of the terminal buds loosely imbricated and frequently ending in sharp, more or less deciduous points; leaf scars crescent-shaped to nearly semicircular, notched at the apex; leaves odd-pinnate with from five to nine (usually seven) leaflets; lateral leaflets stalked, their petiolules 5–10 mm. long, ovate to ovate-lanceolate, rounded and often somewhat unequal at the base, occasionally somewhat narrowed, acute, or acuminate at the apex, 7–16 cm. long, 3.5–7 cm. wide, bright green and glabrous above, much lighter and glaucous beneath and minutely papillose, often with a few hairs along the veins, rather thick and firm in texture, their margin entire to crenate-denticulate; flowers dioecious, the staminate in rather loose panicles, calyx obsolete, stamens mostly two, anthers about 6 mm. long, apiculate; the pistillate in loose panicles with conspicuous bracts, calyx obscurely lobed, persistent in the fruit; samara

---

[*] The Blue Ash, *Fraxinus quadrangulata* Michx. (not included in our key), a large tree characterized by four-angled twigs, occurs in southeastern Wisconsin.

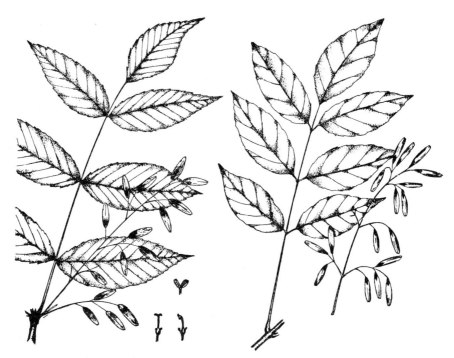

Species of *Fraxinus*: Left, *F. nigra*. Right, *F. americana.*
(Leaves and fruits × 1/2)

2–5 cm. long, narrowly elliptical in outline, 4–7 mm. wide, the body terete and narrowly elliptical in outline, about 15 mm. long, the wing extending only a short distance down the sides. (*Americána*, American.)

In rich upland to lowland woods, white ash is common southward but infrequent and rare within the southern border of Minnesota. It is occasionally planted. It is distributed from Nova Scotia to Iowa and Nebraska and southward to Florida and Texas. The wood is light brown, close-grained, hard, strong, and elastic. It is used in the manufacture of agricultural implements, for oars, handles of tools, furniture, and the interior finish of buildings.

RED ASH, *Fraxinus pensylvanica* Marsh., Arb. Am. 51, 1785

A tree up to 20 m. in height and a trunk diameter of 1 m.; the bark of the trunk grayish-brown, rather prominently ridged, but not quite so rough as that of the white ash; first-year twigs terete, pubescent, grayish-brown; lateral buds broadly ovoid, somewhat compressed dorsally, dark brown and scurfy; terminal buds conical, the two outer scales generally overtopping the next pair of scales and only partially covering them, dark scurfy-brown and more or less pubescent along the middle; leaf scars semicircular or broadly crescent-shaped, with the bundle-trace forming an arc above the middle of the scar; leaves odd-pinnate, with from five to nine leaflets and pubescent rachis; lateral leaflets more or less stalked, their petiolules 2–5 mm. long, lanceolate, ovate-lanceolate, or elliptical,

354

somewhat rounded or narrowed at the base, long or sometimes short-acuminate at the apex, 4–11 cm. long, 2–5 cm. wide, the terminal one generally slightly larger and concavely narrowed toward the base; upper surface dark green and glabrous, lower surface lighter green and pubescent, especially along the principal veins; margin entire or entire only toward the base and more or less crenate-serrate above; flowers dioecious, the staminate in short, crowded panicles, stamens two to four, apiculate, calyx obsolete; the pistillate in loose, open panicles, calyx turbinate or campanulate, more or less irregularly toothed or cleft, persistent in the fruit; samara spatulate or narrowly rhombic, rounded, blunt or emarginate at the apex, 3–5 cm. long, 5–8 mm. wide, the body 12–18 mm. long, narrowly fusiform with the wings decurrent one-third to one-half of its length. (*Pensyl-vánica*, Pennsylvanian.)

Red ash occurs mostly on low ground throughout the Upper Midwest. It is apparently much less common than green ash. It is distributed from Maine, west to North Dakota, south to Florida and Texas.

This is a very variable species, with several geographical races, or possibly a group of closely related species, differing in form of leaf, form of fruit, and amount of pubescence. Several of these forms have been given specific or varietal names. The following is fairly well marked.

The wood is like that of white ash, but coarser-grained and more brittle.

GREEN ASH, *Fraxinus pensylvanica* var. *subintegerrima* (Vahl) Fernald, Rhodora 49:159, 1947 [*F. pensylvanica* var. *lanceolata* (Borkh.) Sarg. 1894; *F. lanceolata* Borkh. 1809; *F. viridis* Michx. f. 1813]

A tree very similar to the preceding; young twigs and petioles and rachises of leaves glabrous; lateral leaflets obscurely stalked, or rarely with petiolules 2–4 mm. long; leaflets thin, bright green on both sides, glabrous above, glabrous beneath except for more or less pubescence along the larger veins; apex usually long-acuminate, base narrowed, rarely rounded; margin usually coarsely sharp-serrate to below the middle, less commonly obscurely serrate or nearly entire; flowers and fruit not distinguishable from typical *F. pensylvanica*. (*Subintegér-rima*, almost entire.)

Green ash is common in moist situations throughout the Upper Midwest and is by far the most abundant ash in the area. It is frequently planted as an ornamental tree. It is distributed from Maine west to Saskatchewan, southward to Florida, Texas, and Arizona.

BLACK ASH, *Fraxinus nigra* Marsh., Arb. Am. 51, 1758

A medium-sized to large tree reaching a maximum height of 25m. and a trunk diameter of 6–8 dm.; the bark of the trunk gray and irregularly scaly; lateral buds large, nearly globular; terminal buds pyramidal, angular, bud scales black, somewhat scurfy; leaf scars prominent, semicircular to nearly circular, often deeper than wide, the bundle traces prominent, forming a nearly closed

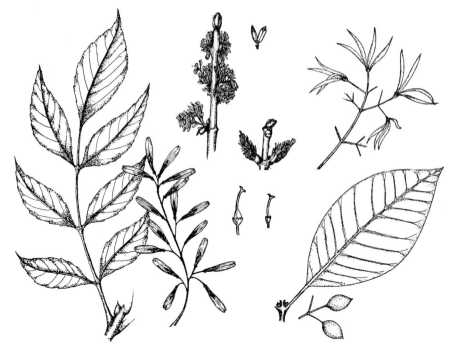

Left, *Fraxinus pensylvanica*. Right, *Chionanthus virginica*.
(Leaves and fruits × 1/2)

curve; twigs very stout, round, much enlarged at the nodes, glabrous, young twigs pale and glabrous; leaves odd-pinnate, leaflets seven to eleven, rachis glabrous except for tufts of brownish-yellow hairs at the base of the leaflets; leaflets sessile, oblong-lanceolate, 7.5–17 cm. long, 2.5–5 cm. wide, the terminal one generally smaller; base narrowed or sometimes slightly rounded, apex long acuminate; upper surface glabrous, lower surface somewhat pubescent along the veins or nearly glabrous, margin crenate or crenate-serrate; flowers polygamo-dioecious, in compact panicles, entirely naked; anthers elliptical, rounded at the apex; the pistillate flowers with rudimentary stamens; samara elliptical or oblong-elliptical, about 4 cm. long and 8 mm. wide, body flat, wing extending to the base, rounded or emarginate at the apex. (*Nigra*, black.)

Black ash is common in low and swampy ground throughout the forested parts of the region, most abundant in the eastern third. It is distributed from Newfoundland to Manitoba, south to Virginia and Arkansas.

The wood is rather soft, coarse-grained, tough, and easily separable into thin layers. It is used for baskets, hoops, splint boxes, and interior finish. The black burls are much sought for by veneer manufacturers.

Chionanthus L., Sp. Pl. 8, 1753

Shrubs or small trees, with simple, entire, opposite leaves; flowers in cymose panicles at the ends of leafy branches, perfect or polygamous; sepals four, small,

356

united; petals four, linear, united only at the base; stamens two, inserted on the corolla tube; ovary two-celled; stigma notched; ovules two in each cell; fruit a drupe, usually one-seeded. (*Chionánthus*, Greek, snowflower.)

This is a genus of about three species, natives of southeastern North America and China. The following species is the only one cultivated in our region.

FRINGE TREE, *Chionanthus virginica* L., Sp. Pl. 8, 1753

A large shrub or small tree 2–8 m. high; twigs grayish olive-green, puberulent or glabrate, with numerous prominent lenticels; leaves mostly elliptic-lanceolate, acute or short-acuminate, rarely rounded at the apex, narrowed at the base, 8–17 cm. long, 4–8 cm. wide, dark green and glabrate above, lighter green beneath and more or less pubescent mostly along the veins, margin entire; petiole about 1 cm. long; flowers borne in loose, cymose panicles on the ends of twigs, which bear much reduced leaves; petals white, linear, 1.5–3 cm. long, 1–2 mm. wide; stamens strongly apiculate; drupe purple, with bloom, ovoid 1–1.8 cm. long, pulp thin covering the large stone. (*Virgínica*, Virginian.)

This tree is occasionally cultivated and is apparently hardy in the latitude of Minneapolis. It is a native of the southeastern United States, and is distributed from New Jersey to Missouri, south to Florida and Texas.

Lilac
Syringa L., Sp. Pl. 9, 1753

Shrubs or small trees with opposite, entire, simple or rarely pinnate leaves; flowers in panicles, from terminal or lateral buds; sepals four, united into a short tubular or campanulate calyx; petals four, united into a tubular or funnel-shaped corolla with a spreading four-lobed limb; stamens two, inserted on the tube of the corolla; pistil of two united carpels; ovary two-celled, with two ovules in each cell; style one; stigma two-lobed or nearly entire; fruit a loculicidal capsule with four narrowly winged seeds. (*Syrínga*, from Greek *syrinx*, a pipe, applied anciently to *Philadelphus coronaria*, probably on account of its hollow internodes, first transferred to the lilac by Dodonaeus. The name is still popularly applied to *Philadelphus*.)

About twenty-eight species, natives of Europe and Asia, are included in this genus. Several species are among our most valuable ornamental shrubs.

KEY TO SPECIES OF SYRINGA

1. Tube of corolla much longer than the calyx; stamens included, nearly sessile.
    2. Mature shoots often without a true terminal bud; panicles on nearly naked shoots from the uppermost buds of the previous year's growth; flowers in May.
        3. Leaves cordate or truncate at the base, 5–10 cm. long, panicles compact....
        ....*S. vulgaris* (p. 358)
        3. Leaves narrowed at the base, smaller, panicles somewhat loose.
            4. Leaves 2–4 cm. long, frequently pinnately lobed; panicles about 8 cm.
            long ....*S. persica* (p. 358)

4. Leaves 5–7 cm. long, not lobed; panicles up to 15 cm. long.........
....× S. *chinensis* (p. 359)
2. Shoots with a true terminal bud; panicles borne terminally on leafy shoots of the current year; flowers in June.
    5. Leaves pubescent on the veins beneath, margins finely ciliate; capsules obtuse ....S. *villosa* (p. 359)
    5. Leaves glabrous beneath, margins not ciliate; capsules acute..........
....S. *Josikaea* (p. 361)
1. Tube of corolla little longer than the calyx, stamens exserted.
    6. Shrub with panicles 8–14 cm. long; leaves mostly narrowed at the base, glabrous
....S. *amurensis* (p. 361)
    6. Small tree with panicles up to 25 cm. long; leaves mostly truncate or rounded at the base, hairy beneath..................S. *amurensis* var. *japonica* (p. 361)

COMMON LILAC, *Syringa vulgaris* L., Sp. Pl. 9, 1753

A large shrub, 2–5 m. high; twigs terete, stiff, olive green, the young growth glandular-puberulent, soon becoming glabrous; buds ovate, somewhat pointed, the terminal bud normally abortive in mature twigs, the growth of the season ending in a pair of lateral buds; bud scales smooth; leaves ovate, 4–10 cm. long, 3–7 cm. wide, base rounded, apex acute, dull dark-green above, somewhat paler beneath, glabrous, margin entire, truncate, or generally slightly cordate; petiole about 2–3 cm. long; panicles commonly in pairs from the pseudo-terminal buds, appearing with the leaves in early spring and blooming about the time that the leaves reach full growth; flowers very fragrant, typically reddish-violet on the outside, paler and more bluish within; pedicels and calyx glandular-puberulent; sepals about equal; corolla tube narrowly cylindrical, about 1 cm. long, lobes ovate, rounded, about 5 mm. long; fruit a flattened, somewhat woody capsule about 1–1.5 cm. long, 5 mm. wide, glabrous, acute. Blooms about May 15 in the southern half of the area, as late as July 15 in the extreme northeastern part. (*Vulgáris*, common.)

Common lilac is a native of eastern Europe. It is one of the most commonly planted of ornamental shrubs, and is perfectly hardy throughout the Upper Midwest, often persisting indefinitely in abandoned dooryards, cemeteries, and hedge rows.

There are many horticultural varieties of the common lilac, some with double flowers. Their color ranges from white through various shades of violet and purple to a deep reddish-purple. The white forms have paler foliage and tend to form taller and less compact bushes.

PERSIAN LILAC, *Syringa persica* L., Sp. Pl. 9, 1753

A shrub 1–2 m. high, with slender, somewhat arching branches; young growth sparsely glandular, puberulent or entirely glabrous; buds pointed, bud scales glabrous; twigs slender, more or less angular, gray or brownish-gray, with well-marked lenticels; leaves simple or some of them often divided or pinnatifid, glabrous; simple leaves lanceolate 2–3 cm. long, about 1 cm. wide, entire, base narrowed, tip acute or somewhat acuminate; lobed and pinnatifid leaves somewhat larger, often irregular; panicles about 8 cm. long, from the uppermost lateral buds and often also from a true terminal bud, less compact than in S. *vulgaris*; flowers fragrant, pale lilac or white; sepals lanceolate; corolla tube narrowly cylindrical, about 1 cm. long, lobes ovate-lanceolate, somewhat acute; capsule quadrangular, somewhat winged, about 1 cm. long, 3 mm. wide, obtuse with a small mucro. (*Pérsica*, Persian.)

Probably a native of Afghanistan and Cashmir, this lilac has long been in cultivation in Persia, whence it was introduced into Europe. The true Persian lilac is rather rarely planted in the Upper Midwest. It is distinctly inferior to the hybrid *Syringa chinensis*, which has more or less usurped its common name.

ROUEN LILAC, *Syringa chinensis* Willd., Berl. Baumz. 378, 1796 [S. *vulgaris* × *persica; S. rothomagensis* A. Rich. 1844]

A shrub 1–3 m. high with slender, somewhat arching branches, the young growth almost glabrous; buds pointed, the bud scales loosely imbricated, glabrous; twigs slender, more or less angular, bright green, becoming olive-brown, with well-marked lenticels; leaves simple, ovate-lanceolate, 5–7 cm. long, 3–4 cm. wide, dark green on both sides, glabrous, entire, tip acute or acuminate, base narrowed; panicles as in S. *persica* but larger, often 14 cm. long; flowers fragrant, reddish-purple, darker than those of typical S. *vulgaris*, corolla tube about 0.8 cm. long, slender, the lobes longer and more pointed than in S. *vulgaris*; fruit not ripening in Minnesota (reported in southern Europe as very rarely bearing capsules similar to those of S. *persica*). (*Chinénsis*, Chinese, an obviously inapplicable name, but the earliest given to this form.)

This hybrid was originally grown in Rouen, France, in 1777. It is much planted as an ornamental shrub and often incorrectly called "Persian lilac." Though somewhat less vigorous in growth than the common lilac, it is a very satisfactory shrub, blooming while still quite small. It blooms about one week later than the common lilac, and in our region appears to be entirely sterile.

Syringa villosa Vahl, Enum. 1:38, 1804

A tall shrub up to 4 m. high, the young growth finely pubescent; buds broadly ovate, pointed, the terminal buds present, much larger than the lateral buds, bud scales finely puberulent; twigs terete, dark gray, puberulent; leaves elliptic to elliptic-ovate, narrowed at the base, apex short-acuminate, 4.5–20 cm. long, 2–11 cm. wide, dark green and glabrous above, paler and pubescent and sparsely villous along the veins, margin entire, ciliate; panicles borne on the ends of leafy shoots, 10–30 cm. long, more or less pubescent; flowers with unpleasant odor; calyx campanulate, 2 mm. long, glabrate, the lobes ciliated; corolla lilac or pale pink, tube narrow, about 11 mm. long, lobes subacute, spreading or somewhat reflexed; fruit obtuse or somewhat acute, straight or slightly curved, smooth or with a few lenticels 1–1.15 cm. long. Blooms in June. (*Villósa*, hairy.)

A native of China and Korea, this species is occasionally cultivated.

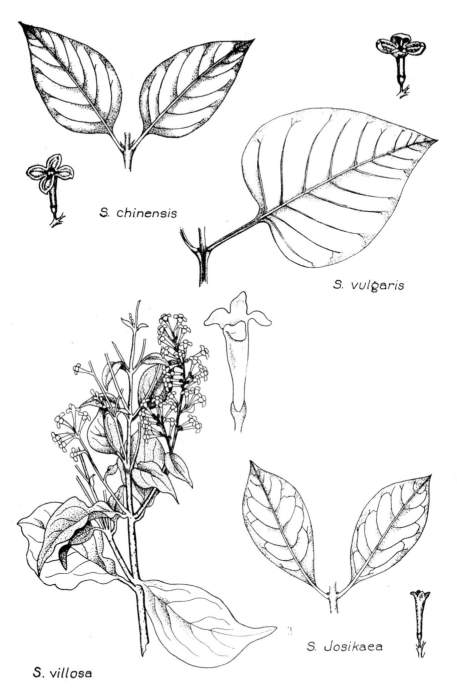

S. chinensis

S. vulgaris

S. villosa

S. Josikaea

Species of *Syringa*

Syringa Josikaea Jacq., Flora., 14:67, 1831

An erect shrub, up to 4 m. high; the young growth yellowish-brown, puberulent; buds broadly ovate, the terminal present, much larger than the lateral ones, bud scales minutely puberulent; twigs terete, somewhat flattened at the nodes, brown or olivaceous, not conspicuously lenticillate; leaves broadly elliptical, base rounded or narrowed, apex short-acuminate, 5–12 cm. long, 3–5 cm. wide, glabrous, dark green above, pale and glaucous beneath, entire, margin sparsely ciliolate; panicles borne at the ends of leafy shoots, 10–20 cm. long, axis puberulent; flowers with a faint but pleasant odor; calyx campanulate, glabrous, 2 mm. long, slightly four-toothed or truncate; corolla deep lilac, tube funnel-shaped, 1–1.5 cm. long, lobes ovate, subacute, about 2 mm. long, somewhat ascending; capsules cylindrical, acute, smooth, about 1 cm. long, 4 mm. in diameter. (*Josikaéa*, named for Rosalia L. B. Josika.)

This native of Hungary and the Erz Mountains is occasionally cultivated. There are several garden forms varying in the color of the flowers. There are also cultivated hybrids of this with the previous species.

Syringa amurensis Rupr., Bull. Phys. Math. Acad. Petersb. 15:371, 1857

A spreading or upright shrub 2–3 m. high, the young growth nearly or quite glabrous; buds obtusely pointed or nearly spherical, the terminal bud abortive; bud scales glabrous, finely and irregularly wrinkled; twigs terete with enlarged nodes, the leaf scars projecting prominently beyond the base of the axillary buds; twigs grayish- or greenish-brown with prominent, round lenticels, the bark soon scaling off and leaving the branches dark brown and cherry-like; leaves broadly ovate to lance-elliptic; base narrowed or rarely somewhat rounded, apex long-acuminate, 4–10 cm. long, margin entire, surface glabrous, the lower surface distinctly reticulately veined; petiole 1–2 cm. long; panicles usually in pairs from the pseudo-terminal buds of the previous season, 8–14 cm. long; flowers, somewhat fragrant, cream-white; calyx campanulate, about 1 mm. long, nearly truncate, or irregularly and shallowly toothed; corolla rotate, about 8 mm. in diameter, tube very short; stamens long exserted; capsule about 1.5 cm. long, 4 mm. in diameter, acute, the surface roughened with numerous lenticels, fruiting calyx very short. Blooms in mid-June. (*Amurénsis*, relating to the Amur River.)

This species is a native of Manchuria, Korea, and the Amur region. It is planted but little in our area, though it is a desirable shrub. The following variety is more frequently planted.

JAPANESE TREE LILAC, *Syringa amurensis* var. *japonica* (Maxim.) Franch. & Sav., En. Pl. Jap. 2:435, 1879 [*S. japonica* (Maxim.) Decne. 1879]

A small tree, 5–10 m. high; leaves more broadly ovate, usually rounded or truncate at the base, 4–12 cm. long, 2.5–8 cm. wide, margin ciliolate, lower surface more or less hirsute; panicles larger, up to 25 cm. long, flowers larger, often over 1 cm. in diameter. (*Japónica*, Japanese.)

This lilac is a native of Japan. It is frequently planted in our area. There is considerable question whether this plant should be regarded as a well-marked geographical variety of *S. amurensis* or as a distinct species.

Forsythia
Forsythia Vahl, Enum. 1:39, 1804

Shrubs 2–3 m. high with opposite, more or less serrate, simple or trifoliolate leaves and showy yellow flowers appearing in early spring before the leaves, each flower from a scaly winter bud, which may be solitary or clustered (two to five) in the axil of a leaf of the previous season; sepals four, united below; corolla campanulate; petals united for about one-third of their length, their tips spreading; stamens two, borne on the base of the corolla; carpels two, united; ovary two-celled, with numerous ovules; style one; stigma two-lobed; fruit a woody septicidal capsule containing numerous winged seeds. (*Forsýthia*, named for William Forsyth, English horticulturist.)

This is a genus of four species, natives of China, Japan, and southeastern Europe. The forsythias are very ornamental garden shrubs, much planted in the eastern and central states. In the Upper Midwest they are entirely hardy but unsatisfactory since the flower buds almost always winter-kill except when they are buried in snow. The following species are occasionally planted, and a few flowers are usually to be found in early spring on the lowest branches.

KEY TO SPECIES OF FORSYTHIA

1. Twigs brown, internodes of branches hollow; flowers bright yellow with orange-yellow stripes in the throat of the corolla.................*F. suspensa* (p. 362)
1. Twigs greenish, usually with lamellate pith; flowers greenish-yellow............
....*F. viridissima* (p. 362)

Forsythia suspensa Vahl, Enum. 1:39, 1804

A shrub about 2.5 m. high; twigs brown with hollow internodes; leaves sharply serrate, some of them usually ternately compound, the simple leaves rounded or broadly cuneate at the base; calyx about as long as the corolla tube, corolla bright yellow with deeper orange stripes in the throat, about 2.5 cm. long. (*Suspénsa*, hanging, referring to the drooping branches.)

This species is a native of China. Two varieties are planted: *F. suspensa* var. *Sieboldii Zabel*, with weak, pendulous branches and a few compound leaves, and *F. suspensa* var. *Fortunei* Rehder, with erect, arching branches and abundant compound leaves.

Forsythia viridissima Lindl., Journ. Hort. Soc. 1:226, 1846

An erect shrub about 3 m. high; twigs olive-green, internodes with lamellate pith; leaves simple, oblong-lanceolate or lanceolate, tapering at the base, entire or somewhat serrate above the middle; calyx shorter than the corolla tube; corolla bright greenish-yellow, 1.5–2.5 cm. long. (*Viridissima*, very green, referring to the branches.)

This species is also a native of China.

NIGHTSHADE FAMILY, SOLANACEAE

Herbs, shrubs, vines, and trees, with alternate, mostly simple, or pinnately compound leaves, and perfect, regular, or sometimes somewhat irregular, solitary or cymose flowers; sepals five, united; petals five, united, mostly folded in the bud; stamens five, inserted on the tube of the corolla, all fertile or, rarely, four fertile and one staminode; carpels two, united; ovary superior, two-celled or, rarely, through secondary partitions five- to eight-celled; style one; stigma two-lobed; fruit a berry or a capsule.

This family includes about seventy genera and seventeen hundred species, of temperate and tropical regions. Most of the species occurring in temperate regions are herbaceous. The following is our only shrubby genus.

Box Thorn
Lycium L., Sp. Pl. 191, 1753

Shrubs or woody vines, mostly poisonous, with small, alternate, entire leaves, commonly with smaller ones fascicled in their axils; twigs often thorny; flowers mostly solitary in the axils of the leaves; calyx campanulate, three- to five-lobed or -toothed, not enlarged in the fruit, persistent at the base of the berry; corolla funnel-form, salver-form, or campanulate, usually five-lobed, tube very short or longer than the lobes; anther sacs longitudinally dehiscent; fruit a berry, usually scarlet. (*Lýcium*, named for the country Lycia.)

KEY TO SPECIES OF LYCIUM

1. Corolla tube longer than the lobes, much narrower below the middle; leaves usually lanceolate....................................... *L. halimifolium* (p. 363)
1. Corolla tube shorter than the lobes, rather wide; leaves rhombic-ovate to ovate-lanceolate... *L. chinense* (p. 364)

MATRIMONY VINE, *Lycium halimifolium* Mill., Gard. Dict. ed. 8, no. 6, 1768 [*L. vulgare* Dunal 1852]

A spreading shrub 1–3 m. high; branches at first upright but later arching or recurving, more or less spiny, light gray and frequently somewhat angled; leaves quite variable, lanceolate, elliptic-lanceolate, or oblanceolate, gradually narrowed toward the base, mostly acute at the apex, 2–7 cm. long, 0.3–2.5 cm. wide, grayish-green, slightly papillose roughened on both sides; petiole variable in length, 2 mm.–2 cm. long; flowers mostly solitary in the axils of the leaves; calyx two- to three-lobed; corolla dull purple, about 1.5 cm. in diameter, the tube longer than the lobes, much constricted below; stamens exserted, filaments ex-

Lycium halimifolium

panded and hairy at the base; fruit oblong, 1.5–2 cm. long, scarlet to orange red. (*Halimifólium*, having leaves like sea purslane.)

This shrub is occasionally planted and is hardy. It is a native of southeastern Europe and western Asia.

CHINESE MATRIMONY-VINE, *Lycium chinense* Mill., Gard. Dict. ed. 8, no. 5, 1768

A low, rambling shrub with arching and often prostrate branches, up to 3 m. long, slightly thorny or unarmed, yellowish-gray, somewhat angled; leaves variable, rhombic-ovate to ovate-lanceolate, acute or obtuse at the apex, broadly to narrowly wedge-shaped at the base, 3–11 cm. long, 1.5–6 cm. wide, bright green and remaining green until late in the autumn, glabrous; petiole not over 1.5 cm. long; flowers solitary or in clusters of two or three in the axils of the leaves; calyx irregularly two- to five-lobed; corolla dull purple-violet, about 1 cm. in diameter, the tube shorter than the lobes, not much constricted, lobes mostly with ciliate margins; stamens long exserted, hairy above the base; fruit ovoid, 1–2.5 cm. long, scarlet or orange-red. (*Chinénse*, Chinese.)

This species is planted chiefly as drapery over walls and sometimes grown on trellises, but it is not truly a vine. It is a native of north China and Manchuria.

BIGNONIA FAMILY, Bignoniaceae

Trees, shrubs, and woody vines (rarely herbs), with opposite or whorled (rarely alternate), simple or pinnately compound leaves without stipules; flowers showy, in clusters, hypogynous, more or less zygomorphic; calyx of five united sepals, often two-lipped; corolla of five united petals campanulate, funnel-shaped, or tubular, more or less irregular, somewhat two-lipped; fertile stamens four or two, borne on the throat of the corolla and alternating with the lateral petals; anthers two-celled, longitudinally dehiscent; pistil compound, consisting

BIGNONIA FAMILY

of two united carpels; ovary superior, two-celled (rarely one-celled) with numerous ovules, placentation parietal or upon the partition wall of the ovary; style one, filiform; stigma with two leaf-like lobes; fruit a two-valved capsule; seeds flat, mostly winged, without endosperm.

This is a family of about sixty genera and five hundred species, mostly tropical.

Catalpa

Catalpa Scop., Introd. 170, 1771

Trees (or shrubs) with large, simple, opposite or whorled, petioled leaves and showy flowers in terminal corymbs or cymose panicles; calyx closed in the bud, splitting irregularly into two lips; corolla tube campanulate, oblique, two-lipped; petals unequal, the upper ones smallest; stamens borne near the base of the corolla, fertile stamens two (rarely four), the anther sacs widely divergent; staminodes three (rarely one); disk nearly obsolete; ovary two-celled; fruit an elongated linear-cylindrical capsule, with loculicidal and septifragal dehiscence; seeds very numerous, flat, strongly winged at the sides and narrowly all around; cotyledons deeply two-lobed. (*Catálpa*, the Indian name for the southern catalpa tree.)

This genus includes about ten species, natives of the eastern United States, the West Indies, and eastern Asia.

KEY TO SPECIES OF CATALPA

1. Capsules 1–2 cm. in diameter; seeds about 2.5 cm. long (exclusive of the hairs); flowers 5 cm. or more in diameter, white with purple markings.
   2. Leaves acute or broadly acuminate; flowers up to 7 cm. in diameter, sparsely spotted ....*C. speciosa* (p. 365)
   2. Leaves narrowly and abruptly acuminate; flowers 5 cm. in diameter, thickly spotted with purple...........................*C. bignonioides* (p. 367)
1. Capsules 0.5–0.8 cm. in diameter; seeds about 1.5 cm. long (exclusive of the hairs); flowers less than 5 cm. in diameter, yellow with orange and purple markings......
   ....*C. ovata* (p. 367)

HARDY CATALPA, *Catalpa speciosa* Warder, *ex.* Engelm., Bot. Gaz. 5:1, 1880

A medium-sized to large tree, in Minnesota 12–20 m. high and about 3 dm. in diameter, but in its native range attaining a height of 40 m. and a trunk diameter of 6–14 dm.; bark grayish-brown with longitudinal, scaly ridges; buds very small, scarcely protruding, bud scales very loosely imbricated, sparingly ciliate; twigs greenish-brown, glabrous, with marked lenticels and very prominent elliptical leaf scars; leaves opposite or in whorls of three, broadly ovate, mostly three-nerved, rounded or cordate at the base, acute or gradually acuminate at the apex, margin entire, 16–30 cm. long, 10–16 cm. wide, bright green above and nearly glabrous except along the larger veins, slightly paler below and pubescent, especially along the veins; petiole about as long as the leaf blade; flowers in flat-topped, cymose panicles; corolla up to 7 cm. in diameter, white, inconspicuously

365

Species of *Catalpa*: Left, *C. speciosa*. Right, *C. bignonioides*.

purple-spotted inside; petals more or less ruffled along the margin, the lower one distinctly notched; capsule 25–40 cm. long, about 1.2–1.8 cm. in diameter; body of seed 25–30 mm. long, 7–9 mm. wide, with tufts of rather coarse hairs, about 1 cm. long. (*Speciósa*, beautiful.)

The catalpa is frequently cultivated in the southern half of the area, but is not reliably hardy north of the Twin Cities. It is a native of bottomlands from southern Indiana to Missouri, south to Tennessee and Arkansas. The wood is light brown, soft, coarse-grained, and very durable in contact with the soil.

CATALPA, INDIAN BEAN, *Catalpa bignonioides* Walt., Fl. Car. 64, 1788[*C. Catalpa* (L.) Karst.]

Differs from *C. speciosa* in the narrowly acuminate leaves, which are frequently indistinctly three- to five-lobed and have an unpleasant odor when crushed, and in the larger panicles of flowers, which are heavily dotted with purple and have two yellow stripes inside. (*Bignonioídes*, bignonia-like.)

This species is occasionally planted, but appears not to be hardy as far north as Minnesota. It is a native of the Gulf states and occurs as far north as Tennessee.

Catalpa ovata G. Don, Gen. Hist. Dichl. Pl. 4:230, 1837

A small to medium-sized tree, in the Upper Midwest rarely over 6 m. high; leaves broadly ovate, frequently somewhat three- to five-lobed, mostly five-nerved, 15–30 cm. long, 15–25 cm. wide, mostly cordate at the base, abruptly acuminate at the apex, finely pubescent with simple hairs, or at length becoming nearly glabrate; petiole 4–14 cm. long; panicle pyramidal, 10–25 cm. long; corolla 2–3 cm. in diameter, pale yellow, with orange stripes and purple dots on the inside; capsule 30–35 cm. long, 6–8 mm. in diameter; seeds, exclusive of the hairs, 12–15 mm. long, 3–4 mm. wide, with tufts of very fine hairs 1 cm. long at the ends. (*Ováta*, ovate, referring to the shape of the leaves.)

A native of China, this species is rarely cultivated in our area, where it seems to be reasonably hardy, but does not reach large size.

MADDER FAMILY, Rubiaceae

Herbs, shrubs, or trees; leaves simple, opposite, or verticillate, mostly with stipules; flowers perfect but often dimorphous, regular; calyx tube adherent to the ovary, its limb variously lobed; corolla sympetalous, campanulate, funnel-shaped, or rotate, four- to five-lobed, frequently hairy within; stamens four or five, borne on the corolla and alternate with its lobes; ovary one- to ten-celled, inferior; ovules one to several in each cavity of the ovary; style short or elongated; fruit a capsule, a berry, or a drupe.

This family is very large, including about three hundred and forty genera and forty-five hundred species, the greater number of which are found in tropical regions. Only one genus of woody plants of this family occurs within our region.

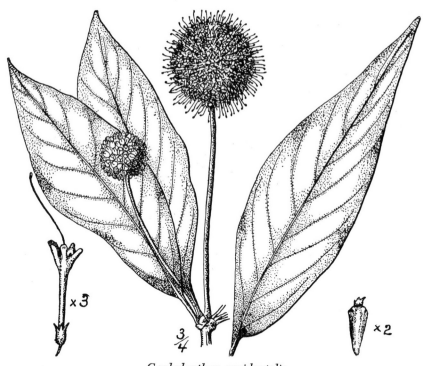

Cephalanthus occidentalis

Buttonbush

Cephalanthus L., Sp. Pl. 95, 1753

Shrubs or small trees, leaves opposite or verticillate, short-petioled and entire; flowers in axillary or terminal heads, small, white or yellow, subtended by bracts; calyx tube short, its limb four-lobed; corolla tubular, with four slightly spreading lobes; stamens four, inserted on the corolla tube, with very short filaments; ovary two-celled, one or two ovules in each cavity; style slender, long-exserted, stigma capitate; fruit splitting into two to four achene-like parts. (*Cephalánthus*, Greek, head flower, referring to the dense inflorescence.)

This is a genus of six species, natives of North America and Asia. The following is the only one occurring in the United States.

BUTTONBUSH, *Cephalanthus occidentalis* L., Sp. Pl. 95, 1753

A shrub 1–3 m. high; branches glabrous; leaves opposite or verticillate, entire, petioled, ovate or oblong-lanceolate, mostly narrowed at the base, acuminate at the apex, glabrous above, glabrous or very sparingly pubescent beneath, 7–14 cm. long, 4–6 cm. wide; petiole 1–2 cm. long; peduncles axillary and terminal, 6–10 cm. long; heads globose, 2–4 cm. in diameter; flowers white, sessile and closely crowded, 8–12 mm. long; styles slender, about twice as long as the corolla; calyx tube surmounting the ovary, persistent; fruit narrowly obconic, 5–6 mm. long. Blossoms in June; fruit ripe in September. (*Occidentális*, Western, i.e., native to the New World.)

Buttonbush grows on banks of streams, in swamps, and on low wet ground. It is common southward, but infrequent northward in the Mississippi and St. Croix River valleys to Taylors Falls, Minnesota. It is distributed from Nova Scotia to Wisconsin and Minnesota, south to Florida, Texas, and Arizona.

HONEYSUCKLE FAMILY, Caprifoliaceae

Shrubs, trees, woody vines, or perennial herbs; leaves opposite, simple or pinnately compound; flowers perfect, regular or irregular, cymose; calyx tube adherent to the ovary, two- to five-toothed or lobed at the top, or the sepals obsolete; petals united into a sympetalous tubular, campanulate, or rotate corolla, five-lobed above, frequently with a sac-like enlargement at the base; stamens five (rarely four), borne on the tube of the corolla and alternating with the lobes, anthers oblong, or narrow and elongated, filaments inserted on the corolla; ovary inferior, two- to five-celled, style slender, stigma enlarged or capitate, two- to five-lobed; ovules one to several in each cell; fruit a one- to several-seeded berry, drupe or capsule; seeds oblong or globose, with small embryo, and fleshy endosperm.

This family includes about ten genera and three hundred species, mostly of the North Temperate Zone.

KEY TO GENERA OF CAPRIFOLIACEAE

1. Leaves compound; flowers small, white, in compound cymes. . . . .
. . . . *Sambucus* (p. 369)
1. Leaves simple.
   2. Flowers in compound cymes; corolla rotate, small; fruit a one-seeded drupe. . .
   . . . .*Viburnum* (p. 373)
   2. Flowers in pairs, or few-flowered racemes or cymes; corolla campanulate or tubular; fruit a berry or a capsule.
      3. Fruit a few-seeded berry, margin of leaves entire (sometimes lobed).
         4. Corolla short campanulate or short funnel-form, regular. . . . .
         . . . .*Symphoricarpos* (p. 378)
         4. Corolla tubular or long campanulate, more or less irregular. . . . .
         . . . .*Lonicera* (p. 381)
      3. Fruit a two-celled capsule, leaves serrate.
         5. Flowers two-lipped, yellow, 1–1.5 cm. long. Native. . .*Diervilla* (p. 389)
         5. Flowers nearly regular, white to rose-pink, about 3 cm. long. Cultivated. . .
         . . . .*Weigela* (p. 391)

Elder

Sambucus L., Sp. Pl. 269, 1753

Shrubs, trees, or perennial herbs; leaves opposite, pinnately compound; leaflets serrate, or sometimes lacinately cut or dissected; flowers small, white, very numerous in compound cymes; calyx lobes or teeth three to five, minute or almost lacking, corolla three- to five-lobed, regular, rotate; stamens five, attached to the base of the corolla, filaments short; ovary three- to five-celled, one ovule in each cavity; style short, three- to five-lobed; fruit a berry-like drupe, containing from three to five one-seeded stones. (*Sambúcus*, the classical name of the elderberry.)

This genus of about twenty species is of wide geographical distribution but most abundant in North Temperate regions. Besides the following, three other species occur in the western part of North America.

KEY TO SPECIES OF SAMBUCUS

1. Pith brown; inflorescence pyramidal, appearing in early spring; fruit red, inedible . . . .*S. pubens* (p. 370)
1. Pith white; inflorescence flat-topped, in midsummer; fruit nearly black, edible.
2. Stems scarcely woody, bark not warty, leaflets mostly seven; stones of fruit mostly four. . . . .*S. canadensis* (p. 372)
2. Stems woody, bark warty, leaflets mostly five; stones of fruit three. . . . .
. . . . *S. nigra* (p. 372)

RED-BERRIED ELDER, *Sambucus pubens* Michx., Fl. Bor. Am. 1:181, 1803

A woody shrub 1–4 m. high; bark gray and warty; young shoots commonly pubescent, with large, brown pith, foliage unpleasantly strong-smelling when bruised; leaflets five to seven, sessile or short-stalked, ovate to ovate-lanceolate, 4–13 cm. long, 2–4 cm. wide, occasionally much larger, base narrowed, rounded or subcordate, mostly unequal, apex acute or acuminate, margin sharply serrate, the teeth rather spreading, upper surface dark green, puberulent along the main veins, otherwise nearly glabrate, lower surface much paler, mostly densely hirsute, rarely nearly glabrous; petiole 2.5–5 cm. long, mostly hirsute, stipules 3–5 mm. long, ovate or ligulate; inflorescence a pyramidal cymose panicle, 4–7 cm. long, 3–5 cm. wide, becoming somewhat diffuse in the fruit; flowers yellowish-white, 3–4 mm. broad, petals reflexed; stamens very short, the anthers about 0.8 mm. long; stigmas nearly sessile, projecting but little above the level of the corolla; fruit bright red, 4–5 mm. in diameter, acid; nutlets dark yellow-brown, finely transversely rugose, 2–2.5 mm. long. Blossoms in April and May; fruit ripe in June and July. (*Púbens*, pubescent.)

This shrub grows on rocky banks and in ravines, woods, and clearings. It is common, especially northward in the Upper Midwest region, somewhat infrequent southward to northeastern Iowa and southern Wisconsin, rare or wanting in the prairie area. It is distributed from Newfoundland to Alaska, south to New England, New Jersey, in the uplands to Georgia and Tennessee, west to Indiana, Illinois, northeastern Iowa, the Black Hills of South Dakota, Colorado, and Oregon. Reports from the Rocky Mountains and the Pacific Coast seem to be due to confusion between this and other related western species.

This is one of a group of closely related species of the northern cool temperate regions, typified by the Old World *S. racemosa* L., with which they have frequently been confused. *S. racemosa* has somewhat smaller and generally glabrous

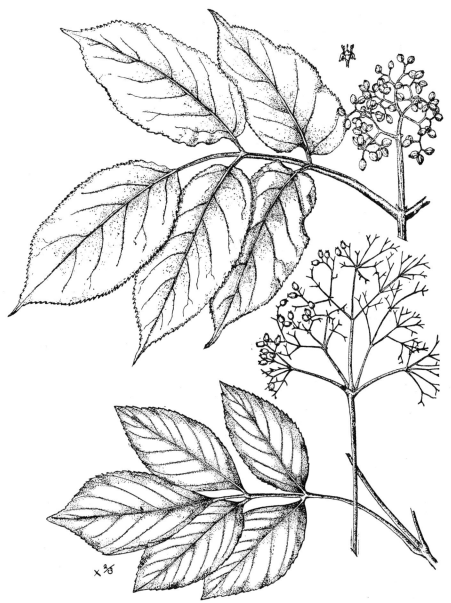

Species of *Sambucus*: Above, S. *pubens*. Below, S. *canadensis*. ($\times$ 2/3)

leaves, with finer appressed serration, smaller and more compact inflorescences, notably larger anthers, and a peculiar, turgid stylopodium, which raises the stigmas considerably above the level of the corolla. *S. racemosa* var. *laciniata* Koch, a cut-leaf form of the European red-berried elder, is occasionally cultivated in Minnesota. A corresponding cut-leaf form of the native elder. (*S. pubens* var. *dissecta* Brit.) has been reported from the Lake Superior region. Its occurrence there is doubtful.

COMMON ELDER, AMERICAN ELDER, *Sambucus canadensis* L., Sp. Pl. 269, 1753

A shrub 1–3 m. high; stems scarcely woody, with nearly smooth, grayish-brown bark and large white pith; leaflets five to eleven, mostly seven, ovate to ovate-oblong or lanceolate, 7–15 cm. long, 3–6 cm. wide, the lower leaflets often showing a tendency to become ternately compound, the base of the leaflets narrowed, rounded, or subcordate, apex long-acuminate, margin sharply serrate, upper surface lustrous, bright green, glabrous except for puberulence along the midrib sometimes extending out along the larger veins, lower surface paler, more or less hirsute along the midrib and larger veins and puberulent along the smaller veins or sometimes nearly glabrous, upper leaflets nearly or quite sessile, lower leaflets with practically glabrous petiolules up to 1.5 cm. long, stipels frequently present; petiole 4–5 cm. long, puberulent along the upper side, stipules mostly wanting; inflorescence a very ample, flat cyme, 10–20 cm. broad; flowers white, 5–6 mm. broad; sepals triangular, nearly as long as the inferior portion of the ovary, petals but slightly reflexed, stamens somewhat exceeding the petals, filaments slender, anthers oblong, about 0.5 mm. long, the upper part of the ovary protruding above the level of the corolla, forming a conical stylopodium, which bears at its summit the completely united stigmas; fruit purplish-black, 5–6 mm. in diameter, edible; stones usually four, flattened, about 3.5 mm. long, rugose-papillose. Blossoms in late June; fruit ripe in August and September. (*Canadénsis*, Canadian.)

Common elder grows in moist, rich soil, chiefly on bottomlands. It is common throughout the southern parts of the area, infrequent northward to southern Manitoba and to the region of Duluth, Minnesota. It is distributed from Nova Scotia to Manitoba, south to Georgia, Louisiana, and Texas. The fruit is used for making pies, jelly, and wine.

S. canadensis var. *laciniata* Gray., the American cut-leaf elder, has the leaflets dissected and compounded. It is occasionally planted.

EUROPEAN ELDER, *Sambucus nigra* L., Sp. Pl. 269, 1753

A shrub closely resembling *S. canadensis*, but taller and more woody and having bark with corky warts; leaflets usually five, the petiolules hirsute, stipels wanting; sepals much shorter than the inferior portion of the ovary, stamens not exceeding the petals, the filaments rather broad; stigmas three, distinct at the top of a conical stylopodium; fruit black, about 7 mm. in diameter, stones usually three. (*Nigra*, black, referring to the fruit.)

This species is seldom seen in our area in the typical form, but horticultural varieties with yellow and with variegated leaves are sometimes planted, as is also *S. nigra* var. *laciniata* L., a form with the leaflets deeply dissected and compounded.

Arrowwood
Viburnum L., Sp. Pl. 267, 1753

Shrubs or trees; leaves entire, serrate, dentate, or lobed, stipules sometimes present, leaf buds naked or with a pair of scales, flowers white, or rarely pink, numerous, in flat compound cymes, sometimes the marginal flowers of the cyme larger and sterile, calyx ovoid or turbinate, five-toothed; corolla rotate or spreading, regular, five-lobed; stamens five, borne on the tube of the corolla, ovary inferior, one- to three-celled, ovule one in each cavity of the ovary; style short, three-lobed or three-cleft; fruit a one-celled, one-seeded, ovoid or globose drupe; stone somewhat flattened and ridged, seed compressed. (*Vibúrnum*, the classical name of the wayfaring tree.)

This is a genus of about a hundred species, of wide geographical distribution. In addition to the following, about fifteen other species occur in different parts of North America.

KEY TO SPECIES OF VIBURNUM [*]

1. Leaves three-lobed, palmately veined.
  2. Flowers all perfect and alike; lobes of leaves shallow, not coarsely dentate.....
    ....*V. edule* (p. 374)
  2. Some or all of the flowers sterile; leaves more deeply three-lobed, coarsely and irregularly dentate.
    3. Marginal flowers large and sterile, central ones perfect, clusters flat-topped.
      4. Lobes of leaves mostly long-acuminate, longer than broad, petiolar glands small. Native...............................*V. trilobum* (p. 374)
      4. Lobes of leaves obtuse to short-acuminate, broader than long, petiolar glands 1 mm. in diameter. Cultivated.............*V. Opulus* (p. 376)
    3. All the flowers large and sterile, clusters spherical. Cultivated.............
      ....*V. Opulus* var. *roseum* (p. 376)
1. Leaves not lobed, pinnately veined, dentate or serrate.
  5. Leaves finely serrate or serrate-dentate (twenty-five or more teeth on each side of leaf); terminal winter buds elongated.
    6. Leaves and inflorescence densely pubescent, winter buds naked. Cultivated...*V. Lantana* (p. 377)
    6. Leaves and inflorescence glabrous, winter buds scaly...*V. Lentago* (p. 377)

[*] Southern Arrowwood, *Viburnum dentatum* L., is not included in this key. It is an upright bushy shrub up to 5 m. high, with close, gray bark; branchlets pubescent, or sometimes glabrate or glabrous; leaves suborbicular to ovate, coarsely dentate, thick and firm, glabrous and lustrous above, glabrous beneath or pilose in the axils of the veins; cymes slender-stalked, 5–8 cm. across; fruit globose-ovoid, about 6 cm. long, blue-black when ripe. A native of the eastern and southeastern United States, it is occasionally cultivated in the Upper Midwest and apparently is hardy as far north as the forty-fifth parallel.

5. Leaves coarsely dentate (mostly fewer than ten teeth on each side of leaf), terminal winter buds short.
    7. Lower surface of leaves densely soft-pubescent; upper petioles not over 7 mm. long . . . . .V. *Rafinesquianum* (p. 378)
    7. Lower surface of leaves glabrous except along the veins and in their axils; upper petioles 8–12 mm. long . . . . . .V. *Rafinesquianum* var. *affine* (p. 378)

SQUASHBERRY, *Viburnum edule* (Michx.) Raf., Med. Repos. 5:354, 1808 [V. *pauciflorum* Raf. 1838]

A low, straggling shrub 0.7–2 m. high, bark grayish, young shoots reddish-brown and ridged; leaves broadly oval or obovate, narrowed, truncate or cordate at the base, mostly with three shallow lobes, dentate, glabrous above, more or less pubescent on the veins beneath, 5–9 cm. long, 4.5–9.5 cm. wide, petioles 1–2 cm. long; cymes few-flowered, about 2 cm. broad, terminating short, two-leaved lateral branchlets; flowers all perfect, 5–6 mm. broad, stamens shorter than the corolla; drupe globose to ovoid, light red, acid, 8–10 mm. long, stone ovate, pointed. Blossoms in June; fruit ripe in August and September. (*Edúle*, edible.)

In cool woods and thickets, squashberry is common in the Lake Superior region, especially in the North Shore area. It is distributed from Labrador to Alaska, south to New Brunswick, northern New England, New York, and the northern parts of Michigan, Wisconsin, Minnesota, and adjacent Ontario and Manitoba; it occurs also in the Rocky Mountains to Colorado.

V. acerifolium L. differs from this species in having the leaves soft-pubescent beneath and the cymes larger (4–6 cm. in diameter) and terminating the principal branches. It has been reported from southeastern Minnesota, but its presence there seems very doubtful. It occurs in central Wisconsin and the northern peninsula of Michigan.

HIGH-BUSH CRANBERRY, PEMBINA, *Viburnum trilobum* Marsh., Arb. Am. 162, 1785 [V. *americanum* of authors, not Miller; V. *Opulus* var. *americanum* Ait. 1789]

A shrub 1–3 m. high, branches nearly erect, smooth and grayish-brown, twigs glabrous; leaves deeply three-lobed, 5–13 cm. long, 4.5–12 cm. broad, cuneate or rounded at the base, the lobes strongly divergent, acuminate to caudate-acuminate, coarsely and irregularly dentate or sometimes almost entire; upper surface dark yellow-green, sparsely strigose; lower surface somewhat paler, with a fringe of stiff pubescence along the larger veins and scattered appressed hairs on the smaller veins, sometimes nearly glabrous; margin ciliate; petiole about 2.5 cm. long, bearing near the upper end two (rarely several) small, stalked glands about 0.4 mm. in diameter; stipules filiform, 3–8 mm. long; inflorescence a flat-topped cyme, 5–10 cm. in diameter; the outer flowers neutral, 1–2 cm. broad, corolla white, nearly wheel-shaped, deeply five-lobed, somewhat irregular; fertile flowers much smaller, 2–3 mm. broad, calyx (best seen just after the

Species of *Viburnum*: Top left, *V. edule.* Top right,
V. trilobum. Bottom, *V. Lentago.*

the corolla falls) forming a collar-like ring about the summit of the ovary, the
individual sepals very short, truncate, often scarcely distinguishable; drupe
bright red, ellipsoid, up to 12 mm. long, sour and bitter but edible when cooked,
stone elliptical, rarely broadly ovate, 1–1.5 mm. thick, convex on the dorsal side,
concave on the ventral. Flowers in May and early June; fruit ripe in September.
(*Trílobum*, three-lobed, referring to the leaves.)

Growing in cool woods and thickets and on shores and rocky slopes, this

375

species is common throughout the coniferous forest of the Upper Midwest, less frequent in mixed and deciduous woods southward to northeastern Iowa, southern Wisconsin and northern Illinois. It is distributed from Newfoundland and Quebec to British Columbia, south to New England, Pennsylvania and northern Ohio, Indiana, Illinois, and Iowa; it occurs also in the Black Hills of South Dakota and in Wyoming and Washington.

This species seems sufficiently distinct from the European *V. Opulus*, of which it is usually regarded as a variety. Besides the differences in the shape and pubescence of the leaves, there are marked differences in the calyx and in the stone of the drupe. Specimens from the Pacific Coast appear to belong to *V. Opulus*, rather than to *V. trilobum*.

The fruit is used for making jelly and preserves. "Pembina, borne first by a river, and then given to the town and county, is stated by Keating to be from the Chippewa word for this fruit, *anepemnan*, which name has been shortened and corrupted into Pembina" (W. Upham, *Flora of Minnesota*).

Viburnum Opulus L., Sp. Pl. 268, 1753

A shrub 2–3 m. high, with smooth, grayish branches; twigs glabrous; leaves three-lobed, 3.5–10 cm. long, 4–11 cm. wide, rounded to cordate at the base, the lobes short-acuminate, acute, or somewhat obtuse, coarsely and irregularly dentate or, rarely, the lateral lobes nearly entire; upper surface dark green, glabrous except for a little puberulence along the main veins and sometimes a few strigose hairs close to the margin; lower surface paler, mostly soft-pubescent; margin ciliate; petiole about 1.5 cm. long, bearing from two to several large glands about 1 mm. in diameter; stipules linear, frequently over 1 cm. long; inflorescence nearly flat, 5–10 cm. in diameter; the outer flowers neutral, 1–3 cm. broad, corolla white, nearly wheel-shaped, deeply five-lobed; fertile flowers much smaller, 3–5 mm. in diameter, calyx minute, consisting of five distinct triangular teeth; corolla broad campanulate, the petals reflexed, stamens exserted; drupe round-oval, red, up to 12 mm. long, stone nearly orbicular, flat, less than 1 mm. thick. (*Op'ulus*, classical Latin name for a tree.)

This species is a native of Eurasia, and also probably of Pacific North America. The typical form is occasionally planted, but much more commonly the following variety.

SNOWBALL, GUELDER-ROSE, *Viburnum Opulus* L. var. *roseum* L., Sp. Pl. 268, 1753 [*V. Opulus* var. *sterilis* DC. 1830]

A form with almost spherical cymes, the flowers all large and neutral. Blossoms in June. (*Róseum*, rose-like.)

Snowball is extensively planted as an ornamental shrub and is perfectly hardy. The leaves are likely to be badly infested with aphis, and as a result to curl and shrivel very badly.

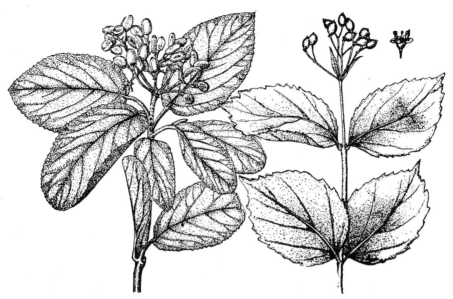

Species of *Viburnum*: Left, *V. Lantana*. Right, *V. Rafinesquianum*. (× 2/3)

WAYFARING TREE, *Viburnum Lantana* L., Sp. Pl. ed. 2, 384, 1762

A shrub or sometimes a small tree, 1–3 m. high; branches brown, young shoots ashy-pubescent, winter buds naked; leaves ovate to ovate-oblong, mostly cordate at the base, blunt or acutish at the apex, finely and sharply serrate or serrate-dentate, densely stellate-pubescent on both sides; petiole 1–2 cm. long, pubescent; cymes short-peduncled, the whole cluster about 6–8 cm. broad; flowers all perfect and alike, 7–10 mm. broad, stamens 6–7 mm. long; fruit oblong-ovoid, flattened, about 1 cm. long. Blossoms in May; fruit ripe in August. (*Lantána*, a genus name of mythological origin.)

This shrub is frequently cultivated and perfectly hardy. It was introduced from Eurasia.

BLACK HAW, NANNYBERRY, *Viburnum Lentago* L., Sp. Pl. 268, 1753

A tall shrub or sometimes a small tree, 3–6 m. high; bark smooth and gray or brownish; winter buds scaly, acuminate; young shoots glabrous; leaves oval or ovate, rounded at the base, acuminate at the apex, very finely and sharply serrate, glabrous on both sides or sometimes slightly puberulent beneath, 4–11 cm. long, 2.5–5.5 cm. wide; petiole about 2 cm. long, often widened and wavy-margined below the middle; inflorescence consisting of from four to six sessile cymes, the cluster hemispherical, 6–10 cm. broad; flowers white, 6–7 mm. broad, stamens about 3 mm. long; drupe oval, bluish-black, 10–12 mm. long, slightly flattened, edible, stone oval, flat. Blossoms in May and June; fruit ripe in August. (*Lentágo*, Latin name of a shrub.)

Black haw grows in rich woods, frequently along banks of streams, and is common throughout the Upper Midwest except northeastward in the region north of Lake Superior. It is distributed from western Quebec to Manitoba, south to New Jersey, upland to Georgia, Ohio, Illinois, northeastern Missouri, South Dakota, and Colorado.

DOWNY ARROWWOOD, *Viburnum Rafinesquianum* Schultes, in Roem. & Schult., Syst. Veg. 6:630, 1820 [*V. affine* Bush 1918; *V. affine* var. *hypomalacum* Blake 1918]

A branching shrub 6–14 dm. high, bark dark-gray, twigs yellow-brown, glabrous, leaves ovate or oblong-ovate, 4–8 cm. long, 2–7 cm. wide, apex acute to acuminate, base mostly cordate, rarely rounded or narrowed, margin coarsely and often sharply dentate with from six to eleven teeth on each side, ciliate; upper surface dark green, glabrous; lower surface somewhat paler yellow-green, more or less pubescent along the principal veins and in their axils, otherwise glabrous; stipules linear, persistent, about 6 mm. long; petioles 5–12 mm. long, those of the uppermost pair of leaves on sterile twigs, mostly over 10 mm.; cymes peduncled, seven-rayed, the rays about 1 cm. long, minutely glandular, the whole cyme 2–5 cm. broad; flowers 4 mm. broad, stamens about 3 mm. long; drupe oval, dark purple, about 8 mm. long; stone flattened, plano-convex, with two marked grooves on the dorsal surface and two obscure submarginal grooves on the ventral surface. Flowers in May and early June; fruit ripe in September. (*Rafinesquiánum*, named for C. S. Rafinesque-Schmaltz.)

Downy arrowwood grows on dry slopes, open woods, low grounds, and barrens, and is common throughout the forested parts of the area. It is distributed from Quebec to Manitoba, south to Georgia, Kentucky and Missouri.

Viburnum Rafinesquianum var. *affine* (Bush) House, Torreya 35:126, 1935

Differs from the preceding in having the leaves glabrous beneath or slightly pilose along the veins. (*Affíne*, related.)

This variety grows in habitats similar to those of the species and occurs throughout the same range, but much less frequently.

Snowberry, Wolfberry
Symphoricarpos Juss., Genera, 211, 1789

Low, upright, branching shrubs; leaves opposite and simple; flowers pink or white, small, perfect, in axillary or terminal clusters; calyx tube short, five-toothed, regular; corolla campanulate or tubular, four- to five-lobed, sometimes hairy on the inside, occasionally gibbous at the base; stamens four or five, borne on the corolla tube; ovary inferior, four-celled, two of the cells containing abortive ovules, the others with a single ovule in each; style slender, stigma capitate or two-lobed; fruit a two-seeded berry, seeds bony.

This genus includes about ten species, natives of North America except for one from China. (*Symphoricárpos*, Greek, clustered fruit.)

KEY TO SPECIES OF SYMPHORICARPOS

1. Corolla 3–4 mm. long; fruit red......................*S. orbiculatus* (p. 379)
1. Corolla 6–8 mm. long; fruit white or pinkish.
    2. Corolla lobes equaling the corolla tube, styles and stamens exserted..........
    ....*S. occidentalis* (p. 379)
    2. Corolla lobes half as long as the corolla tube, styles and stamens included.
        3. Leaves pubescent beneath.
            4. Leaves pale green beneath........................*S. albus* (p. 380)
            4. Leaves whitened beneath............*S. albus* var. *pauciflorus* (p. 381)
        3. Leaves glabrous beneath.................*S. albus* var. *laevigatus* (p. 381)

CORALBERRY, INDIAN CURRANT, *Symphoricarpos orbiculatus* Moench, Meth. Pl. 503, 1794

A low shrub, 0.5–2 m. high, with slender, upright branches, villous to puberulent when young; leaves ovate, elliptic to suborbicular, 1.5–5 cm. long, 1.3–5 cm. broad; dull green above, glaucescent and pubescent beneath, short-acute or obtuse or rounded at the apex; petioles 1–4 mm. long: margin entire, more or less revolute; flowers sessile and in short, dense axillary or terminal spikes; corolla campanulate, 3–4 mm. long, yellowish-white to purplish, sparingly bearded inside; stamens and styles pilose, included; anthers shorter than the filaments; fruit, ellipsoid to subglobose, 5–7 mm. long, coral-pink to purplish-red, crowned by the short, turbinate persistent calyx. Blossoms in July and August; fruit ripe in September and October. (*Orbiculátus*, round, referring to the frequently suborbicular leaves.)

Coralberry grows in open woods and thickets and on banks. It is occasionally cultivated and possibly is native in the southwestern part of Minnesota. It is distributed from Florida to Texas, north to Pennsylvania, Ohio, Indiana, Illinois, and South Dakota.

WOLFBERRY, *Symphoricarpos occidentalis* Hook., Fl. Bor. Am. 1:285, 1833

A low, erect shrub, 3–10 dm. high, more or less freely branching, spreading freely by the root and often forming dense colonies; young twigs puberulent, light reddish-brown, slender, but mostly over 1 mm. in diameter, the bark of the older stems gray and shredded; leaves rather thick, ovate, entire or more or less deeply round-lobed, especially on young shoots, 3–11 cm. long, 1.5–7 cm. wide; base rounded or narrowed; apex acute to rounded, mucronate; upper surface dark dull-green, sparingly strigose pubescent or, more frequently, glabrate except along the midrib and close to the margin, lower surface paler bluish-green, thinly pubescent at least along the veins; margin somewhat revolute; petiole 4–10 mm. long, pubescent; flowers in short dense terminal and axillary spikes, the peduncles usually very short or nearly wanting, rarely 1–3 cm. long; flowers sessile, the bracts and bractlets broadly ovate, ciliate; calyx mostly regularly five-toothed, the sepals ciliate; corolla pinkish, heavily bearded within, short funnelform, 6–9 mm. long, the petals somewhat longer than the tube; stamens somewhat exserted, anthers over 2 mm. long; style exserted, the exposed portion gla-

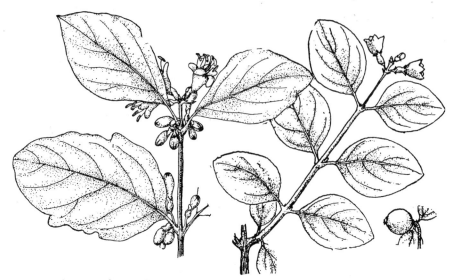

Species of *Symphoricarpos*: Left, *S. occidentalis*. Right, *S. albus*.

brous, the middle portion varying from entirely glabrous to densely bearded; berry dull white, soon becoming discolored and blackish; seeds plano-convex, 4–5 mm. long, straw-colored, smooth. Blossoms in June and July; fruit ripe in September, often persistent throughout the winter. (*Occidentális*, western.)

Wolfberry, which grows in dry soil, is common in the prairie and hardwood districts, not occurring northeastward. It is distributed from Michigan to British Columbia, north on the plains to latitude 64°, south to Illinois, Kansas, and Colorado.

This is one of the few species of woody plants that grow freely on the open prairies. The leaves are very variable in form and size. Particularly on young shoots from the root, they are often very large and deeply lobed. Whenever the old growth has been destroyed, flowers and fruit are apt to be formed on these first-year shoots. The style of this species has usually been described as glabrous. In two-thirds of the Minnesota specimens examined, its middle portion is strongly bearded, and in half the remainder it bears a few hairs. About the same proportion holds for specimens from other parts of the range. No other characters appear to correlate in the least with this style character.

SNOWBERRY, *Symphoricarpos albus* (L.) Blake, Rhodora 16:118, 1914 [*Vaccinium album* L. 1753; *S. racemosus* Michx. 1803]

A low shrub, 2–6 dm. high or occasionally taller; young twigs glabrous or more frequently, puberulent, light yellow-brown, exceedingly slender, the bark of the older stems gray, becoming blackish with age; leaves thin, ovate, ellipticoblong, or nearly orbicular, 2–5 cm. long, 1–3 cm. wide, base narrowed or rounded, apex acutely or obtusely pointed or rounded, occasionally apiculate but not mucronate; upper surface bright green, glabrous or with a few appressed

380

hairs; lower surface in the typical form paler but not whitened, pilose at least along the veins; margin entire, ciliate; petiole 2–5 mm. long, rarely longer; flowers short-pedicelled, solitary in the upper axils or sometimes also in a terminal, interrupted, spike-like raceme, the bracts lanceolate, bractlets deltoid, scarcely at all ciliate; calyx irregularly five-toothed, the sepals glabrous or more or less ciliate; corolla pink and white, heavily bearded within, campanulate, somewhat gibbous at the base, 4–5 mm. long, the petals shorter than the tube; stamens not exserted, anthers 1–1.5 mm. long; style much shorter than the corolla, glabrous; berry bright white, about 6 mm. in diameter, seeds plano-convex, straw-colored, minutely rough. Blossoms in June; fruit ripe in August. (*Al'bus*, white, referring to the color of the berries.)

Snowberry grows in rocky and dry soil throughout the wooded parts of the Upper Midwest. It is most abundant northward and along the bluffs of the Mississippi. It is distributed from Gaspé and the Hudson Bay region to Alaska, south to Massachusetts, Pennsylvania, Michigan, Minnesota, Montana, Washington, and perhaps California.[*]

Symphoricarpos albus var. *pauciflorus* (Robbins) Blake, Rhodora 16:119, 1914

A dwarf shrub, differing from the species in having the lower surface of the leaves more strongly pubescent and conspicuously whitened. (*Pauciflórus*, few-flowered, the original specimens being without racemes. They are quite as common, however, in this variety as in typical S. *albus*.)

This variety is common in the region of the evergreen forests, particularly in the north central part of the area, infrequent southward. It is distributed from the regions of Lake Superior and Lake Winnipeg to British Columbia, south to Minnesota, North Dakota, Colorado, and Oregon.

Forms intermediate between this variety and the typical species are rather common.

Symphoricarpos albus var. *laevigatus* (Fernald) Blake, Rhodora 16:119, 1914

Often taller than the species, up to 2 m. high, leaves larger, glabrous, those on young shoots often more or less lobed, flowers usually in racemes. (*Laevigátus*, smooth.)

This variety is frequently planted and occasionally escapes. It is native from the Gulf of St. Lawrence south in the mountains to Virginia and occurs also in British Columbia and Washington. The cultivated form came originally from the West.

Honeysuckle
Lonicera L., Sp. Pl. 173, 1753

Erect shrubs or woody, twining vines; leaves opposite, entire; flowers in terminal heads or spikes, or in pairs on axillary peduncles; calyx adherent to the

[*] The California plants seen by the authors appear to belong to a distinct variety.

ovary, its limb usually minute, five-toothed or nearly entire, petals five, united into a more or less irregular corolla; corolla trumpet-, funnel-, or bell-shaped, the tube often gibbous at the base and honey-bearing, the limb five-cleft or two-lipped, the upper lip consisting of four petals, the lower of one petal; stamens five, borne on the corolla tube, alternate with the petals; pistil one, compound, two- or three-parted, ovary inferior, two- or three-celled (rarely one-celled); style one, stigma one, capitate or two- to three-lobed; fruit a berry, usually two- or three-celled, few-seeded; in species with flowers in pairs, the two berries sometimes coalescent. (*Lonicéra*, named for Adam Lonitzer.)

This is a genus of about a hundred species, chiefly of the North Temperate Zone.

KEY TO SPECIES OF LONICERA [*]

1. Flowers terminal, in dense clusters or interrupted spikes; upper leaves of flowering shoots connate-perfoliate, usually vines; subgenus *Caprifolium.*
    2. Flowers long, trumpet-shaped, anthers little exserted. Cultivated...........
    ....*L. sempervirens* (p. 383)
    2. Flowers with a short corolla tube and spreading, two-lipped limb; anthers much exserted. Native.
        3. Margin of leaves parchment-like, not ciliate.
            4. Uppermost perfoliate disk rhombic, not glaucous above; anthers about 2.5 mm. long.
                5. Leaves nearly or quite glabrous; outside of corolla not villous.......
                ....*L. dioica* (p. 383)
                5. Leaves pubescent beneath; outside of corolla villous..............
                ....*L. dioica* var. *glaucescens* (p. 384)
            4. Perfoliate disk nearly orbicular, glaucous on both sides; anthers about 4 mm. long.....................................*L. prolifera* (p. 385)
        3. Margin of leaves green, ciliate.....................*L. hirsuta* (p. 385)
1. Flowers in pairs, on axillary peduncles; none of the leaves connate-perfoliate; mostly upright shrubs; subgenus *Xylosteum.*
    6. Peduncles slender, over 1 cm. long.
        7. Leaves narrowed toward the base; flowers strongly two-lipped...........
        ....*L. oblongifolia* (p. 386)
        7. Leaves mostly rounded, truncate, or cordate at the base; petals nearly equal.
            8. Flowers yellowish, funnel-shaped, petals much shorter than the tube; mature leaves yellow-green, ciliate...........*L. canadensis* (p. 386)
            8. Freshly opened flowers pink or white, the petals spreading, nearly equaling the tube; mature leaves blue-green, not ciliate.
                9. Twigs glabrous; flowers not becoming yellow with age............
                ....*L. tatarica* (p. 388)
                9. Twigs pubescent; flowers becoming yellow with age.............
                ....× *L. bella* (p. 389)
    6. Peduncles less than 1 cm. long.
        10. Flowers white, becoming yellow with age, petals spreading; ovaries distinct.......................................*L. Morrowi* (p. 388)
        10. Flowers yellowish from the first, narrowly campanulate; ovaries completely united...............................*L. villosa* var. *Solonis* (p. 389)

[*] *L. involucrata* (Richards.) Banks (not included in this key) has been reported from the Lake Superior region of Ontario, Michigan, and Wisconsin. We have not seen specimens of it from the area.

TRUMPET HONEYSUCKLE, *Lonicera sempervirens* L., Sp. Pl. 173, 1753

A twining vine 3 m. or more tall; bark pale-brown, shredded; twigs glabrous; leaves elliptic or oblong 4–8 cm. long, 2–5 cm. wide on flowering shoots, often much larger on sterile shoots, the lower short-petioled, the uppermost pair on flowering shoots connate-perfoliate, forming a broad elliptical or rarely rhombic disk; the apex of the leaves rounded, minutely mucronulate; base rounded or somewhat narrowed; margin cartilaginous; upper surface dark green, glabrous; lower surface pale, glaucous, finely appressed-puberulent; inflorescence a peduncled, interrupted spike, often with secondary inflorescences in the axils of the connate-perfoliate leaves; ovary glabrous; limb of the calyx minute, five-lobed; corolla scarlet, often with some yellow, especially within, trumpet-shaped, nearly regular, its tube 4–5 cm. long, about 6 mm. wide at the throat, its limb scarcely spreading, about 5 mm. long; stamens and style barely exserted; berries scarlet. (*Sempérvirens*, evergreen, a character that it possesses in the southern states, but not in Minnesota.)

Trumpet honeysuckle is frequently cultivated as an ornamental vine, blooming in June and at intervals until severe frost in October. It is native from Maine to Nebraska and southward.

Lonicera dioica L., Syst. Nat. Veg. ed. 12, 2:165, 1767 [*L. glauca* Hill 1769; *L. parviflora* Lam. 1783]

A twining vine 1–3 m. high or, frequently, a straggling shrub about 1 m. high; bark grayish, peeling on old stems; twigs glabrous and glaucous; leaves oblong, elliptical, or obovate, 4–8 cm. long, 1.5–3.5 cm. wide on flowering shoots, the lower cordate-clasping, the upper two to four pairs connate-perfoliate, the uppermost pair forming a rhombic or elliptic-oblong disk usually strongly angled at the ends; the apex of the leaves rounded or obtuse, often mucronulate, the upper surface bright green, glabrous, the lower surface pale and glaucous, entirely glabrous or with a few scattered hairs, margin cartilaginous and without hairs; inflorescence a dense, head-like spike, sessile or short-peduncled; ovary glabrous, calyx limb barely 1 mm. long, obscurely five-lobed, corolla yellowish or, more frequently, dull maroon with a yellowish tube, glabrous without, villous within, its tube 7–10 mm. long, gibbous at the base and expanding to a width of about 3 mm. at the throat, its limb two-lipped, cleft into five somewhat unequal linear petals 5–10 mm. long; stamens strongly exserted, the thin filaments hairy; berries red. (*Dioíca*, diocecious, which this plant is not.)

This vine grows on bluffs and rocky banks, and in dry woods and thickets. Typical *L. dioica* appears to reach the northwesterly limit of its distribution in southeastern Minnesota approximately at latitude 45° N. It is of far less frequent occurrence than the following variety, with which it has been confused. It is distributed from Maine and southwestern Quebec to Minnesota, south to Georgia, Ohio, and Missouri.

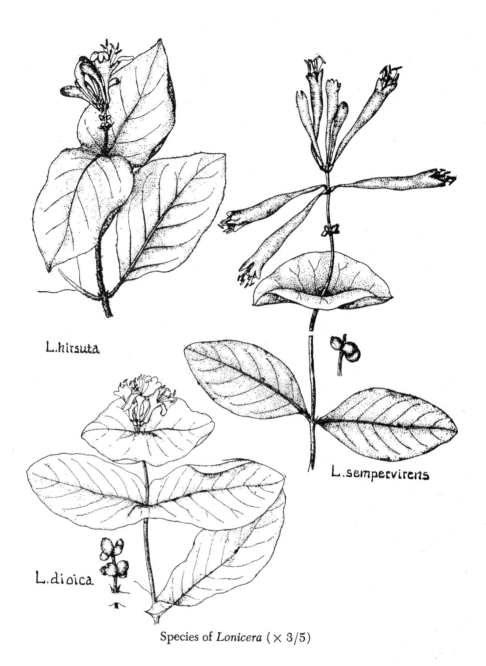

L.hirsuta

L.sempervirens

L.dioica

Species of *Lonicera* ($\times$ 3/5)

Lonicera dioica var. *glaucescens* (Rydberg) Butters, in Minn. T. & S. 289, 1912
[*L. glaucescens* Rydb. 1897]

Leaves ovate to obovate, often only one pair connate-perfoliate, the lower ones narrowed at the base and sometimes short-petioled, glabrous on the upper surface and margin but with the lower surface more or less pubescent, often densely so; flowers more frequently pale yellow; tube of corolla hirsute on the outside, 10–20 mm. long, somewhat more slender than in the type; ovary some-times gland-dotted. Blossoms in May and June; fruit ripe in August and September. (*Glaucéscens*, somewhat blue-green.)

In habitats similar to those of the species, this variety is common through-out the wooded parts of the Upper Midwest. It is distributed from western Que-bec to British Columbia, south to North Carolina, Kentucky, Missouri, and north-eastern Kansas.

The pubescence on the under side of the leaves varies from dense to sparse and even glabrate in late season in some collections. In this respect the variety intergrades in our area with typical *L. dioica*, but is distinguishable by the other characters given.

GRAPE HONEYSUCKLE, *Lonicera prolifera* (Kirchner) Rehder, Rhodora 12:166, 1910 [*Caprifolium prolifera* Kirchner 1864; *L. Sullivantii* Gray 1883]

A twining vine 3 m. or more tall; bark pale brown and glossy, peeling only on the older stems; twigs glabrous; leaves mostly broadly obovate, 3–7 cm. long, 2–4 cm. wide on flowering shoots, the lower narrowed to a short petiole, the upper one to three pairs connate-perfoliate, the uppermost pair forming a nearly orbicular (rarely, slightly rhombic) disk, its ends retuse or sometimes mucronate; the apex of the leaves rounded or obtuse, usually mucronate; the upper surface bright green with more or less glaucous bloom, glabrous; the lower surface pale, very glaucous, appressed-puberulent except in the case of the perfoliate disks, which are usually glabrous; margin cartilaginous and with-out hairs; inflorescence a sessile or short-peduncled spike about 1 cm. long, usually with small secondary inflorescences in the axils of the disk leaves; ovary glabrous; calyx limb about 0.5 mm. long, obscurely five-lobed; corolla pale yellow, glabrous without, pubescent within, its tube 10–15 mm. long, very slen-der and scarcely gibbous below, expanding to about 3 mm. at the throat, its limb two-lipped, cleft into five somewhat unequal linear petals about 8 mm. long; stamens strongly exserted, anthers 3–4 mm. long, filaments and style slightly hairy or nearly glabrous; berry red. Flowers in May and June. (*Prolífera*, pro-liferous, probably referring to the inflorescence.)

Grape honeysuckle grows in woods and ravines and on bluffs and rocky roadside banks. It is infrequent in our area and reaches the northwestern limit of its distribution in Goodhue County of southeastern Minnesota. Reports of its occurrence in Manitoba are doubtfully authentic. It is distributed from southern Ontario to southeastern Minnesota, south to Tennessee, Arkansas, and eastern Kansas.

HAIRY HONEYSUCKLE, *Lonicera hirsuta* Eaton, Man. Bot. ed. 2, 307, 1818

A twining vine about 3 m. tall; bark grayish-brown, soon peeling and exposing the pale-brown inner bark; twigs hirsute; leaves broadly elliptical to orbicular, 5–11 cm. long, 3.5–8 cm. wide on the flowering shoots, the lower short-petioled, the upper one or two pairs connate-perfoliate, the uppermost forming a rhombic (rarely nearly orbicular) disk with mostly acuminate ends; the apex of the leaves very variable, mostly acute or short-acuminate, base narrowed or rounded, the upper surface dark green, finely appressed-pubescent, the lower surface pale, downy pubescent, margin ciliate, not at all cartilaginous; inflorescence a more or less peduncled spike about 1 cm. long, often with sessile or stalked secondary inflorescences in the axils of the disk leaves, peduncles hirsute and glandular; ovary glabrous; calyx limb scarcely 1 mm. long, obscurely five-lobed; corolla pale yellow, pubescent and glandular without, pubescent within, its tube 10–18 mm. long, slender and somewhat gibbous below, expanding gradually into the two-lipped, five-petaled limb of about the same length; stamens strongly exserted, the anthers about 3 mm. long, filaments and style somewhat hairy below; berry red. Blossoms in May and June. (*Hirsúta*, hairy.)

This vine grows on calcareous shores, in thickets and woods, and on bluffs. It is common in the region of the coniferous forests. It is distributed from western Quebec and Vermont to Saskatchewan, south to Pennsylvania, Ohio, northern Michigan, Wisconsin, and Minnesota.

SWAMP FLY-HONEYSUCKLE, *Lonicera oblongifolia* (Goldie) Hook., Fl. Bor. Am. 1:284, 1833 [*Xylosteum oblongifolium* Goldie 1822]

A shrub 5–15 dm. high, bark grayish, twigs puberulent; leaves ovate-lance-olate to oblong, thick, dark green above, pale beneath, finely woolly-pubescent, especially beneath, margin thickened, woolly but not ciliate, apex acute or obtuse, base tapering, length 2.5–10 cm., width 1–3.5 cm.; petiole 2 mm. long or wanting; flowers in pairs in the axils of the lower leaves, peduncles slender, 1–3 cm. long, bracts at the base of the ovaries very minute, or deciduous before the flowers open; ovaries more or less fused; limb of the calyx nearly wanting, having five minute, triangular teeth less than 0.5 mm. long; corolla yellow, often streaked with purple, the tube about 5 mm. long, gibbous just above the base, more or less hairy within and without, limb two-lipped, spreading, about 1 cm. across, the upper lip slightly four-cleft, the lower consisting of a single petal; stamens exserted, the filaments hairy; fruit red or purplish, the two berries nearly distinct or more or less completely united. Flowers in late May and June; fruit ripe in July and August. (*Oblongifólia*, oblong-leaved.)

This shrub grows in bogs, swampy thickets, and wet woods. It is common in the region of the coniferous forests. It is distributed from Quebec to Manitoba, south to Maine, western New York and Pennsylvania, Michigan, northern Wisconsin, and Minnesota.

FLY HONEYSUCKLE, *Lonicera canadensis* Marsh., Arb. Am. 81, 1785 [*L. ciliata* Muhl. 1813]

An irregular shrub, 1–1.5 m. high; bark grayish, twigs glabrous; leaves ovate or lance-ovate, thin, bright green; upper surface glabrous, lower surface slightly

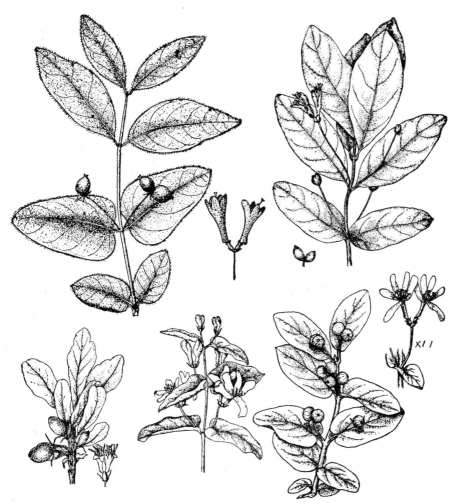

Species of *Lonicera*: Top, left to right, *L. canadensis* and *L. oblongifolia*.
Bottom, left to right, *L. villosa* var. *Solonis*, *L. tatarica*,
and *L. Morrowi*. (× 3/5)

hairy, margin ciliate, apex acute or somewhat obtuse, base acute, rounded, or
cordate, length 2–9 cm., width 1.5–4 cm.; petiole 5–8 mm. long; flowers in pairs,
in the axils of the lower leaves, peduncles slender, about 1 cm. long, bracts
at the base of the ovaries small, the longest lanceolate, about 2 mm. long, the
others about 0.5 mm. long, ovaries separate; limb of the calyx obscurely lobed,
about 1 mm. long; corolla greenish-yellow, funnel-shaped, the tube gibbous at
the base, 1.5 cm. long, expanding gradually into a nearly equally five-lobed limb
about 5 mm. long, slightly hairy within; stamens included; berries separate, red.
Flowers in May; fruit ripe in July. (*Canadénsis*, Canadian.)

Fly honeysuckle grows in cool, moist woods. It is common throughout the
regions of coniferous forest, infrequent and rare southward in deciduous woods

to northeastern Iowa and adjacent parts of Wisconsin and Minnesota. It is distributed from Quebec to Saskatchewan, south to New England, New Jersey, uplands of North Carolina, West Virginia and west to Ohio, Michigan, Wisconsin, and Iowa.

TARTARIAN HONEYSUCKLE, TWIN HONEYSUCKLE, *Lonicera tatarica* L., Sp. Pl. 173, 1753

An upright shrub 1.5–3 m. high; bark light gray, twigs glabrous, green or reddish; leaves ovate, glabrous, or somewhat pubescent beneath, rather thin, upper side dark green, lower paler but not glaucous, margin smooth or with a very few sparse hairs, apex acute or sometimes obtuse, base cordate, length 3–7 cm., width 1.7–4 cm.; petiole about 5 mm. long; flowers in pairs from the axils of the upper leaves, peduncles slender, 1–2 cm. long, bracts at the base of the ovaries partly awl-shaped, about 5 mm. long, partly ovate, less than 1 mm. long; ovaries distinct, glabrous; limb of the calyx with five lanceolate sepals, about 1 mm. long, corolla pink or whitish, the tube gibbous at the base, about 5 mm. long, hairy within, the limb irregularly cleft into five linear or lanceolate lobes, about 1 cm. long; stamens somewhat exserted, filaments hairy; berries slightly united at the base, red. (*Tatárica*, Tartarian, referring to its native land.)

This is a cultivated shrub which often becomes established, at least in the vicinity of cities and villages. It is a native of southeastern Russia and central Asia.

It is hardy and much planted, ornamental both in flower and fruit. Besides the typical form with light-pink flowers, there are forms with white and various shades of pink and crimson flowers.

Lonicera Morrowi A. Gray, Rep. Perry Exped. Jap. 2:313, 1856

A spreading shrub about 2 m. high; bark grayish-brown, twigs finely pubescent; leaves oblong, thick and veiny, dark green above, paler beneath, upper surface finely and sparsely hairy, lower surface hairy, margin ciliate, apex obtuse or rounded, base cordate, length 2.5–5 cm., width 1.5–2.5 cm.; petiole about 3 mm. long; flowers in pairs, axillary, peduncles 7–10 mm. long, bracts small, pubescent and ciliate, the two longest linear, 3–5 mm. long, the others ovate, about 2 mm. long; ovaries separate; limb of the calyx with five obtuse, triangular, ciliate teeth; corolla white, becoming yellow on fading, pubescent, the tube 7–10 mm. long, the limb with five slightly irregular lobes, 8–12 mm. long; stamens exserted, the filaments hairy; berries separate, bright red. Flowers in May and June; fruits from August to late autumn. (*Mórrowi*, named for Dr. James Morrow, a famous traveler in Japan.)

This plant is a native of Japan and is cultivated here. It is very handsome and hardy, ornamental both in flower and fruit and covered with foliage from earliest spring until hard freezing in the fall. It is a very useful plant for untrimmed hedges where there is plenty of space. It grows readily from seed;

it is distributed extensively by birds, and is apt to appear spontaneously in the vicinity of cultivated plants.

× *Lonicera bella* Zabel., Gartenfl. 38:525, 1889 [*L. Morrowi* × *tatarica*]

A more upright shrub than *L. Morrowi*, twigs somewhat pubescent, leaves sparsely pubescent or nearly glabrous, truncate at the base, peduncles about 12 mm. long, bracts nearly orbicular, corolla either pink or white, becoming yellow with age. (*Bélla*, charming.)

This garden hybrid is frequently planted.

MOUNTAIN FLY-HONEYSUCKLE, *Lonicera villosa* (Michx.) R. & S. var. *Solonis* (Eat.) Fernald, Rhodora 27:6, 1925 [*L. caerulea* L. var. *villosa* (Michx.) T. & G. 1841; *Xylosteum villosum* Michx. 1803]

An erect shrub 3 dm. to 1 m. high, with erect or ascending branches; bark brown, much shredded; twigs puberulent and generally sparsely villous; winter buds strongly ascending; leaves elliptical, narrow, oblong or obovate, 2–4 cm. long, 8–16 mm. wide, apex rounded or obtusely angled, rarely somewhat acute, generally mucronate, base rounded, upper surface dark green, more or less strigose-pubescent, sometimes nearly glabrate, lower surface paler with strongly reticulate, prominent veins, villous, margin ciliate, petioles about 1 mm. long, villous; flowers in pairs from the axils of the lower leaves, peduncle 2–8 mm. long, villous, bracts at the base of the ovaries awl-shaped, 3–5 mm. long, hirsute; ovaries of the two flowers completely united, glabrous; limb of the calyx minute, glabrous; corolla pale yellow, narrowly campanulate, glabrous or sparingly pubescent without, villous within, the tube slightly gibbous at the base, about 7 mm. long, the lobes nearly equal, about 5 mm. long; stamens exserted; fruit an oval, bluish-black berry, bearing the scars of the two flowers close together at the summit, edible. Blossoms from late April to early June; fruit ripe in June and July. (*Villósa*, villous; *Solónis*, named for its discoverer, D. Solon C. H. Smith).

This shrub grows in bogs and swamps, on peaty slopes, and in rocky pastures. It is common in the coniferous forest area and southward in some of the outlying tamarack bogs of the region. It is distributed from Newfoundland to southeastern Manitoba, south to New England, Michigan, Wisconsin, and Minnesota.

Diervilla Adans., Fam. 2:157, 1763

Upright shrubs; leaves opposite, serrate; flowers axillary and terminal, cymose or solitary; calyx tube slender and elongated, narrowed below the five persistent sepals; corolla tubular or funnel-shaped, the tube slightly gibbous at the base, five-lobed; stamens five, borne on the tube of the corolla, anthers linear; ovary two-celled, inferior, ovules numerous in each cavity, style long and slender, stigma capitate; fruit a capsule, oblong, slender-beaked or pointed, two-valved. (*Diervilla*, named for Dr. N. Dierville, who brought the plant to Tournefort.)

Diervilla Lonicera

This is a genus of about eight species, two of eastern North America, the others of eastern Asia. The Asiatic species are often regarded as forming a distinct genus, *Weigela*.

BUSH HONEYSUCKLE, *Diervilla Lonicera* Mill., Gard. Dict. ed. 8, 1768

A low, upright shrub, 1 m. or less high; bark grayish-brown, twigs glabrous except for two narrow, hispid lines; leaves ovate or ovate-lanceolate, glabrous except a little rough-hairy along the veins, finely serrate, long-acuminate at the apex, wedge-shaped to rounded at the base, 6–13 cm. long, 2–7 cm. wide; petiole 5–10 mm. long; flowers terminal or axillary, in clusters of from two to six; sepals bristle-like, about 5 mm. long; corolla pale yellow, growing darker with age, funnel-shaped, about 1.5 cm. long, 1.5 cm. in diameter, the free portion of the petals linear. Blossoms in June. (*Lonicéra*, the honeysuckle.)

Bush honeysuckle grows in dry or moist woods and rocky places throughout the forested parts of the Upper Midwest. It is most common northward, less frequent southward to southeastern Minnesota and adjacent parts of Wisconsin and northeastern Iowa. It is distributed from Newfoundland to Manitoba, south to New England, Indiana and Iowa.

The flowers are at first pale yellow, turning to deep yellow, scarlet, crimson, or sometimes maroon.

A variant of the species, var. *hypomalacum* Fernald, which has leaves densely pilose beneath, occurs in northern Wisconsin, northern Minnesota, and adjacent Ontario.

Weigela Thunb., Svenska Vetensk. Acad. Handb. 1:137, 1780

Deciduous shrubs, 1.5–5 m. high; winter buds with several pointed scales; leaves opposite, petioled, serrate, without stipules; flowers rather large and showy, from one to several in axillary cymes; sepals five, distinct or connate below; corolla broadly funnel-shaped, nearly regular; stamens five, shorter than the corolla; style sometimes exserted; stigma capitate; ovary two-celled, elongated; fruit a beaked capsule, opening with two valves; seeds numerous, angular, minute. *Weigéla*, named for C. E. van Weigel, a professor in Greifswald, Germany.)

This genus includes about twelve species of northeastern Asia.

Weigela florida (Bunge) A. de Candolle, in Ann. Sci. Nat. Bot. 11:241, 1839 [*Diervilla florida* Sieb. & Zucc. 1835; *W. rosea* Lindl. 1846]

A shrub 1–2 m. high; bark grayish-brown, twigs hairy in two lines; leaves ovate to obovate, glabrous above, rough-hairy along the veins beneath, finely serrate, acuminate at the apex, wedge-shaped or rounded at the base, 4–7 cm. long, 2.5–3.5 cm. wide; petiole about 2 mm. long; flowers axillary or terminal, in clusters of from one to four; sepals narrow-lanceolate, about 1 cm. long, united for one-third to one-half of their length; corolla broadly funnel-shaped, nearly

Left, *Weigela florida.* Right, *Diervilla Lonicera.*

regular, about 3 cm. long, 3.5 cm. in diameter, the free part of the petals broadly triangular, rose-pink or whitish in some varieties; stigma two-lobed. (*Flórida, flowering.*)

A native of northern China, this very ornamental shrub is much cultivated under the name "Weigela," and is fairly hardy in the Upper Midwest, where it blooms in early June. There are numerous hybrids between this and other related Asiatic species. They appear to be less hardy than W. *florida.*

ASTER FAMILY, Compositae

Herbs, rarely shrubs or trees; flowers in dense heads, surrounded by a calyx-like involucre, the receptacle naked (i.e., bearing only flowers) or bearing scales among the flowers; flowers perfect, monoecious, polygamous or dioecious; calyx adherent to the ovary, the free limb (pappus) variously modified as scales, spines, bristles, plumes, etc., or entirely wanting; petals five, rarely none, united, corolla either regular, tubular, or bell-shaped, or irregular, two-lipped, or flat and ligulate, the marginal flowers of the head often different in form from the central ones; stamens five or none, usually united by their anthers; pistil one, compound; ovary inferior, one-celled, one-seeded; style one, two-cleft above; stigmas two; fruit an achene.

This immense family, the largest of flowering plants, contains about thirteen thousand species. Herbaceous species of this family are very abundant in our flora, especially in prairie regions, comprising such well-known plants as sunflowers, asters, goldenrods, daisies, thistles, and dandelions. Woody plants, on the other hand, are rare and are largely confined to warmer climates, but the

392

following mainly North Temperate genus contains a number of shrubby and half-shrubby species.

Wormwood, Sagebrush
Artemisia L., Sp. Pl. 845, 1753

Herbs or shrubby plants, bitter and aromatic, often canescent or tomentose; leaves alternate; heads few- to many-flowered, pendulous or nodding, in panicles, racemes, or spikes; flowers all tubular, greenish or yellowish; involucre ovoid, oblong, or hemispherical, its bracts imbricated in several series, the outer ones shorter; receptacle flat or convex, naked or pubescent, not chaffy; central flowers perfect, sometimes sterile, marginal flowers usually pistillate and fertile; achenes obovoid or oblong, two-ribbed or striate, with a small, rounded summit and no pappus. (*Artemisia*, the classical Greek name of the wormwood, named for Artemisia, wife of Mausolus.)

This is a genus of about two hundred species, natives of the Northern Hemisphere and southern South America. Besides the following, several herbaceous species occur in Minnesota.

KEY TO SPECIES OF ARTEMISIA

1. Plants 2–5 dm. high, densely silky-canescent throughout; receptacle hairy. Native . . . . A. *frigida* (p. 393)
1. Plants 7–10 dm. high, sparingly pubescent or nearly glabrous; receptacle naked. Introduced. . . . . .A. *Abrotanum* (p. 393)

MOUNTAIN SAGE, *Artemisia frigida* Willd., Sp. Pl. 3:1838, 1804

A low, tufted perennial, 2–5 dm. high, woody at the base, densely silky-canescent throughout, aromatic; leaves 1–3 cm. long, pinnately parted and three- to five-cleft, the divisions linear, the leaves toward the base of the stems with shorter and slightly broader lobes, the upper ones sessile and less divided; heads globose, mostly numerous, in racemes or sometimes paniculate, short-peduncled, about 5 mm. long and 4 mm. broad; involucre hemispheric, bracts oblong, canescent; receptacle villous-pubescent; central flowers fertile; achenes ovate, about 1 mm. long. Blossoms in August and September. (*Frigida*, frosty, referring to the white foliage.)

On dry prairies and dry rocky bluffs and hillsides, mountain sage is common throughout the western parts of the area; it is infrequent in exposed situations to southeastern Minnesota and western Wisconsin. It is distributed from Wisconsin to British Columbia, south to Texas, New Mexico, and Oregon.

SOUTHERNWOOD, *Artemisia Abrotanum* L., Sp. Pl. 845, 1753

A half-shrubby perennial, up to 1 m. high; stems reddish-brown, slightly ridged, puberulent or at length glabrous; branches numerous, short-ascending or erect; leaves 1.5–5 cm. long, glabrous or slightly pubescent, especially toward the base, once to thrice pinnately parted into linear lobes less than 1 mm. wide,

Artemisia frigida. (Single head × 2 1/2, single flower × 10.)

the uppermost leaves frequently entire; inflorescence thyrsoidal, much branched and leafy, heads numerous, in slender racemes, nearly globose, nodding, 2–4 mm. in diameter; involucre hemispheric, somewhat pubescent, the outer bracts lanceolate, the inner oblong-ovate to narrowly obovate with broadly scarious margins, sometimes notched at the tips; receptacle naked; flowers numerous, small, yellowish, the central ones fertile; achenes glabrous, about 0.5 mm. long. Blossoms from September to October. (*Abrotánum*, classical Latin name for this plant.)

A native of southern Europe, southernwood is frequently planted on account of its feathery, fragrant foliage.

Glossary and Index

GLOSSARY

Abruptly pinnate. Pinnate without a terminal leaflet.

Achene. A dry, one-seeded fruit.

Acrid. Sharp, biting, and unpleasant to the taste.

Acuminate. Tapering into a long point.

Acute. Sharp-pointed.

Adherent. More or less grown together.

Adnate. United, grown to, as the inferior ovary with the receptacle.

Aerial. Growing in the air.

Aggregate. Grouped together.

Alternate. With a single leaf at each node.

Anatropous. Applied to an inverted ovule with the micropyle near the hilum.

Annual. Lasting only one growing season.

Anther. The upper part of the stamen containing the pollen.

Apetalous. Without petals.

Apex. The tip or upper end.

Apiculate. Tipped with a small point.

Apocarpous. Having, or consisting of, separate carpels or pistils.

Apopetalous. Having, or consisting of, separate petals.

Appendaged. With an addition or projection.

Appressed. Lying close to or against another part.

Aquatic. Growing in the water.

Aril. The fleshy, often bright-colored, outer coat of some seeds.

Aromatic. Spicy, fragrant.

Ascendate. Having a strong upward direction; said of pedicels of flowers.

Ascending. Growing obliquely upward.

Astringent. With a puckering taste.

Auricle. An appendage more or less ear-like in shape.

Awn. A slender, bristle-like structure.

Awn-pointed. Tipped with an awn.

Axil. The upper angle between leaf and stem.

Axillary. Borne in the axil of a leaf.

Axis. The part of a stem or branch that bears leaves, flowers, or flower parts.

Barbed. With a reflexed point like a fishhook.

Basal. At the base or arising from it.

Beak. An elongated, tapering structure.

Bearded. With hairs or awns restricted more or less to a definite area.

Berry. A fleshy fruit with a thin skin or soft rind, the seeds imbedded in the pulp.

Bifoliolate. Consisting of two leaflets.

Bipinnate. Twice pinnate, i.e., with the primary pinnae again pinnately compound.

Biternate. With three divisions, each subdivided into three leaflets.

Blade. The flat part of a leaf.

Boreal. Northern.

Boss. A raised knob or disk.

Bract. A reduced leaf found below a flower or flower cluster.

Bracteole, bractlet. A small bract or scale on the pedicel below the flower.

Caducous. Dropping off very early compared with other parts.

Calcareous. Containing lime.

Calyx. The outer floral envelope, consisting of sepals; usually green but sometimes petal-like. When only one floral envelope is present, it is considered to be the calyx.

Campanulate. Bell-shaped.

Cane. The elongated new shoot of bushes and shrubs.

Canescent. Gray and hoary in pubescence.

Capitate. Head-like.

Capsule. A dry, dehiscent fruit consisting of two or more carpels.

Carpel. A simple pistil or the unit part of a compound pistil.

Cartilaginous. Firm and tough, like cartilage.

Catkin. A spike-like inflorescence of inconspicuous flowers, usually subtended by scaly bracts, frequently drooping.

Cell. The cavity or chamber of an ovary.

Ciliate. Margined with hairs.

Claw. The narrowed lower part of a petal.

Cleft. Cut about halfway to the middle.

Coherent. United or clinging together.

Compound. Consisting of two or more similar parts united.

Compound leaf. A leaf with two or more completely separate blades or leaflets.

Concrescent. Grown together.

Conduplicate. Folded together lengthwise.

Cone. An elongated axis bearing stamens or ovule-bearing scales, as in the pine; a strobilus.

Connate-perfoliate. Applied to two or more leaves so united that the stem passes through the resulting structure.

Convolute. Rolled up longitudinally.

Cordate. Heart-shaped.

Coriaceous. Leathery in texture.

Corolla. The inner floral envelope consisting of petals, usually bright-colored.

Corymb. A flat-topped or convex flower cluster, blooming first at the edge.

Corymbose. Corymb-like; arranged as in a corymb.

Cotyledon. A seed leaf.

Crateriform. Goblet-shaped or deep saucer-shaped.

Creeping. Growing along the ground.

Crenate. Scalloped; with rounded, shallow teeth.

Crenulate. Finely crenate.

Cuneate. Wedge-shaped.

Cyme. A flower cluster blooming from the apex or middle first, usually somewhat flat.

Cymose. In a cyme; cyme-like

Cymule. A small cyme.

Deciduous. Falling off, usually at the close of the season; applied also to trees and shrubs that shed their leaves in the autumn.

Decumbent. Reclining but with the summit ascending.

Decurrent. Running down the stem, as the base of some leaves.

Decussate. Alternating in pairs at right angles.

Deflexed. Bent down.

Dehiscent. Splitting open, used of pods, etc.

Deltoid. Triangular.

Dentate. Toothed, with the teeth directed outward.

Denticulate. Minutely dentate.

Depressed. Flattened from above.

Dichotomous. Two-forked.

Digitate. Diverging like the fingers of a hand.

Dilated. Broadened.

Dimorphous. Of two forms.

Dioecious. Bearing pistils and stamens on different plants.

Disk. A development of the receptacle at or around the base or summit of the ovary, frequently glandular.

Dissected. Cut or divided into numerous narrow segments.

Divaricate. Widely divergent.

Divided. Lobed nearly or quite to the base or midrib.

Drupe. A fleshy fruit with a pit or stone, such as the plum.

Drupelet. A small drupe.

Elliptic. Of oval outline, broadest about the middle.

Elliptic-lanceolate. Long and narrow, broadest about the middle.

Elongated. Long, drawn-out.

Emarginate. Indented at the apex.

Embryo. The young plant in a seed.

Endocarp. The inner wall of a fruit, as the stone of a plum.

Endosperm. The food supply stored about the embryo in many seeds.

Entire. Without teeth, lobes, or divisions.

Epidermis. The outer layer, the skin of plants.

Epigynous. Borne on the upper part of the ovary; applied also to a flower in which the perianth is so situated.

Even-pinnate. Pinnate without a terminal leaflet.

Exfoliate. To split or peel off, usually in thin layers.

Exocarp. The outer part or wall of a fruit.

Exserted. Projecting beyond the surrounding parts.

Exudation. Sap, resin, or milk that has oozed out, usually dried.

Falcate. Scythe-shaped, curved and flat, tapering gradually.

Fascicle. A cluster, usually dense.

Fascicled. Borne in dense clusters.

Fastigiate. Close, parallel, and upright.

Fertile. Bearing fruit; (of stamens) bearing pollen.

Fetid. Ill-smelling.

Fibrous. Composed of or resembling fibers.

Filament. The stalk of a stamen.

Filiform. Thread-like.

Fimbriate. Fringed.

Flexible. Bending readily.

Floricane. The flowering cane, usually the second year's development of the primocane (*Rubus*).

Flower. An axis bearing stamens or pistils or both, and usually also sepals and petals.

Foliaceous. Leaf-like.

Follicle. A dry fruit of one carpel, splitting on one side only.

Fruit. A developing or ripened ovary, often with other adhering parts.

Genus. A group of related species, as the genus *Ulmus* (elm), the genus *Syringa* (lilac), embracing respectively all the kinds of elm and all the kinds of lilac.

Gibbous. Swollen.

Glabrate. Becoming nearly or quite smooth by the loss of pubescence.

Glabrous. Smooth, i.e., without hairs or any form of pubescence.

Gland. A surface or structure that produces nectar, resin, oil, etc.; often a small appendage or projection.

Glandular. Bearing glands, or gland-like.

Glaucescent. Somewhat bluish or whitish.

Glaucous. Covered with a bloom, a bluish or whitish wax coating.

Globose. Spherical or nearly so.

Clutinous. Sticky, glue-like.

Gynophore. A stalk that raises the ovary above the insertion of the other parts of the flower.

Habitat. The home of a plant.

Hastate. Arrow-shaped but with the basal lobes diverging.

Head. A dense cluster of sessile flowers.

Herb. A non-woody plant that dies annually, at least down to the ground.

Herbaceous. Herb-like.

Hip. The fleshy ripened receptacle of a rose, containing the bony achenes.

Hirsute. With somewhat coarse, stiff hairs.

Hispid. Rough, with stiff, bristly hairs.

Hybrid. A cross between two species.

Hypanthium. In a perigynous or epigynous flower, the cup-shaped, saucer-shaped, or tubular structure that bears the sepals, petals, and stamens.

Hypogynous. Situated on the receptacle beneath the ovary and free from it; applied also to a flower in which the perianth is so situated.

Imbricated. Overlapping like the shingles of a roof; in an imbricated calyx or corolla one sepal or petal must be wholly external and one wholly internal.

Incised. Cut sharply and irregularly, more or less deeply.

Included. Not projecting beyond the other parts.

Indehiscent. Applied to fruits that do not split to liberate the seeds.

Inferior. Applied to an organ situated below another one, especially to the ovary when below the other flower parts.

Inflorescence. A flower cluster.

Infrastipular. Below the stipules at the base of a leaf.

Integument. A protective layer or coat, as the covering of an ovule or a seed.

Internode. The part of the stem between two nodes.

Involucre. The group of leaves or bracts surrounding a head of flowers, as in the sunflower, or sometimes below a single flower or cluster of flowers.

Irregular. Applied to a flower in which the petals are unlike.

Keel. The two fused lower petals of the flower of the pea family.

Keeled. Ridged, like the keel of a boat.

Lacerate. Irregularly cleft, as if torn.

Laciniate. Cut into narrow, pointed lobes.

Lanceolate. Lance-shaped, long and narrow, widest below the middle.

Leaflet. A division of a compound leaf.

Leaf-scar. The scar left by the falling of a leaf.

Legume. A dry, dehiscent fruit of one carpel, splitting on two sides as in the pea and bean pods.

Lenticel. A corky projection or spot on the bark.

Linear. Long and narrow, with the sides nearly or quite parallel.

Lip. The upper and lower halves of an irregular corolla or calyx, as in the snapdragon.

Lobe. Any segment of an organ, especially if rounded.

Lobed. Divided into or bearing lobes.

Loculicidal. Applied to a capsule that splits down the back of the chambers or cells.

Lustrous. Shining.

Membranous. Membrane-like, papery.

Micropyle. The opening through which the pollen tube enters the ovule.

Monoecious. Bearing stamens and pistils in different flowers of the same plant.

Monotypic. Used of a genus containing a single species.

Mounding. Applied to *Rubus* when canes are of low or intermediate stature, overarching, and more or less horizontal.

Mucronate. Tipped with a sharp point.

Nerve. One of the principal veins of a leaf.

Net-veined. With veins running in various directions and connecting with one another.

Nodding. Hanging on a bent peduncle or pedicel.

Node. The part of the stem that normally bears a leaf or leaves.

Novirame. A flowering shoot on a primocane.

Nut. A dry, one-seeded, indehiscent fruit with a stony shell or covering.

Nutlet. A diminutive nut.

Ob-. Prefix meaning reversed or inverted.

Obcordate. Reversed heart-shaped, the point of the heart downward.

Oblanceolate. Reversed lance-shaped, widest above the middle.

Oblique. Slanting.

Oblong-lanceolate. Lance-shaped, but with nearly parallel sides.

Obovate. Reversed egg-shaped, broadest above the middle.

Obtuse. Blunt.

Odd-pinnate. Pinnate with an odd or unpaired leaflet at the tip.

Opposite. (Of leaves) directly across from each other at the same node; (of flower parts) in front of.

Ovate. Egg-shaped in outline.

Ovoid. Egg-shaped.

Ovule. The young unfertilized seed as found in the flower.

Palmate. Spreading from a common center like the fingers of the hand.

Panicle. A compound flower cluster of the racemose type.

Paniculate. In a panicle.

Papilionaceous. Butterfly-like, as the flowers of the pea family.

Papillose. With minute blunt projections.

Pappus. The bristles, hairs, awns, etc., found at the apex of the fruits of asters, dandelions, etc. It represents a modified calyx.

Parcifrond. A long, leafy shoot on a floricane below the ordinary short floral branches, mostly sterile but sometimes bearing flowers.

Parted. Deeply cut.

Pedicel. The stalk of a single flower.

Peduncle. The stalk of a flower cluster or of a solitary flower.

Peltate. Shield-shaped, the stalk attached at or near the middle of the lower surface.

Pendent. Hanging.

Pendulous. Hanging.

Perennial. Lasting from year to year.

Perfect. Having both stamens and pistils.

Perfoliate. Applied to a leaf having the stem apparently passing through it.

Perianth. The floral envelopes, calyx and corolla considered together; used also when the two envelopes are undifferentiated.

Pericarp. The wall of the fruit.

Perigynous. Borne on an hypanthium that is free from the ovary; applied also to a flower in which the perianth is so situated.

Persistent. Remaining after blooming or fruiting.

Petal. One of the parts of the corolla.

Petaloid. Petal-like, brightly colored.

Petiole. The stalk of a leaf.

Petiolule. The stalk of a leaflet.

Pinna. A leaflet of a pinnately compound leaf.

Pinnate. Arranged like the parts of a feather, applied to the veining, lobing, and compounding of leaves.

Pinnately compound. With leaflets on both sides of a common stalk.

Pinnatifid. Pinnately cleft to the middle or beyond.

Pistil. The seed-bearing organ of the flower.

Pistillate. Having pistils but not stamens.

Plumose. Plume-like or feathery.

Pod. A dry, dehiscent fruit.

Pollen. The (usually powdery) material produced in the anthers, consisting of microspores and necessary for the fecundation of the ovules.

Pollen grain. One of the microspores or grains that constitute pollen.

Pollination. The transfer of pollen from the anther to the stigma of the same or another flower.

Polygamo-dioecious. Polygamous and having the perfect and imperfect flowers on different plants.

Polygamo-monoecious. Polygamous and having the perfect and imperfect flowers on the same plant.

Polygamous. Having both perfect and imperfect (staminate or pistillate) flowers.

Polypetalous. Having separate petals.

Pome. A fleshy fruit with a core.

Prickle. A sharp, needle-like or awl-like outgrowth of the epidermis.

Primary. Of the first rank.

Primocane. The first year's cane (usually without flowers) of *Rubus* and similar genera.

Propagation. The process by which new individuals arise or are produced without the use of seed.

Prostrate. Lying flat upon the ground.

Pruinose. Having a waxy, powdery secretion on the surface.

Puberulent, puberulous. Finely hairy.

Pubescent. Hairy.

Pungent. Sharp.

Pyriform. Pear-shaped.

Raceme. An inflorescence consisting of a somewhat elongated axis bearing a succession of axillary, pedicelled flowers.

Racemose. In a raceme or resembling a raceme.

Rachis. The axis of a compound leaf.

Radiate. Like the spokes of a wheel.

Ray. One of the ribbon-like flowers of the Compositae.

Receptacle. The end of a flower stalk bearing the flower parts or, in the Compositae, bearing the flowers.

Recurved. Bent backward or downward.

Reflexed. Abruptly bent backward or downward.

Regular. Having the members of each series alike in size and shape.

Reniform. Kidney-shaped.

Resinous, resiniferous. Bearing resin.

Reticulate. Net-like.

Reticulation. A net-like marking or roughening.

Retrorse. Turned downward or backward.

Revolute. With the margin rolled back.

Rhizome. An underground stem.

Rhombic. More or less diamond-shaped.

Ribbed. Having prominent veins.

Rootstock. An underground stem.

Rostrate. Beaked.

Rotate. Flat and circular in outline; wheel-shaped.

Rudimentary. Imperfectly developed.

Rugose. Wrinkled, roughened.

Salver-form, salver-shaped. With a slender tube, abruptly widened into a flat top.

Samara. A winged fruit, as in the elm and maple.

Scabrous. Rough.

Scale. A minute leaf, also any small, flat, superficial appendage.

Sclerenchyma. Hard, stone-like, or fibrous tissue.

Scurfy. With bran-like scales.

Segment. A part or division.

Segregate. To separate from.

Semiherbaceous. Partly herbaceous, woody only at the base.

Sepal. One of the outer cycle of flower parts, usually green, a division of the calyx.

Septicidal. Splitting through or along the septa or partitions of the fruit.

Septifragal. Where the valves in dehiscence break away from the partitions.

Serrate. Having teeth like a saw.

Serrulate. Finely serrate.

Sessile. Without a stalk, seated.

Seta. A bristle.

Sheath. The part of a leaf or leaf base that clasps or encloses the stem.

Shrub. A woody plant usually less than 20 ft. high and generally with several stems from a common base.

Simple. Consisting of one part, not compound.

Sinuate. With wavy margins.

Sinus. The cleft or recess between two lobes.

Sordid. Dirty in tint, chiefly applied when of an impure white.

Spatulate. Spoon-shaped, shaped like a spatula.

Species. A group of like individuals, as white pine or bur oak.

Spike. An elongated axis bearing sessile flowers.

Spine. A sharp, woody outgrowth of the stem; a reduced leaf or stipule.

Sporangium. A spore-bearing sac or structure.

Spray. A feathery branch.

Spur. A hollow projection from a sepal or petal.

Stamen. The part of the flower that bears the pollen.

Staminate. With stamens but without pistils.

Staminode. A rudimentary stamen that does not produce pollen.

Standard. The large upper petal of the flower of the pea family.

Stellate. Star-shaped.

Sterile. Not producing seeds; (of stamens) without pollen.

Stigma. The portion of the pistil that receives the pollen.

Stipel. A stipule of a leaflet.

Stipulate. Having stipules.

Stipule. A usually small, blade-like structure at the base of the petiole.

Strap-shaped. Long and narrow in outline.

Striate. Marked with parallel lines.

Stolon. A runner or any basal branch that is disposed to root.

Stoloniferous. Bearing stolons.

Strigose. Having appressed, sharp, and stiff hairs.

Style. The stalk-like portion of the pistil connecting the stigma and the ovary.

Stylopodium. An enlargement at the base of the style.

Subcordate. Somewhat heart-shaped.

Submerged. Under water.

Subsessile. Nearly sessile.

Subtend. To stand below on the axis.

Subulate. Awl-shaped.

Sucker. A shoot arising from an underground bud.

Suffrutescent. Slightly woody; woody at the base.

Suffruticose. Applied to a perennial plant that has only the lower part of the stem and branches woody and persistent.

Sulcate. Grooved or furrowed.

Superior. Applied to a part or organ placed above another one, especially to the ovary when it stands above the insertion of the other parts of the flower.

Sympetalous. Having or consisting of united petals.

Syncarpous. Having united carpels.

Teeth. Small projections along the leaf margin.

Tendril. A slender, coiling organ.

Terete. Having a circular cross-section.

Ternate. Of three leaflets.

Terrestrial. On the ground, not water-dwelling.

Thorn. A reduced, sharp-pointed branch.

Thyrse. A contracted, cylindrical or ovoid, usually compact panicle.

Tomentose. Having a dense mat or covering of hairs.

Tomentum. A dense layer of hairs.

Trailing. Creeping along the ground.

Tribe. A group of genera within a family.

Trifoliolate. Consisting of three leaflets.

Truncate. Cut off squarely.

Tubular. Like a tube.

Tundra. An arctic meadow or marsh.

Turion. A first-year cane, as in blackberries.

Twice-compound. With two sets or ranks of leaflets, i.e., with the primary leaflets again compound.

Twining. Winding spirally about a support.

Two-ranked. In two rows.

Umbel. A flower cluster with all the pedicels arising from the same point.

Umbellate. Borne in umbels.

Unarmed. Without thorns, spines, or prickles.

Valvate. Applied edge to edge without overlapping.

Valve. One of the portions into which dry fruits split; a trapdoor-like opening into the pollen chambers of some anthers.

Veins. Threads of fibro-vascular tissue in a leaf or other organ, especially those that branch (as distinguished from nerves).

Vernicose. Shiny, as though varnished.

Verticillate. Arranged in a whorl.

Vestigial. Reduced almost to disappearance.

Villous. Bearing long, soft hairs.

Webby. Bearing a tuft of slender, curly hairs.

Whorl. A group of three or more similar organs, such as leaves, radiating from the same node.

Whorled. Borne in a whorl.

Wing. Any membranous or thin expansion bordering or surrounding an organ; the lateral petals of the flower of the pea family.

Woolly. Covered with long and tortuous or matted hairs.

Zygomorphic. Applied to a flower with petals of different form.

INDEX

INDEX

407

INDEX